THE JOURNAL OF JOHN WODEHOUSE
FIRST EARL OF KIMBERLEY
FOR 1862–1902

THE JOURNAL OF JOHN WODEHOUSE FIRST EARL OF KIMBERLEY FOR 1862–1902

edited by

ANGUS HAWKINS and JOHN POWELL

CAMDEN FIFTH SERIES
Volume 9

FOR THE ROYAL HISTORICAL SOCIETY
University College London, Gower Street, London WC1E 6BT
1997

Published by the Press Syndicate of the University of Cambridge
The Edinburgh Building, Cambridge CB2 2RU, United Kingdom
40 West 20th Street, New York, NY 10011–4211, USA
10 Stamford Road, Oakleigh, Melbourne 3166, Australia

First published 1997

A catalogue record for this book is available from the British Library

Library of Congress cataloguing in publication data
Kimberley, John Wodehouse, Earl of, 1826–1902
The journal of John Wodehouse, first Earl of Kimberley, 1862–1902
edited by Angus Hawkins and John Powell.
p.   cm. – (Camden fifth series; v. 9)
Includes bibliographical references and Index.
ISBN 0–521–62328–6
1. Kimberley, John Wodehouse, Earl of, 1826–1902 – Diaries.
2. Great Britain – Politics and government – 1837–1901 – Sources.
3. Liberalism – Great Britain – History – 19th century – Sources.
4. Liberal Party (Great Britain) – History – Sources. 5. Statesmen –
Great Britain – Diaries.   6. Gladstone, W. E. (William Ewart),
1809–1898.   I. Hawkins, Angus.   II. Powell, John.
III. Title. IV. Series.
DA565.K54A3 1997
941.081'092–dc21
97–32293
CIP

ISBN 0 521 62328 6 hardback

SUBSCRIPTIONS. The serial publications of the Royal Historical Society, *Royal Historical Society Transactions* (ISSN 0080–4401), Camden Fifth Series (ISSN 0960–1163) volumes and volumes of the Guides and Handbooks (ISSN 0080–4398) may be purchased together on annual subscription. The 1997 subscription price (which includes postage but not VAT) is £50 (US$80 in the USA, Canada and Mexico) and includes Camden Fifth Series, volumes 9 and 10 (published in July and December) and Transactions Sixth Series, volume 7 (published in December). Japanese prices are available from Kinokuniya Company Ltd, P.O. Box 55, Chitose, Tokyo 156, Japan. EU subscribers (outside the UK) who are not registered for VAT should add VAT at their country's rate. VAT registered subscribers should provide their VAT registration number. Prices include delivery by air.

Subscription orders, which must be accompanied by payment, may be sent to a bookseller, subscription agent or direct to the publisher: Cambridge University Press, The Edinburgh Building, Shaftesbury Road, Cambridge CB2 2RU, UK; or in the USA, Canada and Mexico: Cambridge University Press, 40 West 20th Street, New York, NY 10011–4211, USA.

SINGLE VOLUMES AND BACK VOLUMES. A list of Royal Historical Society volumes available from Cambridge University Press may be obtained from the Humanities Marketing Department at the address above.

Printed and bound in the United Kingdom by Butler & Tanner Ltd, Frome and London

For Andrew Jones
friend and mentor

CONTENTS

ACKNOWLEDGEMENTS

In preparing this edition we have been helped by many individuals and institutions and we gratefully acknowledge their support. We first wish to thank Lord Kimberley and the Bodleian Library, Oxford, for allowing the journal to be published. Colin Harris and his colleagues in the Modern Papers and John Johnson Reading Room of the Bodleian Library were unfailingly kind and helpful. We wish to thank the University of Oxford, the Institute for the Arts and Humanistic Studies and Penn State Erie, the Behrend College, for financial support. For assistance with various points of research we are grateful to Colin Matthew, Padraic Kennedy, Jean Kennedy of the Norfolk Record Office, Barry Tharaud, Steve de Hart, Dan Frankforter and Kathryn Wolfe. The manuscript itself could not have been prepared without the able assistance of Linda Cox, Liza Denny, Jessica Mann, Wendy Eidenmuller and Brian Sauers. To our families – Esther, Emma and Kate, and Janice, Grady, Tessa and Ellen – our gratitude for their patience and supportive forbearance, *conditio sine qua non*.

Angus Hawkins
John Powell

LORD KIMBERLEY'S FAMILY

On several occasions from the 1860s, Lord Kimberley took time carefully to examine family documents in the muniment room at Kimberley House, and eventually published privately *The Wodehouses of Kimberley* (London, 1887), a straightforward piece of genealogical research based upon family and royal documents, and printed genealogical authorities. In it he suggested the possibility that family honours dated to the reign of Henry I, and tentatively accepted the claim, which some had questioned, that *Frappe Forte* was added to the Wodehouse coat of arms in recognition of service at the Battle of Agincourt (1415). In any case, Kimberley's research was substantial and the general pedigree of the Wodehouses was well established from the fourteenth century onward.

As the Wodehouses were unusually prolific,[1] and clearly proud of their forebears, there were many relatives of collateral branches with the same or similar names, making exact identification sometimes difficult. Even Blomefield, the noted Norfolk genealogist, was not immune to confusion. For the purposes of this journal, however, the following annotated genealogy should provide a reasonably clear guide to the families and family members mentioned. References, unless otherwise indicated, are to Lord Kimberley's page proofs of *The Wodehouses of Kimberley* (Norfolk Record Office).

I. *The Family of John, 2nd Baron Wodehouse (1771–1846) and Charlotte Laura (d. 1845),* da. and heir of John Norris of Witton, Esq. According to Kimberley, the 2nd Baron was an 'active politician on the Tory side, but always supported Sir Robert Peel', giving his 'proxy in favour of the bill for repealing the Corn Laws' (58).

a. Norris John (1798–1819), died without issue.

b. Henry Wodehouse (1799–1834), Lord Kimberley's father. Kimberley had 'no very distinct recollection' of his father except 'that he was a tall, powerfully-built man, a good shot and cricketer, and that he was fond of books' (59).

---

[1] Editors of the *Financial Reform Almanack for 1884* (London, 1884), 36, seeking to expose 'an aristocracy creating and living on *Patronage*', identified 67 Wodehouse relatives who had held 127 offices since 1850, worth £1,296,100.

c. Edward (1802–74), rear-adml., 1838 m. Diana, da. of Col. Thornton of Falconer's Hall, Yorkshire, whose name he assumed, leaving issue.

d. Berkeley (1806–77), major, 8th Hussars; 1837 m. Fanny, da. of Alexander Holmes, Esq., of Curragh, co. Kildare, leaving issue; for 'many years Resident at Zante', Ionian Islands (59).

e. Bertram (1813–56), military officer, died without issue.

f. Alfred (1814–48), Rector of Barnham Broom, 1840 m. Emma-Hamilla, da. of Reginald Macdonald, Esq., who died in 1852. Hamilla and Ernestine-Emma, the younger children of this marriage, were often at Kimberley.

g. Laura Sophia, 1825 m. Raikes Currie, Esq., d. 1869, leaving issue. See below for further family information.

h. Charlotte Laura, m. Rev. Richard Phayre, d. 1878, without issue.

i. Henrietta Laura, m. John David Chambers, Esq.

j. Caroline Elizabeth Laura, m. Mr John Whaites, d. 1856, leaving issue.

k. Emma, d. young from 'a fall through a skylight at Witton' (59).

II.   *The family of Theophilus Thornhagh (sometimes Thornhaugh) Gurdon, Liet.-Col., of Letton, Norfolk, and Anne Mellish.*

a. J. Brampton (1797–1881), 1828 m. Henrietta Susannah, eld. da. of 1st Lord Colborne; educ. Eton and Cambridge; Lib. MP for Norfolk W., 1857–65. His sons, Robert Thornhagh Gurdon (1829–1902) and William Brampton Gurdon (1840–1910), both much involved in Norfolk politics. Robert became a Liberal Unionist and was cr. Baron Cranworth in 1899. William Brampton served as Gladstone's private secretary, 1865–74, and was often at Kimberley.

b. John Gurdon-Rebow (1799–1870), 1835 m. Mary, widow of Sir Thomas Ormsby, and only da. and heir of Gen. Slate Rebow, of Wivenhoe Park, who died in 1842; 1845 m. Georgina, da. of 2nd Earl of Norbury; Lib. MP for Colchester, 1857–9, 1865–70.

c. Philip (1800–74), 1832 m. Henrietta Laura, da. of John Pulteney of Northerwood House, Hampshire; educ. Eton and Cambridge;

rector, Reymerston, Norfolk, 1825–74, of Southburgh, 1828–74, of Cranworth with Letton, 1832–74.

d. Anne (1802–80), 1825 m. Henry Wodehouse. See III below.

III.   *The family of Henry Wodehouse (1799–1834) and Anne (1802–80)*, da. of Theophilus Thornhagh Gurdon of Letton. On their courtship and marriage, see KP1 15/K2/15. Anne's devotion to her sons can be glimpsed in her anniversary journal, begun after Henry's death.

a. John (1826–1902), the subject of this work.

b. Henry (1834–73), educ. Balliol College, Oxford; entered the diplomatic service as attaché in 1855, serving in various capacities in Stockholm, St Petersburg, Constantinople, London, The Hague, Madrid, Vienna, Paris and Athens. Attached to Kimberley's missions to St Petersburg, 1856–8, and to Berlin and Copenhagen during the Schleswig-Holstein crisis, 1863–4. Prone to self-doubt over not 'getting on' in his career. In the fashion of a brother eight years his senior, Kimberley praised his abilities and urged 'a little more energy'. 'You will be very much tired of my sermons, but I know you won't take it ill from me. Let us work together and help each other'. Universally liked in the diplomatic corps, his death from typhoid fever in Athens was particularly regretted by his colleagues. (See *Liberal by Principle*, 8, 9, 10, 79, 83–4; H. Rumbold, *Recollections of a Diplomatist*, 2 vols., London, 1902, 1, 250–2; *Letters from the Honourable Henry Wodehouse, 1870–71*, London, 1874; Kimberley to Henry Wodehouse, 18 Dec. 1860, KP6 MS.eng.c.4476, ff. 12–14.)

c. Annette (1826–33), Kimberley's twin.

d. Laura (1827–35), died while Kimberley was at school in Lyndon.

IV.   *The family of Richard Hobart FitzGibbon (sometimes Fitzgibbon), 3rd Earl of Clare (1793–1864), and Diana (d. 1865), 1st da. of Charles Brydges Woodcock.* FitzGibbon served in Peninsular War with the Grenadier Guards before sitting as Whig MP for Limerick Co., 1818–41; succeeded his brother in 1851.

a. John Charles Henry (1829–54), styled Viscount FitzGibbon; at Christ Church, Oxford, with Kimberley; Lieut. 8th Hussars; killed in the charge of the Light Brigade at Balaklava, 25 Oct. 1854.

b. Florence (1825–95), m. John, 3rd Baron Wodehouse, 17 Aug. 1847.

c. Louisa Isabella Georgina (1826–98), reputed to have 'provided stories for more than one novelist' (*Belfast Weekly News*, 17 April 1902, KP6 MS. c.4484, f. 73); m. Gerald Normanby Dillon. After Dillon's death, m. the Sicilian Marquess della Rochella, spent extravagantly and died penniless under Kimberley's care; buried in the Roman Catholic cemetery at Carisbrooke, Isle of Wight.

d. Elinor (*c.* 1834–?), 1856 m. Francis William Henry Cavendish; in 1865 eloped with Lord Cecil Gordon, who was twice her age and married to her half sister, creating one of the 'grossest cases' that had ever come under the judge's notice (*The Times*, 3 March 1866, p. 9).

V.   *The family of John Wodehouse (1826–1902) and Florence Fitzgibbon (1825–95)*, m. 16 Aug. 1847 at St Peter's, Eaton Sq. The proposal came at the Duchess of Bedford's after only ten days' acquaintance. Lady Kimberley was delicate and frequently dismayed by her husband's political absences. A deep attachment to her kept Kimberley from considering posts abroad after 1858. Scores of references from a wide variety of sources suggest a happy marriage, though he was perhaps more satisfied than she. (For the lone, though haunting, contrary voice, see *CJ*, 75.)

a. John (1848–1932), educ. Eton and Trinity College, Cambridge; spent extravagantly, failed to graduate and filed for bankruptcy in 1872; m. 1875, Isabel Geraldine, da. of Sir Henry Josias Stracey. Despite the disappointments he caused, remained close to his father, both personally and in relation to his position as Liberal agent in Mid and East Norfolk constituencies; county magistrate until removal for personal assault during the campaign against Rider Haggard in 1895. In later years referred to as the 'Labour Earl'. According to the *Norwich Mercury*, however, 'to class him as a modern materialistic Socialist' was 'excruciatingly comical'. Rather, he was 'of an age when peer and peasant stood very close together', a survival 'from a more sincere, more manly, more violent, age' (30 Jan. 1926).

b. Alfred (1856–8), born in St Petersburg; died there, in Kimberley's estimation, from want of adequate medical attention. His death also played a part in Kimberley's attachment to home politics after 1858.

c. Armine (1860–1901), frequently ill in youth, and on the verge of death, 1871–2; educ. privately by Kimberley, with the assistance of a tutor in math; m. 1889 Eleanor Mary Caroline, da. of Matthew

Arnold; asst. private sec. to his father, 1880–5; 1st private sec., 1886, 1892–5; unsucc. contested Isle of Wight, 1895; served on exec. com. of the Eighty Club, 1899; Lib. MP for Saffron Walden div., Essex, 1900–1. His death a particular blow, as he was Kimberley's best companion after the death of Lady Kimberley, and had seemed to be in perfect health.

d. Alice (1850–1937), m. 1872 Hussey Packe of Prestwold Hall, Leics., who unsucc. contested N. div. Leicestershire as a Lib. in 1874 and 1880, and Mid Leicestershire as a Unionist in 1900. Their son, Edward, served as asst. private sec. to Lansdowne at the War Office in 1900, and to Selborne at the Admiralty, 1901–5. Kimberley was a regular Christmas visitor at Prestwold after the death of his wife.

e. Constance (1852–1923), inherited her elder brother's sharp temperament, nevertheless a pleasure to Kimberley, with whom she often travelled; close to her extended family; died unmarried at Beechey Grange, Parkstone, Dorset.

VI.　*The family of Raikes Currie (1801–81) and Laura Sophia (?–1869)* da. of John, 2nd Baron Wodehouse. Theirs was a 'singularly united family', full of happiness and frequent family visits to the Kimberley estate after the marriage in 1825. With Kimberley's father having died in 1834, Raikes Currie became the surrogate, materially assisting his nephew's introduction into the London financial and political world. Currie, a city banker and Lib. MP for Northampton (1837–57) was instrumental in Kimberley's election to the Political Economy Club, in his appointment as under-sec. at the Foreign Office in 1852, and, as late as 1868, in his appointment as Governor of the Hudson's Bay Company. In turn, Kimberley played important roles in the careers of Maynard and Philip Currie. (Bertram Wodehouse Currie, *Recollections, Letters and Journals,* 2 vols., Roehampton, 1901.)

a. George Wodehouse (1826–87), heir to Raikes Currie's interest in Glyn, Mills, Currie & Co, but finding the business tiresome, retired from partnership in 1864; in 1850 m. Elizabeth Vernon, da. of Mr Vernon Smith, later Lord Lyveden. Kimberley wrote upon his cousin's death that he was 'a clever man, excellent in business, who wasted his life and talents'.

b. Bertram Wodehouse (1827–96), partner in Glyn, Mills, Currie & Co. from 1852; almost immediately his father began to withdraw from active affairs of the bank, with Bertram becoming effectively the managing partner; in 1860 m. Caroline Louisa Young, da. of Sir

W. L. Young; member of the Council of India, 1880–95; in the 1890s Gladstone considered him the foremost City authority on banking matters; represented England at the International Monetary Conference in Brussels, 1892; served on Indian Finance Committee, 1893; a firm Liberal and good friend of Kimberley; converted to Roman Catholicism shortly before his death.

c. Maynard Wodehouse (1829–87), educ. at Eton and Cambridge; inherited from his grandmother £5,000 (initially intended for Bertram), on condition that he become a clergyman; appointed to the living of Mentmore by Baron Meyer Rothschild in 1858; and then as rector of Hingham, Norfolk, by Lord Kimberley in 1873; in the following year he m. Lady Mary Cadogan. Kimberley in his journal called him an 'excellent good kind creature, & most active clergyman'.

d. Philip Henry Wodehouse (1834–1906), educ. Eton; joined the Foreign Office as a clerk in 1854, and steadily rose through the ranks; attached to Kimberley's mission staffs in St Petersburg, 1856–7, and in Berlin and Copenhagen, 1863–4; sec. to Salisbury on diplomatic missions to Constantinople, 1876 and Berlin, 1878; asst. u.-sec. at the Foreign Office, 1882–9; perm. u.-sec. at the Foreign Office, 1889–93; amb. to Turkey, 1893–8, to Italy, 1898–1903; cr. Baron Currie of Hawley, 1899; m. 1894, Mary Montgomerie Singleton, whose first husband had died in 1893, and who often wrote under the pseudonym 'Violet Fane'.

EDITORIAL NOTE

The Kimberley Journal is herein fully transcribed. As Kimberley ordinarily wrote in a clear hand, there have been relatively few problems of transcription. The following considerations should, however, be noted:

1. The form and order of the dating has been regularised. This has involved sometimes changing the order of day and month, and sometimes adding the year, to produce the uniform style – '24 May 1864'. Days of the week have not been included unless noted by Kimberley. Because Kimberley often wrote up 'daily' entries after some days had elapsed, he occasionally misdated them. Conflicting days and dates have been adjusted where positive evidence allows.

2. Punctuation and form have in some cases been regularised. Kimberley wrote quickly, and usually with little regard for punctuation. Sentences often end, for instance, with something more like a dash than a full stop, though the latter almost certainly was intended. Also, it is impossible always to determine when a new paragraph was intended. These have sometimes been introduced, but only when the subject matter seems clearly so to dictate.

3. Editorial comment regarding the integrity of the text has been included in brackets. Excisions, particularly for the period 1869–74, have required a certain amount of in-text editorial comment. Also, where ink blots or unreadable words or phrases remain, these have been noted with an in-text – [ill.]

4. Original spellings have been retained. These often reflect conventions of earlier ages, particularly with regard to foreign-language names. Kimberley sometimes misspelled proper names – 'Faussett' for 'Fawcett', 'Jowitt' for Jowett' – usually at a first meeting; he often corrected them in later references. Proper spellings and modern transliterations have been included in the notes.

With regard to notes, every effort has been made to identify persons mentioned in the Journal. Frequently, however, a surname alone has not been sufficient in the context of the entry to make a positive identification. In such cases we have avoided speculation. References to *Hansard* and the *Gladstone Diaries* which are clearly suggested by the dating of Kimberley's own Journal have not been included unless some clarification or substantive issue has required it.

ABBREVIATIONS

a.d.c., aide-de-camp
amb., ambassador
archbp., archbishop
atty. genl., Attorney General
bp., bishop
ch. d. of Lanc., Chancellor of the Duchy of Lancaster
ch. exch., Chancellor of the Exchequer
ch. poor law com., Chairman of the Poor Law Commission
ch. sec. Ireland, Chief Secretary for Ireland
col. sec., Secretary of State for the Colonies
com. works, Commissioner of Works
Cons., Conservative
cr., created
d., died
da., daughter
dep., deputy
dir., director
ed., editor
1st ld. adm., First Lord of the Admiralty
for. sec., Secretary of State for Foreign Affairs
gov., governor
gov.-genl., governor-general
home sec., Secretary of State for the Home Department
India sec., Secretary of State for India
insp.-genl., Inspector-General
judge adv.-genl., Judge Advocate-General
Lib., Liberal
Lib. U., Liberal Unionist
ld. chanc., Lord Chancellor
ld. lt. Ireland, Lord Lieutenant of Ireland
ld. pres. coun., Lord President of the Council
ld. privy seal, Lord Privy Seal
m., married
min., minister
MP, member of parliament
parlt., parliamentary
perm., permanent
post.-genl., Postmaster-General

pr. min., Prime Minister
pres., president
pres. b. of. t., President of the Board of Trade
pres. b. of. c., President of the Board of Control
priv., private
prof., professor
r., reign
Rad., Radical
R.C., Roman Catholic
s., son
succ., succeeded
treas., treasury
u.-sec., under-secretary
war sec., Secretary of State for War

SOURCES

I. Manuscript Sources

AP	Asquith Papers, Bodleian Library
BP	Bright Papers, British Library
BrP	Bruce Papers, Trinity College Library, Dublin
CBP	Campbell-Bannerman Papers, British Library
CdP	Cardwell Papers, Public Record Office
CfJ	Carlingford Journal, British Library
CfP	Carlingford Papers, Somerset Record Office
ChP	Chamberlain Papers, Birmingham University Library
ClP	Clarendon Papers, Bodleian Library
CO	Colonial Office Files, Public Record Office
CP	Currie Papers, Royal Bank of Scotland Archive
CrP	Cromer Papers, Public Record Office
CtP	Courtney Papers, British Library of Political and Economic Science
CvP	Carnarvon Papers, Public Record Office
CwP	Cranworth Papers, Suffolk Record Office
CzP	Curzon Papers, India Office Library
DfP	Dufferin Papers, India Office Library
DkP	Dilke Papers, British Library
DP	Derby Papers, Liverpool Record Office
DvP	Devonshire Papers, Chatsworth, Derbyshire
GBP	Great Britain Papers (Political), Perkins Library, Duke University
GDP	Grant Duff Papers, India Office Library
GP	Gladstone Papers, British Library

GrP	Granville Papers, Public Record Office
HBP	Hicks-Beach Papers, Gloucester Record Office
HfP	Halifax Papers, Borthwick Institute of Historical Research
HGP	Herbert Gladstone Papers, British Library
HmP	Hammond Papers, Public Record Office
HP	Harcourt Papers, Bodleian Library
HrP	Herbert Papers, Public Record Office
KP1	Kimberley Papers, Norfolk Record Office
KP2	Kimberley Papers, National Library of Scotland
KP3	Kimberley Papers, British Library
KP4	Kimberley Papers, Public Archives of Canada
KP5	Kimberley Papers, Cornwall Record Office
KP6	Kimberley Papers, Bodleian Library
KP7	Kimberley Papers, Mr. R.C. Fiske (privately held)
LcP	Larcom Papers, National Library of Ireland
LP	Lansdowne Papers, India Office Library
MBP	Monk Bretton Papers, Bodleian Library
MgP	Musgrave Papers, Perkins Library, Duke University
MlP	Malet Papers, Public Record Office
MP	Morley Papers, India Office Library
MtP	Minto Papers, India Office Library
NP	Northbrook Papers, India Office Library
NtP	Norton Papers, Birmingham Central Libraries
OP	Overstone Papers, University of London Library
PkP	Packe Papers, Leicestershire Record Office
PP	Palmerston Papers, Southampton University Library
RlP	Russell Papers, Public Record Office
RP	Ripon Papers, British Library
RPD	Ripon Papers, Perkins Library, Duke University

RsP   Rosebery Papers, National Library of Scotland

SdP   Sanderson Papers, Public Record Office

SP   Spencer Papers, British Library

WO   War Office Files, Public Record Office

WP   Welby Papers, British Library of Economic and Political
         Science

II. Printed Sources

CJ   A.B. Cooke and J.R. Vincent (eds.), *Lord
                              Carlingford's Journal: Reflections of a Cabinet
                              Minister 1885* (Oxford, 1971)

DD1   John Vincent (ed.), *Disraeli, Derby and the
                              Conservative Party: Journals and Memoirs of
                              Edward Henry, Lord Stanley 1849–1869*
                              (Brighton, 1978)

DD2   John Vincent (ed.), *A Selection from the
                              Diaries of Edward Henry Stanley, 15th Earl of
                              Derby (1826–93) Between September 1869 and
                              March 1878* (London, 1994)

DD3   John Vincent (ed.), *The Later Derby Diaries:
                              Home Rule, Liberal Unionism and Aristocratic
                              Life in Late Victorian England* (Bristol, 1981)

DNB   *Dictionary of National Biography*

EHJ1   D.W.R. Bahlman (ed.), *The Diary of Sir
                              Edward Walter Hamilton 1880–1885* (2 vols.,
                              Oxford, 1972)

EHJ2   David Brooks (ed.), *The Destruction of Lord
                              Rosebery, From the Diary of Sir Edward Ham-
                              ilton 1894–1895 (London, 1986)*

EHJ3   D.W.R. Bahlman (ed.), *The Diary of Sir
                              Edward Walter Hamilton 1885–1906* (Hull,
                              1993)

Gladstone Diaries   M.R.D. Foot and H.C.G. Matthew (eds.),
                              The Gladstone Diaries (14 vols., Oxford
                              1968–94)

Gladstone–Granville
Corresp. 1

Agatha Ramm (ed.), *The Political Correspondence of Mr Gladstone and Lord Granville, 1868–1876* (2 vols., London, 1952)

Gladstone–Granville
Corresp. 2

Agatha Ramm (ed.), *The Political Correspondence of Mr Gladstone and Lord Granville 1876–1886* (2 vols., Oxford, 1962)

Governing Passion

A.B. Cooke and J.R. Vincent, *The Governing Passion: Cabinet Government and Party Politics in Britain 1885–86* (Brighton, 1974)

JE

Ethel Drus (ed.), *A Journal of Events during the Gladstone Ministry 1868–74* (London, 1958)

Liberal by Principle

John Powell (ed.), *Liberal by Principle: The Politics of John Wodehouse, 1st Earl of Kimberley, 1843–1902* (London, 1996)

Notes from a Diary

Mountstuart Grant Duff, *Notes from a Diary* (14 vols., London 1877–1905)

PMP: Gladstone

John Brooke and Mary Sorenson (eds.), *The Prime Minister's Papers: W.E. Gladstone* (4 vols., London, 1971–81)

INTRODUCTION

The first Earl of Kimberley's career is conventionally seen as one thread in the fading pattern of late-Victorian Whig politics. The loyal and able Kimberley, who though talkative talked well, was a permanent feature of Gladstone's[1] governments and his public life is usually woven around those ministerial Whigs, such as Lords Ripon,[2] Clarendon,[3] Spencer[4] and Hartington,[5] who gave administrative weight and social prestige to successive Liberal ministries. Kimberley's historical fate has been to be seen as a capable, obedient, rather dull Whig cypher in Gladstone's calculations. But, in truth, Kimberley was a landed Liberal. Heir to a Tory barony and converted to Liberalism at Eton, neither by blood nor by belief was he part of the Whig brotherhood. Both his career and his Journal are of greater interest and importance than the conventional portrayal of Kimberley would suggest.

John Wodehouse, first Earl of Kimberley, was born in 1826 into the Norfolk Tory gentry. The eldest son of an apolitical father who died when he was eight years old, Wodehouse was a decidedly independent youth, adopting Liberal principles at Eton 'purely from conviction' (6 May 1862). With the death of his grandfather, the second Baron Wodehouse, in 1846, John Wodehouse succeeded to the barony (thereby losing his chance of a Commons career) and in the following year took a first in Classics at Christ Church, Oxford. In 1847, with the help of his uncle and mentor he was introduced to the political world. His first significant involvement was as financial member for the Society for the Reform of Colonial Government, an organisation which included 'men

---

[1] William Gladstone (1809–98), Cons. MP for Newark, 1832, 1835, 1837, 1841–5; Peelite MP for Oxford University, 1847–65; Lib. MP for S. Lancashire, 1865–8, for Greenwich, 1868–80, for Midlothian, 1880–95; Lib. ch. exch., 1852–5, 1859–66, 1873–4, 1880–2; pr. min., 1868–74, 1880–5, 1886, 1892–4.

[2] George Frederick Samuel Robinson (1827–1909), 3rd Earl deGrey, 1859; 1st Marquess of Ripon, 1871; war sec., 1863–6; Indian sec., 1866; ld. pres. counc., 1868–73; Indian viceroy, 1880–4; 1st ld. adm., 1886; col. sec., 1892–5.

[3] George William Frederick Villiers, 4th Earl of Clarendon (1800–70), pres. b. of t., 1846–7; ld. lt. of Ireland, 1847–52; for. sec., 1853–8, 1865–6, 1868–70.

[4] John Poyntz Spencer (1835–1910), styled Viscount Althorp, 1847–57, when he suc. as 5th Earl Spencer, Lib. MP for Northamptonshire, 1857; ld. lt. Ireland, 1868–74, 1882–5; ld. pres. counc., 1880–3, 1886; 1st ld. adm., 1892–5; suc. Kimberley as Lib. leader in the Lords, 1902–5; suc. Kimberley as Lib. leader in the Lords, 1902–5.

[5] Spencer Compton Cavendish, Marquess of Hartington (1857–70), Lib. MP for N. Lancashire, 1857–68, for Radnor Boroughs, 1869–80, for Lancashire N.E., 1880–5, for Lancashire N.E., Rossendale, 1885; Lib. U. MP for Rossendale, 1886–91, when he succ. as 8th Duke of Devonshire; u.-sec. war, 1863–6; war sec., 1866, 1882–5; post. genl., 1868–71; ch. sec. Ireland, 1871–4; Indian sec., 1880–2; ld. pres. counc. 1895–1903.

of all parties' (6 May 1862). Then in 1852 he was appointed under-secretary to the Foreign Office in the Aberdeen coalition government, and principal government spokesman on foreign affairs in the Lords.[6]

Following this auspicious beginning, aged twenty-six, Wodehouse was never far from the centre of political activity. His career was both long and full of important posts. From the time he joined Aberdeen's ministry, he was included in every Liberal government of the last half of the nineteenth century, ending his official career as foreign secretary in Rosebery's ministry (1894–5). In between he served as Minister Plenipotentiary to St Petersburg (1856–58), Lord Lieutenant of Ireland (1864–6), Lord Privy Seal (1868–70), Colonial Secretary (1870–4, 1880–2) and Indian Secretary (1882–5, 1886, 1892–4). Hardly less important with regard to the Kimberley Journal was his service as Liberal leader in the House of Lords (1891–4, 1896–1902).

THE KIMBERLEY ARCHIVE

From the beginning of his political career Kimberley carefully preserved his papers and from 1862 he kept a private journal (hereafter, Kimberley Journal). Just before his death he had thought it best to prohibit publication of any papers for at least fifty years. He nevertheless occasionally allowed edited letters to be published and left the matter after his death entirely to his son's discretion.[7] With a heightened sense of the delicacy of his father's work, in 1901 the second earl refused Lady Dufferin's request to publish letters related to her husband's Indian Viceroyalty.[8] Five years later he did permit Lord Rosebery to read and take notes from a Memoir which Kimberley had written late in life.[9]

The Kimberley archive remained intact and closed to research until 1948, when Lt. Col. G.E. Malet of the National Register of Archives assisted a young South African doctoral candidate, Ethel Drus, in gaining access. At Kimberley Hall she found the papers packed in

[6] On Kimberley's background and early political career see *Liberal by Principle*, 7–24.

[7] Kimberley to Spencer Childers, 20 July 1900, KP1 15/K2/21.

[8] 2nd Earl of Kimberley to Spencer, 20 October 1902, SP K372; cf. A. Lyall, *Life of the Marquis of Dufferin and Ava* (London, 1905). Frederick Temple Hamilton-Temple, 1st Marquess of Dufferin and Ava (1826–1902), had been a contemporary of Kimberley at both Eton and Christ Church, Oxford, gov.-gen. Canada, 1872–8; amb. to St Petersburg, 1879–81; to Constantinople, 1881–4; Indian Viceroy, 1884–8; amb. to Rome, 1889–91; to Paris, 1891–6.

[9] Rosebery to 2nd Earl of Kimberley, 26 October 1906 RP 10120 fols. 33–4. Archibald Philip Primrose (1847–1929), styled Lord Dalmeny, 1851–68, when he suc. as 5th Earl of Rosebery; u.-sec. home office, 1881–3; ld. privy seal and 1st comm. works, 1885; for. sec., 1886, 1892–4; pr. min., 1894–5.

metal boxes, neatly arranged and labelled by the first earl. Among them was a large envelope containing the 'Journal of Events during the Gladstone Ministry' which she subsequently edited for the Royal Historical Society (hereafter, 'Journal of Events').[10]

The break up of the Kimberley archive also began around 1948, when Kimberley's private correspondence as Minister to Russia (1856–8) was acquired by the British Library. In 1972 Kimberley's political in-letters for the period 1891–1901 were sold and eventually found their way into the National Library of Scotland. Later that year a large collection of papers relating to Kimberley's Falmouth property was deposited in the Cornwall Record Office. In 1974 the Norfolk Record Office acquired most of Kimberley's unofficial papers – enough to fill fifteen boxes – including family papers, some early political correspondence and an extensive journal devoted to his reading, kept continuously between 1847 and 1902 (hereafter, Reading Journal). When the remaining Kimberley papers, including most of those associated with his Cabinet career, were being prepared for sale at Sotheby's in 1991, two substantial lots, relating principally to personal property and estate management, and several smaller lots containing letters patent and other collectibles, were auctioned separately.[11] So although the Kimberley archive is now dispersed, each part is accessible and together form an impressive and well-rounded record of a nineteenth-century political life.

THE KIMBERLEY JOURNAL

Among the papers acquired by the Bodleian Library in December 1991 was Kimberley's extensive Journal, kept in five notebooks quarter bound in burgundy leather with marbled boards, and catalogued at the Bodleian Library as:

Ms.Eng.e.2790 (10.9 cm × 18.5 cm) 28 Apr. 1862–10 Oct. 1864 184 leaves
Ms.Eng.e.2791 (11.1 cm × 17.9 cm) 11 Oct. 1864–20 Jul. 1869 236 leaves
Ms.Eng.e.2792 (11.1 cm × 17.8 cm) 11 Aug. 1869–19 Apr. 1881 208 leaves
Ms.Eng.e.2793 (11.3 cm × 17.8 cm) 28 Apr. 1881–7 Sept. 1896 239 leaves
Ms.Eng.e.2794 (11.3 cm × 17.8 cm) 8 Oct. 1896–10 Jan. 1902 248 leaves

Characterised in the Bodleian's catalogue as a 'diary', they are perhaps better described as a journal. Although the notebooks themselves carry

---

[10] Ethel Drus, 'A Journal of Events during the Gladstone Ministry 1868–1874 by John, First Earl of Kimberley', *Camden Miscellany*, 3rd ser., XXI, 1–49.
[11] On the sale see J. Powell, 'Kimberley's Diamonds', *History Today*, March 1992, 3.

no title, Kimberley referred in a later transcription to his 'journal of events', an appellation borne out by the varied nature of the entries.

Kimberley's Journal is comprised of three parts, each reflecting a different phase in his career:

1) *Autobiographical sketch.* Eight days after the first entry of 28 April 1862, Kimberley appended a 'sketch' of his life to that point, which ran to seventy-two manuscript pages, about 4% of the total number of words. Here he briefly recounted the main features of his education, early political training and activity prior to entering Aberdeen's government in 1852. The years as under-secretary at the Foreign Office are mentioned only in passing, perhaps because they were already well documented in official and private sources. The bulk of the sketch is devoted to personalities and activities associated with his ministry to Russia between 1856 and 1858.

2) *Pre-Cabinet entries.* Running from 28 April 1862 until 7 December 1868, when Gladstone offered him the Privy Seal, these entries comprise some 39% of the total number of words. During this period he was ambitious and striving for an invitation into the charmed circle of the Cabinet. As one of the few really active members of the House of Lords, and with more than a decade of government service behind him, Kimberley was in this period close enough to the world of high politics to muse intelligently about them, yet distant enough still to draw a convincing portrait of the extensive political network operating below the cabinet. This part of the journal is highlighted by two unusually comprehensive sections dealing with:

   a. *The special mission to Berlin and Copenhagen.* Between 3 Dec. 1863 and 13 Jan. 1864, when Kimberley kept a daily account of his activities and conversations.

   b. *The Irish Viceroyalty.* From Palmerston's offer of the office on 27 September 1864 until he left Ireland on 17 July 1866, Kimberley kept particularly good records chronicling the relationship between Liberal politics and Irish government. Approximately 11% of the entire Journal is devoted to this period.

3) *Entries after joining the Cabinet.* Running from 7 December 1868 until the final entry of 10 January 1902, three months before his death, these entries comprise approximately 57% of the total number of words.

Although there was no physical alteration in the Journal, the nature of the entries did change. Kimberley is better informed and more cautious from 1869 onward, clearly conscious of the increased importance of his record, and less inclined to record impressions simply as a matter of course. There was a period of transition, when he struggled to find the proper balance between discretion and the need for a record, leading to the striking through of many passages, and the literal excision of many others. For instance, Kimberley removed the first twelve manuscript pages, covering entries for 20 July to 11 August 1869, from the third volume of his journal; and excised some thirty-one of the seventy-two manuscript pages for the whole of 1871. After 1873 excisions are rare, suggesting that he had by then established certain standards for determining what should be included.

It is difficult to say exactly why Kimberley began his journal in 1862. The nature of the entries suggests that it was meant principally as a practical *aide-memoir*. Only with the passage of the major legislation of Gladstone's first ministry did he sense that his record might be important to posterity. In beginning a journal, Kimberley joined in an activity common to many members of both the middle and upper classes. He was well aware of the importance of record-keeping generally. It was of the utmost value in business, he knew, having spent almost twenty years unravelling the financial mess left by his grandfather. In five-and-a-half years as under-secretary at the Foreign Office, and two as minister plenipotentiary in Russia, he had become thoroughly familiar with the uses of varied political records – reports, despatches, circulars, official letters and private letters – each having its own particular purpose.[12] He never could quite convince himself, however, as Gladstone and many others did, that a journal was necessary to moral improvement, and thus he was not committed to accounting for his time. This befits a philosophical utilitarian who believed in the beneficial power of government, who went to extraordinary lengths in doing his official work, but who never went back on what he had done, or asked himself if he might have done better. 'I am satisfied when I have done the very best I could under the circumstances. Perhaps I may say to myself I might have done better, but that doesn't now matter ... It is futile to be crying over the past and I never do it.'[13] With this attitude Kimberley could no more have produced the meticulously detailed Gladstone

---

[12] See, for instance, Kimberley's preparation of 'notes' as well as official despatches and letters while in St Petersburg. Wodehouse to Clarendon, 5 September 1856, KP3 46692, f. 82; also 2 Jan. 1858, KP3 46694, f. 43. The inability of some to produce records also caused problems. See Henry Fitzroy to Wodehouse, 3 Dec. 1853, KP6 MS c.3996, f. 142; also, his record and analysis of Russian finances in E. P. O'Brien (ed.) *Correspondence of Lord Overstone* (3 vols., Cambridge, 1971), II, 750–3.

[13] *Free Lance*, 19 April 1902, c.4484, f. 141.

diary, than Gladstone could have left the gaping holes found in the Kimberley Journal. An essential personality difference is imprinted on every phase of their political lives, from the speeches they wrote, to their means of persuasion and the nature of the journals they kept. In its most elemental form, this distinction can even be found in responses to ordinary events such as the Academy Dinner of 1871, which Kimberley pronounced a 'dismal piece of formal humbug', but which Gladstone found delightful.[14]

The Journal was characteristic of other attempts which Kimberley made at recording his personal views. After marrying in 1847 he kept a Reading Journal in which he faithfully noted titles, publishing information and reflections on his readings. Occasionally he would introduce contemporary events and people, but in the main he dealt with ideas. In the early years Kimberley's record was systematic and comparative, a deliberate attempt to overcome what he perceived as the deficiencies of an Oxford education for a man of ambition entering practical politics.[15] From 1852, however, having finally attained an official position, Kimberley's Reading Journal became principally a listing of what he read, usually accompanied by general assessments, and only occasionally recounting the active engagement with specific passages in the texts which had been characteristic earlier. The minimal record became the pattern and is consistent with other evidence in suggesting that Kimberley's political mind had been made early. Though he continued to record his reading until shortly before his death in 1902, leaving behind a remarkable and instructive record, it was not the record he originally had set out to produce. Similarly, in 1848 he began keeping a commonplace book, but within three years virtually abandoned it, before starting another in 1886 which met with a similar fate.[16] So it was that the Journal, which began as a fairly comprehensive record of his activities, evolved into a more eclectic document, less disciplined, less necessary, but more enjoyable to the author. He set out to produce the journal which he imagined he should, but ended forty years later with the one which reflected his own philosophy of life, with all its strengths and weaknesses.

Although in his Journal Kimberley never strayed from the framework of contemporary events, he generously supplemented this record with historical reflections, political assessments and personal vignettes, a pattern which he would maintain throughout his life. A conversation at a Board of Guardians meeting, for instance, in which it was reported

---

[14] 29 April 1871; *Gladstone Diaries*, VII: 488. Gladstone himself pondered the value of his obsession. See, for instance, the end of vol. VI.

[15] *Liberal by Principle*, 10–11, 12.

[16] See KP1 15/K2/7, 12.

that Gladstone was responsible for Dr Thomson's appointment as Archbishop of York, prompted him to note 'some causes connected with the removal of Sir A. Buchanan' from Madrid during the previous year (10 November 1862). Lord Blachford's death in 1889 reminded him 'of an important era' in his political life, when he took up the seals of the Colonial Office in 1870, and Argyll's death eleven years later caused him to reflect upon his former colleague's lack of influence in Cabinet, and a conversation with Granville upon the matter (1 December 1889, 25 April 1900). In a few cases what appear to be 'daily' entries were in fact accounts written some days later, based upon memory, and perhaps following a look at appointment notebooks, letters and memoranda (see 12 February 1872). Sometimes events occurring over several days were conflated into a single entry without precise dating, and memoranda covering significant periods of time were not uncommon.[17] As a result, days and dates throughout the Journal must be handled with care, though they are in the main accurate.

Apart from the heightened caution regarding Cabinet affairs, the nature of the Journal remained fairly consistent, though the frequency of entries did change. Until the mid 1860s, Kimberley averaged three or four entries per week. After returning from Ireland in 1866, he often maintained this pace during weeks of political activity, but would otherwise allow weeks, and occasionally months, to pass unnoticed. With the press of Cabinet business, the number of entries declined during Gladstone's first administration, though individual entries tended to be longer. The continuation of the Journal at one point seemed in doubt when, uncertain of his political future, disgusted with Tory politics, and having trouble with his eldest son, he made only twenty-one entries in the twenty-nine months between August 1875 and January 1878. After the 1870s, however, he never made fewer than twenty-two entries in a year. For the entire period between 1880 and 1901, he averaged thirty-eight entries per year, predictably concentrated in the first eight months of the year.

THE KIMBERLEY JOURNAL, 'JOURNAL OF EVENTS', AND MEMOIR

Before the sale of the Kimberley papers in 1991 scholars had a reasonably clear view of Kimberley as a departmental administrator, based upon extensive contemporary materials – official records, press reports and significant collections of out-letters, principally to Gladstone,

---

[17] See 15 July 1874, 9 June 1885, 28 June 1885, 18 Aug. 1898.

Clarendon, Russell,[18] Rosebery and Ripon. The letters had a good deal
to say about politics, but still made it difficult to place Kimberley within
a broader context in which bills and elections most often marked the
boundaries of political achievement. Never having competed for a seat
or initiated popular domestic legislation, Kimberley's position in the
Cabinet was by default taken as a reflection of his departmental
competence. This perception was noticeably altered when Ethel Drus
edited Kimberley's relatively brief 'Journal of Events during the Gladstone Ministry' (1958), a fresh 'contemporary' document which demonstrated that Kimberley had been more active in the general business
of the Cabinet than was previously imagined. Presenting Kimberley as
legislative draftsman, inter-party negotiator, and frequent opponent of
Gladstone's foreign and colonial policy, the 'Journal of Events' quickly
became an important source for understanding the process of Cabinet
government during Gladstone's first ministry.

The 'Journal of Events' has been taken to be, as Drus suggested, the
'political diary kept by the first Earl of Kimberley' during Gladstone's
first ministry.[19] This would not necessarily be inconsistent with Kimberley's own admission at the beginning of the 110-page document that
it was 'partly a copy of a Journal which I kept' while in office.[20] But in
fact it was 'partly a copy' in two senses which together undermine the
idea that it was contemporary with the first ministry. First, he copied
only part of the original; second, he added fresh material to the copied
portions. With access to the original journals, we can now see that the
'Journal of Events' was not a contemporary record, but rather a
document written several years later, which reflected the image which
Kimberley wished to leave for posterity, of a ministry which would 'fill
a not unimportant page in English history'.[21] Nor was the 'Journal of
Events' his final 'recollection', for late in life he actually prepared a
Memoir, which differed from both the Kimberley Journal and the
'Journal of Events'.

There were, then, three autobiographical accounts of Kimberley's
life and career, each having its own character and significance as
evidence.

1)   *The Kimberley Journal*, written between 1862 and 1902; comprised
substantially of entries recorded on the day of experience, but heavily

---

[18] Lord John Russell (1792–1878), cr. 1st Earl Russell, 1861; pr. min. 1846–52, 1865–6;
for. sec., 1852–3, 1859–65.
[19] *JE*, vii.
[20] *JE*, 1.
[21] The latter phrase is not present in the Kimberley Journal. Cf. *JE*, 44.

excised for the period of the first Gladstone ministry, occasionally emended and generously supplemented with recollections throughout.

2) *The 'Journal of Events'*, written between 1875 and 1877; based closely upon the Journal, including some verbatim transcriptions, though most entries were at least minimally reworked; passages excised from the Kimberley Journal were revised for inclusion and material added on the basis of memory or other forms of evidence.

3) *The Kimberley Memoir*, mostly written after 1895; a 1,000-page manuscript autobiography based closely on the Journal and including some verbatim entries; included much that had not been written either in the Kimberley Journal or in 'Journal of Events', including direct quotations of conversations occurring decades earlier. The unpublished Memoir has now disappeared, but has been partially preserved in extracts which Rosebery took in 1906 (see Appendix).

Had any one of the three versions of Kimberley's recollections survived alone, it would have been taken as essentially authoritative; as was the 'Journal of Events' so long as it seemed to be the only record left by Kimberley. It is now possible, however, to compare these separate accounts and to assess the particular value of each.

On first reading one is struck by the similarities between the Kimberley Journal and the 'Journal of Events': the Cabinet reports and accounts of parliamentary manoeuvre, reports of Kimberley's multifaceted role as parliamentary handyman, and Cabinet division over colonial and foreign affairs. There are, however, significant differences which subtly alter one's perception of Kimberley, his Cabinet colleagues, and the process of Cabinet government. Although the Kimberley Journal and the 'Journal of Events' are roughly the same length for the period of Gladstone's first ministry, they are substantially different in composition. For instance, Kimberley usually omitted from the 'Journal of Events' material related to his family and estates, routine travel, Norfolk politics and royalty. Kimberley also substantially reduced the number and length of Cabinet reports. The length of these omissions was compensated for, principally, by a dozen extensive reminiscences, reflecting in greater detail Kimberley's role or viewpoint on matters suggested by brief entries, but which were clearly written years later and were often dated.[22]

These later reminiscences change somewhat the character of the

---

[22] See 8 May 1869, 24 Oct. 1869, 14 Dec. 1869, 2 March 1870, 30 June 1870, 13 June 1871, 5 Aug. 1871, 20 April 1872, 25 June 1872, 9 Jan. 1873, 24 May 1873, 6 Sept. 1873.

chronicle, but are for the most part harmlessly transparent. The omissions, on the other hand, are invisible and thus more dangerous. The most important ones have to do with the Cabinet. Accepting the Privy Seal and joining Gladstone's cabinet, Kimberley determined to 'make no note' of what took place there (16 December 1868). He soon abandoned this resolution. Perhaps because he understood the Journal to be a private record for his own use, he eventually gave some account of about sixty Cabinet meetings between 1868 and 1874 (about 25% of the total number of Cabinets). By the end of the first ministry Kimberley knew that he had been part of an historic government. The 'Journal of Events' appears to have been a first attempt at preparing a public account of his life, which such historical importance suggested.

The most delicate operation which Kimberley faced was balancing honesty and the ministry's claims of importance with the potential dangers of revelation. Not surprisingly, accounts of Cabinet deliberations posed the most difficult problem, for they were supposed to be secret, an injunction which Kimberley himself acknowledged as he began his Journal. As a result, only 20% of Cabinet reports included in the original Journal were incorporated into the 'Journal of Events' without significant change. The more sensitive ones he dealt with in one of two ways. First, he completely omitted at least 30% of his private Cabinet minutes from the 'Journal of Events'. In some cases these can now be restored. Often, however, when Kimberley considered material too sensitive, he literally excised it from his original journal, removing anywhere from one line to as many as twelve consecutive pages, or occasionally heavily striking through lines. The most common method of transferring the material, utilised in about half the original Cabinet accounts, was to edit and smoothly rewrite the entry into the 'Journal of Events' before excising unwanted information from the Journal. This leaves the impression in the 'Journal of Events' that entries were full and original, while in fact they were carefully edited, based upon later considerations.[23] Closely related to the sanctity of Cabinet discussion was Kimberley's concern lest he betray the confidence of his Cabinet colleagues, and he therefore sometimes excised sources of information, even when the issues at stake were not strictly related to Cabinet business (see 29 June 1870 and 2 March 1872).

[23] See 29 May 1870, 30 Sept. 1870, 2 Nov. 1870, 27 April 1871, 31 Oct. 1871, 20 April 1872, 26 July 1873. Tantalising clues to the excised material remain. On 8 February 1869, for instance, Kimberley recounted long Cabinet discussions on the Irish Church bill, where no 'violent difference of opinion arise', reported almost verbatim in the 'Journal of Events'. In Kimberley's original journal entry, he continued that Lowe had complained at the end of the Monday Cabinet, 'in a very bitter tone that we had ...'. Not only does Kimberley not tell us in the 'Journal of Events' what Lowe's complaint was, he excises some twelve lines from his Journal so that we may never know.

In preparing his Journal for possible publication Kimberley was also concerned that he might have been unfair in his judgements. Later obituaries were to note Kimberley's confession that he was 'naturally impulsive', a phrase most scholars have taken as a mock admission which rendered his unquestioned self-control all the more impressive.[24] In fact, the Journal demonstrates that he sometimes did question the fairness of what he thought and wrote at a given moment.[25] On a number of occasions he altered or omitted opinions of political figures, though it is not always clear what standards he employed in doing so.[26] Kimberley was more sceptical of Gladstone's leadership than the 'Journal of Events' suggests, describing in the Journal the prime minister's 'habitual austereness' and expressing surprise when Gladstone was 'not on his high horse'.[27] Kimberley was at the time also more concerned about Granville's deficiencies than the 'Journal of Events' suggests.[28] There he straightforwardly expressed his reservations, but probably considered a single collective criticism sufficient to cover a number of individual ones which he had originally recorded.[29] Lowe was significantly, though not totally, written out of the 'Journal of Events'.[30] This probably reflected a combination of factors, including Lowe's declining reputation, and Kimberley's wish both to distance himself from his cantankerous colleague and gently to protect a good friend.[31] Critiques of lesser figures were sometimes omitted as well, probably as irrelevant to the ministry rather than as untrue. The gist of Kimberley's alterations is quietly to suggest a more unified and harmonious Cabinet than actually existed, and thus incidentally to enhance Gladstone's reputation for reconciling party differences.

It is impossible to make the same kinds of comparisons between the

---

[24] *DNB* 23:698.

[25] Cf. entries, for instance, on the Irish, 24 March and 1 April 1866; also see his omission in the 'Journal of Events' of Malmesbury in his list of 25 June 1872.

[26] See 8 Feb. 1869, 20 July 1869, 21 Sept. 1869, 29 May 1870, 14 Feb. 1871, 29 April 1871, 26 July 1873.

[27] See 20 July 1869, 10 July 1873.

[28] Granville George Leveson-Gower, 2nd Earl Granville (1815–91), for. sec., 1851–2, 1870–4, 1880–5; ld. pres. coun., 1852–4, 1859–66; amb. ext. to Russia, 1856; col. sec., 1868–70, 1886.

[29] See 19 June 1869, 7 July 1869, 1 June 1872, 6 Feb. 1873.

[30] Cf. 'Journal of Events' with Journal entries for 4 Feb. 1869, 8 Feb. 1869, 19 April 1869, 21 Sept. 1869, 29 June 1870, 16 Feb. 1874. Robert Lowe (1811–92), educ. Winchester, Univ. College, Oxford; practised law and politics in Australia, 1842–50; returned to London, 1850 as leader-writer for *The Times*; Lib. MP for Kidderminster, 1852–9, for Calne, 1859–67, for London U., 1868–80, when cr. Viscount Sherbrooke; v.p. bd. of trade and paymst.-genl. 1855–8; v.p. com. of council on educ., 1859–64; chanc. exch., 1868–73; home sec., 1873–4.

[31] *Liberal by Principle*, 41, 139. On the general political distancing from Lowe, see R. Shannon, *Gladstone and the Bulgarian Agitation, 1876* (2nd edn, Hassocks, 1975), 118.

original Journal and the Memoir, Kimberley's final attempt at preparing a record for posterity. We now have only the 104 brief extracts which Rosebery took when reading the 'autobiography' in 1906. Some of Rosebery's extracts were summaries of Kimberley's narrative, but many incorporated direct quotes. Despite the limitations imposed by this incomplete record, there are a number of conclusions which may be drawn. First, even in the 1890s, Kimberley never intended to produce an original work. As in the case of the 'Journal of Events', he adhered closely to the Journal as a framework for his Memoir, and occasionally cited material verbatim. Second, the Memoir clearly included material which had never been a part of either the Journal or the 'Journal of Events'. Among the added material reminiscence was prominent. This befits a memoir, but calls into question the degree to which the record can be relied upon as 'contemporary'. In the Memoir Kimberley reflects that on 17 April 1886:

Gladstone sent up a note to the H. of Lords to ask if I would agree to a possible retention of the Irish members at Westminster. With great misgivings I gave way. I have never ceased to regret my weakness on this occasion. Subsequent events proved that I had underestimated my influence with our chief.[32]

This is quite different from the account given in the Journal, where Kimberley seems to have been satisfied that the Government had adopted the best course under the circumstances:

Harcourt ...[33] is now very angry at Gladstone having left open a door to possible reconsideration of the exclusion of Irish members from the H. of Commons. This was done after consulting myself amongst others. Much as I desire to get rid of the Irish members, who are like a cancer eating away our Parliamentary life, I considered that having put in the Bill a provision for bringing them back to the House for a particular case, the amendment of the Irish Gt. Act, we cannot at this stage set our feet down and absolutely refuse any liberty to examine whether other cases may not arise for their presence at Westminster. On the whole in spite of the furious opposition of the London Press and Club society, I think we stand as well as could be expected.

Clearly the Memoir was influenced by the campaigns of 1886 and 1893.[34]

Biographical anecdotes were prominent in the Memoir and also

[32] See Kimberley Memoir, 499.
[33] William Harcourt (1827–1904), barrister; Lib. MP for Oxford, 1868–80, for Derby, 1880–95, for Monmouthshire, 1895–1904; sol.-genl., 1873–4; home sec., 1880–5; ch. exch., 1886, 1892–5; Lib. leader in the Commons, 1894–8.
[34] Governing Passion, 370.

incorporated the wisdom of age. Kimberley reflected in the late 1890s, for example, how 'curious' Gladstone's 'unpopularity' as Liberal leader was in 1867, reinforcing the picture of the prime minister's management skills during the first ministry. In some cases Kimberley restored material originally in the Journal, but which in the 1870s he had left out of the 'Journal of Events'; presumably, with the passage of time, discretion became less necessary.[35]

SIGNIFICANCE OF THE KIMBERLEY JOURNAL

What then is the significance of Kimberley's original Journal for students of Victorian politics? Most importantly, it provides a moderate non-Whig commentary on the workings of Liberal government and opposition for the period from the 1850s to 1890s. Kimberley's opinions and beliefs reflected that moderate bulk of Liberal parliamentary sentiment which was neither Whig nor radical. The Journal is a salutary reminder that the Liberal party was not, *pace* Joseph Chamberlain,[36] simply a two-faction alliance of Whigs and radicals, the creative tension between whom shaped Liberal parliamentary politics. On many occasions Kimberley's Journal articulates the views of that quiet mass of Liberal parliamentarians whose voice was frequently drowned out by polished Whig or earnest radical tones. Described by John Vincent as the 'Liberal plain', such moderate Liberals were not distinguished by social pedigree, doctrinal compulsions, or commitment to particular issues, their names not becoming associated with specific crusades. Rather, the bulk of parliamentary Liberals simply sought the redress of legitimate or historic grievances within a stable social and legal framework upholding the rule of law and the sanctity of property. Thus the material, political and moral progress of the nation was to be secured through responsible reform. Kimberley's Journal speaks for that quiet mass of Liberal opinion excluded by Whig clannishness and wary of radical enthusiasms.

As one of that Liberal generation educated during the 1840s and 1850s, Kimberley's views were shaped by his reading John Stuart Mill,[37]

---

[35] See 28, 29 June 1869.

[36] Joseph Chamberlain (1836–1914), industrialist who became mayor of Birmingham, 1873–5; Lib. MP for Birmingham, 1876–85, for W. Birmingham 1885–1914; Lib. Unionist from 1886; pres. of bd. of trade, 1880–5; pres. l.gt. bd., 1886; col. sec., 1895–1903.

[37] John Stuart Mill (1806–73), philosophical radical famous for his *System of Logic*, 1843; *Principles of Political Economy*, 1848, *On Liberty*, 1859, and *Utilitarianism*, 1863, among others; Lib. MP for Westminster, 1865–8.

Henry Buckle,[38] Adam Smith,[39] James Mill[40] and J.R. McCulloch,[41] though always tempered by Edmund Burke.[42] He did not see himself as a Whig and remained outside that cosy aristocratic coterie. He did not share the Whigs' lofty affectation of the vulgarity of effort, but rather was urged on by his mother Anne Wodehouse to avoid the gentleman's temptation of idleness. Throughout his life he believed that active employment was necessary to every man. Duty and effort were his guides to action and his principles remained largely the product of his youthful Liberalism.

Kimberley observed in his mid-thirties that he liked 'to see a young man begin with rather extreme opinions. They "tone" down fast enough' (3 September 1862). Certainly Kimberley's ardent commitment to free trade shocked his schoolboy contemporaries at Eton and later prompted abuse from his Norfolk neighbours. Free trade and bureaucratic efficiency, at the service of responsible intelligence, formed the cornerstones of his Liberalism. The narrative of modern British history he read as proof of the advance of progress. Like his friend the historian Henry Buckle, whose *History of Civilisation in England* he read in 1857, Kimberley saw liberty as the engine of England's progress. Both his Liberal opinions and patriotic pride were reinforced by direct experience of the 1848 revolutions in the Italian and German states.

After coming down from Oxford he saw free trade and colonial reform as essential to the onward march of enlightened public opinion. His reading of Adam Smith's *Wealth of Nations* and McCulloch's *Principles of Political Economy* in 1851 reinforced his commitment to limiting government interference in economic activity. In March 1851 he was elected to the Political Economy Club. At the same time, through his involvement in the Colonial Reform Association (CRA) with its call for the colonies be left to govern themselves, he sought to overhaul the meddling bureaucracy of the Colonial Office. What Kimberley's close acquaintance and fellow member of the CRA, the philosophic radical Sir William Molesworth,[43] memorably called the 'peculation and plunder' of those in the dark recesses of the Colonial Office, was to be

[38] Henry Thomas Buckle (1821–62), self-trained scholar, best known for his *History of Civilisation in England* (2 vols., 1857, 1861). On the two months which Buckle and Wodehouse spent together, see Alfred Henry Huth, *The Life and Writings of Henry Thomas Buckle* (2 vols., London, 1880), I 30–1.

[39] Adam Smith (1723–90) Scottish economist; laid foundation of political economy with publication of the *Wealth of Nations*, 1776.

[40] James Mill (1773–1836), Scottish philosopher and economist, father of John Stuart Mill.

[41] John Ramsey McCulloch (1789–1864), Scottish economist.

[42] Edmund Burke (1729–97) British politician and writer.

[43] Sir William Molesworth (1810–55), Rad. MP for Southwark, 1845–55; com. works, 1853–5; col. sec., 1855.

forced into the light of open public scrutiny. The young Kimberley was seen more often in the company of radicals such as George Grote,[44] John Bowring,[45] John Bright[46] and Joseph Hume,[47] than with the scions of the houses of Bedford and Devonshire. Following his maiden speech in April 1850 he spoke in parliament during 1850–2 against all vestiges of protectionism, supported the Factories Act of 1850, questioned the expediency of transporting criminals and paupers, and argued for greater colonial autonomy, thinking the Australian Colonies Government bill of 1850 too restrictive and the new constitution for New Zealand too cumbersome.

Kimberley's admiration for John Stuart Mill, like many of his generation, strengthened his belief in the duty of the educated, as much as the propertied, to lead society. Informed intelligence safeguarded social progress and shaped a healthy public opinion. He read with approval Mill's essays on political economy and logic. In 1859 he found Mill's *Essay on Liberty* suggestive. As Kimberley declared to the Northamptonshire Mechanics Institute in 1851, it was through the orderly and earnest performance of their duties as citizens that the educated secured the stability of the country. But unlike Buckle, Kimberley saw liberty and reason as necessary, rather than sufficient, conditions for the security of progress. A strong sense of the practical nature of politics, drawn from Burke, tempered an easy faith in reason as a panacea for the nation's ills. While feelings and dispositions, virtues and vices, played a prominent part in human affairs, it was folly to abandon usage and precedent in the single-minded pursuit of rational solutions. A reign of Neros, he declared, would be no worse than a reign of metaphysicians. A probing sceptical intelligence ensured that Kimberley was no doctrinaire adherent to any one theoretical system. Rather, he found that the pragmatic demands of practical action required the adaptation of theoretical precepts to specific circumstances. There was no point in ruining the country for the sake of an abstract argument. 'Excellent principles', he declared in 1876, 'are of no use unless you can transmute them into action.' Thus Kimberley endorsed Burke's maxim that a disposition to preserve and an ability to improve were the hallmarks of successful statesmanship.

[44] George Grote (1794–1871), Rad. MP for city of London, 1832–41; active in reform agitation; retired to devote himself to history; pub. *History of Greece* (8 vols., 1846–56).

[45] John Bowring (1792–1872), consular agent; Lib. MP for Clyde burghs, 1835–7, for Bolton, 1841–8; gov. of Hong Kong, 1854; lit. exec. of Jeremy Bentham's works.

[46] John Bright (1811–89), Lib. MP for Durham, 1843–7, for Manchester 1847–57, for Birmingham, 1857–85; pres. bd. of trade, 1868–70; Chanc. Duchy of Lanc., 1873, 1880–2; opposed Home Rule for Ireland.

[47] Joseph Hume (1777–1855), Rad. MP for Montrose, 1842–55; staunch advocate of retrenchment.

Kimberley's religious views also framed his youthful commitment to educated reform and rational efficiency. Sound reason should be illumined by Divine revelation. He disliked Tractarianism and Romish practices within the Anglican Church. The Catholic Church itself, susceptible to ultramontanism, promulgated extreme errors and superstitions. On the other hand, he despised evangelical cant and bigotry. He sought an Anglican *juste milieu* in a Protestant national church, free from foreign interference, buttressing the advance of rational progress through the influence of an enlightened public opinion. In 1851 he supported the Oath of Abjuration (Jews) bill on the basis that all religious barriers to the possession of the highest civil privileges should be removed. Burke and broad Churchmanship were incorporated with Millite precepts to define a responsible commitment to Liberal progress. The Journal traces the journey of a moderate Liberal mind through the intricacies of Victorian politics and serves as a memorial to that Liberal 'plain' who neither enjoyed high Whig birth nor embraced radical solutions.

It also provides a view of the political landscape from the perspective of the House of Lords. At one level this was evident in the pattern of the year recorded in the Journal. The intensity and exertions of the parliamentary session, normally from January to early August, were replaced during the late summer, autumn and early winter with the duties of estate management, petty sessions and local social life. Unlike many of his Whig colleagues, Kimberley rarely engaged in the autumnal tour of great country houses that largely comprised their existence outside Westminster and St James'. In 1906 Rosebery recalled that at the end of each session Kimberley would leave for East Anglia, 'remaining in seclusion there till parliament or cabinet called him to London, asking nobody, seeing nobody, indeed repelling visitors' (see Appendix, 488). This was not quite true, though it may have seemed so from the vantage point of high Whiggery. It was the Kimberley estates, family and Norfolk society that occupied his time away from national affairs, and offered him a respite from political cares. For this reason Journal entries during the recess have been retained in this edition so as to give an accurate overall impression of Kimberley's life.

At another level the Journal's observations throw light on the constitutional position of the House of Lords during a period of significant change. Relations with the Commons, party managers and an increasingly democratic electorate, as well as the position of the Lords itself, weave through the confidences of the Journal. The prevailing mood is one of apprehension. In 1863 Kimberley was concerned that the apathy of younger peers was destroying the standing of the Upper House. Neglect of their public duties only rendered the aristocracy the more vulnerable to popular criticism. In 1862 he felt it important to assert and maintain the right of lay Lords to speak on law questions. But the greatest threat to the authority of the mid-Victorian Lords lay not in populist critiques of a hereditary oligarchy. During the 1850s and 1860s the power of the Crown also challenged the authority of both Parliament and the Lords to guide national policy. Only the unexpected death of Prince Albert in 1861, he believed, deferred a dangerous constitutional conflict. The truckling of the elderly Palmerston to the court over foreign policy in 1864 caused Kimberley genuine dismay. The seclusion of the Queen in prolonged mourning, however, allowed Kimberley's profound anxiety about the reassertion of the royal prerogative to abate.

By the 1880s and 1890s Kimberley's constitutional anxieties centred more on the rise of the popular platform as a rival to Parliament's authority. This was a response to the rise of national parties, enjoying mass membership and centralised bureaucracies, as the authoritative expression of the nation's views. Kimberley's own sensibilities were rooted in the mid-Victorian culture of parliamentary government in which sovereignty resided in Westminster. It was in Parliament, not on the hustings, that the nation's interest, national policy and the identity of the government were decided. But by 1884 Kimberley feared that the Commons no longer fulfilled any such useful function, but instead had become 'a mere machine for embarrassing the executive action of the government' (29 March 1894). It no longer enforced economy, but rather promoted extravagance. The speeches of MPs, delivered for the most part to benches almost as empty as those of the House of Lords, with rare exceptions interested no one. It was unable to legislate except on one or two great matters in each session, and then only after the 'most ridiculous expenditure of time in fatuous talk and wrangling'.

Kimberley recognised that the autonomy of Parliament was giving way to the power of the electoral platform. In October 1883 he privately lamented that going 'to the stump' had become increasingly part of the recognised business of politics, more and more indispensable each year as the democracy gained in strength. He regretted that Parliament was visibly losing importance and authority in the country. Thus in old age he saw the rise of popular speaking campaigns, programme politics and party managers in Westminster and the constituencies, supplanting parliamentary autonomy. The political world of the 1890s became an alien and discomforting place far removed from the mid-Victorian assurances of his youth. Kimberley's strong sense of duty meant he was prepared to undertake necessary public speaking and to respond to the party call. But such activity remained a novel, distasteful and unwelcome requirement of late-Victorian public life. Demagoguery was swamping intelligence and property, and seemed to be triumphing over the articulation of enlightened public opinion within Westminster. The

Journal reveals his genuine and profound dismay at the disturbing advance of the democratic machinery of politics.

The Journal also contains important comments on the events and personalities shaping Victorian politics over a fifty-year span. It was written by a man of ambition looking to the centre of political affairs. He openly, if privately, acknowledged his desire for office. In late 1862, with no official duties, he felt foolishly discontented and miserable. Frustrated at vegetating in the country, he was provoked to be shelved in the prime of life. That he was not invited to Granville's opening of the session dinner in February 1863 he saw as proof of going down in the political world. The young Kimberley blamed the official Whig clique for blocking his advancement, it being impossible to 'break through the charmed circle of old men who monopolise office on the Liberal side' (14 April 1863). In April 1864 he railed against worn-out Whig placemen and lamented that his hard-working service to the party had not advanced him an inch (8 April 1864). Thus, even when a junior minister or when engaged in diplomatic missions, Kimberley was keenly following the high political world with an eye toward promotion. And though he usually did not write from the very centre of the political battle, as Gladstone, Chamberlain or Hartington might, he was clearly a part of the ' "inner" political world' which often saw matters very differently than did the press or the public. For example, in October 1884 Kimberley was intrigued to note the different verdicts passed on Lord Dufferin's appointment as Indian Viceroy, the high opinion of Dufferin voiced by the press contrasting with the lower estimate of him held by leading cabinet ministers (8 October 1884).

Kimberley's commentary was informed by his unique position as an observer. He was the only Liberal to serve in all the Gladstone and Rosebery ministries. Others exercised more influence on the Liberal party, and some knew more of the details of clandestine political intrigue. Very few, however, had a longer perspective on the personalities and events shaping political developments. This was reflected in Kimberley's emergence during the 1890s as 'Uncle Kim' to a new generation of Liberals who looked to him less as a political general than as an embodiment of the Liberal tradition; someone who had been with the party from the first and who would remain loyal to its founding ideals, even when they, as younger men, could not. At the time of Kimberley's death in 1902 it made good copy for journalists to remind readers that he had held important government posts while Salisbury was merely writing for the newspapers, and that he was minister to Russia 'before Rosebery had gone to school'. No one tried to elevate Kimberley to the status of Salisbury or Rosebery as a political leader, but all found it remarkable that he had actually *seen* the Revolutions of 1848 and also had survived the rise and fall of Liberal fortunes into the twentieth century.

The commentary provided by Kimberley's Journal is also informed by a strain of intellectual independence devoid of political subservience. He was not told secrets by Palmerston,[48] Russell, Gladstone, Granville and Rosebery. Nor did he attach himself to aspiring Liberal leaders such as Hartington, Chamberlain, Dilke,[49] Harcourt and Morley[50] during the turbulent 1880s and 1890s, when it appeared that Gladstone might at any moment retire. Nevertheless, by the 1880s, Kimberley probably knew more of the whole range of official business of the government than anyone apart from Gladstone and Granville. This, in part, explains the diversity of subjects taken up in the Journal. Those who have accepted the categorisation of Kimberley as a competent but largely apolitical placeholder, will be surprised to find so little mention in the Journal of departmental affairs and so much of party politics.

Although a landed Liberal by conviction, Kimberley's early ministerial career brought him into close association with the Whigs. Youthful acquaintance with radical reform gave way to official contact with Whiggism. In part this sprang from his deep dislike of the Conservative leader Lord Derby[51] and his distaste for evangelical radicalism. His aversion to Protectionism reinforced a deep distrust of Derby. Despite Derby's oratorical talents, Kimberley viewed the Conservative leader as politically dishonest, with rare exceptions ungenerous, and withal unscrupulous. In December 1852 he joined the broad opposition bringing Derby's brief minority government to an end. At Russell's request, and with the help of his uncle Raikes Currie, Kimberley was rewarded with a junior appointment in Aberdeen's coalition ministry. He had hoped for the Vice Presidency of the Board of Trade, a position suited to his practical Liberal interests, but instead he became Under Secretary at the Foreign Office. Despite his never having spoken on foreign affairs, the appointment brought him considerable pleasure. The appointment also bolstered Russell's claim to head a broadly progressive party and answered widespread anxiety about the paucity of young talent amongst the peerage.

[48] Henry John Temple, 3rd Viscount Palmerston (1784–1865), for. sec., 1846–51; home sec., 1852–5; pr. min., 1855–8, 1859–65.

[49] Charles Wentworth Dilke (1834–1911), author and Rad. MP for Chelsea, 1868–86; u-sec. at for. office, 1880–2; pres. loc. govt. bd., 1882–5; public career ruined by being named co-respondent in Crawford divorce case.

[50] John Morley (1838–1923), ed. of *Fortnightly Review*, 1867–92, of *Pall Mall Gazette*, 1880–3; Lib. MP for Newcastle-upon-Tyne 1883–95, for Montrose burghs, 1895–1908; ch. sec. Ireland, 1886, 1892–5; wrote biographies of Burke (1867), Voltaire (1872), Rousseau (1876), Diderot (1878), Cobden (1881), Cromwell (1900) and Gladstone (1903).

[51] Edward George Geoffrey Smith Stanley, 14th Earl of Derby (1799–1869), leader of the Conservatives; pr. min., 1852, 1858–9, 1866–8.

Involvement with foreign policy drew Kimberley into the special administrative preserve of Whiggism. First, briefly under Russell as Foreign Secretary and than after February 1853, under Russell's successor Lord Clarendon, Kimberley established a reputation as a capable and safe pair of hands. His fluency in French, evident intelligence, self-assurance and ready application impressed his colleagues. And while his discontent with Peelite timidity and Palmerstonian bluster in foreign affairs increased, his respect for Clarendon's shrewd handling of foreign policy grew. In the face of Russian aggression in 1853, Kimberley saw Aberdeen's responses as merely cloaking chronic vacillation. Palmerston's pronouncements, meanwhile, seemed empty gestures. As over Italy in 1848 Palmerston 'talked big' and left 'in the lurch those whom his big talk has encouraged to rebellion or resistance' (*Liberal by Principle* p. 77). Palmerston's conservative views on domestic reform exacerbated Kimberley's mistrust. During 1853, Clarendon's far sounder views on foreign policy were hampered. Aberdeen's timidity merely encouraged Russia, Kimberley believed, when more decided action would have forestalled the war that the premier was reluctantly drawn into by 1854. The subsequent mismanagement of the Crimean campaign, moreover, graphically reported in *The Times*, did irreparable damage to the coalition's governing credibility. The damage was heightened, in Kimberley's case, when his brother-in-law and Christ Church friend, Lord Fitzgibbon, was killed in the futile charge of the Light Brigade at Sebastopol. In January 1855 Aberdeen's coalition ministry, under combined radical and Conservative attack, was forced to resign.

In Palmerston's first government, formed in February 1855, Kimberley continued to serve as Clarendon's Under Secretary. His official apprenticeship under Clarendon cemented his respect for Clarendon's industry and astute judgement, Kimberley only regretting Clarendon's tendency to pay too much attention to detail – a trait which Kimberley himself displayed. But, for Kimberley, Clarendon was and remained 'a most kind friend' (23 June 1870). He recognised in Clarendon's pragmatic responses to the realities of European power politics the workings of a practical common sense in the service of British national interests, untainted by Palmerstonian bluster, Peelite vacillation or radical moralising. As Clarendon's protégé, Kimberley's moderate instincts and wish for policies safeguarding Britain's economic pre-eminence reinforced the doctrine of free trade, administrative efficiency, and the nation's identity firmly rooted in her established traditions.

Kimberley's appointment as Minister Plenipotentiary to St Petersburg, following the Treaty of Paris in 1856 which concluded the Crimean War, signalled Clarendon's high regard for Kimberley's abilities. (Granville doubted whether Kimberley would accept the mission because the Foreign Office now seemed the grand object of the young minister's life.) The Journal provides a vivid record of a Russian court struggling with the aftermath of military defeat and diplomatic failure. Kimberley returned from St Petersburg in 1858, resumed the post of Foreign Office Under Secretary in Palmerston's second government in 1859, but resigned upon Russell's elevation to the Lords as Earl Russell and Foreign Secretary in 1861, unwilling to submit to the loss of position.

There followed three years of despondency and frustration. Domestic politics were a 'dead calm' and were 'never duller than in England'. The general preoccupation with Palmerston's health, the premier's unexpected longevity dominating future prospects, was faithfully recorded. In early 1863 Palmerston was looking much older, though in high spirits; by July 1863 he was shaky and unlikely to go on another session; by March 1864 the premier was looking worn-out. Palmerston's slackening grip on life governed political speculation.

With the outbreak of the American Civil War Kimberley observed the instinctive sympathy for the Confederacy, as a property-owning oligarchy, among the English upper classes. In June 1862 news of a Confederate victory was received with great satisfaction, support for the North 'being very scarce' (8 June 1862). Kimberley's own allegiances were with neither combatant. What was welcome was the possibility of the emergence of two or more independent states in North America, Unionist aggression and insolence thus being divided. But it was crises over Poland and Schleswig-Holstein that dominated Kimberley's interests during 1861–4.

Out of office Kimberley's resentment at Whig exclusivity revived. His disagreement with government foreign policy, particularly over Poland and Denmark, sharpened his frustrations. Russell became the principal target of Kimberley's criticism, cabinet disagreements being carefully noted. Both Russell and Palmerston demonstrated a dangerous weakness for pronouncing strong remonstrances against Russian suppression of Polish ambitions for greater independence. But such official declarations, unaccompanied by decided action, Kimberley characterised as contemptible. Russell's subsequent statement of July 1863, that Britain would not go to war for Poland so as to avoid the dangers of a French alliance, only rendered further diplomatic action useless. Similarly, over Prussia's challenge to Denmark's sovereignty in Schleswig-Holstein in 1863/4, Kimberley decried government rhetoric which insinuated much but delivered little. Such imprudence was exacerbated by Russell's habit of acting without Cabinet consultation. Encouraged to speak by Clarendon, Kimberley was glad to show, in May 1863, that disapprobation of Russell's Danish policy was not confined to the opposition. Throughout his life Kimberley firmly believed that to meddle diplomatically, when you did not intend to act, was the height of folly.

Kimberley's Journal and his speeches reveal the depth of Liberal divisions over Russell's Danish policy. Again, Kimberley expressed the discomfort of many moderate Liberals at what was seen as Russell's exalted, yet hollow, language. The government's political response to Kimberley's public criticisms was to bring him back within 'the charmed circle'. In December 1863 Kimberley was passed the poisoned chalice of the Schleswig-Holstein crisis and despatched to Berlin and Copenhagen to mediate a diplomatic settlement. Officially Kimberley was sent as envoy to congratulate Christian IX of Denmark on his succession to the throne, but his real purpose was to attempt to resolve the Schleswig-Holstein question. His mission, predictably, failed. But shortly after his return, in April 1864, he was offered, and reluctantly accepted, the Under Secretaryship of the India Office. Clarendon had urged Palmerston to appoint Kimberley to the Duchy of Lancaster with a seat in Cabinet, but without success. Then, in November 1864, Kimberley was appointed Lord Lieutenant of Ireland. Thus a potentially formidable Liberal critic of government policy was brought safely within the fold. The dangerous and divisive undertows beneath the calm Liberal surface of Palmerston's good-natured insouciance were evident. Again the Journal reveals quiet misgivings beneath loud ministerial statements seeking to provide authority and reassurance, suggesting that Gladstonian zeal and radical enthusiasms were not the only Liberal voices muzzled by Palmerston's longevity.

Kimberley's period in Ireland, from September 1864 to July 1866, proved one of the most successful of his official career. The Journal throws light on the constant frustrations and occasional satisfactions of governing Ireland. Kimberley believed that reconciling the Irish to British rule by reform was a necessary, but inevitably slow and long-term, process. He supported land law reform, Church reform, educational reform, and agricultural improvement through land drainage schemes, combined with firm implementation of the rule of law. He decried the danger of looking too much upon Ireland with English eyes, while remaining insistent that maintaining law and order often required a sharp remedy for a serious disease. His swift arrest of leading Fenians in September 1865, and the raid on the offices of the *Irish People*, averting insurrection, was widely applauded. His impatience with the ceremonies and stifling protocol of the Vice Regal Lodge reinforced his hope that, in due course, the office of Lord Lieutenant might be abolished. The unseemly disturbances common to all Irish assemblies, and the rowdy counterpoint of Fenian hisses to the singing of the National Anthem, were duly recorded. In February 1866 Kimberley suspended Habeas Corpus, made further arrests and on St Patrick's

Day 1866 witnessed a most contemptible rabble hissing 'God Save the Queen' with more vigour than usual. To his Journal, a week later, he confided his deep frustration:

On the whole I think there is no people on the face of the earth more unworthy of respect. They have always been despised by the Englishmen and, as a nation, they have always deserved his contempt. (24 March 1866)

But within a few days Kimberley's equilibrium was restored.

They are an unfortunate people: that is too true but it is mean to cast upon them imputations for faults which we have aggravated by evil treatment. I don't absolutely despair. Perseverance in fair just government must produce its effect in the end; but Englishmen must be persuaded to treat Irishmen as Irishmen and not as Englishmen. This last folly will pass away, and there will be slow but certain improvement, that is my faith. (1 April 1866)

Thus a conscientious Liberal English mind, caught between the rule of law and remedial reforms, grappled with the intractability of Irish grievances.

Kimberley's labours were increased by the tactlessness and indiscretion shown by Robert Peel (eldest son of the Conservative premier) as Chief Secretary of Ireland until December 1865.[52] In September 1865, for example, Peel engaged in a foolish fracas with a fellow traveller in a railway carriage (30 September 1865). Kimberley found his colleague utterly wanting in judgement. He was, Kimberley observed, quick-witted, clever, vigorous and a source of weakness to any administration of which he was a member (8 December 1865). 1865 was a year, the Lord Lieutenant concluded, of much activity and anxiety. Kimberley had no higher regard for Peel's successor, Chichester Fortescue, whose entry to the cabinet he blocked.[53] An Irish Chief Secretary in Cabinet would become, for all practical purposes, Kimberley believed, the head of the government of Ireland. The Lord Lieutenant would revert to being 'a mere useless appendage – a sort of Lord Mayor' (14 February 1867). Kimberley saw Fortescue's political success, moreover, as less due to his talents than to the over-arching ambition of his wife, the hostess Lady Waldegrave, whose gatherings at Strawberry Hill were famous occasions. It was Lady Waldegrave,

[52] Sir Robert Peel (1822–95), Lib.-Cons. MP for Tamworth, 1850–80, for Huntingdon, 1884–5, for Blackburn, 1885–6; ch. sec. Ireland, 1861–5; eld. son of the prime minister. On the general contempt for Peel's abilities, see DD1, 201.

[53] See 14 May 1866. Chichester Samuel Fortescue (1823–98), Lib. MP for Louth, 1847–74, when created Baron Carlingford; u.-sec. col., 1857–8, 1859–65; ch. sec. Ireland, 1865–6, 1868–71; pres. bd. of trade, 1871–4; ld. privy seal, 1881–5; ld. pres. counc., 1883–5.

Kimberley believed, who wore 'Fortescue's breeches'. 'She is making a sad fool of herself, and will do her husband a world of harm.' None the less, despite the inadequacies of his colleagues, Kimberley was pleased in May 1866 to receive many compliments on his management of Irish affairs. That same month he was delighted to be informed of his elevation as the first Lord Kimberley.

Kimberley's record of the Reform debates of 1866–7 does little to modify, though much to illustrate, our understanding of events as drawn from studies by Maurice Cowling and F.B. Smith.[54] After defeat of the Liberal Reform bill in June 1866, Kimberley favoured dissolution, but after a 'week passed in the strongest uncertainty', Russell and Gladstone decided to resign (18 June 1866). He believed Derby's pure Tory Cabinet, moderate Liberal dissidents having declined to join the new Conservative government, would not last long. The July 1866 reform riots in Hyde Park he judged 'a melancholy affair' for bringing the people into collision with the police (24 July 1866). His Journal betrays no deep class anxieties brought on by such demonstrations. Rather, the meetings revealed the utter incapacity of the lachrymose Spencer Walpole,[55] Derby's Home Secretary, and refuted 'the calumnies of Lowe, Elcho etc. who declared the working man took no interest in reform' (24 July 1866). The reform demonstrations of February 1867, which Kimberley watched from the windows of the Traveller's, seemed 'a flat affair'. 'Some of the processionists, e.g. the tailors, were respectable artisans but there were many dirty boys and rabble. All together a failure' (11 February 1867). It was on the complex and rapid turn of parliamentary events that Kimberley's mind focused.

Disraeli's unscrupulous cynicism and opportunism, Russell's failure and unpopularity, and deepening Liberal suspicion of Gladstone, were recurrent themes in Kimberley's Journal during 1867. The Liberal opposition, broken and demoralised, became prey to the manoeuvrings of a contemptible Conservative ministry. Kimberley feared that it was Disraeli's conduct, rather than that of the popular demagogues, which would 'stir up at last a democratic agitation which will carry a democratic bill' (16 February 1867). Although such an outcome might be 'better even than the present cowardly false line which the House takes on all questions home and foreign, faithfully reflecting the opinions of the middle classes, the always cowardly, ease-loving bourgeoisie. A strong infusion of working class men into the constituency is the only remedy' (16 February 1867). When, in conversation with Gladstone and

[54] Maurice Cowling, *1867: Disraeli, Gladstone and Revolution* (Cambridge, 1967) and F.B. Smith *The Making of the Second Reform Bill* (Cambridge, 1966).

[55] Spencer Walpole (1806–1898), Cons. home sec., 1852, 1858–9 and 1866–7. Allegedly cried when confronted by Reform League representatives over Hyde Park riots.

the Commons Liberal whip, Henry Brand, in February 1867, Kimberley spoke in favour of household suffrage 'Gladstone looked astonished and said that he did not wish to go so far. It is said he is rather alarmed at the progress of "democratic" ideas in our party' (27 February 1867).

Secure in his own Liberal beliefs on reform, Kimberley watched with deep distaste the parliamentary mêlée of 1867. Derby's statements he found degrading and contemptible. When the Conservative Reform bill was presented to the Commons in 1867, he observed, that never was 'there ever a more pitiable exhibition of imbecility and levity in dealing with a mighty question' (5 March 1867). Yet, following the failure of Gladstone's amendment to the measure in April, it was also clear that Gladstone was 'very unpopular as leader' (12 April 1867). Gladstone's excessive vehemence alienated supporters. 'His very honesty is now a hindrance to him' (9 July 1867). By mid-May 'the opposition party [was] shattered to pieces' as Disraelian suppleness exploited Liberal disarray (10 May 1867). Disraeli's acceptance of the radical Hodgkinsons' amendment to the Conservative measure, incorporating a uniform household suffrage in borough constituencies, left Kimberley in dismay.[56] 'The Tories say they prefer this to last year's bill because the lower you go the more ignorant and dependent the voters will be! Thus it seems if you dig deep enough you come to a lower stratum of dirt which is Tory dirt. A truly noble creed for the gentlemen of England' (18 May 1867).

Kimberley's Journal also provides insight into that more neglected arena of reform debate in 1867, the House of Lords. A meeting of Liberal peers on 19 July 1867 demonstrated Russell's isolation, widespread opposition to Lord Grey's motion,[57] and general uncertainty as to the best course to adopt. Subsequent Lords debate merely left 'the impression that the House swallows the bill as a bitter dose and that ministers are dishonest politicians, and somewhat sore at being told so' (23 July 1867). Lord Cairns'[58] successful Conservative amendment, supported by *The Times*, which safeguarded Tory representation in large cities by giving each elector only two votes in three-member

---

[56] Grosvenor Hodgkinson (1818–81), Lib. MP for Newark-upon-Trent, 1859–74, moved his amendment on 17 May. It abolished compunding (whereby, landlords paid the rates for their tenants, thereby disfranchising them). This made household suffrage in the borough constituencies a reality and removed the legal obstacle to small tenants seeking the vote. 3 *Hansard* 187 (17 May 1867); 720–6; Smith, *The Making of the Second Reform Bill*, 196–202; Cowling, *1867: Disraeli, Gladstone and Revolution*, 267–86.

[57] Henry George Grey, 3rd Earl Grey (1802–94), col. sec., 1846–52; pub. *Colonial Policy of Lord John Russell's Administration* (1853).

[58] Hugh MacCalmont Cairns (1819–85), Cons. MP for Belfast, 1852–66; ld. chanc., 1868, 1874–80; cr. Baron Cairns of Garmoyle, Antrim, 1867, Viscount Garmoyle and Earl Cairns (UK peerage), 1878.

constituencies, divided Liberal peers. Russell, Clarendon, Argyll[59] and others supported it. Granville opposed it. A hesitating Kimberley, with Lords Halifax and Lyveden, abstained. Tory peers saw it as a 'contrivance to check democracy', while Kimberley disliked it for being a theoretical device. 'Philosophers have ever been bad constitution makers from Plato down to Sieyès, and this philosophical scheme of Lowe, Mill and the philosophers of the House of Commons I believe proves no exception to the rule' (30 and 31 July 1867). As the Lords' debate drew to a close Kimberley regretted that it was evident that there were not above a dozen really Liberal peers in the House. After Parliament was prorogued and the Conservative Reform Bill passed Kimberley found solace in shooting bucks on his Norfolk estate.

In 1868 Kimberley welcomed Gladstone's proposal to disestablish the Irish Church. Not only did the reform have intrinsic merit, as the least objectionable of options available, but it also provided a clear litmus test for Liberal loyalty. The defeat of the government on the Irish church question in April 1868, by a margin of 60 Commons votes (270–330), fulfilled all expectations. 'The Liberal party is resuscitated. We have a policy and a leader, and justice to Ireland will, if we honestly, justly persevere, become something more than a mere party cry' (4 April 1868). It became clear that the Government would not resign. 'They will remain and be dragged together with their party through the mire until the name of Dizzy will stink in the nostrils of the nation and the Conservative party will cease to exist.' Kimberley counselled patience to his colleagues. 'You must get the confidence of the nation before we can put an end to the present reign of trickery. A premature attack will spoil all. Our great object must be to restore a better tone to politics and some strength to the Executive' (4 April 1868). Kimberley's Journal reveals how rapidly Irish disestablishment provided a powerful restorative tonic to a demoralised and divided opposition. Irish disestablishment did as much to pacify the Liberal party as fulfilling Gladstone's declared hope of pacifying Ireland.

In retrospect historians have seen Disraeli's opposition to disestablishment in 1868 as predictable. From Kimberley's Journal it is apparent how uncertain Liberals were that Disraeli would, indeed, adamantly oppose Irish disestablishment. Kimberley reminds us how shaken were Liberal nerves, in the immediate aftermath of Disraeli's triumph over reform, and how uncertain the party landscape had become. Liberal 'dissension has brought the country under the dominion of the unscrupulous adventurer who is now at the head ... He has

---

[59] George Douglas Campbell, 8th Duke of Argyll (1823–1900), ld. privy seal, 1853–5, 1859–60, 1860–6, 1880–1; post.-genl., 1855–8, 1860; India sec., 1868–74; opposed Home Rule, 1886, 1893.

dragged Englishmen through the dirt and will drag them through more still, until too late their eyes will be opened to their miserable folly and baseness. Meanwhile fraud reigns triumphant' (5 March 1868). In May 1868 Kimberley feared Disraeli would play the same game on Irish disestablishment as over reform. 'He will announce a measure to reform the Irish Church. The radicals would say that we had better let him bring in his measure' (11 May 1868). Disraeli's service to Liberal unity, by opposing any reform to the Irish Church, was as great as that of Gladstone. Even after the Liberals' resounding electoral victory in November 1868, a Liberal majority of 384 MPs facing a reduced Conservative party of 274 MPs, Kimberley remained uncertain about the future. The Conservative opposition will be 'neither powerless nor discouraged' (25 November 1868). Moreover, Gladstone's pamphlet *A Chapter of Autobiography*, justifying his conversion to Irish disestablishment, and speeches in Lancashire did not increase Kimberley's confidence in Gladstone's judgement and discretion. 'I shall be surprised if a ministry formed by [Gladstone] lasts long' (25 November 1868). Kimberley's Journal warns against attributing to contemporaries the certainty granted by hindsight. Gladstone's triumph, as the saviour of the Liberal party in late 1868, became easier to appreciate in retrospect.

When Gladstone formed his first government in December 1868 Kimberley became Lord Privy Seal. The Home Office might have been his, he was told, if he had been in the House of Commons. Most importantly, however, the appointment brought Kimberley for the first time into the cabinet. Aged forty-two he officially entered the 'charmed inner circle'. Then in June 1870 Kimberley moved to the Colonial Office when Lord Granville succeeded Lord Clarendon as Foreign Secretary. Thus in his Journal Kimberley provides an invaluable inside record of the achievements and failures of Gladstone's reforming ministry for the whole period from December 1868 to February 1874. It reveals Kimberley's role in persuading Gladstone to persevere with the Irish Church bill in 1868 when, in the face of fierce Lords opposition, the prime minister was contemplating abandoning the measure. It confirms the serious, if short-lived, rifts in the Cabinet caused by the Irish Land Act of 1870 and Kimberley's consistent support for the legislation. Kimberley's concern at Gladstone's timorousness in negotiating with the United States over the *Alabama* claims are noted. And the Journal indicates how Kimberley's colonial policy, after June 1870, was, as Ethel Drus observed, at once more vigorous and conciliatory than that of his predecessor. Kimberley supported the annexation of the Fiji Islands as Crown Colonies and the strengthening of British influence on the Gold Coast and in Malaya. At the same time he supported Australian control of their tariff policy. In the last resort the principle of colonial autonomy was even more important that the principle of free trade.

The Kimberley Journal, in contrast to his later 'Journal of Events', also reveals more readily the recurrent unease during 1868 to 1874 over Gladstone's leadership. The more polished 'Journal of Events' smoothed over the rough edges of ministerial disquiet at Gladstone's excited volubility and fervour. For example, in February 1870 Kimberley, recorded in his Journal that Gladstone was in a 'Fools Paradise' in his thinking on Ireland (21 February 1870). In the Journal of Events this view was tempered to Gladstone entertaining 'happy delusions'. Kimberley always admired Gladstone's political courage while often mistrusting his methods. Again, it was easier to appreciate in retrospect the collective achievement and shared commitment of Gladstone's first administration. Despite Kimberley's careful subsequent excisions, the Journal still betrays those ministerial misgivings which persisted in Cabinet discussion, while at the same time acknowledging the absence of any credible challenger to the premier's authority. By 1869 Russell was decrepit, by 1870 Clarendon was dead, and prior to 1868 Granville had established his well-deserved reputation for compliance. Cabinet harmony rested on a realistic appreciation of Gladstone's indisputable authority as well as ministerial common purpose.

What the Journal of Events did judiciously to modify the original judgements of the Journal with regard to Gladstone was also more broadly true. Discrete revision was applied to Kimberley's opinions of ministerial colleagues, such as Chichester Fortescue and his wife Lady Waldegrave, fellow peers, such as Lord Gosford and Lord Westbury, and to comments on the contemptibility of Irish politicians and their supporters. The Journal's record of Earl Russell's 'shambling talk and sad twaddle' on May 1870 became 'maundering' in the Journal of Events. The reference in the Journal on 24 June 1871 to the 'sulky seclusion of the Queen and the silly frivolous debauched life of the Prince [of Wales]' was omitted altogether from the Journal of Events. Likewise, during the Franco-Prussian War in 1870, Kimberley's description of the North Germans as a 'hateful race' in the Journal (7 September 1870) was moderated to their being 'a very disagreeable race' in the Journal of Events. Innumerable and deft editorial touches softened the vivid, harder-edged, more vituperative tone of the original Journal entries in accord with the gentler sensibilities of recollection.

In his valuable analysis of Gladstone's first ministry J.P. Parry has located policy debate in a broad cultural context of intense religiosity.[60] With Gladstone as premier and given the deep moral dimension of

[60] J.P. Parry, *Democracy and Religion: Gladstone and the Liberal Party, 1867–1875* (Cambridge, 1986).

Victorian views on public issues, such an approach is both important and suggestive. It is also worth noting, however, that from his Journal during this period emerges Kimberley's attempts to act in a rational non-sectarian manner, so as to secure the policy he believed best-suited to the national interest. Kimberley saw his Christian beliefs as a private, not a public, matter, although his dislike for Catholic superstition and ultramontanism, on the one hand, and evangelical cant on the other, continued. In May 1870 he recorded his response to debate on the Deceased Wife's Sister bill. 'Tedious dissertations on Leviticus. How can a rational man argue with fanatics who believe that Leviticus is binding on Englishmen?' (19 May 1870). Kimberley saw the Liberal party as less a moral coalition than an association of progressive opinion, safeguarding social and political improvement within the framework of the rule of law and propertied intelligence. His official responsibility for colonial affairs and contribution to foreign policy debate only encouraged him to look askance at sectarian enthusiasms. While intense religiosity was undoubtedly part of the public context of legislative debate in the early 1870s it does not always provide a sure guide to the intentions of individual ministers such as Kimberley.

Recent historical writing on the late 1870s, particularly by T.A. Jenkins, has re-examined the basis of an essentially Gladstonian reading of Liberal politics from 1874 to 1880, based on certain assumptions.[61] First, following Gladstone's resignation as party leader in 1875 the Whig duumvirate of Lord Hartington in the Commons and Lord Granville in the Lords proved hesitant and ineffective. Second, Gladstone's ability to rouse the moral passion of popular Liberalism, as shown during the Bulgarian agitation of 1876 and Midlothian campaigns of 1879–80, demonstrated his unchallengeable status as the true embodiment of Liberal belief. Third, this status ensured Gladstone's return to the premiership as party leader in 1880 and a restoration of the natural Liberal hegemony that had characterised electoral politics since 1846. Each of these assumptions has recently come under question. Kimberley's Journal throws further light on the revision of the Gladstonian myth.

In Kimberley's eyes Granville was far from being an ineffective party leader. In February 1876 he believed Granville made an admirable speech in response to the Royal Address (8 February 1876). In June 1877 Kimberley judged the debate on the government's Burial bill to be 'uncommonly well managed by Granville from the first' (17 June 1877). Again, in February 1880, Granville made an excellent speech on the Address (15 February 1880). Clearly, when he chose, Granville was capable of providing effective leadership to Liberals in the Lords.

---

[61] T.A. Jenkins, *Gladstone, Whiggery and the Liberal Party, 1874–1886* (Oxford, 1988).

Similarly, Kimberley thought Hartington did well as Liberal leader in the Commons, particularly considering that 'our party is so demoralised that, were he a heaven-born leader, he could do little at present to mend our fortunes'.[62] In November 1876 Kimberley agreed entirely with Hartington's cautious line over the Bulgarian issue. Moreover, Gladstone's dramatic hijacking of the Bulgarian agitation in late 1876 left Kimberley largely unmoved. In July 1876 Kimberley had judged Disraeli's government to be 'masters of the situation' and the autumn 'was spent very quietly and happily at Kimberley' (3 July 1876 and February 1877). At precisely the moment Gladstone was whipping popular Liberal opinion into a virtuous passion Kimberley was happy in quiet seclusion to attend to his Norfolk estate.

Kimberley's Journal in April and May 1877 then confirms the deep reluctance among leading Liberals to support Gladstone's anti-government resolutions on the Bulgarian issue. At a meeting of the late Liberal Cabinet on 28 April 1877, from which Gladstone was absent, only W.E. Forster, radical MP for Bradford, supported the resolutions. Bright was deputed to dissuade Gladstone from proceeding. Gladstone 'thinks nothing of disburdening his own conscience and is blind to the disastrous effects this will produce' was Kimberley's private assessment. 'The whole Liberal party, as far as I can hear, with the exception of a few radicals, strongly disapprove any parliamentary action at this moment on the part of the opposition' (28 April 1877). Kimberley believed the wave of feeling which had swept the country the previous autumn was spent and no common opinion existed among Liberals on the issue. Well might Gladstone record in his own journal: 'Such a sense of solitary struggle I never remember.' Following the failure of his Commons resolutions Gladstone was, Kimberley happily noted in June 1877, in a quieter mood.

Two points are worth making. First, Gladstone was not regarded by Kimberley or other leading Liberals in 1876–7 as the exclusive embodi-ment of Liberal belief. Second, the quieter opposition strategy adopted by Hartington and Granville was not simply a confession of personal incompetence. Rather, it appeared the most astute course to adopt in the face of serious Liberal differences over the Bulgarian question. Hartington and Granville offered calm moderation in contrast to the excited unpredictability of Gladstone, who might become a prisoner of the radicals.

Just as Gladstone's return from retirement to the Liberal leadership was not until early 1880 irresistible, nor was the Liberal electoral landslide of April 1880 anticipated. On 20 March Kimberley thought the outcome quite uncertain, the most likely result being a tie, with

---

[62] *Liberal by Principle*, 141.

Conservatives holding half the Commons seats and the Liberals, alongside seventy Home Rulers, in a miserable position. Popular jingoism and a vague terror of Gladstone, Kimberley thought, might keep the Conservatives in office. As it was, the elections proved such prognostications utterly wrong. Liberals gained their largest Commons majority since 1832, a boon which Kimberley ascribed to the economic recession.

Gladstone's second government never enjoyed the congeniality of the first. Kimberley surprised Gladstone by declining the Indian Vice-royalty, but agreed to join the new Liberal Cabinet by accepting the Colonial Office. Prior to the election Kimberley feared that the Liberal party consisted of mere fragments. Moreover, he believed that Ireland was a growing threat which would immediately require a new coercive bill from the Liberal government. After April 1880 Kimberley's anxieties were confirmed. Ireland divided the Liberal Cabinet, ministers such as Kimberley and Hartington favouring the firm restoration of the rule of law in the face of increasing agrarian violence, while others like Gladstone and Chamberlain were seeking remedial reforms. Kimberley was scornful of those who hoped to win over Irishmen with easy conciliation without an accompanying resort to coercion, and his reputation as a successful Irish Lord Lieutenant lent weight to his opinions in Cabinet discussion. But his concerns over the divisive nature of Irish policy increased. In July 1880 he feared an imminent schism between Whigs and radicals leading to an early break up of both the government and parliament. Lord Lansdowne's[63] resignation in July 1880 in protest over the government's Compensation for Disturbance bill, aimed to check Irish evictions and extend compensation to tenants, signalled the outrage of landowners at concessions to Irish insurrection. In his Journal Kimberley ascribed the haste of the Irish Chief Secretary, W.E. Forster,[64] to his lack of nerve and excessive sensitivity in the face of Irish invective. Forster's bill was overwhelmingly rejected by the Lords in August 1880. Kimberley despairingly concluded in his Journal: 'we are going the usual weary round and in due time shall have to recur to the old coercive policy' (2 and 3 August 1880).

The Irish difficulty seems hopeless. Turbulence and disrespect of law have been bred in them for generations till they have become part of Irish nature. Our philanthropists cannot see that no remedial measures can for generations produce a change in the character of men, any more than you can by good feeding suddenly change the character of a sheep or ox. That is no reason for

[63] Henry Charles Keith Petty-Fitzmaurice (1845–1927), suc. as 5th Marquis of Lansdowne, 1866; gov.-genl. Canada, 1883–8; viceroy of India, 1888–93; war sec., 1895–1900.

[64] William Edward Forster (1818–86), Lib. MP for Bradford, 1851–86.

not taking measures to improve the breed, but it is a reason for unlimited patience. Coercion by itself is of little use. (8 November 1880)

By September 1880 what Kimberley described as a 'most wearisome session' had ended. And, while the Irish Disturbance bill had been 'a blunder', Hartington had 'led admirably and risen immensely in general estimation' (5 September 1880). From late August to early September Gladstone was absent from Westminster on a recuperative sea trip.

During a quieter 1881 session the government passed an Irish Coercion Act (empowering the Lord Lieutenant to arrest on warrant individuals suspected of acts of violence or intimidation) and a revised Irish Land Act (based on a Royal Commission and establishing a judicial machinery to fix fair rents, and confirming the rights of tenants to fixity of tenure and entitlement to sell their interest in their tenancy). Over the Land bill Kimberley believed Gladstone's skill and calmness, in the face of provocation from Salisbury, had averted a clash between the Commons and the Lords. Kimberley welcomed the arrest of Charles Parnell[65] in October 1881, only regretting Forster's lack of vigour in not arresting other leading agitators. But by April 1882 he feared some of his Cabinet colleagues were 'in the old Fool's paradise of soothing, conciliation, etc., as a remedy for the woes of Ireland, superseding the necessity for the hateful coercion. Why can't they see both are necessary?' (22 April 1882). When the Home Secretary William Harcourt, following the savage murder in May of the new Irish Chief Secretary Lord Frederick Cavendish,[66] swung from talk of conciliation to breathing nothing but blood and thunder while bringing forward his Crimes Act, Kimberley was equally scathing about Harcourt's apparent belief that dark conspiracies engrained in the habits and character of the population could be swiftly eradicated (7 May 1882). Only the sustained and patient application of reform, accompanied by firm maintenance of the rule of law, could remedy the Irish situation.

Alongside Irish tribulations Kimberley's Journal records the persistent sense of instability that afflicted Gladstone's second Cabinet. Rumours of resignation, including erroneous reports of Kimberley's own imminent departure in May 1882, hung around the actual comings and goings of ministers. In May 1881 Lord Carlingford entered the Cabinet as Lord Privy Seal, succeeding Argyll who, like Lansdowne, had opposed the Irish Land bill. In May 1882 Forster resigned in protest over Gladstone's negotiation of the Kilmainham Treaty releasing Parnell from prison. In July 1882 Bright resigned over the government's Egyptian policy,

---

[65] Charles Stewart Parnell (1846–91), Home Rule MP for Co. Meath, 1875–80, for Cork, 1880–90; leader of the Irish Nationalists.
[66] Frederick Charles Cavendish (1836–91), younger brother of Lord Hartington.

and Kimberley found himself acting Chancellor of the Duchy of Lancaster in conjunction with being Colonial Secretary. In December 1882 Kimberley moved to the India Office, releasing a Cabinet place for the Liberal convert Derby at the Colonial Office. At the same time Hartington succeeded Hugh Childers[67] as Secretary of State for War, Childers became Chancellor of the Exchequer and the radical Sir Charles Dilke President of the Local Government Board. Surrounding such ministerial rearrangements was constant speculation over Gladstone's anticipated retirement.

Fluctuations in Gladstone's health were a common preoccupation as a barometer of political prospects. In April 1882 Kimberley notes that Gladstone was looking 'worn and dispirited'. On medical advice in January 1883 Gladstone went to Cannes, not returning to England until the beginning of March. All this was, Kimberley felt, 'very serious' (5 February 1883). Amid such uncertainty no single measure provided a legislative centrepiece to government business in the 1883 session. Kimberley found the concluding weeks of the session an unedifying spectacle. 'The House of Commons after wasting months in idle questions and personal bickerings, "rushed" through a number of important bills, the House of Lords being thus practically set aside' (25 August 1883). A sense of Liberal unease and parliamentary malaise prevailed.

The Journal provides little record of Kimberley's official activities at either the Colonial Office or the India Office after 1880. Entries comment on general political issues, most often Ireland, and incidents of wider interest. Reading the Journal, therefore, gives little impression of the increasing official burden under which Kimberley laboured. The interrelation of colonial and foreign policy between 1880 and 1882 required a close working relationship with Granville, particularly over African affairs. Policy in Southern Africa dominated the Colonial Secretary's attention. Lord Carnarvon's[68] confederation policy was continued, despite Liberal backbench condemnation, the embarrassment caused by the revolt of the Boers in December 1880, and defeat at Majuba Hill in February 1881. Kimberley favoured a decisive military suppression of the Boer revolt, but acquiesced in Gladstone's more conciliatory policy embodied in the Convention of Pretoria of August 1881, granting the Transvaal independence under a general claim of British suzerainty. Thus a policy of imperial consolidation, protecting Britain's strategic position in Cape Colony, was aligned with

[67] Hugh Culling Eardley Childers (1827–96), Lib. MP for Pontefract, 1860–85, for S. Edinburgh, 1886–92; 1st ld. adm., 1868–71; chanc. duchy of Lanc., 1872–3; war sec., 1880–2; chanc. exch., 1882–5; home sec., 1886.
[68] Henry Howard Molyneux Herbert, 4th Earl of Carnarvon (1831–90), u.-sec. for col., 1858–9; col. sec., 1866–7, 1874–8; ld. lt. of Ireland, 1885–6.

the promotion of self-government generally. Kimberley refused to annex Namaqualand and Damaraland in South-west Africa, or the Cameroons in West Africa. At the India Office, after December 1882, he grappled with Lord Ripon's aggressive promotion of local self-government and native judicial control, which he supported in principle but frequently felt compelled to curb on the grounds of 'sound administration'. Fear of Russian aggression along the Afghan frontier heightened international tensions during 1883–5.

But the Sudan crisis and parliamentary reform dominated Journal entries during 1884. Over the Sudan Kimberley regretted that circumstances were forcing England into arbitrary involvement. In order to support the reckless General Gordon[69] they would have to fight the Sudanese, with whom they had no quarrel, and support 'the rascally Egyptians, whose cowardice and cruel government have been the cause of the whole calamity' (13 May 1884). The Liberal Reform bill of 1884, equalising the county and borough franchise by proposing a household county suffrage, highlighted the government's weakness in the Lords. By late 1881 Kimberley feared that there were only forty peers, who were not placemen, who could be counted on loyally to support the ministry. In July 1884 the Lords rejected the Liberal Reform bill by 205 to 146 votes. This was a damaging blow to an administration that Kimberley believed was already tottering. But, in fact, it paved the way for a settlement of the crisis in November 1884, in which Liberal franchise reform was secured through Gladstone's private negotiation with Conservative leaders over redistribution. As Kimberley noted, a redistribution bill was negotiated with opposition leaders 'without any serious difficulty' (27 November 1884). Thus equalisation of the borough and county suffrage was accompanied by adjustments to constituency boundaries which gave comfort to the Conservatives.

The reshaping of the electoral regime during 1884–5, however, also brought politicians to the threshold of an unfamiliar world. While Gladstone relapsed in early 1885 into talk of imminent retirement, the Liberal Cabinet grappled with difficulties over the Sudan, Irish coercion, a budgetary deficit, and Chamberlain's call for tax reform to mitigate the inequities of land ownership. On 8 June 1885, following a Commons defeat in the budget debate, Gladstone's second government resigned. Kimberley saw the budget defeat as unnecessary and solely due to Hugh Childers' temper and obstinacy. At the same time, Kimberley recognised the advantage to the Liberals of going out over the budget when the government was on the point of falling to pieces over Ireland.

In looking over the record of the 1880–5 Liberal government Kimberley believed the 1884 Reform Act to be a 'brilliant success', which,

---

[69] Charles George Gordon (1835–85), gov.-gen. Sudan 1877–80.

with the redistribution Act, were 'great and solid achievements'. The 1881 Irish Land Act he also considered a 'well conceived measure' carried against parliamentary opposition with firmness and decision (28 June 1885). However, he judged W.E. Forster the worst Irish Secretary he had known – a significant distinction when one remembers his low opinion of Robert Peel and Chichester Fortescue. Lord Spencer, on the other hand, he considered a good Lord Lieutenant who had conducted himself admirably. Foreign affairs had been the weak point of the ministry, Egypt and the Sudan being 'the chief cause of our ruin'. Colonial affairs had been less prominent, though South Africa and the Pretoria Convention had excited popular interest. Hartington's handling of the Afghan crisis he judged to have been satisfactory. Gladstone's authority in his Cabinet after 1880 had been less complete than in 1868–74. Hartington, Harcourt and Chamberlain had all, in their separate ways, Kimberley noted, exercised much influence in Cabinet. The least influential minister was Childers, 'who seldom expressed an opinion, and, when he did, was usually so indistinct and muddled that it was difficult to know what he meant'. Rosebery, who had also said little, remained 'a dark horse'.

Like other British politicians in 1885, Kimberley recognised Ireland as the 'pivot on which the political future turned' (13 October 1885). In October 1885, conversation with Derby touched on the probability of a Liberal schism should Gladstone embrace Irish Home Rule. In 1886 such prognostications proved all too true as Gladstone, leading his third Liberal government from February to July 1886, split the Liberal party over his unsuccessful Irish Home Rule bill. On the day he joined his third Gladstone Cabinet Kimberley noted that there were 'long faces everywhere, except in the Parnell camp'. Appointed to the India Office Kimberley loyally supported Gladstone during 1886, as Hartington, Joseph Chamberlain and others committed themselves to Unionism. Thus Kimberley's Journal records events from within the Gladstonian Home Rule camp.

In 1871 Kimberley had declared that Home Rule simply meant separation from England, 'and when we are such fools as to assent to that, we deserve to be kicked by every nation in the world'.[70] But by 1886 he had accepted Gladstone's argument that the Irish problem demanded urgent action. For Parliament to carry on the government of the Empire some *modus vivendi* with Parnell had to be achieved. This was all the more true after the general election of 1885, held under the terms 1884–5 Reform and Redistribution Acts, which returned eighty-six Irish Home Rule MPs to the Commons. Acknowledging that no completely satisfactory arrangement with the Parnellites was possible,

---

[70] *Liberal by Principle*, 130.

Kimberley also believed that some arrangement must be achieved if parliamentary government were to be carried on. The Long experience of Irish politics had convinced him that no middle ground between coercion and Home Rule was possible, and that whichever party attempted a settlement would be harmed. By 28 January 1886, with the Conservatives out of office, Kimberley was prepared to examine any scheme for bringing peace, though he disliked the 'whole business', for the party was now bound to travel an impossible path.[71] After much Cabinet discussion, Gladstone's Home Rule bill was introduced on 13 March, leading, as Kimberley had foreseen, to a dramatic split in the Liberal ranks. Still, in the final weeks leading to the vote, and then in the run-up to the election, he was optimistic that Liberal Irish policy had 'more life in it' than their opponents imagined.[72] On the morning of 8 June, Gladstone's measure was rejected by the Commons by 341 to 311 votes and the Cabinet promptly decided to dissolve. At the subsequent election Gladstonian Liberals won only 190 seats, and their Irish Nationalist allies 85, while 316 Conservatives and 79 Liberal Unionists were returned. On 20 July Gladstone's government resigned.

Having reluctantly accepted the necessity for Home Rule, Kimberley believed that Liberal fortunes were largely tied to its success. While in opposition from 1886 to 1892, Kimberley unswervingly supported Home Rule, speaking often out of Parliament on its behalf and apologising to Gladstone when he could not do more. He believed that Gladstone's policy had been 'most beneficial to the relations between England and Ireland', demonstrating the sympathy of a part of the English people for Irish aspirations and paving the way for Home Rule in the near future (29 September 1886). Even the Conservatives, Kimberley noted, while embracing Unionism, were now speaking of the desirability of reforming local Irish institutions. 'They will do in two steps what we proposed to do in one.' In fact, for the remainder of Kimberley's life, Parliament declined to take the second step towards Irish autonomy, leaving Liberals in a precarious position, too far advanced to retreat yet too weak to press vigorously forward.

Not only was the party weakened by the withdrawal of the dissentient Unionists, but those that remained were divided over both policy details and political tactics. Kimberley himself, despite agreeing with the necessity of a Home Rule measure, often disagreed with Gladstone. Kimberley consistently opposed the retention of Irish members at Westminster, for instance, and repeatedly told Gladstone why, though

[71] *DD3*, 59.
[72] *Liberal by Principle*, 186; also Kimberley to Grant Duff, 12 March 1886, copy, MS. eng. c. 4223, f. 23; Kimberley to Grant Duff, 18 June 1886, GDP 1, 40.

he could see plainly enough that it might be politically necessary to retain them.[73] The larger mistake, in Kimberley's estimation, was tactical. On 29 September 1886, he confided to his Journal his belief that it had been wrong to overthrow Salisbury's Conservative government in January 1886. Prior to this precipitous act the Liberal party had been agreed that the best policy was not to drive the Conservatives out of office until they brought forward their own Irish policy. The Conservatives 'must have foundered on that rock and we should probably have had the inestimable advantage of uniting all sections of Liberals against their measures'. This was exactly the line which Kimberley had taken upon first learning of Gladstone's intention to bring forward a measure. In December 1885 Kimberley was pushing what Derby considered the sensible line that, with the Conservatives in office, the Liberals were not called upon for an opinion at present and had better offer none. After the Hawarden Kite on 17 December 1885, which gave public notice of Gladstone's conversion to Home Rule, Kimberley insisted that any commitment by the Liberal party either for or against should be avoided. In opposition after 1886, Kimberley continued to urge silence regarding details of a future Home Rule plan, in the hope that Conservatives would fail in what must have been an impossible task.[74] The problem created by precipitously ousting the Conservatives from office in January 1886 was then compounded, in Kimberley's judgement, by Gladstone's decision not to take Chamberlain into his confidence. For all of these disagreements, however, Kimberley marvelled that his Liberal colleagues could visualise anyone better able to grapple with the intractable problem than Gladstone and was dismayed by the tepidity of front bench support.

In August 1892 Kimberley entered Gladstone's fourth Cabinet, returning to the India Office and holding the Presidency of the Council. A second attempt in 1893 to establish Home Rule for Ireland, though approved by the Commons, was overwhelmingly, and not surprisingly, rejected by the Lords. As Kimberley noted, however, Argyll and Rosebery 'ingeniously avoided saying much in support of the bill' (5 Sept. 1893) – personally understandable under the shadow of a 419 to 41 massacre, but none the less ominous for the future of the Liberal party. Gladstone was old and declining, his 'big bill' had been defeated, and unenthusiastic Home Rulers were freed to pursue those alternative objectives which they secretly cherished. In the Cabinet of 23 February 1894 the Prime Minister announced his intention to resign, heightening tensions which had smouldered in the Liberal party since Gladstone's conversion to Home Rule.

---

[73] *Liberal by Principle*, 183–5, 198–9, 205–6.
[74] Journal, 26 Jan. 1887, 9 Feb. 1891; see also *Liberal by Principle*, 188, 194, 196.

Lord Rosebery thus inherited a party divided over policy and unsure of its own identity. He appointed Kimberley to the Foreign Office, despite the objections of Harcourt and Morley, who thought it undesirable to have both the Prime Minister and the Foreign Secretary sitting in the Lords. Kimberley's suspicion that such protests reflected the cantankerous Harcourt's own frustrated aspirations were pointedly accurate. As Foreign Secretary Kimberley was beset by both the inherited difficulties of defining a diplomatic role for Britain in Europe and by the lack of party unity. The Anglo-Belgian Treaty of 1894 irritated Harcourt, for instance, as much as it did France and Germany. As Kimberley noted in his Journal, he had fallen victim to the kind of administrative trust which Gladstone had always fostered in his Secretaries of State:

The fact is I found the matter in progress: I trusted to Rosebery and Anderson & thought I had done a pretty stroke of business. Imperfect knowledge & blind trust in other people, these are the reasons for my fiasco, but they are no valid excuse for my blunder. (22 June 1894)

Failure here determined Kimberley to proceed cautiously in the future. Thus, although he and Rosebery worked cordially together and generally agreed on foreign policy issues, it was difficult for the Prime Minister silently to pursue foreign policy objectives as he had characteristically done during the final Gladstone ministry.[75] This caution, so characteristic of Kimberley's political method, yielded neither dramatic diplomatic successes, nor disastrous blunders. The failure to join Russia, Germany and France in coercing Japan to moderate her claims against China following the Sino-Japanese War (Aug. 1894–April 1895), for instance, appeared to be a modest defeat, just as rapprochement with Japan proved to be a small tactical step in Britain's diplomatic reorientation.

Politically, Kimberley was able for fifteen months to keep the smouldering mistrust between Rosebery and Harcourt from erupting into Liberal self-immolation, but he could do no more. In June 1895, much to the relief of most party members, the Liberal government resigned following a snap Commons vote on the peripheral issue of army stocks of cordite explosives. A dissolution called by Salisbury in July 1895 led to what Kimberley characterised as 'the complete smash of our party at the elections' (21 July 1895). Only 177 Liberal MPs were returned to face 340 Conservatives, 71 Liberal Unionists and 82 Irish Nationalists. Kimberley's desolation found an immediate personal target in Harcourt, whose behaviour had infuriated Kimberley in Cabinet.

[75] *Liberal by Principle*, 40.

Harcourt was 'utterly without principle, an arrant coward and a blustering bully', combining 'every quality which unfits a man for the conduct of the affairs of a country' (21 July 1895). In despondency Kimberley concluded that 'in the present state of the Liberal party it is much the best for the country that the Tories should be in power' (15 August 1895).

Kimberley's Journal thereafter records the increasingly bleak existence of the Home Rule Liberals in the Upper House during the 1890s. In 1887 only forty-three peers in the Lords had supported Gladstone over Home Rule, a small minority which nevertheless had been given lustre by experienced followers such as Granville, Kimberley, Spencer, Ripon and Rosebery – a front bench without a following. By 1897 Gladstone had retired, Granville had died and Rosebery had withdrawn from active leadership. Liberals could then count only 25 supporters in a chamber of 565 peers. In October 1896, Kimberley earned the dubious distinction of being selected to succeed Rosebery as Liberal leader in the Lords. What a 'miserable position, almost absurd', Kimberley reflected, ' to be a leader with a handful of (at most) forty men to lead' (18 Oct. 1896). Succeeding Rosebery moreover required Kimberley to work with Harcourt, as Liberal leader in the Commons, in whom he had no confidence. Harcourt's odious temper had not improved since the Rosebery ministry, and made 'all business relations with him detestable'. Kimberley and Harcourt worked together surprisingly well, but Kimberley did it only for the good of the party and could not regard his position as anything other than a disagreeable duty. Upon Harcourt's retirement as Liberal leader in December 1898, Kimberley personally welcomed Campbell Bannerman's[76] emergence as leader, though it brought no unity and little strength to a party in rapid decline. 'It is really a farce to pose as a leader when I have only about 15 followers who attend the House when whipped', he lamented (8 Aug. 1900). Thus had Gladstone's aristocratic Liberal juggernaut of 1869–70 come to a stand-still, leaving Kimberley to wonder impotently at the dismal prospects of the party (21 Feb. 1900, 25 June 1901, 17 July 1901).

The frequent valedictory Journal entries for the 1890s marked a sense of decline. The death of his beloved wife in May 1895, and of his youngest son in April 1901, made the political fight seem less worthwhile. The loss of so many influential colleagues progressively marked the decline of a Liberal party struggling to cope with the mixed legacy of Gladstone's leadership. With the death of Lord Granville,

[76] Henry Campbell-Bannerman (1836–1908), Lib. MP for Stirling burghs, 1868–1908; ch. sec. Ireland, 1884–5; war sec., 1886, 1892–5; Lib. leader in the Commons, 1897; pr. min., 1905–8.

Kimberley lost 'an excellent and constant friend' (31 March 1891). No man, Kimberley felt, could give better advice or discern the wisest course of action. Although Granville was not always equal to realising his suggested aims, inattention to detail was no bar to Granville's achievements as the tactful arbiter of Liberal high politics, built upon his wide popularity and social finesse. Similarly, Lord Derby's death in April 1893 removed another good friend and Cabinet colleague who had embodied many of the best qualities of Liberalism under Gladstone. 'No man saw both sides of a question so clearly or could state the arguments pro and con with such perfect impartiality' (22 April 1893). Yet it was precisely Derby's clear vision that exacerbated his besetting weakness of indecision. Intellectual integrity, Kimberley believed, had sapped Derby's administrative effectiveness. Yet men like Granville and Derby had flourished under Gladstone's leadership, as had Kimberley himself. When Gladstone died in May 1898, Kimberley keenly felt the loss of the man whose powers of speech, organisation and leadership had been so instrumental in both fashioning the Liberal party and in destroying it. He was quick to refute allegations of Gladstone's dictatorial style of governing, and glad when others recognised the great truth which held so much promise for the Liberal party in the halcyon days of the seventies. 'I never did business with any man who was more patient, less meddlesome, and more ready to listen to the arguments of those who disagreed with him', Kimberley recalled (20 May 1898).

In April 1900 the death of the Duke of Argyll further symbolised the fate of the Liberal party. Three years Kimberley's senior, Argyll was the last surviving member of Aberdeen's coalition Cabinet of the 1850s, remembered for his 'cocksureness' and propensity to harangue his colleagues, 'with a touch of the Presbyterian preacher'. Argyll's death broke the last living link with the world in which both Kimberley and the Liberal party had formed their political identities. It was proving Kimberley's unkind fate to outlive both his contemporaries and the political creed to which he had committed himself. No wonder that he sometimes reflected upon the quiet life that he might have had in enjoying the natural pursuits of farm and field. As Liberal woes multiplied, Kimberley took solace in the company of his children and grandchildren, and in the friendship of Lords Ripon and Spencer, who had travelled so much of the same road. But as Kimberley wrote in his Memoir, a 'strong sense of duty' had always been the 'touchstone' of his life. When the end came on 8 April 1902, Kimberley was still in harness, dutifully leading the small band of Liberal Lords to nowhere.

Influential memorials such as *The Times* obituary and his entry in the *Dictionary of National Biography* portrayed Kimberley as a devoted Gladstonian Whig who focused his talents on departmental labours. Vicary Gibbs in Cokayne's *The Complete Peerage* characterised Kimberley as 'one of the few peers who blindly followed Gladstone'. Thus posterity rewarded loyalty with a simplistic caricature. Kimberley's Journal reveals a more complex reality and a broader field of political endeavour, corroborating the view of Liberal MP and fellow Cabinet member George Shaw-Lefevre,[77] that 'in proportion to his real weight in the inner circle of the party', no one was 'so little known' to its rank and file.[78]

---

[77] George John Shaw-Lefevre (1831–1928), Lib. MP for Reading, 1863–85, for Bradford, 1886–95; suc. as Baron Eversley, 1906; post.-genl., 1884–5; 1st comm. works, 1892–4; pres. loc. govt. bd., 1894–5.

[78] *Liberal by Principle*, 2.

JOURNAL:
6 MAY 1862–10 JANUARY 1902

6 May 1862. 48 Bryanston Sqre. Before commencing this journal I will shortly sketch my life up to this point. I was born Jany. 7, 1826 in Baker Street. My father died of a cold after an illness of only four days in the spring of 1834. I remember little of him except that he was very kind to me, and that he was fond of cricket & shooting. My mother devoted herself to the education of my brother & me, and I can never repay her affection & care. I married my dearest wife on Aug. 16, 1847, having proposed to her after only ten days acquaintance. *The* question was put at a breakfast at the Duchess of Bedford's at Camden Hill.[1]

When nine years old I was sent to school at Lyndon in Rutlandshire. The Rev. T. Kerchever Arnold,[2] the master of the school was an accomplished scholar, indeed too much so to teach little boys. He had bad health, was very irritable, and sometimes too severe, but he was a just man & his pupils respected him. I am grateful to him for two things, for having extirpated in me a vile habit of falsehood and for having compelled me to be accurate in my lessons. He punished me both with the birch & cane, & whatever may be said in favor of 'moral suasion' as contrasted with corporal punishment, I must admit that the latter was effectual in my case. I disliked being flogged, & took care afterwards at Eton to avoid it by attention to lessons & discipline. My dislike however was more to the degradation than the mere bodily pain.

From Lyndon when 12 years old I went to Eton to the Rev. E. Pickering's, a worthy excellent man.[3] I was tolerably successful in scholarship at Eton, indeed I was 'sent up for good' more than 20 times. I was rather a big boy of my age, & was therefore never much bullied, but I hated school, & there is no period of my life to which I look back with less satisfaction. I remained at Eton till I was '6th form', having been placed on going to Eton in the remove. At the age of 17 I left Eton, & then travelled on the Continent for some months with the Rev. Constantine Frere, a good scholar & a good man, perhaps not so good a bear leader.[4] At the age of 18 I went to Christ Church

---

[1] Francis Russell, 7th Duke of Bedford (1788–1861) m. Anna-Maria Stanhope, 1808.

[2] Rev. T. Kerchever Arnold (1800–53), rector of Lyndon, Rutlandshire, 1839–53: miscellaneous writer.

[3] Rev. Edward Hayes Pickering (1807–52), asst. master, Eton.

[4] Rev. Constantine Frere, tutored Kimberley in Europe prior to the latter going up to Christ Church.

Oxford. There I lived with a 'fast' set, but being ambitious, I read hard during the latter part of my residence, & thanks to the admirable coaching' of the Revd. H. L. Mansel (the well known author since of the Bampton Lectures &c.)[5] I obtained a first class in classics at Easter 1847.

After my marriage I passed the winter in Italy. I was always ambitious of making a figure in the political world, but I found it a sad 'damper' on my ambition to be placed in the icy cold atmosphere of the House of Lords at 21. What would I not have given to have been able to try my fortune in the H. of Commons? I determined however to make the best of my position, & soon began to take some part in the debates. My maiden speech was made on the 12th of April 1850 on the 3rd reading of the Convict Prisons Bill. I remember there were not more than 10 or 12 peers present. Lord Derby who whatever faults he possesses, is generous towards very young aspirants complimented me tho' I spoke from the Govt. side. I did not get much encouragement from my supercilious exclusive friends the Whigs. I adopted Liberal principles purely from conviction. Indeed I was a Liberal when a boy at Eton, & I remember very well shocking the august assembly of 'Pop' by defending in a set speech the execution of Charles I.[6] My only supporter was the eldest son of General Peel.[7] I was however no great admirer of Lord John Russell's Government which was in power when I entered political life, & I remember that I declined I forget in what year to move the address, not wishing to identify myself too closely with the measures of the Govt. But I was a steady supporter of the Administration on most questions. The only important question, as far as I now remember, on which I differed very strongly from the Govt. was on their Italian policy. I had witnessed Lord Minto's[8] famous progress thro' Italy in 1847–48, and I declined to vote against the motion hostile to Govt. made by Lord Brougham.[9] I did not vote at all. I was in the country at the time, & in answer to a letter from Lord Grey asking for my vote I declined to go up to town, saying that if I did I must vote against Govt. I voted for the Govt on the Greek question (Pacifico's case) & entirely approved Lord Palmerston's policy in spite of the brilliant speech of Lord Derby, the most brilliant speech

[5] Henry Longueville Mansel (1820–71), philosopher; scholar and tutor at St John's College, Oxford from 1844. See entry for 10 Aug. 1871.

[6] Charles I (1600–49), King of England, executed during the Civil War.

[7] Robert Kennedy Peel (1825–63), son of Jonathan Peel (1799–1879), maj.-genl. from 1854; war sec., 1858–9, 1866; Cons. MP for Huntingdon, 1818–68.

[8] Gilbert Elliot, 2nd Earl of Minto (1782–1859), ld. privy seal, 1846; prevailed on King of Naples to grant Sicily a separate parliament.

[9] Henry Peter Brougham, Baron Brougham and Vaux (1778–1868), ld. chanc., 1830–4; reformer who sat constantly in supreme court of appeal and in judicial committee of privy council; strenuously opposed repeal of navigation acts, 1849.

I think I have ever heard.[10] In this debate Ld. Canning[11] after speaking for about 10 minutes suddenly broke down, turned as white as a sheet, & sat down. Colonial questions at that time excited much attention, & frequent debates. I sometimes spoke on these subjects against Lord Grey's measures.

I was a member of the 'Colonial Reform Association', a society comprising men of all parties, amongst others Molesworth, Joseph Hume, Cobden,[12] Spencer Walpole, Roebuck,[13] Lord Naas,[14] Adderley,[15] Horsman.[16] The society lasted but a short time.[17] It caused much annoyance however to the Govt. & put the finishing stroke to the liberation of the Colonies from the incessant meddling of the Colonial Office.

Since Lord Grey's administration there have been no colonial questions, because the colonies are now wisely left to govern themselves. Roebuck was wonderfully 'cantankerous', whenever he attended the Council of the Society of wh. I was a member, & wh. by the by was in fact the Society as I never heard of any 'tail'. Joseph Hume & I were the Finance Committee,[18] & we got on very well together. Hume

[10] For a vivid description of the Don Pacifico debate see *DD1*, 20–2.

[11] Charles John Canning, 2nd Viscount and 1st Earl Canning (1812–62), post.-genl., 1853–5; gov.-gen., then viceroy of India, 1855–62; cr. earl, 1859.

[12] Richard Cobden (1804–65), leader of the anti-corn law agitation; Rad. MP for West Riding Yorkshire, 1847–57, and for Rochdale, 1859–65.

[13] John Arthur Roebuck (1801–79), MP for Sheffield, 1849–68, 1874–79; moved for committee of inquiry into conduct of Crimean war, leading to Aberdeen's resignation.

[14] Richard Southwell Bourke (Lord Naas), 6th Earl of Mayo (1822–72), Cons. MP for Kildare, 1847–52, for Coleraine, 1852–57, for Cockermouth, 1857–69; ch. sec. for Ireland, 1852, 1858, 1866; viceroy of India, 1869–72.

[15] Charles Bowyer Adderley, 1st Baron Norton (1814–1905), Cons. MP for Staffs. N., 1841–78; pres. b. of t., 1874–78; cr. peer, 1878.

[16] Edward Horsman (1807–76), Whig MP Cockermouth, 1836–52, for Stroud, 1853–68, for Liskeard, 1869–76; ch. sec. for Ireland, 1855–7; with Lowe formed 'cave of Adullam' against Reform bill of 1866.

[17] The first 'preliminary' meeting of the Society was on 3 Jan. 1850, while final minutes recorded were for a meeting of 30 June 1851. Other founding members of the Society included Francis Baring (chair.), Thomas Milner Gibson, M.J. Higgins, Lord Kinnaird, Lord Lyttelton, F.A. McGeachy, Joseph Napier, Francis Scott, H. Ker Seymer, John Simeon and Augustus Stafford. Lord Naas joined on 9 March 1850.

[18] Writing more than a decade later, Wodehouse's memory failed him with regard to the Finance Committee, which was at first composed of Wodehouse, Simeon and McGeachy. McGeachy appears to have been inactive, leading to Adderley's 'appointment' to the committee. Wodehouse was a member of several other committees, however, and was frequently working with Adderley, Molesworth, Hume and Simeon. Together these members formed the active core of the Society. Detailed minutes of the Society's business can be found in NtP 2735. For the founding prospectus of the CRS, see 'The Society for the Reform of Colonial Government', 29 Jan. 1850, KP6 MS.eng.c.3995, ff. 110–11. See too William S. Childe-Pemberton, *Life of Lord Norton, 1814–1905: Statesman & Philanthropist* (London, 1909), 75–83.

was one of the most muddle headed men with whom I ever transacted business. His dogged perseverance, & a certain appearance of candor & honesty gained him his reputation such as it was. Walpole showed himself unmistakeably to be a very weak man in deliberation, but a more honest & admirable politician does not exist. The most valuable acquaintance which I formed by my connexion with this society was Molesworth's. It continued till his death. Molesworth was a first rate specimen of the doctrinaire statesman. He always wrote his speeches before he delivered them, & I remember on one occasion he had a pile of *printed* copies of his speech on his table the day before it was delivered in the House of Commons.

I was from the first an ardent free trader, & I incurred a good deal of obloquay in my own county (Norfolk) on account of some speeches which I made in Parliament, denying that agricultural distress had been caused by the repeal of the corn laws.[19] Whilst I am on the subject of free trade, I may mention a circumstance which made a great impression upon me as a boy. I met at dinner at Raikes Currie's Grote, Charles Buller,[20] & other Radical M.Ps at the time when Peel[21] brought in his new sliding scale, & they all declared that from expressions which Peel had let fall, they had no doubt he intended eventually to repeal the corn law. I was introduced to Peel only a few days before his death. I heard one of his last speeches, & I remember that arguing in favor of a change in the settlement laws he said 'he was credibly informed that at present in many parishes the labourers lived at such a distance from their work that they were compelled to go to their work upon donkeys', whereupon there was a loud & very insulting cry from the opposition benches (where Peel sat) of Oh! Oh! donkeys, donkeys! Peel did not look at all disturbed but when the noise stopped, repeated very blandly 'Yes Sir upon donkeys'. Peel's manner of speaking was very measured & pompous.

In 1852 when Lord Derby's first Government was formed, I took an active part in opposition. On one occasion I went too far in an attack on Lord Derby, alluding to his political conduct in throwing over protection on taking office as inconsistent with his personal honour.[22] I never saw Derby so angry. I of course had to withraw the expression which was decidedly unparliamentary, but I retain my opinion unchanged that nothing could be more mean than to drive Peel out of office on the question of Protection, to keep up an opposition for five years on the ground that protection was essential to the prosperity of

[19] See 3 *Hansard* 114 (18 Feb. 1851), 797–801; (20 March 1851), 218–20.
[20] Charles Buller (1806–48), Lib. MP for Liskeard, 1832–48; judge adv.-genl., 1846; ch. poor law com., 1847.
[21] Sir Robert Peel, 2nd Baronet (1788–1850), pr. min., 1834–5, 1841–6.
[22] 3 *Hansard* 123 (22 Nov. 1852), 290–3.

agriculture, to take all possible advantage of the protection cry at the hustings, & then quietly to kick away the ladder by which he had mounted to the leadership of the Tory party. The only mistake was the word personal; I meant & ought to have said 'political' honour.

When the Govt. of Lord Aberdeen[23] was formed in December 1852, I was appointed Under Secretary for Foreign Affairs, this office being selected, I suppose, for my debut because I had never expressed an opinion in public on foreign affairs, & had given them less attention than any other class of political business. The office I wished for was that of Vice President of the B. of Trade. I served under Lord John Russell for a few months & then under Lord Clarendon till 1856, when on peace being made with Russia I was appointed Minister at St Petersburg. I remained at Petersburg exactly two years from June 1856 till May 1858. I told Lord Clarendon on accepting the post that I would not stay more than two years, & it was already known to him that I should resign in the spring of 1858, when the fall of the Palmerston Govt. caused me to resign at once as I did not wish to serve under Ld. Malmesbury.[24] My reception at St Petersburg was, as might be expected immediately after the war, very cold. When the Emperor received me at the audience to present my credentials,[25] he put on a very stern look, & said in a tone almost offensive that he hoped to forget what had passed during the war, but that it must be very long before Russia could forget the atrocities committed by the English on the coast of Finland. I saw this attempt at bullying must be resisted at once, & therefore replied that it would be better to abstain on both sides from referring to the events of the war, as if atrocities were to be discussed, I too should have something to say which it might not be agreeable to H. My. to hear. I felt excessively angry, & if the Emperor had pursued the conversation further I should have told him plainly what we thought in England of the barbarities committed on our wounded by Russian soldiers before Sevastopol. Our interview passed off otherwise without any incident, & the manner of the Emperor was except on this one point, mild and courteous. On the very few other occasions when I conversed with him, he said little on politics. He has the air of being 'bored' by his position. Naturally an amiable well meaning man of average abilities, he has a burden on his shoulders which he is scarcely

[23] George Hamilton Gordon, 4th Earl of Aberdeen (1784–1860), for. sec., 1841–6; pr. min., 1852–5.

[24] James Howard Harris, 3rd Earl of Malmesbury (1807–89), for. sec., 1852, 1858–9; ld. privy seal, 1866–8, 1874–6.

[25] Aleksandr II (1818–81), r. 1855–81; m. 1841, Maria da. of Grand Duke Louis II of Hesse-Darmstadt. On presentation of Wodehouse and other English representatives to the Emperor, see E. Fitzmaurice, *The Life of Granville George Leveson Gower, Second Earl Granville, 1851–1891* (2 vols., London, 1905), I, 186, 189–94.

equal to support, & I doubt much whether he will be able to carry through the great reforms which he has undertaken without a catastrophe. He is a tall man not handsome but well set up & military looking. Scandalous stories were rife as to his private life, he was said to be constantly drunk & to spend his time with mistresses. I took some pains to discover the truth & as far as I could find out these stories were gross exaggerations. Occasional orgies there may have been with the Adlerbergs & the other court minions, but at all events the orgies were private & the mistresses were never obtruded on the public. One of the maids of honour a Princesse Marie Dolgoroukow was commonly said to be a mistress of the Emperor. She was rather a handsome girl, & the Emperor's attentions were certainly rather marked. Whether she really was his mistress I don't know, but I must relate a piece of scandal which went the round of Petersburg Society about this girl & which may serve as a specimen of the sort of stories which passed current there.

A new Maitre de Police at St Petersburg had been appointed, Count Schouvalow, the town was very much puzzled to account for the appointment having been given to the Count who had only the rank of Colonel, as it had been usually held by a General Officer. The following explanation was quickly invented. The Princesse M. Dw., it was said, was in the family way by the Emperor: it was necessary therefore to marry her forthwith to some one: Count S. had been selected as the happy man, the reward was the Police mastership. The Count, however, having got the office declined to perform the marriage part of the bargain. I don't believe the lady was ever in the family way, but the story was devoutly believed for some time, & people used to look narrowly at the poor girl to see whether she showed any signs of a big belly.

I saw but little of the Empress. She is a quiet, ladylike woman without much pretension to good looks. She had the reputation of being very 'dévote'; at the Coronation she kissed the holy pictures in the Church where the ceremony took place, with great show of fervour. I was present at the coronation at Moscow & the fetes which followed it. Nothing could be finer than the court pageants, but nothing wearies me so much as a succession of big shows and I was not in the humour to enjoy anything at Moscow, as I was in much anxiety about my dear Florence whom I had left at St Petersburg, far advanced in the family way. She was safely delivered of a boy on the 9th. Novr. (1856). We named him Alfred. The poor little fellow died to our extreme grief, of a cold on the 9th of Feby. 1858. My wife was attended in her confinement by one Wrangel a German doctor. I was not much impressed with his skill or knowledge; but he evidently rated himself highly, as I heard he was much discontented with the fee of £50 which

I gave him, double Locock's[26] fee! It was no thanks to him but to an English monthly nurse, Mrs Baker, whom we engaged to come out from England that my poor Flo: got safely thro' her trouble. I attribute the loss of our boy partly to climate, but more to our having foolishly attempted at first to bring him up by hand.

To return to the Imperial family. The Grand Duke Constantine[27] seemed to me a vain man, impatient & haughty in his manner, but endowed with considerable abilities, & very anxious to gain information from any quarter. The Grand Duchess is a singularly beautiful woman. Of the Grand Duke & Grand Duchess Nicholas[28] nearly the contrary may be said. He is heavy & stupid; she ugly and uninteresting. The Grand Duke Michael[29] was but just grown up; he married whilst I was at Petersburg. He struck me as a very pleasing gentlemanlike young man, his wife, a Baden princess, I saw but once, & the only thing I remember of her was that she was amiable in manner & that she spoke English extremely well. The Grand Duchess Marie is so well known, & her husband, who is called the 'Grand Duke' Strogonoff that I need say very little of them. Count Strogonoff who was her lover and equerry during her first husband the Duke of Leuchtenberg's life, is now her husband & equerry, but in public he appears only as the equerry. The G. Duchess did not dare to avow her marriage during the Emperor Nicholas' life. She is a very clever agreeable woman with the remains of great beauty.

The other members of the Imperial family, resident at the capital, were the Empress Dowager,[30] a vain frivolous old lady who spent huge sums of money in travelling about Europe in state for health, but who fortunately for the Russian Treasury died soon after I left Russia; the Grand Duchess Catherine, daughter of the Grand Duke Michael with her heavy German husband from Mecklenberg Strelitz; & the Duke of Oldenburg & his family of whom it is enough to say that they were North Germans, slow in mind & body but quiet good natured people enough.

The Russian court was an odd mixture of easy manners & stiff etiquette. The Emperor drove about the streets in a droshky with no servant but the coachman, & went sometimes to evening parties in

---

[26] Sir Charles Locock (1799–1875), obstetric physician; first physician-accoucheur to Queen Victoria, 1840.

[27] Konstantin Nikolaevich (1827–92), second son of Tsar Nicholas I; commanded Russian fleet in Baltic during Crimean War; gov. of Poland, 1862–3.

[28] Nikolai Nikolaevich (1831–91), third son on Tsar Nicholas I; commanded Russian army of Danube in Russo-Turkish War, 1877–8.

[29] Mikhail Nikolaevich (1832–1909), fourth son of Tsar Nicholas I; pres. of privy council of state from 1881.

[30] Alexandra Fyodorovna, Empress Dowager, widow of Nicholas I.

private houses where he mixed in society without any form. On the other hand the etiquette of court presentations was rigid. A ridiculous instance of it occurred to me when I was presented to the Grand Duchess Marie. It is necessary that a foreign Envoy should be presented separately to every member of the Imperial family, male & female. My wife having to go to Peterhof to be presented to the Empress, I accompanied her to the palace. I was not to go with her to her audience of the Empress. To this she proceeded alone, & after her audience she was invited to stay to luncheon. I meantime was served with an elaborate luncheon by myself in another room, & after luncheon the Grand Duchess Marie who had been eating her luncheon in the room where my wife was with the rest of the Imperial family who were all assembled for some Imperial birthday, drove off to her own country house several miles distant. I duly followed in a Court carriage, & was in due form presented. Etiquette would have been outraged if I had been presented to the G Duchess anywhere but in her own house. The foreign ministers were never asked to dinner at Court, except the Prussian Minister[31] on account of the family connexion between the Emperor & the King of Prussia & the French Ambassador, M. de Morny,[32] whom the Imperial Court were most anxious to curry favor with. On the whole very little civility was shown at Court to the diplomatic body, much less than is shown to that body at the English Court.

I shall give a sketch of my colleagues, but first I must mention the odd way in which my wife made acquaintance with the Tsar on the occasion above alluded to at Peterhof. After her audience of the Empress she was sitting down waiting for luncheon to wh. she had been invited, & amongst several officers who came & sat down beside her to talk to her was the Emperor. After he was gone she asked who the tall officer was & to her astonishment was told who he was. The Emperor afterwards rallied her good humouredly on her not having known him.[33]

My principal colleagues were of course the Rps. of the Great Powers, M. de Morny, Count Valentine Esterhazy,[34] & M. Werther. Monsieur de Morny, the French Ambassador, is the type of the Imperialist French adventurer, a cold cunning man of the world, vulgar, insolent, & intensely conceited. I conceived an extreme dislike for him, the more intense probably because my diplomatic position obliged me to remain

---

[31] Baron Karl von Werther, Prussian minister to St Petersburg.

[32] Charles Auguste, Duc de Morny, half-brother of Napoleon III; pres. of the Corps Legislatif, 1854–65.

[33] An eminently repeatable anecdote which improved with age. Cf. Kimberley Memoir, 489, F. Levenson Gower, *Bygone Years* (London, 1905), 217.

[34] Valentin Esterhazy, Austrian amb. to St Petersburg.

on as good terms as possible with him. The obvious aim of the Court & all connected with it was to sow dissensions between N.B. of France & England, with this end all possible contrast was made between M. de Morny & me; every civility & honour which cd. gratify his vanity, was heaped upon him, whilst I was subjected to as many & as open slights as they dared venture upon. My obvious policy & duty was to frustrate their attempts & I flatter myself I did so most completely. Indeed I must have dissembled my dislike for the Frenchman pretty effectually as I remember that one day after his departure when I happened to say to my wife that I had seldom met any man whom I disliked so much, she expressed her surprise at this discovery of feelings wh. she had never suspected. But though I refrained from quarrelling with Morny, I never pretended to be intimate with him, or to like him. That would have been dishonorable.

The French Secretary of Embassy M. Baudin[35] was a very different man from his chief. I knew him well when he was Secretary of Embassy in London, & a more honest, upright, Frenchman I have never known. He is a Protestant. He now holds the appointment of Envoy at Stockholm. Morny hates England, & made no concealment of his hatred. I must add however that in spite of the abject flattery which he received from the Russians, he despised them, more than they deserved perhaps. Behind his back the courtiers repaid him for his contempt by saying biting things of the 'vulgar upstart'. What Jonathan would call 'quite a sensation' was created in society by what the Russians considered an unheard of breach of good manners committed by Morny at a ball at the French Embassy at which the Emperor was present. The Emperor himself retired early, immediately upon which the Ambassador & his suite disappeared for a few moments, & divested themselves of their uniform coats, so that when they returned to the ball room they wore ordinary dress coats & waistcoats with uniform trousers. They certainly looked absurd enough, but the Russians took grave offence at it wh. was much more absurd. To mark their disgust very few Russians appeared at the next reception at the Embassy.[36] Some very harmless things which Morny did were considered by the Russians to indicate his meanness. Amongst others he was very much blamed for having condescended to show to a Russian friend some carriages which he wanted to sell!

Morny's chief political object whilst he was at St Petg. appeared to be to establish a close friendship between the French & Russian

---

[35] Jean Baptiste Baudin. On his friendship with Wodehouse, see Baudin to Wodehouse, 28 June 1856, KP6 MS.eng.c.4009, ff. 11–12.
[36] For elaboration on the sartorial indiscretion, see Wodehouse to Clarendon, 28 Feb. 1857, KP3 Add. MS 46692, f. 302.

Courts & to injure Austria. He used to say to me, there are only three Great Powers as for those Germans Bah! they count for very little now in Europe. England, France & Russia should make a close alliance, & they can dictate to the world. In order to buy the friendship of Russia France was ready to let Russia by a side wind get rid of some of the most onerous conditions of the peace of 1856. How far France would have gone in this direction, it is impossible to say as the firm attitude of our Govt. & of Austria entirely frustrated the designs of Russia. We had many very stormy discussions with the Russian Govt. during the first year after the peace, & my position & duties were critical & anxious. We certainly gained a complete diplomatic victory of which Lord Palmerston & Ld. Clarendon had a right to be proud. My Austrian Colleague who died poor fellow of Bright's disease in 1858, was a very agreeable man, a thorough gentleman, & what is rare in a foreign diplomatist, impervious to Court flattery. Austria was the *bête noire* of Russians at that time in consequence of her treachery & ingratitude as it was termed to Russia, in not having sided with Nicholas against the Allies. She met with the usual fate of trimmers; Russia hated her, & France despised her. But however much the Russians abused Austria, they could not dislike Ct. Esterhazy. It was universally admitted that his personal popularity had alone rendered it possible for him to remain at St Petersburg to the close of the war. He acted most cordially with me in the discussions about the execution of the terms of peace notwithstanding the rather lukewarm support of his Govt.

He told me a curious anecdote of the insolence of the Emperor Nicholas. There was a close intimacy when he arrived as Envoy, between Austria & Russia, & Nicholas was immensely gracious. Whenever you have any difficulty, he said, 'don't go to Nesselrode,[37] but apply direct to me for an audience'. The Crimean war came, & with it difficulties enough. Now is the time thought Ct. Esterhazy, to see the Emperor. After many fruitless applications he at last succeeded. He was very badly received. At the close of the audience wishing to know whether the Emperor wd. receive him in future, he reminded HMy. of his intimation that he was to apply direct for an audience, and asked whether in future he should apply thro' the Minister for Foreign Affairs. '*Demandez à mon valet de pied*' was the reply. The Russians who were in terrible dread of Nicholas during his life, avenged themselves by 'kicking the dead lion' pretty freely. Every one at court was open mouthed about his tyranny & insolence.

I cannot better describe the feelings of the Russians towards the Austrians than by narrating the witty reply made by a Russian to the

[37] Se p. 55.

question asked by some one at a dinner party 'why the Emperor of Austria bore the title of '*Sa Majesté Apostolique*', 'because he is in direct descent from Judas Iscariot'. My poor friend Esterhazy was just about, when he died, to marry the rich widow of Prince Kotchoubey. There had been a long flirtation between them but it was said that the lady, who was a 'grande dame' in Russian society, could not resolve upon her third marriage, since by Russian law only three marriages are permissible. Her first husband was Prince Bieloselzki. Of my Prussian colleague I need only say that he was a thorough North German, honest & heavy. He had a heavy, sentimental, Secretary Baron Werthern. My other colleagues were Baron Adelswärd, Minister of Sweden, Count Munster of Hanover, Baron Plessen of Denmark (who had married a Russian wife & become more Russian than the Russians) Baron de Braye of Bavaria, Marquis Sanli of Sardinia (who has since been given his passports by the Russian Govt. a just end of the tortuous policy of Sardinia as to the peace of Paris, a policy of subserviency to Russia in the hope of turning her hatred of Austria to account,) M. Regina of the two Sicilies, M. de Jonghe of Belgium, M. de Gevers of Holland, M. de Koneritz chargé d'affaires of Saxony, M. de Lobstein of Wurtemberg, M. de Moira of Greece was Minister from Portugal, M. Isturitz & the Duke d'Ossuna from Spain, Mr Seymour or Governor Seymour,[38] as the Yankees called him, from the United States. This worthy gentleman held but little communication with the natives as he could not speak a word of any language but his own.

M. Regina[39] had a very pretty wife, whom he had just married. She was his niece, & a dispensation had therefore to be procured from Rome. Pending the arrival of the document, the most important part of the marriage ceremony was so effectually performed that the lady found herself in the family way, & matters at length had advanced so far, that as Madame Regina said 'it became serious. I determined therefore to go to Rome myself to press for the dispensation. *Enfin j'ai vu le Saint Père, mais avant que je l'ai dit un mot, le Saint Père s'est ecris Ah! Madame Je vois qu'il est bien temps*'. The dispensation was not further delayed, & the lady's honor was saved.[40] She told the story herself with perfect naivete.

M. de Morny married a pretty Russian, the Princess Troubetzkoi, & soon after left Petersburg. The Princess Troubetzkoi was brought up at the Smolna Convent, a sort of fashionable foundling Hospital.

My political business was of course carried on with the Minister of

[38] Horatio Seymour, gov. of New York, 1853–5, 1863–5; Democratic candidate for President.
[39] Gennaro Capeche-Galeota, Duke of Regina.
[40] Cf. Kimberley Memoir, 489.

Foreign Affairs, Prince Gortchakow.[41] Prince G. is a man of unquestionable ability, but irritable, hasty, & devoured by a ridiculous &
insatiable vanity. He was violently opposed to the peace. I would
sooner, he said, have cut off my right hand than have signed it. His
passion was to 'briller', & for the sake of an opportunity of displaying
himself to advantage as a despatch writer, he would sacrifice much.
Still I think he had the interests of his country at heart. His manner &
tone were sometimes insolent but like all bullies he soon drew in his
horns when met with firmness. We had many sharp encounters in
words, but I must do him the justice to say he bore no rancour, & he
was more truthful than most Russians. He was a disagreeable Minister
to deal with on account of his vehemence & hot temper, but on the
other hand his hastiness & imprudence gave a great advantage to a
foreign diplomatist. It was always easy to draw him into avowals, & his
bluster, tho' very loud at times, 'broke no bones'.[42] I preferred him
greatly to his 'adjoint' M. Tolstoy,[43] who under many professions of
friendliness concealed a mean & arrogant temper, a combination of
qualities analogous to the communion of cowardice & bullying.

   Prince Gortchakow's passion for 'orders' was incredible, & led him
sometimes into foolish actions. He was very anxious for the Neapolitan
order (I don't remember what it is called) & he conveyed a hint thro'
M. Regina to King Bomba[44] that he might as well send it to him. But
Bomba said he would wait till Gortchakow had done something to
deserve it.[45] When he was heaping daily abuse upon Austria, he
nevertheless accepted with joy the order of St Stephen & but the most
conspicuous instance of his order mania occurred in the case of the
Turkish Medjidie. Riza Pasha had arrived from Constantinople as
Turkish Minister, & brought the Medjidie with him for G. After he
had called on G., & asked for his audience of the Emperor, news
arrived by telegraph that the Russian Minister at Cpl. had broken off
relations with the Porte on account of some disagreement about the
Principalities. Thereupon Riza Pasha called again on G., & said he
supposed the audience must be suspended, & that G. would of course

---

[41] Prince Aleksandr Mikhailovich Gorchakov (1798–1883), Russian foreign minister,
1856–82. Wodehouse's business can be closely followed in his correspondence with
Clarendon (BL Add. MSS 46692–4) and Hammond (PRO FO 391/3); and in other
correspondence, memoranda and papers relating to his ministry in St Petersburg (KP6
MSS.Eng.c.4008–11).

[42] Wodehouse was rather more critical at the time, reflecting the heat of their mutual
antagonism. See Wodehouse to Clarendon, 22 Nov. 1856, KP1 Add. MS 46692, ff. 144–
5.

[43] Dimitri Aleksandrovich Tolstoi, Russian for. u.-sec.; min. of public instruction, 1866–
80.

[44] Ferdinand II (1810–59), King of Naples r. 1830–59.

[45] Cf. Kimberley Memoir, 489.

not wish for the present to have the order. 'Yes' was the answer, 'we must put off the audience, but you may as well send me the order—'[46]

Gortchakow's vanity extended even to his personal appearance. He is singularly ugly. 'You would hardly have believed', he said to me one day, 'that I was a very handsome young man.' I could hardly resist the temptation to answer 'no, I really should not have thought it.' He got up very early in the morning & worked his secretaries very hard, dictating a great number of despatches. He generally received me in a long & very dirty black dressing gown, which made him look like a decayed old verger in one of our cathedrals.

Count Nesselrode,[47] the celebrated foreign Minister, of Nicholas' reign, had quite retired from affairs. He was hospitable & kind to us, agreeable & chatty in conversation, & apparently gay & cheerful. He does not give the least the impression of half civilization which is the characteristic of Russians, but of a man born (wh. he was) & educated in the West. His intellect seemed quite unimpaired by age. Count Orloff[48] on the contrary was a Russian to the back bone, a massive but brutal sensual looking man. I could understand that he had been a fit instrument of Nicholas' brute force policy.

Russian society did not please me. Much flattery & much back biting make the staple of ordinary Petersburg talk. There is a great superficial cleverness, but from defective education, an extraordinary want of sound knowledge.[49] On first making the acquaintance of a Russian gentleman I generally thought him intelligent, but nearer acquaintance invariably lowered my opinion. Their knowledge of foreign languages which is in the West thought so surprising does not seem to me to prove superior cleverness so much as is commonly supposed. It is rather the natural result of their education. They learn no Greek & little Latin, & scarcely any history or philosophy. Their whole attention is

[46] Kimberley, always wary of pretension, enjoyed recounting a similar story regarding Prince Metternich. Late in life, as Metternich prepared for an audience with the King of Denmark, he was unable to find the insignia of the Danish Order of the Elephant. According to Kimberley, 'Metternich ordered [his valet] at once to buy, borrow, or steal another set. This the one valet did, and Metternich, conspicuously adorned with the insignia of the Order, presented himself before the King. He then, to his dismay, found that His Majesty had summoned him for the purpose of presenting him with the Order of the Elephant, that being one of the very few European Orders which had not already received.' *Reminiscences of Lord Kilbracken* (London, 1931), 203. See too Kimberley to Cardwell, 23 Oct. 1870, CdP 30/48/31, ff. 77–8, 94; *JE*, 33.

[47] Karl Robert, Count Nesselrode (1780–1862), member of the Congress of Vienna; Russian chancellor who negotiated the Treaty of Paris ending the Crimean War.

[48] Prince Aleksei Fedorovich Orlov (1787–1862), engaged in negotiations following the Crimean War.

[49] For a more favourable view of Russian society, laced with biographical observations on a variety of lower-level diplomats, see Henry Wodehouse's letters to his mother, KP1 15/K2/20.

given to modern languages (with the exception of officers who are trained in mathematics & engineering in order to qualify them for the scientific military corps). They usually begin four languages at once, Russian, which they speak to their serfs, German wh. they speak to their hired upper Servants who come mostly from the German provinces belonging to Russia, English which they pick up from their nurses but which few have more than a smattering of, & French which is the language of polite society. Russian however is beginning to be spoken sometimes in society. Limit the education of a native of any country in the way in which the Russian gentleman's education is limited, & I believe he will learn modern languages quite as well & as quickly.

I heard a good deal about spies in Russian society but I was I suppose too stupid to be conscious of their operations: at all events they caused me no annoyance.[50] I had an amusing conversation once with a lady whom I had been warned against as a Govt. spy. She mentioned to me an absurd story which was current in Petersburg as to my having bribed the Secretary to the Committee which had been appointed to settle the new tariff. The story was this. The Moscow manufacturers who were hostile to the new tariff had sent a deputation to Petersburg to press their views on the Govt. This deputation offered a bribe to the Secretary to advise the postponement of the threatened reductions. The Secretary refused the bribe & denounced the deputation. The deputation however threatened such awkward revelations, if pressed that the Govt. thought it better to hush the matter up, & not to punish the bribers. But how to account for the secretary having refused the money. The Moscow men hit on this explanation. The English Minister who was instructed to move heaven & earth to get the new Tariff of cotton duties through, had offered a much larger bribe.

As the lady seemed particularly anxious to draw me into conversation on this subject, I resolved to gratify her curiosity. I accordingly talked mysteriously about the unlimited means of which I disposed & the wide spread secret agency which I had established. All this being darkly shadowed out roused the lady's curiosity to the uttermost. At last I suddenly burst out laughing, & looking her full in the face, asked her what she would not give, to know whether I was in jest or earnest.

Letters passing through the post office are habitually opened & read. Unfortunately one day the opened despatches were replaced in the wrong envelopes, so that the Austrian Minr. received the Prussian

---

[50] Wodehouse was, of course, spying as well. See Clarendon to Wodehouse, 29 Oct. 1856, 4 Feb. 1857, KP3 Add. MS 46692, ff. 110, 263; Wodehouse to Clarendon, 12 June 1857, KP3 Add. MS 46693, f. 112; Wodehouse to Clarendon, 12 Dec. 1857, KP3 Add. MS 46694, ff. 14–19; Wodehouse to Hammond, 23 May 1857, 10 Oct. 1857, HmP FO 391/3.

Despatch & vice versa. The Wurtemberg chargé d'affaires told me that the Govt. had remonstrated with him for sending his despatches through the Post, as they did not wish their own Post Office authorities to see their contents. They were full of Court scandal sent for the edification of the Wurtemburg Royal family. The Grand Duchess Olga is wife to the Crown Prince.

We had a very good house,[51] the Hotel Lazareff in the Michel's Platz, & a pretty villa (the second year of our residence) the smaller Villa Laval in the islands, but we were heartily glad to leave our grandeur & return to comfort at home. It may be worth mention that we paid for our house *2000 silver Roubles per annum including firing & water. The house was beautifully furnished.

[Undated mem:] *This must be wrong. If I remember rightly we paid £1750 per ann: K[52]

I occasionally made excursions into the country to shoot bears & elks. We went to considerable distances sometimes from the capital. The condition of the peasants varied very much in different villages. Some seemed tolerably well off, others in abject misery. They are by no means a heavy stolid people, but humorous & noisy like the Irish. Many of the men are well grown & handsome, but the peasant women, whom I saw, were universally hideous. In winter when men & women are clad in fur caps, sheepskins, & high boots, there is nothing but the beard to distinguish the sexes.[53]

The curse of the country is the peculation of the Govt. officers, & the corruptness of the Law Courts. Unless the Law Courts are thoroughly reformed & some degree of honesty infused into the administration, the emancipation of the serfs will benefit the country but little.

Every one admits the corruptness of the judges. I was much struck by an observation on this subject of Ct. Pierre Meyendorf,[54] one of the most honorable & distinguished of the servants of the Imperial Crown. He was deploring to me the corruptness of the judges. How could the country improve whilst the courts were venal. I asked him whether looking back over a series of years he could see no improvement. He thought a moment & said 'Yes I do not think the members of the Senate, the highest Court, can now be bought. Formerly all the judges not excepting the highest, had their price.' Another grievous evil is the

---

[51] For a sketched floorplan and further description, see John Wodehouse to Anne Wodehouse, 29 Sept. 1856, KP1 12/K2/18; Henry Wodehouse to Anne Wodehouse, 2 Nov. 1857, KP1 15/K2/20.

[52] Cf. Wodehouse to Raikes Currie, 11 Oct. 1856, KP1 3/1, where he indicated £1,950, less £300 for leasing a portion to Kers.

[53] Cf. Wodehouse to Clarendon, 31 Jan. 1857, KP3 Add. MS 46692, f. 259.

[54] Count Peter von Meyendorff, diplomatic adviser to Nicholas I.

delay of justice caused by the cumbrous forms and interminable appeals. The political administration is equally slow & cumbrous. Of all delusions I know none greater than that a despotic Govt. is necessarily prompt because unencumbered by the forms wh. hamper a constitutional Govt. A Govt. like that of France which has at its command an admirably organized machine of administration may be prompt but the Russian Govt. which is omnipotent in theory, in practice is involved in a web of circumlocution which would put to shame the most ingenious red-tapest in the West. It takes months to get an answer on the most trifling detail of business from some provincial Govt. a few hundred miles from the capital.

As to the law suits they quite beat our Court of Chancery. Here is an instance. A gentleman living in a remote part of the country obtained leave from a neighbour to hire one of his serfs as wet-nurse to his child. Some time after the two gentlemen quarrelled & the proprietor of the serf out of spite suddenly withdrew his permission to her to act as wetnurse. The child was seriously ill in consequence, & the father commenced an action for restitution of his child's nurse against his quondam friend in the provincial court. The cause was carried from court to court by appeal & lasted many years. At length the Supreme Court at St Petersburg gave final judgment, & a young gentleman serving in the cadet corps at the capital was astonished one day by receiving formal notice that the cause had been decided & that his wet nurse was ordered to return to him forthwith.[55]

Count Panin,[56] a morose, disagreeable man, but said to be a man of ability was, & I believe still remains Minister of Justice. He was very unpopular, & had the credit of being the chief of the reactionary party. His office gives him a wide power of interference with the course of justice, & he had exercised that power in a manner which made him generally hated. The courts of justice in Russia will never be improved until there is publicity & a regular bar. At present there is neither. I remember hearing of the astonishment of Lord Wensleydale[57] when he visited St Petg. on being told that there were no law courts nor lawyers in our sense of the words. There are not even chamber advocates. When I wanted an opinion as to a point of Russian law for the information of my Govt. I did find a retired 'Consciller' who professed to have studied law, but I was obliged ultimately to apply to the Ministry of Justice for the opinion. The Senate of which one branch sits at Moscow, & another at St Petersburg, & which is something like

[55] Cf. Kimberley Memoir 489–90.
[56] Viktor Nikitich Panin, min. of justice, 1841–62.
[57] Sir James Parke, Baron Wensleydale (1782–1868), raised to the king's bench, 1828; transferred to the exchequer, 1834.

our Privy Council combining political functions with judicial, was presided over by Count Bloudoff, the father of the Secretary Legation in London now Minister for Russia at Athens. Count B. enjoyed a good reputation as an honest & capable man. I might write much more on the subject of Russia, but I could write little which may not be found in ordinary books of travel.

The Russians have in my judgment many amiable & some great qualities. They are obliging, cheerful companions; they are persevering & courageous, and are generally quick & intelligent; above all they are imbued with a strong love of fatherland; but on the other hand they are exceedingly untruthful, they are arrogant to their inferiors cringing to their superiors; & they are entirely without the Western principles of honour or chivalry. Want of opportunity to learn has made this knowledge of those who are educated very superficial & has left the mass of the people half barbarous. I believe the Crimean War (which did them far more injury than was supposed in Western Europe) has been the commencement of a new era in their history. They have seen clearly that the military policy of Nicholas was a mistake & that before they can really take up a great position in Europe, they must be civilized. The first step in this direction has been taken by the Emperor by the emancipation of the serfs: the rest must follow in time. But meantime Russia's power of interference in Europe is completely paralysed. She cannot pursue her plans of aggrandisement in Turkey & even in Eastern Asia tho' by the acts of Ct. Mouravieff, a great territory on the Amour has been added to her Empire, sound thinking Russians recognise the impossibility of any further advance for the present. The Crimean war must therefore be pronounced to have answered its purpose. It has rescued Turkey from all immediate danger from Russia & it has removed the nightmare of Russian preponderance which weighed upon Germany & in some degree upon all Europe.

Russia civilized might no doubt be still more formidable than Russia semi barbarous, but before the civilization of Russia is completed many years must pass, & who can tell what changes may take place. At all events the Russia of Nicholas is a dream of the past.

I must add two anecdotes one showing the immoveability & stupidity, the other the slowness of the Russian administration. The first is that Macaulay's History[58] had been placed on the list of prohibited Books in Nicholas time, but in the present Emperor's reign a Russian translation of Macaulay had been allowed to be published. No order however had been made rescinding the prohibition of the English

---

[58] Thomas Macaulay's *History of England* was published in three stages: vols. I & II in 1848; vols. III & IV in 1855; vol. V in 1861.

version so that the English version was prohibited, the Russian version allowed!

The other is as follows. An English gentleman called upon me at one day [sic] & asked my assistance in the following circumstances. He had come all the way from Australia in order to marry a Russian lady, but to his dismay on his arrival he found that no marriage could be solemnized during Lent which had just commenced. He was pressed for time, having engagements in Australia; could I get leave for him to be married before the expiration of the 40 days? I applied accordingly, tho' I told him I was sure it was no use, to the Russian Gt. Some time after the gentleman sought an interview with the Greek Archbishop who told him it was quite out of the question to grant his request. He found out however that there was nothing to prevent the Protestant ceremony at the English Church from being gone through, leaving the Greek ceremony to be performed after Lent. Being thus half married he persuaded the lady to postpone indefinitely the Gk ceremony, & to proceed at once on their wedding tour. But here a fresh difficulty arose. Every one, travelling in Russia, must have a Russian passport. The happy couple not being married in the eyes of the Russian law, could not have a joint passport as man & wife, & the lady objected to the scandal of a passport describing her as a spinster. I could suggest no remedy, but I gave them a passport as man & wife which would become available as soon as they crossed the Russian frontier, & away they went. On Good Friday I recd. an answer from the Russian Foreign Office, expressing regret that the gentleman's request could not be granted.[59]

After my return from Petersburg in June 1858, I made one or two slight speeches in the H. of Lords.[60] On March 8, 1859 I brought the question of the 'Charles et George' in rather a long speech under the notice of the House. On June 17 Lord Derby's Govt resigned, & Lord Palmerston's 2nd administration being soon after formed, I accepted the post of Under Secretary at the Foreign Off: with charge of the foreign business in the House. After the peace of Villafranca, when a Conference was proposed of the European Powers at Paris, I was appointed 2nd English Plenipotentiary, Lord Cowley[61] being first. I had

[59] See M. A. Biddulph to Wodehouse, 8 March 1867, KP6 MS.eng.c.4009, ff. 21–2.

[60] On 17 June Wodehouse spoke on the slave trade, on 2 July in favour of the Church Rates Abolition Bill, on 23 July in favour of the Marriage Law Amendment Bill, and briefly interposed in favour of the second reading of the Government of New Caledonia Bill.

[61] Henry Richard Charles Wellesley, 1st Earl Cowley (1804–84), amb. to Paris, 1852–67; conducted negotiations following the Crimean War. On circumstances surrounding the appointment of Wodehouse, see *Liberal by Principle*, 32; Clarendon to Duchess of Manchester, 16 Dec. 1859, in *'My Dear Duchess': Social and Political Letters to the Duchess of Manchester, 1858–1869* (London, 1956), 83–4.

gone so far as to engage rooms at Paris but the Conference never took place, much to my joy, as I had no fancy for the business. It would have led to no good. In July 1861 Lord John Russell being made a Peer I resigned my office, tho' requested by Lord John to retain it. After having had charge of the business for two years in the House I could not submit to the loss of position.[62] In 1860 I was offered the Govt. of Madras, in 1861 of Canada & in 1862 that of Bombay, all wh. I declined.[63]

28 April 1862. Monday. Went to the Grove and stayed till Thursday. Private theatricals on Monday & Wednesday. Lord Clarendon told me that so far was it from being true that Prince Albert[64] had originated the Great Exhibition which is to be opened on the 1st of May, that the Queen had herself told him (Lord Clarendon) that the Prince was very reluctant to give the scheme the sanction of his name. He was persuaded at last, but had grave doubts of the expediency & success of the project. It is evidently a job of Dilke, Coles & co.[65]

Ld. Granville was I know averse to it, as he told me he was sorry I had put my name down as a Guarantor, as he had hoped the plan would fall through.

Lord C. blamed the management of the Liberal party at elections. How could the Govt. expect to retain offices if seats were lost as of late by pure stupidity or carelessness.

1 May 1862. Thursday. Came back to London. Did not go to the opening on the Exhibition. From what I hear it was on the whole a failure.

5 May 1862. Monday. Spoke in the House in favor of 3rd reading of Land Transfer Bill as it was announced that there was no division, and the hour of dinner was nearly arrived, besides the subject being uninteresting, it is not surprising that I did not produce much effect.

[62] Expanding on his rationale for resigning, see Wodehouse to Raikes Currie, 13 July 1861, in *Liberal by Principle*, 88–9.

[63] On these offers, see Wood to Wodehouse, 5 Sept. 1860, KP6 MS.eng.c.4475, ff. 16–17; Palmerston to Russell, 19, 20 July 1861, RiP 30/22/21, ff. 508–9; Newcastle to Palmerston, 27 Aug. 1861, in John Martineau, *Life of Henry Pelham, Fifth Duke of Newcastle, 1811–64* (London, 1908), 303. There was also talk of his going as ambassador to Constantinople. *Liberal by Principle*, 282.

[64] Albert Francis Charles Augustus Emmanuel of Saxe-Coburg-Gotha (1819–61), prince consort of England, m. Queen Victoria, 1840.

[65] Sir Charles Wentworth Dilke (1810–69), commissioner; Sir Henry Cole (1808–82), on managing committee. For a concise treatment of problems related to the exhibition, see Thomas Prasch, 'International Exhibition of 1862', in (J. Findling, ed.) *Historical Dictionary of World's Fairs and Expositions, 1851–1988* (New York, 1990), 23–30.

My main object was to indicate the right of a 'lay' lord to speak on law questions. Surely lay lords ought not to abandon their right of discussing vital questions connected with land.

11 May 1862. Sunday. M. Marliani called upon me. He has come over to negotiate a Treaty of Commerce between Italy and England. Had a long talk with him about Italian affairs. He thinks the Italians ought to give up all pretension to Rome. He argues that it would be impossible for the King of Italy & the Pope to exist side by side. The Pope, aided by the intrigues of foreign powers would make the Govt. of the King impossible. The Emperor of the French should, he thinks, declare to Italy that he never in any circs. will permit Rome & the Patrimony of St Peter to be annexed to the Italian Kingdom. Then the Italians seeing that Rome was out of their reach would gradually accustom themselves to doing without it, & another capital, perhaps Florence would be chosen.

12 May 1862. Monday. Lord Clanricarde[66] made a violent speech about the navigation of the Shannon. Lord Granard[67] seconded, equally violent. Govt. angry with Lord G. who they say has been made Lord Lieutenant of his county, & is now angry because he can get no more. It seems he wrote to the D. of Newcastle[68] asking for a Colonial appointment, and the Duke did not answer his letter.

13 May 1862. Tuesday. Repeal of declaration reqd. of persons holding office Mr. Hadfield's[69] bill proposed by Lord Taunton,[70] opposed by D. of Malborough.[71] I a short speech in support. Bill lost.

15 May 1862. Thursday. Dined with Mr. Legh[72] M.P. for Lancashire where was told that Lady Selina Vernon on being asked how she could

---

[66] Ulick John de Burgh Canning, 1st Marquess of Clanricarde (1802–74).

[67] George Arthur Hastings, 7th Earl of Granard (1833–89).

[68] Henry Pelham Fiennes Pelham Clinton, 5th Duke of Newcastle (1811–64), war & col. sec., 1852–4; sec. war, 1854–5; col. sec., 1859–64.

[69] George Hadfield (1787–1879), Rad. MP for Sheffield, 1852–74.

[70] Henry Labouchere, 1st Baron Taunton (1798–1869), col. sec., 1855–8; raised to peerage, 1859.

[71] John Winston Spencer Churchill, Marquess of Blandford (1822–83), Cons. MP for Woodstock, 1844–5, 1847–57, when he succ. as 7th Duke of Marlborough; ld. pres., 1867–8; ld. lt. of Ireland, 1876–80. In his Memoirs, Kimberley called Marlborough at Eton an 'ill conditioned disagreeable fellow'. See herein, 492.

[72] William John Legh (1828–98), MP for S. Lancashire, 1859–85; cr. Baron Newton, 1892. On the connection between the two families, see Thomas Wodehouse Legh, 2nd Baron Newton, *Restrospection* (London, 1941), 8.

marry Bidwell, such a bad man, replied 'because I could not bear to meet both my husbands hereafter'.[73]

17 May 1862.   Saturday. Dined with Lord Palmerston. H Ldp in high exultation at Dizzy's foolish speech about 'bloated armaments.'[74]

18 May 1862.   Sunday. M. Marliani called again. Expressed astonishment at finding Englishmen so little aware of the insuperable difficulties in the way of Rome becoming the Italian capital: thinks the Catholic powers would not allow the Pope's temporal power to be abolished. If the French were to leave Rome, the Pope would enter into no arrangement with Victor Emmanuel but wd. leave at once, perhaps go to Venice. He maintains that Naples is not an insurmountable difficulty. The nobles & middle class are thoroughly corrupt, but the masses are only brutal through ignorance, want of civilization.

19 May 1862.   Monday. Went to Kimberley.

20 May 1862.   Tuesday. Returned to town.

22 May 1862.   Thursday. A fire in my home in B. Sqr. Discovered about 4 P.M. and, happily put out without serious damage. Caused by a beam being too near the kitchen chimney, it began in the garret & extended to nursery.

23 May 1862.   Friday. Asked to shoot in the rifle match between the Lords & Commons. Declined – rifle shooting is not my forte. Ld. de Grey tells me that Sir G. Lewis[75] has commenced the study of Chinese. He says the D. of Cambridge[76] who is Tory in his opinions, is frantic at the speech of Dizzy on the 'bloated armaments'. That speech however & the warnings from below the Gangway have had their effect & Govt. is preparing reductions. Not too soon.

Met 'Delane' of the Times[77] big with the 'melancholy' news of a fresh Confederate defeat.

---

[73] Lady Selina had first married G.E. Vernon, then John Junior Bidwell senior f.o. clerk, 1859–72. Cf. Kimberley Memoir, 490.

[74] Benjamin Disraeli, 1st Earl of Beaconsfield (1804–81), ch. exch., 1852, 1858–9, 1866–8; leader in commons, 1858–9; pr. min., 1868, 1874–80; accused the government of warlike expenditure in time of peace bringing on a heavier burden of taxation. 3 *Hansard* 166 (8 May 1862), 1403–28.

[75] Sir George Cornewall Lewis (1806–63), ch. exch., 1855–8; home sec., 1859–61; war sec., 1861–3; political theorist.

[76] George William Frederick Charles, 2nd Duke of Cambridge (1819–1904), comm.-in-chief from 1856.

[77] John Thadeus Delane (1817–79), ed. of *The Times*, 1841–77.

24 May 1862.   Saturday. At Lady Palmerston's in the evening. Lord P. on my congratulating on the Slave Trade Treaty with the U.S. 'we must now get the right of search from France.' He seemed to think this wd. not be very difficult.

25 May 1862.   Sunday. Went with Henley to Eton. Airlie appeared yesterday at dinner at my house graced with his new order of the 'Thistle'.[78]

26 May 1862.   Monday. Signed at Coverdale's a codicil to my will.

27 May 1862.   Tuesday. Lord Clarendon mentioned the anecdote told in Guizot's last volume of Memoirs of Lady Holland & the picture.[79] Lord C. said neither he nor Lady C. could remember the circumstance.

Lord C. also said that Guizot was not correct in representing the demand for Napoleon's bones as having been made in the first instance through himself. The proposal came first in a letter from Thiers[80] to Ld. Melbourne,[81] Ld. M. showed it to the cabinet who after some discussion agreed that the request might be granted. Ld. Clarendon suggested that the D. of Wellington[82] ought to be asked. Lord. M. assented & told Ld. C. to speak to the Duke about it.

The Duke's reply to Lord C's inquiry whether he saw any objection to giving up the bones, was 'No! No! You had better give them up, but I will tell you what will happen. They will say we gave them up because we were unworthy to keep them, & they will be more insolent than ever. I shan't care a two-penny d–m.'—

Why does Lady Selina Vernon marry Mr. Bidwell?

Because she wants a 'rake' to get rid of her weeds.

Lord Chelmsford[83] told us the following story today *à propos* of a very deaf witness on the Noxious Vapours Committee. Lord Ellenborough[84] said to a witness–'Why witness you don't know the A, B, C. of the

[78] Anthony Henley (1825–98), Lib. MP for Northampton, 1859–74; cr. Baron Northington, 1885; David Graham Drummond Ogilvy, 7th Earl of Airlie (1826–81). Both were with Wodehouse at Eton and Christ Church, and remained his lifelong friends. See Wodehouse's estimate of Airlie, herein, 324.

[79] François Pierre Guillaume Guizot (1787–1874), French historian.

[80] Louis Adolphe Thiers (1797–1877), French historian, leader of Lib. opposition, 1863–70.

[81] William Lamb, 2nd Viscount Melbourne (1779–1848), pr. min., 1834, 1835–41.

[82] Arthur Wellesley, 1st Duke of Wellington (1769–1852), commanded army of the Netherlands in defeat of Napoleon, 1815; com.-in-chief, 1827–8, 1842–52.

[83] Frederick Thesiger (1794–1878), 1st Baron Chelmsford; atty.-genl., 1845–6, 1852; ld. chanc. 1858–9, 1866–8.

[84] Edward Law, 1st Earl of Ellenborough (1790–1871), gov.-genl. of India, 1841–4; pres. bd. of cont., 1858.

matter.' 'My Lord,' observed the foreman of the jury, 'don't you see that the witness is D, E, F.'

28 May 1862.   Wednesday. Dined at Grillion's, afterwards to a party at the Speakers & to the 'Cos'.

30 May 1862.   Friday. Finance Debate in H. of Ld., Carnarvon made a very good speech.

31 May 1862.   Saturday. Apponyi[85] dined with us, a dull dinner. Madame A. said that Anatole Dernidoff who is just dead, had an income of 4 million francs.

1 June 1862.   Sunday. Dined with B. Currie at Wimbledon & saw the charming site of his new house in Coombe Wood. A bullet recently came thru' the window of his nursery, & lodged in the wall just over the bed where his baby was asleep. Pleasant neighbors the volunteers!

2 June 1862.   Dined with the Corks.[86] Amongst other people that fat vulgar Lady Cowper[87] with her ugly daughter–very full of her importance. Lord Broughton[88] came to dinner by mistake, & never found it out. Lord Canterbury[89] who sat next to me, loud in abuse of Disraeli, his party leader.

3 June 1862.   Tuesday. Heard Lord Palmerston announce that he should meet Walpole's resolution as a vote of no confidence. Nothing could be more cool, & perfectly poised than his manner. He was very well recd.

Walpole as usual showed he had no backbone. Nothing could be weaker than his conduct, & manner.[90] B. Osborne's[91] happy definition of his manner in speaking is 'that he reminds him of a high stepping hearse horse'.

---

[85] Rudolphe, Count Apponyi (1812–76), Austrian amb. to London, 1856–71; to Paris, 1871–6.

[86] Richard Edmund St Lawrence Boyle, 9th Earl of Cork and Orrey (1829–1904).

[87] Anne Florence, wife of Francis Thomas de Grey, 7th Earl Cowper.

[88] John Cam Hobhouse, Baron Broughton de Gyfford (1786–1869), pres. of bd. of cont., 1835–41, 1846–52; friend of Byron and executor of his estate.

[89] Charles John Manners-Sutton, 2nd Viscount Canterbury (1812–69), died unmarried and succeeded by his brother, John Henry Thomas.

[90] Walpole's motion, on government expenditure, placed the House in an embarrassing position. On Walpole's weakness, see *DD1*, 186–7.

[91] Ralph Bernal Osborne (1808–82), Lib. MP for Chipping Wycombe, 1841, for Middlesex, 1847, 1852, for Dover, 1857–9, for Liskeard, 1859–65, for Nottingham, 1866–8, for Waterford, 1869–74; sec. of admiralty, 1852–8.

I heard for the first time Mr. Stansfeld[92] speak. He is an interesting looking, young man with a pale face, & long black hair. More of an Italian than an English type. He looks the follower of Mazzini.[93] A studious earnest manner, clear diction, perhaps rather pompous. He will make a figure in the world of politics.

De Grey told me that Lewis & others in the Cabinet did not wish to raise the point of confidence. They would have moved the previous question, but Gladstone insisted on the direct issue. The result proved he was right. The defeat of the Opposition was complete. Of all Dizzy's fiascos this is the worst. Nevertheless Stansfeld's motion may do good. The Govt. ought to take warning. With such a fearful calamity as impends over us in the North, economy is an absolute necessity, & the nation will insist upon it.

In the House of Lords I took some part in the Committees on the Scotch Public Houses Bill, vainly endeavoring to persuade the Scotchmen to modify some of its absurdities. It is in part a Maine Liquor Law.[94]

4 June 1862. Wednesday. Did not go to the Derby. Saw the very curious collection of art objects lent to the Kensington Museum.

5 June 1862. Thursday. To Eton. A miserable rainy day.

6 June 1862. Friday. Put away my correspondence with Cardwell[95] & Brand[96] about the "Southrepps" living. C's conduct was weak & shabby. If the living was promised to Prince Albert's nominee why not say so at once, if not actually promised why not give it to Suffield's[97] brother, & say when asked by the Court, it was given away? As it is, a Liberal Minister gives a valuable living to a Tory parson, personally obnoxious to the inhabitants of Southrepps & to the principal landowners (liberals)

---

[92] James Stansfeld (1820–98), Lib. MP for Halifax, 1859–95, put forward a motion calling for greater government economy, which was defeated by 367 to 67 votes. On the impression left by Stansfeld, see too T. A. Jenkins, *The Parliamentary Diaries of Sir John Trelawny, 1858–65* (London, 1990), 208–9.

[93] Giuseppe Mazzini (1805–72), Italian republican, associated with all major revolutionary movements between 1830 and his death.

[94] In 1851 the US state of Maine enacted legislation prohibiting the production and sale of alcoholic beverages.

[95] Edward Cardwell (1813–86), pres. b. of t., 1852–5; ch. sec. Ireland, 1859–61; col. sec., 1864–6; war sec., 1868–74; cr. viscount, 1874.

[96] Henry Bouverie Brand (1814–92), Lib. MP for Lewes, 1852–68, for Cambridgeshire, 1868–84; parlt. sec. to treas., 1859–66; speaker of House of Commons, 1872–84; cr. Viscount Hampden of Glynde, 1884; succ. as 23rd Baron Dacre, 1880.

[97] Charles Harbord, 5th Baron Suffield (1830–1914), of Gunton Park, Norfolk; intimate friend of Edward, Prince of Wales.

in the district. Givyn, the new parson is Sir W. Cubitt's[98] son-in-law, and the hand of C. Grey[99] is manifest in the business.

His Grace of Argyll told me this afternoon that there had been considerable hesitation as to how Walpole's motion should be met, but Palmerston insisted on meeting it directly as a vote of want of confidence. The Whig clique were evidently for weak temporising as usual.

7 June 1862. Wednesday. I heard yesterday that Hammond[100] proposed that the D. of Cambridge in the absence of the Queen should receive the Pasha of Egypt. It is a pity that he should be recd. less well here than at Paris.

Met Prince Gorchakow, son of the Russian Foreign Minister at Lady Londonderry's[101] at dinner. He is just arrived as 2nd Secy. to the Russian Embassy. Had a long conversation with General Peel on the possibility of reductions in the expense of the army, which he doubts except perhaps as regards stores. It is evident he has no sympathy with the assailant of 'bloated armament'.

8 June 1862. Sunday. Dined at Brunnow's[102]–met several Russians; amongst others, General Betancourt, & Princess Tcherkow a pretty agreeable woman.

At the Cos: the news of a Confederate victory at Winchester U.S. published in the second edition of the Observer was brought by Bruce,[103] & received with great satisfaction by all present. Sympathies with the North are very scarce.

10 June 1862. Tuesday. Heard last week of the death in Syria of poor Buckle, the author of 'Civilization in England'. I made Buckle's acquaintance accidentally in 1843, when travelling with a tutor (C. Frere) in Germany.

He was a man of extraordinary power of acquisition & memory, but excessively rash, over confident & arrogant. Not an 'original' genius, but there was something resembling originality in the fearlessness with

---

[98] Sir William Cubitt (1785–1861), engineer and partner, Messrs Ransome of Ipswich; consultant in development of major English and European railways and waterworks.

[99] Charles Grey (1804–70), genl., 1865; priv. sec. to Prince Albert, 1849–61 and to Queen Victoria, 1861–70.

[100] Edmund Hammond (1802–90), perm. u.-sec. for for. aff. 1854–73.

[101] Roman Catholic wife of Frederick William Robert, 4th Earl of Londonderry (1805–72). On the strain of madness in the family, see *DD1*, 219.

[102] Ernest Philip Ivanovich, Count Brunnow (1797–1875), Russian amb. to London, 1840–4, 1858–64.

[103] Henry Austin Bruce (1815–95), Lib. MP for Merthyr Tydvil, 1852–68 for Renfrewshire, 1869–73; u.-sec. for home off., 1862–64; home sec., 1869–73; ld. pres. coun., 1873–74; cr. Baron Aberdare, 1873.

which he attacked known opinions. His premature death is a serious loss to literature.

12 June 1862. Thursday. Heavy rain all day. To Admiralty & saw Adml. Eden[104] about Harry's nomination as cadet.

13 June 1862. Friday. To T. Baring's[105] magnifcent fête at the Crystal Palace. Saw the fountains play & Blondin[106] walk the rope. The ease with which he walks is such that I did not even feel an emotion.

I saw him afterwards in a room; a very weather beaten ugly little man with his wife on his arm a tidy looking woman, who looked greatly proud of her husband being the 'lion'.

18 June 1862. Wednesday. Dined at Grillion's—a very pleasant dinner. Was photographed at Heath's for Lord Overstone,[107] & the day before at Hughes' in the Strand for Black[108] the publisher. My face seems to be in request.

19 June 1862. Thursday. Assisted in a little 'bait' of the D. of A. about the Red Sea telegraph Bill.[109] The Treasury management of telegraphs is a job which it is not easy to fathom. Camperdown's[110] pertinacity was very amusing, & I must add effective.

20 June 1862. Friday. Sat for a 'drawing' to Richmond[111] for Sir Thos.

---

[104] Henry Eden (1797–1888), adm. lord, 1855–8; rear-adm., 1854; adm., 1864.

[105] Thomas George Baring, 1st Earl of Northbrook (1826–1904), Lib. MP for Penryn and Falmouth, 1857–66, when he succ. as 2nd Baron Northbrook; u.-sec. for India, 1859–64; Viceroy of India, 1872–6; 1st ld. adm., 1880–5.

[106] Charles Blondin (pseud. of Jean François Gravelet) (1824–97), French tightrope walker who several times had crossed Niagara Falls in the 1850s.

[107] Samuel Jones Loyd, 1st Baron of Overstone (1796–1883), city banker, author and early Kimberley supporter. See O'Brien (ed.), *Correspondence of Lord Overstone*, I, 750–8; Currie, *Recollections*, I, 425–6.

[108] Adam Black (1784–1874), owned bookselling firm in Edinburgh, where he was a Lib. MP, 1856–65.

[109] The order for the third reading of the Red Sea and India Telegraph bill was discharged and the bill re-committed. Argyll observed that objections to the bill had been made for giving the sanction of parliament to the new, as well as the old, company. Because of this he proposed that the first three lines of the 1st clause be omitted and new lines inserted. Wodehouse and the Earl of Camperdown, Lord Redesdale, Lord Lyveden and Earl Grey, refused to accept this change until the new text was set out in a clear and intelligible form. As a result the bill was resubmitted to a Committee of the whole House. 3 *Hansard* 167 (19 June 1862), 728–30.

[110] Adam Duncan-Haldane (1812–67), Lib. MP, 1837–52, 1854–9; succ. as 2nd Earl Camperdown, 1859.

[111] George Richmond (1809–96), portrait painter and sculptor.

Acland[112] who has collected a series of portraits of members of 'Grillion's Club'. Richmond talks well. My mother has a watercolor of myself & my brother when boys by Richmond.

21 June 1862.   Saturday. Richmond again. Dined at the D. of Newcastle's. The Duc d'Aumale[113] whom we met there, told me he knew the 'Baron' whose daughter came over in man's clothes to see the Exhibition.(rcd: Police Reports) He was an Orleanist by politics, a retired officer of the French army.

Lord Grey told me that when the repeal of the Navigation laws was before Parliament in 1849, two thirds of Lord John Russell's Cabinet (who proposed the bill) were against the measure.[114] So much for Whig love of Free trade.

Lord Grey complained of the inferiority of men of the present day. Neither the bar, the Church (witness the sermons, witness E. James,[115] Digby Seymour[116]&c) nor politics produced any remarkable men. I contested the justice of this remark, except perhaps as regards the bar (whose character is certainly low): as to the degeneracy of politicians and of which Lord G. finds proof in the dulness of our debates, I think this dulness arises simply from the absence of exciting political questions.

26 June 1862.   Thursday. Debate on Fortifications began by Airlie in a very weak tedious speech wh. drove every one out of the House. Lord Grey also tedious & less forcible than usual. I had intended to speak in support of the Govt. but as there were only 7 or 8 peers left after Lord Grey's speech I went away in disgust. Lord Ellenborough & others would have spoken if there had been an audience. Then one reads the newspapers that 'the debate in the Lords was a far better one than in the Commons'– The debate!! 6 or 7 peers versus the red benches.

On Tuesday some skirmishing about the Public Houses Scotland Bill in which I took part.

27 June 1862.   Friday. The Govt. in difficulties in both houses. Billy

---

[112] Sir Thomas Dyke Acland (1809–98), Lib. MP for W. Somerset, 1837–41, 1885–86; for North Devonshire, 1865–85.

[113] Henri Eugene Philippe Louis d'Orleans, Duc d'Aumale (1822–97), 5th s. of Louis Philippe.

[114] On Wodehouse's determination to repeal the Navigation laws, see Currie, *Recollections*, I, 243.

[115] Edwin John James (1812–82), barrister and Lib. MP for Marylebone, 1859– 61; bankrupt and disbarred for unprofessional conduct, 1861.

[116] William Digby Seymour (1822–95), barrister and Lib. MP for Sunderland, 1852–5, for Southampton, 1859–65; bankrupt and censured by benchers of Middle Temple, 1859.

Cowper in a scrape as usual,[117] and in our House an open question between the Treasury and Admiralty as to Kutch prize money, wh. the latter say ought to be given, the former refuses.

Went to the magnificent show of cattle at Battersea.

Curious stories afloat as to Lord Canning's will. It is said to have been made 8 years ago, & to leave everything to Ld. Hubert de Burgh[118] without any provisions for or mention of Lady Canning. May not this be, because the relations between Lord & Lady C. were bad when the will was made? It is notorious that C. was not very faithful to Lady C. & that before they went to India they were not always on the best terms.

30 June 1862. Monday. Began to sit on a tedious Ry. Committee. Myself (for the first time) Chairman with Lords Nelson,[119] Granard, Cremorne,[120] Abinger.[121] Nelson is the talkative member, Cremorne the sleepy, & Granard & A. the silent members.

1 July 1862. Tuesday. Committee again.

2 July 1862. Wednesday. Do.

3 July 1862. Thursday. Do. passed the Stafford & Uttoxeter Ry. Bill.

4 July 1862. Friday. Committee. Went to a fête at Orleans House. The worst managed entertainment I ever saw. A fight like that at a Railway Station when an express train arrives for scraps of food.

5 July 1862. Saturday. Meant to have gone to Eton but prevented by the rain which has been incessant for the last month.

6 July 1862. A fine day. Went to Eton with Flo: the girls & Henry to see Johnny of whom Johnson gave a good account.   ·

7 July 1862. Monday. Threatened with an opposition to the 3rd

---

[117] William Francis Cowper, (1811–88), Lib. MP for Hertford, 1835–68; comm. works, 1860–6; raised to peerage as Baron Mount-Temple, 1880. In difficulties in the Commons over the Thames Embankment Committee. 3 *Hansard* 167 (27 June 1862), 1138–50.

[118] Hubert de Burgh Canning (1832–1916), second son of 1st Marquis of Clanricarde; entered dipl. service, 1852. With the death of his elder brother in 1867, became heir to the marquisate; succ. in 1874. In 1862 he assumed the additional surname of Canning, by royal license, as heir of his maternal uncle, 1st Earl Canning.

[119] Horatio, 3rd Earl Nelson (1823–1913).

[120] Richard Dawson, 2nd Baron Cremorne (1817–97), cr. Earl of Dartrey, 1866.

[121] William Frederick Scarlett, 3rd Baron Abinger (1826–92).

reading of Stafford Uttoxeter Bill, to be led by Ld. Chelmsford on the ground that the running clauses are unfair to the North Western & N. Staffordshire Railways. The matter was however arranged by two slight amendments.

[8 July 1862].   Tuesday. Committee. dined at Orleans House.
Wednesday Do.
Thursday Do.–Yesterday we rejected unanimously the "Wellington & Cheshire Ry." bill. (for a Railway from Market Leighton to Potteries) Our main reason the opposition of Lord Crewe[122] who showed that a more convenient line could be made without annoyance to him. We had previously on Friday last passed the Market Leighton and Wellington Line having refused to hear the London & North Western opposition on the ground of competition. We have now begun our last bill the Hull & Grimsby 'so called' Ry. really a line from Wakefield to Doncaster & to join line from Grimsby.

11 July 1862.   Friday. Committee.

12 July 1862.   Saturday. Went with Johnny to Lord's to see Eton & Harrow match. Eton won.

13 July 1862.   Sunday. A fine day!

14 July 1862.   Monday. Committee every day this week till Friday when we unanimously passed the Grimsby Bill, striking out all the running powers over other lines. The 'amenities' of Conmel were rather amusing. Mr. Merewether on Mr. Burke his opponent (for the bill) observing that he had a lively imagination as to facts, rejoiced that Mr. Burke's imagination was equally fertile but unfortunately for those who heard him, not lively. The learned Counsel who had been unsparing in their personal attacks on each other, informed us at the close that they were about to dine together at Greenwich. So much for the invectives of Counsel. They really acted their indignation very well. Wm. Harcourt who was junior Counsel for the bill, disappointed me. He was often slow & tedious, tho' occasionally he made his point well.
    On Tuesday (I touch on one of the other days in this week) I moved an amendment in the Copyright Bill bringing pictures &c. under the International Copyright Act 1844.

16 July 1862.   Wednesday. Dined with Lord Donoughmore.[123] Met

---

[122] Hungerford Crewe, 3rd Baron Crewe (1812–93).
[123] Richard John Hely-Hutchinson, 4th Earl of Donoughmore (1823–66).

Montalembert[124] who talked very agreeably. He speaks excellent English. In the evening Storey[125] the American sculptor came in. He is a strong 'Northerner' in politics. We had a long conversation. He defended the North with moderation. Spoke with great bitterness of the 'Times' & 'Saturday Review' & I grieve to say stood up for that wretch Butler.[126] Storey is a short, good looking man, with an intelligent bright face. His Yankee twang & angularities worn off by residence in Europe.

Donoughmore praised Carnarvon highly—said he would be the future leader of the 'Tories'; of Stanley[127] he spoke very depreciatingly; would make us a present of him.

Montalembert spoke with the utmost bitterness of the French Emperor & all belonging to him. He said the sympathies of the French were with the Northern Americans, because the Emperor's sympathies were with the South. I doubt both the fact & the reason. He defended the Orleans princes who have been in the Northern army. The French like to see them fighting no matter where.

We did not allude to the Italian question. Persigny,[128] he admitted was logical in his treatment of the press, but blundering.

18 July 1862. Friday. Said a few words in the House on the conduct of the Canadians. De Grey told me he had suggested to Lewis to withdraw the troops into the fortresses of Quebec & Halifax announcing that we should not attempt if attacked in the winter to do more than defend these fortresses, but he could not persuade him.

19 July 1862. Saturday. A sitting at Richmond's.

21 July 1862. Monday. To a party at Lord Palmerston's where amongst other Royal personages I saw Prince Carignan,[129] a stout uninteresting looking man. Had a curious conversation with Brunnow about precedence of ambassadors. He said that the true cause of the disinclination

---

[124] Charles Forbes, Comte de Montalembert (1810–70), journalist and politician; entered French House of Peers, 1835; champion of R.C. interests, and opponent of Napoleon III after 1851.

[125] William Wetmore Story (1819–95), lived in Rome from 1856, becoming intimate friends of Robert and Elizabeth Browning.

[126] Benjamin Franklin Butler (1818–93), American lawyer, army officer and politician; arbitrary rule as military governor of New Orleans in 1862 led to widespread charges of corruption.

[127] Edward Henry Stanley (1826–93), Cons. MP for Lynn Regis, 1848–69, when he succ. as 15th Earl of Derby; col. sec., 1858, 1882–5; for. sec., 1866–8, 1874–8; joined Liberals, 1882; led Lib. U. in the Lords, 1886–91.

[128] Victor Fialin, Duc de Persigny (1808–72), amb. to London, 1855–8, 1859–60; min. of inter., 1860–3.

[129] Of Savoy.

of the Emperor Nicholas to receive ambassadors at his court was that they took precedence before the Duke of Leuchtenberg & other not 'Royal' princes who had married Russian Grand Duchesses. Brunnow said that as he could not give preceedence to the Princes of Leiningen at our Court, he avoided going to Court when they were there.

23 July 1862. Wednesday. Richmond finished my picture yesterday. I am only tolerably satisfied with it. We went to Kimberley to-day; Ernestine[130] with us.

28 July 1862. Monday. The R. Curries came.

29 July 1862. Warre came.

30 July 1862. Wednesday. Edmund Wodehouse,[131] son of Sir Philip, who is going circuit for the first time, came for a night on his way to Ipswich.

1 August 1862. Friday. R. Curries went. We enjoyed their visit much. R. Currie who has not been here for some years thinks the park almost too much grown up with the trees which he says have made great progress since his last visit.

Dear Johnny came home today with a very good report from Eton, except as to arithmetic in which I fear he is as stupid as his father.

4 August 1862. Monday. Warre went. He is slick, indolent & good tempered, as when he was with us, as attaché, at St Petersburg. He saw 'Bull's run' & fully confirms the panic of the Yankees. The Yankees, he says, hate us, but he agrees with me that we shall find the Confederates at least as disagreeable if they establish their independence. My sympathies are with neither party, but I wish for the breakup of the Union. If the Union had lasted, the insolence & aggressive temper of the Americans would have led to war with England before long. Two or more independent States in N. America will balance each other, & give Europe less trouble. The Yankees know that this is the general feeling of Englishmen; hence their anger against us.

Warre is attached to Lord Lyons' Legation.

Went to the Workhouse.

---

[130] Ernestine, sixth child of Wodehouse's paternal uncle, Alfred Wodehouse, who had d. in 1848.

[131] Edmond Robert Wodehouse (1835–1914), only son of Sir Philip Wodehouse; priv. sec. to Kimberley, 1864–6, 1868–74; MP for Bath, 1880–1906, Lib. then Lib. U. from 1886. One of 18 Lib. to vote for Jessie Collings's amendment in 1886.

9 August 1862.   Saturday. Attended Committee at Norwich Castle. On Thursday Aug 7 Parliament prorogued. Rolfe bought 100 wethers for me (shearlings) 34/6.

13 August 1862.   Wednesday. Weighed the 'family'

	stone–	lbs
Baby (Armine)	2	2
Constance	4.	4
Alice	6.	7
Johnny	5.	13
Ernestine	7.	10
Florence	7.	13
Self	13.	1

16 August 1862.   Saturday. The 15th anniversary of my wedding day. Gave dear Flo a pair of enamelled earrings.

18 August 1862.   Monday. To Union Workhouse.

19 August 1862.   Tuesday. To Wymm. Petty Sessions. Very little business. Bought 50 half bred ewes from Rolfe. Saw 'Rosa's' comet.

20 August 1862.   Wednesday. Began harvest–barley. Mlle. went away for a holiday.

28 August 1862.   Thursday. Went to Letton to luncheon. Met there Sir G. Nugent[132] &c. On Monday–at the Union House, the Parochial Asst. Act adopted unanimously on my proposal, William Robert Cann (of Carick) seconding. Requested George Forrester to suggest to Mr. Robert James Tunaley not to persevere in being candidate for appt. of medical officer, as could not support him after his forced resignation of that office some 14 years ago. F. since told me that Tunaley has withdrawn.

29 August 1862.   Friday. Target shooting at 200, 3 shots, 5 points, 3 hits; at 500, 7 shots. 3. 3 hits (all at 3rd class target).

1 September 1862.   Monday. At Union Bd. resolution on Par: Asst. Act confirmed unanimously & David Watkins Hughes elected parish doctor *viz* Lewis dead. Tunaley who announced himself a candidate resigned

[132] Sir George Nugent, West Harling Hall, Thetford.

at my recommedation & that of others. His former compulsory resignation (in 1849?) the reason.

3 September 1862.   Wednesday. P. Gurdon[133] brought over a Hungarian
Ct. Brunswick with his wife, & his wife's brother. An intelligent agreeable
man.

9 September 1862.   Tuesday. Went to Airlie's Glenisla to hunt. Deerstalking ten days with poor success. Killed one stag, a middling beast
with an indifferent head ten points. Also two hinds & a nobber. Had
nothing but wild shots except at one stag wh. I wounded but lost in
the wood, till the last day of my visit when had two good chances at
fair stags & missed them both. Only three other stags were killed during
my visit, one by Mr. Carnegie, one by Stanley of Alderley,[134] & one by
Airlie. Airlie had good sport before my arrival. Saw however much
fewer stags than usual, accounted for partly by two successive bad
winters, partly by the Queen's forest being left quiet this year.

Mr. Carnegie is a Forfarshire laird (lately in the army & wounded
at Delhi) with £4000 a year about to marry Miss Rait a pretty little
niece of Airlie's.

Hatty Russell[135] at Glenisla on a visit, coming from Loch Inver, lent
to the E. Russells[136] for three months by the D. of Sutherland.[137] She
says Lady W. Russell[138] & Odo Russell[139] are both Catholics. Her
account of the present D. of Bedford[140] is that he remains, as before
his father's death on the 3rd floor in Belgrave Sqre., seldom stirs out
but attends to business. Mr. Jowitt[141] [sic] & Lyulph Stanley[142] also there
on a visit. Jowitt the (perhaps) only liberal & agreeable don I ever met.
Lyulph S. a clever young man, & will be very pleasant when he has
rubbed off a little juvenile conceit, which however is pardonable, as he

[133] Philip Gurdon, a maternal uncle.

[134] Edward John Stanley, 2nd Baron Stanley of Alderley (1802–69), post.-genl., 1860–
6. For Wodehouse's political assessment, see entry for 11 Aug. 1869.

[135] Probably Lady Henrietta Russell, wife of Lord Henry Russell and sister-in-law to
the 7th Duke of Bedford and Lord John Russell.

[136] Lord Edward Russell (1805–87), adm., 1867; son of John Russell, 6th Duke of
Bedford.

[137] George Granville William Leveson-Gower (1828–92), 3rd Duke of Sutherland.

[138] Lady Wriothesley Russell, da. of Lord William Russell; m. 1829 the Rev. Lord
Wriothesley, Canon of Windsor and Chaplain to Prince Albert.

[139] Odo William Leopold Russell, 1st Baron Ampthill (1829–84), amb. at Berlin, from
1871. On Wodehouse's assessment of Odo Russell, see entry for 27 Aug. 1884.

[140] William Russell, 8th Duke of Bedford (1809–72), recluse; d. unmarried.

[141] Benjamin Jowett (1817–93), Oxford prof. from 1855; master of Balliol, 1870–93.

[142] Lyulph Stanley (1839–1929), fellow of Balliol from Nov. 1862; succ. as 4th Baron
Stanley of Alderley, 1903. On his radicalism, see N. Mitford (ed.), *The Stanleys of Alderley:
Their Letters between the Years 1851—1865* (London, 1968), xii.

has just taken a first class at Oxford. He is a staunch Northerner which is singular and a finer Radical. I like to see a young man begin with rather extreme opinions. They 'tone' down fast enough.

I met two Germans at Peterboro', where we dined at the same table in the coffee room. They were on a farming tour in England. Their names–Julius Frommel, & Otto Mugel–intelligent men, & evidently well up in the business of farming.

24 September 1862. Wednesday. Returned home, & found dear Flo: & all well.

30 September 1862. Tuesday. Mr. & Mrs. Dodson[143] came.

3 October 1862. Friday. Henley came. Had many conversations on politics & religion. Dodson as usual paradoxical, Henley loud & positive. Henley however is improved by contact with the world since he is M.P. & has become more liberal and large minded.

Partridge shooting very bad; our best day 30 braces on Cunningham's farm.

7 October 1862. Tuesday. Dodsons went. I like Mrs. Dodson much– pretty & good rather weak in character & superstitious, that is to say thoroughly feminine both in her faults & merits. How much pleasanter a wife & a friend than a 'maitresse femme' like Lady Airlie![144]

13 October 1862. Monday. Henley went. Attended Bd. of Guardians, afterwards to Letton with Flo: to see Robert Gurdon's bride. Bride, daughter of Sir Wm. Miles.[145] She made a very favorable impression upon us which was fully confirmed by what we saw of her at a dinner at Barnham parsonage on the following Thursday, & at a luncheon visit wh. she paid us on the next day (Friday). Without being pretty she is pleasing, & she talks like a quiet sensible woman. I think he is fortunate in his choice. Her fortune is but £5,000, but as my uncle settles £10,000 a year upon them, this does not matter.

[143] John George Dodson (1825–97), Lib. MP for E. Sussex, 1857–74 for Chester, 1874– 80, for Scarborough, 1880–4; fin. sec. treas., 1873–4; pres. loc. govt. bd., 1880–2; chanc. d. of Lanc., 1882–4; Lib. U. from 1886; with Wodehouse at Eton and Christ Church; 1st Baron Monk Bretton, 1884.

[144] Henrietta Blanche, Lady Airlie (1829–1921), was the third child of the 2nd Baron Stanley of Alderley. According to Mitford, she became, like her mother, a 'tartar to her relations in old age.' *Stanleys of Alderley*, xiii.

[145] Robert Thornhagh Gurdon (1829–1902), Lib. MP for S. Norfolk, 1880–5, for mid-Norfolk, 1885–92, 1895; Lib. U. after 1886; cr. Baron Cranworth, 1899. M. Harriet Ellen, 6th da. of Sir William Miles (1797–1878), Cons. MP for Somerset E., 1834–65.

16 October 1862. Thursday. To Quarter Sessions at Norwich. Ph: Gurdon's (& Lord Sondes')[146] motion for making Mitford & Launditch a highway district carried nem: con. also Mr. Blyth's for making Docking a highway district. The feeling was decidedly favorable to the new Act which by degrees I have no doubt will be put in force in the whole county.

My mother came to us on a visit this week.

20 October 1862. Monday. Attended Union House.

21 October 1862. Tuesday. At Wymm. petty Sessions. Visited Wymm. Prison.

25 October 1862. Saturday. To Norwich.

28 October 1862. Tuesday. Henry came on a visit, not looking I am sorry to say, at all well.

29 October 1862. Wednesday. Admiral W.[147] & Cecilia[148] came on a visit–& went on Saturday. Henry went on Tuesday Nov. 4

My mother who went away for a few days to Harling, came back & left on Monday Nov: 3.

Henry seems on the whole reconciled to going back to Cple.[149]

8 November 1862. Saturday. Attended meeting of Chairman of Parochial Assessment Committees at Norwich. Mr. William Howes presided. After much discussion resolutions proposed by Mr. Howes adopted unanimously.

10 November 1862. Monday. Ernestine went away. Attended Bd. of Guardians. Met Sir John Walsham Poor Law Inspector there. He says it is reported that the appointment of Dr. Thomson[150] to be Archp. of York is attributed to the influence of Gladstone in the Cabinet.

I may note here with reference to official appointments some causes

---

[146] George John Milles, 4th Baron Sondes (1794–1874).

[147] Edward Thornton-Wodehouse (1802–74), 3rd son of John, 2nd Lord Wodehouse; rear-admiral.

[148] Cecilia Wodehouse, eld. da. of Edward and Diana Thornton-Wodehouse.

[149] On H. Wodehouse's doubts, see J. Wodehouse to H. Wodehouse, 1 Aug. 1861, KP1 15/K2/19.

[150] William Thomson (1819–90), chapl. to Queen Victoria, 1869; opposed *Essays and Reviews* (1860) with *Aids to Faith* (1861); bishop of Glouchester and Bristol, 1861; archbp. of York, 1862.

connected with the removal of Sir A. Buchanan[151] in 1861 from Madrid. It was popularly ascribed to an intrigue to find room for Elliot,[152] Lord Russell's brother-in-law. What really happened was this. When it was determined to raise the Mission of Petersbg. to an Embassy, it was thought objectionable to make Sir J. Crampton,[153] my successor in the Mission an ambassador on account of his having married Miss Balfe, the opera singer. Lord Russell therefore determined to move Buchanan to St Petg. as Ambassador & send Crampton to Madrid. Crampton was told he was to come away, & a minute was sent out by Lord R. appointing Buchanan, Lord P's & the Queen's sanction having been obtained. But Hammond & I persuaded Lord R. that Buchanan was not the best person for Ambassr. at Petg.

I need not give my reasons which were partly that I thought Buchanan had made a mess of the Madrid Mission, partly that the Russians like a Lord, & that I thought Napier[154] would please them better. The result was the appt. of Napier to Petg., Crampton to Madrid, & Buchanan to the Hague. Buchanan's friends made a great noise at his ill treatment as they termed it, but B. himself like a canny Scotchn. held his tongue, & is now rewarded for his discretion by getting the new Berlin Embassy for which he is certainly far more fit than that pompous busybody Lord A. Loftus.[155]

10 November 1862.   Monday. Attended Board of Guardians.

15 November 1862.   Saturday. At Committee Norwich Castle.

17 November 1862.   Monday. At Bd. of Guardians.

18 November 1862.   Tuesday. At Wymm. Petty Sessions. No business.

22 November 1862.   Saturday. At Norwich Castle Committee. Saw O. Taylor[156] & signed Bond for Hamilla's[157] Administration. Conversation

[151] Andrew Buchanan (1807–82), min. to Prussia from 1862.

[152] Sir Henry George Elliot (1817–1907), amb. at Constantinople, 1867–77, at Vienna, 1877–84.

[153] Sir John Fiennes Twisleton Crampton (1805–86), min. plen. and envoy ext. at Hanover, 1857–8; min. plen. to Russia, 1858–60; min. to Madrid, 1860–0.

[154] Sir Francis Napier, 1st Baron Napier and Ettrick (1819–98), amb. to St Petersburg, 1860–4; amb. to Berlin, 1864–9.

[155] Augustus William Frederick Spencer Loftus (1817–1904), amb. to Prussia; amb. to Russia, 1871–9. Cf. Derby's view of the 'pompous and tedious' Loftus. *DD2*, 18, 42.

[156] John Oddin Taylor, Norwich solicitor; Liberal agent in E. Norfolk during the 1850s and 1860s.

[157] Hamilla Wodehouse, Wodehouse's cousin, whose parents had died in 1848 and 1852. Sister to Ernestine Wodehouse, previously mentioned.

with him as to Harvey[158] the banker's wish to be made a baronet. Harvey called at Kimby. on Friday Oct 31, & asked me if I would recommend him to Lord Palmerston for a baronetcy. He vaunted his wealth his influence etc etc. I asked him if he was a Liberal. He said frankly enough No, but he wished to keep out of politics. He wd. be satisfied with a baronetcy. If he could not get it otherwise, he should come in for Norwich or the county & I suppose force his way to the dignity he covets. I gave him a civil answer but declined to write to Lord P., as I could not recommend a non-Liberal. Today he coolly writes to me enclosing a petition to the Queen which he requests me to forward to Lord P. I have declined (Sunday Nov. 23) on the grounds stated by me at our interview. Harvey is evidently a mean sod who is afraid to risk his money bags by taking part in politics, tho' he wants to be made a bart. to gratify his petty vanity. He came over from Wymm. in a fly to the Lodge & walked up to the House. I asked him how he had got here, & his explanation was that he did not like to drive up to the House in a fly–! This little incident describes the mean vulgarity of the man better than volumes. Taylor quite against his being a bart.

24 November 1862.   Monday. To Union House.

25 November 1862.   Tuesday. Dillons[159] came, & Rochfort, & Windm. Baring & wife.[160]

26 November 1862.   Wednesday. We killed 7 woodcocks in Wildman Coves &c.

27 November 1862.   Thursday. B. Gurdons[161] came. Pouring Rain. Could not shoot in Forehoe.

28 Nov 1862.   Friday. Dillon, Rochf., Graves Browne, Baring & self shot in Forehoe.

29 November 1862.   Saturday. W. Barings & Gurdons went. Mrs W. Baring who was a Miss Ponsonby, plain & amiable.

[158]   Robert John Harvey, of Harvey and Hudson's Crown Bank.
[159]   Gerald Normanby Dillon and Louisa, Kimberley's sister-in-law.
[160]   William Bingham Baring, 2nd Baron Ashburton (1799–1864), pres. of Geographical Society, 1860–4.
[161]   J. Brampton Gurdon (1797–1881), Lib. MP for Norfolk W., 1857–65.

1 December 1862. Monday. To Union House: where draft order from Poor Law Bd. reassessment approved.

3 December 1862. Wednesday. Rochfort & Dillons went. The weather very fine for planting during the last fortnight. Planted two oaks at the end of terrace, an oak & walnut below Flo's garden: & filled up the alder corner of boat house plantation with horse chestnut.[162]

6 December 1862. Saturday. To Castle at Norwich. Visited 123 prisoners.

7 December 1862. Sunday. A letter from old Hammond, asking me whether it was true I was vegetating in the country, & Sunday new appointments & changes set me thinking of my prospects. I am foolishly discontented & miserable about them. In fact I am selfishly ambitious instead of trying humbly to do my duty.

It is provoking to find myself shelved in the prime of life, when I feel energy longing for action, but I must & will brace myself up to a contented performance of daily duties, hum-drum & unexciting tho' they be.

13 December 1862. Saturday. Visited Norwich Castle.

15 December 1862. Monday. To Union House, where Assessment Committee elected Directors. W. R. Cann, Rev. Charles Beauchamp Cooper, William Hurnard, John Cann, Edmund Larke & self Guardians J. Twaites, R. Smith, Cobon, Rising, John Howlett (of Bowthorpe), & Fryer.

16 December 1862. Tuesday. To Wymm. Petty Sessions.

20 December 1862. Saturday. Visited Norwich Castle.

22 December 1862. Monday. First meeting of Assessment Committee. I was elected Chairman. My proposals as to deductions &c adopted after a long discussion unanimously. Howlett (of Bowthorpe) however objected to the standard of Schedule A.

23 December 1862. Tuesday. Planted three 'Wellingtonias' in Falstaff wood. Yesterday planted in same wood 12 'Douglass' and in the garden a Wellingtonia, two '*Parvapo*', one 'Thuja gigantea', two 'Thuja borealis'. Also made a little nursery near the gate going from the Falstaff to Sand

---

[162] See below, 23 Dec. 1862. On the status of wood plantation on the Kimberley estate, see unpublished 'Tree Condition Survey' of Kimberley Park held by Mr. Ronald Buxton.

pit close, in which planted 8 Wellingtonias, intending to keep them there for a while & plant them out when larger.[163] All these pines were from Waterer of Bagshot. F. Cavendish & Elinor[164] came here on a visit to day.

He looks ill, poor fellow.

27 December 1862.   Saturday. Visited Castle. Attended Committee County Bill &c.

29 December 1862.   Monday. To quarterly meeting of Bd. of Guardians at Wymondham. Julian Fane[165] & Henry came & stayed till Thursday. Julian the same as ever perhaps more absent. He says the Austrian Govt. are much perplexed by the demands of Bohemia.

1 January 1863.   Thursday. Another New Year. The past year has been a year of peace & quiet happiness to me, but of disappointment to my political hopes. I see no prospect of employment this year. Politics never were duller in England. Prosperity except in Lancashire, & general acquiescence in what is; this is the sum of our domestic position. Even garotting stirs us up only to the point of naming a Commission to inquire. Such a dead calm must presage some storm.

3 January 1863.   Saturday. Attended Police Committee at Norwich. For want of anything else to do I grind away at county & parochial business. Is my destiny to do this for the rest of my life!

5 January 1863.   Monday. Meeting of Assessment Committee. Altered scale of deductions on house property. I foolishly at our first meeting acquiesced in too low a scale. It is scarcely high enough as now fixed.

6 January 1863.   Tuesday. Attended Hingham School Trust meeting.

7 January 1863.   Wednesday. Attained my 37th year. I am getting old, & tho' I have worked hard, I may say from my youth up, I seem to make no progress. I thank God for the good health, & many blessings I enjoy, & I trust (whatever my yearnings after political work may be) I am cheerful & contented.

---

[163] See above, 3 Dec. 1862.
[164] Francis William Henry Cavendish and Elinor, Lady Wodehouse's sister, had married in 1856.
[165] Julian Henry Charles Fane (1827–70), sec. of leg. St Petersburg, 1856–8; first sec. at Paris, 1865–7.

Marked trees in New Wood.

9 January 1863. Friday. Cavendishes went away.

12 January 1863. Monday. To Union House.

13 January 1863. Tuesday. To Dereham to attend meeting of Scarning School Trustees.

17 January 1863. Saturday. Attended Castle Committee at Norwich.

19 January 1863. Monday. To Union House.

21 January 1863. Wednesday. Dear little Johnny went back to Eton. A tremendous storm of wind with rain & lightning last night. This winter has been remarkable thus far for mild weather & wind. I measured lately the girth of the great Ash Tree in the Park near Gelham's Wood. 25 feet in girth five feet from ground.

26 January 1863. Monday. To Union House.

31 January 1863. Saturday. To Norwich Castle.

2 February 1863. Monday. Union House Assessment Committee.

4 February 1863. Wednesday. Moved to London. Granville omits me in his dinner for the Speech, the first time for many years; a sign how I am going down in the political world. The more reason for exertion. Met Sir A. Buchanan at dinner at my Mother's. He says Pam is not over-pleased with Lord R's Danish policy. I am not surprised at it. He does not think any serious crisis impending at Berlin, angry tho' the Liberals are. Reeve[166] whom I met at the Cos; in the evening says that when Lord R. was at Gotha, he was talked over by Crowe & Ward (blind guides both) on the Danish question.[167] How easily the little man is talked over by the first person he meets. H. appd. to the Hague, of wh. I am glad.

A poaching affray in the Wildman plantation on Tuesday night in

---

[166] Henry Reeve (1813–95), man of letters, ed. of *Edinburgh Review* from 1855.

[167] Joseph Archer Crowe (1825–96), *Times* correp., 1857–9; cons.-genl. for Saxony, 1860–72; John Ward (1805–90), cons.-genl. at Hamburg to the Hanse Towns, 1860–70. Palmerston found them intolerably pro-German. See pp. 151–2 of Keith A.P. Sandiford, *Great Britain and the Schleswig-Holstein Question, 1848–64* (Toronto, 1975), which serves as the best published guide to the details of British diplomacy in the Dano-Prussian controversies of 1862–4.

which Jacob Reid who was alone was severely beaten by two scoundrels; we believe Barnard, & Lincoln from Morley. They have been arrested by the police.

5 February 1863. Thursday. To the H. of Lords at 4 o'clock to see the P. of Wales take his seat. I was much pleased with his appearance & manner. He looked a quiet, pleasing, gentlemanlike young man, with a thoughtful & almost melancholy expression of countenance. Some said he was nervous, but it did not strike me that he was more so than was natural, & tho' his shyness was evident, there was nothing awkward in it. His accent is slightly German.

At the meeting of the House Lord Dudley[168] moved the address. Very vulgar in speaking of the P. of Wales whom he bestowed in his presence with the most fulsome praise, otherwise a not unsuccessful speech. Lord Derby made one of his happiest light speeches. Lord R. heavy in reply. I said a few words. I was anxious to take the opportunity of expressing my disapproval of the Danish policy of Lord R.

6 February 1863. Friday. Dined with political Econ: Club.[169] Sir S. Northcote[170] very heavy in opening a discussion about maritime rights. Was introduced to Mr. Wilkinson,[171] ex M.P. for Lambeth, & just defeated for Reigate by Mr. Gower.[172] He says bribery won the election.

7 February 1863. Saturday. Breakfasted at Grillions where Sir E. Head[173] elected.

8 February 1863. Monday. [*sic*] Dined with de Grey. Met Gen. Romley, recently returned from Canada. He thinks it absurd to attempt to defend the Canadian frontier by sending out a few thousand men from England. He said that McClellan[174] pointed out to him the folly of exposing our little force to an attack from an overwhelming American army. We only placed a temptation in the way of any unscrupulous Govt. at Washington which might wish to gain an easy triumph at our

[168] William Ward, 1st Earl of Dudley (1817–85).

[169] On Wodehouse's election to the Pol. Econ. Club, see *Liberal by Principle*, 12.

[170] Sir Stafford Northcote, 1st Earl of Iddesleigh (1818–87), Cons. MP for Dudley, 1855–7, for Stamford, 1858–66, for N. Devon, 1866–85; pres. b. of t., 1866–7; ch. exch., 1874–80; treas., 1885–6; for. sec., 1886–7; cr. peer 1885.

[171] William Arthur Wilkinson (1795–1863), Lib. MP for Lambeth, 1852–7.

[172] Granville William Gresham Leveson-Gower (1838–95), Lib. MP for Reigate, 1863–5; returned in 1865, but election declared void.

[173] Sir Edmund Walker Head (1805–68), gov.-genl. of Canada.

[174] George Brinton McClellan (1826–85), genl.-in-chief of Union troops in American Civil War, 1861–2.

expense. Genl. R. thinks the proposed Railway thro' Canada a mistake.
It could not he says, be kept open in winter.

9 February 1863.   Tuesday. [*sic*] Alice & Constance to a dance at the
de Greys, with which they were delighted.

10 February 1863.   Wednesday. [*sic*] Dined at Stanley of Alderley's.

14 February 1863.   Saturday. Flo & I to Eton to see Johnny. In the
evening to the Palmerstons. Pam looks very much aged since last Session
but seems in high spirits. Introduced to the Princess Obrenowitch of
Servia: a fine barbarian looking woman. She was a Hunyadi, a
Hungarian family. Sir Hamilton Seymour[175] & I talked of Kinglake's
book.[176] We agreed it was a 'sensation' history—He thinks as I do that
plain warning given by us early in the business to Czar Nicholas would
have prevented the war.

15 February 1863.   Sunday. Called on Baroness Lionel Rothschild[177] who
told me a long winded story of Disraeli going every year to visit one
Mrs Williams, a very old miserly woman who lives at Torquay, & who
it is thought will leave him her money. The old lady, it seems, insisted
on making his acquaintance, as being his devoted admirer, & Dizzy
has improved the occasion.[178]

Poor little Yarde, Flo's maid, died at 10 o'clock this evening in our
house. She was completely deformed & it seems her deformity increasing
the action of the heart was impeded fatally. She had been ailing, yet
was well enough to dress Flo: this morning. The doctor however told
us when he saw her in the middle of the day that she could not live
long. She was near dying a year ago. Her deformity was caused by
lace working at Honiton when very young.

[175] Sir George Hamilton Seymour (1797–1880), env. extr. to St Petersburg 1851–4 and
Austria, 1855.

[176] Alexander William Kinglake (1809–91) barrister; Lib. MP for Bridgewater, 1857–
65; publ. *Invasion of the Crimea* (8 vols., 1863–87).

[177] Charlotte, wife of Lionel Rothschild, chief manager of the Rothschild banking
house in England. After election to parliament in 1847, and repeatedly thereafter, Baron
Rothschild had been denied a seat in parliament for refusing to take the oath, but was
finally seated in 1858. One of Wodehouse's earliest speeches in the Lords had been in
favour of the Oath of Abjuration Bill. 3 *Hansard* 118 (17 July 1851), 875–7; *Liberal by
Principle*, 25.

[178] On Mrs Brydges Willyams, see R. Blake, *Disraeli* (London, 1966), 414–21.

17 February 1863. Tuesday. Normanby[179] on the Pope in the H. of L.; more twaddling than ever.

18 February 1863. Wednesday. To see the Cavendishes at Woodlands.

19 February 1863. Thursday. A talk in the H. of L. about Prison Discipline commenced by Carnavon, in which I took part.

20 February 1863. Friday. Ellenborough on the Poles. Whilst on foreign affairs, I may note here that I was told on the best authority that Lord Russell wanted in the autumn to mediate between the North & South in the American civil war. The French proposal really arose from suggestions from our F.O. But when the matter came before the Cabinet, they declined to interfere. Hence no little annoyance at Paris. Johnny's Sleswig escapade[180] (his despatch was dated Gotha!) was also unsanctioned by the Cabinet, & disapproved by Lord P., and it is pretty clear that the Despatch proposing to cede the Ionian islands was going faster than some of the Cabinet approved. Altogether the little man seems to be taking the bit between his teeth.

Lord Chelmsford's last pun. Some one coming up to the H. of Lords from the Commons on the night when the vote for the P. of Wales' allowance was proposing, said, 'no one was objecting but Sir H. Willoughby'[181] on wh. Lord C. said– 'The Prince will hardly care to have his countenance'. Sir H. is a singularly ugly man.

23 February 1863. Monday. To the Lyceum with Johnny to see the 'Duke's Motto'. Fechter's[182] action good but on the whole I was disappointed. The plot is childish & the dialogue without point. The 'sensation' scenes which are worthy of 'Astley's' are the chief attraction.

25 February 1863. Wednesday. To the Levee held by the P. of Wales– a prodigious squeeze.

26 February 1863. Thursday. Heard that Johnny was ill–measles coming.

1 March 1863. Sunday. Went to see Johnny.

[179] Constantine Henry Phipps, 1st Marquis of Normanby (1797–1863), amb. to Paris, 1846–52; min. to Florence, 1854–8.
[180] Of 24 Sept. 1862. Note, especially, the possible influence of Morier. Sandiford, *Schleswig-Holstein Question*, 53–5.
[181] Sir Henry Pollard Willoughby (1796–1865), Cons. MP for Evesham, 1847–65.
[182] Charles Albert Fechter (1824–79), German actor and dramatist who moved from Paris to London in 1860, leasing the Lyceum, 1863–7.

3 March 1863.   Tuesday. To Committee on Prison discipline.

4 March 1863.   Wednesday. Dined with the Russells. Talked to Brunnow about Poland. B. says the measures which have caused the insurrection were the work of Wielopolski,[183] himself a Pole, who 'led away' the G. Duke Constantine—not very difficult I suspect where work so congenial to a Russian was to be done. B. professes to treat the insurrection lightly. On Monday I saw Prince Perre Dolgoroukow.[184] He has been obliged to leave Brussels, being threatened with a prosecution, he says, for publishing his *'verite sur le Russe'*. Of course he's violent against the Russian Gt. He expects a revolution in Russia & the establishment of a Constitution: the dreams of an exile. The Russian 'Liberals' would give up Poland, he thinks, being convinced that Russia cannot be free whilst she treads down Poland. He ascribes the recent measures to Wielopolski.

I made the acquaintance last Saturday of the new French Ambassador, Baron Gros,[185] a tall, quiet, 'un'-French looking man.

5 March 1863.   Thursday. Committee Prison Discipline.

6 March 1863.   Friday. Committee of which I am Chairman (Lord Hawarden,[186] Wynford,[187] Cremorne, Congleton[188]) on Edinbro Water Works.

7 March 1863.   Saturday. To the War Office to see the procession of the P. of Wales & Ps. Alexandra. The procession a very shabby affair: for accounts of the enormous crowds, and the prodigious enthusiasm of John Bull *vide* the penny-a-liners passim. This demonstration however proves indisputably the great popularity of the Crown, arising entirely from the domestic virtues of the Queen & the late Prince Consort. The Queen is said to be somewhat jealous of the extraordinary affection displayed to the Prince & Princess. If this is true, she greatly mistakes the popular feeling which was essentially a feeling of regard for her, & her family as representing her virtues.

---

[183] Marquis Wielopolski, Russian gov.-genl. Poland.

[184] Petr Vladmirovich Dolgorukov (1817–68), genealogist and author. Exiled from Russia for publishing *The Truth about Russia* (1860). He eventually settled in England, and asked Wodehouse to recommend a bank. Wodehouse suggested Curries & Co., writing to Bertram Currie that though the Russian exile was 'clever' and 'unscrupulous', he knew of no reason why Currie should not *'receive* his money'. 'He lived in the highest Russian society in St. Petersburg when I was there.' 31 March 1863, CP.

[185] Jean Baptiste Louis, Baron Gros.

[186] Cornwallis Maude, 4th Viscount Hawarden (1817–1905).

[187] William Samuel Best, 2nd Baron Wynford (1798–1869).

[188] John Vesey Parnell, 2nd Baron Congleton (1805–83).

It seems that the Queen wanted the marriage to be as private as possible & that she was really the cause of the shabbiness of the procession, & the slights put upon the Corporation of the City. But I doubt this, & am more disposed to attribute the mismanagement to the incapacity of Sir George Grey, the Home Secretary.

9 March 1863.   Monday. My select Committee passed Edinburgh Water Works Bill unanimously. Refused a *locus standi* to Gt. Westn. and North Western, who opposed Hoylake Ry. Bill, which therefore was referred to Ld. Redesdale,[189] as unopposed.

10 March 1863.   Tuesday. Marriage of the Prince of Wales. I did not go out to see the illuminations.

11 March 1863.   Wednesday. Select Committee met at 12 o'clock. Went into case of Isle of Wights Railway. Admitted Cowes & Newport Ry. Company's *locus standi*.

12 March 1863.   Thursday. Passed Isle of Wights Raily. except that part which authorized a tramway to be made to Ryde Pier. The Committee all thought that the tramway would be useful to the public, & that the opposition of the Ryde Commissioners was selfish & foolish, but as the Ry. Company had made an agreement in 1859 with the Commissioners not to make a tramway, which agreement is recorded in the Companys Act of 1860 we did not think we should be justified in setting aside that agreement, before even the railway authorized by the Act of 1860 has been constructed. The opposition to the Londonderry (Seahorn to Sunderland) Ry. being withdrawn, the business of the Committee was concluded. I afterwards attended the Prison Discipline Committee & Lord Grey's Committee (at 4 o'clock) on Charging settled Estates for Railways.

14 March 1863.   Saturday. Played Tennis with Fletcher (even) & beat him. On Thursday, I forgot to mention, we went to ball at the Stanley's of Alderley, where were Prince & Princess Christian, father & mother of the Princess of Wales.

The Princess Christian not particularly good looking, though of course the newspapers make her a miracle of middle aged comeliness.

Flo: not well today.

16 March 1863.   Monday. Poor Flo: in bed with the measles.

[189] John Thomas Freeman-Mitford, 2nd Baron Redesdale (1805–86); ch. of comm. and dep. speaker of the Lords, 1851–86.

17 March 1863. Tuesday. Prison Committee. Went to the House of Commons & heard Forster propose Game Laws Committee. The squires impatient & violent. As was to be expected Forster & the Govt. who supported his motion, were beaten. Can anything be stupider than Sir G. Grey's conduct? Last Session if he had proposed inquiry, he might have succeeded in preventing the Game Bill. This Session when it is obviously too late, he supports a motion for inquiry.

Poor Flo: very ill today.

18 March 1863. Wednesday. Flo: much better. Attended Committee on charging settled Estates etc. Lord Romney[190] is in the chair. I had a curious conversation some days ago with Lord Clarendon about Poland & Prussia. The Govt., he told me, have determined not to fall into the snare set for them by Louis Napoleon. They see plainly that if they unite with France in remonstrating with Prussia, they will be placed in a most awkward dilemma if L.N. improves the occasion into a war for the Rhine. A mild remonstrance will be made by us singly at Berlin & Petersburg. Palmerston wanted a stronger reference to the Treaties of Vienna than that decided on by the Cabinet. I don't see how the Govt. could have acted otherwise with prudence. Every one must abhor the Russian oppression in Poland, but if we are not prepared to make war against Russia to compel her to restore Poland to independence, strong remonstrances are out of place, & only make the remonstrants contemptible. And it cannot be the interest of England to join France in a Polish crusade against Germany & Russia.

Lord C. said he had had some very serious conversations with Crown Princess of Prussia as to the position of affairs at Berlin. The Princess said that the Crown Prince was much alarmed at the position of danger in which he might be placed by the King's abdication, unless he was left full discretion as to his policy as his successor, & that he had declared that in no case would he undertake the duties of Sovereign unless his father in abdicating declared his positive resolution never afterwards to interfere in any way directly or indirectly in public affairs. The Princess said her husband was fully convinced of the necessity of governing upon constitutional principles. Dined at Grillion's; afterwards to Cos.

19 March 1863. Thursday. To Marylebone Vestry.

22 March 1863. Sunday. To Zoological Gardens, where we saw the Prince & Princess of Wales. I ought to have mentioned that on Friday

---

[190] Charles Marsham, 3rd Earl of Romney (1808–74), Cons. MP for W. Kent, 1841–5, when he succ. to peerage.

I went to an evening party at St. James' Palace in honour of the Prince & Princess.

23 March 1863. Monday. Committee on Charging entailed estates. Derby one of the Enclosure Commissrs. gave unfavourable evidence. He is evidently dead against all new facilities for improvement. I thought he talked a great deal of nonsense.

23 March 1863. Tuesday. Prison Committee. One thing is proved by the evidence we have had: that we want a new Home Secretary who has some backbone, & new inspectors of prisons, endowed with a few grains of common sense.

24 March 1863. Wednesday. Agreed unanimously to report in favour of charging Entailed Estates for Railways.

25 March 1863. Thursday. Prison Committee.

26 March 1863. Friday. House adjourned for Easter Recess. Dined at Polit: Economy Club where we had an animated discussion introduced by John Mill on the question what is the best definition of productive & unproductive labour & prod: & unprod. consumption. His definition was, labour employed in producing something which has exchangable value, & which is not consumed in the act of production. I made the acquaintance of Mr. Faussett[191] [sic], the blind man who has been lately Liberal candidate for Cambridge. He spoke well in the discussion.

Flo: has been suffering terribly from sore eyes, but is now, I hope, recovering.

27 March 1863. Saturday. Played Tennis.

29 March 1863. Sunday. Walked with B. Currie & Johnny to Zoolog: Gardens.

1 April 1863. Wednesday. To meeting of Senate of London University. Yesterday I had a long conversation with Prince Dolgoroukow. I could not gather from him any very definite opinion as to the prospects of the Polish Insurrection. On the whole however I think he expects that it will soon be mastered by the Russians.

---

[191] Henry Fawcett (1833–84), prof. of pol. econ. at Cambridge, 1863–84; Rad. MP for Brighton, 1865–74.

4 April 1863. Saturday. Had a long conversation with Dr. Foster[192] of the 'Liberation' Society. Agreed to move the 'Qualification for officers' bill in the H. of Lords tho' I told him the bill has no chance of passing. We talked much of the Dissenters in Norfolk who are much dissatisfied & no wonder with Colonel Coke's[193] votes. I told him plainly I could not help them, & that I only supported Coke on the principle that half a (Liberal) loaf is better than no bread.

I went one day this week to the Polytechnic with Johnny where I saw a capital optical illusion by Prof. Pepper. The Professor's harangue was intolerably tedious & his jokes almost as oppressive as the atmosphere of the crowded room, but the 'ghost' which he evoked was a first rate spectre. By the aid of ventriloquism it would be easy to make the ghost speak. The exhibition would then be perfect.

7 April 1863. Tuesday. To Minley, where we stayed till Saturday. A very pleasant visit. On Thursday a dance where I met Kingsley.[194] He takes too unfavorable a view of the N. Americans. Was introduced to Lord Dorchester[195] one of those pillars of the State who discharge their duties by never (as he said himself) attending the House of Lords. How can that institution last if the Peers show that they attach no value to their legislative rights?

We walked over to the new 'Convict Lunatic Asylum', a huge building or rather group of buildings with palatial looking terraces— a fine view. It is not quite finished: 180 of 'Jebb's[196] pets' are working there, two of whom asked us for 'baccy'-villainous sleek looking scoundrels. I don't wonder it is difficult for them when let loose on 'ticket of leave' to find honest employment. Their looks would drive off any one.

14 April 1863. Tuesday. House of Lords met after recess. Heard of Sir G. Lewis' death. A great loss to the Liberal party & to the country. Many speculated as to his successor. De Grey seems the favorite. I fear there can be no opening for my return to office. I must work on perseveringly & hope for a turn of luck some day. There will be one decided advantage to all men below forty if de Grey is appd. It will

[192] Dr Charles James Foster, ch. of the parlt. comm. of the Liberation Society. On the activities of the society, see Jenkins (ed.), *Trelawney Diaries, 1858–65*.

[193] Wenman Clarence Walpole Coke (1828–1907), Lib. MP for Norfolk East, 1858–65. Opposed the ballot.

[194] Charles Kingsley (1819–75), chaplain to Queen Victoria, 1859; prof. of modern history, Cambridge, 1860–9; novelist.

[195] Guy Carleton, 3rd Baron Dorchester (1811–75).

[196] Sir Joshua Jebb (1793–1863), insp.-genl. of military prisons from 1844; developed progressive system of incarceration; designed Portland Prison.

break through the charmed circle of old men who have so long monopolized office on the Liberal side.

15 April 1863. Wednesday. Dined at Grillion's–afterwards to Cosmop:– I mentioned to Lord Stanhope[197] that my uncle Rebow[198] had been reproached at the Colchester elections with his descent from Colonel Gurdon who commanded a Parliamentarian regiment at the siege of Colchester! A curious example of the permanence of political enmities.

16 April 1863. Thursday. Attended Committee on Prisons. Also Committee on the Chancellor's Bill for sale of Chancellor's livings. I pointed out the inexpediency of giving power to owners of estates for life to burden the inheritance in order to purchase advowsons. My remarks seemed to meet with concurrence.

Said a few words in the hour in favour of second reading of "Alkali Works Bill" I heard a part of C. of Exchequer's Speech.

17 April 1863. Friday. Weather so warm that we partly left off fires.

20 April 1863. Monday. De Grey appointment to War Off: announced. Ld. Hartington to be under Secretary. De Grey's appt. generally approved. If Cardwell had had any merit he could not have been passed over. He has shown himself wonderfully proficient in the art of sinking. It was rumoured that if de Grey had not succeeded Lewis, Ld. Clarendon would have returned to Office but he could not have been War Secy. Would he have accepted the Privy Seal if Argyll had gone to the India Off. I doubt it.

Fortune seemed to have played me a scurvy trick when I lost my Under Secretaryship by Lord Russell becoming a Peer, but it has turned out a kind of negative luck, as it would have been very mortifying to have had de Grey put over my head: & I could have had no cause to complain, much less have resigned in consequence. How curious that all the office holders in the H. of Lords (except the Household) should be in the Cabinet. The five under secretaries in the Commons.

Hartington's appointment is chiefly notable, as showing that tho' a young man may spend his time in riot & debauchery, yet if he shows a spark of ability & is connected with one of the great aristocratic

---

[197] Philip Henry Stanhope, 5th Earl Stanhope (1805–75), historian and Peel's executor; published, among others, *History of England from Peace of Utrecht to Peace of Versailles, 1713–83* (7 vols., 1836–58). On Stanhope as historian, see Peter Marsh, 'Prime Ministerial Exemplar: Studies of Pitt the Younger by Victorian Statesmen', *Nineteenth-Century Prose* 22 (Fall 1995), 115–28.

[198] John Gurdon Rebow (1799–1870), Lib. MP for Colchester, 1857–70; Kimberley's maternal uncle. Upon marriage added 'Rebow' to the patronymic Gurdon.

families, he has the door always open to political office.[199] Ld. Hartington it is said has abilities, but above all he is the son of the D. of Devonshire. Bow down ye ignoble hard working members!

22 April 1863. Wednesday. Johnny went back to Eton. Stansfeld appointed junior Lord of the Admiralty. What an instructive sequel to Hartington's appt.

Met at Cos: White[200] Vice Consul at Warsaw & Oliphant,[201] both just come from Poland. Their account is that the insurgents persevere in hope of aid from France. White says the Duke Constantine is a well meaning but weak man. The disorganization of the Russian army he ascribes to the dissemination of Herzen's[202] opinions amongst the officers. The men have been warned by the Govt. against their officers, & now will not obey them. Saw also [*space left blank*] a German right hand man of D: of Saxe Coburg. He has been to see the Queen at Windsor. His acccount of K. of Prussia deplorable. The King thinks there is no alternative but Bismarck[203] or the fate of Louis 16!

23 April 1863. Thursday. Sharp conversation in House of Lords about America. I said a few words which were well received.

24 April 1863. Friday. Moved second reading of Qualification for Officers Abolition (Mr. Hadfield's annual) Bill.[204] Spoke, I think with fair success, for 1/4 of an hour. Ld. Derby moved this day six months & in fact admitted that there is no valid ground for opposing the Bill. He went off upon the usual Church buncombe in default of reasons. The grievance is certainly small but the grounds of opposing its removal still smaller or rather nil. How foolish Churchmen are to give battle on such ground to the Dissenters! The Bill was rejected–69 to 52.

---

[199] Spencer Compton Cavendish, Marquess of Hartington (1857–70), Lib. MP for N. Lancashire, 1857–68, for Radnor Boroughs, 1869–80, for Lancashire N.E., 1880–5, for Lancashire N.E., Rossendale, 1885; Lib. U. MP for Rossendale, 1886–91, when he succ. as 8th Duke of Devonshire; u.-sec. war, 1863–6; war sec., 1866, 1882–5; post. genl., 1868–71; ch. sec. Ireland, 1871–4; Indian sec., 1880–2; ld. pres. counc., 1895–1903. On the misunderstood nature of Hartington's 'riot & debauchery', see Patrick Jackson, ' "Skittles" and the Marquess: A Victorian Love Affair', *History Today* (Dec. 1995), 47–52.

[200] William Arthur White (1824–91), vice cons. at Warsaw from 1861; then consul at Danzig, 1864–75.

[201] Laurence Oliphant (1829–88), novelist and war correspondent; visited Poland Moldavia and Schleswig-Holstein in 1863.

[202] Aleksandr Herzen (Yakovlev) (1812–70), Russian writer and political activist.

[203] Otto Eduard Leopold von Bismarck (1815–98), Prussian amb. to Russia, 1859, to France, 1862; pres. of Prussian cabinet and for. min., 1862–71; German chanc., 1871–90.

[204] George Hadfield (1787–1879), Rad. MP for Sheffield, 1852–74, introduced bill to repeal oath to support the Anglican Church upon taking up certain ministerial offices. See 3 *Hansard* 170 (24 April 1863), 658–60. Defeated in the Lords by 69 to 52 votes.

I attended the Committees on Prison Discipline, the Chancellors Bills & Railways this week.

27 April 1863. Monday. Smith of Truro came about Falmouth business. He gives a flourishing account of Falmouth. The Railway, & Docks making rapid progress, and a Hotel Company formed with a capital of £20,000 of which no less than £14,000 paid up! They have purchased of my Trustees 3 acres of land at £500 an acre. It seems probable I may have to decide shortly to take the property off the Trustees hands. I am told it will be a mine of wealth to me. I foresee little but a mine of trouble.

A short debate in the Lords on the report of the Committee in favour of charging settled Estates for making Railways. I made a few remarks supporting the report.

29 April 1863. Wednesday. Sent Cheque to Oddin Taylor for £415, price of four cottages and of land in Wicklewood. These cottages are a bad purchase but I am determined by degrees to buy up the miserable cottages in Wicklewood & make them decent habitations. I am convinced there is no better charity.

Dined with Beaumonts[205] & met here the Princess of Servia, a beautiful woman wife of Michel Obrenowitch[206] the reigning Prince (born Hunyadi a Hungarian family). I sat next to her at dinner. We talked of Turkish politics. She complains bitterly that England prevents the Christians from obtaining redress of their grievances. Her grand object is to get the Turks out of Belgrade. One cannot but sympathize with the Servians. I tried to her [sic] why the policy of England is so Conservative in the Levant, but with little effect.

2 May 1863. Saturday. Breakfasted at Grillions. Arthur Mills[207] elected. Much discourse of Gladstone's proposed Income Tax on Charities. The Bp. of Oxford[208] said that Gladstone interpreted the Text 'Charity never faileth' to mean that Charity is a never failing source of revenue.

I attended Committees on Prisons, on the Sale of Chancellor's Livings Bill and Metropolian Railways this week. In the Committee on the Chancellor's Bill a curious point arose on Thursday. Lord Derby proposed a clause to add certain Livings (of higher value) to the

---

[205] Wentworth Blackett Beaumont (1829–1907), Lib. MP for Northumberland S., 1852–85, and for Northumberland Tyneside, 1886–92; cr. Baron Allendale, 1892.

[206] Michael Obrenovic (1825–68), prince of Serbia, 1839–42, deposed, 1860–8; assassinated.

[207] Arthur Mills (1816–98), barrister; Cons. MP for Taunton, 1852–3, 1857–65, for Exeter, 1873–80. Son-in-law of Sir Thomas Dyke Acland.

[208] Samuel Wilberforce (1805–73), Bishop of Oxford, 1845–69.

Schedule of Livings to be sold. Lord St Leonards[209] objected that the consent of the Crown had not been obtained. On this there was a discussion & it was suggested that we should pass the clause subject to the Assent of the Crown. Lord Eversley[210] & others objected, because it is open to any member of Parliament to make any proposal he pleases affecting the prerogative of the Crown, & the House may adopt the proposal without the previous consent of the Crown. That consent must be signified in the House at any time during the passage of the Bill through it, & if not given, the Bill is null, & void. But the consent of the Crown cannot be signified to a select Committee. The Chancellor & Granville seemed not a little embarrassed. Ultimately the Chancellor did what was very irregular. He asked us our opinion (which except St Leonard's was in favor) of Lord Derby's Clause, it being understood that nothing should be recorded in the minutes, but that he should ascertain the pleasure of the Queen before we went further. The fact was, I heard afterwards, that the Queen had very reluctantly given her consent to the Bill, & that the Chancellor has doubts whether she will agree to Derby's addition. Of course he ought to have ascertained the Queen's wishes before anything was said about it in the Committee.

6 May 1863.   Wednesday. Played Tennis at Hampton Court with Ponsonby. Dined at Grillion's Club 50th Anniversary dinner.

7 May 1863.   Thursday. Voted for Clause in Corrupt Practices Bill proposed by Lord Lyveden[211] excluding Agents from voting. We were beaten. Afterwards voted with majority against Govt. to omit clause enabling a borough to be disfranchised for 5 years.

8 May 1863.   Friday. Lord Shaftesbury's[212] motion on Poland. Lord Russell made an excellent speech, but the positon of the Govt. is really untenable. How can we gravely ask Russia to put the Govt. of Poland in the hands of the Poles when we know that the only use the Poles will make of their official position will be to separate Poland from the Czar's rule?

---

[209] Edward Burtenshaw Sugden, Baron St. Leonards (1781–1875), ld. chan., 1852. According to the *DNB*, 'almost infallible as an oracle of law'.

[210] Charles Shaw-Lefevre, Viscount Eversley (1794–1888), speaker of the House of Commons, 1839–57; eccl. commissioner, 1859.

[211] Robert Vernon Smith, Baron Lyveden (1800–73), Lib. MP for Tralee, 1829–31, for Northampton, 1831–59; pres. bd. of cont., 1855–8; raised to the peerage in 1859; father-in-law of George Wodehouse Currie, Wodehouse's cousin.

[212] Anthony Ashley Cooper, 7th Earl of Shaftesbury (1801–85), philanthropist; Lib. MP 1826–51, when he succeeded to the earldom.

Attended Prison Committee & Metropolitan Ry. Do. this week.

10 May 1863.   Sunday. Dined with Lady Waldegrave. The lady spoke with very faint praise of de Grey's appointment; evidently she is mortified that C. Fortescue is still no more than an Under Secretary.[213] Wednesday Dined at Grillion's & to Cos:

14 May 1863.   Thursday. Flo: went to Eton to see Johnny. Flo: & I were vaccinated. The unusual prevalence of small pox has led many to take this precaution.

I forgot to note that on Sunday I went with G. Currie & Airlie by the Metropolitan Ry. to the City. I had not been before by this new line. It seems to be admirably constructed & worked. We looked at the proposed site of the viaduct over Ludgate Hill, admired St. Paul's, peeped into the venerable Temple Church, condemned as mean & ugly the new Temple Library, & having passed our afternoon pleasantly finished by a walk in the Park.

On Thursday the Prison Committee considered Ld. Carnarvon's proposed heads of report. We had a long discussion from twelve till past five o'clock. I divided the Committee against the proposal to put a mark on felons convicted a second time.

contents	*not-contents*
Carnarvon	Eversley
Dudley	Cathcart[214]
Wensleydale	Romney[215]
Lyveden	Salisbury[216]
St Germans[217]	Wodehouse

The numbers being equal I carried it against the proposal. It was afterwards agreed (very irregularly I think) that this Division should not appear in the minutes that we might seem unanimous.

15 May 1863.   Friday. Debate in our House on Holstein & Sleswig question, introduced by Lord Ellenborough, who did not speak so well as usual, was nervous and rather confused. Lord Russell followed and

---

[213] In 1863 Frances Elizabeth, Lady Waldegrave (1821–79), married Chichester Fortescue, Lib. MP for Louth, 1847–74; u.-sec. col., 1857–8, 1859–65; ch. sec. Ireland, 1865–6, 1868–71; pres. b. of t., 1871–4; ld. privy seal, 1881–5; ld. pres. counc., 1883–5.

[214] Alan Frederick Cathcart, 3rd Earl Cathcart (1828–1905).

[215] Charles Marsham, 3rd Earl of Romney (1808–74).

[216] James Brownlow Cecil, 2nd Marquess of Salisbury (1791–1868).

[217] Edward Granville Eliot, 3rd Earl of St. Germans (1798–1881), ch. sec. Ireland, 1841–5; ld. lt. Ireland, 1853–5.

adroitly seized some weak points in Ld. E's speech but could make but a lame defence of his own policy. Lord Derby spoke after him– admirably. I rose with Lord D. after Lord R.; of course had to give way. When Lord D. had finished, I ventured to speak after him (a great piece of audacity in so young a man. I am only 37, & but partially gray & bald). Lord Clarendon encouraged me to speak, & I managed to persevere for 20 minutes. Lord C. good naturedly complimented me on my performance, but I am not blind enough not to see that it was a poor affair. However I am glad I spoke as at all events it served to show that the disapprobation of Lord R's foolish despatch of Sept 1862 is not confined to the oppositon. I doubt if any one not a German, or connected with Germans, defends it. How difficult it is to find an opportunity to speak in the House of Lords. Lord Derby, Lord Ellenborough, Lord Grey, & some Minister usually occupy the time between 5 & 7 when foreign affairs are debated, after which the House breaks up for dinner.

16 May 1863.   Saturday. Flo: was to have gone to the Drawing room. I foolishly advised her not to go on account of the crowd–at the last moment when she had begun to dress. She was much vexed.

I dined with Bille the Danish Minister. He thinks there will be war between France & Russia & Prussia about Poland, before the year is out. He says the Danes earnestly hope for such a war, & that Lord Russell by his anti-Danish policy must drive Denmark into the arms of France.

18 May 1863.   Monday. Committee–

D. of Manchester[218]
Lord Shrewsbury[219]
Lord Camoys[220]
Lord Dufferin[221]

& myself, Chairman met to consider Chatham & Dover Railway Bill, & some other Bills. There had been a great stir about the Ludgate Hill Company's Bill which was also referred to us, but this bill was

---

[218] William Drogo Montague, 7th Duke of Manchester (1823–90).
[219] Henry John Chetwynd-Talbot, 18th Earl of Shrewsbury (1803–68).
[220] Thomas Stonor, 5th Baron Camoys (1797–1881).
[221] Frederick Temple Hamilton-Temple Blackwood, Lord Dufferin (1826–1902), Irish baron cr. Baron Clandeboye in U.K. peerage, 1850; u.-sec. for India, 1864–6; u.-sec. to War Office, 1866–8; ch. d. of Lanc., 1868–72; cr. earl, 1871; gov.-genl. Canada, 1872–8; amb. at St Petersburg, 1879–81; amb. at Constantinople, 1881–4; viceroy of India, 1884–8; cr. marquess of Dufferin and Ava, 1888; amb. at Rome, 1889–91; amb. at Paris, 1891–6.

withdrawn. The clause in the Lond: C. & Dover Ry. Bill prolonging for two years their compulsory powers as regards the line over Ludgate Hill was also withdrawn, so that there was no opportunity of discussing the merits of the viaduct, etc. The L. C. & D. Ry. fall back upon their Act of 1860 by which they obtained powers to make the line over Ludgate Hill . Those powers expire in August, & they have given the requisite notices for the land. Whether they have means to complete the purchase may be doubted. We passed the remainder of their Bill— also a Mercantile Marine Liverpool Assocn. Bill.

19 May 1863.   Tuesday. Committee met & passed the Victoria Station & Pimlico Bill. Our work was over at 12.30. My arm is much swollen & inflamed from the vaccination. Dined with Ld. Clanricarde.

Interesting Debate on Ebury's[222] motion to amend Act of Uniformity. Bshp. of Canterbury[223] made a very weak speech: the Bp. of London[224] the best I ever heard made by Bishop.

20 May 1863.   Wednesday. Went to Academy Exhibition. Not much pleased with anything except Millais'[225] two pictures of children, & Stansfield's[226] 'After the Battle of Trafalgar'. The portraits as numerous as & even more horrible than usual.

23 May 1863.   Saturday. House of Lords adjourned on Thursday till Monday week. Ld. Clarendon tells me that Ld. Palmerston is very hot about Poland, will not hear of Ld. Ellenborough's plan of making 'Congress' Poland independent under the D. of Leuchtenberg. Lord P. says the Govt. believe that France will not move without England in matter of Poland. Lord P. according to Lord C. is rather despondent about Greece, the throne of which Pr: Willm. of Denmark has not yet consented to take, C. says the Princess of Wales spoke to him the other night at Marlboro' House about her brother & said she disapproved his acceptance of the Greek Throne. She complained of Lord Russell's having announced that the Prince had accepted when he knew it was not the case: said she had told Lord R. so. The Ministry have managed this Greek affair badly from the first.

---

[222] Robert Grosvenor, 1st Baron Ebury (1801–93), Whig MP for Chester, 1826–47, for Middlesex, 1847–57, when he was cr. Baron.

[223] Charles Thomas Longley (1794–1868), archbp. York, 1860–2; of Canterbury, 1862–8.

[224] Archibald Campbell Tait (1811–82), bp. London, 1856–68; archbp. Canterbury, 1869–82.

[225] John Everett Millais (1829–96), painter and pres. of the Royal Academy.

[226] Clarkston Stansfield (1793–1867).

25 May 1863. Monday. Went on a visit to the Carnarvons' at Highclere, a most beautiful place, but I don't like the House which is externally Barry's.[227] Lord & Lady Chesterfield,[228] H. Forrester,[229] Lady M. Charteris,[230] C. Greville,[231] Mr & Lady S. de Veux,[232] Cyril Graham,[233] Lord St Asaph[234] & others were there. A pleasant party. Delane ('Times') there the first day. He thinks as does H. Greville[235] that the civil war in N. America will last a long time. I think so too.

C. Graham's account of Turkey is discouraging, but I am by no means convinced by the 'anti Turk' party that the Turkish Empire is near its fall, or that we ought to cease to pursue our policy of keeping things quiet in the East. Where no one can forecast the future, 'better to bear the ills we have &c. &c.'

28 May 1863. Thursday. Returned to London.

31 May 1863. Sunday. After great heat on Saturday, a cold raw wind today. Result: I caught a bad influenza cold. Lord Clarendon showed me to-day a curious letter from Ld. Cowley, expressing a strong opinion that nothing but the Mexican entanglement has kept the Emperor from a war in favour of Poland. Lord Cy. thinks that the result of the Paris elections if unfavourable to the Emperor will compel him to resort to war to divert public attention from home affairs. He expects, he says, war before the year is out. The Empress, it seems, wants to go on a sort of pilgrimage to the Holy Places!

2 June 1863. Tuesday. Had a last sitting from Richmond for my Grillion portrait. Flo: saw it, & thought it a good likeness.

3 June 1863. Wednesday. Soames' Bill lost in H. of Commons. I hear a strong pressure was put on members who have Dissenting Constituents.

[227] Sir Charles Barry (1795–1860), architect; occupied in building the Houses of Parliament, 1840–60.
[228] George Augustus Frederick Stanhope, 6th Earl of Chesterfield (1805–66).
[229] Probably Alfred Henry Forrester (1804–72), artist and illustrator; worked for *Punch* and the *Illustrated London News.*
[230] Lady Margaret Charteris (1834–1915) da. 2nd Earl of Glengall; m. 1858 Lt.-col. Richard Wemyss-Charteris.
[231] Charles Cavendish Fulke Greville (1794–1865), clerk to the privy counc., 1821–59.
[232] Sir William Henry Des Voeux and Lady Sophia Catherine, da. 7th Earl of Coventry.
[233] Cyril Graham (1834–95), attached to Lord Dufferin's mission to Syria, 1860–1; priv. sec. to Carnarvon as col. sec., 1866–7; lt.-gov. Grenada, 1875–7.
[234] Bertram Ashburnham, Viscount St. Asaph (1840–1913), succ. as 5th Earl of Ashburnham, 1878.
[235] Henry William Greville (1801–72), gentleman usher at court.

I tried to play Tennis but obliged to give it up as my vaccinated arm is not yet well!

4 June 1863. Thursday. Went to Marylebone Vestry & told Mr. Carr that when my term is over (next May) I do not wish to be re-elected. I find I can hardly ever attend now that the day is changed from Saturday to Thursday.

5 June 1863. Friday. Went to Salt Hill for Eton '4th of June'– a miserable wet day.

6 June 1863. Saturday. Returned to town & dined at Lord Palmerstons (Queen's birthday dinner).

7 June 1863. Sunday. Conversation with E. Ellice[236] ('the Bear') about the influence of the Crown, which he thinks as I do has increased, is increasing, & ought to be diminished. We were led to this subject by my observing upon the outrageous vote which is to be asked of the H. of Commons for the Glass House at Brompton. £484,000 for that monstrous eye-sore! The job will be done, as the leaders on both sides wish to curry favour with the Queen, which can only be done by carrying out every project, real or supposed of Prince Albert. Ellice told me that when the late Ld. Campbell[237] was appointed Cr. of the Duchy of Lancaster, Prince A. proposed to make Lord Hardwicke[238] amongst others one of the Council of the Duchy. Lord H. naturally objected as he belonged to the Opposition, and amongst other things asked how the Church patronage was to be given away. Oh said the P., 'I want to get some energetic men without distinction of party on the Council in order to improve the Duchy property, & you need not trouble yourself about the Church patronage. I have made arrangements for that'. That is to say, he meant to dispose of them himself. The attempt failed in consequence of the resistance of Ld. Campbell. The object however was constantly kept in view by the P. who was determined to weaken the Govt. by parties, & if he had lived, would I believe have brought about a serious conflict between the H. of Commons & the Crown, in which, if he had chosen his time well, I am not sure the H. of Commons would have been victorious.

A remarkable instance of the encroachment of the P. in the rights of

---

[236] Edward Ellice (1781–1863), Lib. MP for Coventry, 1831–63; dep. gov. Hudson's Bay Co.

[237] John Campbell, 1st Baron Campbell (1779–1861), ch. d. of Lanc., 1846; ld. chanc., 1859.

[238] Charles Philip Yorke, 4th Earl of Hardwicke (1799–1873), rear-admiral, 1854; admiral, 1863; post.-genl, 1852; ld. privy seal, 1858–9.

the Ministers to give away the Church patronage of the Duchy occurred in the case of the living of Southrepps (or Northrepps?) last year, which is a Duchy living, & became vacant by the death of Archdeacon Glover. Suffield (backed by every Liberal of mark in Norfolk) asked Cardwell to present it to his brother, & considering that the living is close to Gunton & that S. paid a larger sum at the last election to bring in Coke, his claim was a strong one. The living was given to a high Tory clergyman. (Personally obnoxious to Suffield & the parishioners) for whom P. Albert had obtained the promise of it. The Queen asked Cardwell not to disregard the known wish of P. Alb: & Cardwell who is wretchedly weak, gave way. This is an example of what may be done by persevering encroachments, when a weak minister can be got hold of.[239]

11 June 1863.   Thursday. Attended Committee on Telegraphs Bill.

12 June 1863.   Friday. Saw 'Finesse' at the Haymarket. Lady D's play. A poor affair, only made tolerable by the admirable acting of the Wigans[240] & Buckstone.[241]

14 June 1863.   Sunday. At Cos: Much talk about the monstrous Brompton job. I fear Court influence will carry the day, & Coles & Dilke will reign triumphant over us.[242]

15 June 1863.   Monday. To Kimberley & Flo: to see C. at St Leonards. Walked across the mud to the island in the Lake which is quite dry. Sixty men at work digging out the mud. The usual doleful accounts as to the effects of spring frosts on fruit &c. &c. The young trees planted in the autumn & winter have done well.

17 June 1863.   Wednesday. Returned to London.

18 June 1863.   Thursday. Lord Portman,[243] one of the Commissioners of the 1851 Exhibn. told me that he & others of the Commission wanted to dissolve the Commission & hand over the land (subject to mortgages) to the Govt. I could guess he said who the opponents were. No doubt the Court.

[239] Cf. entry of 6 June 1862.
[240] Alfred Sydney (1814–78) and Leonora (1805–84) Wigan, husband and wife actors.
[241] John Baldwin Buckstone (1802–79), comedian; manager of the Haymarket, 1853–76.
[242] See entry for 28 April 1862.
[243] Edward Berkeley Portman, 1st Viscount Portman (1799–1888).

20 June 1863.   Saturday. Fortescue's Cos. party at Strawberry Hill.

22 June 1863.   Monday. Attended during this week sittings of the Prison Committee, & the Metropolitan Railways Committee. Carnarvon does not manage his Committee successfully. His draft Report is written in an inaccurate slip-slop style, & he shows a want of 'backbone' in defending it. The D. of Richmond[244] who is a hard, shrewd, persevering man of business worries C. as a dog worries a rat, always however with courtesy & good temper, which makes it the more difficult to shake him off.

The promised debate on Brazil in our House was a lame affair, tho' Lord Malmesbury made one or two good points. The Govt. ought I think to have proposed to submit the whole question to arbitration. If Brazil had refused, no one could have blamed a resort to reprisals.

Committee on the 'Telegraphs Bill' which I attended again, settled the amendments. We have taken all the sting out of the Bill.

24 June 1863.   Wednesday. Flo: went to Eton to see 'Winchester Match'.

26 June 1863.   Friday. Went to Guard's Ball at the Exhibn. Building. Talked to Bn. Brunnow about Poland. He complained bitterly of our hostility to Russell: inveighed against Layard[245] for his manner in speaking of Russia in the H. of C. He admitted however that Mouravieff, who commands in Lithuania, is not 'un homme de bien,' & said he was selected because he would treat the rebels with unsparing severity, not caring what Western Europe thought or said of him. He is the late Minister of Domains, not the Mouravieff of Kars nor the Govn. Gol. of Siberia.

I hinted that it was the conduct of such men as Mouravieff which roused the indignation of Europe, & would someday plunge Russia into terrible calamities. He replied that Russia was hated by the rest of Europe, & it was of no use to try to become less unpopular.

The answer to our last proposals, he thought, would be a long time coming: we had taken 7 weeks to prepare our despatch, they might fairly take as long to prepare their answer. They must first endeavor to satisfy their neighbours Austria & Prussia. Does this mean 'to detach Austria from France & Engd.'? Probably. Afterwards I spoke to Lord

---

[244] Charles Henry Gordon-Lennox, 6th Duke of Richmond (1818–1903), Cons. MP for W. Sussex, 1841–60; succ. as Duke, 1860; pres. b. of t., 1867–9; leader of Cons. party in Lords from 1868.

[245] Sir Austen Henry Layard (1817–94), Lib. MP for Aylesbury, 1852–7, for Southwark, 1860–70; for. u.-sec., 1852, 1861–6; excavated Nineveh in 1840s.

Grey, who as usual is against all interference abroad. Lord Stratford[246] on the other hand said to me that he believed that such a strong diplomatic pressure may be put upon Russia by the three Powers that in her present state of weakness she will yield without war to all our demands. I said to Lord Grey that I had much confidence in Palmerston's well known ability to drive the coach along the edge of the precipice without upsetting it. 'Yes,' he replied, 'but John Russell is on the box too, & is sure to upset it.' There is a growing feeling that we are drifting into war with Russia.

28 June 1863.   Saturday. Heard Faust the new opera at the H. Th.

29 June 1863.   Monday. Went to a very pleasant concert at the Duke d'Aumale's at Twickenham. Attended this week Committee, moved by Lord Dunoughmore, on Raily. Companies Borrowing Powers arising out of the affair of the Northpool Railway, & also the Metropolitan Raily. Committee on Friday to consider our report.

30 June 1863.   Tuesday. Dined with Ld. Stanley. Met the Grotes & A. Stanley.[247]

1 July 1863.   Wednesday. Dined with Somers. A Confederate officer named Robinson, a Virginian came in after dinner; a quiet, gentlemanlike young man. I asked him his views on Slavery. He said he had little personal interest in Slavery, being the owner of only three old women, but he had no hesitation in telling me that after much reflection & some doubt on the subject he had come to the deliberate conclusion that Providence had ordained the events now taking place in America in order that the Confederate States might prove to the world the beneficial effects of the institution of Slavery! I said I admitted that if I were a Southern man I should consider immediate emancipation out of the question, but that I thought as soon as the war was over, measures should be passed for preventing slaves from being sold away from the estates to which they belong (as a first step to the improvement of their position).[248] I was glad to find that he concurred in this view.

2 July 1863.   Thursday. Redesdale being unable from illness to attend the House today, I was much to my surprise asked to take the chair in

[246] Stratford Canning, 1st Viscount Stratford de Redcliffe (1786–1880), began dipl. career in 1807, amb. to Constantinople, 1842–58.

[247] Probably Frederick Arthur Stanley (1841–1908), Lord Stanley's brother, who suc. as 16th Earl of Derby upon Stanley's death in 1893; married Clarendon's daughter.

[248] Cf. Wodehouse's notes on *Uncle Tom's Cabin*, KP1 15/K2/6, 54.

Committees of the whole House. I was rather puzzled by so novel a position, & made more than one blunder. Fortunately there was very little business.

4 July 1863. Friday[*sic*]. A rumour that Lord Russell has resigned? Can there be any truth in this? It may be connected with a story which Lord Taunton told me that the Queen and(?) Lord Palmerston had been putting a check on Lord R's Polish enthusiasm.

5 July 1863. Sunday. It is still rumoured that there is a 'crisis' in the Cabinet: but I don't believe there is any foundation for the rumour.

6 July 1863. Monday. Report of Carnarvon's Committee[249] at last agreed to.

8 July 1863. Wednesday. A dinner at home. Ct. Dmitry Nesselrode dined with us: Also Lady E. (Tatty). One of her sayings as to not asking people to dinner who don't ask her in return is becoming proverbial– 'cutlet for cutlet is my rule'. She told a particular friend that she could not ask her daughter to her balls, because she (the friend) never gave so much as 'a tea'.

10 July 1863. Friday. Johnny came up for the Eton & Harrow match & stayed till Monday morning. I spoke in the House very briefly on Japan. Carnarvon introduced the subject in a long speech which wearied the House but is read by the public & applauded by the newspapers. I respect his determination to be heard. I thought however both his speech & Grey's weak in argument. I should have liked to follow Grey, but the D. of Somerset stepped in. Of course I had to give way, & I got a very poor 'innings'.

12 July 1863. Sunday. Went to Wimbledon to dine with B. Curries. Saw & was much pleased with the charming little house which they have nearly finished building in Coombe wood.[250] Very hot weather.

13 July 1863. Monday. Interesting Debate in the H. of Lords on Poland. I should have spoken if I could have got an opportunity but as usual Lord Grey, Lord Russell & Lord Derby monopolised the debate. Poor old Brougham spoke or rather attempted to speak for his whole set of false teeth tumbled out & after trying for nearly five

---

[249] Carnarvon's committee convened to examine the subscription to formularies of faith by fellows and tutors of Oxford University.
[250] Coombe Warren, Kingston.

minutes to put them in again, he went on mumbling without them. I never saw a more painful spectacle. Lord Russell's declaration that in no event will we go to war for Poland, seemed to me excessively imprudent, & will render our diplomatic action, almost useless. The 'Post' writes so fiercely against Lord R. that rumours prevail that he & Pam are at two about Poland, Pam preferring a more decided policy. The other day the 'rumours' were in the contrary sense. Probably the present story is nearest the truth.

16 July 1863.   Thursday. We settled the report of the Committee on Metropolitan Railways.

17 July 1863.   Friday. Met R. Currie & Mr. Jones at 29 Cornhill about Falmouth. Determined not without misgivings to take the estate & charges off the hands of the Trustees next January. The immediate effect on my income will be a loss of something over £100 per annum, but ultimately I think there must be a gain to me in the transaction, & there will be a great satisfaction in paying all my Grandfather's liabilities in full, & relieving the Trustees from further responsibility.

19 July 1863.   Saturday. [*sic*] Went with a large party to see the outlets of Metropolitan Main Drainage at Barking. Dined in the North Reservoir. The brick work is admirable. I observed that near London the river stunk abominably.

21 July 1863.   Monday. [*sic*] The Russian answer about Poland is a complete 'fin de non reçevoir'. Everything depends on the conduct of Austria. If she remains firm we shall avoid a war. From Apponyi's language today in a conversation I had with him I augur well.

21 July 1863.   Tuesday. Attended Committee on Railway Debentures. Agreed on our report.

22 July 1863.   Wednesday. Went to Kimberley. Thus ends for me this Session, which has been dull for every one, & to me most discouraging. Ld. Palmerston seems very shaky. I don't think he will go through another Session.

27 July 1863.   Monday. Attended at workhouse. Johnny came home, a few days earlier than the holidays, on account of a bad eye. Very dry weather. The Lake fills very slowly, after being emptied for mud to be taken out. I calculate that the mud accumulates at the rate of one foot in ten years. The new Home Farm buildings are making progress.
   Twenty eight fawns this season: four of which drowned in ditches in

Cascade Plantation one born dead, remain eleven bucks, ten does marked, two not marked, six unknown.

28 July 1863.   Tuesday. Parliament prorogued.

29 July 1863.   Wednesday. Heard of Ld. Normanby's death, which will not be much regretted. His latter public career was a melancholy spectacle. He was a man of small capacity who by persevering importunity & toadying occupied many high places of trust. The [*ill.*] will now be without a representative in the House of Lords.

1 August 1863.   Saturday. Attended Norwich prison Committee. Fewer prisoners than this day last year.

4 August 1863.   Tuesday. Killed two Bucks, the first since the reestablishment of the deer. Both came from Studley.[251] I meant to have killed one of them at the end of this month, but by a curious mistake, the deer being very much alike in appearance, I killed the second buck with my second barrel, mistaking it for the buck which I had fired at and wounded with my first barrel. What was still more singular the Buck I first shot at was not the one I intended to kill now, though its death was fixed for a few weeks hence. I was 'up a tree,' whose leaves must be the excuse for my bungling vision. The bucks were very fat weighing 10 Stone 5 lb. & 10 stone clean.

5 August 1863.   Wednesday. Ernestine came.

8 August 1863.   Saturday. Attended Norwich Gaol Committee. Talked with Mercury Bacon[252] about Norwich manufacturers. He asserts they make large profits, but that the wages of the weavers are miserably low. The last is true enough; I doubt the first except in a few cases.

10 August 1863.   Monday. Began cutting wheat. To workhouse. Very fine hot weather.

15 August 1863.   Saturday. To Norwich Castle Committee.

16 August 1863.   Sunday. Sixteenth Anniversary of my marriage with my dearest wife. Celeberated it by eating the first haunch of venison from our Park. Gave my darling 4 lockets for our 4 children's hair. She gave me a pretty set of studs.

---

[251] De Grey's country seat.
[252] Richard Noverre Bacon, editor of the Liberal weekly, *Norwich Mercury*.

17 August 1863. Monday. Finished carting wheat. The weather so dry that the wheat shelled much. This eveng. weather changed, & some rain.

18 August 1863. Tuesday. Began to cut barley. The yield of wheat promises to be enormous. Barley good also Turnips suffer horribly from grub.

22 August 1863. Saturday. To Norwich Castle Committee.

24 August 1863. Monday. To workhouse.

25 August 1863. Tuesday. Went with Flo: to Lowestoft to look for lodgings. A bare ungenial looking place. Finished harvest this morning. In the afternoon heavy rain. My corn staked in splendid order.

31 August 1863. Monday. To workhouse.

1 September 1863. Tuesday. Killed on Runhall Lands the miserable number of six brace of partridges.

4 September 1863. Friday. A still worse bag on the Hardingham Hall farm. One old red leg!, & Barley's four brace, & a hare.

5 September 1863. Saturday. To Norwich Castle.

7 September 1863. Monday. To workhouse Mrs Brewster, our new housekeeper came. Wages £50.

8 September 1863. Tuesday. Practice at target. Hit bull's eye at 500 yards.

12 September 1863. Saturday. To Norwich Castle.

14 September 1863. Monday. Mrs. R. Currie, Maynard & P. Currie, H. Hutchinson & Warre came on a visit.

15 September 1863. Tuesday. Mother came. Shot with Hutchinson on Home Farm—23 brace 1/2, self 15 1/2.

16 September 1863. Wednesday. Shot with H. & Graves Browne on Cunningham's, Matthews & R. Smiths 36 brace self 15 br.

17 September 1863. Thursday. The whole party to Norwich to hear

'Elijah', a fine performance. The alterations in St Andrew's Hall mean, & vulgar.

18 September 1863. Friday. Shot with Hn. over Rolfe's–23 br:1/2 Self 16 br:–Flo: to hear 'Messiah'.

19 September 1863. Saturday. Visitors went: some yesterday. Johnny caught two pike of 14 & 9 1/2 lbs. Altogether he & I took 7 fish. One day last week we laid out 4 dozen trimmers in Hingham Sea Mere, only took one perch.

21 September 1863. Monday. To workhouse first meeting of Asst. Committee. Re-elected Chairman.

Sold 100 lambs at 33/– the pick of 125. Rams to ewes to-day. 110 ewes. Two r.& a lamb r. to come in later.

22 September 1863. Tuesday. To volunteer meeting at Letton.

23 September 1863. Wednesday. Went with Johnny to London. We nearly had a bad accident with the pony phaeton going to Wymondham. Prince the new pony kicked & plunged furiously whilst I was lighting a cigar, & my Lady holding the reins. Johnny & I dined at the Traveller's under the new rule admitting strangers, & he went off after dining in pretty good spirits to Eton.

24 September 1863. Thursday. Flo: went with Alice & Constance & Ernestine to Cromer; I to de Grey's at Studley, where I found Lord John Hay,[253] Mrs. G.G. Glyn,[254] Mr. & Mrs Cameron, (a rich vulgar Canadian shipowner with a Yankee wife from New York), the latter a ladylike unassuming woman with the usual nasal twang. Doyle[255] the artist and B. Viner[256] completed the party.

25 September 1863. Friday. Went out shooting with Mr. Cameron & killed 39 brace Self 25 brace. De Grey came out in the afternoon.

26 September 1863. Saturday. De Grey, Cameron, a neighbour & self shot 59 brace (self 25 brace).

[253] Lord John Hay (1827–1916), Lib. MP for Wick, 1857–9, for Ripon, 1866–71.

[254] Wife of George Grenfell Glyn (1824–87), banker; Lib. MP for Shaftesbury, 1857–73, when he succ. as 2nd Baron Wolverton; Lib. chief whip, 1867–73; sec. to treas., 1868–73. In 1864 the firm of Glyn, Mills & Co. consolidated with Raikes Currie's private bank. See 'Curries & Co. in the Nineteenth Century', *Three Banks Review* (June 1964), 52–4.

[255] Richard Doyle (1824–83), illustrator and caricaturist.

[256] The Rev. B. P. Viner, Canadian priest then visiting England.

27 September 1863. Sunday. To Church in the morning at the Minster, a dilapidated building which is repairing under the direction of Scott. In the afternoon walked to Fountain's Abbey. Had much talk with Mr. Cameron on American affairs. He thinks the North will persevere till they have exterminated all the South even whites, & that they will succeed in reconstituting the Union by parcelling out the land among Northern Whites. When the conscription & bounties fail in procuring sufficient soldiers, the North will grant to every man who serves for a certain period a piece of confiscated Southern land, & thus by degrees the whole country will be transferred to Northern hands. He did not explain what was to be done with the Negroes. The war would last, he said, over another President's term. The next President would be a Democrat. Canada, he declared, wd. defend herself to the uttermost against Yankee aggression. Mr. C. resides at New York, & is a shrewd man of business. He mentioned that the Canadian Minister Macdonald[257] is married to a wife from the Southern States, & that her animosities are converting him to British sympathies, his leaning having been rather to an annexation policy.

Doyle & I had some 'chaff' about the old monks of Fountain's Abbey. He as a good Catholic stood up manfully for them.

28 September 1863. Monday. Osborne (S.G. O's[258] son) de Grey's private Sec: came on Saturday. He de Grey & I killed to day 37 brace of partridges. I killed 14 1/2 brace.

29 September 1863. Tuesday. A school feast at the Abbey.

30 September 1863. Wednesday. De Grey, Osborne & self killed 60 brace of partridges-self 25 brace. Colonel Shadwell & wife came. The Canadian American who had boasted of his walking & shooting is utterly sown up, & can neither walk nor shoot.

1 October 1863. Thursday. De Grey, Osborne, Shadwell, & self killed about 100 head, pheasants, hares, & partridges. I killed 13 braces of the latter.

2 October 1863. Friday. Went to Kimberley, slept there & on Saturday Oct 3 to Cromer stopping at Norwich on my way to attend Castle Committee. Lady de Grey told me that the Pss. of Wales is with child. From what de Grey said about the Ironclads, it seems that the Govt. have not quite made up their mind on account of the difficulty of

---

[257] John Sandfield Macdonald (1812–72), pr. min. of Canada, 1862–4.
[258] Sidney Godolphin Osborne (1808–89), philanthropist and miscellaneous writer.

getting evidence that they are ordered for the Confederates, but it is clear that they contemplate stopping them.

4 October 1863.   Sunday. Went to Cromer Church which is restoring.

5 October 1863.   Monday. Bathed to day, & the following day.

7 October 1863.   Wednesday. To Witton.

8 October 1863.   Thursday. To Gunton to shoot. Five guns. Suffield, Major Reilly, W. Baring, R. Burroughes, & self. 67 brace, self 11 1/2.

9 October 1863.   Friday. Went with Sir F. Buxton²⁵⁹ & C. Buxton²⁶⁰ to N. Walsham Agricultural Meeting. At the dinner I made a speech which was well received. In going over my Estate at Witton on Wednesday, I remarked the very satisfactory growth of the firs in Barton Wood.

10 October 1863.   Saturday. To Gunton to shoot. Suffield, R. Burroughes, Major Reilly & self killed 99 brace 1/2–birds very wild. Self 27 brace 1/2. The keepers say the birds did not breed well.

12 October 1863.   Monday. Went to London on my way to Cornwall.

13 October 1863.   Tuesday. To P. D. Smith's²⁶¹ at Truro where I stayed three nights.

14 October 1863.   Wednesday. We spent this & the following day in looking over my property at Falmouth. The docks are a fine work, & I am altogether satisfied that the prospects of the town & of my property connected with it are much improved. The Leases on three lives run out during the last 14 years have averaged 50 years 3/4, I wish I could introduce leases for fixed terms of 60 years.²⁶² No sewerage, I find in the town! I desired Smith if we build terraces near the new hotel to insist on their being provided with proper sewerage. The new hotel, for which I have sold 4 acres, is building fast. The railway renders the

---

²⁵⁹ Sir Thomas Fowell Buxton (1837–1915), Lib. MP for Lynn Regis, 1865–8.
²⁶⁰ Charles Buxton (1823–71), Lib. MP for Newport, 1857–9, Maidstone, 1859–65, for E. Surrey, 1865–71.
²⁶¹ P. D. Smith, of Smith & Paul's, Wodehouse's Cornwall solicitors.
²⁶² On the inequities (and iniquities) of the 'three life' lease system prevalent in western Cornwall in the 1860s and beyond, see 'The Bitter Cry of Cornish Leaseholders', [188?], KP6 MS.eng.d.2491.

Arwenack property quite independent of the Basset property which formerly as it were barred the entrance to the town.

I am glad I determined to pay off the mortgages and to resume possession. The arrangement with the Trustees, R. Currie & J. H. Gurney[263] is going on. I am to raise £40,000 on Witton.

16 October 1863.   Friday. Went to Pencarrow, Lady Molesworth's.[264] On my way, stopped at Lord Vivian's[265] (Glynn) for luncheon.

17 October 1863.   Saturday. A queer party at Lady M's. Madame de la Grenée [?] & Mlle. Olga, her daughter. Col: Airey,[266] a tame cat of 'Andalusia's', Williams an extraordinary piano-forte player, Eastlake a clever son of the painter,[267] & Hickes a most facetious teller of stories in Cornish dialect.

Pencarrow is a very comfortable plain house with small but very pretty gardens & pleasure grounds, laid out by the late Sir W. Molesworth. The country round hilly & very bleak. We drove 11 miles to Hell Bay, near Padstow, on the North Coast, a fine rugged coast with terrible rocks, Madame de la Grenée is a Russian by birth, widow of a French diplomatist, a most wearisome woman with cleverness & information enough to keep up a perpetual stream of small talk: her daughter a clever rather pretty girl.

19 October 1863.   Monday. Went with the La Grenée & daughter to Port Eliot Lord St Germans'. Port Eliot is a fine old place, formerly an Abbey. It rained all the afternoon I was there so that I saw its beauties through a mist. Poor old St German's seems very much aged & spoke in a melancholy way of the children he has lost. W. Ponsonby[268] & Lady Louisa were there.[269] The latter, the mother of 8 children, is as

[263] John Henry Gurney (1819–90), Norwich banker; Lib. MP for Lynn Regis, 1854–65.

[264] Andalusia, Lady Molesworth. After Sir William's death in 1855, she lived thirty-three years at Pencarrow, where she reigned 'alone – but never lonely'. See Alison Adburgham, *A Radical Aristocrat, Sir William Molesworth of Pencarrow and his Wife Andalusia* (Padstow, 1990), ix.

[265] Sir Charles Crespigny Vivian, 2nd Baron Vivian (1808–86), ld. lt. of Cornwall, 1856–77.

[266] Sir James Talbot Airey (1812–98), served at Cabul, in Gwalior campaign and in the Crimea; lt.-genl., 1877.

[267] Sir Charles Eastlake (1793–1865), pres. of the Royal Academy.

[268] The Hon. and Rev. Walter Ponsonby (1821–1906), 7th Earl of Bessborough after the death of his brother in 1895.

[269] Lady Louisa Eliot, m. Walter Ponsonby in 1850.

ugly, jolly & good-natured as ever. Eliot,[270] the secretary of Legation, was there. We had much talk about Brazil. I am more than ever convinced from what he said, that our late proceedings there were a great blunder. It seems there was clear evidence that the chaplain & other officers were the worse for drink & had insulted passers by before they reached the guard-house. Eliot is going pro temp: to Washington instead of Stuart.

The Archbishop of Canterbury & two daughters came to stay at St Germans. The Archbishop seems a mild mannered pleasant man. After dinner he stood up at the piano-forte with his two daughters & sung a glee! His voice melodious, tho' somewhat feeble from age. Is there any previous instance of an *Archevêque chantant*.

20 October 1863. Tuesday. To London. Dined at the Travellers' with Henry who is over from the Hague on leave. He has been lately in the North of Italy. He found Venice incredibly deserted & dismal; Milan full of liveliness & joy. Afterwards with H. & Warre to the Strand Theatre where saw a bad burlesque of the Duke's Motto.

21 October 1863. Wednesday. To Kimberley. Flo: came from Cromer with Ernestine & the children. All well. Heard in the evening by telegraph that Lord Clare[271] is dangerously ill.

22 October 1863. Thursday. My dear wife went off to London to see her father. A great disappointment to us both to be separated again after so much absence from each other. Went to Norwich to Qr. Sessions where no important business: afterwards to meeting at J. O. Taylor's about proposed N. Walsham Railway. Suffield, Sir J. Preston,[272] Blake Homfray,[273] H. N. Burroughes[274] & others present. We had had a previous meeting at N. Walsham on the 9th at which George Butler Bidder director of the Gt Eastn. Ry. & Sinclair engineer were present.

[270] Henry Eliot (1835–1911), served in RN, 1848–53; foreign office, 1855–81, when he succ. as 5th Earl of St Germans.

[271] Richard Hobart FitzGibbon, 3rd Earl of Clare (1793–1864), served in the Napoleonic wars; MP for Co. Limerick, 1818–41; ld. lt. Co. Limerick, 1831–48, 1851–64.

[272] Sir Jacob Henry Preston, DL of Norfolk, of Beeston Hall, Beeston St Lawrence, Norwich.

[273] Robert Blake Humphrey. DL of Norfolk, of Wroxham House, Wroxham; active Cons.

[274] Henry Negus Burroughes (1791–1872), Cons. MP for Norfolk E., 1837–57, when he retired. On Wodehouse's role in electing a Liberal to replace Burroughes, see KP1 3/2; *Liberal by Principle*, 11–12. Cf. *The Poll for a Knight of the Shire for the Eastern Division of Norfolk ... and an account of the Position of the Parties between the Contests of 1837 and 1858* (Norwich, 1858), ix–xxii, where Wodehouse's potential influence in local politics is suspected, but never traced.

The proposal is that the line should be made via Wroxham. 14 miles to cost £120,000, of wh. £30m to be found by district, £30m by Gt E. Ry., £30m by Sir S.M. Peto[275] contractor, & £30m raised by debentures.

I promised to take £500 in shares. Suffield £3000. Suffield, Sir J. Preston, & I consented to be provisional directors. The first call on shares will be 8 perct. Returning in the dogcart with R. Gurdon, & my groom, Petersburg, my old horse, took fright going down Earlham hill, & ran clear away nearly to the top of the hill near Mr Scott's. We fortunately stopped him without any harm to man or beast. The groom, sitting behind, was thrown out but not hurt.

23 October 1863. Friday. Lambert tells me that a buck has gored a poor doe to death, & a fawn has drowned.

26 October 1863. Monday. To workhouse. Flo returned. Her father better.

27 October 1863. Tuesday. My mother & Henry came.

28 October 1863. Wednesday. Shot thro' Wymondham Slips with Henry. 34 hares, 12 pheasants, 9 rabbits, 1 woodcock the first this year.

29 October 1863. Thursday. To Assessment Committee.

30 October 1863. Friday. On Cubitt's farm with Henry. Torrents of rain all day: Killed 8 brace & 1/2. Self 3 1/2. Arthur Eden came.

31 October 1863. Saturday. To Norwich Castle Committee. Attended meeting at J. O. Taylor's as to E. Norfolk Railway. Eden told me to day the history of St Clair, the attaché. It seems that Madame Kisseleff wife of Kisseleff who was Russian Ambr. at Paris finding herself with a child, not her husband's, induced a niece who lived with her to marry a Mr St Clair on condition that she took this child for her own. St Clair is the genuine produce of the marriage so brought about. Madame K. is the lady so notorious as a gambler at Homburg. Very high wind.

2 November 1863. Monday. Henley, Rochfort, & George Currie came. Very rainy. Shot with Henry & Eden over Cunningham's &c. 8 brace 1/2. self 3 1/2.

3 November 1863. Tuesday. Shot Carlton cover, & Calry Meadow: self,

---

[275] Sir Samuel Morton Peto (1809–89), contractor; Lib. MP for Norwich, 1847–54, for Finsbury, 1859–65.

Eden, Hy., Henley, Rochfort– 76 Ph: 56 H: 3 R: 4 P: 1 wild Duck. Total 140.

4 November 1863.   Wednesday. Henry went. Same party shot Crownthorpe Carr & Watergate. 65Ph: 23 H:—1R. 10 P: —total 99.

5 November 1863.   Thursday. Began to shoot in Reed Meadow: Obliged to give up on account of torrents of rain. Mr Withers (Coverdale & Co.) came to search for deeds respg. Witton for mortagages of 40m. to London Ass: Cy. & said he had found all he wanted.
   Killed in Reed Meadow Wood H.7.Ph:3 R:19 = 31 [*sic*].

6 November 1863.   Friday. G. Currie went. A very fine day. Henley, Rochfort, Eden & self shot thro' Reed Meadow wood, Forehoe &c. H.69. Ph:(almost all cocks) 118. R.40. Woodcock 1. Total 228. Altogether this week 514 head. There is more game than I expected. My mother & Ernestine went to-day.

7 November 1863.   Saturday. All the party went away. Flo: & I left very happy alone. A wet day. Went over Lake with King: full of weeds, which were cut & have sunk. Must rake great part of it. Saw several coots on the water. Our wheat setting finished all but an acre. The mangold partly carted away.

9 November 1863.   Monday. To Union House.

14 November 1863.   Saturday. To Norwich. Attended public meeting at Swan as to N. Walsham etc. Railway. Suffield in the Chair. I explained the business to the meeting. Oddin Taylor also said a few words. The meeting was fairly attended, & went off well. Afterwards to Castle Committee.

16 November 1863.   Monday. To Union House.

17 November 1863.   Tuesday. To Wymondham Petty Sessions: afterwards inspected Wymondham Bridewell.

18 November 1863.   Wednesday. To Ketteringham to shoot. Lord Braybrooke,[276] Vernon, Col: Brett, Sir J. Boileau,[277] & self killed 255 head. Dined at Km.

---

[276] Charles Cornwallis, 5th Baron Braybrooke (1823–1902).
[277] Sir John Peter Boileau (1794–1869), archaeologist; v.p. Society of Antiquaries, 1858–62, 1863–7; Norfolk County magistrate.

19 November 1863.   Thursday. Mr Wright (Wright and Mansfield) came to advise as to re-decorating the house.

21 November 1863.   Saturday. Shot 13 partridges on Cunningham's farm, & Twaites'.

23 November 1863.   Monday. To workhouse.

25 November 1863.   Wednesday. Went shooting to Howlett's wood &c.

26 November 1863.   Thursday. Attended assessment Committee. Decided against Mr Larke's appeal. Adjd. to Jan: 14. Dillons came.

27 November 1863.   Friday. Dillon & I killed 30 hares 30 rabbits 16 Ph: 1. P. in Wymondham strips & Gelham's. Total 77.

28 November 1863.   Saturday. Dillon & I killed in Carlton wood & Calry Meadow. 29 Ph: 13 H. 6 R. 2 P.— T.50.

30 November 1863.   Monday. To workhouse. Windham Barings came.

Tuesday.   Baring, W. Vernon, Dillon & self shot in Falstaff wood.

Wednesday.   Baring, Dillon & I shot in Wildman wood. A terrific gale began about 4 o'clock with a squall such as I never before saw in England & a deluge of rain.

3 December 1863.   Thursday. Gale still raging. Much damage done all over the country. This morning greatly to my surprise, a messenger came with a letter from Lord Russell asking me to go on a special Mission to Copenhagen. I replied at once by telgph. in the affirmative. I don't like the business and I have little hope of success, but I think it is my duty to go if the Govt. think I can be of use. The worst of is I must leave dear Flo: & the children: just at Christmas too. I went up to London this afternoon by train.

4 December 1863.   Friday. Went to Pembroke Lodge, where Lord Russell and I had long conversation as to Danish question. The gist of the matter seems to be that our Govt. stands by Treaty of '52 but wishes to get the Danes to make concessions to Germany without our pledging ourselves to support Denmark in case these concessions fail to satisfy Germany.
   I saw Lord Clarendon in the evening at the Travellers'. He told me that the Queen was very strong on the German side, that there had

been a sharp correspondence between Her & Lord R. on the subject. Lord C. has just come from Windsor where he says he found great excitement. The Crown Princess of Prussia & her husband on one side & the P. of Wales & his wife on the other sustain opposite parts with great vigour. General Grey for Germans, Phipps[278] for the rising Sun. Grey's infuence appears to be growing daily more inconvenient.

5 December 1863.   Saturday. Saw Lord Palmerston at Cambridge House. He was looking extremely well. He takes part with the Danes more than Lord Russell. In the afternoon went to Windsor. I no sooner arrived there than General Grey came to my room, & talked violently on the German side for half an hour. He evidently gives the Queen very bad advice. Dined with Crown Prince & Princess, & the Princess Helena. The Gladstones & the household also dined. The Queen still dines alone.

6 December 1863.   Sunday. Went to Kimberley in the evening. In the morning attended services in the Royal Chapel. Genl. Grey came to me and said that the Queen wished that part of my instructions to be changed which desired me to tell German Govts. if they would not accept reasonable conditions that HM's Govt. would be free to adopt whatever course the interests &c. of England demanded; The Queen he said would never consent that England should go to war with Germany to support Danes. I told him that I understood my instructions to be that either party which should refuse reasonable terms must be responsible for the consequences. Genl. Grey asked me to tell Lord R. this as it would save the Q. the trouble of writing. I replied that I was not the Q's Minister & that I could not undertake to be the channel of any communications between H.M. & Lord R. Genl. G. talked in favour of the Scandinavian idea &c. I gave him my mind very plainly about court intrigues in favour of Germany. Soon afterwards I had my audience of The Queen. She was looking better & more cheerful than I expected. She spoke reasonably on the Danish question, only urging that pressure should be brought to bear on Denmark as well as on Germany. The drift of what I said was that I should strive to be impartial. With this assurance she seemed pleased, as if she had been told I was a furious Dane. She talked at some length of the recent losses of public men, especially of Lord Elgin,[279] & this naturally brought in the late Prince Consort. She mentioned the dangerous position of the King of Prussia, & spoke in terms of condemnation of the Prince

---

[278] Sir Charles Beaumont Phipps (1801–66), priv. sec. to Prince Albert from 1847; keeper of the queen's purse from 1849.

[279] James Bruce, 8th Earl Elgin (1811–63), Viceroy of India, 1862–3.

of Augustenburg.[280] The interview lasted about an hour, the Queen standing all the time. My impression was very favourable both of the knowledge & fairness of H. M.

I then saw the P. of Wales & the Princess. The latter is evidently not looking well on account of being in the family way, but her beauty is immensely exaggerated. She is nice looking nothing more.

7 December 1863.   Monday. Spent this day very sadly at home.

8 December 1863.   Tuesday. I & dear Flo: went to London. Dined at Pembroke Lodge, & told Lord R. what passed between me & the Queen. The gist of my interviews with Lord Russell is contained in a mem: of what passed on Dec. 4.– His Lordship as usual was rather vague in his instructions. He is evidently bitten by Morier's very clever but unfair pamphlet 'The Dano-German Question &c.'. I hear that this pamphlet is taken for Gospel at the Court. I can't conceive what business an English Secretary of Lgn. has to write anonymous partizan pamphlets.[281]

9 December 1863.   Wednesday. In the morning to the F.O. where I saw Lord Russell; also Brunnow & Bernsdorff.[282] Brunnow was as slimy as usual. It is evident that Russia is deeply offended with France on account of the Polish affair. Brunnow is anxious I should not be in a hurry at Copenhagen– *'Surtout n'estranglez pas cette négotiation mon cher'* – Bernsdorff of course was brutal & disagreeable. *'On vous croit bien Danois ‡ Berlin'* – The devil may not be so black as he is painted was my reply.

Started this evening for Berlin via Dover & Calais taking with me Henry, Philip Currie & Sanderson.[283] Dear Flo: came with us to the Railway Station.

10 December 1863.   Thursday. Arrived at Cologne where we slept at Hotel Royal.

11 December 1863. Friday. Saw Sir H. Howard[284] at Station at Hanover.

---

[280] Prince of Augustenburg (1818–1906), succ. as Christian IX, King of Denmark and Norway, r. 1863–1906.

[281] Sir Robert Burnett David Morier (1826–93), held various diplomatic appointments at German courts, 1853–76; min. to Portugal, 1876–81; to Spain, 1881–4; amb. to Russia, 1884–93. On future results of the disagreement between Wodehouse and Morier, see *Liberal by Principle*, 278–9.

[282] Albert Bernstorff (1809–74), Danish min. to London.

[283] Thomas Henry Sanderson (1841–1923), junior f.o. clerk, 1859–66; priv. sec. to Derby, 1866–8, 1874–8; and to Granville, 1880–5; perm. u.-sec., 1894–1906.

[284] Sir Henry Francis Howard (1809–98), British amb. to Hanover, 1859–66.

Lodged at Berlin at Hotel Royal. Saw Sir A. Buchanan[285] at Embassy immediately on my arrival.

12 December 1863. Saturday. Had long interview with Baron Bismarck, for three hours and a half. Bismarck gave me the impression of a cunning, unscrupulous man. He spoke however with frankness on the quarrel with Denmark; & it is evident that he will hold back the king if he can. At dinner at Sir A. Buchanan's I met Ct. Enlenberg, the Minr. of the Interior. He spoke with the utmost contempt of the Prussian Lower Chamber. I also met Count Karolyi[286] who was most violent on the Sleswig: Holstein question. I had some conversation with Bn. Nothomb the Belgian Minister, but he said nothing worth repeating. Quaade, the Danish Minsr. made a very favourable impression upon me. He says he has written to Copenhagen to urge a change of policy. M. d'Oubril, the Russian, seemed a poor creature. In the evening we went to a party at Pcs. Talleyrand's. The French ambassador, a dapper little man with a pretty wife, a daughter of the Russian brandy farmer, Bernadaki.

13 December 1863. Sunday. The King appointed 1 o'clock to day to see me. H.My. dispensed with Sir A. Buchanan's introduction of me on the ground that I had been presented to him when Crown Prince at Potsdam when I was on my way to Russia in 1856. The King was very polite but I soon found that not much impression could be made upon him. I tried him on every tack. He seemed rather frightened at the idea of an occupation of Dantzic by the French but the prospect of loss of the Palatinate by Bavaria I fancied, did not affect him much. He talked much of the dangers of revolution in Germany. '*Ici*' he said '*nous sommes en pleine révolution*'. He assured me that he was beset with letters of the most pressing kind from his friends & relatives in Germany entreating him not to abandon them, (in other words to save their thrones by robbing Denmark). The King kept his temper, admirably tho' I confess my remarks were hardly of a soothing nature.

14 December 1863. Monday. Started for Copenhagen. Dined at Hamburg, & saw Ward our Consul General. He is a strong 'German' We talked a good deal about the differences betn. Denmark & Germany. He declared that the Holsteiners were to a man against the Danish connexion, & that nothing, but Sleswig-Holstein under Augustenberg will satisfy Germany. I believe he is not far from right. The Germans

---

[285] Andrew Buchanan (1807–82), British amb. to Spain, 1858–60; amb. to Prussia, 1862–4.
[286] Count Aloys Karolyi, Austrian min. at Berlin.

are mad about Sleswig-Holstein, & they will end by bringing the whole ponderous machine of Fatherland down by the run.

15 December 1863. Tuesday. Arrived about 11 o'clock at Copenhagen. Went at once to the Hotel, the Phoenix, an indifferent Inn; a peculiarity in Denmark is the beds, in our Inn only 2 feet & 1/2 wide tho' longer than German beds. Paget[287] took me to the Ministry for For: Affairs where I saw Mr. Hall.[288] He was formerly a professor. A difficult man to do business with on account of his vague way of talking. I am told he is hot-tempered. With me he was courteous, & never lost his temper. He combines the ministry for F. Affs. with the Presidency of the Cabinet and is perhaps the most popular man in Denmark.

16 December 1863. Wednesday. Saw M Dotique[?], the French Minister, Baron Nicolai the Russian, M d'Ewers the special Russian Envoy, & Count Hamilton the Swedish Minr.

I soon found there was nothing to be done with Dotique. He has his instructions not to help in settling the quarrel betn. Denmark & Germany it suits his master better that it should go on. Dotique is a dirty old Frenchman who has been here 20 years & during that time is said never to have stirred two miles out of the town. He has never been away on leave. He is however by no means without acuteness, & has a prodigious power of getting rid of an awkward question by talking generalities with immense volubility. He is unmarried & passes his time in smoking all the morning & playing whist all the evening. Ewers is one of the chief ridacteurs in the Russn. F. Off. He was for many years secretary here in the Russn. Legn., afterwards Ch:d'aff: in Brazil. A keen witted, dry, decided, man. He acted throughout this business most cordially & loyally with me. Bn. Nicolai was formerly first Secry. in London; a quiet, sensible gentlemanlike man. Hamilton is a great friend of the King of Sweden & occupies an influential position in his own country. He has fanned the Scandinavian flame here, & I suspect has 'promised' more than he is able to perform.

17 December 1863. Thursday. General Fleury[289] arrived last night to congratulate the King on his accession. The General called on me this morning. He professed great frankness. The Emperor L. N. 'goes in' it seems for 'nationalities' & will not support Denmark. As we would not agree to his Congress, he will not assist in any negotiations here. I persuaded Fleury however to ask for instructions to join Ewers & me

---

[287] Augustus Berkeley Paget (1823–96), min. at Copenhagen, 1859–66.
[288] Carl Hall (1812–88), Danish pr. min., 1857–9, 60–3.
[289] Comte Emile Felix Fleury (1815–84), brig. genl.; a.d.c. to Napoleon III.

in pressing this Govt. to revoke the Constn. of Nov: 18. In the evening I had my formal audience of The King at Christianborg to present my letters of credence, and afterwards of The Queen. The courtiers seemed in great confusion, & the whole affair badly organized. The King does not live in the Christianborg Palace.

18 December 1863. Friday. I may mention at once the various other Royal Audiences which I had to go through. The Landgrave of Hesse, an old beau, father of The Queen, very adverse to Constitutions & such new fangled follies; the Pr. Fred: Will: of Hesse brother to The Queen, a not over wise middle aged man with a handsome wife; the old Queen Dowager widow of last King but one, and a toothless old lady, the Princess Caroline, widow of Pr: Ferdinand uncle of the late King. The reigning Queen is an agreeable mannered woman with a very sly expression. She spoke to me very plainly of her hope that we should put the 'screw' strongly on The King's Govt.

19 December 1863. Saturday . We all went to Roeskilde to attend the Funeral of the late King. We were about three hours in the cathedral which was horribly cold. The Cathedral is an old gothic church in a plain style of brick. The service was a series of songs and a long sermon in Danish from the Bishop. The procession was rather imposing. I was placed between Ewers & Fleury, who seemed *bon enfant* enough & talked cheerily about English horses.

20 December 1863. Sunday. Today Ewers & I had an interview with Hall at which we told him that our Govts. advised abrogation of Constn. of Nov: 18 He received the communication courteously but I have no expectation that he will follow our advice. Fleury went in after us. It is said he did not really back our advice, but my belief is that he did, though his tone may have given Hall some encouragement.

21 December 1863. Monday. We dined with The King to day. A State dinner at 1/2 past five o'clock. Atrocious food. After dinner The King avoided speaking to Ewers and me evidently fearing that the Danes would watch him. The Queen said a few words to me, urging me to put a strong pressure on the Ministry. The Rigsraad was dismissed to day with a message from The King which amounts to a rejection of our advice. I talked with Bille an old Admiral who has just resigned the ministry of Marine and with Mr. Wolfhagen the Minr. for Sleswig.

22 December 1863. Tuesday. Wolfhagen whom I met yesterday looks what I am told he is a very weak man. To day I dined with Paget & met Hall to whom I talked very seriously about the dismissal of the

Rigsraad. Paget has heard that the King never signed the message but it appears that he did sign it tho' after much opposition. This measure puts an end I fear to our hopes of stopping the Germans. If the Rigsraad had been kept sitting, the Constn. might perhaps have been revoked. Fleury went away yesterday. He would not even stay to dine with The King.

23 December 1863. Wednesday. This morning Paget & Ewers met the King. It seemed that he was bent on changes of policy. I determined to ask for interview of H.My. I dined with Nicolai & at 9 o'clock went by appt. to the Palace. The King was very civil & asked me to sit down. I remained an hour. He seemed calm & collected. He told me Andre whom he had asked to take Ministry had declined. However he was determined to adopt a *'politique paisible'* & to convoke Rigsraad. I advised him to keep strictly within constitutional limits. After seeing me he saw Hall who it seems refused to convoke Rigsraad, & in consequence offered his resignation.

24 December 1863. Thursday. Hall came this afternoon to my hotel and told me he had resigned office. We had a friendly conversation. He admitted that it might be an advantage for The King to have another Minister, as he is *'suspect envers l'Allemagne'*, but he is strongly against not calling back the Rigsraad, and gives some good reasons why it is now too late to propose to them to repeal the Constn. Why did he advise the dismissal of the Rigsraad?

25 December 1863. Friday. Oxholm[290] came this morning to see me, & told me that he had undertaken to sign the Decree convoking the Rigsraad if The King could find no one else. He seemed very anxious to avoid being Minister, & on my telling him that as far as I was concerned I did not consider The King bound to convoke the Rigsraad, he looked immensely relieved. Telegram from home telling me to suggest conference arrived whilst I was talking to O. to whom I communicated it confidentially requesting him to let The King know of it.

26 December 1863. Saturday. Oxholm came, & said the convoking of Rigsraad was given up. No new Ministry formed. King had determined to assemble at the palace in the evening a few leading members of the Rigsraad of all parties & went with Ewers to Hall to communicate suggestions as to Conference. Hall looked as if he was put out at this suggestion coming after his resignation. He immediately started

[290] Waldemar Tully d'Oxholm (1805–76).

difficulties! The Conference at Palace ended in nothing. Hall, Kruger, Andre, Bp. Monrad[291] amongst others are said to have assisted.

27 December 1863. Sunday. Dined with Dotique French Minister. A bad dinner. No new Ministry formed. Various rumours flying about. Some say it was decided last night that Hall should remain with Quaade as new Minister for Foreign Aff; Prince Frederick of Hesse called on me, & said he thought Bluhm[292] would form Ministry. Every day brings this country nearer war, & it seems as if no man has the courage to come forward to save the country from ruin.

28 December 1863. Monday. Dined with Mr. Hage, a queer & very bad dinner. After dinner we smoked in a room which was like the black hole at Calcutta. I met here Mr. Krieger, the Chief Judge with whom I had a conversation yesterday. He was formerly a minister and is a hot Dane, determined to oppose all concession to Germany. Mr. Vedel the Under Secretary also dined here. He seems a man of some sense. Hall was amongst the guests & actually recd. during dinner the letter from the King announcing that his resignation was definitively accepted. Afterwards in the evening to Paget's where Count Dauneskiold brought me a message from the King that he had sent for Bishop Monrad who had consented to form a new Cabinet.

29 December 1863. Tuesday. Nothing particular occurred to day. I hear that the Bishop quoted the instances of Fleury, Mazarin, Talleyrand & Richelieu as precedents which would warrant his taking charge of the Foreign Office. He has the reputation of a sly ambitious ecclesiastic.

30 December 1863. Wednesday. Ewers having recd. instructions to act with me and to Conference we went together to see the Bishop. He speaks bad French, and has the true bland ecclesiastical manner. He was very warlike however, & talked confidently of the chances of Denmark finding some way out of the scrape, tho' he admitted that the Germans would probably occupy all the mainland. To night we hear that the P. of Augustg. has arrived at Kiel.

31 December 1863. Thursday. Bishop Monrad has nearly formed his Ministry. The King goes to Sleswig tonight. Ewers & I had audiences of leave. The K. recd. me in plain clothes, was very civil, & asked me to sit down. I told him plainly I expected nothing now but war. I saw

---

[291] Ditlev Gothard Monrad (1811–87), bp. of Lolland-Falster, 1849–54; Danish educ. min., 1859–63; minister pres., 1863.

[292] Christian Albrecht Bluhme (1794–1866), minister pres. and for. min., 1864–5.

Hamilton & Vedel in the course of the day. The French, it seems, refuse the Conference. There is nothing more to be done here & I have telegraphed for leave to depart.

So ends the year 1863. I am away from all I love at home. May God bless & preserve them. This has been a strange year for me; very quiet at first, & now all this racket & responsibility. I have this comfort; if I have done many things during it which I could wish undone, I have not been idle or wasteful of my time. My appetite for political distinction has, I think, diminished, & I feel more contented at the possibility of passing the rest of my days as a quite undistinguished country gentleman. Just as I begin to feel this, I am summoned again to action, perhaps my career may yet not be a failure. I was even I hear talked of for Gov. Genl. of India, a great post indeed, but even if I could have imagined myself fit for it, I am quite determined not to separate myself from my wife & family, even were that most glittering of prizes within my grasp.

1 January 1864. Friday. New Govt. nearly formed. Monrad, Prime Minister & F. O. provisionally. Lundby War Lutke Marine. Fenger finance but without a seat in cabinet wh. he will not retain for fear of offending Hall. Engelstoft, a Bishop Culter, Casse Justice. Quaade is not far from Berlin & will be offered F.O.– Sleswig Minr. not named yet.

2 January 1864. Saturday. I had a very satisfactory interview with Quaade, but I fear he will not take F.O. on account of his eyes. He speaks like a man who has been out of Copenhagen. In the afternoon Quaade begged me to go to Monrad. I was in a shooting jacket, just proceeding to the ice to skate. However I went as I was, & had an hour & 1/2 with the Bp. I think I made some impression upon him, but he was very obstinate at first. He certainly talked of assembling the Rigsraad!

3 January 1864. Sunday. Went with Ewers to Bp. Monrad at 1 o'clock. Long interview with him, Quaade being also present. The Danish Govt. will propose mediation. This is a wise decision.

In the evening whilst I was at dinner the Bishop came in great trepidation on account of Dotique's language. It seemed that D. on being informed of the decision as to mediation talked very big. I talked much bigger, & so did Ewers. We ended by somewhat convincing the Bishop that it was no use to offend two Great Powers in order to avoid offending one.

4 January 1864.   Monday. The Bishop is still a little shaky, but I think we have now fairly pinned him to mediation. We sent off telegrams with his consent last night announcing it. In the evening at 8 o'clock Ewers & I went to the F.O. & talked for some three hours with the Bishop & Quaade about possible plans for re-arranging the Danish Constitution. We had a very nice *petit souper* with Champagne, & we all smoked cigars during the whole interview. Capital skating now on the canals around the town.

5 January 1864.   Tuesday. The mediation proposal sent off at last. I saw Dotique in to day. He professed not to mind what had been done. The Bishop was evidently too much frightened. The fact is D. who has not been at Paris for 20 years, gets very little information from his Govt. of what is going on & he fancied that the Emperor still insisted on his Congress. I gave him a hint that he was rather *arriere*.

6 January 1864.   Wednesday. Skated round the town to day. Did no political business. I have seen three sights since I have been here, Thorwaldsen's Museum, The Scandinavian Museum, the Rosenborg Castle, all admirable especially the first & second. Professor Worsaae[293] has the care of the last, & Prof: Thornson, the very type of an old antiquary of the second. This evening after dining at Pagets, we went to Count Dauneskiold's, a very tiresome tea party. With joy we are preparing to depart to morrow evening. No post for three days from England. We suppose the Sleswig Holsteiners have stopped it.

7 January 1864.   My birthday. This day I am 38 years old. May this year be as happy as the last.

I don't think I have written what I think of Hall. If I am not mistaken, he is a regular 'Don', clever, obstinate, pedantic, exactly fitted to ruin a country for the sake of an argument. The Bishop last night asked me whether if the Danish Gt. bought an iron plated ship at Glasgow & they could not get it finished before war broke out, they would be allowed to take it out of port. I declined to give opinion, but advised him to refer the matter to Bille who might take legal advice in England.

I saw Bishop Monrad & Quaade in the course of the day. They still seemed shaky as to sending off their despatches to Vienna & Berlin for mediation, but I think I ended in persuading them. This evening I left Copenhagen, & proceeded with Ewers to Eckenfiorde in a steamer which the Govt. placed at our disposal. From Eckenfiorde we went Friday Jan 8 (some 16 miles) in carriages to Kiel. There we stopped at

---

[293] Jens Jacob Worsaae (1821–85), Danish historian and archaeologist.

the Railway Hotel some hours waiting for the train to Hamburg. The doors of the Hotel were guarded by some ill looking Sleswig-Holsteiners in plain coats with tricolor ribbons in the button holes. They were armed with rusty muskets.

The Prince of Augustenburg was living in the Hotel. To my surprise I found Oliphant here, very 'thick' with the Pretender and a furious Sleswig-Holsteiner. We slept at Hamburg. From what I could learn, the excitement tho' great is slightly on the wane.

9 January 1864. Saturday. Started for Brussels in the evening. In the morning Currie & I skated on the Alster. The Elbe is frozen but a passage is kept open for the steam ferry to Hamburg. We stopped 3 hours at Hanover & were regaled in a sumptuous manner by Sir H. Howard.

10 January 1864. Sunday. Arrived in the afternoon at Brussels. Went to call on Ld. Howard de Walden,[294] & by mistake walked into the house of Mr. Sanford the U. S. Minister. Afterwards saw Ld. Howard.

11 January 1864. Monday. By train to Paris. On my arrival found a telegram that Lord Clare died yesterday (at 1/4 before 6) & that I am executor (with Mr Huthchinson). Called on Lord Cowley.

12 January 1864. Tuesday. Saw Drouyen de Lhuys[295] by appt. at 2 o'clock. He talked long & wordily about the unfriendly relations between Engd. & France. France, he said, had been put in 'quarantaine'. He said the French Gt. hesitated to take active steps in the Danish affair. If they joined us in urging the Diet to agree to a conference, they wd. expose France to an impertinent rebuff, which coming after the Polish rebuff could not be borne; if they threatened Germany they could not back out, & a war with Germany was 'la grande guerre' which they did not want. The Polish fiasco evidently rankles in his mind. As to the Congress, he said he never expected it would meet, & tho' he used some fine phrases in defence of it, it was clear he cared nothing about it— 'no child of his'. It was very difficult to extract any reasoning out of his clever talk. He was positive— not to expose France to a second rebuff tho' how he meant to avoid it he did not explain. But his complaint as to our conduct in the Polish matter has, I must admit, some foundation & he is right in pointing out the objections to menaces followed by eating humble pie.

[294] Charles Augustus Ellis, 6th Baron Howard de Walden (1799–1868), min. to Belgium, 1846–68.

[295] Edouard Drouyn de Lhuys (1805–81), French for. min., 1862–6.

In the morning I saw Count Moltke, the Danish Envoy, & it was agreed between Cowley him & me that he should present without delay the Danish despatch asking for mediation, which I brought with me last night from Copenhagen. I started this evening for London & arrived there on the morning of 13 January 1864.

Wednesday, and found, thank God, my dearest wife & the children all well. So ends my mission to Copenhagen, without much result, tho' I effected I think, all that was possible, and the formation of a new Danish Ministry of which I was the indirect cause together with the proposal for a mediation is not an altogether unimportant result.[296] At all events I have the consolation of knowing that I spared no pains to carry out my instructions.

In the afternoon I went to Richmond, & rendered to Ld. Russell an account of my stewardship. From his language I gathered that he & Lord Palmerston are opposed by a party in the Cabinet who are for peace at any price. I told him that the moment seemed to me to be fast approaching when we could not, consistently with the dignity and honour of this country, continue our diplomatic action unless we were prepared if necessary to support our views by force.

14 January 1864. Thursday. I saw Lord R. again today at the F.O.

Lord Clare's death from the account I have recd. from Flo: seems to have been very shocking. A series of fits terminated his illness.

15 January 1864. Friday. Called on Coverdale to day, who told me my mortgage business will cost me £1000. Pleasant! Lady Hesilrige[297] died in her 90th year on Jan 3 at 23 Upper Brook St. & was buried at Kensal Green Cemetary.

16 January 1864. Saturday. Attended Lord Clare's Funeral at Kensal Green Cemetary at 12 a.m. My wife, Lady Louisa Dillon, Lady Elinor Cavendish, Mr Dillon, Mr Cavendish, Johnny, Chas. & Augustus Dillon, & Reginald Cavendish, Mr Leman, and Mr Hunt were mourners. After the ceremony we all returned to Lord Clare's house & heard the will read by Mr. Leman. Lady Clare & Lady Isabella FitzGibbon were also present.

18 January 1864. Monday. Johnny went back to Eton.

[296] A fair estimate of a failed mission. According to Sandiford, 'Wodehouse did not have the slightest chance of averting the federal execution.' *Great Britain and the Schleswig-Holstein Question*, 79.

[297] Last surviving da. of John, first Baron Wodehouse, by Sophia, only child of the Hon. Charles Berkeley.

23 January 1864. Saturday. Did very little this week but attend to the business of Ld. C's Executorship. Saw Mr. Gibson who of course is very pacific about Holstein.

24 January 1864. Sunday. Went to Windsor to dine and sleep. Saw Genl. Grey who I observe has somewhat moderated his language about the Danish Question, tho' his bias is still strongly German.

Before dinner I had my audience of The Queen. The Queen sat during the audience. She looked well & cheerful. Her language also was moderate. She wished she said for a Conference. I can see she has been much prejudiced against Monrad. Her fear now is that there may be a revolutionary movement in the minor German States.

25 January 1864. Monday. Went to Frogmore to see the Prince of Wales. The Prince spoke very strongly on the Danish side. Afterwards I walked to Eton to see Johnny & I returned to town in the afternoon.

26 January 1864. Tuesday. Called on Lord Palmerston whom I found sitting with de Grey. Lord P. seemed anxious to know in what disposition I found the Queen. I said she was I thought much perplexed but on the whole rather more moderate in her views than when I saw her before I started. 'We have made some impression upon her I hope,' was the reply. Lord P's language was, as I expected, favourable to Denmark. Afterwards I walked with de Grey in the Green Park & had a long talk. He is for strong measures.[298] The whole affair has I fear been mismanaged, Lord P. & Lord R. have been overborne by their pacific colleagues backed by the mischievous influences of the Court; the result has been a miserable vacillating undignified policy. We have either done too much or too little. We should never have made such angry remonstrances to Germany, if we meant to go no further. A policy of interference is intelligible, & perhaps would have been the best in this question. We might have said that as France & Russia were not disposed to aid us in enforcing the Treaty of 1852, we did not feel bound to enforce it alone. On the other a timely intimation to Germany that she wd. have to deal with us as well as Denmark might perhaps have prevented war. The half-hearted policy which we have pursued has alienated our friends has not deterred our enemies, & has brought us into contempt. It will not improbably drag us into war. If Hall had been an able statesman instead of an obstinate narrow-minded professor, he would have said, I will propose to the Rigsraad to repeal the Constn. of Nov. 18, if England will promise armed assistance to repel an attack on Sleswig. In this way our Govt would at all events have been

[298] Cf. Kimberley Memoir, herein, 490.

compelled to declare itself and very possibly the resistance of our Court might have been overcome by the argument. 'If we now promise aid, the Danes will promise repeal of Constn., & we shall thus prevent war.' But Hall lost the favourable moment, and the concession since made as to the Constn., like all the Danish concessions, has come too late.

27 January 1864.   Wednesday. Dined with Lord Palmerston.

4 February 1864.   Thursday. Parliament met. An amusing speech from Lord Derby; an effective reply from Lord Russell; an inaudible speech from Ld. Sligo[299] the mover of the Address. Altogether the Govt. came off well in both houses. The absurd scandal about Ld. Palmerston was dissipated by the withdrawal of the suit by O'Kane to day.[300] The object seems to have been to extort money.

7 February 1864.   Sunday. Poor Amy Gurdon died last night.

9 February 1864.   Tuesday. Met R. Currie at Cornhill about Falm: business.

12 February 1864.   Friday. My dear little Army who has been very ill for several days with a feverish attack and an inflammation of the ears, better this morning, thank God.
Last night I had some talk at the H. of L. with the Chancellor. According to him the Cabinet would have sent a fleet to Kiel and 10,000 men to the Dannewerke if the weather had permitted.[301] Why did they not send them to Tonning? He lamented the evil influence of the Court, & the crooked policy of France. It is clear that Austria & Prussia completely hoodwinked our Govt.

13 February 1864.   Saturday. Went to Lady Palmerston's in the Evening. Apponyi whom I talked to for some time is evidently much afraid of Prussian designs on Holstein.

14 February 1864.   Sunday. Took a long walk with de Grey, & talked about politics home & foreign. De Grey is getting rather Conservative in his views. He foresees a Coalition betn. moderate Whigs & Conservatives. He told me he feared Palmerston would make Sir R. Peel a

[299] George John Browne, 3rd Marquis of Sligo (1820–96).
[300] Palmerston having been cited as co-respondent in a divorce suit brought by an Irish journalist.
[301] Cf. Kimberley Memoir, herein, 490.

Cabinet Minister! (as a reward for his brilliant performance at Tamworth last autumn?)

In the evening I went to the Cos. where I met Wade[302] the Chinese Secretary and Bernardi, the agent of Augustenberg. Bernardi professes to believe that the Prussians have no designs on the Duchies. He evidently however dreads Napoleon & a Confederation of the Rhine.

17 February 1864. Wednesday. Hutchinson & I signed at my house the necessary papers for Probate of Lord Clare's Will.

22 February 1864. Monday. A short debate in the House of Lords on Penal discipline, in which I said a few words.

29 February 1864. Monday. Said a few words on 'Insane Prisoners Bill' 2nd reading.

2 March 1864. Wednesday. Attended Levee held by the Prince of Wales. Dined at Grillion's, where I was introduced to Mr. Gathorne Hardy[303] with whom I had some conversation as to penal Discipline. Afterward, to the Cosm;– Lord Stanley and Forster very strong against war for Denmark. Lord S all for a peace policy. We want, he says, another Sir R. Walpole for Minister. Forster says that England North of the Trent would pull to a man for peace.

9 March 1864. Wednesday. Dined with Lady Waldegrave. Ld. Grey there. After dinner talked of Danish affairs. The Earl fiercely warlike! A curious instance of the contradictory spirit of the man. The violent opponent of the Crimean War, because it was not the business of Engd. to protect weak states against strong states, is now frantic in favour of war, because it is our duty to protect weak states. Witness his speech in the H. of Lords' last night. Ellenborough was wonderfully eloquent. He takes a more favourable view of the negotiations in wh. I was engaged then Grey. He told me that he was convinced that if Talleyrand had been in Lord Russell's place, he might have written more mellifluous despatches but could not have prevented war. I had some conversation this morning at the Traveller's Club with Azeglio, the Italian Minister about the articles in the Morning Post on the Danish Question. Az: thinks that Ozartoriski & the Poles are the real inspirers of those articles. He also thinks the Porte is subsidized by the French Govt. Both

[302] Sir Thomas Francis Wade (1818–95), member of Peking legation, 1861–71.

[303] Gathorne Gathorne-Hardy (1814–1906), Cons. MP for Leominster, 1856–65, for Oxford U., 1865–78; home sec., 1867–8; war sec., 1874–8; Indian sec., 1878–80; ld. pres. counc., 1885–92; cr. Viscount Cranbrook, 1878, Earl of Cranbrook, 1892.

suppositions are not unlikely.[304] It is certain however that Borthwick[305] is closeted nearly every day with Lord Pam.

11 March 1864.   Friday. Went to the City & signed at the London Assurance office the Mortgage of Witton for £40,000, which I deposited at Curries. Soon, I hope, I shall wind up the Falmouth business.

12 March 1864.   Saturday. Dined at Marlborough House. After dinner went to the smoking room with the P. of Wales, Prince John of Glucksburg, brother to the Princess, & Lord Shelburne. We smoked & talked of the Danish war till 1/2 past 1 o'clock. The old Duchess of Cambridge (who dined) very Danish in her talk.

15 March 1864.   Tuesday. Said a few words on the 2nd. reading of the Malt for Cattle bill, deprecating agitation against the Malt Tax.

18 March 1864.   Friday. Two very bad nights for the Govt. in the H. of Commons. Stansfeld acted very unwisely in allowing Mazzini to continue to make use of his house, & still more so in not at once explaining & apologizing in a frank & straightforward manner. The Govt. get more shaky daily.[306]
   Johnny came home on Thursday.
   Parliament adjourned to day.

19 March 1864.   Saturday. Dined at Lord Palmerston's I thought Lord P. looking more worn and out of spirits than I had ever seen him.

21 March 1864.   Monday. Went to Kimberley.

22 March 1864.   Tuesday. Spent the day with Forrester, looking over the new farm buildings &c. The lambing very prosperous. A horribly cold day.

23 March 1864.   Wednesday. Saw J. O. Taylor in the morning, & had long talk as to our unsatisfactory election prospects in E. Norfolk, and about East Norfolk Ry. I advised that we should proceed with bill & encounter the opposition of Burroughes & Co. Went back to London.

---

[304] On Wodehouse's early agreement with the elder Azeglio's moderate revolutionary ardour, see Wodehouse, Notes on Books, KP1 15/K2/6, p. 5.
[305] Algernon Borthwick (1830–1908), succ. father as editor of the *Morning Post* in 1852; purchased same in 1876; Cons. MP for South Kensington, 1885–95; cr. Baron Glenesk, 1895.
[306] See entry for 8 April 1864.

27 March 1864.   Sunday. Easter Sunday.

31 March 1864.   Thursday. Went to the Adelphi to see Miss Bateman[307] in 'Leah'. She is a tragic actress of real genius, & we were much delighted with the performance. The other actors miserably bad.

2 April 1864.   Saturday. Went to Minley & passed two very pleasant days there with my dear old Uncle & Aunt.

3 April 1864.   Monday. Heard of D. of Newcastle's resignation, & the appointments of Cardwell & Ld. Clarendon. My hopes of office were too small (notwithstanding the rumours current) for me to be really disappointed; nevertheless I admit I feel much discouraged at the very low state of my political prospects. I seem to labour on uselessly without success, reward, or reputation.

7 April 1864.   Thursday. Gladstone propounded his Budget. His speech said by those who heard it to have been rather tedious; but his measures seem to be generally approved.

8 April 1864.   Friday. People talk a great deal of the extraordinary Memorandum, evidently, written by the Queen herself, which appeared in the 'Times' on Wednesday.[308] It is a foolish act on her part, and is universally so regarded by those who understand anything of the relations of the Court with the Govt. The general public which knows about as much about the mysterious power exercised by the Crown, as about the Mikado of Japan, is simply puzzled. The fact is that the Queen meddles far too much with foreign affairs & indeed with all affairs. She is the unconscious tool of Leopold[309] & other intriguing potentates with whom she has family connexions, & with whom she keeps up an incessant correspondence. Leopold's advice is no doubt on the whole wise but there are others such as the D. of Coburg who are not wise, & at all events they are not Englishmen & of course don't act on English principles of policy. At some not very distant day there will be serious trouble from this cause. A young Baron Stockmar has, I

---

[307] Sidney Frances Bateman (1823–81), playwright and actress.

[308] Refuting the prevailing idea that she was 'about again to hold levees and drawing rooms in person, and to appear as before at Court balls, concerts, &c.' *The Times*, 6 April 1864, p. 9.

[309] Georges Chrétien Frédéric, Leopold I (1790–1865), fourth son of Francis Frederick, Duke of Saxe-Coburg-Saalfield; chosen first King of the Belgians in 1831; uncle of Queen Victoria.

hear, taken the place of the old Fox.[310] I know of no proof so striking of Palmerston's intellectual senility as his truckling to the Court.

Lord Clarendon came to me to day in the House of Lords, and assured me with much apparent goodwill that when asked to take the office vacated by Cardwell, he had recommended me strongly for the place.[311] He expatiated much on my claims, & declared that Lord Palmerston fully recognized the tact & ability I had shown in my Danish Mission &c. &c. &c. &c. &c. &c. &c. All this may go for what it is worth–which is very little. It is however worth this much that it proves that I am not considered wholly unfit for office, and if ever the list of worn out Whig placemen should be so diminished that a place should go begging, & if there should be no Billy Cowper or Bob Peel or other favored incompetency ready to fill the place–in short if the nature of Whigs should be altogether changed, I might be employed. It is a brilliant prospect no doubt. Ld. Clarendon said that Palmerston hinted that Lowe's & Peel's claims were a serious obstacle.[312] A more serious obstacle to my mind is the obstacle raised by keeping incompetent worn out men like G. Grey in office. I met Lowe on Saturday April 9 at the meeting of a Committee of the Senate of the Lond. Univ. He is intensely disgusted at not being promoted. I don't know whether R. Peel is angry but I think he will be in the Cabinet ere long, at least if he commits a few more follies, & disgusts a few more Irish men, if any remain to be disgusted. Ld. Clarendon professed that he had accepted office with immense reluctance, only because he believed that the ship was sinking. Now that the prospects of the Govt. were so much improved (since Stansfeld's resignation)[313] he regretted that he had accepted.

I dined at (Lionel) Rothschild's to night where I met, for the first time, the Prince de la Tour d'Auvergne, the new French Ambassador. He made a very favourable impression upon me. He asked if I was to attend the Conference to which I could answer no with the more confidence that Ld. Clarendon told me he is to 'assist' Lord Russell. Of course the French Ambr. stood up for the French plan. He professed a great desire for the union of France & England in the Conference. He advocated a division of Sleswig, but the German part not to become Federal territory but to be administratively united to Holstein. But I don't think from his tone the opposition of the French to the acquisition of Kiel by the Confedn. will be very strong.

[310] Christian Freidrich, Baron von Stockmar (1787–1863), Coburg advisor to Victoria and Albert.

[311] For Clarendon's recommendation, see *Liberal by Principle*, 35.

[312] Cf. Wodehouse to Raikes Currie, 9 April 1864, in *Liberal by Principle*, 95–6.

[313] For allowing Mazzini's supporters to use his house as a post office. See entry for 18 March 1864.

Poor Mrs. Robert Gurdon died to day 3 weeks after her confinement.[314]

11 April 1864. Monday. Commenced sitting on 'Bute Docks' Committee with Lord Granard, Ld. Ravensworth,[315] De Tabley[316] & Strathspey,[317] myself chairman.

Garibaldi[318] arrived in London. In the evening debate in the Lords on Ld. Stratheden's motion about Danish question, I spoke after Lord Derby. Altogether it was a very tedious debate. Ld. Grey made one of the most ineffective speeches I ever heard from him. Derby showed plainly enough that he has no intention of attacking the Govt. about Denmark.

12 April 1864. Tuesday. To St. James' Theatre, where we saw a very stupid piece the 'Silver Lining', vulgar as well as stupid.

13 April 1864. Wednesday. Johnny went back to Eton.

15 April 1864. Friday. Dined with Panizzi[319] at the British Museum to meet Garibaldi. The hero of the day is a younger looking man than I expected; very quiet composed in his manner a fair complexion, not at all 'Italian' looking. Lord Shaftesbury told me he had written to Persigny to reassure the Emperor thru' him, as to the Garibaldi demonstrations!– and had a most satisfactory answer, with 'vu et approuvé' from the great man.

19 April 1864. Tuesday. We threw out the 'Bute Docks' Bill four to one. Ravensworth the one. The main objection wh. weighed with me was the Board of Trade Report pointing out that the proposed works would damage the navigation. The evidence was not sufficiently strong to render it prudent to disregard this Report. I also thought that there were objections to the non-parliamentary East Dock obtaining a new access without being opened to the public.

20 April 1864. Wednesday. We finished the other bills (wh. were of small importance) referred to the Committee. We passed a Welsh

---

[314] Harriet Ellen Gurdon, 6th da. of Sir William Miles.

[315] Henry Thomas Liddell (1797–1878), Lib.-Cons. MP for Liverpool, 1853–5, when he succ. as 2nd Baron Ravensworth.

[316] George Fleming Warren, 2nd Baron De Tabley (1811–87).

[317] John Charles Ogilvie-Grant, 7th Earl of Seafield (1815–81), sat as Baron Strathspey.

[318] Giuseppe Garibaldi (1807–82), Italian patriot and revolutionary.

[319] Anthony Panizzi (1797–1879), chief librarian of the British Museum, 1856–66; KCB, 1869.

Railway Bill, the Llandilo Ry., and the Railway Passenger's Assurance Amending Act.

21 April 1864. Thursday. Received from Ld. Palmerston the offer of the Under-secretaryship at the India Office. I was very reluctant to accept it. The position of Under Secretary is so very unimportant that it is most discouraging to me to have offered to me such an appointment. More than eleven years ago I accepted the Under Secretaryship of the Foreign Office, a decidedly better post. All my hardworking service has not advanced me an inch. However after taking counsel with Lord Clarendon & others who all advised me to take this step, I have decided to accept. At all events I shall make it a little more difficult for my Whig friends to get rid of me.

22 April 1864. Friday. I called on Lord Palmerston & told him that I had made up my mind after much hesitation to take the under-secretaryship. He professed himself sorry that he had nothing better to offer me &c. Afterwards I went to the India Office, and arranged with Wood[320] to commence work on Monday. It seems that there is very little to do, and the under-secretary is, I am told, a mere cypher.

Still I shall have a good opportunity of learning an important branch of our administration, and as I am to begin again as an under-strapper, I may as well learn to strap a new horse; and as the employment is not dignified, I am glad it is light.

23 April 1864. Saturday. I hear that C. Fortescue is not a little discontented at his treatment. It seems it was understood that he was to succeed Lowe, but it is supposed that Palmerston forgot what had been determined when he appointed Bruce. The other members of the Govt. seem to have been much annoyed at Bruce's appointment. Certainly he has been wonderfully lucky. Granville, I hear, knew nothing of the intention to appoint Bruce!

We dined at Lord Palmerston's to day. In the evening I was introduced to Baron de Beust,[321] a lively looking man. I also saw Quaade & Krieger who seemed as might be expected, not a little depressed. The Conference[322] really meets on Monday. There is no doubt that departure of Garibaldi was greatly desired by the government. On Friday he came to the H. of Lords. On his entering the Bp.

---

[320] Charles Wood (1800–85), Lib. MP for Grimsby, 1826, for Wareham, 1831, for Halifax, 1832–65, for Ripon 1865–6, when he was created Viscount Halifax; 1st ld. adm., 1855; India sec., 1859–65; ld. pr. seal, 1870–4.

[321] Count Friedrich Ferdinand von Beust (1809–86), pr. min. of Saxony, 1853–66.

[322] Conference of parties to the London Treaty, seeking repeal of the Danish constitution in return for postponement of Prussian occupation.

of Oxford went to him and in an ostentatious manner shook hands
with him. Bath therupon (who has resigned his office of whip to the
Opposition in consequence of Ld. Derby meeting Garibaldi at Stafford
House) went to the Bishop, & expressed to him his astonishment that
'he had shaken hands with the champion of revolution & infidelity!'[323]
Bath says he shall represent to the Library Committee the impropriety
of Sir. A. Clifford conducting Garibaldi to a place.[324]

25 April 1864. Monday. Attended at India Office. Sir C. Wood
introduced me to the Councillors.

28 April 1864. Thursday. Gave evidence before House of Commons
Committee on East Norfolk Railway. Sir S. Goldschmidt in the chair;
I moved amendment on 3rd reading of Ld. Westmeath's bill, as to
punishment of rape by whipping. The bill was originally to give judges
power at their discretion to order whipping. In Committee the whipping
was made compulsory. I moved to make it discretionary as at first, and
on a division carried it 55 to 20. I also answered two questions of Lord
Ellenborough's, one whether the seat of Govt. in India is to be removed
from Calcutta, the other as to Mr Beadon's[325] indiscreet proceedings
about the former burning Hindoo bodies at Calcutta. I was nervous &
rather indistinct.

   We had a dinner party in the evening; & were well satisfied with
Mrs. Leonard our new cook.

5 May 1864. Thursday. I attended the Indian Council for the first
time. The position of the Under Secretary with regard to the Council
is anomalous & absurd. He sits, but can neither speak nor vote.

9 May 1864. Monday. The armistice between Denmark & Germany
announced to the great dismay of the opposition. It seems that the
Austrians had at last got a strong hint from our Govt. that they would
not be allowed to join the Prussian fleet in the Baltic. It is very lucky
for Govt wh. would have I believe been driven out by a storm of
indignation if the Conference had broken up without doing anything.
The news of the defeat of the Austrian ships by the Danes was received
with almost frantic cheering by the House of Commons. I presided this

---

[323] John Alexander Thynne, 4th Marquess of Bath (1831–96). See too *DD2*, 218; Cf.
Kimberley memoir, herein, 491.
[324] Sir Augustus Clifford (1788–1877), usher of the black rod, 1832–77; Malmesbury,
Memoirs of an Ex-minister (new edn, London, 1885), 593–5.
[325] Cecil Beadon (1816–81), lieut. gov. of Bengal, 1862–7.

morning at the giving away of the prizes to medical students at University College, & made a short speech.

11 May 1864. Wednesday. Gladstone's liberal speech gave a smart shock to the (liberal?) party. It was on Baines'[326] motion for lowering suffrage in boroughs.

13 May 1864. Friday. Quaade, the Danish Envoy, & others dined with us. De Grey told me that he believes there is an intrigue on foot to make over Holstein and South Sleswig to Oldenburg, Oldenburg in return to cede a piece of territory to Hanover, & Hanover to cede a Naboth's vineyard[327] to Prussia. Of course France will be indemnified by a 'rectification' of territory on the Rhine. A very pretty project! It seems that Apponyi waived his right of speaking first in the Conference on the part of Germany to Bernstorff. Austria is evidently in the mess she deserves to be in. The Danes say they would rather leave Holstein & South Sleswig outright than agree to a 'personal Union' of the Duchies.

14 May 1864. Saturday. Went to Bertram's charming villa at Coomb and stayed till Monday, on Sunday Pierre Dolgoroukow dined there. He spoke in praise of Prince Alex; Gortchacoff though, he said, he (G) was too old to favour reform in Russia. The G Duke Constantine he looked upon as a 'faux Libéral' & therefore the greatest obstacle to reform. On Sunday we drove over to Hampton Court & saw the splendid horse chestnuts in Bushy Park. The weather extraordinarily hot.

19 May 1864. Thursday. Merivale[328] told me that at the Literary Fund Dinner last night Lord Russell was received with hisses.

22 May 1864. Sunday. Met Brunnow at the Zoologl. Gardens. He thinks that the Danish Question will end by the separation of S. Sleswig & Holstein from Denmark and a popular vote to determine who is to rule over the severed territory. He said (in which I agree with him) that the Govt. here would have been changed if no armistice had been concluded. *'Ce sont de vos anciens amis, les ministres actuels et j'ai ete bien aise qu'ils aient obtenu l'armistice. J'ai fait actuels mon possible pour eux'.*

---

[326] Edward Baines (1800–90), ed. of *Leeds Mercury* from 1818; Lib. MP for Leeds, 1859–74.

[327] Naboth's vineyard, adjacent to royal lands, was coveted by King Ahab of Israel. His queen, Jezebel, plotted Naboth's death so that Ahab might take the vineyard. See II Kings 9:25–6.

[328] Probably Herman Merivale (1806–74), u.-sec. for India, 1859–64, and miscellaneous writer.

The idea of Russian diplomacy being guided by personal friendship for our ministers is rather too good.

24 May 1864.   Tuesday. Signed a new will.

25 May 1864.   Wednesday. Went with Henley & Airlie by rail to the Derby. An immense crowd. Blair Athol won. It was said that if Lord Westmorland's[329] horse Birch Broom had won, he would have won for his owner £70,000. As it was, they say he won £5,000.

26 May 1864.   Thursday. Dined with Lord Russell where we met Messrs. &c. Beust, Balan, & Biegeleben. The last has the reputation of being very clever. Like all dinners at Lord R's, it was intensely dull. A story is going that some one, on Balan's (Balaam's) name being mentioned, said *'Ou doue est l'asse.'* whereupon Mussuns, not understanding what was said, observe *'C'est l'ambassadeur'* – i.e. Bernstorff; — 'very appropriate' I say.[330]

Ld. Ellenborough in asking a question to night about Denmark alluded to the Queen's German partialities. Of course Lord Russell gave the usual answer that H.M. had always followed advice of her Ministers &c. &c. &c. Nevertheless it is an understood fact that the Queen has exercised a most pernicious and un-English influence in this unfortunate business. If Palmerston were not so old, he would have resisted, but he can have no future, and therefore he does not dare to threaten resignation. How can a Cabinet carry on a negotiation with Germany with any chance of success when the Queen carries on a tumultuous correspondence with the King of Prussia, assuring him that in no case will she consent to war between England & Germany? This correspondence was at length stopped by Palmerston's interference but the mischief was already done. Meanwhile Lord Derby has been also muzzled by fear of offending the Court, so that altogether the Crown and its Continental Advisers have the game in their own hands.

28 May 1864.   Saturday. Sir C. Wood mentioned that both Palmerston & Lord Russell had opposed the plan of transporting our troops to India thro' Egypt for fear of offending France. Truly we do sing a small note now a days. However [?] fortunately the aged men were overruled by Wood & the D. of Somerset.

---

[329] Francis William Henry Fane, 12th Earl of Westmorland (1825–91), succ. to Earldom, 1859; retired from army as col. 1860, having served in India and the Crimea.

[330] Balaam was a heathen diviner, who first respected God's prohibition from helping the Moabites against Israel. Finally giving way to King Balak's entreaties, Balaam rode toward the Moabite court. During the course of the journey, Balaam was verbally rebuked by his ass for resisting the plan of God. See Numbers, chaps. 22–5.

4 June 1864.   Saturday. Went to Salt Hill with Flo: & the girls & stayed till Monday. Wonderful to say brilliant weather for the Eton Boats. We enjoyed ourselves with Johnny very much.

5 June 1864.   Sunday. Pulled up to Surley in the afternoon with Johnny.

6 June 1864.   Monday. It seems that the Conference settled nothing on Saturday. Despatches from the Russn. Govt. have fallen into the hands of our Foreign Office showing that Russia has all along been playing a double game. She has assured Prussia that her advice not to dismember Denmark given out of deference to the western Powers means nothing. She has concluded an alliance with Austria & Prussia; the terms, A. & P. to support R. in Poland. P. to support A. in Italy. P. to be allowed her own way in Denmark. This was reported some months ago in the foreign newspapers. This evening in the H. of Lords I took part in the discussion about the public schools. Carnarvon made a very priggish speech in favour of Eton Dons, and against change. He got I am happy to say no encouragement from anyone whose opinion has weight.

7 June 1864.   Tuesday. I moved 2nd reading of C. Villier's[331] 'Union Assessment Committee Act Amendment Bill'; a bill for giving the Committees power to appear at Special & Qr. Sessions to defend their decisions when appealed against.

11 June 1864.   Saturday. The state of foreign affairs is alarming. Wood who belongs to the peace party in the Cabinet told me that Lord Russell was the originator, not Lord Palmerston of the intimation to Austria that the junction of the Austrian & Prussian fleets would be prevented by England. Palmerston only spoke to Apponyi after a communication had been made by Lord R. at Vienna. Wood also said that Lord R. had without consulting the Cabinet committed us to the proposal (singly) of the line of the Schler without the concurrence of France. Lord R. was for our single action in the winter, but he (Wood) proposed & carried joint action with France. There are rumours that the opposition mean to try a want of confidence vote. Lord Grey whom I met at Airlie's this afternoon thinks the present most unpleasant position of the Govt. ascribable to the divided opinions of the Cabinet, one party for peace the other for war. He compared the situation, justly I think, to that of the Aberdeen Cabinet before the Crimean War.

[331] Charles Pelham Villiers (1802–98), Lib. MP for Wolverhampton, 1835–98; pres. poor law bd., 1859–66.

If the Conference breaks down the country will be instensely mortified, & will vent its anger in some way—either by turning out the Govt., or by war. Oliphant says, if there is war, The Queen will abdicate. I doubt this, but her blind obstinancy has certainly grievously aggravated the difficulties of the Govt.

14 June 1864. Tuesday. Carried Union Asst. Act Amdendment Bill thro' Committee after a tedious opposition from Lord St Leonard's who has a grievance against an Assesst. Committee which he thinks has rated his property too high.

18 June 1864. Saturday. The Govt. narrowly escaped destruction last night on a motion about the Ashantee war.[332] I think they would hardly have been sorry if they had been beaten, & could have escaped by resignation their increasing difficulties.

It is probable that if the Conference breaks up the Cabinet will break up also, as they are utterly divided. Gladstone, Milner Gibson, Cardwell, Granville, Wood & Villiers are for peace at any price; Palmerston, Russell, the Chancellor, Somerset, de Grey, Stanley, Argyll for war. I am not sure as to Sir G. Grey and Clarendon.[333]

Went with Flo: to the Cavendishes at St Leonards & stayed till Monday.

22 June 1864. Wednesday. Appointed at Hutchinson's request The Revd. G. Francis Popham Blyth of Whitton Lincoln to be my Chaplain. Interview with Leman. Our Executor's account goes on well. The sale of pictures at Christie's on last Friday went off admirably. Ld. C's 39 pictures fetched £6772.[334] I hear that Lord Hertford[335] bought the 'Grange'. I bought the 'Groigione' [?] & 'Caracei'[?] very cheap; they had no authentic pedigree.

At the Cos; this evening great excitement at the breakdown of the Conference. Curiously enough C. Mills[336] told Wood and me this morning that Rothschild had favourable news & was buying largely. He was probably misled by a telegram from Grammont at Vienna, forwarded by Cowley. According to Layard, Lord R. has already committed Govt. to action in the Baltic.

---

[332] Sir John Hay calling upon parliament to 'avenge the blood of their brothers' who had died in the 'fetid swamps of Central Africa' for the government's want of foresight. The motion against the government was beaten 233 to 226. *The Times*, 10 June 1864, 8.

[333] Cf. Kimberley memoir, herein, 491.

[334] For an account of the sale, see *The Times*, 18 June 1864, 14.

[335] Richard Seymour-Conway, 4th Marquis of Hertford (1800–74).

[336] Charles Mills (1825–95), brigade commander in Crimea; held various military posts in South Africa.

25 June 1864. Saturday. The Conference sat for the last time to day; the Cabinet was in anxious deliberation to day and yesterday.

27 June 1864. Monday. Ministers announced in both Houses a peace policy. Ld. Palmerston spoke very well I was told except in the passage about Copenhagen. This was clumsily put and ill-received. Ld. Clarendon told me that the Cabinet voted 8 to 7 in favour of alluding to the contingency of interference if Copenhagen is in danger; he himself in the minority.

Ld. Russell gave a clear narrative of events but spoke in a feeble voice, & the allusions to danger to us from the N. Americans and to our commerce &c. was singularly ill-timed and injudicious.

29 June 1864. Wednesday. Disraeli gave notice yesterday of a vote of Censure. Govt. say that on counting noses they have a majority of 23 in the House; but if the Catholics go against them, as is rumoured how then? The impression however is that they will win.

Poor Lady Clare had a stroke of paralysis last night.

4 July 1864. Monday. Rumours more unfavourable to Govt. G. Clive[337] won't vote for Gt. because he was not made Irish Secretary!!! Enfield[338] because he refused Lordship of the Admiralty & has been offered nothing since. H. Grenfell[339] because he is a crotchetty angular man who thinks himself cleverer by far than he is. F. Goldsmidt[340] because he wanted war; Berkeley[341] because his father was made a Peer &c. & c. &c., and the son thinks jobbing should extend to the next generation & wants place. He is offended at not being made Lord of the Admiralty the other day, & so on.

7 July 1864. Thursday. Signed the Release of the Falmouth Trustees. J. H. Gurney, R. Currie & G. Currie. They re-convey what remains of the Estate to me. A very satisfactory termination of 18 years trouble and uncertainty. All creditors of the Estate have been paid in full, and tho' at present I am not a gainer, I have a good prospect of ultimately making the Estate pay. The forbearance & patience of the numerous

---

[337] George Clive (1806–80), Lib. MP for Hereford, 1857–69, 1874–80; u.-sec. home o., 1859–62.

[338] George Stephens Byng, Lord Enfield (1830–98), Lib. MP for Tavistock, 1852–7, for Middlesex, 1857–74; succ. as 3rd Earl of Strafford, 1886.

[339] Henry Riversdale Grenfell (1824–1902), Lib. MP for Stoke-upon-Trent, 1862–78.

[340] Sir Francis Henry Goldsmid (1839–78), Lib. MP for Reading, 1860–78.

[341] Charles Paget Fitz-Hardinge Berkeley (1830–1916), Lib. MP for Gloucestershire 1862–5; succ. as 3rd Baron Fitz-Hardinge, 1896.

incumbrancers has been most remarkable. The incumbrances at my Grandfathers death were upwards of £140,000!.

8 July 1864. Friday. The end of the great debate on the vote of Censure on the Danish Question. Govt. won by 18 in the Commons, by 4 of Peers present but beaten by 9 on present & proxies. Our division was a remarkably full one. 345 Peers present or by proxy, 44 paired = 389, which leaves very few Peers unaccounted for. Both Houses divided at the same moment, but Commons' Division was known to us before we had finished taking proxies. We cheered manfully when the numbers present were announced. I never heard so much cheering in our House. The debate suffered from the absence of Derby whose gout is very bad. Malmesbury was as feeble as usual. Argyll spirited but somewhat too 'cocky', Clanricarde not a bad speech. Clarendon very weighty & effective. Chelmsford the usual *nisi precis* oration. I followed & spoke for half an hour, I am told effectively. Carnarvon, not so good as usual. Lord Russell rather feeble, Grey ditto. Granville a very neat reply. On the whole we had much the best of the Debate. I never saw such excitement, as followed the tidings of the result in the Commons. Up to the last moment it was very doubtful whether we should reach 10. The debate in the Commons altogether was brilliant except perhaps the last night. Pam, I heard, made a very poor speech. It is evident he is worn out.

The Govt. would not have come off so victoriously had it not been that the Opposition offered no programme, nothing in short but themselves to the country. The issue was 'men' not 'measures' an issue unfavourable to Dizzy & Co. Besides the alliance with the Brass Band is hateful to the Tory gentlemen. So ends this sharp 'faction fight' as Argyll justly called it, leaving the Govt. stronger than they have been for some time.

Dear Johnny came up to day for the Eton & Harrow match & stayed till Monday.

Lord C. remarked to me during the Debate on Denmark that it was amusing to hear Lord Russell refuting in his speech all his own arguments (in the Cabinet) for war.

10 July 1864. Sunday. Prince Pierre Dolgoroukow called and told me that he had heard from good authority in Russia that the negotiations between Russia & Austria had ended in Russia giving Austria her pledge for Poland but refusing it for Italy. Nothing, he says, is in writing, I believe he is right. Mr. Pepoli the Italian Minr. at Petersburg taking leave lately of Gff it seems some rather sharp words passed. Pepoli complained that Gff was less friendly to Italy. Gff replied– To tell you frankly 'Turin c'est Paris?'

Nothing interesting to note this week. The Tories are wonderfully down in the mouth & politics as dull as ditchwater.

16 July 1864. Saturday. All the gossips astir about the disgraceful marriage of Ld. H. & Lady F. Paget.[342] The very night before she kept up the pretence she was going to marry Mr Chaplin.[343]

21 July 1864. Thursday. Opposed 2nd reading of Poisoned Flesh &c. Bill, which is in fact a fox preserving Bill. The fox-hunters were too strong for me & beat me 31 to 18.

22 July 1864. Friday. I moved amendments in the same bill & carried them on a division. The bill now is confined to prohibiting poisoned flesh & meat & won't interfere with the poisoning rats & other vermin.

23 July 1864. Saturday. Went to the Ministerial Fish Dinner.

25 July 1864. Monday. Moved Poor Removal Bill, declaring residence in the Parish of settlement to count towards the three years residence in a Union which makes a pauper irremovable. Lord Redesdale made some opposition. I doubt if the Bill would have passed if more attention had been drawn to it.

27 July 1864. Wednesday. Moved 2nd reading of the Bill for relief of casual poor in the metropolis. A sharp oppositon but carried it through without a division. The temporary duration of the bill saved it. The fact is C. Villiers is culpably indolent in his department, & ought to have brought the bill in earlier in the Session.

28 July 1864. Thursday. The Casual Poor bill passed. We had a sharp affair about the Railway Facilities bill. The Commons amendments only coming up this evening, Redesdale who wanted to destroy the Bill, objected that no time was left to consider them. On a division however we carried our point; & 'considered' the amendments by disagreeing to all but but one. The fear was that the Bill was answered in the Queen's Speech, (already settled in Council for to morrow) as one of the achievements of the Session. Donoughmore went to the Commons to get a Tory to count out the House but luckily could not

---

[342] Henry Weysford Hastings, 4th Marquess of Hastings (1842–68), married Lady Florence Paget (1842–1907) and ruined himself on the turf.

[343] Henry Chaplin (1840–1923), Cons. MP for mid-Lincolnshire (Sleaford), 1868–1906, for Wimbledon, 1907–16; pres. bd. agric., 1889–92; pres. loc. govt. bd., 1895–1900. For Chaplin's revenge, see entry for 23 May 1867.

find one, so the Commons cr. M. Gibson & some ten men 'not insisting' on their amendments we passed the Bill.

Johnny came home.

29 July 1864.   Friday. Parliament prorogued.

30 July 1864.   Saturday. Jones came, and I signed the Falmouth Trustees' Account. So ends that business after 18 years of difficulties.

Dear Johnny showed us a very pretty little copy of English verses which he had written in his collections. He has not got a high place (38th) in 5th form Examinn. but I am happy to say Johnson reports him to have been a very good boy.

3 August 1864.   Wednesday. Went to Kimberley & found everything in a lamentable condition from the great drought.

10 August 1864.   Wednesday. Began harvest on the Home Farm.

12 August 1864.   Friday. Presided at meeting at Norwich to give away prizes &c. to candidates at the Univy. Local Examinations.

16 August 1864.   Tuesday. Our 17th anniversary of our wedding day which we passed in great peace & happiness. Gave dear Flo: a black Cashmere shawl.

20 August 1864.   Saturday. To Norwich Castle. Hamilton came on a visit. Constant rumours in newspapers that I am to succeed Ld. Carlisle[344] as Lord Lieut: in Ireland.[345] I don't think there is much probability that it will be offered to me. If it were, I should accept it, as anything is better than remaining Under Secretary all one's life, but the post is not a pleasant one, especially with Peel for Secretary.

22 August 1864.   Monday. Yesterday a thunderstorm & change of weather. Went to day to Board of Guardians at Wicklewood.

26 August 1864.   Friday. Finished harvest; corn got up in excellent order.

[344] George William Frederick Howard, 7th Earl of Carlisle (1802–64), ld. lt. Ireland, 1855–8, 1859–64.

[345] On 12 Aug. 1864, Delane had observed in *The Times* (p. 6) that 'happily now and then a good man' was not placed 'so entirely to his liking as to shirk an untried burden'. The position was first offered to, and refused by, the Duke of Devonshire and Lord Bessborough.

29 August 1864. Monday. Attended Asst. Committee. Jodrell's appeal put off for 14 days.

3 September 1864. Saturday. Cavendishes came. Johnny began partridge shooting on the 1st. To Norwich Castle. Last years crop on farm; average of 11 cw. wheat 14 cw. barley.

9 September 1864. Friday. Attended Licensing meeting at Wymm.

12 September 1864. Monday. To Union workhouse. Jodrell's appeal heard before Asst. Committee.

13 September 1864. Wednesday. Cavendishes went. Yesterday my uncle Berkeley W.[346] & Charles W.[347] my ward came on a visit. Charles who is going to Queensland as a colonist, next month, has grown a very nice lad.

22 September 1864. Thursday. Attended first general meeting of East Norfolk shareholders at Norwich; Suffield in the chair. J. O. Taylor says we shall have a fight next election for East Norfolk.

Johnny went back to Eton to day & Flo went to London with him and stayed till Saturday.

24 September 1864. Saturday. Little Army's 4th birthday.

27 September 1864. Tuesday. Received a letter from Lord Palmerston, offering me the Lord Lieutenancy of Ireland.[348] Answered that I would accept. This is not at all the office I coveted, but is a great advancement; and I could not hesitate as to accepting it. I feel sure however that the office ought to be abolished. What I should like, would be that I should be the last Ld. Lieut; & should aid in my own abolition. Dear Flo: does not at all fancy being a Vice-Queen, but I have no doubt she will face it bravely when the time comes. Henley came yesterday on a visit.

28 September 1864. Wednesday. My mother came on a visit.

---

[346] Berkeley Wodehouse (1806–77), maj. 8th Hussars; British res., Ionian Islands; younger brother of Wodehouse's father.

[347] Charles Wodehouse, son of Rev. Alfred Wodehouse and Emma-Hamilla Macdonald; brother of Hamilla and Ernestine, *see above*, x, 73, 78.

[348] Palmerston wrote that it had first been offered to Bessborough 'as an Irishman', though Wodehouse was the best Englishman, and would at all events possess an advantage over most Irishmen, of being unconnected with Irish land and party politics. Palmerston to Wodehouse, 25 Sept. 1864, KP6 MS.eng.c. 4475, ff. 31–2. On Lady Wodehouse's distress, see Henry Wodehouse to Anne Wodehouse, 13 Oct. 1864, KP1 15/K2/20.

1 October 1864.   Saturday. Henley went away. I went to Norwich.

3 October 1864.   Monday. Went to London to Home Office where I found that I have £290 to pay to a grateful country for my patent. Returned by the express to Ky.

10 October 1864.   Monday. My mother went away.

11 October 1864.   Tuesday. Went up to London.

18 October 1864.   Tuesday. Brady[349] the Irish Chancellor & Sir Bernard Burke[350] Ulster King at Arms called on me. The former rather a vulgar looking little man did not impress me very favourably. Sir B. B. is the type of a herald; a fussy important little man full of gules & or & argent in his talk.

19 October 1864.   Wednesday. Brand called on me. He says there are only 25 Irish Liberal members. We are in a prodigious turmoil engaging servants & ordering our outfit for Ireland. The mummeries are not only absurd but extravagantly costly.

1 November 1864.   Tuesday. To Windsor to be sworn a P.C. & declared Ld. Lieutenant of Ireland. The Q. very gracious. At my audience she spoke of the abolition of the Ld. Lieutenancy; to which she is opposed, but she gave no reason except the objections of the Dublin tradesmen. I told her I was in favour of abolition. She said it would never do for it to be a settled arrangement that one of the Royal family should go over every year to hold a court. This would only be perpetuating the distinction between the three Kingdoms in another form. She spoke with much dislike of the Irish character, tho' she admitted the great and faithful services of the Irish soldiers.

As we returned in the Railway I had a long talk with Cardwell. He thinks the R. Catholics in Ireland are better inclined to Govt. than they were. Monsell[351] he considers their leader now, and he says Monsell saved the Gt. on the Ashantee vote. Buchanan had his audience on going to Petg. which he don't like at all.

2 November 1864.   Wednesday. A long interview with Ld. Clarendon at Grosvenor Crescent. He gave me some curious details as to his

---

[349] Maziere Brady (1796–1871), Irish ld. chanc., 1846–52, 1853–8, 1859–24 July 1866.
[350] Sir John Bernard Burke (1814–92).
[351] William Monsell (1812–94), Lib. MP for Limerick, 1847–74; v.p. b. of t. and paym.-genl., 1866–8; u.-sec. col., 1868–70; post.-genl., 1871–3; cr. Baron Emly, 1874.

acceptance of the Ld. Lieutenancy in 1846. The D. of Bedford was named for the post but his reluctance was so great that Ld. C. from actual pity for him consented to give up his office of Bd. of Trade & go to Ireland.

5 November 1864.   Saturday. Took my leave of the India Office; my actual tenure of the Under Secretaryship terminated on Tuesday the day of my Patent being signed. Julian Fane told me a curious story of Morny. An English speculator on hearing that Florence was to be the next capital of Italy sent a telegram to buy up all the house property for sale at Florence; answer the D. de Morny had bought up everything a week before.

6 November 1864.   Sunday. Walked with de Grey. He wants information about Greer brothers the late M.P. for Devon, & Presbyterian Assembly with reference to vacancies of army chaplaincies, Hibernian school, clothing of Police. Told me that the Archbp. of Armagh's[352] plan for transferring revenues of rich to poor livings and otherwise reforming Irish Church was backed by Pam but opposed by the rest of the Min: especially Gladstone, & so fell to the ground.

7 November 1864.   Monday. To Holyhead.

8 November 1864.   Tuesday. To Kingstown in a special steamer, made my public entry into Dublin. Busily engaged all this week in receiving the various addresses of congratulation, the heads of departments, and in establishing ourselves at the Viceregal Lodge.[353]

16 November 1864.   Wednesday. Played my first game of rackets. Saw I. the Agent for elections. Our prospects are not bright. He thinks the Catholics as bitter against us as ever.

17 November 1864.   Thursday. A long morning at the Dublin society's Exhibn. Dined with Sir G. Brown.[354] Yesterday after dinner here Archp. Trench[355] touched on the national education question. He is I fear bitter with the denominational idea. He seems a heavy awkward man.

---

[352] Joseph Dixon (1806–66), archbp. of Armagh, 1852–66.
[353] In his memoir, Wodehouse recounted the absurdity of the lord lieutenant riding into Dublin all booted and spurred, as if spontaneously assuming the office. See Kimberley memoir, herein, 491.
[354] Sir George Brown (1790–1865), fought in the Peninsular War and Crimea; lt.-genl., 1851; commdr.-in-chief, Ireland, 1860–5.
[355] Richard Chenevix Trench (1807–86), archbp. of Dublin, 1864–84.

Of the men I have seen Larcom[356] & Graves[357] please me most, the former a thoroughly practical, able permanent servant of Govt; the latter that rare phenomenon a liberal clergyman. Sir G. Brown is fine old soldier.

18 November 1864. Friday. The Duke of Leinster[358] & others came with address from the Agricultural Society.

24 November 1864. Thursday. Deputations daily. They are unmercifully but deservedly quizzed by the London newspapers. Ld. Leitrim[359] called to day, full of his grievances against Ld. Carlisle & the police. Dined with the Ld. Mayor.[360] Made a speech which I think was successful. I was very well received. Peel made rather too party a speech. The chief of the MacSwineys was magnificent as Ld. Mayor. I was pleased to see so many R. Catholic priests present. Dr. Russell[361] the head of Maynooth to whom I was introduced made a very favourable impression on me. A calm benevolent looking ecclesiastic.

25 November 1864. Friday. A command night at the Theatre.[362] The audience enthusiastic. Some 'Fenian' hisses when 'God save the Queen' was played but drowned in cheers by the well-disposed.

26 November 1864. Saturday. Long talk with Peel about drainage Question. Agreed to recommend Govt. to advance money for the arterial drainage.[363] A tiresome fussy little man named Vesey Fitz-Gerald[364] bored me to death with his impertinent talk.

[356] Sir Thomas Aiskew Larcom (1801–79), maj.-genl., 1858; perm. u.-sec. for Ireland, 1853–68. On Wodehouse's favourable estimate of Larcom, see Wodehouse to deGrey, 7 Dec. 1864, in *Liberal by Principle*, 99–100.
[357] Charles Graves (1812–99), dean of Castle Chapel, 1860; dean of Clonfert, 1864; pres. of Royal Irish Academy, 1861; bp. of Limerick, 1866–99.
[358] Augustus Frederick Fitzgerald, 3rd Duke of Leinster (1791–1874), premier lord of Ireland.
[359] William Sydney Clements, 3rd Earl of Leitrim (1806–78). On Leitrim's notoriety as a disreputable landlord, see Wodehouse to deGrey, 11 Feb. 1865, RP 43522, f. 31; E.D. Steele, *Irish Land and British Politics* (Cambridge, 1974), 72.
[360] Peter Paul McSwiney, Lord Mayor of Dublin.
[361] Chalres William Russell (1812–80), pres. of Maynooth College from 1857.
[362] Theatre Royale.
[363] For an account of the recommendations, see Wodehouse to Grey, 8 Dec. 1864, in *Liberal by Principle*, 101–2.
[364] William Robert Seymour Vesey-Fitzgerald (1817–85), Lib.-Cons. MP for Horsham, 1852–65, 1874–5.

28 November 1864. Monday. To Lord Castlerosse's[365] at Killarney where we stayed till Thursday. Dr. Moriarty[366] the R.C. Bp. of Kerry dined with us on Monday; a quiet sensible man who pleased me much. He has the reputation of being the only moderate man amongst the R.C. prelates.

Lord Cloncurry[367] & his wife staying in the House. He a thorough Tory, hating Popery & Whigs as authors of all evil, but a cheery genial kind of man; she very handsome. James O'Connell,[368] the brother of the Liberator also dined; an honest looking old Irish Squire. We went out shooting both days, but found few woodcocks.

2 December 1864. Friday. Went to the Exhibition to a Christy's Minstrels Performance, a vulgar affair which it was a mistake on my part to patronize.

3 December 1864. Saturday. Macdonnell[369] a keen sharp man the Head of the Educn. Bd. dined here, & Brewster,[370] genial & pleasant as ever.

5 December 1864. Monday. To the Philharmonic Concert; a dismal business.

6 December 1864. Tuesday. Saw Donelly[371] the Registrar Genl., an intelligent man; and Gregory[372] M.P. for Galway about his report on the Dublin institutions.

7 December 1864. Wednesday. Mr. Reynolds the late poplin manufacturer called here with his son who wants to be made a Resident Magistrate. He is now a Clerk in the Constabulary. Made no promises, but said he should be considered with others.

10 December 1864. Saturday. Went over the Hibernian school. A clean well-arranged establishment. The boys look happy and well cared for.

---

[365] Valentine Augustus Browne, Lord Castlerosse (1825–1905), cr. 4th Earl of Kenmare, 1871.
[366] David Moriarty (1814–77). Bitterly opposed Home Rule and all movements against the government.
[367] Edward Lawless, 3rd Baron Cloncurry (1816–69).
[368] Sir James O'Connell (1786–1872). On Wodehouse's regard for O'Connell, see Wodehouse to Russell, 1 Oct. 1865, RiP 30/22/15f, ff. 8–9.
[369] Alexander Macdonnell (1794–1875), resident com. of the bd. of ed. 1839–71.
[370] Abraham Brewster (1796–1874), Irish ld. chanc., 1867–8. On Wodehouse's high opinion of Brewster, see Wodehouse to Larcom, 2 Aug. 1866, LcP 7694.
[371] William Donelly (1804–79).
[372] William Henry Gregory (1817–92), Lib.-Cons. MP for Galway Co., 1857–72.

12 December 1864. Monday. Went over the museum of Irish Industry, presided over by Sir R. Kane,[373] which corresponds in some measure to the Geological Museum in Jermyn Street.

14 December 1864. Wednesday. Henry came on a visit. Went to Dublin Society's fat cattle show. Some fair beasts but nothing very good.

16 December 1864. Friday. Johnny arrived from school.

20 December 1864. Tuesday. Distributed prizes at Hibernian School. Made a short speech which was tolerably successful.[374] The boys looked nice, sung well, & cheered in capital style. Went the same day to Moore Abbey.

21 December 1864. Wednesday. Shot in the woods near the House. In the evening theatricals Everard[375] & S. & F. Ponsonby admirable.[376] Lady Ormonde a visitor, pleased me much. She is still very handsome, & seems a clever woman.

22 December 1864. Thursday. Shot a large number of rabbits & 21 cocks. A ball in the evening. Drogheda[377] & his wife are good natured hospitable people but their mode of living is dirty and uncomfortable. Lord & Lady Erne,[378] two very stiff old people, & Ld. & Lady Cloncurry were there.

23 December 1864. Friday. Returned to the Lodge.

24 December 1864. Saturday. Distributed prizes in Art Department of the Dublin Society. The usual busybodies in bald heads and white sticks[?]–smirking prize winners–a speech from Dt. E. &c.[379] Truly buncombe reigns paramount here.

---

[373] Sir Robert Kane (1809–90), pres. of Queen's College, Cork, 1845–73; dir. Museum of Irish Industry from 1846.

[374] 'There is no lesson more necessary than this', Wodehouse observed from experience, 'that you should not be discouraged, but persevere, and you may be assured that the reward will come at last ... some attain distinction early, while others that have risen but slowly, attain that distinction afterwards.' KP6 MS.eng.b.2408, f. 13.

[375] Captain Walling Everard, a.d.c. in waiting; eventually asst. priv. sec. to Wodehouse.

[376] Probably Spencer Ponsonby, entered FO, 1840; priv. sec. to Palmerston, 1846–51, to Granville, 1851–2, to Clarendon, 1852–7; and his elder brother, Frederick Ponsonby, who succ. as 6th Earl of Bessborough in 1880.

[377] Henry Francis Seymour, 3rd Marquis of Drogheda (1825–92).

[378] John Critchton, 3rd Earl of Erne (1802–85).

[379] George Woods Maunsell complained of the recent withdrawal of government subsidies to the Society. KP6 MS.eng.b.2408, f. 14.

28 December 1864. Tuesday. Dined with Ld. Chancellor. An atrociously bad dinner.

30 December 1864. Thursday. The meeting called by the mayor McSwiney at the Rotundo to form a new Assocn. went off very tamely & peacably. I had great doubts as to the propriety of attending some private theatricals at the Mansion House this evening. I accepted the invitation before the day of the meeting was fixed, and it looked very like a trap laid by McSwiney.

However after consultation with the Chancellor and Attorney Genl.[380] who were both asked to the theatricals & Lawson[381] & Larcom, it was decided that I shld. go. I have no doubt the decision we came to was right as to have excused ourselves wd. have given far too much importance to the meeting. A captain Elphinstone who was to act first lover thought differently & called off very unfairly at the last moment, alleging objections on the part of his father M.P. for Portsmouth.[382] However another lover was procured at short notice, and the theatricals went off very well.

31 December 1864. Saturday. F. Ponsonby came for a night on his way to London. Thus ends 1864, an eventful year, as far as concerns me. I have much reason to be contented, and happy. I wish I could be more active & energetic, & use better the opportunities so largely given me for doing useful work.

I omitted to mention that an influential deputation Latouche,[383] Guinness,[384] Codd,[385] & others representing the Grand Canal Company, the Dublin Chamber of Commerce, and the Limerick Chamber of Commerce waited on me to-day to remonstrate against any interference with the Shannon Navigation. McKerlie was present.

2 January 1865. Monday. Sir R. Griffith[386] came. We had a long talk about drainage, buildings and valuations.

[380] Thomas O'Hagan (1812–85), Irish atty.-genl., 1861–3, Feb. 1865; Irish ld. chanc., 1868–74, 1880–1.

[381] James Anthony Lawson (1817–87), sol.-genl., 1861–5; atty.-genl., 1865–6; Lib. MP for Portarlinton, 1865–8; justice of the common pleas, Ireland, 1868–72; Irish Church com., 1869.

[382] Sir James Dalrymple-Horn-Elphinstone (1805–86), Lib.-Cons. MP for Portsmouth, 1857–65, 1868–80.

[383] William Digges LaTouche, ch. Grand Canal Company.

[384] Benjamin Lee Guinness (1798–1868), brewer and restorer of St. Patrick's Cathedral, 1860–5; cons. MP for Dublin, 1865–8.

[385] Francis Codd, sec. Dublin Chamber of Commerce.

[386] Richard John Griffith (1784–1878), ch. bd. of wks., 1850–64.

John Ball also called & announced that his father[387] meant to resign his Judgeship shortly. Note I have made no bargain with him, nor promise that I will appoint the Judge's son, the registrar to be Resident Magistrate. Now that he has resigned unconditionally, I may consider favourably his wishes. Dined with literary Club.

4 January 1865. Wednesday. Saw Captain Whitly, the very able & intelligent director of Prizes. Mr. Joynt called; talked about drainage. He is in favour of charter to Catholic University. Told him to sound cautionary as to giving the Queen's University powers like those of the London University.

5 January 1865. Thursday. To Meath Hospital Function– opening of Smyley ward. Speech &c. &c. The new children's ward interested me much.

6 January 1865. Friday. Went over Mountjoy Prisons. Male & female. On plan of Pentonville, well managed comfortable establishments. Women only allowed by doctors to be in separate confinement 4 months! Sleep–1/2 past 8 to 7, for winter; to 5 summer. Singular fact. Irish convict women break out less than English. Separate confinement men–9 months, if good conduct. What is to be done with life sentence convicts? Whitly suggests some separate settlement in some island near home.

7 January 1865. Saturday. I enter on my 40th year. If I am spared another two years may I pass it better than the last two.

9 January 1865. Monday. Interview with the Chancellor who presses me to recommend O'Hagan to succeed Ball.

10 January 1865. Tuesday. Long interview with the Attorney General, as to his claims to be made Judge. A most perplexing business. Wrote to Ld. P. recommending O'Hagan; but with misgivings.

11 January 1865. Wednesday. Went over Heytesbury Refuge for Protestant female Convicts, and Smithfield Intermediary Prison. At the latter met Organ;[388] had long talk with him; he anticipates no difficulty in working supervision of convicts. Two (the first to be supervised under

---

[387] John Thomas Ball (1815–98), judge of the Consistorial Court until his resig. in 1865; sol.-genl. Ireland, 1868; atty.-genl. Ireland, 1868, 1874–5; Cons. MP for Dublin University, 1868–75,when he was appointed Irish ld. chanc., 1875–80.
[388] Inspector of Released Convicts.

the new system) have just notified themselves from England. The refuge is very small as there are only on an average 45 Protestant female Convicts in Ireland. Eight there when I went to see it.

12 January 1865. Thursday. To Miss Kirwan's remarkable convent Refuge for F. Convicts at Golden bridge. About 60 there. Mrs. Kirwan, a Sister of Mercy, & superior of the whole of the Dublin Convents manages this with other Sisters of Mercy. She is a lady of good family in Galway & undertook this benevolent work in pursuance of a vow made in sickness. She borrowed £5000 to build. The women under no restraint outwardly. Only two escapes. No *recidives* allowed. I was much pleased & interested. The women executing contract for 10,000 army shirts. Mrs. K. says they are very ignorant when they come. She selects them from Mountjoy. Many emigrate, & do well. Those staying at home not so well. Wants gratuities maintained for emigration. At Heytesbury Refuge it is thought that the gratuities are too large.

18 January 1865. Wednesday. Sent for the Chancellor to speak to him about the Registrarship of Judgments; a nice little job which he was about to perpetrate quite quietly. His son (a questionable character) was to be made Registrar without waiting for the decision of the Treasury on the proposed consolidation of the office with the Registrarship of Deeds.

19 January 1865. Thursday. A most tiresome man, a Sir Malby Crofton, bored me for an hour with his sorrows on account of not being made Dep: Lt. for Sligo.

20 January 1865. Friday. Went over the Exhibition building which promises to be very handsome & useful.[389] Johnny went back to Eton.

21 January 1865. Saturday. A Council.

22 January 1865. Sunday. A very sharp frost. We skated on Viceregal Pond.

23 January 1865. Monday. Visited the 'Mater Misericordia' Hospital, a noble institution lately built by the Sisters of Mercy.

25 January 1865. Wednesday. Moved into the Castle.

26 January 1865. Thursday. Lord Mayor's dinner; a horribly tedious

[389] See entry for 6 May 1865.

affair; a vile dinner and tiresome speeches which lasted from 7 to 10 o'clock! It was appropriately wound up by a drunken speech from Butt[390] M.P. for Youghal. Skating every day this week. Sunday a complete thaw. On Saturday to museum of Irish industry, where I made a speech.

30 January 1865. Monday. Long talk with Peel who seems more pacified now about O'Hagan's appt.– We agreed that there should be no superannuations for medical officers, on the ground that there is no good reason for different systems in Ireland & England; that there should be a bill for carrying out the recommendations of the Belfast Commissioners i.e. for extending constabulary to Belfast as at Cork; that there should be no new Irish peer created as there are now three extinctions of pre-Union peerages–whichever way the law is, the H. of Lords guided by the Tories would surely reject any Peer created on the ground of a post Union extinction; that on the grounds stated in Hancock's able report there shall be no grant proposed for poor Law schoolmasters or medical officers, and that I shall write to Granville strongly opposing the amalgamation of the Museum of Irish Industry with the Royal Dublin Society. In the afternoon to Molyneux Blind Asylum a very good Protestant blind asylum managed by Lady Campbell. Cost per head about £18 per annum.

31 January 1865. Tuesday. My first Levee; well attended.

1 February 1865. Wednesday. My first drawing room–a prodigious labour. I kissed 570 ladies. Some of the affectionate creatures kissed me![391]

2 & 3 February 1865. Thursday and Friday. On each day a dinner of 50 persons. Hard work. On Friday went over Trinity College. Some very curious old MS. in the Library. Two bibles I saw said to be 1000 yrs. old, beautifully illuminated.

7 February 1865. Tuesday. Our first ball which went off very well. Heard to day of the mysterious disappearance of Elinor.[392]
  During this week I went to the Irish Academy, & to see St Patrick's Cathedral; also over the Kildare St. Club.

---

[390] Isaac Butt (1813–79), prof. of pol. econ., Trinity College, Dublin; MP for Youghal, 1852–65; defended Fenian prisoners, 1865–8; MP for Limerick, 1871–9; founder of Irish Home Rule party, 1870–9.
  [391] On Lady Wodehouse's distaste for the drawing room, see R. A. J. Walling, *The Diaries of John Bright* (New York, 1931), 325.
  [392] See entry for 17 Feb. 1865.

14 February 1865. Tuesday. Went over Charlemont House with Ld. Charlemont,[393] a curious old House with fine Library (1st Folio Shakespeare, 1st ed. Ariosto & some valuable MS. Irish), and a few good pictures. Several admirable Hogarths, splendid busts of the first Pitt, & of Ld. Chesterfield by Wilton.[394] Saw two of the flags of the Volunteers. Ld. C. is about to sell the house. It is in a dilapidated state not having been inhabited for 60 years; but it is an historical relic I should be loth to give up were I the owner.

15 February 1865. Wednesday. Went for a night to Castle Forbes. Lord Granards. Lady G. a nice little woman with £8000 a year, which has quite set Lord G on his legs.

The excitement of the people at Mullingar to see me was wonderful. One would think that Westmeath instead of being one of the most disaffected was the most loyal Co. in Ireland. Ld. Granard's village Newtown Forbes was full of People & illuminated.

16 February 1865. Thursday. We had some very pretty woodcock shooting. I killed 5 couple out of 15 1/2 couple.

17 February 1865. Friday. Returned to Dublin last night; found a letter from F. Cavendish announcing that Elinor certainly eloped with Lord C. Gordon, & that he is taking steps for a divorce. Her conduct is as inexplicable as disgraceful.[395]

20 February 1865. Monday. Went to Kilruddery, a charming place of Lord Meath's near Bray to shoot. Killed 8 woodcocks, the whole bag 16.

In the evening to a conversazione of physicians, a curious proceeding, the reverse of amusing.

21 February 1865. Tuesday. Levee–happily a small one.

22 February 1865. Wednesday. Drawing room.

23 February 1865. Thursday. Dined with the Archibishop, a dinner in honour of Mr. Guinness.[396]

---

[393] James Molyneux Caulfield (1820–92), Lib. MP for Co. Armagh, 1847–57; succ. as 3rd Earl of Charlemont, 1863.

[394] Joseph Wilton (1722–1803), sculptor to George III.

[395] See entry for 2 March 1866.

[396] See entry for 31 Dec. 1864

24 February 1865.   Friday. To the opening of St Patrick's a fine ceremony but the Archbishop's sermon was wholly inaudible where we sat.

27 February 1865.   Monday. To Marlborough Street Schools. Very 'smart' looking schools. The boys principally I was told children of small tradesmen. The first class answered wonderfully cleverly.

2 March 1865.   Thursday. Went to Lord Powerscourt[397] where we shot 13 fallow deer in his beautiful deer park.

6 March 1865.   Monday. Sir H. Brownrigg[398] came to me to announce his resignation. He was much overcome, & shed tears. A regular and efficient policeman; he has done his work honestly & well, as far as the discipline and management of his force goes, but he has alienated the magistracy, made his force unpopular, and his retirement is an advantage to the public service, especially at this moment when a Parliamentary inquiry is threatened. He put his retirement entirely on the ground of health.

7 March 1865.   Tuesday. Poor Mr. Senior[399] killed by a railway train. His own headstrong obstinacy seems to have been the cause of the catastrophe. He was an able man & is a loss to the public service.

8 March 1865.   Wednesday. Went in the evening to the Young Men's Xtian Association to hear a lecture on the English languages by Archp. Trench. The lecture was able but ill-delivered; the proceedings altogether singular. They began with prayers and a hymn, then the lecture then, a speech from me, then the doxology & the blessing. I confess I thought the mixture a strange one. There was a Fenian or two in the Gallery who called out how about the Irish language. Perhaps the prayers were useful as preventing the unseemly disturbance common to all Irish assemblies.

9 March 1965. Thursday. A visit from Alderman Reynolds. This vulgar noisy & pretentious, but clever man wants Senior's place!

11 March 1865.   Saturday. A Deputation from the Ballast Board to state their apprehensions that Kingstown may becomome a great commercial Port and supplant Dublin. Their arguments seemed to me fallacious. I said that nothing could be done at present as the case apprehended

---

[397] Mervyn Wingfield, 7th Viscount Powerscourt (1836–1904).
[398] Henry J. Brownrigg, insp.-genl. of the constabulary since the 1840s.
[399] Irish poor law com.; brother of Nassau W. Senior.

had not arisen. When it did arise, I would fairly consider anything they had to urge. McKerlie, & Lefanu were present. I forgot to mention that on Thursday we had private theatricals at Charlemont House. Lady C. as Peg Woffington really acted admirably specially in the pathetic scene. Burn also excellent in Betsy Baker. Lady Rachel B.[400] I thought rather a failure. Albert W.[401] & Harbord[402] as footmen, and Walmsley as a black page inimitable.

13 March 1865. Monday. In daily communication with Mr. Power the P.L. Commissioner on the difficult point of filling up Senior's place. Peel happily consents to R. Catholic but who is to be the man?

14 March 1865. Tuesday. Dined at Catch Club. Too long an affair to be pleasant.

My lady went to the opera which she says was good. Norma. Titien & c. The first night we went it was absurdly bad. The tenor in dumb show in Lucrezia Borgia, diversified with hideous cries & songs from the Gallery between the Acts. One would have supposed the audience to have been savages just caught.

17 March 1865. Friday. St Patrick's day. The Castle Grand scene went off very peacefully, and 'dully'. The ball in the evening was very well attended, & the company universally decorous. So ends the 'Castle Season'.

19 March 1865. Monday. A numerous deputation from the Corporation of Dublin &c. on the Catholic oath. I gave them a cautious answer.

20 March 1865. Tuesday. Went with my lady to the Criminal Lunatic Asylum at Dundrum, a clean cheerful house. We saw numerous murderers– a captain of a ship who murdered 7 seamen, a man who cut his mother's head off &c. on the whole they looked quiet but excessively villainous. The presence of my lady it was said calmed them, as they behaved better than usual. One woman I saw with her hands tied. She had throttled one woman in the asylum, & has a marked homicidal mania, a propensity to throttling– O'Dell the barrister who shot the bailiff lately was there–a dirty depressed looking man. The belief is that he is now quite sane but was perhaps mad when he committed the murder from excessive drink.

---

400 Lady Rachel Butler.
401 Albert J. Wodehouse, a.d.c.
402 Hon. Ralph Harbord (1833–78), 6th son of 3rd Baron Suffield.

21 March 1865. Wednesday. To some amateur theatricals at the Queen's theatre, bad on the whole even for amateurs.

22 March 1865. Thursday. Moved to the Lodge, to our great joy— I have at last settled the appointments consequent on Senior's death and Brownrigg's retirement. Flanigan would have been a better working man than Bellew but the latter is a moderate man who will not give trouble.[403]

28 March 1865. Monday. Marcus Brownrigg the new Asst. Inspector General called on me. He is a sharp clever policeman.

29 March 1865. Tuesday. To the R. Hibernian Academy; very few good pictures. Had to buy two pictures of indifferent merit by Irish artists by way of patronizing native art.

30 March 1865. Thursday. At length a warm spring day.

31 March 1865. Friday. Catterson Smith[404] began his portrait of me. Flo: went to London this evening, & had a calm passage.

3 April 1865. Catterson Smith again. Dined with Literary Club; a bad dinner.

8 April 1865. Saturday. Flo: returned with Johnny.

12 April 1865. Wednesday. Poor Bob Williams, my comptroller died of a heart complaint. He was a thorough Welshman; hot, peppery, a good fellow & an honest gentleman.

13 April 1865. Thursday. Petition in favour of Lynch, a parricide in Cork, condemned to death. I never saw a stronger case for capital punishment if there is to be capital punishment in any case. I refused the petition.

14 April 1865. Friday. Kennedy returned yesterday for Louth.[405] This is a disappointment for the Tories.

15 April 1865. Saturday. George Currie came on a visit.

---

[403] Bellew also had recommendations from Palmerston, Russell, Clarendon and Brand. Wodehouse to Grey, 24 March 1865, KP6 MS.eng.c.4023, f. 164.

[404] Stephen Catterson Smith (1806–72), pres. of Royal Hibernian Academy, 1859–64.

[405] Tristram Kennedy (1805–85), Lib. MP for Louth, 1865–8.

19 April 1865. Wednesday. Went to the Dublin Cattle show. In the evening to distribution of prizes. Made a speech. Lord Clancarty & others long & tedious.

20 April 1865. Thursday. To Punchestown races. A charming day, and excellent amusement. On Tuesday that intolerable bore, and empty headed coxcomb Vesey FitzGerald paid me a visit to tell me that he could have returned Mackenna[406] for Tralee but he preferred Mr. O'Donoghue[407] because Mackenna was a low fellow whilst he (V.F.) was 9th in descent from the Earl of Desmond. I told him we cared little for either O'D: or Mack. *Arcades ambo.* He had also returned Kennedy for Louth! &c. &c. &c.

25 April 1865. Monday. To the Glasnevin Gardens. Fine palm houses.

26 April 1865. Tuesday. Amateur play. Plot & Passion. Leeson most absurd as the lover. Lady Charlemont acted very well.

27 April 1865. Wednesday. News arrived of President Lincoln's[408] assassination.

31 April 1865. Saturday. To Maynooth College. The building very handsome that is the new part by Pugin.[409] Accommodation for between 500 & 600 students. Grant £28,000 per ann: Students free except £8.8 entrance fee and clothes: appointed by R.C. Bishop of dioceses to each of which a fixed number of nominations allotted. Dunboyne students £60 per ann: for 3 years. These Dunboyne Studentships founded by a Lord Dunboyne[410] at the beginning of this century. Lord D. was R.C. Bishop of (Cork?) his elder brother dying, he became a peer, abjured R. Catholicism, married, had no children, on his death bed recanted again; & left his property to Maynooth. Will disputed, confessor examined & committed for contempt of court for not revealing death bed confssn. the end a compromise between Maynooth & the heir.

4 May 1865. Thursday. Went to Drogheda to open the Whitworth

---

[406] Joseph Neale MacKenna (1819–1906), Lib. MP for Youghal, July 1865–8, 1874–85; unsucc. contested Tralee, Feb. 1865.

[407] Daniel O'Donoghue (1833–1889), Lib. MP for Tralee, 1865–85.

[408] Abraham Lincoln (1809–65), pres. of US, 1861–5.

[409] Edward Welby Pugin (1834–75), architect noted for extensive work on R.C. cathedrals.

[410] John Butler, by courtesy 12th Lord Dunboyne (1716–1800), R.C. Bishop of Cork, 1763–86; succ. to peerage, 1785.

Hall & turn the sod of the new water-works. The Mayor Matthews[411] a worthy man and a Liberal with Mr. Whitworth[412] took me round the town in an open carriage. The waterworks reservoir is to be about 2 miles from the town. I visited Whitworth's new cotton weaving factory. It will employ 600 hands. The work will be weaving coarse cotton shirting for India & China. I had much talk with Whitworth a shrewd Lancashire manufacturer who drops his h's and speaks with a Lancashire burr. His father came from England to Drogheda many years ago as a merchant: failed & became clerk of the Bd. of Guardians.

Young Whitworth was brought up but not born at Drogheda. He has made a very large fortune in Lancashire. He told me the wages of factory workers (of whom there are about 1200 now making coarse linen fabrics) were not more than four shillings a week at Drogheda on an average! At Manchester the same labour cost 13/– to 16/– per week. He predicts a scarcity of hands in the English cotton districts; hence the advantage of resorting to Irish labour.

The dampness of the climate in Ireland he said was a sensible advantage in cotton weaving and the absence of frost. Coal can be supplied at Drogheda at 15/– or 16/–, and every year economy of fuel is greater.

Many Manchester men had come over & were present at the luncheon in the Whitworth Hall where of course I made a speech. There were large but orderly crowds and I was very well recd. The Whitworth Hall is a sort of Mechanics Hall which Mr. W. has built at his own expense & presented to the town. The site was given by Mr St George Smith an old man more than 80 years of age a Tory formerly a fierce opponent in local matters of Whitworth's father. Dr. Dixon the R.C. Primate was at the luncheon, a quiet amiable unaffected looking man–also Ld. Gormanston[413] & Lord Athlumney.[414] Altogether it was a very satisfactory day.

5 May 1865. Friday. Catterson Smith finished my portrait after 16 sittings. It seems to me very successful.

6 May 1865. Saturday. Arranged with Colonel Lake that every possible precaution should be taken to protect the Prince during his visit here.[415]

[411] Joseph Matthews.
[412] Benjamin Whitworth (1816–93), Lib. MP for Drogheda, July 1865–9, 1880–5, for Kilkenny city, 1875–80.
[413] Edward Anthony John Preston, 13th Viscount Gormanston (1796–1876).
[414] Sir William Meredyth Somerville, Baron Athlumney (Irish), Baron Meredyth (UK) (1802–73), ch. sec. Ireland, 1847–52.
[415] During the International Exhibition of Arts and Manufactures, which opened in Dublin on 9 May.

At all times there is some ground for precaution here, but especially just now after the murder of Lincoln. Such crimes are contagious.

7 May 1865. The Fenians attempted a mass meeting at Clontarf– a wretched failure but neither the police nor constabulary was as much on the alert as I would wish–

Yesterday I heard of a squabble between Peel & Gladstone about the Belfast Bill which the Treasury insist at the last moment on mutilating. It seems they had high words in the H. of Commons. The fact is the Treasury is overbearing & encroaching & Peel has no tact or discretion. I have poured a can of oil on the troubled waters.

We went to Church at St Werberg's today for a charity. St Werberg's is the parish Church of the Castle and this is an annual function to get money for St. Werberg's schools. The Ld. Lt. draws!

8 May 1865. Monday. An agony of preparation for the Prince of Wales. I think all will go off well, notwithstanding anonymous threats and warnings. The Prince arrived this afternoon. We went to meet him at Kingstown, the Chancellor, Sir George Brown, and most of the members of my household. I was in plain clothes. My lady received the Prince at the door. In the evening we had a ball and a small evening party.

9 May 1865. Tuesday. Opening of Exhibition. The crowds in the streets received the Prince on the whole well, but far from enthusiastically. There was a good deal of hissing. Some people ascribed this to our being in close carriages, but yesterday when we passed through the town in open carriages from the Westland Row Station I heard quite as much hissing. The close carriages were unavoidable, as we went in state. Besides we should have run the risk of rain, and have had our uniforms covered with mud in an open carriage. The ceremony of the opening was really fine, and very well managed. In the evening we had a large dinner, and then went to the Lord Mayor's Ball, which was one of those ridiculous entertainments which newspaper writers call magnificent because five times as many people were asked as could stand comfortably in the rooms. The self complacency of the Lord Mayor[416] (who is a harmless well-meaning Quaker) was most amusing. He asked, it is said, 2500 people. Many of the guests were three or four hours in the street on their way to the Ball, some never arrived at all.

10 May 1865. Wednesday. Review in the Phoenix Park at 3 o'clock.

[416] Sir John Barrington.

Immense masses of spectators. Some discontent was caused by an erroneous announcement in a newspaper that the review was to be at 11 o'clock. It had been settled a week ago that 3 should be the hour, but of course the newspapers ascribed the careless blunder to 'officials'– any one but themselves. Probably more ridiculous mistakes are made by newspaper writers and correspondents than by any other class of men existing. It is very funny to hear them prate of their infallibility.

The Prince was better received at the review than on any other occasion, and as he left the ground there was some enthusiasm shown. I heard that one of the 5th Dragoon Guards who was keeping the ground, hearing a man hiss said, 'I'll teach you to hiss you ──' and gave him several blows in the face with the hilt of his sword.

We dined afterwards with Sir G. Brown.

11 May 1865. Thursday. We went in open carriages to see the Exhibition in the morning and to St Patrick's Cathedral. The people of whom there were a good many assembled at some points received the Prince, especially at St Patrick's Cathedral. The mob there was rather uproarious in their greeting, and I was glad when we got away from them. In the evening we had a ball at the Lodge.

12 May 1865. Friday. To Powerscourt in open carriages and afterwards to Kingstown where we dined on board the yacht & took leave of the Prince. My horses fearfully done up. They went nearly 40 miles with but little rest. Two I was obliged to leave a night at Kingstown.

The general impression left on my mind by the Prince is that he is very self indulgent, and un-intellectual, but that he has a sound understanding and is kindly disposed to those with whom he comes in contact. He spoke sensibly of Ireland, & seems to wish to conciliate the Irish. At times he has something of the sullenness of his father but he is generally lively & talks with some animation. I am sure a Royal visit here is productive of much good. The Prince of Leiningen who came in command of the Royal Yacht seems an amiable soft sort of man. H.R.H. of Cambridge who was also here was in great good humour, & very obliging & kind throughout the business. We took every precaution as regards detectives &c. but nothing unpleasant occurred, and the visit certainly passed off on the whole much to my satisfaction.

In the evening after the Prince's departure we went to a ball for the Academy of Music in the Exhibition Building, a cold and comfortless but according to the newspaper scribes most 'brilliant' entertainment. The weather bad throughout the week.

14 May 1865. Sunday. Johnny went back to Eton.

15 May 1865. Monday. To Howth Races. We were caught in a tremendous hail storm just as we arrived on the ground. The hail stones as big as marbles.

17 May 1865. Wednesday. To Trinity College sports. A pretty sight. Crowds of people.

19 May 1865. Friday. A command night for Wigan. Mrs. Wigan excellent in the poor nobleman. The audience civil & loyal. No hisses when 'God save the Queen' was played, which is very unusual here. Mr. McGee[417] called on me to day. His history is curious. He was deeply concerned in the rebel folly of 1848, was Editor of the 'Nation', emigrated to the U. S., was four years editor of a paper there, left the U.S. for Canada, & is now a very loyal subject of the Queen, member for Montreal & Minister of Agriculture. He has come over here as Commissioner to the Dublin Exhibition, but his visit to London has for its object to arrange in conjunction with other Canadian delegates the terms of the proposed North American Colonial Confederacy. He thinks notwithstanding the opposition of New Brunswick the Confederacy will be established. At all events he said (& I quite agree with him) Canada cannot long remain as she is. Either she must form a Confederacy with the other colonies or be annexed to the U. S.

Mr. McGee has just made an excellent speech at Wexford, his native town, on Irish affairs, and we had a long talk on Irish matters. He thinks Dublin improving, but has not seen enough of the country generally to express an opinion as to its condition. The continuance of the emigration he deems inevitable.

His political views were as follows. Irish patriots must accept the Union as an accomplished fact & endeavour to work out the Irish problem by constitutional means. I asked him whether the question of the abolition of the Established Church exerted much interest amongst the mass of the Irish Catholics. He said no; that the education question was more urgent. In his opinion some change must be made in the national school system. He instanced Upper Canada where it had been found necessary to grant the R. Catholics the liberty to have denominational schools, supported by the State. The result he stated had not been prejudicial to the common schools; on the contrary it had the effect of preventing proselytism in those schools, as they had to compete with the exclusively Catholic schools for popular favour, and in many cases the Catholics preferred the common school. He

---

[417] Thomas D'arcy McGee (1825–68), member of Montreal assembly, 1858–62; pres. counc., 1864. Assassinated 7 April 1868. On Wodehouse's particular interest in the McGee case, see extensive newscuttings in KP6 MS.eng.d.2447.

anticipated the same results from such a change (if made) in Ireland.

Could he, I asked, suggest any plan for reconciling the Irish to England? He replied that a Commission composed of eminent Irishmen to enquire & report generally what changes in the law are necessary might perhaps do good. The Fenians were also discussed. He said their numbers & influence in Canada were greatly exaggerated. He does not regard their conspiracy as really formidable.

The danger to peace in the U.S. would arise, he said, from that part of the army (150,000 men by his reckoning) recruited from the large towns. The men from the land states would be soon absorbed in the population. Mr. McGee is a R. Catholic–a thorough Celt in appearance, but has not much brogue.

23 May 1865. Tuesday. Went to charades at the Attorney Generals. Very hot, but clever acting by Mr. Lawse.

24 May 1865. Wednesday. Celebration of The Queen's Birthday. Review in the morning which I attended, & large dinner to official people.

25 May 1865. Thursday. Attended a ridiculous function called a conversazione for St Vincent de Paul's charity.

26 May 1865. Friday. A cricket match between Birkenhead & Viceregal Club won by latter in one innings.

30 May 1865. Tuesday. Went with Mr. Murray to Lusk farm. A very talkative agricultural superintendent. Mr Gallagher showed us over. The men sleep associated in a corrugated iron hut, no police protection. Some 50 or 60 men working at drainage and agriculture, all convicts no convict dress. Of 1400 men who have passed thro' this establishment only six have absconded. The drainage work is severe, the land being a wet moor. The soil good however & grows fine crops, no notice had been given of our visit and the establishment was in every respect in good working order.

31 May 1865. Wednesday. Received deputations from the College of Physicians, the Dublin University, & the Queen's Univ: praying me to order reconsideration of the order of the Poor Law Board, admitting Irish Apothecaries to poor law medical appointments. Long argument with Dr Corrigan, Dr Bently, Dr Stokes &c.– Corrigan is a clever arrogant man. I pulled him up more than once. They maintained that the apothecaries' examination is a farce, and that the 'order' will provide cheap & bad doctors for the poor. The fact is the physicians have got a monopoly in Ireland, and naturally want to keep it. The 'general practitioner' so useful & universal in England is unknown here. The 'order' will introduce him. I gave its opponents no hope of reconsideration.

In the evening gave a dinner to some of the people connected with the Exhibition. Baron Donnafugate Italian Commissr., (from Sicily) gave a bad account of affairs in Sicily. He says the Sicilians sigh for English Govt. & he fears a counter revolution. They want autonomy under our protection. The very thing the Ionians have just cast away as oppressive. Dr. Adamson the Canadian Commissioner and Dr. Honeyman Nova Scotia also dined. They were very full of their gold discoveries.

That charming old lady Pamela Lady Campbell sat next me. We talked of the Napiers. She said Wm. Napier[418] was not a pleasant man, too overbearing & eaten up with vanity but that Charles[419] was everything that was charming.

1 June 1865. Thursday. Dined with Lord Gough.[420] The old lion seemed uncommonly well, & drank his claret like a man of 30.

2 June 1865. Friday. Went to the Exhibition; and had a long examination of the Canadian Nova Scotian and Indian departments.

5 June 1865. Monday. Sir Hugh Rose[421] came to see me. He looked worn & tired, but not more than I expected after 7 years in India.

7 June 1865. Wednesday. Visited the interesting Reformatory at Glencree. Rode down. Father Lynch who manages the establishment a quiet intelligent but determined looking man. Glencree was formerly a barrack, a station in the rebellion of /98. Peeped also at the lovely Lake of Bray, where Sir P. Crampton[422] built his surgery.

On Tuesday I also inspected the Constabulary Depot in Phoenix Park, very crowded. The Board of Works have managed to combine extravagance, incompleteness, & inconvenience with marvellous skill.

[418] Sir William Francis Napier (1785–1860), fought in Peninsular War; wrote *History of the War in the Peninsula* (6 vols., 1828–40); made general and knighted, 1848.

[419] Sir Charles James Napier (1782–1853), fought in Peninsular War and in US, 1813; maj.-genl., 1837; conquered Sind, 1843; lt.-genl., 1846.

[420] Sir Hugh, 1st Viscount Gough (1779–1869), fought in Peninsular War; maj.-genl., 1830; commdr.-in-ch. in India, from 1843; fld. marshal, 1862.

[421] Sir Hugh Henry Rose (1801–85), served in Crimea and during Indian mutiny; commdr.-in-ch. India, 1860–5; commdr.-in-ch. Ireland, 1865–70; cr. Baron Strathnairn, 1866; genl., 1867; fld. marshal, 1877.

[422] Sir Philip Crampton (1777–1858), surgeon at Meath Hospital from 1798. Lodge on Lake Bray presented for services to the Powerscourt family.

It may be worth while to note that on June 3 I received a Tel: from Sir G. Grey announcing the birth of a Prince.[423] I went to the Ld. Mayor, the Ld. Chancellor & Sir G. Brown informing them. No salute was fired. On the birth of the Pr: Victor a salute was specially ordered from the Horse Gds. None ordered on this occasion.

12 June 1865.   Monday. Long conversation with Col: Wood[424] concerning the Constabulary. The efficient Cy. Inspectors he says are only four! Manby, Duncan, Hill and another. He is naturally sore at the attacks on the Constabulary in Parliament.

Yesterday I answered J. O Taylors's suggestion that E. Wodehouse should be 2nd candidate for E. Norfolk. It would not do. I should be suspected tho' unjustly of having intrigued to get Coke[425] out of the way to put in one of my own family. I should not like that a 'Wodehouse' should play the 2nd fiddle to Buxton's first, and I could not nor could E. W. afford to keep the seat if won. Moreover it is too illiberal a constituency for him and a debut there would embarrass his career.[426]

Mr Abbott the Subdean committed suicide. The cause, poor man, pecuniary losses.

14 June 1865.   Wednesday. With Flo: to Marlborough St. Schools. Examination of teachers to whom I said a few words. They answered well.

15 June 1865.   Thursday. Dined with the Benchers. The first Ld. Lieut: it is said who has done so since Ld. Strafford[427] *−abrit omen.* A fair dinner, many legal lights present, benchers, barristers, attorneys.[428]

17 June 1865.   Saturday. Inspected the Dublin City & Artillery Regiments. They looked well & their Colonel Latouche was worth going a mile to see. A very fat man on a dancing cart-horse.

19 June 1865.   Monday. To Carton on a visit. The party consisted of Ld. & Lady Cloncurry, & Mr Kane besides of course the Duke & Lord & Lady Kildare. The Duke is really the most charming old man

---

[423] George Frederick Ernest Albert, succ. as George V, 1910.

[424] Col. John Stewart Wood, insp. genl. of police.

[425] Wenman Clarence Walpole Coke (1828–1907), Lib. MP for Norfolk E., 1858–65.

[426] Two cons. were elected on 20 July, Edward Howes and Clare Sewell Read. On the 'extraordinary mess' made by the Liberals in both East and West Norfolk, see Robert Gurdon to Wodehouse, Aug. 1865, KP1 3/1.

[427] Sir Thomas Wentworth, 1st Earl Strafford (1593–1641), ld. lt., 1640–1; sent to the Tower and executed.

[428] For the list of 'legal lights', see KP6 MS.Engl.b.2048, f. 52.

I ever met. He talked much of the state of the country which he thinks improving–still he admits that there is a disaffected feeling abroad amongst the people, & he complains that notwithstanding all the money he spends amongst them, their conditon remains very poor. Want of industry & activity– want of perseverance is their character. He is against long leases, says he never knew a lessee for a long term improve his land. They let their interest to midddleman. In 1848 he was unpopular, & the Govt. he told me, tho' he never knew it, ordered a policeman to watch him constantly for fear of an attempt upon him. He is a most excellent landlord, & if a resident FitzGerald can't acquire the affections of this people who can?

Lord Kildare though very shy & retiring is very intelligent & liberal-minded. He told me that Lord Carlisle was much vexed that Lord Palmerston made Trench Abp. of Dublin, he wanted too to make Graves a Bp. Carton is a charming house & place, & we passed two very agreeable days, the weather wonderfully hot.

22 June 1865.   Thursday. Returned home.

23 June 1865.   Friday. A council for revoking the proclamations in Mayo, Galway, & Monaghan.[429]

24 June 1865.   Saturday. Went with Dr. Nugent to visit the Richmond Lunatic Asylum, & the private asylum at Drumcondra kept by the nuns of St Vincent de Paul, and the 'Quaker's Retreat' on the Donnybrook road. The Richmond asylum is the asylum for Dublin Cy. Wicklow, & I think Meath. It was quite full–upwards of 750 patients male & female. In the exercising ground the male lunatics were walking in procession to tunes played by a lunatic band, who played I must say, in indifferent time. Altogether the patients seemed quiet & con-tented. None were in constraint.

The Private asylums were a far sadder sight. Whether the mind is more affected by the spectacle of insane persons belonging to one's own class, or whether patients of the higher classes are more sensitive and excitable or private asylums are less well managed, I can't say, but the patients seemed far more irritable and uneasy, & the general aspect was more saddening than in the public asylum.

At Drumcondra I saw a poor young girl recently admitted running wildly round a yard. They said she never stopped night or day; yet they had more hope of her than of the melancholy cases. I was shown

---

[429] Under provisions of the Peace Preservation Act (19th and 20th Vict., c. 36 (1856)). See Grey to Wodehouse, 21 June 1865; Wodehouse to Grey, 22 June 1865, KP6 MS.eng.c.4027, ff. 82–94.

a lady who fancies herself the Queen. This lady on the occasion of a visit of Lord Carlisle asked to see the Ld. Lieut. On Lord Carlisle being pointed out to her, she said in a loud voice— You're Carlisle– 'I don't want you, you're of no use– send me Clarendon. I want to see Clarendon–' The Quakers' retreat pleased me much more than Drumcondra. There is more space and air & the patients seemed calmer & more composed. Dr Nugent told me that not seldom the keepers of asylums went mad. I am not surprised at it.

26 June 1865. Monday. Gave a dinner to Sir Geo: Brown on his departure. A worthy old man– & fine specimen of a British soldier. Yet he is a martinet and unpopular as a commander. No one would suppose it from his demeanour in private society. He is very sorry to go.

27 June 1865. Tuesday. Went to Adare, Lord Dunraven's[430] and stayed till Friday. The House, a modern one, very handsome, especially a beautiful gallery 120 ft. long. The House has only been finished two or three years. It has been entirely built & furnished with oak carving, carved chimney pieces &c. by workmen of the neighboring village! The ruins of three Abbeys and of the castle of the Desmonds are very curious and perfect. They are close to the house–

I met here Major Gavin[431] and Mr. Russell[432] the two members for Limerick city; the R. C. Bp. of Limerick, Dr. Butler;[433] Moriarty RC Bp. of Kerry; Aubrey de Vere,[434] & the Cloncurries– & Sir Dd. Roche, Sheriff of the Cy. Major Gavin is a heavy man, Russell a rather vulgar but shrewd looking Limerick flax spinner. It is said he may lose his seat for incivility in not replying to his constituents' letters. A. deVere, a clever 'young England' sort of man, a follower of W. Monsell, became a R. Catholic. He is of the sentimental, aesthetical turn of mind which is closely allied to superstition– clever, amiable but priestridden. Very much the same may be said of Ld. Dunraven but he is a harder cast of man. He made strenuous efforts for many years, efforts bordering on persecution to convert wife & family to Popery. To their great credit they have resisted all his endeavours. Lady Dunraven is a clever

[430] Edwin Richard Windham Wyndham-Quin, 3rd Earl of Dunraven and Mount-Earl (Ireland) (1812–71), Cons. MP for Glamorganshire, 1837–51, when he succ. as Irish earl; cr. Baron Kenry (UK), 1866.

[431] George Gavin (1810–80), Lib. MP for Limerick, 1859–74.

[432] Francis William Russell (1800–71), Lib. MP for Limerick, 1852–71.

[433] George Butler (1819–90), vice-princ. of Cheltenham College, 1857–65; princ. of Liverpool College, 1866–82; canon of Winchester from 1882.

[434] Aubrey de Vere (1814–1902), poet and miscellaneous author; reluctantly supported union; convert to R.C., 1871.

woman, & Adare[435] the model of an obstinate man. Constant passive resistance has given him a singular air of stubborness. With all this marvellous to say they remain a united & I believe happy family. The governess turned R. Catholic to curry favour with Ld. Dunraven & was ordered to teach the girl Popery! A priest in the house! altogether a melancholy example of a sensible good hearted man led by superstition & bigotry. Happily he has found the priests too encroaching even for his taste. He told me that the superior of the Franciscans coolly demanded as of right restitution of one of the ruined abbeys to the order. This Lord D. boldly refused. I say boldly, for it is an act of remarkable boldness in a man of his creed & temperament.

I had a long talk with the Bp of Limerick. He was furious against Lord Derby for his speech on the Oaths Bill. He is evidently much more favourable to us and will do all he can for Russell & Gavin in Limerick. He & Lord Dunraven both agreed that the Fenians were increasing in numbers in Limerick both county and city.

30 June 1865. Friday. Returned home. Stopped in Limerick for an hour & drove round the town with the Mayor. It looked rather cleaner I thought than ten years ago, but very little doing in the port. We visited the manufactory of Tait the army clothier, who employs a thousand hands. The work people, chiefly women, looked well dressed & well fed. We also saw poor FitzGibbon's monument on the Bridge. A very graceful statue by Macdowell, with Crimean (Russian) cannon on each side.[436]

3 July 1865. Monday. Saw Professor Sullivan of the R. Catholic Univ:– an intelligent & liberal minded man. He spoke strongly of the importance of strengthening the lay R. Catholic element against the ecclesiastical Body, and contended that we ought for that purpose to encourage the R. C. Univ: which he regards as essentially a lay body. I forgot to mention that on my way from Limerick I went to the town of Tipperary, a poor looking town of one street.

---

[435] Windham Thomas, Wyndham Quin, Lord Adare (1841–1926), succ. his father as 4th Earl of Dunraven, 1871.

[436] Patrick McDowell (1799–1870), sculptor and member of the Royal Academy from 1846; sculpted the European group of the Albert Memorial. By May 1855 more than £1,000 had been raised to erect the statue in memory of John Charles Henry Fitzgibbon, Lady Wodehouse's brother, who had been slain at the Battle of Balaclava while serving with the 8th Hussars. The monument was badly damaged by an IRA bomb in 1929, and replaced with a bronze group commemorating Republicans who fought in the war of independence, 1916–22.

On the controversy surrounding the original placement of the Fitzgibbon monument, see N. Lenihan, *Limerick, its History and Antiquities* (Cork, 1866), 513.

4 July 1865. Tuesday. Saw the oily President of Belfast Q. Coll: who professes himself not adverse to our University policy.

Went to Kilruddery Lord Meath's[437] on a visit till Friday. We met there Mr. Tighe and Lady Louisa Tighe, and Sir Stephen Glyn.[438]

6 July 1865. Thursday. Drove in pouring rain to the 'Seven Churches'– Lord Meath thinks the disaffection amongst the peasantry wide spread. He does not believe they are less disloyal than formerly, only more quiet for want of leaders. He ascribes their disloyalty not to grievances but to the old feeling of hatred to the Saxon, as the conqueror of Ireland. The dissolution of Parliament took place to-day.

8 July 1865. Saturday. The Hibernian School sports cut short by a lamentable accident–a boy killed and three injured by an explosion of fireworks.

10 July 1865. Monday. Drove to Mrs. White's villa at Killakra from which there is a lovely view of the bay of Dublin. Met there the rival candidates for Dublin Cy., Taylor,[439] White,[440] & Hamilton.[441] The first elections took place in London to day.

11 July 1865. Tuesday. To Rehoboth Protesant Reformatory, and the girls [reformatory] in Cork Street– small well managed institutions. Some of the girls looked intelligent and of a decent class; others had a low degraded look, evidently of the true criminal class: but the former predominated.

13 July 1865. Thursday. Sir H. Rose arrived. To day the first polling for Irish boroughs; the Attorney Genl. returned.

Visited the Schools at the Baggot Street Convent of Mercy of which Mrs. Kirwan is supervisor. Very large schools–almost 1000 girls & boys. The monitor class examined in our presence. They had evidently learned by rote a prodigious number of answers to questions but when taken off their own prepared ground they seemed helpless & ignorant. One girl gave the answer to the wrong question, mistaking her turn. The little children looked happy & healthy. The arithmetic of the

---

[437] William Brabazon (1803–87), Whig MP for Dublin Co., 1830–2, 1837–41; succ. as 11th Earl of Meath, 1851.

[438] Stephen Richard Glynne (1807–74), Cons. MP for Flintshire, 1831–47; Gladstone's brother-in-law.

[439] Thomas Edward Taylor (1812–83), Cons. MP for Co. Dublin, 1841–83; parlt. sec. to treas., 1866–8; ch. d. of Lanc., 1868–9, 1874–80.

[440] Charles William White (1838–90), Lib. MP for Tipperary, 1866–75.

[441] Ion Trent Hamilton (1839–98), Cons. MP for Co. Dublin, 1863–85.

monitors seemed very good, and they read well & distinctly. Altogether I should think it was a fair average school. Henry came to day. He is looking well & in good spirits.

15 July 1865. Saturday. The elections still raging in all directions. On the whole they are going well for us, especially in Ireland.

17 July 1865. Monday. Henry went away this evening.

18 July 1865. Tuesday. News by telegraph of our defeat in E. Norfolk.[442]
I omitted to mention that on last Sunday week, the historian Ranke[443] who is married to a sister of Dean Graves dined here–a queer little, fidgety man, full of Sleswig Holstein nonsense, but full too of cleverness– German professor's cleverness. He talked much & wildly about politics. Prussia he hopes will make a compact with France, and (in return for the Rhine provinces?) get a large slice of Austria which is to be destroyed! I am not quite sure whether the Professor specified the Rhine provinces as the French share, but obviously there is nothing else to offer.
Pim,[444] the new member a quiet intelligent looking Quaker, & the Ld. Mayor came this morning to press me to reprieve Kilkenny the man who is to be hung on Thursday for murdering a girl at Palmerstown. I refused, the crime was atrocious and the Executive Govt. must not take upon itself to set aside the law, because the community have a repugnance to death punishments. That is for Parliament to consider. It is clear that the feeling against death punishments is increasing. Townley's case of course was thrown in my teeth.[445] Sir G. Grey's weakness has done great harm.

20 July 1865. Thursday. To a dinner at the Exhibition, bad eating & speechifying in which I had to take a part. Guinness in the chair. He seems a quiet man, not very intelligent at least as to politics. His remedy for the ills of Ireland, a law punishing those who by word incite others to wrong doing! He could suggest nothing else. The Airlies came on a visit to day.

[442] Where Cons. Edward Howes and Clare Sewell Read defeated Sir Thomas Beauchamp and Wenman Coke.
[443] Leopold von Ranke (1795–1886), founder of modern school of objective historical writing; prof., Univ. of Berlin, 1825–71.
[444] Jonathan Pim (1806–85), Dublin merchant and manufacturer; Lib. MP for Dublin City, 1865–74.
[445] Victor Townley, Derbyshire murderer who committed suicide in Feb. 1865 by jumping from the staircase of Pentonville Prison.

24 July 1865. Monday. Elections over in Ireland on Saturday, in England to day. Our gains very considerable, more than I expected here. White lost his chance for Dublin by an imprudent Sunday meeting, and the defection of Sir C. Domvile. That high minded Barast on the day before the election wrote to St Lawrence[446] a letter which St L. showed me, saying that if I would oblige him, (that is recommend him for a Peerage of the U. Kingdom or a P.C. !) it was not then too late for him to influence his tenantry in White's favour, tho' he himself must vote for Taylor & Hamilton as he had promised them! What inconceivable baseness and treachery; worthy of the old times.

25 July 1865. Tuesday. Airlies went to Killarney.

26 July 1865. Wednesday. Saw Peel on his way from Valencia (where he had been for the laying the cable) to England.

27 July 1865. Thursday. Saw Att: & Sol: Genl. & afterwards Barry. Settled that Barry[447] (who had resigned Law Advisership on going to stand for Dungarvan for fear of the holding the office disqualifying him for the H. of Comms.) cannot hold that office as an M. P. Agreed that the office should remain vacant till after the coming trials in August.

31 July 1865. Monday. My mother came on a visit.

2 August 1865. Wednesday. Luncheon at Kingstown Regatta, a most tiresome & useless function. Maynard Currie here.

3 August 1865. Thursday. Dined with the Lord Mayor. Speeches &c. Supposed to be in honour of the Yacht Club.

4 August 1865. Friday. Johnny came home. Saw Bruce & had a long talk with him about the University scheme.

8 August 1865. Tuesday. Wrote to Sir G. Grey recommending prohibition of importn. of cattle into Ireland. The Lord Mayor came to me on this to day. Great alarm exists lest the disease should extend to Ireland. Lady Molesworth came on a visit to day.

---

[446] William Ulick Tristram St. Lawrence (1827–1909), state steward to ld. lt. Ireland, 1855–8, 1859–64; Lib. MP for Galway, 1868–74, when he succ. as 4th Earl of Howth.
[447] Charles Robert Barry (1824–97), crown pros. for Dublin, 1859–65; Lib. MP for Dungarvan, 1865–8; Irish sol. gen., 1868–70.

9 August 1865. Wednesday. Saw Lord Naas[448] who entirely agrees with me as to the prohibition of importn. of cattle & is going over to London to urge it upon Govt.

10 August 1865. Thursday. Breakfast at Kilruddery, a melancholy function. Pouring rain.

11 August 1865. Friday. Sir H. Rose sworn in at a Council. Col. Dunne & others came about cattle disease.

12 August 1865. Saturday. Numerous deputations on the subject of the cattle plague, urging prohibition.

14 August 1865. Monday. Knighted Sergeant Howley.

15 August 1865. Tuesday. Went to Mr Bagwell's[449] at Marlfield for the Cattle show at Clonmel. The Bagwells are quiet unpretending people, and we enjoyed our visit. The show yard was dry & pretty. The pigs admirable–oxen and sheep good–horses indifferent.

On Wednesday August 16 the 'banquet' took place Lord Waterford[450] (in the chair) made a silly speech. I was obliged to snub him gently. It was amusing to see with what faint cheers the guests received my allusion to the revoking the proclamation in Tipperary. After clamouring against it in Parliament they are not I suspect altogether pleased at being taken at their word. This was the anniversary of my wedding day: the first I have passed away from home for a long time.

18 August 1865. Friday. The cattle Show Ball. On Thursday I inspected the local institutions, jail, poor house, lunatic asylum. The two last good–the first under repair and alteration. A stupid gaol governor–
I had much talk with Mr. Bagwell on Irish Affairs. He complained of want of attention to Ireland–said he left the Treasury because his advice was never taken, thinks the Ld. Lieutenancy should be abolished, an Irish Secretary appd. in the Cabinet–told me there were many Fenians in Cork & Tipperary and that people were getting alarmed about them. Lord & Lady Doneraile were at Marlfield.

---

[448] Richard Southwell Bourke, Lord Naas (1822–72), ch. sec. Ireland, 1852, 1858–9, 1866–8; Cons. MP for Kildare, 1847–52, for Coleraine, 1852–7, for Cockermouth, 1857–67, when he succ. as 6th Earl Mayo; viceroy of India, 1868–72. On Wodehouse's assessment of Mayo's character, see *JE*, 27.

[449] John Bagwell (1811–83), Lib. MP for Clonmell, 1857–74.

[450] John De la Poer Beresford, 4th Marquis of Waterford (1814–66), succ. 1859.

19 August 1865.   Saturday. Returned to Dublin.

21 August 1865.   Monday. All this week very busy about the Cattle
Plague. Govt. at last gave way, if they had resisted, every Irish M. P.
would have opposed us. Sir G. Grey displayed great obstinacy, and
his obstinacy only equalled the weakness of his arguments against
prohibition.[451]

25 August 1865.   Friday. To the theatre— saw Sothern[452] in Garrick, very
clever.

26 August 1865.   Saturday. Interview (one of many) with Bruce re
University. The Catholic Bps. seem inclined to agree to some reasonable
plan.

28 August 1865.   Monday. Went to Johnstown Castle, Lady Esmonde's
where we stayed till Wednesday. Johnstown Castle is a building in what
C. Connellan[453] correctly terms 'florid Cockney'. The Lady *[veuve]*
Grogan Morgan now married to Sir T. Esmonde[454] is on a piece with
the Castle—foolishly vain, purse-proud, vulgar but energetic— a dreadful
old woman. Sir T. Esmonde an old man of 80 shrewd, pleasant,
gentleman-like. The late Mr Grogan Morgan's father was hanged on
Wexford Bridge for the part he took in the rebellion of /98, and Sir
T. Esmonde's father for the same crime was hanged on Carlisle Bridge
in Dublin. Curious coincidence. The Grogan Morgan Estates were
confiscated but restored. Lord Granard, J. Esmonde[455] M. P., and
Lawrence (Grey Livingstown) were the party. I went to Wexford, a
poor town. Passing the Slane on the road from Enniscorthy. I saw the
Crimean monument, an 'old' Irish Tower. What an anachronism!
    On Wednesday as we returned, we had luncheon with the new M.
P. for Wexford Sir J. Power,[456] a fussy little director of the Railway.

    [451] On Wodehouse's role in securing the prohibition of cattle imports from the United
Kingdom, ordered by Grey on August 25, see Wodehouse to Palmerston, 22 Aug. 1865,
PP GC/WO/5/1–4; Wodehouse to Russell, 22 Aug. 1865, R1P 30/22/28, ff. 264–6;
Grey to Palmerston, 26 Aug. 1865, PP GC/GR/2574/1–3; and general papers relating
to cattle plague, KP6 MS.eng.b.2047, ff. 1–108.
    [452] Edward Askew Sothern (1826–81), actor, born in Liverpool; made his mark in the
United States.
    [453] Corry Connellan, sec. to Lord Carlisle as Viceroy.
    [454] Sir Thomas Esmonde (1786–1868), Liberal MP for Wexford, 1841–6. Earlier in the
year, Wodehouse had written that the Esmondes were 'an influential Roman Catholic
family who had been steady supporters of the govt. in spite of priestly intimidation . . .'.
16 March 1865, KP6 MS.eng.c.4023, f. 9.
    [455] John Esmonde (1826–76), Liberal MP for Waterford, 1852–76.
    [456] Sir James Power (1800–77), Lib. MP for Wexford, 1835–47, 1865–8.

1 September 1865.   Friday. Mr Organ came to propose a statue to Lord Carlisle–promised him £5.

4 September 1865.   Monday. I ought to have mentioned that at Wexford I saw the Jail, very well arranged–on the separate system, but the greater part of the inmates lunatics. This will be remedied when the lunatic asylum now in progress near Enniscorthy is opened.

Went to day to Sir John Stewart's at Fincoul Lodge a shooting lodge about nine miles from Armagh. The peasantry lit bonfires on the hills in my honour. We stayed here till Friday, & went grouse shooting each day. Ridiculously bad sport. First day I killed 3 brace, the other days less. A fine tract of moors where one would expect plenty of game. The country is rugged hilly– Lord Granard was there. Major Knox[457] M.P. for Dungannon dined one night.

8 September 1865.   Friday. Went to Derry thro' Omagh the latter a poor country town of some 3 or 4000 inhabitants. Saw in three hours, at railway speed, all the lions of Derry, the Magee College, the Gaol, lunatic Asylum, model school, George's Institution (a school) the cathedral, & [*ill.*]. Afterwards luncheon with the Dean. The situation of the town is most striking–met Sir W. Heygate the M.P. for Derry Co.[458] whom I used to know as Heygate major at Eton. He is married to a lady of property near Derry. He has grown very grey. Sir Hervey Bruce M.P. for Coleraine[459] and Heygate accompanied us part of the way to the Great Causeway which we reached late, passing along Lough Foyle, thro' Colerain and Port Rush. The sea was calm–we rowed into the two principal caves, round the magnificent rocks, and landed on the causeway, a curious freak of nature. Slept at Sir E. Macnaghten's[460] and next day went to Belfast.

9 September 1865.   Saturday. Galloped through the sights of Belfast in 3 or 4 hours. Saw the Jail, Lunatic asylum, and the Queen's College, a noble building & went over Mr. Mulholland's[461] great flax spinning & weaving manufactory which employs 2100 hands.

Belfast is a clean and thriving town. What a disgrace that it should be torn to pieces by turbulent factions who on the pretence of religion violate every principle of Christianity. Could they be worse if they were pagans? Returned to Dublin this evening & found all well.

[457] William Stuart Knox (1826–1900), Cons. MP for Dungannon, 1851–74.
[458] Sir Frederic William Heygate (1822–94), Cons. MP for Co. Londonderry, 1859–74.
[459] Sir Henry Hervey Bruce (1820–1907), Cons. MP for Coleraine, 1862–74.
[460] Sir Edmund Charles Macnaghten (1790–1876), Cons. MP for Antrim, 1847–52.
[461] Andrew Mulholland (1791–1866), cotton and linen manufacturer; mayor of Belfast, 1845.

12 September 1865.   Tuesday. Received a deputation about County Cess who stated their case singularly ill.

13 September 1865.   Wednesday. A deputation headed by Sir R. de Burgo[462] about fish presses—the whole bother caused by the stupidity of Mr. Lane, one of the Fishery Commissioners.

14 September 1865.   Thursday. Consultation at the Lodge between Rose, Larcom, the Att: Genl. & me, when we determined to arrest the Fenians in Cork & Dublin simultaneously to morrow night. Rose was only taken into counsel as to any military measures which might be necessary. The Att: Genl. Larcom & I are responsible for the decision come to.

Went to Howth.

15 September 1865.   Friday. Bathed at Ireland's Eye. Johnny, &c. Cetto, and I off some very sharp rocks. Met the Beaumonts at Howth. The Castle very curious—part of it now inhabited being the original Danish Castle taken by Sir Almericus Tristram,[463] Lord Howth's[464] ancestor from the Danes in 1177. The Barony has descended in direct line ever since.

The red deer [*ill.*] on Ireland's Eye. Lord H. told us that one when swimming to land had been carried out to sea, & taken 16 miles from land. We saw Lord H: stud of brood mares, & hunters, & walked to the top of the hill where the view is superb. The whole hill except about 150 acres near the sea which his ancestors granted to a monastery, belongs to Lord Howth.

This night the arrests of Fenians were made, as arranged, in Dublin and Cork.[465]

16 September 1865.   Saturday. Returned to Dublin. A Privy Council, at which we proclaimed Cork County.

---

[462] Richard de Burgho (1821–73), of Limerick.

[463] Actually, Sir Amoricus Tristram.

[464] Thomas St. Lawrence, 3rd Earl of Howth (1803–74), Irish peer; ld. lt. Co. Dublin; son-in-law of 13th Earl of Clanricarde.

[465] Having watched the Fenians for months, on 1 Sept. Wodehouse informed Russell that he was 'quite prepared to run some risk of exceeding the law' if it were necessary to obtain 'tangible proofs' of the treasonable activity he was sure was taking place. On developments leading to the arrests of 15 Sept., see Wodehouse to Russell, 1 Sept. 1865, R1P 30/22/28, ff. 269–70; Wodehouse to Grey, 3 Sept. 1865, copy, PP GC/GR/2577/encl. 2; Wodehouse to Grey, 12 Sept. 1865, copy, PP GC/GR/2578, enc. 1; Wodehouse to Grey, 16 Sept. 1865, PP GC/GR/2579, enc. 2; Leon Ó Broin, *Fenian Fever, An Anglo-American Dilemma* (New York, 1971), 8–29.

18 September 1865. Monday. All this week very busy with Fenian business. Went to Swifts Lunatic Asylum, where I saw a poor old lady who fancies herself Lady Normanby; also to Stevens' Hospital.

25 September 1865. Monday. Last week Peel came over.

26 September 1865. Tuesday. This evening, Flo: having heard of the dangerous illness of her mother went to London.

29 September 1865. Friday. Lady Clare died at 8 a.m. in Bryanston Sqre. She had been suffering poor woman for nearly five years from a succession of paralytic strokes. Her last months of life were very melancholy and suffering. She was once a beautiful woman by all accounts, and if she committed one great fault,[466] she expiated it by a subsequent life passed chiefly in retirement, & with the strictest propriety. She retained to the last a singularly sweet smile. Poor Lady: her misfortunes were many. May she rest in peace.

We had a Council to day and proclaimed certain districts in Tipperary &c.

30 September 1865. Saturday. Peel has got into a foolish fracas with a Mr. Gray in a railway carriage. A most trumpery affair, but a 'rowdy' Chief Secretary is a discredit to the Govt.–

2 October 1865. Monday. To London by evening mail with Johnny.

3 October 1865. Tuesday. Opened & read Lady Clare's will.

4 October 1865. Wednesday. Funeral of Lady Clare at Kensal Green Cemetery. Attended by Flo: Louisa, Dillon, Johnny, Charley Dillon, Hutchinson, and myself: Johnny went back to Eton.

5 October 1865. Thursday. Very busy yesterday afternoon & this morning arranging about poor Lady Clare's effects &c. Henry in London on his way to Madrid in good health and spirits. Saw Hammond, Baring, and Romaine[467] whilst I was in London.

---

[466] Presumably involving the scandal which led to the dissolution of Lady Clare's marriage to Maurice Crosbie Moore in 1825, which enabled her to marry the 3rd Earl of Clare. Wodehouse apparently announced his intention to marry by suggestion to his mother that she would find three 'insuperable objections to her future daughter-in-law; 1st that her mother had run away; 2nd, that her sister had run away; 3rd, that she was an Irishwoman'. Cited in A.M. Stirling (ed.), *The Letter-Bag of Lady Elizabeth Spencer-Stanhope* (2 vols., London, 1913), II, 216–17.

[467] William Govett Romaine (1815–93), barrister; second sec. to admiralty, 1857–69.

6 October 1865.   Friday. Flo: & I returned to Dublin.[468]

11 October 1865.   Wednesday. Attended the ceremony of giving degrees of the Queen's Univesity in St Patrick's Hall. Very mean of Govt. not to give the Univ: a House. My speech was pretty well received. There were some slight hisses when I spoke of the plan for letting in the students from the Catholic Univ: to degrees. After nearly six weeks uninterrupted dry weather, at length we have rain.

14 October 1865.   Saturday. Ld. Charlemont came to say he wd. accept the Riband of St P. His hesitation arose from his fear that the Fenian trouble might cause rents to be ill paid. He reports great terror amongst the Northern Protestants who expect every day to be massacred by their R. Catholic neighbours! Mr Verner, son of Sir H. Verner Orange M.P.[469] for Armagh has sold off & left the country. Others contemplate following his example. They have evidently a bad conscience. Lord C. asked to be made a P.C. One thing at a time my Lord! I held out no hope to him of P.C.ship.

17 October 1865.   Tuesday. F. Cavendish consents to take back his wife. Perhaps the best thing he can do. She professes great penitance.[470]

18 October 1865.   Wednesday. This afternoon news arrived by telegraph that Lord Palmerston is dead. A great event. If ever a man could be pronounced fortunate both in his life & death Lord Palmerston is the man. He has died after a very short illness, in the full possession of his faculties, in the zenith of his force and power. His last letter to me was written on the 9th, approving very highly of my measures against the Fenians. How I shall miss his powerful support in the H. of Commons. Peel thinks the Duke of Somerset[471] will succeed him, that Granville will go to Paris, Sir G. Grey retire. I don't believe this. Lord Russell will I believe be Prime Minister but he has grown very old, much altered since I last saw him.

   If Sir G. Grey retires Bruce ought to be his successor. I fear whatever else happens, I have no chance of getting home. Flo: prays daily for our release, but at all events I could not go away till this Fenian business is settled.

[468] Recording impressions of a lengthy conversation with Wodehouse while in transit on board the *Connaught* was John Thadeus Delane. See Arthur Irwin Dasent, *John Thadeus Delane, Editor of 'The Times': His Life and Correspondence* (2 vols., London, 1908), II, 142–4.

[469] Sir William Verner (1782–1871), Cons. MP for Armagh Co., 1832–68.

[470] See entry for 17 Feb. 1865.

[471] Edward Adolphus Seymour (1804–85), MP for Okehampton, 1830–4, for Totnes, 1834–55, when he succ. as 12th Duke of Somerset; 1st ld. adm., 1859–66.

24 October 1865.   An extraordinary mess made by Lady L.D.[472] of an attempted reconciliation between F.C. and his wife.

Lord Russell is the new Premier, Lord Clarendon goes to the F.O. I wonder whether those old stagers Grey & Wood will go on. Unless the ministry gets fresh strength in the H. of Commons it can last but a very short time.

1 November 1865.   Wednesday. Delane the Editor of the 'Times' dined with us. He is hostile to Lord Russell: wishes Gladstone to be Premier:[473] does not believe in a do nothing policy: in short seems determined to create a storm–all I suppose in Lowe's interest. He has been travelling for some time in the S.W. of Ireland, and says the improvement of country and people is everywhere great.

2 November 1865.   Thursday. Went to Clondalkin to see the round Tower: a very perfect one.

3 November 1865.   Friday. Met Delane at the Exhibition. He says he hears the D. of Somerset has resigned and that the ministry may after all break up. Peel is evidently very uneasy. He has not mentioned to me the offer Ld. R. made to him of a Viscountcy, a pretty high bid. How can he remain after such an unmistakeable hint? He has suddenly become quite Liberal–! is all in favour of the Univ: scheme, is for appointing Catholics, putting down orangemen &c. &c. ! ! !

5 November 1865.   Sunday. Went to Christchurch, where the singing was admirable, a horribly tedious sermon.

11 November 1865.   Saturday. Stephens,[474] the Head Centre of the Fenians, taken.

12 November 1865.   Sunday. An attempt in Dame Street to shoot two detectives.

13 November 1865.   Monday. The Court of Common Pleas stopped

---

[472] Louisa Dillon.

[473] According to Delane, Wodehouse believed that the Queen ought to have sent for Gladstone rather than Russell, and that the Liberals 'ought to have a long banishment from office, and only return when the old batch are fairly out of the way'. Dasent, *Life of Delane*, II, 150; cf. entries for 18, 24 Oct. 1865.

[474] James Stephens (1825–1901), a founder of the Irish Republican Brotherhood; Head Centre, 1858–66; founded *Irish People*, 1863. On Stephens' revolutionary activities, see D. Ryan, *The Fenian Chief* (Dublin, 1967).

Luby's suit against me.[475] Peel tells me it is quite true that Lord Clarendon paid £7000 to stop the suit against him about the 'World'. He mentioned to me that C. Justice Monaghan[476] had told him at dinner the other day that when Lord Russell proposed the Eccles: Titles Bill Lord Clarendon resigned & was only persuaded to stay on clauses being put in which he (Monaghan) framed, providing that only the Att: Genl. shall prosecute which has rendered the Bill inoperative.

14 November 1865.   Tuesday. Dr. Russell came about Maynooth repairs.

15 November 1865.   Wednesday. Received a threatening letter the second of the kind from the Fenians.[477] Those amiable patriots are sowing such missives broadcast just now. The magistrates, detectives, newspaper Editors &c. &c. &c. are to be doomed. A pleasant and inviting country! No wonder Irish men who have anything to lose, would rather live anywhere than in Ireland, and that Englishmen despise a race whose chief weapon is the assassin's bullet.

18 November 1865.   Saturday. Peel announced to me his resignation. He did not tell me the circumstances himself but from another source I learned that he recd. a letter yesterday from Lord Russell offering him the Chancellorship of the Duchy without a seat in the Cabinet. I infer from what Peel said, that he means to refuse the offer unless with the Cabinet. Rumours to day of an outbreak in Dublin. I don't believe them but I have written to Rose that we must omit no precaution.

22 November 1865.   Wednesday. Went to Bessborough–a beautiful park, & comfortable House.

23 November 1865.   Thursday. Visited Malcolmson's[478] superb linen & cotton factory at Portlaw which employs 1600 hands. In the morning saw Piltown a model village belonging to Ld. Bessborough. Some cottages we saw showed (with their gardens) that Irishmen & women can be neat & tidy under favourable circts. Also went to a national

---

[475] Thomas Clarke Luby (1821–1901), briefly imprisoned following abortive uprising of 1848; co-editor of the *Irish People*; arrested during govt. raid of 15 Sept. Luby sought damages for unlawful entry into the newspaper's offices. Wodehouse to Clarendon, 11 Nov. 1865, C1P, C99.

[476] James Henry Monaghan (1804–78), ch. just. common pleas, 1850; com. of natl. ed., 1861.

[477] Wodehouse later told Margot Asquith of a letter which began: 'My Lord, we intend to kill you at the corner of Kildare Street; but we would like you to know that there is nothing personal in it!' M. Bonham Carter (ed.), *The Autobiography of Margot Asquith* (London, 1962), 100–1.

[478] William Malcolmson.

school where the children answered & read well. The Irish children are much sharper than English. Why is there always a screw loose somewhere in Irish heads? Lord B. has 14 such schools on his admirably managed Estate. In the morning received an address from the Commissioners of Carrick on Suir, a poor & very disaffected town. The trade to it which formerly came up the Suir has left it since the railway was made to Waterford. At Carrick Malcolmson has recently built a linen factory employing 600 hands.

24 November 1865. Friday. 'Dies nefastus.' Went to Waterford, on arriving just as I was about at the station to receive an address from the Corporn. , I received news that Stephens had escaped about 2 this morning from Richmond Bridewell. A most disastrous event. I had little stomach after such a piece of intelligence for functions. However, I duly went through the pig-killing and bacon curing establisht. of Messr. Richardson where they kill & salt some 20 or 30,000 pigs per annum for the London market, also the Model School, Lunatic asylum, and Gaol. Afterwards Malcolmson took us down the noble river as far as Duncannon fort. Then a 'luncheon' at 5 o'clock, a speech & home.

25 November 1865. Saturday. Returned sorely crestfallen to Dublin.

28 November 1865. Tuesday. Peel told me he had declined the Duchy because unaccompanied by the Cabinet. He would have taken the Poor Law Board, he says, or any place with work to do, without the Cabinet. He professes to intend to support the government (for the present I suppose.) Went this evening to the Statistical Society, still out of sorts about Stephens, & made a poor bungling speech.[479]

29 November 1865. Wednesday. Went to Mountjoy Prison to see that our birds (if we catch them) are properly caged.

'Pagan' O'Leary now under sentence at Mountjoy for 7 years for trying to make Fenians of soldiers at Mullingar entered himself in the prison register as a 'Milesian Pagan and hereditary rebel'.[480] He declined to attend any religious worship but being put on bread & water for infringing the rules of the prison said his parents were R. Catholics & that he would go to mass. He was convicted under the name of 'Murphy'–

---

[479] On Wodehouse's assessment of the value of statisitical inquiry, see his speech of 24 Nov. 1864, in KP6 MS.Engl.b.2048, f. 9.

[480] Patrick O'Leary. The Pagan; in charge of enticing soldiers to join the Fenians, was arrested in November 1864 and convicted of tampering with the allegiance of the troops. See J. Devoy, *Recollections* (New York, 1929), 133–9.

Mrs. William Wodehouse died this day at 10 Green Street, Grosvenor Sqre.

1 December 1865. Friday. Luby convicted. Sentence 20 years Penal Servitude.

6 December 1865. Thursday. O'Leary convicted.[481] 20 years.

8 December 1865. Friday. Peel called to take his leave. I have managed to get on with him without quarrelling for a year, but his departure is a great relief to me. His utter want of judgment, & above all his 'inconséquences' makes him a very undersirable colleague. He is quick-witted, clever, & vigorous but will always be a source of weakness rather than strength to any Govt. with which he allies himself.

10 December 1865. Monday. Chichr. Fortescue and Lady Waldegrave arrived yesterday. I saw Fortescue to day. We had a full explanation about his wish to be in the Cabinet & my objection to such an arrangement.[482]

11 December 1865. Tuesday. O'Donovan (Rossa) convicted.[483]

12 December 1865. Wednesday. The Special Commission went to Cork.

15 December 1865. Friday. Johnny came home, & H. Hutchinson came with him on a visit.

25 December 1865. Monday. Great alarm that there will be a rising to night. The Govt. is beset with applications for troops from the South of Ireland. At Dublin we are obliged to be on the watch. All as yet is quiet, and I believe it will remain so though if we had not taken precautions the Yankee Irish might have been mad enough to attempt some outbreak.

28 December 1865. Thursday. Investiture of Ld. Charlemont as a K.P. The ceremony was in Patrick's Hall, & thanks to Flo's excellent arrangments was a brilliant success. Cork has been staying with us for

---

[481] John O'Leary (1830–1907), ed. of *The Irish People*; arrested 1865 and sentenced to twenty years in prison, released and exiled, 1874. See Marcus Bourke, *John O'Leary: A Study in Irish Separatism* (Tralee, 1967), 89–95.

[482] See entry for 14 May 1866.

[483] Jeremiah O'Donovan Rossa (1831–1915), business manager of *The Irish People*; sentenced to twenty years in prison; released and exiled, 1871.

the investiture. He is to be the new Master of the Buckhounds, a good appointment.

Corry Connellan torments me daily about the mess at Richmond Prison. I never saw such a coward. I forgot to mention that on Thursday the 21st I distributed the prizes at the Hibernian School and on Saturday the 23rd the prizes at the Art School of the Dublin Society. Nothing worth remark on either occasion.

1 January 1866. Monday. Thus begins a new year. This past year has been a year of much activity and anxiety to me. I have reason to thank God for giving me strength to meet the many difficulties by which I have been beset. The year which opens promises to be even more anxious. May His providence guide & protect me, & mine.

2 January 1866. Tuesday. Went to Kilronan Castle, Mr & Lady Louisa Tansons's and stayed till Friday. A pretty place, & some fair shooting. Met Sir Rowland Blennerhasset here, M.P. for Galway,[484] a dreamy Newmanite with some cleverness & much conceit. All the world talking of the ridiculous cock & bull story of our having been shot at.[485]

9 January 1866. Tuesday. Went to Lord Granard's, where we had a pleasant party. The 'duffer' was there in great force. Not many woodcocks. The best day 19 1/2 couple.

12 January 1866. Friday. Returned from Granard's, discovery of pikes and bullets in Dublin.

13 January 1866. Saturday. We proclaimed the city and county of Dublin, and the remainder of Tipperary & Waterford Cies.[486] The alarm felt is general, much of it exaggerated, some well-founded.[487]

20 January 1866. Saturday. Hard at work all this week at questions about troops, proclamations &c. &c. Johnny went to Eton on Friday.

[484] Sir Rowland Blennerhasset (1839–1909), Lib. MP for Galway, 1865–74, for Kerry, 1880–5.

[485] Wodehouse wrote to his mother that the story originated in 'a silly mistake of the engine driver who mistook a blow from a fallen telegraph post for a shot', suggesting the tension which then existed in Dublin. Wodehouse to Anne Wodehouse, 9 Jan. 1866, KP1 15/K2/18. On the threat of assassination generally, see Wodehouse to Raikes Currie, 23 Dec. 1865, in *Liberal by Principle*, 108; Kimberley to Clarendon, 30 April 1866, C1P, C99.

[486] On the proclamations, see Wodehouse to Russell, 14 Jan. 1865, R1P 30/22/16a.

[487] See Wodehouse to Raikes Currie, 23 Dec. 1865, in *Liberal by Principle*, 108; Wodehouse to Russell, 18 Jan. 1865, R1P 30/22/16a; correspondence in KP6 MS.eng.c.4039/4040.

The D. & Duchess d'Aumale here this week on a visit to Fortescue. Fortescue & Lady W. much disgusted at Goschen's appointment.[488]

24 January 1866.   Wednesday. Migrated to Castle.

26 January 1866.   Friday. Interview with Mr. Russell & Capt. Stackpoole[489] and Mr. Barry as to Mr. Macdonnell want to be a R. M. promised a favourable note. Mr. M. the son of a merchant at Limerick a R. C. Saw F. Ponsonby, talk about Fenians in Wicklow.

27 January 1866.   Saturday. Last sitting of Catterson Smith to touch up picture. He decidedly improved it by deepening the colour of the eyes which were too indistinct. I rather like the picture. It is hard & cold but free from affectation or vulgarity.

29 January 1866.   Monday. Dined with Chancellor, where I met a number of Irish members. Judge Keogh[490] who was there is in a perfect panic about the Fenians; talked wildly about the decline of British power &c. &c. I never met such a coward.

30 January 1866.   Tuesday. First levee attended by about 1000 people— a wearisome business. Lord Mayor's dinner. My speech went off well, and I was extremely well received. Fortescue was not so warmly received as I expected, but he made an excellent speech. I had some difficulty in persuading the Ld. Mayor (one Mackey a seedsman a good sort of man)[491] to propose his health which was not on the list of toasts. It would have been a great fiasco to have omitted it.

31 January 1866.   Wednesday. Drawing Room—about 1150 people. All kinds of rumours of a Fenian outbreak to night. We took special precautions & had dragoons to keep the streets especially.

1 February 1866.   Thursday. Parliament met. As we feared a riot on account of our stopping the Fenian bazaar at the Rotundo which was to have taken place to day. But all was quiet. We had a double escort for the Lord Mayor's dinner.

---

[488] As Chancellor of Duchy of Lancaster.

[489] William Stacpoole (1830–79), capt. of Clare militia, 1855–65; Lib. MP for Ennis, 1860–79.

[490] William Nicholas Keogh (1817–78), Irish sol.-genl., 1853–5; Irish atty.-genl., 1855–6; judge of the court of common pleas from 1856. In a panic because he had received threatening letters. Wodehouse to Clarendon, 11 Nov. 1865, C1P C99.

[491] Sir James William Mackey.

3 February 1866.   Saturday. A deputation from the loyal meeting held at the Rotundo. The meeting had a narrow escape of being an exclusively Tory assemblage which would [have] had a very bad effect, but we persuaded our friends to attend.

5 February 1866.   Monday. To Moore-Abbey.

6 February 1866.   Tuesday. Snipe shooting. Mr. Wray & I killed 11 couple & 1/2. The Queen opened Parliament for business.

7 February 1866.   Wednesday. Back to Dublin.

8 February 1866.   Thursday. Smart debate in the Commons on Ireland. Our Atty. Gen: seems to have acquitted himself well.

10 February 1866.   Saturday. A council at which we proclaimed Roscommon, Wicklow, Armagh, Wexford, and rest of Longford & Cavan.

14 February 1866.   Wednesday. After consulting Fortescue and the Chancellor and Sir H. Rose wrote to Govt. recommending suspension of the Habeas Corpus Act.

15 February 1866.   Thursday. Went to Kilruddery to shoot with Musters,[492] Arkwright,[493] Boyle.[494] Saw only 4 woodcocks. Shot 1 woodcock, 1 snipe, 1 rabbit!

16 February 1866.   Friday. Heard from Govt. that notice would be given to night of a bill to morrow for suspension of the H. C. Act. On receiving telegram consulted with Chancellor & Fortescue & decided on arrests this night.

17 February 1866.   Saturday. Arrests made early this morning, very successfully without disturbance. Susp: Act passed through all its stages to day & recd. Royal Assent.

25 February 1866.   Sunday. The whole of the past week incessantly engaged in determining against whom warrants should be issued & in negotiations about the University Question. One of the hardest week's work I ever did.

---

[492] Lt-Col. Henry Musters, master-of-the-horse.
[493] Capt. Henry Arkwright, a.d.c.
[494] Capt. Edmund J. Boyle, a.d.c.

26 February 1866.   Monday. Heard of poor H. Herbert's death.[495]

27 February 1866.   Tuesday. Levee. Great indignation of 'Irish Times' because I did not wait for people who were late.

28 February 1866.   Wednesday. Drawing room with what 'Irish Times' calls a limited attendance—a lie, there were as many as usual.

1 March 1866.   Thursday. Heavy fall of snow last night. Fortescue & Lady Waldegrave went to England yesterday. Strange vain woman Lady W., full of overweening conceit—utterly without tact, but wonderfully courageous and energetic. She is as bitter as wormwood against every one because *il care sposo* is not in the Cabinet. She vows she will put him in or upset the Govt., which she fairly believes she can do whenever she pleases!

2 March 1866.   Friday. F. Cavendish's divorce,[496] as the Judge justly said one of the grossest cases he had known, & I may add one of the most inexplicable. Poor Elinor deserves her fate but she is indeed to be pitied.

10 March 1866.   Saturday. Nothing particular to note this week, overwhelmed with business connected with the arrests under the H.C.S. Act. I think Larcom will break down altogether.

16 March 1866.   Friday. St Patrick's Ball. It was well attended though there were foolish people, it is said, who stayed away for fear of the Fenians.

17 March 1866.   Saturday. St Patrick's day. The usual guard mounting went off without anything remarkable. The usual dirty ragamuffins danced & yelled. Perhaps they hissed 'God Save the Queen' with somewhat more vigour than usual. A most contemptible rabble. Many people thought there was to be a row.

My poor Flo: quite knocked up & laid up with a bad sore throat & cold.

---

[495] Henry Arthur Herbert (1815–1866), ch. sec. Ireland, 1857–8; Lib. MP for Kerry, 1847–66.

[496] Cavendish v. Lady Elinor Cavendish and Lord Cecil Gordon. Verdict for petitioner and assessment of damages on co-respondent of £10,000. *The Times*, 3 March 1866, 9. On Lady Elinor's 'bitter repentence', see her letter to Kimberley, 26 Feb. 1883, KP1 15/K2/21. See entry for 17 Feb. 1865.

20 March 1866. Tuesday. Torrents of rain, horribly cold 'March' weather.

22 March 1866. Thursday. Moved to Lodge. Very bad, wet, cold weather.

23 March 1866. Friday. Johnny came home.

24 March 1866. Saturday. Heard that Stephens had arrived at Paris. I can't say much for our police. Stephens will come back again, and yet do harm. The Fenians however can never now really make a great coup. The complete unveiling of their whole scheme is fatal to them. No people but the Irish could be such egregious fools as to be led by such phantoms. On the whole I think there is no people on the face of earth more unworthy of respect. They have always been despised by the Englishman and as a nation they have always deserved his contempt. 'Unstable as water, thou shalt not excel' should be their motto.[497]

25 March 1866. Sunday. Caught a cold coming into the house tho' it was well aired. Had a good deal of fever and have been ill all this week.

1 April 1866. Easter Sunday. My remarks about Irishmen on the other side of the page are unfair and unjust. They are excusable only on account of the bilious condition of my mind & body when I wrote them. I recant. They are an unfortunate people: that is too true but it is mean to cast upon them imputations for faults which we have aggravated by evil treatment. I don't absolutely despair. Perseverance in fair just Government must produce its effect in the end; but Englishmen must be persuaded to treat Irishmen as Irishmen and not as Englishmen. This last folly will pass away, and there will be slow but certain improvement. That is my faith.

12 April 1866. Thursday. Debate on Reform Bill began. Govt. says it will have 15 majority. Graves is to be Bishop of Limerick. I am very glad of it. He is the most liberal minded clergyman I ever knew & altogether admirably qualified for the mitre.[498]

---

[497] However, cf. entry for 1 April 1866. On Wodehouse's ambivalent attitude toward the Irish, see J. Powell and P. Kennedy, 'Lord Kimberley and the Foundation of Liberal Irish Policy: Annotations on George Sigerson's *Modern Ireland*, 1868', *Irish Historical Studies*, forthcoming 1998.

[498] See Wodehouse's glowing recommendation to Gladstone, knowing that he took 'much interest in these appointments'. Kimberley to Gladstone, 10 April 1866, GP 44224, ff. 46–50.

17 April 1866. Tuesday. Went to Punchestown Races a very amusing day, a large and orderly crowd.

20 April 1866. Friday. Johnny went back to Eton. Friday division on Reform Bill. Govt. a majority of 5. I think they must resign. At all events they can never recover such a blow. The fact is a certain number of old Whigs don't want Reform at all altho' they dare not say so, and none of the Tories want Reform, altho many of them pretend they do. The sooner this hollow insecure state of things ends the better for all parties. Lowe's speech might have satisfied a Tory such as Perceval or Eldon. It is the most Tory speech delivered in Parliament in my time.[499]

21 April 1866. Saturday. Govt. decided not to resign. On the whole I think they were right. The dissentients asked for the Redistribution Bill. It is fair they should have an opportunity to recant.

Poor Flo: was woefully disappointed. She positively cried when she heard that ministers would not resign. I must say I am weary to death of this place, and should be only too glad of a decent pretext to get away.

5 May 1866. Saturday. Went with Flo: to London, sleeping Friday night at Holyhead. Very busy all this week. Went to Windsor where I've slept a night & dined *tête a tête* with The Queen–viz: H.M., the Princess Helena, Lady Churchill, A. Paget, Genl. Grey and selves– dreadfully formal. After dinner the Queen went away, and we passed the evening with the household. The Queen looking very well, talked a great deal.

Saw Lord Russell, Sir G. Grey & most of the other ministers. All agree we must renew the H.C. Susp: Act. Asked Lord R. to make me an Earl. He was very civil but gave no promise. Received many compliments on my management of Irish affairs.

Went to the Prussian Legation, a party. Every one seems to expect war. Apponyi & Azeglio openly say they wish it. Gladstone was very friendly about Irish affairs, earnest for our Land Bill, promised to give it his attention next to the Reform Bill.

14 May 1866. Monday. I received a letter from Lord Russell announc- ing that the Queen had consented to make me an Earl.[500] Flo: was delighted. I am pleased too. It is a recognition of my services and in a

---

[499] On Robert Lowe's infamous speech of 13 March, see J. Winter, *Robert Lowe* (Toronto, 1976), 212–15. Spencer Perceval (1762–1812) and John Scott, 1st Earl of Eldon (1751–1838), were adamant opponents of early reform.

[500] Russell to Wodehouse, 14 May 1866, KP6 MS.eng.c.4475, f. 66.

manner which I like, because it is not a mere personal honour but confers dignity on my family. Much discussion ensued as to the title. Lord Russell suggested 'Norwich', & I agreed to this but on inquiry found that the Howard family had claims to this title and that it would give offence if I took it. So I determined on Kimberley. Some of my family especially the Curries wanted me to keep the title 'Wodehouse' and have Viscount Kimberley for second title, but I preferred another name. A surname is not well fitted to serve as a title unless indeed it is very celebrated like Russell or Canning. Now though my family is very respectable and provincially famous, it has never acquired any national or historical fame. I shrewdly suspect the true reason for the eagerness of some Wodehouses for Earl Wodehouse arises from their fear that the world will not so easily recognise their connection with the Earl of Kimberley.[501]

Went to Kimberley to day & stayed till Wednesday. Found things working well & much pleased with the new front to Matthew's farm house at Kimberley.[502] It does Boardman, the architect great credit. Decided not to dig out the river. The mud after all as I saw it with the water let off is not so deep and it will do to leave it some time longer.

I attended most nights at the H. of Lords whilst I was in London. Spoke one night on the Land Bill. If I had been silent, it would have been said that Fortescue and I disagreed upon it. Lord Russell sent for me one morning & said that Fortescue pressed hard to be put in the Cabinet. I stood firm; if they wished me to resign, I was ready I said to do so at any time: indeed should be only too glad to get away, but I declined positively to remain if the Chief Secretary were in the Cabinet. My influence would be gone and my power of usefulness irretrievably weakened. The fact is 'Frank Waldegrave' who wears Fortescue's breeches is frantic to be in the Cabinet. She is making a sad fool of herself, and will do her husband a world of harm.[503]

On Friday we dined with the P. of Wales. H.R.H. talked briefly about a toothache from which he was suffering. Immediately after dinner he smoked cigarettes in the dining room. He offered old Ld.

---

[501] See Rosebery's notice of this 'unusual' piece of vanity, Kimberley Memoir, herein, 491.

[502] For a good visual record of farm architecture on the Kimberley estate, see sales catalogue, *The Earl of Kimberley's Estate*, Jacobson-Stops & Staff, 1958.

[503] Fortescue felt that he could 'fairly expect' Wodehouse to take the handsome and friendly course of waiving his objections. Fortescue to Kimberley, 30 May 1866, KP MS.eng.c.4047, ff. 95–9. On the oddly recurring collision of ambitions between the two, see Wodehouse to Russell, 21 Nov. 1865, R1P 30/22/15g, f. 112; Wodehouse to Clarendon, 5 Nov. 1865, C1P C99; Wodehouse to Russell, 12 Dec. 1865, R1P 30/22/15h, ff. 62–3; Kimberley to Fortescue, 1 June 1866, KP6, Ms.eng.4048, ff. 8–9; Dasent, *Life of Delane*, II, 161; Extracts, Kimberley memoir, herein; *CJ*, 153–8; Carlingford Journal, CfP 63688.

Delawarr[504] one! The Princess looks very thin & bored. The Princess Mary fat as ever and cross because Teck flirted with other women after dinner. After dinner a concert and as we had to start by the mail train at 7.30 we got little sleep.

19 May 1866.   Saturday. Returned to Dublin, & found the children all well. We brought Hamilla[505] with us. Ernestine's marriage with Mr Marshall[506] at which we were present took place at St Mark's Church on Thursday the 17th. He seems a quiet sensible man, & she is very fortunate in making so good a match. We had a great family gathering at the wedding. The day I was at Kimberley Tuesday the 15th news arrived that the cattle plague had broken out in Co. Down. I have been immensely busy all this week in consequence. I think we have a fair chance of checking it, but already there is a senseless clamour against our measures of precaution.

26 May 1866.   Saturday. Review in Phoenix Park in honour of Queen's birthday and the usual full dress dinner.

28 May 1866.   Monday. I wonder when my Earldom will be gazetted. I have paid my fees & begin to think I shall never get my money's worth. The trial of Macarthy the soldier for Fenianism commenced to-day.[507] I am sorry to say there are still signs of life in this wretched conspiracy. On the Sunday after I returned a miscreant tried to assassinate the informer Warner at Howth. Happily he was caught and every such attempt puts another nail in the coffin of the conspiracy. When conspirators become assassins, they cease to be politically formidable.

29 May 1866.   Tuesday. Received the news that I was gazetted Earl of Kimberley last night. I will strive not to disgrace my new name.

1 June 1866.   Friday. Rain at last. Ball at the Lord Mayor's a very scrubby assemblage.

[504] George John Sackville-West, 5th Earl Delawarr (1791–1869).
[505] Hamilla, fifth child of paternal uncle, Alfred Wodehouse.
[506] John Marshall, 2nd son of Henry Cowper Marshall, Westwood Hall, Leeds.
[507] Kimberley paid particular attention to the trial of Sergeant Macarthy of the 64th Regiment, fearing that military authorities in England were 'not awake to the very dangerous character of the attempts of the Fenians to undermine the loyalty of the Irish soldiers'. Kimberley to Russell, 6 Jan. 1866, R1P 30/22/16a; Wodehouse to Clarendon, 29 March 1866, C1P 99C; Kimberley to Rose, copy, 17 June 1866, KP6 MS.eng.d.4048, 134.

3 June 1866. Sunday. A most wearisome sermon from the Dean of Dromore[508] or Drone-more, as we have christened him. This man thinks himself fit to be a Bishop!

4 June 1866. Monday. Political crisis again, no one seems able to form an opinion of the result, but it is clear that Gt. is in great peril. Declared the infected district of Brennan free from disease. I think we have 'stamped' it out.

5 June 1866. Tuesday. The opposition completely handled by the withdrawal of Captn. Hayter's amendt. last night.[509]

7 June 1866. Thursday. To night the opposition suffered two severe defeats. If Ministers are firm they may carry their bill.

8 June 1866. Friday. Seven virulent cases of cattle plague reported from near Lisburn, at Drumla. The culpable folly of those who tried to induce people to believe the Drennan cases not cattle plague is producing its effect. Cases are concealed and the efforts of Govt. are rendered fruitless.

The Dean of Elphin[510] came to day to press his claims for a Rt. Magistracy for his son a Bishopric for himself &c. I rather like the man, but I don't think he is fit for a Mitre but he might get a better Deanery of which I gave him hopes.

9 June 1866. Saturday. Went to St Columba's Coll: an attempt at a public school, established about 20 years, same time as Marlborough, but has not thriven much. There are only 53 boys. The largest number ever there about 70. A sensible master, Langden. A very pretty spot. The school looks Puseyitish which I suspect is the true cause why it does not thrive.

14 June 1866. Thursday. Went to Mountjoy, saw the caged Fenians. The arrangements for safety good. The Governor told me that one of the Gleeson's is 6 feet 7 high, a stupid giant. The men he said were not any of them of a superior class of society but sharp cunning villains,

[508] Daniel Bagot.

[509] Arthur Divett Hayter (1835–1917), ret. as capt., Grenadier Guards, 1866; Lib. MP for Wells, 1865–8, for Bath, 1873–85, for Walsall, 1893–5, 1900–5. Secretly encouraged by Disraeli, the young Whig Hayter moved a hostile motion against the government's redistribution scheme. See F. B. Smith, *The Making of the Second Reform Bill* (Cambridge, 1966), 98–102.

[510] William Warburton.

some of them. Those I saw in the exercising ground looked thorough Yankee rowdies.

The Fenian raid into Canada of which we have news to day will be a wretched fiasco and help to bring the conspiracy into hopeless discredit.[511] Dublin is much excited about the Westmoreland Street fire.

15 June 1866. Friday. A public meeting to get a subscription for a statue to Lord Carlisle where the adage 'de mortuis nil nisi bonum' was copiously illustrated. The fact is he was a very accomplished, amiable & kind hearted man, but weak, and second rate as a politician.[512] But he deserves a statue at least as much as Lord Eglinton.[513]

18 June 1866. Monday. Dunkellin's[514] rating clause carried against Govt. (315–304). The rest of the week passed in the strangest uncertainty whether Ministers will resign or not. The Queen neglecting her duties at Balmoral, a Continental war just broken out, everything & every body in perplexity & doubt. My own voice would be for dissolution. The most humiliating position would be to go on neither resigning nor dissolving.

21 June 1866. Thursday. My Lady presented new colours to the 24th at the Curragh. She was very nervous but got through it well. For the first time for weeks a fine day.

24 June 1866. Sunday. Corry Connellan here for two nights. Most amusing.[515] At last a hot day.

26 June 1866. Tuesday. Ministers resigned and Lord Derby sent for. The whole week consumed in rumours and negotiations.[516] Fine hot weather all the weak.

---

[511] In a private letter to Hammond, Kimberley added that it would show that 'Stephens' influence with the Brotherhood' was not small, and would 'confirm the Canadians in detestation of them, and force the United States Gt. to act against them to some extent'. 14 June 1866, HmP2.

[512] See too Kimberley's mixed estimate of Carlisle in Powell and Kennedy, 'Lord Kimberley and the Foundations of Liberal Irish Policy', *Irish Historical Studies* forthcoming.

[513] Archibald William Montgomerie, 13th Earl of Eglinton (1812–61), Irish viceroy for ten months during 1852–3, and for sixteen months during 1858–9; cr. 1st Earl Winton in U.K. peerage, 1859.

[514] Ulick Canning de Burgh, Lord Dunkellin (1827–67), lt. col., Coldstream Guards; Lib. MP for Galway bor., 1857–9; Galway co., 1865–7.

[515] Connellan reported to Clarendon that Kimberly had been asked to stay on as Lord Lieutenant. 'Had I been asked,' Kimberly wrote to Clarendon, 'my answer would have been unequivocal refusal.' 4 July 1866, CIP MS.Clar.dep. c. 99, f. 197.

[516] On negotiations, see *DD1*, 225–6.

1 July 1866.   Sunday. No new Govt. yet formed. It is believed we shall have a pure Tory Cabinet: so much the better: it can't last long. Dean Graves consecrated Bp. of Limerick last Friday. On Tuesday we went to the Curragh Races: wretchedly bad. On Wednesday dined in Trinity College Hall. To day went to St Werberg's Church to draw a congregation for a collection for the parish schools: an absurd annual function. The Dean of Cork (Magee) preached an excellent sermon.

6 July 1866.   Friday. The new Ministers appd., Lord Abercorn[517] Lord Lieut:

16 July 1866.   Monday. Farewell levee at 3 o'clock at Castle. A very small knot of Fenians hissed me just opposite the old 'People' office. Much respect shown by people generally.[518] A good many attended the levee.

17 July 1866.   Tuesday. Left Ireland. Many people in the streets and at Kingstown. I could not but be much pleased at the general respect shown at our departure. We had a lovely passage slept at Holyhead, and arrived in London on Wednesday July 18 after a most prosperous journey. I have indeed deep reason to be thankful that my Irish administration has been brought to a close with so much honour, and I hope with some advantage to the country.

23 July 1866.   Monday. Took my seat as Earl in the House, introduced by Ld. Clarendon & Ld. Granville. The Reform riot in Hyde Park.[519]

24 July 1866.   Tuesday. The park again in the power of a mob. Called on Ld. Abercorn. I found him just returned from the park where he had stones thrown at him.

This Reform riot was a melancholy affair, as it brought the police in collision with the people, & demonstrated the utter incapacity of the Home Office. Grey or Walpole I think the difference would have been small tho' the former would not have made the ridiculous exhibition of weakness made by the latter in the H. of Commons, & to the Beales'

[517] James Hamilton, 2nd Marquis of Abercorn (1811–85), Irish ld. lt., 1866–8, 1874–6; raised to the dukedom, 1868. The post had first been offered to Manners. See C. Whibley, *Lord John Manners and his Friends* (2 vols., London, 1925), II, 136–40.

[518] Even moderate nationalists were, however, glad to see Kimberley go, having consistently criticised him for harsh treatment of Fenians and use of coercion. See doggeral from *Nation*, 11 Aug. 1866.

[519] After the Reform League was denied access to Hyde Park, the railings were pushed over and some 200 people injured. See D. Richter, *Riotous Victorians* (Athens, Ohio, 1981), 51–61.

deputation. Grey has the meantiers of a stateman at all events. Walpole would be contemptible as Mayor of a small town. He is the type of the 'worthy & excellent' but most feeble Justice. But the demonstration was justifiable in itself to disprove the calumnies of Lowe, Elcho[520] &c. who declared the working men took not interest in Reform. It settled that question at all events.

6 August 1866. Monday. Spoke in the H. of Lords on the 2nd reading of the H. Corpus Bill. My speech was well received tho' I don't suppose many of their Lps. much liked what I said, in their hearts.

9 August 1866. Wednesday. Went to Kimberley. For many days was inundated with articles in Irish newspapers, talking more 'Hibernica', a most exaggerated view the one side of the wisdom, the other of the utter folly & iniquity of my speech on Irish affairs. They cannot digest wholesome truth. Such things go like whiskey, to their heads at once.

9 September 1866. I have spent a month here very happily & find myself much too lazy to record the little daily incidents of my life.[521]

15 September 1866. Saturday. After some suspense heard from Smith that the Liberal Electors of Falmouth had determined to select as their candidate *vice* T. G. Baring (now Ld. Northbrook), Jervoise Smith[522] the banker. They would not have Edmond Wodehouse (tho' some were favorable to him) because they feared Falmouth would be looked on as a pocket borough. Of course the true & simple reason was that they think they will be able to get more out of a London Banker than out of me. Fitness in a candidate is the last thing electors think of. If they are too respectable to take the bribe directly, they are in their hearts just as anxious to make money of their votes by the indirect method of bleeding a rich candidate in the guise of contributions for improvements &c. There is very little difference as far as purity of election goes between those middle class borough-mongers & J. Smith who pockets £5. At all events a wide extension of the suffrage will make this branch of the trade less easy.

Heard to day the melancholy news of the death of my old friend Sir

---

[520] Sir Francis Wemyss-Charteris-Douglas, Lord Elcho (1818–94), leading Adullamite; succ. as 10th Earl of Wemyss, 1883.

[521] Or to return correspondence. Apologising to Larcom for his sloth, Kimberley maintained that he was 'too lazy to do anything but walk about in the open air shooting a stray wild duck or looking after my harvest which is much better fun than looking after Fenians'. 2 Aug. 1866, LcP 7694.

[522] Jervoise Smith (1828–84), partner in banking firm of Smith, Payne, and Smiths; Lib. MP for Penryn, 1866–8.

Archibald Campbell,[523] a good amiable fellow. I am deeply grieved for him.

1 October 1866. Monday. Went to Studley and stayed till Friday. Met Wm. Harcourt & R. Doyle there and Sir Chas. & Lady Douglas.[524] Sir Chas. a former private Secretary of Lord Ripon, a dull man.

6 October 1866. Saturday. Attended meeting at Norwich to establish a Chamber of Agriculture. C. Read[525] M.P. in the Chair. This movement evidently directed against the landlords, the way to render it innocuous and useful if possible is for landlords to take part in it.

8 October 1866. Monday. This week Henley, Rochfort & Dodson came on a visit, and on Saturday my mother. Nothing worth recording. Henley becomes less Radical daily–he & Dodson as argumentative & contradictory as ever. We carried this day the final vote to bring this hundred under the Union Rating Bill. The usual narrow minded pig-headed opposition which is the characteristic (unavoidable) of all local boards more or less, but we carried it, not because of any greater enlightenment in the majority over the minority but because Wymondham hopes to gain some petty advantage by the change.

18 October 1866. Thursday. Yesterday went to Ketteringham to shoot. Met there F. Walpole,[526] Fellowes of Shotesham,[527] Sir H. Durrant (half an idiot) & P. Amherst, shooting not very good. I knocked down a woodcock, the first I have seen this year. Attended Qr. Sessions.

20 October 1866. Saturday. Much shocked to hear of poor Arkwright's death. What can induce people to risk their lives to say they have been up a hill. How many more victims will the snows of Mont Blanc overwhelm?

[523] Sir Archibald Islay Campbell (1825–66), Cons. MP for Argyleshire, 1851–7; contemporary of Kimberley at Eton and Christ Church. See John Wodehouse to Anne Wodehouse, Feb. 1843, in *Liberal by Principle*, 55.
[524] Sir Charles Douglas (1806–87), priv. sec. to Lord Ripon, 1830–4; Lib. MP for Warwick, 1837–52, for Banbury, 1859–65.
[525] Clare Sewell Read (1826–1905), prosperous Norfolk tenant farmer; Cons. MP for Norfolk E., 1865–8, for Norfolk S., 1868–80, for Norfolk W., 1884–5.
[526] Frederick Walpole (1822–76), Cons. MP for N. Norfolk, 1868–76.
[527] Robert Fellowes (?–1869) of Shotesham park.

30 October 1866.   Lord Albermarle[528] his daughter, Mr. & Mrs Legh,[529] Wm. Harcourt, R. Doyle, and E. Wodehouse came to us for the Festival.

31 October 1866.   Went to Norwich. Heard Costa's 'Naaman':[530] finely performed. All Norwich in excitement for the visit of the P. & Princess of Wales, D. of Edinburgh, & Queen of Denmark. The Norwich people out of sorts because the P. of Wales did not look graciously enough at them. H. R. H. has not the talent of pretending to look pleased. When he is bored, he looks it. Not a good quality in a Prince. In the evening to a ball at Cossey. The Prince took me to the smoking room, & asked me to advise him how he could avoid going with the Crown Prince of Prussia to Petersbg. for the Princess Dagmar's marriage. I told him he had better not make a difficulty if pressed to do it. He fancies it is a dodge of Bismarck's to secure the Crown Prince a good reception. I doubt Bismarck caring a fig about either Prince. He also asked me what sort of people the Russians are. I said they were touchy, & advised him to be particular about 'petits soins'.

Query. Was not the whole conversation a pretext to get out of the ball room to smoke? Ld. Stafford must have spent a heap of money on this visit which he can ill afford.

1 November 1866.   Thursday. Shot thro' the Forehoe wood.

2 November 1866.   Friday. Do. the Wildman & Alma & New Wood.

3 November 1866 Saturday. Attended meeting to settle rules of new Chamber of Commerce.

I forgot to mention that on Oct 25 I went to dinner of N. Walsham Agric: Society. A succeessful 'jáu baterie' as Suffield appropriately called it. The farmers in particularly good humour. From this to Nov 14 led a very quiet life at home attending to Assessment Committees, petty sessions & such small matters.

27 November 1866.   Tuesday. Went on a visit to Raby. We met there

---

[528] George Thomas Keppel (1799–1891), Lib. MP for E. Norfolk, 1832–5, for Lymington, 1847–50; priv. sec. to Lord John Russell, 1846; succ. as 6th Earl of Albermarle, 1851.

[529] In 1856 William John Legh m. Kimberley's cousin, Emily Jane, da. of Rev. Charles-Nourse Wodehouse, Can. of Norwich, and Lady Jane Wodehouse.

[530] Sir Michael Costa (1810–84), dir. of music at Covent Garden theatre from 1846; composed the oratorio 'Naaman', 1864; resident in England from 1829.

Ld. & Lady Morton,[531] Ld. & Ly. Durham,[532] Ld. Garlies,[533] Mr Tomline, Capt. Ellis, & Mr Wells. The Castle is a splendid building, more picturesque and imposing than Windsor tho' of course not so large. No one could be more anxious than the Duke & Duchess to amuse their guests. The shooting was good, the best day 580 head (9 guns). All that was wanting was a tolerable cook, drinkable wine, attentive servants, & a comfortable bed.[534] I had a good deal of talk with Mr. Tomline about politics. He thinks the Govt. won't bring in a Reform Bill, and that the Tories despairing of office will become Radical, and run a-muck.

2 December 1866.   Saturday. Returned home.

14 December 1866.   Johnny came home, very much grown.

1 January 1867.   Tuesday. A new year! The old year has been in many ways a happy and prosperous one for me. May I improve my opportunities, & do my duty better, more energetically and with a single mind in the year which now opens.

A very hard frost and heavy fall of snow last night. Johnny & I shot seven wild ducks to day.

2 January 1867.   Wednesday. To Holkham[535] on a visit till Saturday. The party the Prince & Princess of Wales, D. of Edinburgh,[536] D. & Duchess of Sutherland,[537] Dunmores,[538] Powerscourts,[539] Suffields, Lord Huntly,[540] an inpertinent young puppy from Cambridge and many others.

Thursday was the great days' shooting. We killed 1683 head 16 guns. A stupid massacre on the whole, and horribly cold. The Ladies including the Princess picknicked in a tent, & walked about in the snow (the Princess in a sledge) to see the shooting. A very unfeminine proceeding. The Prince of Wales looked very ill. He is ruining his health as fast as he can—eats enormously, sits up all night, smokes incessantly, drinks continually 'nips' of brandy, he has only to add as I fear he will gambling and whoring to become the rival of the 'first gentleman in Europe'– It will be an evil day if this should be the result of his present

---

531 Sholto John Douglas, 19th Earl of Morton (1818–84).

532 George Frederick D'Arcy Lambton, 2nd Earl of Durham (1828–79).

533 Lord Garlies, title by which 9th Earl of Galloway (1800–73) sat in Lords.

534 This sentence quoted verbatim in the Kimberley Memoir, herein, 492.

535 Holkham Hall, country seat of the Dukes of Leicester.

536 Prince Alfred Ernest Albert, Duke of Edinburgh (1844–1900), succ. as D. of E., 1866.

537 George Granville William Leveson-Gower, 3rd Duke of Sutherland (1828–92).

538 Charles Adolphus Murray, 7th Earl of Dunmore (1841–1907).

539 Mervyn Wingfield, 7th Viscount Powerscourt (1836–1904).

540 Charles Gordon, 11th Marquess of Huntly (1847–1937).

utterly foolish frivolous life, but it seems inevitable. The Princess is a pretty amiable lady.

In the evening one night we had a dance but this was too quiet for the Prince who prefers some romping game. We had a specimen of this the next night. It was a melancholy exhibition—at once puerile and *mauvais* too. Add to this that the other chief amusement was putting brandy cherries &c. in tail pockets, Harvey sauce in flasks &c. and you have a picture of the tom foolery which we very unwillingly took some part in. Ld. Leicester would have stopped it if he could, but he could do nothing but look on in disgust & contempt.

The frost continued all this week, the thermometer at Kimberley marking one night four degrees below zero.

I omitted to mention that I had some slight conversation with the Prince on political matters enough to show me that he is becoming unmistakeably Tory. The D. of Edinburgh behaved quietly enough.

7 January 1867. Monday. Another year of my life ended. To day I am 41 years old. Would that I could indeed 'grow in grace as I grow in years'. To day George Currie & Evy and on Tuesday Arthur Eden came on a visit. Eden is very cheery & very little changed: just a trifle grey. We shot thro' the woods this week but killed not much game.

On Saturday our party broke up. On Friday 11 Jany. it began to snow. On Monday we went to Letton & returned home on Wednesday on the afternoon of which day & following night there was a very heavy fall of snow. All the roads quite blocked up. The snow at least a foot or 14 inches deep even where not drifted. Johnny could not go back to Eton till Saturday when with great difficulty we got to Wymondham with four horses.

The snow, the deepest I ever saw here, was full a foot deep even where not drifted. We had a very heavy flood on its departure. So great were the drifts in places that traffic was quite stopped. The wife & children of Mr Johnson of Yaxham who had been to a party at Mr. Raikes' could not get home till Saturday, and then only on horseback. They were obliged to take refuge at B. Broom Rectory.

5 February 1867. Tuesday. Went to London for the meeting of Parliament. Nothing worth notice in the debate on the address. Lord Russell made a bilious unwise speech.

11 February 1867. Monday. Saw the Reform demonstration from the windows of the Travellers'—the procession about one hour & 1/4 passing. It was a flat affair. Some of the processionists e.g. the tailors were respectable artizans but there were many dirty boys & rabble. Altogether, a failure. But not so geat a failure as Disraeli's speech in the evening in the H. of Commons, which was dull, empty, and pompous–a total failure in matter and manner.[541]

12 February 1867. Tuesday. The Fenian attempt at Chester[542] absurd tho' it may seem was I believe connected with the simultaneous outbreak in Kerry. The information of the Govt. must have been bad or their foresight none: else how on the eve of an outbreak could they have announced with a flourish of trumpets the non-renewal of the H. Corpus Suspension Act?

14 February 1867. Thursday. Lord Naas goes off in hot haste to Dublin. What is the good of a Lord Lieutenant if on an emergency whilst Parlt. is sitting the Chief Secretary must leave his duties in London? The fact is a C. Secretary in the Cabinet is the head of the Govt. of Ireland, and the Lord Lieut: a mere useless appendage–a sort of Lord Mayor. The common sense course is to abolish the Lord Lieutenancy.

16 February 1867. Saturday. Great perplexity as to the course of the Liberals on the Reform resolutions.[543] The honest course & best in itself would be to propose as an amendment that the resolutions are too vague to afford a basis for a bill, but our party broken and half hearted, fearing a dissolution, won't support I am afraid, this view. The other alternative seems unavoidable to discuss and try to amend the resolutions. No good result seems probable. If the Liberal party with all the advantage of office and with a large nominal majority could not carry a bill how can the same party divided and disorganized carry a bill in opposition. Yet that is in fact what they are asked to do by the Government. The position of Ministers is most contemptible, but that of the whole H. of Commons is not much better. I greatly fear the dishonest conduct of the House will stir up at last a democratic agitation wh. will carry a democratic bill. Better even that than the present cowardly false line which the House takes on all questions home & foreign, faithfully reflecting the opinions of the middle classes, the always cowardly, ease loving bourgeoisie. A strong infusion of working class men into the constituencies is the only remedy.

22 February 1867. Friday. Debate in H. of Lords on Land Tenure in Ireland raised by L. Clanricarde. I spoke shortly. The Irish landlords

---

[541] Cf. Malmesbury's assessment that Disraeli had 'dissatisfied the House by too long and ambiguous a speech'. *Memoirs of an Ex-Minister: An Autobiography* (new edn, London, 1885), 627.

[542] To seize arms and ammunition stores at Chester Castle.

[543] Kimberley wrote to Larcom that 'men's minds are wholly occupied with Reform'. 18 Feb. 1867, LcP 7593.

are obstinately bent on preventing useful legislation on this subject. They are not without some excuse, having the unreasonable Celtic tenant to deal with; but some remedy must be tried.

Dined with T. Baring: the best dinner and best served entertainment I ever saw. Met there Adams[544] the U.S. Minister, a dry quiet man with some dignity of manner. His wife vulgar as Yankee women usually are.

25 February 1867.   Monday. The Ministry at last make up their minds to announce a definite place for reform. For the last two days they have been in a miserable state of indecision, balancing between household suffrage & plurality of votes and £6 rating &c. Their position becomes more despicable daily.

26 February 1867.   Tuesday. Gladstone's meeting went off I hear well but some grumbling at Ld. Russell's presence. His determination to remain at the head is a stumbling block to many Liberals. Monday. The Habeas C. Susp: Bill moved in our house. I drew attention to the foolish popularity hunting speech at Galway of the Irish Atty. General Michael Morris. I might have been more severe but an occasion of this kind is one on which party attacks should be abstained from.

27 February 1867.   Wednesday. See last paragraph. Ministers at length compelled to bring in a bill for Reform. I heard Disraeli make the announcement. He looked dejected and beaten. His party disgusted and sullen. A decisive measure from the Opposition was all the encouragement he got. The bitterest enemies of the Tories must be satisfied with the retribution which has fallen on them for their factious conduct last year. As for the adullam faction, it is no where. I called on Gladstone last Friday to talk about Irish land bills.[545] He is disposed to run our scheme against Naas'. Brand came in & we began to talk of Reform. I spoke in favour of household suffrage. Gladstone looked astonished & said he did not wish to go so far. It is said he is rather alarmed at the progress of 'democratic' ideas in our party.

3 March 1867.   Sunday. News that Peel, Cranborne[546] & Carnarvon have resigned.

---

[544] Charles Francis Adams (1807–86), US min. to Great Britain, 1861–68.

[545] See *Liberal by Principle*, 42.

[546] Robert Arthur Talbot Gascoyne-Cecil (1830–1903), Cons. MP for Stamford, 1853–68; India sec., 1866–7, 1874–6; for. sec., 1878–80, 1885–6, 1887–2, 1895–1900; pr. min., 1885–6, 1886, 1887–92, 1895–1902 succ. as Viscount Cranborne, 1865, as 3rd Marquis of Salisbury, 1868.

4 March 1867. Monday. No explanation in the House of Commons because the leave of the Queen (so Cranborne said) had not been given to reveal the Cabinet secrets. Dizzy dropped a few strange words about reverting to their 'original plan'! A full revelation on the other hand in our house never did I hear a more degrading contemptible statement than Lord Derby's.

He talked of the resolutions as a 'tentative process'. Well might Grey call this fishing for a policy. Carnarvon made a poor nervous speech, as if he was begging Derby's pardon for leaving them.

5 March 1867. Tuesday. A full disclosure in the House of Commons. Was there ever a more pitiable exhibition of imbecility and levity in dealing with a mighty question.

6 March 1867. Wednesday. A formidable outbreak in Ireland. A pretty commentary on the popularity hunting speeches & vacillating policy of this wretched Government.

8 March 1867. Friday. A debate in our house raised by Argyll on the Cretan papers. Argyll made a fine but most indiscreet speech. I said a few words to show that his former colleagues are not as imprudent as he is. His views are those of an enthusiast not of a statesman.

9 March 1867. Saturday. Long talk with little Sullivan our Ex Irish Solr. General. He takes a gloomy view of the S. of Ireland. He says Morris is utterly unfit for his post: Blackburne[547] infirm & unimportant: Abercorn does no political work. Naas however has a head on his shoulders. The new appointments of Cabinet Ministers are truly brilliant! The Dukes of Buckingham[548] and Marlborough are shining lights indeed.

12 March 1867. Tuesday. Began to sit on a Select Committee on Railway Bills &c.

18 March 1867. Monday. 2nd reading of Reform Bill. Gladstone made a brilliant & destructive onslaught on the Bill. Dizzy's opening speech tame: his announcement of dual voting received with deep groans by the opposition. I did not stay till Cranborne & Lowe's speeches.

[547] Francis Blackburne (1782–1867), ld. chan. for Ireland, 1852, 1866–7.
[548] Richard Plantagenet Campbell Temple Nugent Brydes Chandos Grenville, 3rd Duke of Buckingham and Chandos (1823–89), pres. of council, 1866–67; col. sec., 1867–8; gov. of Madras, 1875–80. Even Disraeli considered Buckingham a poor second. W. Monypenny and G. Buckle, *Life of Disraeli* (6 vols., London, 1910–20), IV, 504–5.

19 March 1867.   Tuesday. Went to the Queen's Court with Flo: & was presented.

21 March 1867.   Thursday. Finished Select Committee.

22 March 1867.   Friday. Went to Levee.

23 March 1867.   Saturday. This whole week spent by the Liberal party in trying to reconcile their differences. Gladstone & all the leaders, rightly as I think, wished to oppose the 2nd reading but were obliged to give way to the objections of the malcontents 100 or 120 in number among whom Enfield made himself very prominent. Gladstone was at first as was not surprising intensely disgusted with his half hearted cowardly followers. At the levee he said to me with an air of great vexation 'If the party won't support me I shall go back to Italy & give up the game'. After the meeting at his house he was somewhat appeased.
   What a spectacle the H. of Commons presents!

Monday March 25 and Tuesday– 25.   Debates in H. of C. on Reform. On Tuesday night Disraeli made a brilliant speech, coolly professing himself ready to yield anything. His policy is to force the oppositon to produce some competing plan, & he reckons on our dissensions which are palpable, to find a way of safety for the Ministry.

26 March 1867.   Wednesday. Dined at Grillions, where I made the acquaintance of Dizzy. He appears very little worn by business or age. He was full of exultation & sarcasm.

30 March 1867.   Saturday. On Thursday night I made a few remarks in the H. of Lords on the Ecclesiastical Titles Bill. It is well to get clear of all entanglement with that escapade of Lord Russell before the Irish Church Question comes up for serious discussion.

5 April 1867.   Thursday. Heard a portion of Disraeli's Budget speech. Very well received by our side, sullen silence on the Tory side.

7 April 1867.   Saturday. To Eton to see Johnny. Yesterday dined at Pol: Econ: Club. Took part in the discussion Irish Land Tenure. I defended the Govt. measure of last year. Mill & Bagehot[549] & Dufferin agreed with me.

---

[549] Walter Bagehot (1826–77), ed. of *Economist*, 1860–77.

8 April 1867. Sunday. At Cosmop: Extraordinary disorganization in the Liberal party exists according to some. Sixty or seventy opposition will, it is said, vote with Government. All sorts of gloomy reports are flying about. The French Emperor said to pass his days crying partly over his diplomatic failures, partly over the ill health of the Prince Imperial. I don't believe it. The Princess of Wales' leg so bad that it will have to be amputated, which I also don't believe, tho' I fear she is not doing well.

Lord Clarendon says the true explanation of the state of the Liberal party is that given him by an Italian Radical statesman of the difficulties of the Italian Parliament 'Sono tutti castrati'. Lord C. gave me a curious account of his conversation with the Emperor L. N. when he went to Paris in 1864 to try to induce him to join us in supporting Denmark. He absolutely refused, giving exactly the reason which Drouyen de Lhuys gave me when I saw him at Paris on my way home from Copenhagen. Our unsteady conduct in the Polish business, the impossibility of efficient aid from England to France in a war with Germany, the fear that we should not agree that the French should have the Rhine frontier as the prize of victory.

It is difficult now to say which has made the greatest diplomatic blunders during the last 3 years, England or France or which has lost weight & reputation the most. The influence of both is incalculably lessened.

12 April 1867. Friday. Government victorious over Gladstone's amendment on personal rating 288–310. More than 40 of our men voted against us 19 stayed away. As many of those who did vote with us, voted against their convictions, it is fortunate we did not win. Gladstone should have persisted in fighting on the 2nd reading if he wanted to upset the bill. But the bill is so craftily framed that his opposition could scarcely have been successful however conducted. He is I fear very unpopular as a leader.[550]

Johnny came home today.

18 April 1867. Thursday. Johnny confirmed at St James' church by Bp of Oxford.

23 April 1867. Tuesday. Went with Johnny to Truro. Stayed with the Smiths who were as kind & hospitable as usual. Wednesday and Thursday passed these days at Falmouth, looking over my property. The town much improved. Had a meeting of the Mayor, A. Fox &

---

[550] Late in life, Kimberley recalled how curious it was 'now to reflect upon his unpopularity as leader'. Kimberley Memoir, herein, 492. See too entry for 9 July 1867.

other members of Chamber of Commerce. Some dismay at Govt. decision that the packets are to call at Plymouth. The worst business is the docks. The breakwater is seriously damaged by the gale and the Cy. have no money to repair it.

On Thursday evening went to Penzance.

26 April 1867.   Friday. Went in such rain as one only sees in the West to the Logan rock & Lands' End. The coast scenery superb. Returned to Truro, where we 'did' a volunteer function, amateur concert, & bazaar, & I made a speech, the usual 'buncombe' suited to these occasions.

27 April 1867.   Saturday. Returned home & found Flo. & the children all well & delighted with their trip to Eastbourne.

4 May 1867.   Saturday. Delane told me at Lady Molesworth's the astonishing news that Walpole had 'caved in' about Monday's meeting in the Park.[551]

6 May 1867.   Monday. Beales triumphant.

9 May 1867.   Thursday. Ld. Cowper in a rather heavy bungling speech attacked the Ministry for their conduct in the Hyde Park matter. Derby in reply announced that the Cabinet was responsible, but that he had thrown Walpole overboard. His imbecillity is almost beyond belief. The loss of a man so utterly incapable must be a gain to the Ministry.

10 May 1867.   Friday. The majority of 66 in favour of the Govt. last night settles the question of the Reform Bill for this session. The opposition party is shattered to pieces. Gladstone's excessive vehemence in this last debate was a sad mistake in tactics. But in the main he is right, tho' this cynical unbelieving H. of Commons won't follow him. The Tories are now quite delighted. Personal payment of rates is the expedient by which they claim to have saved the Constitution!

All this week the weather has been oppressively hot. On Wednesday Johnny & I went to Cambridge to engage lodgings for him.

18 May 1867.   Saturday. Dizzy having accepted the principle of Hodgkinson's amendment now discovers that he was always for uniform household suffrage![552] Thus after all the Radicals have their way. The

---

[551] Of the Reform League. Described in *Annals of our Time* as 'orderly as an Exeter Hall meeting', 774–5.
[552] See p. 25, herein.

Tories say they prefer this to last year's bill because the lower you go, the more ignorant and dependent the voters will be! Thus it seems if you dig deep enough you come to a lowest stratum of dirt which is Tory dirt. A truly noble creed for the gentlemen of England.

21 May 1867.   Monday. Heard Lowe denounce the Tories. They visibly winced, and well they might, under the well laid on lash.

23 May 1867.   Wednesday. The Derby. The weather now cold as mid-winter. Snow sleet & a bitter N.Easter. Mr Chaplin said to have won £120,000; Ld. Hastings to have lost ditto. Every one will be glad that the former has this sweet revenge for Lord H's shabby conduct about Lady F. P.[553]

26 May 1867.   Saturday. Discussed at dinner at Ld. Clarendon's with Ld. C., Gladstone and Sir G. Grey the question of hanging Burke. They were all strongly against. I differed.[554] I don't believe the disaffected Irish will be conciliated by this sentimental clemency, and the ignorant peasantry will attribute our merciful policy merely to fear of the U. States. But it would no doubt have been better to try the prisoners for treason-felony. The question would then never have arisen. As it is, as usual, the Govt. by 'caving in' at the last moment have shown that they have no foresight, and no authority.

28 May 1867.   Monday. Spoke on the H. Corpus Susp. Bill. Derby said the Irish Church is no grievance. Note that for future use.

1 June 1867.   Friday. Moved 2nd reading of O'Loghlen's[555] bills, oaths & c. My speech which was a short one, well received. Lds Courtown,[556] Bandon[557] &c. talked some foolish twaddle, & the bills were read 2nd time.

4 June 1867.   Tuesday. I hear old Brougham who has just arrived in London, is quite childish. An old friend of his said to him don't you remember me, Mr. B——. Ld. B. anwered Mr. B— is dead. On Mr. B— controverting this, Ld. B. got quite angry: & said 'Pray don't dispute with me a fact wh. is within my personal knowledge.'

---

[553] See entry for 16 July 1864.
[554] On the danger posed by Michael Burke, leader of the Fenian raid in Canada, see Kimberley to Clarendon, 4 June 1866, C1P C 99.
[555] Sir Colman Michael O'Loghlen (1819–77), Lib. MP for Co. Clare, 1863–77.
[556] James George Henry Stopford, 5th Baron Courtown (1823–1914).
[557] Francis Bernard, 3rd Earl of Bandon (1810–77).

12 June 1867. Wednesday. To Minley & stayed till Saturday. Abraham Hayward[558] there, made a pitiable exhibition of conceit, and talked too much to be witty.

19 June 1867. Wednesday. Fakenham (see below).

24 June 1867. Monday. Debate in the House of Lords on Irish Church. I spoke in answer to Lord Cairns.[559] My speech was well received, & I was much complimented by my friends but there was not much in it. I have not studied the question deeply enough to make a really good speech. My answer to Cairns was well enough as a debating reply but something more is required to make an impression on the public mind.[560] The division did not fairly represent opinions in the House, as Ld. Grey, furious at finding people argue with him, forced a division, when it had been agreed that we should not divide. A more cantankerous useless man does not exist. All his powers are thrown away, and his influence is absolutely nil in the House & scarcely anything out of it. It is evident I fear that public opinion is unfavourable to endowment of the Catholics. If so, nothing will remain but to adopt the voluntary system. The policy of the English Episcopalians is short sighted. If they wish to preserve the English Establisht. they should strengthen the principle of endowments.

29 June 1867. Saturday. Have attended numerous meetings of Clanricarde's Land Tenure Committee. A worse Chairman than C. it wd. be difficult to find.

I have forgotten to note my journey to Fakenham where on June 19 I presided at the dinner of the Norfolk Agricultural Assn. I made a speech of more than an hour which was well received, considering that I was not very complimentary to my bucolic audience. There were over 200 persons at the dinner. I slept at R. Hamond's. Went to Eton to-day.

4 July 1867. Thursday. Heard Verdi's new opera 'Don Carlos' at Covent Garden; a gloomy, dull opera.

9 July 1867. Tuesday. Ld. de Grey told me that the D. of Cambridge had expressed himself in the strongest terms of condemnation at the

[558] Abraham Hayward (1801–84), essayist who wrote widely for the *Quarterly Review*, *Edinburgh's Magazine* and *Fraser's Magazine*.

[559] Hugh MacCalmont Cairns (1819–85), Cons. MP for Belfast, 1852–66; ld. chanc., 1868, 1874–80; cr. Baron Cairns of Garmoyle, Antrim, 1867, Viscount Garmoyle and Earl Cairns (UK peerage), 1878.

[560] On the nature of Kimberley's oratory, see *Liberal by Principle*, 28, 47–50.

Queen's not entertaining the Sultan[560a] and her general neglect of her public duties. By Gd. said H. R. H. she ought to abdicate! She is certainly unpopular in London, and I hear the mob begins to speak very disrespectfully of her.

We had a sharp and interesting discussion in the Select Committee on Proxies &c. Ld. Redesdale stated all the stock Tory arguments if arguments they can be called. Ld. Shaftesbury blurted out that if the Lords did not get rid of proxies the Reformed H. of Commons might do it for them, much to the horror of the Tory peers. Ld. Stanhope was absurdly pompous, & priggish. Ld. Malmesbury characteristically foolish and weak. He advised us to decide the question without reference to opinion out of doors, or in the House of Commons! But the weight of argument went so much against proxies that they were condemned by 12 to 4. Malmesbury notwithstanding his bold speech abstained from voting!

The Reform bill went through the Committee in the H. of Commons to day. I met Lowe at dinner at Airlie's. He thinks Gladstone loses ground daily. I fear it is so. His very honesty is now a hindrance to him. Our prospects as a party are decidedly bad. And I even doubt whether they will mend in the new Parliament.

11 July 1867. Thursday. Committee on Oaths Bill & Transubstantiation Bill, passed after a foolish attempt of Ld. Chelmsford to substitute for verbally making the declaration against transubstantiation &c. a subscription to it. We had an unexpectedly good division on Lyveden's motion to admit R. Catholics to Lord Lieutenancy of Ireland (69 to 55), tho' of course we were beaten. Westmeath made a speech of frantic violence & nonsense.

15 July 1867. Monday. Reform bill passed in H. of Commons. The world all half mad about the Sultan's visit.

17 July 1867. Wednesday. Heard Nilson[561] sing in 'Don Giovanni'. She has a very pretty but not a rich voice. With the aid of a fair young face she has made a most favourable debut in London.

18 July 1867. Thursday. Saw the Sultan pass on his way to Guildhall. The only view I am likely to have of him as happily I am not going to any of the fêtes.

[560a] Abdul Aziz (1830–76), first sultan of the Ottoman Empire, r. 1861–76, to visit Western Europe. A series of state functions during July included trips to Covent Garden, the Crystal Palace, and the Guildhall, and a ball given at the India Office.

[561] Christine Nilsson (1843–1921), Swedish soprano and violinist.

19 July 1867. Friday. Meeting at Lord Russell's. This was a meeting to consider what course should be taken on the Reform Bill. It was attended by the Dukes of Somerset, Devonshire, Argyll, Cleveland, Lords Russell, Halifax, Taunton, Lyveden, Cranworth, Granville, Clarendon, de Grey, Stanley of Alderley, Spencer, and myself. Lord R. declared his intention of proposing the £4 franchise even though he stood alone. General chorus of disapprobation. The principal subject of discussion was Lord Grey's resolution. This Lord R. had to a certain extent promised to support. The D. of Somerset was strongly against it, & declared that whatever others did, he would speak & vote against it. It was in his opinion a dishonest resolution and he should say so in the House. The Dukes of Argyll, Devonshire, Cleveland all against it. Granville spoke against it, but said ultimately he would vote for it. Clarendon against. I gave my own opinion against. In short the predominant feeling was against. Lord Taunton the only one heartily for it. The general opinion in the party was found to be so much against it that all idea of supporting it was eventually abandoned.

20 July 1867. Saturday. Saw the Sultan at Buckingham Palance.

22 July 1867. Monday. Second reading of Reform Bill in House of Lords. Ld. Derby's speech very tame. Ld. Grey broke down in the middle of a very common place speech. Carnarvon was admirable. Granville spoke well, but made some egregious mistakes in good taste: in fact his jokes were almost vulgar. There were however some happy colloquial hits.

23 July 1867. Tuesday. Adjourned debate. Shaftesbury began with a very eloquent alarmist speech. Argyll made a capital attack on Ministers. Cairns a very ingenious apology for them: but he was too long & rather wearied the house. The 'Dukes' were as heavy & dull as could be desired by us discontented Whigs. Ld. Camperdown[562] made a neat maiden speech. Morley[563] a pretty speech but in rather too humble & feminine a tone. Altogether the debate left the impression that the House swallows the Bill as a bitter dose and that Ministers are dishonest politicians, and somewhat sore at being told so. But they have the Tory majority behind them, & the bill is perfectly safe. Nor could the Liberal party honestly attack it.

[562] Robert Adam Philips Haldane-Duncan (1841–98), succ. as 3rd Earl of Camperdown, 1867.
[563] Albert Edmund Parker, 3rd Earl Morley (1843–1905), u.-sec. war, 1880–5; first com. of pub. wks, 1886; resigned over Home Rule.

25 July 1867.   Thursday. I moved Oxford & Cambridge Tests Abolition Bill.[564] I cannot flatter myself that my speech was very effective, but I got through tolerably and was well beaten on a division as I expected. Lord Russell spoke in a very spirited manner, better than I have heard him for some time. My interview last Saturday with the Sultan was of the briefest. A certain number of ex-ministers &c. were invited by Musurus[565] to attend. If Musurus had been there, he would have explained to the Sultan who we were. But poor Madame Musurus' sudden death at the Ball at the India House on Friday night of course prevented him from attending, and as Fuad Pasha[566] knew scarcely any of us by sight & had probably not heard the names of the greater part of us before, the affair passed off nearly in dumb show. The Sultan is a short dark handsome intelligent looking man. It is a great pity he can only speak his own language. I heard a characteristic story about Ld. Cardigan. When the Sultan bowed to him amongst the rest, Fuad mumbling something as he did at each presentation about the Sultan being glad to see him, Ld. C. called out in great dudgeon I led the charge at Balaclava. Lord Bradford attended as Lord Chamberlain but I suspect his explanations which were very curt were limited by a narrow stock of French words.

29 July 1867.   Monday. Committee on the Reform Bill. Lord Derby being ill with the gout, Malmesbury took the lead & made himself most ridiculous. The Duke of Marlborough not much better: and altogether the sorriest exhibition of Ministerial incompetence I ever saw. Such blundering, ignorance, and awkwardness would have been discreditable to parish vestrymen. Lord Halifax made a good speech in proposing his resolution but of course we were beaten (not in debate but on the division). I tried to speak but the house would not hear me, preferring to hear Lord Fortescue who punished them well by inflicting upon them sundry other dull boring speeches in the course of these discussions. I must take it as a wholesome warning not to speak too often. After the rejection of Ld. Halifax's motion Lord Cairns proposed to raise the lodger franchise from £10 to £15. Malmesbury forthwith assented with hardly a word of explanation. We strongly remonstrated but in vain. It was carried aginst us on a divison; ditto Harrowby's motion to raise the copyhold & leasehold franchises & Cairns' to University residents the borough franchise. Ministers were insolent as well as idiotic. One of our leaders asking the opinion of the Gt. on some

[564] See 3 *Hansard* 189 (25 July 1867), 75–6; C. Harvie, *The Lights of Liberalism, University Liberals and the Challenge of Democracy, 1860–86* (London, 1976), 88–91.

[565] Constantine Musurus (1807–91), Turkish amb.

[566] Mehmet Fuad Pasha (1814–69), Turkish for. min., 1852–3, 1853–5, 1858, 1867–8; grand vizier, 1861–8.

clause, the D. of Marlborough had the impudence to say 'You will see when we divide'!

30 July 1867. Tuesday. To night in Committee Cairns' 'minority' clause carried by a large majority. I never was in greater doubt in my life which way to vote. My inclination was against the proposal but when I found that Lord Russell, Argyll, Ld. Clarendon, de Grey, D. of Somerset & Stanley of Alderley were all for, I felt great reluctance to separate from them. Granville voted against. Finally just before the division I resolved to stay out with Ld. Halifax & Ld. Lyveden & not to vote. On reflection I am very glad I did not vote for but the abstaining from voting is rather a weak course, and my opinion being against the proposal on the whole, I should have done better to vote against. Lord Stanhope made a smart speech in favour, and the speaking for was unquestionably superior to the speaking against; but in the absence of Lord Derby there was no one to argue the case on the Govt. side. Dizzy was in the House, & did not look pleased at the result. The Tory peers showed clearly enough why they voted for it. They looked on it as a Tory contrivance to check democracy. I don't suppose if Lord Derby had been present he could have defeated Cairns but the majority would have been smaller.

31 July 1867. Wednesday. The 'Times' sings a paean over Cairns' or rather the Times' victory. It is pretty evident that Walter's seat for the three cornered constituencey of Berkshire is the prize for which the Times is contending with such frantic violence.[567] But this minority dodge will be found unacceptable to the mass of the English people, and the idea of stemming the democratic tide by such paper contrivances seems to me preposterous. Philosophers have ever been bad constitution makers from Plato down to Sieyès, and this philosophical scheme of Lowe, Mill and the philosophers of the H. of Commons will I believe prove no exception to the rule.[568]

1 August 1867. Thursday. Lord Derby came down to the House looking very ill and weak and with one arm in a sling. His presence was very necessary. By unsparing use of the whip he managed to defeat Grey's motion on re-distribution by a narrow majority. If those Tories who

---

[567] In a series of articles in *The Times* supporting cumulative voting. If adopted the system would allow John Walter (1818–94), proprietor of *The Times*, to be elected. Lib. MP for Nottingham, 1847–59, for Berkshire, 1859–65, 1868–85.

[568] On 30 May 1867, Mill had argued for proportional representation: 'the majority should be represented by a majority, and the minority by a minority'. See B. Kinzer, A. Robson and J. Robson, *A Moralist in and out of Parliament: John Stuart Mill at Westminster, 1865–1868* (Toronto, 1992), 100–7.

promised Grey had voted with him the Govt. would have been beaten. The present redistribution cannot stand. We have at all events the satisfaction of knowing that we are free from all responsibility for the failure to settle this part of the question. I got an opportunity of making a short statement of my views.

2 August 1867.   Friday. The important question of this evening was the voting paper clause proposed by Lord Salisbury. I spoke & voted against it. It was carried by a large majority. The bill went thro' Committee to night.

5 August 1867.   Monday. On the report Lord Derby wisely gave up the alteration in the Lodger clause, thus avoiding an inevitable defeat in the H. of Commons.

6 August 1867.   Tuesday. The bill read a third time, after some croaking speeches of no importance. On the whole I think the Lords have displayed creditable ability in these debates except on the Govt. side where Cairns, a host certainly in himself, alone defended the Bill, the rest of the Tory peers in the absence of Lord Derby being quite incapable of debating the measure. The strong Conservative feeling of both sides of the House was strongly marked. Great & I think unfounded terror was manifested, and it is evident that there are not above a dozen really Liberal peers in the House.

7 August 1867.   Wednesday. Went down to Kimberley. On reflection I think I have been tolerably active in politics this session and without achieving any marked success have fairly maintained my position. I was asked to take charge of the Church Rates Bill but declined thinking I have done enough in that direction lately. I don't want to appear always in a position of prominent antagonism to the Church. The bill (for the abolition) was moved by Ld. Morley and rejected.

10 August 1867.   Saturday. Lambert killed a black buck weighed 11 st. 4 clean. He came from Elmham, got away soon after his arrival & was retaken in Falstaff wood, for wh. reason we christened him the 'Falstaff' Buck.

12 August 1867.   Monday. Attended Board of Guardians as Chairman for the first time.

14 August 1867.   Wednesday. Attended opening of the Workman's Industrial Exhibition in Norwich at St Andrew's Hall. Prodigiously hot.

Made a speech, perspiring freely. The Mayor, Watson[569] & the Sheriff Clabburn[570] also harangued.

16 August 1867. Friday. Began harvest on the home farm. The twentieth anniversary of our wedding day, which dear Flo. & I passed with great content & happiness.

20 August 1867. Tuesday. My Uncle Rebow and his two little girls came & stayed till Thursday. They are self-willed spoiled little minxes.

21 August 1867. Wednesday. Parliament prorogued.

26 August 1867. Monday. Started for Glenisla, slept at Edinburgh, & arrived at the Tulchan next day. The weather throughout my visit was most unfavourable for deerstalking. The hills were only clear for two days. I got but one stalk at a stag which I killed; a small beast weighing but 9 stone 4. Lord Wemyss killed a stag with a fair head weighing 14 st. 6 lb. No other deer were killed during my stay. The grouse were abundant, tho' all around they have died off. Lord Wemyss is a wonderful old man in point of bodily vigour. He is 72 years old, hunts his own hounds, & walks on the hills like a young man. He went down a very steep place to stalk his deer, a feat not unattended even with some risk.

Jowett & Mr. Roundell[571] & Maude Stanley[572] were the other visitors. Mr. R. told me the Oxford Univ: Reformers mean to agitate for the complete opening of the Universities, including the College endowments to all religious persuasions. He is a quiet man with more in him than appears at first sight.

6 September 1867. Friday. Left Glenisla, slept at York & arrived home on Saturday night where I had the delight of finding my dearest wife & the children all well.

11 September 1867. Wednesday. Went to Witton on a visit till Saturday. On Tuesday Sept 10 Lambert killed a buck weighing 10 st: 13 lbs.

---

[569] Frederick Elwin Watson.

[570] William Houghton Clabburn.

[571] Charles Savile Roundell (1827–1906), priv. sec. to ld. lt., Earl Spencer, 1869–71; Lib. MP for Grantham, 1880–5, Skipton, Yorkshire, W. Riding, 1892–5. On Kimberley's favourable estimation of Roundell, see Kimberley to Spencer, 12 January 1869, in *Liberal by Principle*, 115–16.

[572] Maude Stanley (1832–1915), younger sister of Lady Airlie.

17 September 1867.   Tuesday. My mother, Henry, Leeson & Philip Currie came on a visit.

24 September 1867.   Tuesday. Lambert killed (by mistake) a six year old [five off] buck weighing 9 st. 13 lbs. The weights of the deer are extraordinary this year. All clean weights.

1 October 1867.   Tuesday. Henry & my mother came back from Letton and stayed till the following week (Wednesday).

12 October 1867.   Saturday. Attended Agricultural Chamber at Norwich. Discussion on employment of women & children in agriculture. I said a few words. Nothing very notable except a very silly speech from Leman the W. Norfolk yeoman.

15 October 1867.   Tuesday. Took dear Johnny to Cambridge. We had luncheon with Philip Frere who has married a plain but amiable mannered wife. He has poor fellow a disease of the lungs wh. would make most men hesitate to beget children. He has four.

We visited Dr. Thompson,[573] the master of Trinity, a keen witted man with the manners of a gentleman, which is not always the case with college dons. We bought Johnny his outfit of *[ill.]* &c. & his gown, & left him duly installed in his lodgings in Jesus Lane. I earnestly pray he may do well but his character is unformed, & his loose indolent habits make me tremble for the future.[574]

17 October 1867.   Thursday. Attended Qr. Sessions.

21 October 1867.   Monday. Johnny's first start at Cambridge has been bad. He has failed to pass the matriculation Examn. He is to try again. I am not surprised. He knows scarcely any Greek and that little very imperfectly.

1 November 1867.   Hutchinson came for a couple of days. He is the most cheery old parson I know: quite the old school. He is a thorough gentleman which becomes rarer in modern parsons every day.

5 November 1867.   Tuesday. A very fine black buck killed in a fight with another buck.

---

[573] William Hepworth Thompson (1810–86), canon of Ely, 1853; master of Trinity College, Cambridge, 1866–86.
[574] On the realization of Kimberley's fears, see entries for 20 June 1868, 14 May 1870, 28 May 1871, 1 Jan. 1872. Lady Kimberley to Alice Packe, 14 Oct. 1872, PkP 1749/38/8.

A few days ago put two Egyptian & two barnacle geese in the Lake, sent me by Lord Wemyss.

12 November 1867. Sunday. S. Ponsonby, G. W. Currie and his wife & Henley came on a visit.

13 November 1867. Wednesday. Lady Leicester & Lady M. Coke & Col. Calthorpe[575] & his wife and Edmond Wodehouse came. Johnny came on Monday from Cambridge for a week, having (happily) passed his matriculation Examn. wh. he failed in at first going up. We shot the woods and found but little game, except in the Forehoe. On Saturday our visitors departed.

Evy Currie[576] has, foolish woman, become a Roman Catholic, the usual end of silly women, who have no sober ideas about religion, or indeed in her case about anything.

19 November 1867. Tuesday. Went to Quiddenham stayed till Friday. A dull party, bad cook, and bad shooting. This day Parliament met. I don't even go up unless something unexpected occurs. There is nothing to vote about, & the House evidently heard me oftener than it liked last session; so I shall keep quiet. Besides in the present most uncertain state of politics it is wiser to observe rather than act.

23 November 1867. Saturday. The three Fenians hanged at Manchester.[577] I am glad the Govt. had the firmness not to resist their punishment. A mawkish feeling has seized some part of the English people with reference to Fenianism which may do great harm. I believe it was an enormous error not to hang the Fenian raiders in Canada. Disguise it as we may, the true cause of our lenity was a shameful one, fear of the United States. It was also, I think an error not to hang Burke. Either we have no right to hold Ireland in which case we ought to recognize its independence at once, or we have a right to hold it. In the latter case we are bound to enforce the law against all Irish traitors. If the infliction of death can be avoided, so much the better, but can it? Can a Govt. which allows men who come over from a foreign country and raise an insurrection to escape the extreme penalty, inspire that wholesome fear which will deter others from similar attempts. I think not. The natural Irish party will continue to hate us, at all events

---

[575] Somerset John Gough-Calthorpe (1841–1912), col. 5th Dragoon Guards, 1866; maj.-genl., 1870; lt.-genl., 1881.

[576] *Née* Vernon, m. George Currie, 1850.

[577] On 23 Nov., for the murder of a policeman. Cf. Kimberley to deGrey, 25 Nov. 1867, in *Liberal by Principle*, 112.

for a long time to come, whatever we do. But we may inspire them with fear. Hitherto the Irish have feared England, tho' they have hated her. By this fear we have been enabled to keep some order in Ireland. If they neither love nor fear us, how can we govern them? To give up Ireland is in my mind utterly out of the question. It would be base and wicked to abandon the Northern Irish and the other Protestants & to leave the island a prey to civil war. It would indeed be impossible, for Englishmen & Scotchmen could not look on and take no part in such a struggle. Moreover an indepedent Ireland would be hostile to us in time of war. We should be compelled to reconquer the island. We must keep our hold on her, cost what it may, and the cost will be, as it ever has been, heavy.

26 November 1867.   Tuesday. Shot at Letton. A good day 405 head. Saw my poor cousin Charlotte I fear for the last time.[578]

3 December 1867.   Tuesday. Went on a visit to Wivenhoe till Friday. Met Sir C. Rowley a genial old man, Mr. Western a priggish provincial, and Mr. Augustine & wife. We had two days fair shooting.

7 December 1867.   Saturday. Parlt. adjourned. What a wretched fiasco Lord Russell's resolutions on education were! He was warned of his folly in prematurely forcing on the question: but nothing can control his senile vanity. Gladstone exhibited a sage self control. If only he will be patient till his time comes, we shall soon be rid of this feeble Govt. They have one able man Lord Stanley who does his work well.

8 December 1867.   Sunday. Bitter N. E. gales & some snow during all this week. To day a considerable fall of snow.

12 December 1867.   Thursday. Johnny came home.

26 December 1867.   Thursday. Went to Ketteringham to shoot.

1 January 1868.   Wednesday. Another year begins. What can I say of the past year? Have I made progress in anything? I doubt it. May the coming year be one of earnest work. I thank God for the many blessings I have enjoyed during the year past. May he pardon my many sins & shortcomings.

On this day Admiral W.,[579] Cecilia & Lizzy W. & Francis a friend of

---

[578] See entry for 12 Jan. 1868.

[579] Edward Thornton Wodehouse (1802–74), rear-adml.; Kimberley's paternal uncle. Cecilia and Anne-Elizabeth-Laura were the admiral's daughters.

Johnny's came on a visit. The F. Boileaues[580] came next day & all stayed till Saturday. Sir H. Durrant,[581] an almost idiot, & his wife a rather vulgar little woman dined here on Thursday.

12 January 1868.   Sunday. Nothing to record the past week. Frost & snow and foggy weather, unusually combined, have made the past 3 weeks singularly disagreeable. Poor Charlotte Brooke died yesterday.

28 January 1868.   Tuesday. Shot two does through the haunch, a singular shot, the ball after passing thro' one deer, hit another some fifteen yards to the left having glanced off a bone of the first deer. The second one was not got till some days afterwards.

30 January 1868.   Thursday. Johnny went to Cambridge.

31 January 1868.   Friday. A tremendous gale from Friday to Saturday evening, not much damage done here.

12 February 1868.   Wednesday. Went to London.

16 February 1868.   Sunday. Nothing stirring in town. Lord Derby's illness has apparently stopped all political business.

24 February 1868.   Monday. Went to a small meeting at Gladstone's house to talk over Irish affairs. Most of the members of the late Cabinet were there, besides Fortescue, Brand, Glyn, & myself. We all agreed that religious equality should be established in Ireland; and that a regular endowment of the three Irish Churches could not be proposed with any chance of success. Some of us were in favour of giving some portion of the revenues of the Irish Church to the different denominations. Lord Russell I except of course as he has a plan of endowment to which he is committed. All of us felt that he has caused much embarrassment by his premature announcement of a cut & dried plan. It was also agreed that an 'instruction' should be moved on the Scotch Reform Bill to provide the 7 seats by disfranchising 7 English boroughs.

In the H. of Lords we had a discussion on the Land Tenure in Ireland in wh. I took part: & afterwards a debate on the 2nd reading of the Habeas Corp: Susp: Bill. Lord Russell spoke with unusual vigour. Ld. Malmesbury made a pitiful figure as leader! of the Govt. At Gladstone's we all agreed not to go beyond Fortescue's Land Bill.

[580] Sir Francis George Manningham Boileau (1830–1900), son of Sir John Peter Boileau.
[581] Sir Henry Durrant, of Scottow, Norfolk; m. Alexandrina Barton, 1863.

25 February 1868.   Tuesday. Lord Derby resigned office.

5 March 1868.   Thursday. Heard ministerial explanations in both houses. Nothing remarkable except the vigorous & bitter attack of Lord Russell on the Govt. of 'deception': a most just description of them. I believe we have now the most mischievous Govt. wh. has ruled this country since Lord North. The Liberals have themselves to blame. Their dissension has brought the country under the dominion of the unscrupulous adventurer who is now at the head. What care does Disraeli for [sic] the reputation of England, or for the institutions of England? He has dragged English gentlemen through the dirt & will drag them through more still, until too late their eyes will be opened to their miserable folly & baseness. Meantime fraud reigns triumphant. May not Cranborne be the Jew's nemesis?

8 March 1868.   Sunday. Campbell Wodehouse[582] died at Norwich after a lingering illness. He is to be buried at Kimberley. He leaves no children.

10 March 1868.   Tuesday. Heard Maguire's speech on Ireland: a windy piece of Irish rhetoric.[583]

13 March 1868.   Friday. Argyll's attack on Dizzy came off in our house. It was very cleverly done. Cairns' reply is much admired, I hear, by his friends, but it was not (nor could it well be) anything more than a neat advocate's reply on behalf of a client who has no case. I doubt however the policy of Argyll's assault. It looks too like mere party bitterness and it loses half its effect by Dizzy not being in the House where it is made. But I see nothing unfair or unjust in such a criticism of a Minister's conduct. A party leader's political character must always be open to public debate.

14 March 1868.   Saturday. Bright's splendid speech last night the general topic of conversation. We are making progress in the H. of Commons, but the position of affairs is altogether uncertain till Dizzy has spoken. Will he throw over Mayo, Hardy, &c. as he did last year?[584] Not yet I think.

[582] Campbell Wodehouse (1826–68), rector of Alderford, Norfolk; collateral cousin.

[583] John Francis Maguire (1815–1872), Lib. MP for Dungarvan, 1852–65, for Cork, 1865–72; proposed a motion for a committee on the state of Ireland, describing constitutional liberty there as on a par with Morocco and Abyssinia. 3 *Hansard* 190 (10 March 1868), 1288–1314.

[584] Gathorne Hardy and Lord Mayo were known to be the staunchest defenders of the Church of Ireland in the cabinet.

17 March 1868. Tuesday. Dined at Willis' Rooms at 'Festival' of St Patrick's Assocn., the Prince of Wales presiding. He spoke remarkably well without any pretension just as an English gentleman should speak on these occasions. I proposed his health. After dinner I had some talk with him. He is evidently with the Tories at heart, & can't bear Gladstone.

20 March 1868. Friday. I was shown at the House of Lords the resolution on the Irish Church wh. Gladstone is to move. It is very stringent and I fear it will alarm some of our friends. But every possible course is open to objection. A mere abstract resolution would have been justly condemned as a factious party move. I am convinced that it is right to take decided action on the Irish Church Question. Some test must be applied to our so-called party that we may know before the elections who are & who are not our friends. We shall at all events unite all who are really Liberals: and what is much more important we shall now have a plain object in view worth fighting for.

21 March 1868. Saturday. Went to Cambridge to see Johnny, dined in the Hall at Trinity: an excellent dinner; after dinner to the combination room where were five or six dons who seemed more rational men than such men usually are. They still booze over strong Sherry and Port! In another generation they will arrive at Claret. Then we went to the 'Athenaeum'. This superb name is assumed by a club of some 25 undergraduates in two rooms over a shop! Then I smoked a cigar, & then home.

22 March 1868. Sunday. The town full of gossip about the opposition move. The quidnuncs at Lady Waldegrave's and Brooks' say we shall win. It is too early to prophesy. I note that Gladstone's speech in the late Irish Debate (altho' his declaration against the Irish Church gave much satisfaction to our party) is not considered to have been one of his happiest efforts. Dizzy was singularly dexterous in his 'chaffing' speech. Grievous heartburnings about the meeting at Gladstone's house. The Tory whip puts a spy near the house to see who goes in and out, & then sends the list to the papers—so they say: and it looks as if it were true. Dirty work.

3 April 1868. Friday. Had an interview with Sir C. Lampson,[585] which decided me to accept the Governorship of the Hudson's Bay Company. I fully explained to him that tho' I expected no change of Govt. till

[585] Sir Curtis Miranda Lampson (1806–85), advocate of the Atlantic cable; dep. gov. of Hudson's Bay Company.

next year, I am a candidate for office and the Cy. wd. of course lose my services if I should be offered a place in a Liberal Cabinet, a contingency which I regard as possible yet very uncertain. Sir C. L. said that the directors had fully considered this point, and thought it would be advantageous to the shareholders to have my assistance if only for a few months, as I should become acquainted with the affairs of the Compy. and might be of service in seeing that justice is done to them in their negotiations with Canada and the U. States. On this clear understanding I accepted the proposal to become Governor.[586] I am indebted entirely to the kindness of Raikes Currie & B. Currie for this offer. I think the business will be interesting and £1000 per ann: is not to be wholly contemned.

4 April 1868. Saturday. This morning the Govt. were beaten on the Irish Church question by 60, 270–330, a crushing majority. The club gossip to day is that Dizzy was half drunk. It seems he drank three strong glasses of brandy & water during his speech, & became quite confused and maudlin after the middle of his oration. He certainly talked arrant nonsense about the conquest of England & Ireland by the Normans, & Dutch!, and Cromwell, and ended by a ridiculous accusation in the Whalley style[587] that Gladstone is leagued with the Jesuits. No one expects the Ministry to resign. They will remain &: be dragged together with their party through the mire until the name of Dizzy will stink in the nostrils of the nation, and the Conservative party will cease to exist. Meanwhile we have dealt the death-blow to the Irish Church Establishment. The Liberal party is resuscitated. We have a policy and a leader, and justice to Ireland will if we honestly persevere, become something more than a mere party cry. There is a healthy resolve amongst us not to make any direct attempt to oust the Govt. We must get the confidence of the nation before we can put an end to the present reign of trickery. A premature attack would spoil all. Our great object must be to restore a better tone to politics, and some strength to the Executive.

I omitted to mention that a few days ago Archbishop Manning[588]

---

[586] On the circumstances surrounding Kimberley's administration, see E.E. Rich, *Hudson's Bay Company, 1670–1870* (3 vols., New York), III, 878. However, note numerous errors in the paragraph of biography. Cf., on various points, *Liberal by Principle*. Correspondence and papers relating to company business may be found in KP6 MS.eng.c.4072–3.

[587] John Whalley (1653–1724), described in the *DNB* as a 'quack', selling universal medicines and astrological works, and publishing a 'libellous weekly journal', *Whalley's News Letter*, from 1714.

[588] Henry Edward Manning (1808–92), ultramontane Roman Catholic archbishop of Westminster, 1865; cardinal, 1875; published Feb. 1868, *A Pastoral Letter ... Quinquagesima Sunday.*

called upon me to explain certain amendments in Ld. Devon's poor law bill wh. I have undertaken to move. We had a long conversation on Irish affairs. The impression he left on me was that he is a thorough specimen of a polished Jesuit, a bland insinuating man of the world intent on improving every opportunity to advance the influence of his Church. Perhaps his fault is that he is too specious. I need not record what he said about Ireland. Is it not written in his recent pamphlet?

9 April 1868. Tuesday. Saw Graves the Bp. of Limerick. We had a talk about the Irish Church. He has made up his mind that the fall of the Establishment is inevitable.

13 April 1868. Easter Monday. Went with Johnny to see c/y Portrait Gallery at Kensington. To my surprise saw a picture of 1st Lord Wodehouse by Sir Wm. Beechey belonging to Mr. Wm. Wodehouse wh. I did not know existed.[589]

15 April 1868. Wednesday. Easter week. Went to Kimberley with Johnny who caught in the river a pike weighing 14 lb:

17 April 1868. Friday. Attended a meeting at Norwich to form a new Liberal Registration Society. I was in the chair: a talkative unsatisfactory meeting. F. Boileau showed himself wild & impractical & occupied most of the time with a foolish scheme for choice of candidates.

18 April 1868. Saturday. Returned to London with a horrible toothache, from which I have been suffering more or less for the last three months. Had the enemy taken out, a monster with huge fangs.

22 April 1868. Wednesday. Dear Alice confirmed by Dr. Anderson, retired Bp. of Rupert's Land at St Mary's Church. The Bp's address very poor & dull.

24 April 1868. Friday. Elected Governor of Hudson's Bay Compy. Attended special meeting of Board & sworn in.

27 April 1868. Monday. Saw D. of Buckingham, Adderley, & Elliot at Col: Off: on H. Bay affairs. D. of B. showed me the draft of a bill & his Desp: to Lord Monck.[590] Did not go into question of terms, but

[589] Sir William Beechey (1753–1839), portrait painter to Queen Charlotte. On the portrait of Wodehouse, see Currie, *Recollections*, I, 5.

[590] Charles Stanley Monck, 4th Viscount Monck (1819–94), Lib. MP for Portsmouth, 1852–7; gov.-genl. of Canada, 1861–8; cr. UK peerage 1866.

pointed out possible necessity of some security against undue interference of Canada with free Trade.

28 April 1868.   Tuesday. Attended meeting of the H. B. Board.

30 April 1868.   Thursday. Govt. beaten on Gladstone's first resolution
by 65.

4 May 1868.   Monday. Dizzy announced that he would not resign. I
heard his speech: he spoke calmly & clearly with the exception of that
part which related to The Queen. He bespattered her with fulsome
flattery and left I thought purposely a doubt as to whether he had
power to dissolve in any case. Gladstone followed & spoke temperately &
well.

11 May 1868.   Monday. On Thursday Gladstone's resolutions all passed
without division, almost without discussion. Then followed a scene of
violence discreditable to both sides. All this confusion is the result of
the unscrupulous attempt of Dizzy to govern without a majority in the
H. of Commons. There has been much talk of a vote of want of
confidence. In my judgment we shall make a great mistake if we try it.
It is not certain we should succeed at all, but we should certainly have
a much smaller majority than on the Resolution. This would be
equivalent to a defeat. Dizzy would dissolve at once appealing to the
country against the factious conduct of the oppoosition. Our game is
to facilitate winding up the business & an appeal as soon as possible to
the new constituencies. I am not by any means certain we shall have
better success in the new parl. but our best chance is to leave matters
as they now stand & not to worry the Govt. any more. We have at all
events a clear issue on which to go to the country. What I fear is that
Dizzy will play the same game in the new Parliament as in this. He
will announce a measure to reform the Irish Church. The Radicals will
say we had better let him bring in his measure. We shall be able to
mould it as we wish and it will be far easier to pass what we want with
Dizzy in office than Dizzy in opposition.

12 May 1868.   Tuesday. The answer to the Address on the Irish Church
delivered. I was present. There was some cheering on our side. This
puts an end I hope to the schemes of a vote of want of confidence.
      It is said Dizzy will not oppose the Suspensory bill! on ground that
it will suit his intended measures as well as ours– I made some remarks
in the House on the Poor Law this evening which were well received.

17 May 1868.   Sunday. With Dodson to Hampton Court & Bushy

Park. The chestnut trees in great beauty. Spoke to Gladstone yesterday at the Airlies' breakfast. He said truly– people say why do we, the majority allow a Govt. in a minority to go on! but are we in a majority except on the Irish Church question? If ministers facilitate the discussion of his bill, he thinks matters will go on quietly: if not, that there is no alternative but a direct attack. He did not seem to be anxious to attack if it can be avoided.

29 May 1868.   Friday. Presented two petitions in favour of removal of Univ: Tests, a dull debate followed. The political situation seems at length clearly defined. We wait for the new constituencies to pronounce their decision. The fact is the result of an appeal to the new constituencies would be doubtful, a defeat ruinous, & victory embarrassing; but if we can win in the new Parliament, our prospects will be excellent. Violent attacks on the Govt. will not help, perhaps damage our cause. You could not mistake the disgust with which Bouverie's[591] rabid speech was heard by the whole house.

What a queer episode. Rearden's question about the Queen![592] Of course he was howled down, yet the general and well founded opinion is that the Queen culpably neglects her public duties. Rearden, unfortunately for him, does not know that there are many things wh. every one thinks but no sensible man will say.

I hear that miserable man Lord Hastings is not yet utterly ruined.[593] For the sake of the peerage wh. he disgraces the sooner he disappears from public view, the better. His wife who is separated from him is ruined by her own debts. Her jewels were sold for a song the other day. I wonder if the story is true that Chaplin proposed Ld. H's expulsion from the Jockey Club as a defaulter. A sweet revenge!

1 June 1868.   Monday. Went to Minley & stayed till Thursday. The weather very dry.

2 June 1868.   Tuesday. Drove to Wellington Coll: & to Beauwood, an enormous new house wh. Walter the proprietor of the 'Times' is building.

6 June 1868.   Saturday. Attended a curious function, the yearly despatch of the H. Bay Compy. Ships to York in Hudson's Bay. Two ships were

---

[591] Edward Pleydell Bouverie (1818–89), Lib. MP for Kilmarnock, 1844–74.

[592] Denis Joseph Rearden (1817–85), Lib. MP for Athlone, 1865–8, asked whether the Queen's delicate health, which prevented her carrying out her public duties, required her abdication. 3 *Hansard* 192 (22 May 1868), 711–12. Cf. entry for 9 July 1867.

[593] See entries for 16 July 1864, 23 May 1867.

all. We breakfasted at Blackwell went down to Gravesend in a steamer, then on board our ships, signed formally their sailing orders, mustered the crew, gave the boatswains a guinea each, and after a run down the river, returned to Greenwich to drive. The usual fish & speechifying. The day was fine & very enjoyable.

12 June 1868. Friday. Johnny came home.

14 June 1868. Sunday. Johnny, Henley, & I went to Windsor, rowed up to Bouvery Weir & bathed. On Friday we settled the Church Rates Bill in the select Committee. Cairns acted very fairly, threw over the High Ch: party much to the disgust of Sam Oxon & Co.,[594] & with his help we made the bill a really liberal measure. Will Gladstone acccept it, as amended?

20 June 1868. Saturday. Very unhappy at Johnny's failure to pass his college examination. Will he ever be roused to real exertion? I doubt it. I fear he has a feeble will. Yet he has ability and an excellent disposition.

23 June 1868. Tuesday. Settled finally report of Hudson's Bay Cy. A bad dividend will put the shareholders out of humour; at all events it is not my fault.

25 June 1868. Thursday. Debates in the H. of Lords on Irish Church Bill. Ld. Granville made a first rate speech, far the best I ever heard him make. Ld. Grey crossgrained and ineffective. Ld. Malmesbury ludicrously feeble. Ld. Clarendon was powerful on the effect produced abroad by the maintenance of such an injustice as the Irish Ch: but the conclusion of his speech was somewhat drawn out & tedious.

Ld. Derby made a regular Church & state party Speech. I thought his reference to the Coronation oath most improper. He not obscurely advised the Queen to oppose her conscientious scruples to the wishes of her people & Parliament. I essayed a reply to Derby. On the whole I did pretty well, but all the arguments on our side were completely exhausted by previous speakers.

26 June 1868. Friday. Debate in H. of Lords continued. Carnarvon

---

[594] Samuel Wilberforce (1805–73), bp. of Oxford, 1845–69, was a highchurchman and close ecclesiastical acquaintance of Gladstone. In committee on Gladstone's Church Rates bill, Lord Cairns ammended the measure with the support of the low church bishops, in a manner which pleased Dissenters, the existing rating system being preserved, less its compulsory aspect.

made a bitter attack on the Govt. Ld. Salisbury a very telling speech against the bill, far superior to Derby's. The D. of Somerset made a strange jocular! (fancy the Duke jocular) speech, more against than for the bill. The truth is he does not like Gladstone or the bill & expects not to be in the next Liberal Ministry. Many people thought he was drunk, & Derby observed, (Ld. Cork having spoken before) that we had had the Cork and had now the Bottle, but I dined at de Grey's with him & we walked down to the House together, & I can vouch he was sober as a judge.

29 June 1868.   Monday. A rather wearisome night. Argyll not quite so good as usual, too long & laboured. The Bp. of Oxford answered him in a low serio-comic style very unworthy of his office & abilities.

Ld. Russell made a feeble speech. Then Ld. Cairns summed up (as he would have done in a great appeal case) at prodigious length, three mortal hours. His points were admirably put, but he wearied his audience & I think the cheers wh. greeted the close of his speech arose as much from relief that it was ended as from the effect of the speech. Just before 3 o'clock we divided– 97 contents, 192 not conts. –95. There were 27 pairs besides.

Ld. Suffield was going to vote against us! but I persuaded him by pointing out that such a vote would be quite inconsistent with supporting our candidates in Norfolk, to stay away. We had not many deserters, the most notable Lds. Dudley[595] & Dartrey, & Vernon.[596] The second might have at least had the grace not to vote, considering that Ld. Russell made him an Earl only the other day.

3 July 1868.   Friday. A curious scene in the H. of Lords yesterday. Ld. Beauchamp[597] moved to replace in the Boundary bill most of the Clauses struck out by the Select Committee in the H. of Commons. We objected that Dizzy had said that the bill was 'settled' & that therefore the Govt. could not support B. without breach of faith. Ld. Malmesbury said the Govt. were not bound: that what Dizzy said only meant that the bill was settled so far as concerned the H. of Commons. A warm discussion ensued, and at last Lord Russell said that he & his friends would not stay to discuss the amendt. after so gross a breach of faith on the part of the Govt., and left the house followed by most of the opposition peers. Argyll who had a speech to make cd. not forego the pleasure of making it & stayed behind with one or two others. This

---

[595] William Ward, 1st Earl of Dudley (1817–85), Peelite.

[596] Augustus Henry, 6th Baron Vernon (1829–83).

[597] Frederick Lygon, 6th Earl of Beauchamp (1830–91), Cons. MP for Tewkesbury, 1857–63, for Worcestershire, 1863–6.

'secession' was not an act of momentary ill temper as has been supposed but was done on deliberate calculation. Ld. Portman suggested it, & after some doubt & discussion amongst the Peers on the front bench his suggestion was adopted.

The movement was singularly successful. The debate after our departure was adjourned, and to night the Govt. announced that they had discovered that if any amendments, likely to be disputed in the Commons were made in the bill, the bill cd. not pass in time to enable Parlt. to be dissolved in the autumn. Singular that they did not know this last night! still more so, that they allowed the D. of Montrose,[598] one of the Ministers, to give notice of an amendment in the Scotch Reform Bill wh. for similar reasons he was obliged to withdraw.

6 July 1868.   Monday. Some of the supporters of the Ministry forced divisions on the amendments wh. at the desire of the Govt. Ld. Beauchamp & the D. of Montrose had withdrawn, & we had the intense amusement of seeing the Ministers vote with us against them! Never did I see men look more crest-fallen.

7 July 1868.   Tuesday. The annual meeting of the H. Bay Company– a warm business. One Thorne a discontented shareholder pitched into the Board. A 3 pr. ct. dividend–*hinc illae lacrymae.* The management of the negotiation will be very ticklish.

Rose the Canadian Finance Minister who is over here, does not give a hopeful account of our prospects of getting fair terms from Canada.

11 July 1868.   Saturday. Since the Irish debate the H. of Lords has been very waspish. A sharp altercation between Carnarvon & the Chancellor about the West India Bishop's bill went altogether in favour of the former.

I take no notice of the hard words which Derby & others addressed to us on our secession. Being utterly in the wrong, and compelled to give way, they tried to cover their retreat by volleys of abuse. Edmond W. & R. Gurdon had a queer little squabble this week about their precedence as candidates for N. Norfolk in wh. the latter displayed a petty spirit.

Wednesday July 15 and July 16. Prodigiously hot. The drought extra-ordinary.

Friday July 17 & July 18. Irish burials bill of wh. I have taken charge

---

[598] James Graham, 7th Marquess and 4th Duke of Montrose (1799–1874), post.-genl., 1866–8.

read 2nd in spite of Abp. of Armagh's[599] opposition. The Govt. meant to support him in smothering bill in select Committee, but dare not after his foolish speech. They revenged themselves by carrying a foolish amendment against me on Friday.

22 July 1868. Wednesday. Went all of us to Kimberley. Prodigious heat & drought; no rain at K. (except a shower on June 4) since May 17!.

24 July 1868. Friday. Shot a Buck, a small one weighing only 8 1/2 stone. Harvest began generally in this district last Monday, & on the home farm.

31 July 1868. Parliament prorogued.

8 August 1868. Saw Mr. Tillett at Norwich.[600] He is determined to persevere in standing for Norwich. On the whole I think the Whigs wrong in not supporting him. He is decidedly the working man's favourite, & in towns like Norwich the moderate Liberals must whether they like it or not consult the wishes of the working men. They cannot yet make up their minds to the transfer of power which has been made by the Reform Act. Harvest finished on the home farm on Monday last!

16 August 1868. Sunday. Our wedding day, very happily passed, but rather gloomy at the prospect of our separation to morrow, Flo. & the children to Cromer, Johnny & I to Vienna. Some rain at last. Ten days after this the drought nearly as bad as ever.

17 August 1868. Monday. Started with Johnny for Vienna.

5 September 1868. Saturday. Returned home. We went by way of Calais, Brussels, the Rhine, Munich where we stayed a day, to Vienna, & returned by Ischl, Munich, Strasburg, & Paris. Vienna is vastly improved by the demolition of the fortifications & the new Boulevards. Nothing struck me as much changed in the outward appearance of Germany. The same slow well to do middle class, and dirty toiling peasant women, the same greasy food & indifferent wine; fewer pipes, more cigars. Our countrymen & women on their travels as absurd & vulgar as ever. The [*ill.*] larger & much dearer.

---

[599] Marcus Gervais Beresford (1801–85), archbp. of Armagh, 1862–85. See 3 *Hansard* 193 (17 July 1868), 1862–3.

[600] Jacob Henry Tillett (1818–92), solicitor; twice mayor of Norwich; Lib. MP for Norwich, 1870–1, 1875, 1880–5.

12 September 1868.   Saturday. Attended a discussion on local taxation at the agricultural chamber at Norwich. Nothing worth hearing.

18 September 1868.   Friday. To London. Conference with the D. of Buckingham, (Adderley, & Elliot) on the proposed transfer of the Hudson's Bay territory to Canada. The Duke spoke sensibly, & showed acquaintance with the business; in short acquitted himself better than I expected.[601] Elliot is his prompter. Adderley hardly said a word. Lampson was with me & gave me excellent support. He thinks Reverdy Johnson, the new U.S. Minister has made a mistake in Sheffield in speaking in so cordial tone of England. He has outrun the feeling of the U. S. people which tho' more friendly to us, is not yet cordial. A more reserved tone would have been wiser. Rain at last. The country was suffering fearfully from the drought.

22 September 1868.   Monday. This week on Tuesday Leeson & M. Currie came & on Wednesday F. Cadogan[602] & Lady Adelaide C. & Edm. Wodehouse. No turnips, the birds all driven, bad sport.

6 October 1868.   Tuesday. Attended H. B. Board.

7 October 1868.   Wednesday. To North Walsham for agricultural dinner. Noisy demonstrations on behalf of candidates who were present. Lacon[603] looked like a man about to be hanged, but many of the farmers (shame upon them) cheered him when he spoke. I stayed at Witton two nights. Ld. Suffield was violent against Bright in conversing with me on politics. I never heard a man express so silly unreasoning a hatred against a public man. Suffield as he grows older, seems to me to grow more prejudiced & obstinate: the result no doubt of living so much amongst thick headed squires & farmers.

17 October 1868.   Saturday. Sent to London and had an interview of three hours & 1/2! with the D. of Buckingham on the Hudson's Bay business. Elliot is the only man at the Col: Off: who understands the business. He has as much brain as Bucks & Adderley combined, & to spare.

20 October 1868.   Tuesday. To London. Attended meeting of H. B. Bd.

    [601] Cf. Rich, *Hudson's Bay Company*, III, 881–2.
    [602] Frederick William Cadogan (1821–1904), Liberal MP for Cricklade, 1868–74; m. 1851 Adelaide, da. of 1st Marquis of Anglesey.
    [603] Edmund Henry Knowles Lacon (1807–88), brewer and banker; Cons. MP for Yarmouth, 1852–7, 1859–68, and for North Norfolk, 1868–85.

24 October 1868.   Saturday. To London. Conference with the D. of B. Unsatisfactory. I expect the negotiations will be broken off. Canada evidently wants to get the territory for nothing. Adderley is in the hands of the Canadian delegates, & the D. of B. has no real opinion of his own. But I don't think if the Company stand firm, their possessions will be handed over to Canada without a fair compensation.

27 October 1868.   Tuesday. To London. Attended Board. Agreed to letter to the Col: Off: The only unreasonable man was Hamilton who talked much nonsense.

29 October 1868.   Thursday. To Letton till Saturday, a dull party. Young Ross (the rifle shooter) a rather vulgar man, and Garnett who married Miss Custance a very snobbish man much up on shooting party with R. Gurdon.

31 October 1868.   Saturday. Attended a public meeting at Norwich to get funds for Hospital. Not many people there. Also attended meeting of the Registration Society. Much discussion about candidates for S. Norfolk. None are to be found. We are now feeling the full effects of the wretched fiasco at the last Election.[604] I don't know which was most to blame, Ld. Suffield, W. Coke, or Tillett. Each in his way acted most unwisely.

10 November 1868.   Tuesday. Went to Tacolnestone[605] to shoot. Much talk with F. Boileau about Hudson's candidature for S. Norfolk. I would give him some slight aid so as to keep his friends in good humour. He will do much to break down Read's prestige, and will not win.[606]

11 November 1868.   Wednesday. Parliament dissolved. I hope we may get a more honest H. of Commons than the last. We can't get a more (politically) base & dishonest House.

24 November 1868.   Tuesday. Went to London to attend half yearly meeting of Hudson's Bay Company. The shareholders were very discontented, but I got through pretty well.[607] To day Albert Wode-

---

[604] In the Norfolk, East election of July 1865, Lord Suffield with little consultation refused to throw over the unpopular Wenman Coke. For a full report of the 'extraordinary mess', see Robert Gurdon to Kimberley, [Aug. 1865], KP1 3/1.

[605] Sir John Peter Boileau's country seat.

[606] In the election on 21 Nov., H.L. Hudson received 1,679 votes; Conservatives C.S. Read and E. Howes received 3,097 and 3,055, respectively.

[607] Rich, *Hudson's Bay Company*, III, 883.

house,[608] Hutchinson, Johnny, & G. Currie came on a visit.

25 November 1868.   Wednesday. Lord & Lady Chelsea[609] came & stayed till Saturday. He seems clever with a certain acid flavour in his talk which seasons it. She is a very pleasant well bred woman. His Toryism is strong.

25 November 1868.   Thursday. The North Norfolk polling to day.[610]

Walpole	2642
Lacon	2574
Wodehouse	2237
Gurdon	2081

Yarmouth caused our defeat. Apart from Yarmouth Wodehouse was one ahead of Walpole. It is not a little disgraceful that a notorious briber, such as Lacon, should be one of the members for this county. But the 'dog returns to its vomit' is eminently true of Yarmouth.

The general result of the elections is decisive of the fate of the ministry, but the violent opposition of the clergy to the Liberals has made its mark on the elections, & Gladstone will face an opposition neither powerless nor discouraged. His chapter of Autobiography[611] & his twelve speeches in Lancashire have not increased my confidence in his judgment, and discretion. I shall be surprised if a Ministry formed by him, lasts long.

2 December 1868.   Wednesday. Disraeli resigned. He took every one by surprise. It was certainly both a wise and dignified act. He avoids an inevitable defeat, retires without having to declare, except in vague terms his future policy, & prevents much waste of time in Parliament and embarrassment to his successors.

3 December 1868.   Thursday. Gladstone sent for to form a Ministry.

7 December 1868.   Monday. I was beginning to despair of being included in the Govt. when just as I was starting for London to attend the H.

---

[608] Albert Wodehouse (1840–1914), capt.; son of Kimberley's uncle, rear-adm. Edward Thornton-Wodehouse.

[609] George Cadogan, Viscount Chelsea (1840–1915) s. as 5th earl Cadogan 1873, u-sec. War 1875–8, u-sec. Colonies 1878–80, Ld. Privy Seal 1886–92, Ld. Lt. Ireland 1895–1902, m. Lady Craven 1865.

[610] *McCalmont's Parliamentary Poll Book* (8th edn, Brighton, 1971) places the numbers at 2,630, 2,563, 2,235 and 2,088.

[611] Explaining at length his *volte-face* on the established church. 'A Chapter of Autobiography', *Gleanings of Past Years* (7 vols., London, 1879), VII, 97–151.

Bay Cy. meeting to morrow I received a telegram from Glyn telling me that Gladstone wished to see me this afternoon.

I saw him at 1/2 past 4. He offered me the office of Privy Seal which I at once accepted, saying I had no pretension to pick & choose & that I was much pleased to be promoted to the Cabinet & to serve under him. He said nothing could be more handsome on my part; that I was quite fit for any of the more important offices, but that he could not give any more such offices to Peers. For example, the Home Office was still unfilled and I should have been a very fit man to hold it, but it must be held by a member of the Commons.

8 December 1868. Tuesday. Attended H. Bay Board for the last time & made my bow. The Company is in a mess. The feeling of the public, fomented by lying articles written in the Canadian interest, is so adverse to the 'monopoly' that I fear the shareholders will not get fair terms.[612] The Company's territorial rights ought certainly to be extinguished but it will be grossly unjust not to fully compensate the shareholders.

I had a long talk in the evening at the Travellers' with Lord Stanley. He seemed to regret not having joined the Liberal party when Palmerston offered him office. 'If it had not been for my father' was his expression.[613]

9 December 1868. Wednesday. The new Ministers including myself sworn in at Windsor to-day. Bright by the Queen's desire (*mero motu*) made his affirmation without kneeling.

10 December 1868. Thursday. Parliament opened by Commission. I was one of the Commissioners. I hear that Fortescue (whom 'Jezebel his wife stirred up'[614]) has made an egregious fool of himself,[615] pressing for the Colonial Secretaryship, and complaining bitterly because he has only got the Irish Secretaryship! A post at least equal to his merits & capacity.

Lord Halifax called yesterday to ask me about the Lord Lieutenancy. He really was offered it with a seat in the Cabinet. He left me apparently intending to refuse but he evidently had some doubts, & was not at all offended at the proposal.

---

[612] On 'lying articles', see John S. Galbraith, *The Hudson's Bay Company as an Imperial Factor, 1821–1869* (New York, 1977), 420.

[613] Palmerston had offered the Colonial Office in Oct. 1855. Gladstone considered the 14th Earl's influence 'monstrous'. *DD1*, 136–9; L. Tollemache, *Talks with Mr. Gladstone* (3rd rev. edn, London, 1903), 21; considerably expanded in *JE*, 1.

[614] I Kings 21:24.

[615] This phrase omitted from *JE*.

11 December 1868. Friday. Long talk with Ld. Spencer who is the new Lord Lt. I fancy he is rather afraid of the 'Walrus'. The appointment was in doubt between him and Dufferin. The latter I believe was thought too yielding & not 'great man enough'– Vernon Harcourt told me he declined the Judge Advocate's place, because it would throw him out of his profession. He was quite right. Returned to Kimberley.

15 December 1868. Tuesday. Attended first Cabinet.

16 December 1868. Wednesday. Returned to Ky. I shall make no note of what takes place in the Cabinet. [*Four lines here crossed through.*]

Saw Dufferin who does not conceal his great chagrin at not getting the Lord Lieutenancy.[616] He thinks Ireland should be governed by Irishmen. I combated this as against the principles of the Union. My view is that Irishmen should have their fair share in the Imperial Government i.e. in the Cabinet, not be relegated to mere provincial that is subordinate posts. The misfortune is that we have no Irishman in our party in the House of Commons except C. Fortescue (& he is rather weak) fit for the Cabinet: in the Lords Monck & Dufferin are the only Irish peers who could be thought of. It is singular how little Parliamentary eminence is found amongst Irishmen just now on the Liberal side.

Parliament formally addressed in a Queen's message to day by Lord Commissioners to day. The house afterwards adjourned.

22 December 1868. Tuesday. Went to London to attend Cabinet. Returned Wednesday.

29 December 1868. Tuesday. Cabinet again. Went to Londn. & returned same day.

30 December 1868. Wednesday. Edm. W., Sir C. Lampson, Mr. Locke, son of M. P. for Southwark[617] came on visit Thursday. P. Gurdon & two daughters do. J. O. Taylor came to consult me as to N. Norfolk petition.[618] I said I could not promise to subscribe to the expenses nor take upon myself any responsibility as to the petition as I was not ready to put forward a candidate in the event of success. I thought Edm. W. would agree in this, wh. on consulting him I found was the case. But, if others thought fit to decide to petition, as a political move I approved

---

[616] He accepted the Chanc. of the Duchy of Lancaster.

[617] John Locke (1805–80), Liberal MP for Southwark, 1857–80.

[618] Seeking to unseat the two Conservatives elected on 23 November, for employing proscribed canvassers; see correspondence and related papers in KP1 3/1.

of it. We shall now see if Ld. Leicester[619] & the rest will put their hands in their pockets the petition having been urged on the responsibility of the Election Committee. I am not sure what day I saw Taylor but I think on Friday Dec: 18.

Ld. Spencer offers Edm. W. to be his private Secretary.[620] This E. W. refused, & I think rightly. The position is disagreeable & he has nothing to gain but the salary by going to Dublin.

1 January 1869.   Another year. What can I say as to the past year? Much I have done wh. I regret. I have enjoyed many & most undeserved blessings. May my retrospect of another year, if I am spared so long, show some real improvement in my life. I see on looking back that I have unconsciously used nearly the same expressions as I did last New Year! Does that not show how little progress I have made except in years?

16 January 1869.   Saturday. Went to Osborne, being asked to dine & stay one night. It is a very thoughtless proceeding to ask a man for Saturday night to a place from which he can only get away by train on Sunday which gets to town late at night. The Queen was very cheerful & gracious. No one at dinner but Princess Louisa, the household & myself. On Sunday morning we had prayers in the house & in the afternoon I went back to London with Sir W. Jenner[621] the court physician a pleasant man enough. Osborne seems a charming villa but it rained hard nearly all the time I was there: so I saw little of its beauties.

26 January 1869.   Tuesday. Came to London, & on the following day Flo. & the children came.

2 February 1869.   Tuesday. *[This entry excised from journal.]*

3 February 1869.   Wednesday. Sheriff pricking dinner at de Grey's. Some of the excuses rather comical.

4 February 1869.   Thursday. Council at Osborne: a dreary sham. Dined with Gladstone. It was to have been a Cabinet dinner but many did

---

[619] Thomas William Coke, 2nd Earl of Leicester (1822–1909), ld. lt. Norfolk, 1846–1906.

[620] Edmond Wodehouse having been an unsuccessful candidate for North Norfolk in the November election, see Kimberley to Raikes Currie, 5 Aug. 1868, and notes in *Liberal by Principle*, 113.

[621] William Jenner (1815–98), established distinct identities of typhus and typhoid fevers.

not come. Bright sat, looking very unhappy, between Lowe & Bruce. I don't think Lowe & Bright exchanged one word. I heard a story which we believe to be true, that...

[Several lines removed, as verso of entry for 2 February 1869.]

... his intention to resign; that Ld. Derby on hearing of it, strongly advised them to stay in but in vain.

5 February 1869.   Friday. At dinner at Ld. Dartrey's to day, Ld. Stanley said to me that he knew we had not yet considered the Irish Church bill in the Cabinet. Of course I admitted nothing; but it is true enough. How did he know it?

Monday Feb: 8 and Tuesday Feb: 9.   On these two days we settled in the Cabinet the bases of the Irish Church Bill. The subject was discussed on Monday for the first time. There was a long discussion on each day, no other question being mentioned. No discussion or violent difference of opinion arose; but on Monday at the end of the Cabinet Lowe who had said little or nothing complained in a very bitter tone[622] that we had

[Some twelve lines here removed.]

... discussion was that Gladstone's plan was adopted without much...
[verso of previous excision missing.]

16 February 1869.   Tuesday. Parliament met. Very dull debates on Address. Cairns in the H. of Lds. seemed nervous & embarrassed as leader of opposition.

17 February 1869.   Wednesday. First meeting of Committee of Cabinet on Irish Church Bill. We sat five hours.

Thursday and Friday.   Two long sittings. The bill, drawn in Ireland, will require thorough recasting. The Committee consisted of Gladstone, Bright, Lowe, the Chancellor,[623] Granville, & myself assisted by the

---

[622] See introduction.
[623] William Page Wood, 1st Baron Hatherley (1801–81), Lib. MP for Oxford, 1847–53; ld. chanc., 1868–72.

Attorney & Solicitor General[624] the Atty. Genl. for Ireland,[625] Thring,[626] & Law,[627] an Irish draughtsman.

17 February 1869. Wednesday. My dear Aunt Sophy (Mrs Raikes Currie) died at a little after 8 o'clock P.M. at 17 Hill Street. She was not thought to be seriously ill till one o'clock when suddenly she began to sink. The cause was heart disease. I deeply regret her. A kinder & more right minded woman never lived. All who knew her, loved her.

22 February 1869. Monday. Finished in Committee the Irish Ch: Bill. It is I think a good sound scheme.

26 February 1869. Friday. Moved 1st. reading of Bruce's Habitual Criminals Bill. Spoke for an hour. Bill well received, rather too well by the Tories. I had only heard on Monday that I was to have charge of this bill. So I had little time to prepare myself.

1 March 1869. Monday. Heard Gladstone's most admirable speech explaining the Irish Ch: bill. It was very well received. He spoke for 3 hours and avoided his usual diffuseness. Nothing could exceed the skill with which he divided the subject and marshalled his arguments. My only fear is that the scheme is too tender to the Church.

3 March 1869. Wednesday. Alice presented at Court. She looked very nice.

5 March 1869. Friday. 2nd reading of Bruce's bill. A dry discussion: favourable to the bill.

14 March 1869. Monday. Bruce's bill thro' Committee after nearly five hours discussion.

[24] March 1869. Wednesday. 2nd reading of Irish Church Bill this morning at 3.A.M. 368–118 – a larger majority than was generally expected. Bright made a superb speech. Ball a very successful speech but its success must have been much owing to manner. I read it carefully, & it is not remarkable as a piece of argument. Sullivan a clever reply to him. Lowe's speech seems to have been thought a

---

[624] James Anthony Lawson had been both Atty.-genl. and Sol.-genl. for Ireland. See entry and notes for 30 Dec. 1864. Also, cf. *JE*, 2.

[625] Edward Sullivan (1822–85), Lib. MP for Mallow, 1865–70, Irish atty.-genl., 1868–70.

[626] Henry Thring (1818–1907), Parliamentary couns. to Treasury.

[627] Legal adv. to ld. lt. Ireland.

failure. It is full however of subtle argument. Roundell Palmer made the best speech against the bill.[628] Disraeli was wonderfully ingenious but his discordance from real Tory sentiment was never more apparent. His speech points to general endowment which the genuine Protestant Tory abhors.

An article on the difference between Belgium & France in the 'Times' this morning treating the apprehensions of a serious difficulty as chimerical is remarkable as showing how the public may be led entirely astray by newspaper writers. Doubtless the 'Times' know perfectly well the true state of the case which is that the difference is essentially political, that France seeks to obtain an exclusive political influence over Belgium, that this railway question is a mere pretext; that it is a glaring example of uncalled for interference in the internal affairs of a weak state by a powerful neighbour; that every Govt. in Europe has been seriously alarmed; & that but for the good offices of England the affair might have led to a rupture, but it is far more political to make the public believe that the quarrel is a mere dispute about railway tariffs, & so the 'Times' pooh poohs (very judiciously) the 'alarmists'.

Belgium certainly has behaved imprudently. She should have taken her precautions immediately after the outrageous interference by France with the Luxembourg Govt. in a similar affair. As it is she has managed to give the Emperor a public slap in the face wh. of course he resents.

30 March 1869. Tuesday. Went with Johnny for two days to Kimberley. Found Oldfields cottage in flames on our arrival, stayed there till 11 PM in a biting North Wind & caught a bad cold.

6 April 1869. Tuesday. House of L. met after recess yesterday. To day the 'Criminals Bill' passed without much trouble thro' report.

10 April 1869. Saturday. Met Lord Lawrence[629] at de Grey's. Talked to him about our relations with Afghanistan. He said he thought in the improbable event of a Russian attack on India, the Afghans would certainly be against us whatever we did, that they would be tempted by the prospect & tradition of plunder in India. Our proper course was to keep quite clear of Afghanistan & if attacked to await our enemy in the plains. Our subsidies &c. to the Ameer he looked on as useful to quiet public feeling in India but for no other purpose.

14 April 1869. Wednesday. Council at Windsor. Costa knighted. He

---

[628] Roundell Palmer objected to disendowment, but was prepared to support disestablishment.

[629] John Laird Mair, 1st Baron Lawrence (1811–79), viceroy of India, 1863–9.

appeared like a true foreigner in dress coat &c. i.e. *en frac.*

19 April 1869. Monday. I hear that Mrs. Lowe is much offended that the Q. has not asked her to Windsor. It will be supposed she says that there is something against my character; but I am as free as any one from any such imputation – not that I had not plenty of opportunities in Australia![630]

29 April 1869. Wednesday. Attended a Council at Osborne. De Grey told me that the Queen speaking to him about Ireland, said she feared Fortescue was not a 'very strong man'. Unhappily this is the universal opinion.[631]

7 May 1869. Friday. Another Irish 'row' in the H. of Lords. Granville defended Bright with inimitable tact. I said a few words in reply to Cairns wh. were well received.[632]

8 May 1869. Saturday. My colleagues are very gloomy about our relations with the U. S.[633] All agree that we could not defend Canada, & that our aim must be her independence. But meanwhile? The U. S. seems determined to humiliate us, and our means of damaging them are small, whilst they can wound us in every part of the world, as well as destroy our trade. For all this I am convinced that our only policy is to show a firm front, to make no further concessions, and to fight to the last if we are attacked. Unscrupulous as the Americans are they will hesitate before they attack us.[634]

10 May 1869. Monday. A very long & wearisome debate in the Lords on the Scotch Education Bill. Argyll at first completely lost his temper & I thought we were in a mess, but he recovered himself, & with de Grey's help who in Granville's absence played the part of leader with such dexterity, he pulled the Bill thro' Committee. The Opposition showed a bitter animus against us & damaged the bill considerably. Denominationalism for ever was their cry, & they rallied all the fanatics and priest ridden peers. R. Catholics voting *en masse* with them. But even, as amended, the bill is a step in the right direction.[635]

[630] A story tastefully excluded from *JE.*
[631] This entry omitted from *JE.*
[632] This entry omitted from *JE.*
[633] On 13 April 1869 the American Senate rejected the Johnson–Clarendon convention as a basis for resolving differences between the two countries.
[634] Cf. *JE*, where this entry is considerably expanded with a reflection from 1874.
[635] This entry omitted from *JE.*

13 May 1869. Thursday. A bitter attack from Ld. Russell on our Irish policy[636] was followed by one of the most disgraceful speeches from Lord Derby that I ever heard even him make. He did not scruple to compare Bright to the Mayor of Cork! altogether a most unseemly exhibition of malignant party hatred.[637] I was put up to reply. A decent regard for Derby's age & position prevented me from expressing all the indignation I felt, but I believe I did make some impression on the House.

As to Lord R., irrepressible vanity and anger at not having been consulted as to our course on the Irish Land Bill were I suppose the motives which impelled him to lead the Tory opposition for once. All the efforts known of our enemies have failed to drive us into the suicidal folly of attempting a land Bill this year. Bright's speech was of course imprudent but it is simply ridiculous to attribute, as the D. of Abercorn did, the Irish murders to the speeches of Gladstone, Bright & Bruce, and as to the land agitation it is sufficient to observe that it is full 20 years old.

14 May 1869. Friday. I have not noticed the great Mayor of Cork question.[638] At first we intended only to prosecute him but when we found that the prosecution wd. not take place till November, we changed our minds on the Irish Atty. Genl.'s advice. Brought in the 'O Sullivan disability Bill'. The rest is public history.

[Date and portion of line excised.] ... we discussed a curious piece of intelligence (a canard in my opinion) which Childers recd.[639] *[Four full pages here excised.]*[640]

24 May 1869. Monday. The N. Norfolk petition decided against us.[641] As I expected. The case was very weak except on the one point of the employment of Preston, a scheduled man. The Judge (Blackburne's) remarks upon Laine must make Norfolk proud of its representative! My aunt (Mrs. Edward Gurdon) who has been very dangerously ill with inflammation of the lungs & fever is I rejoice to say a little better.

27 May 1869. Thursday. Returned to London from Kimberley. Not

---

[636] Russell criticised the government for delaying on Irish Land reform and pointed to the increase of crime in Ireland.

[637] On 27 April 1869 the Mayor of Cork, Daniel O'Sullivan, praised the attempt to assassinate the Duke of Edinburgh at Melbourne.

[638] Stemming from O'Sullivan's incendiary remarks in his speech of 27 April lauding assassination as a patriotic tool. O'Sullivan resigned on 11 May 1869.

[639] See *Gladstone Diaries*, VII, 68.

[640] *JE* records no entries between 13 May and 19 June 1869.

[641] See entry for 30 Dec. 1868.

sorry to leave the country in such cold, wet, cheerless, weather as we have had in Norfolk.

19 June 1869.   Saturday. This morning at 3 o'clock we divided in the H. of Lords on the 2nd reading of the Irish Ch: Bill.[642]

Contents	179
Not-contents	146
	33
Pairs were 9 =	18?
Tories voted with us	32
Liberals against	2

About 60 Tory peers who might have voted were absent, & about 10 Liberals.

Immediately after the division Ld. Salisbury said to de Grey & me 'we have given you more than we intended'. The fact is they meant us to win by 7 or 8 but with so many peers uncertain they dare not withdraw their men, & hence a majority much larger than they wished. The debate was most brilliant; the best I ever heard in the H. of Lds. The best speeches were the Abp of Canterbury's,[643] the Bp of Peterborough's[644] & St David's[645] & Bp of Derry's[646] & Ld. Salisbury's. Argyll & the Chancellor also both spoke very well.

Granville was excessively nervous and awkward but in the important parts of his speech he was very weighty & judicious, especially as to the amendments & the position of the House. The Bp. of Peterborough's most brilliant speech began unfortunately with allusions to the 'howls' in the H. of Commons, but after that it was a continued triumph of rhetoric. He is a most consummate actor, & the great charm of his speech was the tone of his voice, his humour, & his attitude. His humour is in the truly Irish vein half comic, half sentimental. Poor de Grey had empty benches to speak to after this display. Lord Derby's was a very painful exhibition. He is like the old toothless lion. His voice was feeble, he lost the thread of his argument, & nearly burst into tears. On the other hand Lord Russell was quite himself again full of dry sarcasm & quaint historical allusions. The Bp. of Derry's was an orange platform speech, powerful but coarse, & slightly vulgar. St Davids' speech as a piece of argument was admirable, unsurpassable.

[642] See Parry, *Democracy and Religion*, 283.
[643] Archibald Tait (1811–82), archbp. of Canterbury, 1869–82.
[644] William Connor Magee (1821–91), dean of Cork, 1864–8, dean of Chapel Royal, Dublin, 1868–8; bp. of Peterborough, 1868–91.
[645] Connop Thirwill (1797–1875), bp. of St David's, 1840–75.
[646] William Alexander (1824–1911), bp. of Derry, 1867–93.

How weak of the two English Archbp. not to vote. The Archp. of Canterbury spoke excellently, but his speech was directly in favour of 2nd reading. Nothing weakens the Church more than this weak trimming. My own performance was not particularly successful. The dinner hour and empty benches took all the go out of me. Cairns does not shine as a leader. Instead of . . . us at once *[Seven lines here excised.]*

22 June 1869. Tuesday. The Pasha of Egypt arrived. There was the utmost difficulty in getting the Q. to lodge him in Buckingham Palace. *[Some seven lines here excised, verso of entry for June 19; see above.]*[647]

. . . Lord Gosford, who two or three weeks ago took the riband of St Patrick, did not vote with us on the Irish Ch: Bill, what meanness!

25 June 1869. Friday. Breakfasted with Granville to talk over Irish Church Bill amendments. Fortescue, Monck, Camperdown, Atty. General Sullivan, Dr. Hancock,[648] Argyll were there. (Constance confirmed).

26 June 1869. Saturday. Cabinet at 12. No difference of opinion about Irish Church Bill. We are to oppose the amendments in the H. of Lords, but Gladstone will make certain concessions on minor points if necessary viz 1. lump sum of £500,000 for private endowments

2. add 7 per ct. to commutation where 4/5ths of diocese commute 3. reckon as permanent curates only those who are so returned under Church Temporalities Act
4. Glebe houses gratis to Church
5. £50,000 to Church body for expenses

Gladstone not favourable to concurrent endowment. To attempt to carry it through the Commons wd. he thinks break up our party. Bright of same opinion. We agreed that it should be opposed in the Lords' yet so as to leave the question open for further consideration, if carried against us. The feeling of the Cabinet however against such a total change of policy.

28 June 1869. Monday. Garden party at Buckingm. Palace. The general impression seems to be that the D. of Cleveland's[649] amendt. for giving glebes to the R. Catholics and Presbyts. will be carried.
    Ld. Westbury gave up proceeding further with his Copyright Bill in

---

[647] This passage combined with entry of 19 June in *JE*.
[648] William Neilson Hancock, superintendent of jud. and criminal statistics office, Dublin.
[649] Harry George Powlett, 7th Duke of Cleveland (1803–91) Lib. MP for Durham, 1841–59, for Hastings, 1859–64, when he succ. as Duke of Cleveland.

the Select Committee this morning. He is evidently much cast down by the rascally conduct of his son, & I suspect that Graves the print seller who is the real mover of the Bill has told him that with the amendments I have carried the Bill will no longer answer his purpose.[650]

29 June 1869. Tuesday. Committee on I. Ch: Bill. On the whole the evening favourable to Govt. − Sir C. O Loghlen[651] told me yesterday he believed 95 of the Irish members would vote for D. of Cleveland's amendment. The Bp. of Oxford 'pitched into' his brother of Lichfield[652] with unsparing severity. He was delighted to show that he is still (non-obstante Magee) cock of the episcopal walk. Bp. Lichfield talked wretched nonsense. The chief feature of the evening was the petty venom of the 'holy' Westbury.[653]

30 June 1869. Wednesday. Went to Hypothec Committee.

Thursday & Friday. Irish Church Bill in Committee.

5 July 1869. Monday. And Tuesday. Irish Ch: Bill in Committee. Granville's perseverance thro' all those nights in spite of a fit of gout was most heroic. The debates were very exciting. The opposition being all powerful have knocked the bill to pieces. How will it end?

7 July 1869. Wednesday. The Granville Murray fracas. I trust that he will be fairly shown up at last.

[Four pages here excised. Ed.]

... All the Ministers were for resisting concurrent endowment, or rather no voice was raised in its favour, because all believed the H. of Commons & country to be against it. Gladstone seemed in good humour & confident. We hear that Salisbury says he must have two millions for the Church, our concessions will give nearly one million. Won't the Church party close with the bargain! I think, probably.[654]

12 July 1869. Monday. Third reading of Irish Church Bill. The clause excluding Irish Bps. restored. Lord Stanhope's concurrent endowment clause carried 114/121 7 majority. The heat intense. After speaking I felt nearly suffocated. There is an extraordinary infatuation in the

[650] See expansion of this passage in the Kimberley Memoir, herein, 492–3.
[651] Sir Colman O'Loghlen (1819–77), Home Rule MP for Co. Clare, 1863–77.
[652] George Augustus Selwyn (1809–78), bp. of Lichfield, 1868–78.
[653] The second and final sentences of this passage omitted from *JE*.
[654] In *JE*, this passage combined in entry for 1, 2, 5 July.

House in favour of this scheme of giving glebes to the Catholics. It is an utterly impracticable proposal. Stanhope's amendment was drawn up by Tighe Hamilton[655] (as I am informed): and the clause was certainly as muddle headed a performance such as our world expect from T. H.

Thursday & Friday.   The Commons threw out the Lords amendments adopting the changes we proposed.[656]

17 July 1869.   Saturday. Gladstone told us *[Two words struck through.]* that he had been in negotiation with the Abp of Canterbury & had hinted that we might go as far as 12 per ct. addition to the Commutation money, and suggested an arrangement as to the insertion of words in the 68th Clause (the course ultimately adopted). The Queen he said was quite satisfied that the bill must pass & only anxious that as much money as possible should be got for the Church. She has pressed the Abp to bring about a compromise.[657]

20 July 1869.   Tuesday. An extraordinary scene of excitement in the H. of Lords on the I. Ch: Bill, on Granville moving that the H. shd. not insist on its amendments. When I entered the H. de Grey told me that Gladstone had determined to throw up the bill if the amendment on the preamble was carried against us, & said that Granville wished us to see Gladse. immediately & try to persuade him not to persist in this determination. Both de Grey & I were strongly impressed with the folly of throwing up. We thought that the whole of the amndt. should be gone through and no final decision of the Govt. taken till we had the general result before us. This was also Ld. Clarendon's[658] opinion. On our way to find Gladstone we met Bright whom we endeavoured to persuade to our view. We then went to the H. of Commons, & found Gladstone in one of the small rooms behind the Speakers' chair. Bright was present, & Bruce & Glyn also came in. Gl: was obstinately bent on throwing up the Bill at once. I combated his arguments. He replied with all his habitual austereness. De Grey took the same view as I did even more strongly. Bright was moderate evidently inclining to our side. Glyn supported G.; Bruce who is a cypher in such discussions said little. At last Gl: said, I am not convinced but as there is this difference of opinion we must have a Cabinet to decide: &

---

[655] William Tighe Hamillton, Irish barrister. On the Stanhope amendment, see Parry, *Democracy and Religion*, 284–5. Cf. S. Walpole, *The Life of Lord John Russell* (2 vols., London, 1889), II, 436.

[656] See 3 *Hansard* 198 (16 July 1869), 122–3.

[657] *JE*, 16 July, omits forms of the compromise.

[658] Not mentioned in *JE*.

Granville must adjourn the debate to night after the first division against us. We went back to the House & told Granville. Cairns was speaking. When he had spoken some time, Granville said I was to reply. This I did ineffectively enough, as I had only heard part of Cairns' speech (which was very powerful). On the surplus point I did not attempt to answer him. In fact no answer was possible after Gladstone's extraordinary statement in the H. of Commons that the principal might be applied for Irish purposes of any kind.

[Loose sheet]
Earl of Kimberley. Diary, 1869. July 20, 1869 continued will be found at the beginning of the next volume.
Annotated in K. hand – No: it is not there. K.

[First twelve pages of the second volume excised, and the following partial paragraph on page 13 marked through: 'preventing this folly if luckily de G. had not asked whether the Q's pleasure had been taken. This not having been done, they were obliged to give in.'][659]

11 August 1869.   Wednesday. Parlt. prorogued. I attended as one of the Commissioners. Went, all of us, to Kimberley, to my great joy.

I have not noted in its place the death of Ld. Stanley of Alderley. I lost in him a kind friend. The public who estimate a statesman's career in England almost exclusively by his skill in speech, held 'Ben' Stanley too cheap. He was a bad speaker, & therefore of course newspaper editors concluded that he was as their phrase runs, a 'fifth rate' politician, jobbed into office merely to please influential Whig friends. The truth is that S. was a man of uncommonly shrewd sense, utterly devoid of humbug, & pretension, a thorough Liberal especially in Church matters, and foreign politics, an entirely honest & trustworthy man: worth incomparably more as a member of a Cabinet, than such a man for example as Ld. Lytton,[660] a rhetorician & a novelist, but without a single quality of a statesman, or his brother Sir H. Bulwer, tricky, scheming, unscrupulous, & therfore very dangerous.

How amusing it is to read the newspaper comments on the Queen's speech. 'It is a very ill-written speech' true enough; 'therefore it cannot be Gladstone's'. Utterly mistaken. Every word of it was written by him. The Cabinet induced him to omit two or three phrases which were peculiarly absurd, but put nothing in.[661] Any one who knows G. at all,

---

[659] Entries of 22 July, 9 Aug. in *JE* no longer extant in the Kimberley Journal.

[660] Edward George Earle Lytton Bulwer-Lytton, 1st Baron Lytton (1803–73), novelist and Cons. MP for Hertfordshire, 1852–66; col. sec., 1858–9. Lytton and Bulmer not mentioned in *JE*.

[661] This sentence omitted from *JE*.

knows that marvellous as is his ability, the one thing he is most unlikely to do well, is to write a Queen's speech.

16 August 1869.   Monday. Passed our wedding day anniversary peacefully & happily together. Harvest began to-day. The weather cold & uncertain.

24 August 1869.   Tuesday. A buck weighing 11 St 5 (clean) killed to day. He was an 8 yr. old buck.

27 August 1869.   Friday. Went to Glenisla & stayed there till the 10th of Sept: The weather beautiful but I was unlucky with the deer. I missed two good shots; killed one stag, with a royal head, but a small head, and a light beast (13 st 1 lb). The last day I hit two fine deer right & left, but got neither. They escaped into the wood. One with 10 points was found next day: the other a very large stag (royal) was not seen again. Johnny killed a stag of no particular mark. Jowitt was at Glenisla, & made much pleasant talk.

13 September 1869.   Monday. Lady Palmerston died. I saw her not long before I left London. She was in full possession of her faculties (at 83) & very eager about the Irish Church & land questions. She was quite certain that Palmerston would never have abolished the Ch: Establishment. I think he would, as usual, have gone with the times.

Another buck killed here of great size 11 st: 9 (with the skin 12 lbs) he weighed as much as a fair stag. All our cattle ill with foot & mouth disease.

20 September 1869.   Monday. The bucks get bigger & bigger. A black fellow weighing 12 st. 1 killed to day.

21 September 1869.   Tuesday. The Lowes came and stayed till Saturday. Lowe is much frightened at the extravagant demands of the Irish tenant right party. Their demands are certainly alarming. It would be folly to give way to them. How to produce a good land measure puzzles me utterly.[662]

23 October 1869.   Saturday. Henry and my mother left us, having stayed a fortnight.

24 October 1869.   The newspapers announce the death of Lord Derby, yesterday morning. I cannot say I think as a statesman he is a loss to

---

[662] This entry omitted from *JE*.

this nation, tho' no one would dispute the brilliancy of his talents. I never can forgive him for the (politically) dishonest course he took both as to Protection & Reform. He & Disraeli[663] together have ruined the Tory party, the former the instrument, the latter the guiding mind. Lord Derby was as far as my experience goes and I have sat opposite to him for 20 years generally an ungenerous and unscrupulous opponent. I have seen some but rare exceptions. No speaker whom I ever heard so continually & glaringly misrepresented what his opponents said. His eloquence was sometimes touching, more often he was rather the brilliant slashing debater than the polished orator. Of late years he grew careless & slovenly in his speeches & evidently did not give himself the trouble to prepare his matter. The best speech I ever heard him make was on the 'Pacifico case' when he attacked Lord Palmerston. He seemed to me to act always on impulse with a reckless turf-spirit if I may use the term. The noblest passage in his life was I think his management of the relief of the cotton distress.

It is curious to note that Lord D. always showed nervousness when about to speak, & often during his speeches (if you watched him closely). He was excessively sensitive when attacked by others, tho' unsparing in sarcasms on friend & foe. You could invariably know by the working of his countenance & his gestures what impression the speech of another was making on his mind.[664]

26 October 1869. Tuesday. Went to London to attend a Cabinet at wh. nothing important took place.

28 October 1869. Wednesday. A deep fall of snow. Curious to see the geranium flowers peeping out of the snow, & the leaves all on the trees.

31 October 1869. Saturday. Another cabinet. The Atty. Genl. for Ireland (Sullivan) attended & expounded his Irish land scheme, extension of the Ulster tenant right to the whole of Ireland. He stated his case most ably & the Cabinet broke up more than half convinced. Then in a few days came a mem: from Fortescue intended to embody Sullivan's views, but ill-drawn. At the next cabinet a much less favourable feeling was shown to the plan, & we are now at sea again. Nevertheless something like Sullivan's plan will be adopted. Gladstone is inclined to it and he will carry the Cabinet where he pleases.[665]

10 November 1869. Our cabinets ended to day for the present. Nothing

---

[663] Not mentioned in *JE*.
[664] This entry much expanded in *JE*.
[665] Gladstone not mentioned in this passage in *JE*.

of consequence was decided at them except a reply to the U. S. despatch on the Alabama claims. What a miserable spectacle Ireland presents. Is there a native in the world so generally odious? Wretched weakness in action, contemptible vapouring in speech, & cowardly assassinations seem to be the chief characteristics of the native Irishman. I had forgotten slavish bigotry which is another pleasing trait.

Time alone can show whether past mis-government is so far the cause, that perseverence in just Government will improve the race. There are Irishmen (& not a few) who are bright exceptions, why may not the race be gradually raised to their level? But it will take many generations to accomplish.[666]

11 November 1869. Thursday. Flo. & I went to town on Tuesday & came home to day.

27 November 1869. Saturday. Ld. Chelsea, Ld. & Lady Albermarle, & Lady Augusta Keppel, Mr. Lawley, Mr. Lascelles, & Johnny left us to day after a visit wh. went off pleasantly. Henry stayed on till Monday.

I went to a meeting to day of a Committee at Norwich about the G.E. Railway. We were appd. at a county meeting last Saturday, where I attended & spoke.

Since I wrote about the Irish p. 28 &c.,[667] the Tipperary ruffians have elected as their member, the rowdy felon O'Donovan Rossa, a most fit and proper representative of them.

30 November 1869. Tuesday. To Woodrising to shoot: a dismally cold day. I went on to Letton where we stayed till Friday. Snow and miserable weather all c/y week.

7 December 1869. Tuesday. To London. Attended cabinets on Tuesday, Thursday & Friday. The Irish Land Bill not discussed in consequence of Fortescue's absence in Ireland. It was folly in him not to come over. On Friday night I returned home. Nothing of any importance was done at these Cabinets.

On Tuesday the 14th December went again to London. Cabinets on Tuesday, Thursday & Friday. On Tuesday we made some progress with the Irish land. On Thursday Gladstone had so bad a cold that he could not be present: we did nothing.

On Friday a very long Cabinet at Gladstone's House. It was agreed that a bill should be drawn up, but several important points were left

---

[666] This passage expanded and combined with discussion of Land bill in *JE*, 14 Dec. 1869.

[667] Entry for 10 Nov. 1869.

undecided. Cardwell & Lowe strongly object to payments to tenants for good will, where no custom can be proved, except where the tenants hold very small occupations. Will they give way? There is no hope of a bill wh. will be satisfactory to the Irish tenants. They clamour for what no honest Govt. can concede. But our measure may if carried satisfy English feelings of justice to Ireland, & possibly lay the foundation for peace hereafter. But I am far from sanguine. An appeal to force seems the ultimate end to wh. the Irish are determined to push their grudge against us. It is a melancholy prospect. We must hold the island by sheer force if all measures of justice & conciliation fail.[668]

There was sad news last week of the illness of the Duchess of Argyll. The poor Duke, who was in London (she at Inverary), when he heard it fainted away. She has had a paralytic stroke.

17 December 1869. Friday. Johnny came of age.

18 December 1869. Saturday. Back to Kimberley.

24 December 1869. Friday. A fall of snow. Sharp weather till the 31st.

31 December 1869. Friday. We gave a very successful tenants' ball in honour of Johnny's coming of age. About 130 people present.

1 January 1870. Saturday. On looking back at the past year I have the satisfaction to think I have not passed it idly. It has been to me & mine a happy & prosperous year, & I earnestly hope that a sense of so many blessings given to one so unworthy will make me more careful how I live.

[Six pages here excised.][669]

... On the whole I think we decided rightly as to Irish Crime to postpone actions till we see what effect our Land Bill produces. I fear the first effect will be disappointment & increased discontent.[670]

6 February 1870. Monday. I had a long walk to day with Dufferin. He has seen the Land Bill, & approves it generally.

On Sunday I walked with Goschen & talked about local Taxation. He wants to make owners pay half the rates: & brings some strong

---

[668] This entry expanded in *JE.*

[669] *JE* records no entries between 19 Dec. 1869 and 5 Feb. 1870.

[670] Cf. *JE,* for 5 Feb., where Kimberley admits that, from the vantage point of 1875, he was 'unduly alarmed'.

arguments in favour of such a measure. It is evident to me that landowners will have a hard fight to defend themselves against the attacks which will be made on their present rights. Landed property is in too few hands in England, & the landlords being so small a number are in an unsafe position. I have no doubt the possession of landed property will every year become less desirable, that is, of land not occupied by the owner. Gradually the tenant will oust the landlord of the land, just as the copyholder ousted the Lord of the Manor. Irish landlords will, if they are wise, avail themselves of the provisions in our bill to sell to their tenants and even in England prudent men will avoid possessing large tracts of land let to tenants.

I shall certainly avoid all increase of my estate, & shall watch closely the course of events so as to sell at the proper moment if needful. I am far from expecting any violent measures, and I believe the general result will be good for the nation. I write only as a landowner, not as a statesman who is bound to consider the welfare of the whole community.[671]

9 February 1870. Went to Osborne for a night. The Queen, notwithstanding her neuralgia, looking very robust & well, & apparently in good spirits.

12 February 1870. Saturday. At the Cabinet to-day Fortescue attempted to get rid of Bright's clauses in the Land Bill. I thought it a scurvy proceeding in Bright's absence.[672]

14 February 1870. Monday. Lowe, Fortescue, the Atty. Genl. for Ireland (Barry),[673] O'Hara an Irish lawyer, & myself met at Thring's office to revise the Land Bill, & insert the last decisions of the Cabinet. We got hopelessly puzzled in trying to frame a clause providing for compensation to sub-tenants.[674] The Bill is sound in its main features, but the details want more consideration.

15 February 1870. Tuesday. I heard a part of Gladstone's speech. He was clear, and successful: not equal, I think, nearly to his Irish Church speech last year. In fact he understands the subject less.[675]

---

[671] See Kimberley's reflection from 1875 in *JE*, 5 Feb. 1870.
[672] This passage omitted from the *JE*. Bright's clauses provided provision for land purchase.
[673] Charles Robert Barry (1824–97), Lib. MP for Dungarvan, 1865–8; Irish sol.-genl., 1868–70.
[674] This sentence omitted from *JE*.
[675] This passage expanded in *JE*.

19 February 1870.   Saturday. Gladstone proposing to release O'Donovan Rossa! (on condition that he leaves the U. Kingdom). It would be a grievous mistake to release any Fenians at this juncture. *[About three lines struck through in this passage.]*

21 February 1870.   Monday. The great & undiscriminating approval of our Land Bill begins to cool. In Ireland, as I fully expected, there is much disappointment. No measure (not robbing the landlords of their property) would satisfy the Tenant right party: and a measure which satisfies them would disgust every other Irishman. In fact no measures can satisfy Irishmen: they can only lay the basis for slow improvement in the temper of that most wayward people: & so Gladstone will find out. Now he lives in a fool's Paradise,[676] imagining that his measures will produce a speedy change.

22 February 1870.   Tuesday. Johnny told us to our infinite amazement that he has proposed marriage to Miss Bentley daughter of Mr Bentley, who is a brewer at Bantrey & father of a college friend of his. I of course could not consent.

2 March 1870.   Wednesday. Spoke to Ld. Granville about state of Ireland. He advised me to see Gladstone. I found Gladstone in the afternoon at home. He was very determined against the Susp: of the H. C. Act, & said that Bright would resign.[677]

5 March 1870.   Saturday. Hartington, Fortescue, the Atty. Genl. for Ireland & myself met at the Irish office to consider finally the measures for repression of crime in Ireland (apart from the H.C. Susp: Act) which we could recommend to the Cabinet. We had been appd. a Committee for this purpose.

[676] 'Fool's paradise' becomes 'happy delusion' in *JE*. See Parry, *Democracy and Religion*, 292.

[677] Cf. the broad expansion in the *JE*, where Kimberley suspects that Gladstone's vehemence is 'greatly due to the fear of losing Bright' if a vigorous course were taken. 'I made the best fight I could.' Kimberley wrote, 'but it is impossible to get the best of Gladstone in argument. His ingenuity in shifting his ground, and in probing every weak point in his adversary's armour render him almost invincible. Unfortunately he is often led astray by his own subtilty, and thus gives exaggerated weight in council to arguments useful perhaps in debate but more plausible than sound. I have heard that Palmerston one day when he had been sorely tried by Gladstone's dialectics said to a friend 'you remember that anecdote about Pitt when he was asked what was the first quality of a statesman. He answered "patience": and the second? patience. & the third? patience. But Pitt did not know Gladstone!'

[Two pages here excised.][678]

... Hartington & myself were appd. a Committee to draw up suggestions for the Bill. Practically they were arranged by F. & me, & the Atty. & Solr. Genl. for Ireland. The first sketch was drawn by Barry. The press clauses were suggested by Lowe, & arranged by a Committee consisting of the Chancellor, Fortescue, Lowe, Cardwell & myself with the Irish Solr. Genl. (Dowse).[679]

Dowse seems a sharp, ready man.

On March 17 Mr Charles Wodehouse died at Lowestoft. (formerly Prebendary). A worthy, & pleasant man, self tormented by an over scrupulous conscience.

I heard yesterday of poor Charles Hogg's death of fever at Calcutta.

30 March 1870.[680] Wednesday.   Went to Brighton to see Mrs Walker's school. On Tuesday the Irish Peace Preservation Bill read 2nd in H. of Lords. I spoke with tolerable success. The oppositon peers were very mild. It looks as if the Tory party had adopted the policy of the 'Quarterly Review', supposed to be Ld. Salisbury, namely to support the Whigs & wait for a split between them & the Radicals, hoping then to form a strong coalition between moderate men on both sides. They may win if they are patient. There are already evident signs of dissensions between the Govt. & the extreme Left in the H. of Commons. Irish education will probably [be] the rock on wh. we shall wreck.[681]

General Grey's death is the event of the week. It will of course be very difficult to find a discreet man to fill his post: but it is easy to conceive that his successor may fill the post better. The General was a crochetty wrong headed politician like his brother, Ld. Grey. On foreign politics he gave the Queen bad advice. He had a strange dislike of the French alliance, and a regular John Bull suspicion of everything French. Nor was he always prudent. He had latterly made a foolish stir about 'John Brown' talking more than was wise about that silly scandal & even refusing to acknowledge J.B's touch of the hat.[682] This is said to have annoyed the Queen.

1 April 1870.   Friday. An explosion of Radical discontent on the Irish

---

[678] Presumably regarding Gladstone's giving way over possible use of a coercian act. Cf. *JE.*

[679] Richard Dowse, Irish sol.-genl., 14 Feb. 1870 to 6 Feb. 1872.

[680] Dated 29 March in *JE.*

[681] See Parry, *Democracy and Religion,* 299.

[682] John Brown (1826–83), was Queen Victoria's favourite servant and confidant, their close relationship becoming the subject of rumour.

University question. The Land Bill drags heavily along. I hear C. Fortescue, as was to be expected, gives Gladstone but little aid.[683]

3 April 1870. Sunday. Mr William Wodehouse my Great Uncle died this morning in Green Street. He had been parlaysed for many years, & had lived entirely in London. He was singularly like my Gt Gd. father in face, a slow, dogged man, very crusty at times, but he was useful in his day as rector of Hingham, & magistrate, & chairman of our Bd. of Guardians, & always irreproachable in his conduct public & private. His death had been long expected.

11 April 1870. Monday. Went to K. & stayed till 26th. Beautiful spring weather.

26 April 1870. Tuesday. Heard the news of the cruel murder of Vyner, Herbert, Lloyd, & Ct. Boyl by Greek brigands. Saw de Grey who is much & very naturally hurt at a conversation with Gladstone who *proh pudor*! took up the cudgels for the miserable Greek Govt.[684] This is to be Philhellene with a vengeance.

7 May 1870. Saturday. Found out that Johnny has incurred heavy debts.[685]

14 May 1870. Saturday. Have been very busy all this week in the unpleasant work of settling Johnny's debts. He has drawn Bills, which amount to between £9000 & £10,0000. We expect to settle them for about £8,500. There are also some tradesmen's bills. This money has been principally squandered in betting on horse races. It is surprising that he should have made such a fool of himself in spite of my constant warnings. 'Naturam expellar funca' &c. Note. They turned out to be £11,000 wh. I paid!

[Four pages here excised.][686]

[683] *JE* excludes the first sentence of this entry and adds, 'the loss of Sullivan is irreparable'.

[684] Vyner was de Grey's brother-in-law. Gladstone believed that the press generally had been 'most precipitous and & unjustifiable abt. the Greek Govt'. See *Gladstone Diaries*, VII, 283 n. 8; also correspondence of 14 April to 16 May 1870 in CIP, Clar. dep. c. 499, ff. 90–132.

[685] The beginning of a series of revelations which led to Lord Wodehouse's bankruptcy, filed 1 Jan. 1872. See KP1 28/4.

[686] Presumably on the withdrawal of troops from the Australasian colonies. Cf *JE*, May (sic) 13.

19 May 1870. Thursday. Debate on Deceased wife's Sister Bill.[687] Tedious dissertations on Leviticus. How can a rational man argue with fanatics who believe that Leviticus is binding on Englishmen? I made a few observations in support of the bill.

The Chancellor must really be slightly crazy on this subject. In his pamphlet[688] he says he would rather see 30,000 armed Frenchmen landed at Dover than that the bill should pass. It will however certainly pass after the division of to night, our excellent Chancellor's opposition notwithstanding.[689]

28 May 1870. Friday. I moved 2nd reading of Ecclesiastical Titles Repeal Bill. Nothing remarkable in the discussion except that Lord St Leonard's who will be 90 next Feby. made a speech one hour long. In body the old man is wonderfully vigorous, but his rambling or rather shambling talk was sad twaddle. Lord Russell was as actively vicious against his friends as usual.

One meets everywhere in the town the K. of the Belgians[690] who looks an amiable dull man.

29 May 1870. Saturday. We have had curious discussions...

[Parts of three lines struck through.]

... on the Suez canal, & the route to India in case of war. Childers is hot for neutralization of the canal on the basis of a free passage for troops & war vessels of all belligerents. Gladstone acutely observed that this meant that we were to have a free use of the passage under the guise of a general freedom. Of course as long as we were masters of the sea on the other side the canal would be a mere trap for our enemies. There is no harm in trying for this neutralization but I expect other nations will say 'don't you wish you may get it' – In case of a great war between us & France or France & the U. S. combined, it will be a race to get possession of Egypt. If we manage well, we ought to get there first – from India – But we ought I think to keep our stations on the Cape route such as Mauritius secure from sudden attack, as in spite of all our efforts we may lose the command of the Mediterranean the loss of wh. would render the Suez route useless. How great a blunder Palmn. made in opposing the Suez Canal scheme! When I was Under Secretary at the F.O. I wrote a mem: pointing out

[687] Legislation to allow marriage with a deceased wife's sister not passed until 1907.

[688] William Page Wood, *A Vindication of the Law Prohibiting Marriage with a Deceased Wife's Sister* (1861).

[689] In *JE* in 1875 Kimberley added: 'I was quite wrong here. The bill seems farther than ever from passing.'

[690] Leopold II (1835–1909), r. 1865–1909.

the objections to that policy. It was sent to Pam who honoured my arguments with an elaborate answer.[691] I was unconvinced then, & unhappily it is now clear that for once the great master of foreign policy was utterly wrong.

3 June 1870.   Friday. Johnny & I went to Weymouth.

4 June 1870.   Saturday. Passed the day in seeing the Fortifications, breakwater & Prison at Portland. We had for cicerone Col: Belfield the Commandant of the Engineers, who was very civil to us. The fortifications & breakwater are a very fine work. Amongst the convicts we saw several Fenians, amongst others Luby, O'Leary & McCafferty. They looked well and defiant. The Governor Capt. Clifton said they were quite unmanageable. In my opinion they ought to be kept in a separate prison & treated differently from ordinary convicts. It is quite sufficient punishment to impress on them without inflicting on them the degradation of mixing them with the ordinary convicts.[692]

6 June 1870.   Monday. Went to Truro and stayed with Smith till Thursday. On Tuesday & Wednesday went to Falmouth. Several houses building & the place is evidently improving.

9 June 1870.   Returned to town.

[Four pages here excised.][693]

23, 24 June 1870.   Committee in Lords on Land Bill. Salisbury violent, carping & peevish. O'Hagan[694] at first talked vaguely & seemed to be of no use to us, but later on he spoke to the point: he is evidently popular in the house, and an acquisition to our bench. Our minority stuck well together spite of repeated defeats. On the last night the opposition was disorganized, & the leaders quarrelling with each other.
   On Monday morning I was shocked at the news of Ld. Clarendon's death. He was sitting by me in the House on Thursday, & I observed to him that he looked very ill, & asked why he did not go home.[695] He said he had had diarrhoea for five days. Soon after, he went away, & I never saw him again. I deeply lament his loss. He was ever a most

[691] Corresp. untreated.
[692] Note expansion in *JE*.
[693] No entries are recorded in *JE* between 3 June and 24 June.
[694] Thomas O'Hagan, Baron O'Hagan (1812–85), Irish ld. chanc., 1868–74; Lib. MP for Tralee, 1865–8; cr. UK peerage, 1870.
[695] This passage dated 'June 27' in *JE*, where it begins: 'I was shocked this morning at the news of Clarendon's death.'

kind friend to me. His character has been so fully drawn in the newspapers than here is little to add here.

One peculiarity has escaped notice. He was a pessimist (of the Melbourne school) as to human nature, & often in private very bitter in his remarks on those he disliked. His good nature was not the good nature of a weak man, and it is no detraction from his character to say that he had that spice of 'devil' in him without which no one can attain the high position he held. Granville will no doubt succeed him at the F. Off: & Fortescue at the Col: Off.

29 June 1870.   Thursday. Henley married to Miss Jekyll. I went to the church and breakfast at Sir F. Goldsmid's,[696] the latter very gorgeous of course as becomes a rich Hebrew. The lady is good looking, (nothing more,) and quiet & pleasing in manner.

When I went to the H. of Lds. I heard to my surprise that Gladstone wished to see me to morrow (for the purpose as I learnt confidentially from Lowe & de Grey)[697] of offering me the Colonies.

30 June 1870.   Friday. Saw Gladstone at 11 o'clock. He offered me the Col: office in the kindest & most flattering terms. Granville has the Foreign Office, Halifax becomes Privy Seal,[698] and Forster gets a seat in the Cabinet. I hear that Lady Waldegrave demanded the colonies for Fortescue & got a flat refusal. She is I am told, frantic with spite & rage. What a foolish woman! She has done poor F., who is a good fellow, infinite harm.

I am naturally much pleased at my promotion, but it really pains to me that F. should have exposed himself to such a rebuff. He has no real reason to complain. The Irish Secretaryship is more important just now than the Colonial, and it would have been impossible to fill the post adequately if F. had left it, as Forster, the only fit man, cannot leave the Education Dept. I am heartily glad he enters the Cabinet.

I got the Ecclesl. Titles [Repeal] Bill very quietly thro' Committee to day, having agreed privately with Cairns to accept his amendments with some alterations. O'Hagan & Bowyer preferred Cairns' words to ours.[699]

6 July 1870.   Wednesday. Sworn in at Council at Windsor as Secy. of State for the Colonies.

---

[696] Francis Goldsmid (1808–79), Lib. MP for Reading, 1860–78.

[697] Lowe and de Grey not cited as sources in *JE*.

[698] See Kimberley's estimate of Halifax in *JE*.

[699] Final sentence excluded from *JE*, while adding that 'its original enactment was a mistake'. Kimberley had been outspoken in favour of the measure in 1850–1, but by the mid-sixties had come to regret his support. See *Liberal by Principle*, 68–70; 3 *Hansard* 186 (28 March 1867), 711–12.

7 July 1870.   Thursday. Attended at Colonial office first time.

8 July 1870.   Friday. Irish Land Bill read 3rd time. Great excitement about the Spanish (Hohenzollern) question.[700]

15 July 1870.   Friday. News of the determination of the French to make war on Prussia.[701]

[Six pages here excised.][702]

... The question of asking for men & money from Parlt. was easily disposed of. I observe that Childers is decidedly French in his leanings.

To the Lord Mayor's dinner afterwards, where Gladstone made a most funereal oration.[703]

1 August 1870.   Heard of poor Chucky Dillon's death last Saturday at the Isle of Wight.

11 August 1870.   Thursday. Went to Ky. Parliament prorogued yesterday.

7 September 1870.   Went for two days to Witton. With this exception we have stayed quietly at home. The accounts of the war make one shudder.[704] We shall I hope firmly resolve to persevere in our strict abstention from all interference nothwithstanding the senseless alarm of our now of part of our press.

The siege of Paris if pressed to extremity may either break the spirit of the turbulent Parisians, or end in excesses as bad as those of the reigns of terror. The North Germans are socially a hateful race, but their supremacy would be less dangerous to Europe than that of France. But I see no good to come from this war, which will throw Europe back 20 years.

What a year of calamities public & private. The war, the loss of the *Captain*,[705] in private the sudden deaths of C. Dillon, Mrs. Farquhar,

---

[700] In late 1869 Prince Leopold of Hohenzollern (1835–1905) was secretly offered the throne of Spain. Bismarck pressed his claim while France fiercely opposed it.

[701] On 12 July, France demanded that Prussia endorse Prince Leopold's withdrawal of his claim to the Spanish throne. On 19 July France declared war on Prussia.

[702] These pages almost certainly having to do with the 'important decisions taken for the "situation"' on 30 July. *Gladstone Diaries*, VII, 335. In *JE* long entries for 16 and 22 July 1870 are on Canada and the attempted suicide of Sir Robert Hervey.

[703] Gladstone himself characterised it as a 'peaceful speech to a warlike company'. *Gladstone Diaries*, VII, 335.

[704] On 2 Sept. 1870 Napoleon III surrendered to the Prussians at Sedan. Bismarck demanded Alsace and Lorraine, and laid siege to Paris.

[705] HMS *Captain*, an iron-clad turret ship, capsized on 7 Sept., causing more than 450 fatalities.

and many more misfortunes mark this as the 'blackest' year in my lifetime hitherto.

30 September 1870.   Friday. To London...

[More than one line struck through.]

... Gladstone proposed that we should address a remonstrance to Germany against the annexation of Alsace & Lorraine contrary to the wishes of the inhabitants on the ground that it has become the practice in Europe not to annex territory without the consent of the population, witness the plebiscites in Savoy &c. &c.

Granville was entirely of an opposite opinion.

[Two pages here excised, followed by this lightly crossed through: 'seemed somewhat vexed at these two questions being decided against him'.]

... Spencer and even Fortescue were against the release of the Fenians till we see whether the autumn passes quietly in Ireland.[706]

6 October 1870.   My cousin Col: Edwin Wodehouse died suddenly at Portsmouth, and October 12 my uncle John Rebow died at Wyvenhoe.

11 October 1870.   Johnny returned from America after a very successful tour.

20 October 1870.   Thursday. Suddenly to London for a Cabinet at wh. we resolved to make an appeal to Germany to grant & France to accept an armistice.

2 November 1870.   Came to London. A cabinet at which nothing particular took place. A long talk in the evening with Persigny. He lays all the blame of the misfortunes of France on the Emperor & Empress, the former for refusing to follow his (Persigny's) advice and put down the Republican party by a new coup d'etat, the latter for refusing to make peace as Regent & use Bazaine[707] & his army to restore the Empire.

Persigny says he was all against the war & that he strongly advised Gramont & the Empr. to accept the ... of Prussia ..

[Some five lines here excised.]

... Persigny's language is most extravagant & violent, his policy utterly

---

[706] Final passage omitted from *JE*.

[707] Achille Bazaine (1811–88), head of French army in Mexico, 1863; appt. marshal, 1864; command. main French armies during Franco–Prussian War.

unscrupulous but there is force in what he says from his point of view.

10 November 1870. The Russian despatch, delivered by Brunnow,[708] yesterday was considered by the Cabinet. Granville was for consulting the other signatory Powers...

[Some five lines here excised, verso of excision from November 2; see above.][709]

... rejoinder to Gortchacow's answer[710] to Granville's Desp. we are to consider the draft on Monday.

26 November 1870. Back to Kimberley.

28 November 1870. Monday. To London for a Cabinet. We settled the draft of answer to Gortchacow without difficulty.[711]

30 November 1870. Wednesday. Cabinet. Cardwell explained his proposals for the army.[712] I think them quite sufficient. They were generally approved. Much discussion whether we should go into Conference at once, or delay. On the whole we were for going on. The difficulty is France, who of course wants to get us into war. My theory of the situation is this. Bismarck & Gortchacow (Arcades ambo) had an understanding when the war broke out. Russia to keep Austria in check, Prussia to favour Russian desire to set aside the 1856 Treaty. When France collapsed, Gff was afraid that Bismarck would play him the same trick as he played France after Sadowa. Seeing that c/y Prussians were unexpectedly held at bay by Paris, Gff seized the opportunity, much to Bismarck's annoyance to take a decisive step as to the Black Sea. Bismarck can't wish to quarrel with Russia, but still less does he wish a war now to break out between England & Russia, which might bring some aid to France. He therefore temporises, & will try to smooth the matter down.[713]

14 December 1870. Wednesday. To London. *[One line here struck through.]* Luxembourg affair. The Prussian note on the face of it seems to go no further than to complain of non observance of the duties of neutrality, &

[708] Ernest Philip Ivanovich, Baron Brunnow (1797–1875), Russian amb. to London, 1858–74.

[709] Fuller entry in *JE*.

[710] Renouncing the covenants of 1856 restricting Russian rights in the Black Sea.

[711] Accepting a conference in London to determine questions of unilateral treaty changes. This entry omitted from *JE*.

[712] See *Gladstone Diaries*, VII, 409–10.

[713] Excepting the brief mention of Cardwell's army measures, this Cabinet report was omitted from the *JE*.

does not in terms imply a renunciation of the Treaty.[714] But is doubtless intended to prepare the way for the annexation of the Duchy to Germany. We had not much difficulty in agreeing on the answer to the Prussian note.[715] The rest of a long sitting was spent in discussing whether the navy should *[Several words ill. as a result of striking through on previous page of journal.]* Granville was mildly for, Gladstone violently against. He argues that the present position of France renders our naval position relatively much stronger than it was last year. On the other hand it was admitted on all hands that every day increases the danger of our being engaged in war. There is force in Gladstone's argument, & it prevailed. Nevertheless the country will be dissatisfied I think if the navy is not increased. But nothing would satisfy the unreasoning clamours for armaments. The newspapers are stark mad on the subject. I hailed with joy the sensible speech of Lord Derby. What has become of our boasted common-sense if we are to raise armies sufficient to enable us to send expeditions to the Continent fit to cope with the monstrous armies of the Continental nations? At no period of our history have we attempted this since the Plantagenets. A strong fleet, an army of sufficient force to meet an enemy who landed 80 or 100,000 men on our shores with a militia reserve is enough to satisfy all but prestige hunting scribblers. But I fear the sight of blood will be too much for John Bull, and that he will rush madly into war, like his ancestors. Men like dogs can't keep quiet long when a fight is going on.

17 December 1870. Saturday. Cabinet. We discussed withdrawal of remaining troops from Canada: the upshot was that the Cabinet on the whole wished them withdrawn but left the 'when' very much to my discretion & Cardwell's. The rest of the sitting spent in discussing how to get France to the Conference, & how to proceed when it meets. Went back to Ky.

21 December 1870. Wednesday. It began to freeze & snow.

Xmas Eve. Tremendously cold. At 6 on Xmas morning the thermometre marked 6 1/2 below zero of Fahrenheit under a tree 4 ft. from ground. Very heavy snow. This great frost lasted with a slight thaw one day till Saturday, Jan. 14. 1871.

---

[714] Accusing Luxembourg of breaking neutrality in contravention of the 1867 Luxembourg Treaty.

[715] Expressing great concern about Bismarck's circular. See *Gladstone Diaries*, VII, 416–17. This discussion of the Luxembourg Treaty omitted from *JE*.

5 January 1871. Thursday. I got a bad chill in a snow storm which brought on 'tic' in my face, & made me extremely ill.

18 January 1871. Wednesday. We all went to London.

9 February 1871. Thursday. Parliament met. The Queen opened in person. She did not wear her robes but had them put on the chair behind her, an absurd sight.

14 February 1871.[716] Wednesday. Put the final touches in *[Several words heavily struck through.]* Cardwell's bill.[717] Hartington was strongly for applying the ballot wherever the militia quota is below the numbers fixed by Parliament. I alone supported him.

Long discussion on Spencer & Hartington's proposal to suspend H.C. Act in Westmeath. Fortescue, Bruce & I supported H.[718] The rest silent or adverse. I suppose by dint of hammering we shall convince Gladstone and Granville as we did last year, that the preservation of life is a duty wh. a Govt. is bound to discharge even at the risk of violating the constitutional liberties of Irishmen: but we want Thor's hammer for the purpose.

[Some three lines here excised.]

... & Lorraine. Wants us to protest against cession against will of people. Cabinet not with him. How can we safely take this ground? Witness Bessarabia in 1856, Oude &c. &c. &c., Ireland, the S. States of America. The wishes of the inhabitants are an important but...

[Some three lines here excised, the verso of above excision, as well as a similar amount at the top of the following page.]

... Prussia as to all *[ill.]* demand of an indemnity of six milliards from France. Experienced financiers such as L. Rothschild[719] and K. Hodgson[720] say France could not raise more than 120 millions sterling, but of course much depends on the time of payment. We decided to send a civil remonstrance, which...[721]

---

[716] 15 Feb. 1871 in *JE* and in *Gladstone Diaries*, VII, 449.

[717] The Army Regulation bill reorganised the armed forces, creating a new reserve force and abolishing the purchase of commissions.

[718] Fortescue and Bruce not mentioned in *JE*.

[719] Lionel Rothschild (1808–79), chief manager of Rothschild banking house in England; Lib. MP for London, 1858–79.

[720] Kirkman Daniel Hodgson (1814–79), gov. Bank of England; Lib. MP for Bristol, 1870–8.

[721] In *JE* Kimberley adds how curious it was that these predictions were 'falsified by the event'.

[Some three lines here excised, verso of previous page.]

... I forgot to chronicle that Constance was duly presented at Court on Tuesday.

25 February 1871.   Saturday. Much talk at the Cabinet about the mess we are in as to the Westmeath Committee. The decision at the Cabinet to refer the question to a secret Committee was taken[722]
...

[Almost a full page excised.]

... speech for so *[ill.]* ordinary an invasion of the liberty of the subject...
[Verso of previous excision.]

... conspiracy. This is a chronic disease & the remedy must be one of some duration. It seems better that the circumstances should be fully examined by a Committee before such extreme measures as a suspn. of the H.C. Act are adopted. It amounts to this, that arbitrary imprisonment will become part of the ordinary system of Irish Government, for what is good for Westmeath will be good for any other county when agrarian crime breaks out.

The Commons were greatly alarmed at the notion of a secret Committee; so we resolved to propose to leave the secresy to the discretion of the Committee. On the motion itself as thus amended we shall stand firm, & treat it as a vote of confidence. The fact is we are undergoing the usual fate of administrations. We have had our youth & manhood, & are becoming elderly, next year, if we survive as long, we shall be decrepit – at least we shall be thought to be, which is the same thing.

We have done handsomely what we were brought in to do. The Irish Ch: & Land Bills, & the Education Bill are great achievements. War & foreign affairs are uncongenial to Gladstone, & he will never shine when they.... .

[Some dozen lines here excised.]

... The conclusion of peace makes affairs flat for the moment: but it is no better than a truce: and Europe will long rue the violence...

[Verso of previous excision.]

---

[722] With local suspension of Habeas Corpus if the case warranted. See Parry, *Democracy and Religion*, 318–19; Kimberley to de Grey, 20 Feb. 1871, in *Liberal by Principle*, 124–5.

... Mazzinian *[ill.]* But Goschen[723] is also I suspect the stronger man. Went to Windsor for the night. The Queen spoke to me at some length about public affairs. She said amongst other things that she wished Gladstone would take rather a higher tone about foreign affairs, in wh. I entirely agree with H. M.. She expressed much sympathy with the Emperor L. N. He had committed she said great faults but he was much to be pitied. The Empress had much to answer for in the encouragement she had given to extravagance & luxury, tho's she had behaved with dignity in her misfortunes. She hoped that one good result of the fall of the Empire would be that the luxury of Paris would no longer be an evil example to society in England, the tone of which had much deteriorated of late.[724]

I was much struck by the good sense, & ability of her observations.

16, 17 March 1871.   Thursday & Friday. Long Cabinets on negotiation with the U. States. *[One line heavily struck through.]* ... strongly against the proposed declaration binding the ...

[Two pages here excised.][725]

21 March 1871.   Tuesday. Went to marriage of Ld. Lorne & Princess Louise at Windsor a very pretty sight.[726] The Queen looked pleased, the Prince of Wales sulky ...

[Some half-dozen lines here excised.]

17 April 1871.   Returned to Ky. where we stayed a fortnight. I ought have noticed the opening of the Albert Hall at wh. I was present. It was successful so far as a fine sight goes: but what good the Hall can be unless it is turned into a Circus I can't imagine.

27 April 1871.   Thursday.

[The following two-and-a-half pages excised.]

[723] George Joachim Goschen (1831–1907), Lib. then Lib. U. MP for City of London, 1863–80, for Ripon, 1880–5; for Edinburgh E., 1885–6; for St. George's Hanover Square, 1887–1900, when he was cr. Viscount Goschen; pres. poor law bd., 1868–71; 1st ld. adm., 1871–4; chanc. exch., 1887–92.

[724] In a similar vein, see Lady Kimberley's advice to Alice not to read 'any French novels ... Their tone is false and their sentiment bad.' PKF DE 1749 38/3.

[725] No entries in *JE* between 9 March and 21 March.

[726] Princess Louise, Queen Victoria's third daughter, married the Marquess of Lorne, eldest son of the Duke of Argyll.

... Licensing Bill to wh. I was always opposed is enough to[727] destroy us utterly.[728]

Dizzy knows what a prodigious advantage the rage of the publicans gives the Tory party. But our misfortunes are not all of our own making. The singular bad luck of having to oppose increased estimates to meet a war Expenditure for which the nation clamoured under the influence of the despicable panic of last autumn, when the hot fit was beginning to cool down, and to provide the ways & means when the cold fit has come on, is the true explanation of our discomfiture. If the war between France & Germany were still waging, we could have carried fresh taxes easily enough. Whatever fresh taxation we proposed there would have been a savage cry against us.

29 April 1871. Saturday. Dined for the first time at the Academy dinner. I don't care if it is the last for a more dismal piece of formal humbug I never 'assisted' at.[729] Army went to Mr Worsley's school on Wednesday. I believe the practice of not giving the Cabinet an opportunity of altering the Budget arose when Gladstone was C. of the Exch: under Palmerston. He & P. were always quarreling, & P. used to intrigue to upset his budgets. So to prevent this he kept them till the last moment when discussion was impossible. But the practice is a foolish one, & especially so in a Cabinet which has such able financiers as Cardwell, Stansfeld,[730] Goschen, & Halifax. If we could have debated Lowe's budget, we should probably have produced something better.

4 May 1871. Thursday. Alas! Blackest of days. My darling Army's illness began at school.[731] Flo. brought him home helpless in the carriage.

6 May 1871. Saturday. At the Cabinet to day decided to abandon 'Local Rating' & 'Licensing' Bills. On Tuesday May 2 I moved second reading of Westmeath Bill. The Bill well received.[732]

[727] The previous eleven words seem to have been added as a summary of the previous excisions, as it flows smoothly into the final three words. Cf. *JE*, 27 April 1871.

[728] The Home Secretary, H. A. Bruce, proposed in his licensing bill to prevent any increase in the number of public houses. The long-term security of publican's licenses was also left in doubt. The bill alienated the 'drink interest' in the country.

[729] Cf. Gladstone attending with 'much interest and delight'. *Gladstone Diaries*, VII, 488.

[730] Stansfeld excluded as an 'able financier' from the *JE* because he failed to live up to expectations. See entries for 3 Dec. 1873, 21 Feb. 1874.

[731] For details, see Kimberley to Raikes Currie, 10 May 1871, in *Liberal by Principle*, 125–6.

[732] This entry omitted from *JE*.

8 May 1871. Monday. University Tests Bill in Committee in H. of Lords.[733] Ld. Salisbury made a laboured speech with little of his usual incisiveness, & sarcasm. The debate went very favourably for us, & the smallness of the majorities by which we were beaten indicates a speedy victory over our opponents. In fact this new test against infidelity is absurd. Ld. Rosebery made a clever speech with a good deal of sub-acid humour, unusual in a young man.[734]

19 May 1871. Friday. Our poor little Army who seemed to be getting slowly better during the last ten days, attacked with dreadful tetanic convulsions. May God have mercy upon us.

28 May 1871. The week now ended has been made infamous for ever in the annals of France by the scenes of unheard of wickedness & cruelty which took place on the taking of Paris by the Versailles party. Hell seems to have broken loose in that accursed city. The fiendish atrocities of the Communists are rivaled almost by the cruelty of the party of 'order'. Words are wanting to describe such horrible events.

Alas! my foolish son has again plunged into wild debt. He says he owes £5000. His ruin is inevitable. This only was wanting to make our cup of bitterness full. I can endure it: but my poor wife! It cuts me to the heart to see her despairing grief.

29 May 1871. Monday. Went to Falmouth to lay the first stone of a new landing place. The function followed by a dinner went off well and the people seemed pleased and happy.

31 May 1871. Wednesday. Returned to find unspeakable woe in my home. Poor Army had another fearful fit this evening.

13 June 1871. Tuesday. Univ: Tests Bill finally agreed to in H. of Lords. I was told that all the Tory leaders were against further resistance but were forced by Ld. Salisbury to make a fight. They were evidently very half hearted about it.

Yesterday we had a long debate on the Washington Treaty.[735] I had a very bad cold, and spoke with difficulty but I managed to say what

---

[733] Abolished those religious subscriptions which effectively restricted the governing of Oxford and Cambridge Universities to Anglicans.

[734] This entry omitted form *JE.*

[735] Cf. *JE,* where Kimberley gives 'some account of the origin and progress of the negotiation which ended in the Treaty'.

was necessary. Sir J. Rose[736] who was present told me he thought the debate wd. have a useful effect in Canada.

17 June 1871. Saturday. Both at this Cabinet and at the Cabinet last Saturday we were chiefly occupied with the Army Bill...

[Most of the page excised.][737]

... Australian Inter colonial trade *[ill.]* The Cabinet...

[Verso of previous excision.]

24 June 1871. Saturday. Gladstone has a scheme for abolishing the Irish Ld. Lieutcy. and getting the P. of Wales to reside a couple of months, the Dublin season, in Ireland. I am for the plan: but can H. M. & H. R. H. be brought to it? I fear they are too blind to the dangers ahead, and too selfish to sacrifice a moment's personal convenience for any national purpose. What could Odger[738] & Co. desire better for their ends than the sulky seclusion of the Queen, & the silly frivolous debauched life of the Prince.[739]

The old sports of bull-baiting & cock fighting were far better than this cruel & contemptible 'amusement' of pigeon slaughtering. Faugh! Sport!

8 July 1871. Saturday. Dear Army began to mend, thank God, last Tuesday. Went on Friday to the P. of Wales' Garden party at Chiswick where I saw the Prince & Princess of Prussia.[740] The latter grown much older in appearance: the former looking wonderfully well, a fine soldier like man.

15 July 1871. Saturday.

[Several lines here excised.] ... D. of Cambridge's position & conduct much discussed. He has been playing a miserable shilly shally game. At one time telling us he wd. support us, at another pleading the impossibility of doing so without departing from his neutrality. His speech yesterday was rather more in our...

[Verso of previous excision.]

---

[736] John Rose (1820–88), first min. of finance for dominion of Canada, 1867–8; resigned office and settled in England, 1868.

[737] There are no entries in *JE* between 13 June and 24 June.

[738] George Odger (1813–77), Cornish shoemaker and secretary of the London Trades Council, 1862–77.

[739] In the *JE*, the two previous sentences become 'I should much doubt it.'

[740] Prince Frederick of Prussia and Princess Victoria, eldest daughter of Queen Victoria.

... evidently politic in us to accept it as favourable. But it was really a paltry performance. 'Let me be Commander in Chief for the rest of my life and I will do anything you please: only don't ask me to express any decided opinion for fear I should offend some one'. It would be a happy result of the whole business if we were to get rid of him. We are resolved if the Lords pass the Resolution to abolish purchase by Royal warrant leaving it to the Lords to determine whether they will then persevere in opposition to the Bill which secures the over regulation prices to the officers. I expect their Lordships will be somewhat astonished at the result of their proceedings. The resolution does not destroy the Bill. If we cannot get the Lords' assent to this Bill, we shall probably bring in another dealing only with over regulation prices, & ask a vote for regulation money.

17 July 1871. Monday. The H. of Lords passed D. of Richmond's amendt. to the Army Bill by 155 to 130 – (40 Lords also paired).[741] Northbrook made an excellent speech in moving the bill: Argyll a slashing speech on the last night. Derby's speech very clear & able but out-heroding Herod in its democratic spirit, & abject humility to the constituencies.

[Six pages here excised.][742]

31 July 1871. Monday. The vote of censure carried against us in the H. of Lords by majority of 80.[743] A foolish move. Such a vote utterly disregarded by the Govt., serves no purpose but to proclaim to the world the impotence of the House. Cairns made a very able speech, as did Argyll. It has been assumed out of doors that the Royal Warrant was specially due to Gladstone, the imperious Minister! The fact is that it was much more the work of Cardwell. After all the discussions on it, I feel quite certain that it was the least bad course. The folly & faction of the opposition brought the matter into a position from which there was no escape without some violence to the H. of Lords. Cairns, it is generally believed was entirely opposed to the rejection of the Army Bill, but unluckily the D. of Richmond was once in the army, & the prejudices of the Guards Club clung to him, & made him combine with Salisbury on this occasion.

---

[741] Charles Henry Gordon-Lennox, 6th Duke of Richmond (1818–1903), Cons. leader in Lords, 1870–76; mediator in franchise bill crisis, 1884; his motion called for a Royal Commission to review proposed army reforms, 3 *Hansard* 207 (17 July 1871), 1792–1870.

[742] There are no entries in *JE* between 17 July and 31 July.

[743] Motion expressing the view of the Lords, as proposed by the Duke of Richmond, that the government's handling of the Army Regulation bill was damaging to the independent action of the legislature. 3 *Hansard* 208 (31 July 1871), 459–539. Lord Russell voted against the government.

What a vast amount of nonsense has been talked about the British officer. The officers of the Artillery & Engineers I have always found well-informed men, taking real interest in their profession. The officers of the purchase corps (with many exceptions of course) have always seemed to me as a rule the most ignorant idle prejudiced set of men in this country. The fact is there has been no real professional spirit amongst them. They know nothing of science and despise it accordingly; and educated scientific men despise them accordingly, & avoid the profession. I anticipate the greatest good from the abolition of the purchase abuse. That it has died hard, can be no surprise.[744]

5 August 1871. Saturday. After all we shall get the Ballot[745] through the H. of C. next week. Gladstone is violent against the H. of Lords, because it is supposed they will reject the Bill. It is no doubt excessively foolish, but the lateness of the Session is a decent excuse. Salisbury appears to be deliberately working...

[The following four-and-a-half pages excised.][746]

... completely incapacitated him for his duties as *[One word heavily struck through.]*

10 August 1871. Thursday. The Ballot very quietly extinguished in the H. of Commons. Even...

[Verso of previous half-page excision.]

... Poor Mansel died very suddenly last week. He was a very able thinker, hard, logical, & unbending in argument. In private life a kind amicable man. Outwardly his appearance & manner was rather mean and vulgar. He did not therefore take in the fastidious London society which cares only for superficial literary graces, nothing for mere intellect & thought. Mansel's clerical profession cramped his mind. He was naturally a thorough skeptic & was perpetually seeking by ingenious reasoning to reconcile skeptical premises with orthodox conclusions, in which of course he necessarily failed. His Toryism as in many other men, arose really from his profound scepticism. He could not believe in progress.[747]

15 August 1871. Tuesday. Went to Kimberley.

[744] In the *JE*, Kimberley reflects that no measure had cost so much effort, or been so worthy, 'not even the disestablishment of the Irish Church'.
[745] The Ballot bill replaced open voting in parliamentary and municipal elections with voting by secret ballot.
[746] Fuller entry in *JE*.
[747] On Kimberley's previous relations with Mansel, see p. 44 above.

10 September 1871. Sunday. Poor Army after 24 days cessation of his fits had them 14 successive nights. Now he has had two nights of quiet, but we live in miserable anxiety.[748]

20 October 1871. Friday. Went to London all of us.

21 October 1871. Saturday. A desultory Cabinet. The

[Ten lines here excised.]

31 October 1871. Tuesday. Brisk discussion in the *[Partial line excised.]* French Treaty.[749] Gladstone, Granville, Lowe, & myself for letting it go. Fortescue strongly *[One line excised.]* ... to & fresh ... bargain on worse terms for five years. Bright...

[The following two-and-a-half pages excised.][750]

31 November 1871. Saturday. Returned to Kimberley.

11 December 1871. Monday. To London for Cabinets. Stayed with my Mother till...

[Some dozen lines here excised.]

... in the army. Goschen had some difficulty with Gladstone who pressed for larger reductions, but *[ill.]* gave way before...

[The following four-and-a-half pages excised.]

1 January 1872. The past year has been the most unhappy in my life. My poor Army's dreadful illness, & Johnny's wretched extravagance & folly have been enough misery to wear out my wife & me. Flo. holds out bravely but she leads a melancholy life. I strive to forget my sorrow in business: but the burden is heavy, & at times I faint under it. May the good God in his compassion grant us a happier future.

18 January 1872. Went to London.

27 January 1872.

---

[748] For a fuller account, see Kimberley to Monk Bretton, 4 Sept. 1871, MBP.

[749] To determine the parameters of commercial relations between Britain and France upon the expiry of the 1860 Cobden–Chevalier Treaty.

[750] There are no entries in *JE* between 15 Aug. 1871 and 18 Jan. 1872.

[Half-page dealing with Cabinet disposition on Washington Treaty heavily struck through. The following two pages excised.]

12 February 1872. Monday. Attended on Saturday the dinner to Mr. Verdon.[751] The Alabama case the great topic of discussion. Ripon & Forster were for allowing the U. S. case to go to the arbitrators, we making a protest against the indirect claims and declaring that we would not pay them if awarded against us. Granville also inclined to this course: but the rest of us were strongly against this course: & we prevailed. Granville's illness unlucky. It was no doubt the cause of no steps being sooner taken to protest against the U. S. case. The sad news received to day of Ld. Mayo's assassination.[752]

Went to the H. of C. to look at Brand sitting as Speaker. He looked very small in the Chair. Gladstone talks wildly about the Collier business,[753] says if we are accused by the H. of C. he would consider himself bound not only to resign office but his seat!

19 February 1872. Monday. Splendid majority of 27! for Govt. on the Collier business so we have escaped but narrowly. The majority in the Lords was a surprise to us & our opponents. They expected to beat us by 30 votes. The fact is we had a bad case. There was no job intended, nor any bad intention, but it was straining the Act, and a blunder.[754]

22 February 1872. Northbrook has accepted India. He is the best man available. Dufferin, 'the next choice' has not *backbone enough for such a post. The office would have been offered to me if my colleagues had not known that I could not for domestic if for no other, reasons accepted it.[755] It is a high compliment that they should have thought me the best man for such a great employment. It is a dazzling prize, but I prefer my position at home. A Cabinet Minister has really a higher employment than the Viceroy, & tho' it looks such a fine thing to govern 130 millions of Indians, it is a much finer thing to govern 32 millions of Englishmen with the general control of the whole of our vast Empire India included.

[751] Royal Agent to Fiji.

[752] Reflecting five years later in the *JE*, Kimberley adds 'a few words as to his character'. He was a man of 'sound sense and independent character' but in no way 'a man of first rate powers' as the press was suggesting.

[753] Surrounding the temporary appointment of Sir Robert Collier, then atty.-genl. to a superior court position merely for the purpose of qualifying him for a salaried position on the judicial committee of the Privy Council.

[754] See expansion in *JE*, where Kimberley acknowledged Collier's fitness.

[755] See *Gladstone–Granville Corresp. 1*, II, 307–8.

[Later, undated annotation:] *We were quite wrong in thinking this. K.[756]

27 February 1872. Wednesday. Thanksgiving for P. of Wales went to St Paul's. The whole affair a great success. The new Speaker (Brand) strutted up the nave with an air of dignity really wonderful in the little man.

Why are Gladstone & Lowe impervious to reason about the Thames embankment?[757] The opposition threaten a serious attack. If we behave like rational men we may easily parry it, but it will not [be] the fault of G. & L. if we do not get into a serious difficulty. It is all very well to set forth the legal theory of the Crown lands, that they are the private property of the Sovereign, bound for the life of the Sovereign to the nation. The nation will never understand this fine drawn theory. In the eyes of the people it is national property, & practically they are right. Whether a slice worth £100,000 of this property should be given to the metropolis is another question in doubt.

2 March 1872. Saturday. Granville[758] told me that when he saw the Queen yesterday he congratulated H.M. on the courage she displayed on the occasion of O'Connor's attack on her.[759] 'Oh,' she said 'to tell the truth I was horribly frightened'. But she really seems to have behaved admirably, & who would not have been frightened at having a pistol presented at one's head?

Gladstone, Lowe, & Cardwell make no secret of their colonial policy, namely to get rid of the colonies as soon as possible; and Cardwell thinks the Australian demands as to tariffs[760] a good occasion for bringing matters to a point! I am quite persuaded that the Australian colonies & Canada will become independent States: but to drive them into independence seems to me the utmost folly. Let it come of itself if it must, but I for one will be no party to any step which shall make them separate in anger. At present they have no wish to separate, & tho' the Australian colonies pursue a policy which is going straight in that direction, they would indignantly resent our casting them off. The telegraph will bring them somewhat closer for a time.

20 April 1872. The Australian matter I settled at last,[761] & yesterday

---

[756] This annotation not included in *JE*.

[757] Government proposed that the Metropolitan Board of Works appropriate land reclaimed from the Thames. See *Gladstone Diaries*, VIII, 100.

[758] Granville's name omitted in *JE*.

[759] On 29 Feb. 1872, O'Connor, a Fenian, pointed an unloaded pistol at the Queen in her carriage, demanding the release of Fenian prisoners.

[760] The power to levy intercolonial tariffs.

[761] On Kimberley's negotiations with Gladstone, see *Liberal by Principle*, 37. W. D. McIntyre, *The Imperial Frontier in the Tropics, 1867–75* (London, 1967), 211, 246–59.

the despatch went. The Canadian question is also clearing itself, so that I am in smoother water so far as colonial politics are concerned. But I have a far worse difficulty thrown on my hands in the Licensing Bill.[762] On Saturday last it was suddenly proposed by Bruce to the Cabinet that I should bring in the Bill. On Tuesday a Committee of the Cabinet met Cardwell, Lowe, Goschen, Hartington, self. We found that Bruce had actually not read his bill through! We decided on some serious alterations. On Tuesday Ap. 16 I brought in this well digested measure. On Wednesday I spent the whole day with Thring endeavouring [to] reduce the bill into shape. I never could have imagined that any one could have put together such a heterogeneous mass of...

[The following four pages excised.]

... note, assenting to one presenting the case, without prejudice, they gave every very sulkily after much discussion & we agreed to present the case, & to the form of protest which was to accompany it.[763]

16 May 1872.   Thursday. Went to Kimberley and stayed till May 30. Beautiful weather.

1 June 1872.   Saturday. We seem to have arrived at the final crisis of the Alabama affair. On Tuesday last we were summoned to a Cabinet and on Thursday night we had a Cabinet at Gladstone's 'room' in the H. of Commons (a closet a few foot square) which lasted from 10 till nearly 1 o'clock. Roundell Palmer,[764] and the Law Officers were present.

Palmer drew up a new article which we proposed by telegraph instead of the article amended by the U. S. Senate. The alteration made by the Senate made that latter article clearly inadmissible.

To day a most unsatisfactory answer from Fish. Another amended article proposed by us. Our last amendment I think a very fair & reasonable proposal. Here I must [mention] a most extraordinary blunder in this matter. When the original 'supplemental Treaty' was drawn up, Granville who besides being very deaf has a slipshod way of doing business, which I for my part cannot admire, left it to Argyll to take down in writing the words agreed to by the Cabinet. It seems

---

[762] A modified version of Bruce's 1871 bill which only regulated the granting of new licenses and restricted the opening hours of public houses.

[763] Cf. the extended account in *JE*, where in 1877 Kimberley reflects on the 'imprudence of Bruce's management of the question', but suggests that it had 'worked well'. Kimberley presented the Licensing bill to the Lords on 16 April 1872. 3 *Hansard* 210 (16 April 1872), 1311–27.

[764] Roundell Palmer (1812–95), entered Parliament as a Cons. gradually moving into the Lib. camp; MP for Richmond, 1861–72, when cr. 1st Baron Selborne; ld. chanc., 1872–4, 1880–5.

(I had this from Granville himself) that after the Cabinet was over Granville being not quite sure of the exact words himself, requested Argyll to communicate with Tenterden, the Under Secretary, & see that the version to be telegraphed to the U. States was correct. Unfortunately Argyll by mistake substituted at the end of the article the words 'the President shall not make any claims, &c. for the words agreed to by the Cabinet which were that the indirect claims 'should not be entertained by or before the Tribunal at Geneva'! Of course the latter words were open to some of the objections on the score of ambiguity made against the article as actually transmitted. What a mode of doing business! Imagine the Foreign Secretary not himself taking down words so vitally important, or if he trusted any one else to write them down, not himself remembering the words, and imagine also the F. Secretary understanding the affair so badly or treating it so negligently that he could not prevent so flagrant a blunder in his own office. Yet Granville is a very able man in many ways, and shrewd & ready when he fairly gives his mind to the business before him. But he is essentially a hand to mouth man who trusts to the chapter of accidents, and never reasons out any matter completely or goes into it enough to master its details. His want of knowledge of the details of the affairs he has to manage & is the cause of his comparative weakness as a departmental Minister, by comparative I mean, as compared with his admirable sagacity and tact as leader of the H. of Lords.

9 June 1872. Sunday. Last week was eventful and exciting. Our fruitless negotiations with Washington have been unceasing. On Tuesday Ld. Russell made his long threatened motion.[765] Granville spoke with remarkable force & vigour. Derby and Cairns came forward as the advocates of the U. S. Govt. The latter who is always the advocate, & cannot in a speech forget for a moment that he holds a Tory brief, did not surprise me, the former did. I thought he would have been able in a crisis of this kind to prefer his country to party. As the debate went on it became obvious that the motion would be pushed to a division & carried against us by a large majority; and Ld. Granville wisely determined on proposing adjournment wh. after a noisy scene was agreed to.

20 June 1872. Thursday. Cabinets & debates have been so incessant that I have never had a moment to write in this Diary. We seemed last

---

[765] Calling for postponement of the Geneva tribunal until the U.S. withdrew its call for 'indirect claims' for compensation. 3 *Hansard* 211 (4 June 1872), 1095.

week on the verge of a break up of the Government.[766] After we had agreed to decline to put in our summary of arguments at Geneva & to make an application for an adjournment, Gladstone insisted on the door being left open for further concession, & for putting in the summary under protest, if the arbitrators declined they could not adjourn if our summary was not put in. On this a most decided division of opinion manifested itself in the Cabinet. Granville evidently would have given way in the last resort sooner than break up. I was one of those who opposed Gladstone. The feeling of the Cabinet was decidedly against him but he was obstinate, & it seemed as if we must come to a rupture when Granville suggested that we might instruct Tenterden to telegraph for further instructions if 'anything unforeseen occurred'. Gladstone wanted to give contingent instructions to put in the summary. However we all agreed to Granville's suggestion, our side very readily because it was pretty nigh certain there would not be time to give fresh instructions, & we were perfectly satisfied that the matter should be in the hands of R. Palmer who had expressed the strongest opinion against putting in the summary (the Law officers both concurring). The question has now happily taken another turn & the danger is past for the moment: but I am more than ever convinced that Gladstone cannot safely guide the foreign relations of this country.

With great difficulty the majority of the Cabinet have hitherto controlled him, but our course and above all our tone in foreign questions has been very unsatisfactory. As long as Clarendon lived, his authority kept things straight. Granville is far too nonchalant & yielding and were it not that neither he nor Gladstone can carry the Cabinet as far as they wish, they would long ago have utterly disgusted the country. As it is there is a deep feeling of distrust of the government as regards foreign affairs: & even when we are right, we manage to leave an impression of vacillation & truckling. We shall I believe after all creep through this wretched 'Alabama' business.

As to ballot and such minor matters, are not our debates written in the pages of the newspapers? There is nothing worth recording here about them.

Thank God. dear Army suddenly became well yesterday. Dare we hope that his recovery will be permanent. It is like a miracle.

25 June 1872. Tuesday. Henry married to day to Miss Mary King[767] at St Philip's Church Kensington.

[766] Over the terms of the Geneva tribunal established to settle U.S. claims for compensation from Britain for supplying the warship *Alabama* to the Confederacy during the American Civil War. See *Gladstone Diaries*, VIII, 145–68.

[767] Mary Livingston King, of Sandhills, Georgia. In writing prior to the marriage, her father thanked Kimberley for the 'ready' confidence with which you welcome an alliance

Much to my astonishment Gladstone to day offered me the G. C. B. I declined it, having no love for decorations, nor any wish to be classed with Malmesbury, Pakington, & R. Peel.[768] I have always thought it a mistake to give the 'Bath' for party services. What one party regards as merit, is demerit in the eyes of the other.[769]

27 June 1872. Thursday. Announcement in Parlt. that we have got rid of the indirect claims. 'All's well that end's well'!

6 July 1872. Saturday. Discussed *[Partial line excised.]* what should be done if the Lords insist on their optional ballot amendment.[770] Resignation we rejected at once: but we were all for dissolution, either immediately, or at the beginning of next year after an autumn session in November supposing the Bill should be then again rejected. The opinion of the experts was that we should lose 25 or 30 seats but should have a majority of about 25 if we dissolved immediately. If we had an autumn session we should have a very fair chance of carrying the bill, and if not a much more favourable dissolution. We were generally for the Autumn session plan, but of course the final decision was adjourned till after Monday. It was agreed that if as we feared the majority against us in the optional ballot was larger, we could not take the Bill again to the H. of C. but must throw it up at once. We determined in that case however to adjourn the House after the vote to take time for Consideration.

8 July 1872. Monday. All our expectations as to the Ballot Bill happily falsified by a majority of 19 in our favour.[771] To the last moment we were not sure of the result as we cd. not tell how many Tories would vote with us or stay away. It is a heavy blow to that part of the Opposition, which wanted to appeal to the country & hoped to destroy

between our families, and promised £400–500 per annum and an inheritance of not less than £10,000. 'You are aware,' King added, 'that our disastrous Civil War left us only the wreck of fortunes once possessed.' KP6 MS. eng. C. 4470, f. 57. Cf. Henry Wodehouse's letter to his mother saying 'I am very much in love with a young lady. She has not much money and no particular connection in the way of family.' 24 April 1872, KP/15/K2/20.

[768] Malmesbury omitted from this list in *JE*.

[769] Cf. in *JE*, Kimberley's long digression on his disdain for 'orders'.

[770] Amendment introduced by the Duke of Richmond on 17 June 1872 to allow the voter, if he wished, to mark his ballot paper before the officials in the polling station. On 28 June the Commons rejected the optional ballot amendment. Gladstone learned on 3 July that Richmond intended to persevere with his amendment in the Lords.

[771] Richmond's optional ballot amendment was rejected by the Lords by 157 to 138 votes. See B. Kinzer, *The Ballot Question in Nineteenth-Century English Politics* (New York, 1982), 239–43.

the Govt., but I suspect Disraeli never approved the optional Ballot, nor wished any serious attack to be made on the Govt. What a coward Derby is! He never has said a word altho' he voted with his party throughout these discussions.[772]

10 July 1872. Wednesday. Last night at Lord Dudley's Ball Mr. Packe[773] to our great joy proposed to Alice, & to day she gave him her answer, yes. It is a very happy event.

10 August 1872. Saturday. Parliament prorogued. I was very near having to read the Queen's speech. The Chancellor, poor man, is too blind, and he asked me to read it which I had promised to do, when I espied Granville who was not expected as we were five without him, & handed over the speech to him. There has really been nothing worth recording this last month.

14 August 1872. Wednesday. Alice married to Hussey Packe at St George's Hanover Sq. A marriage which gives us all the greatest pleasure.

17 August 1872. Saturday. Went to Kimberley. I was very much knocked up by heat and over-work and so ill that I was only just able to attend the wedding. Country air & rest soon set me right.

10 October 1872. Went to London for several Cabinets principally about the French Treaty. I never saw a worse drawn draft. The F. O. had apparently forgotten that we have colonies. Two days discussion convinced us that we could not stipulate for imports into our colonies. So we determined to leave them out. Granville in the middle of this went off to Walmer & coolly requested a Committee of the Cabinet to make the necessary alterations in his absence! So Childers, Halifax & I with Mr. Herbert[774] of the Col: Off: & Mr. Kennedy[775] of the F. O. met in Granville's rooms in the F. O. & drew up the most favoured nation clause which has been adopted. We did not deal with the other clauses. Mr. K. seems to me very helpless, & the whole affair a discreditable muddle. We did little else at the Cabinet beyond vague

---

[772] For Derby's disquiet at having to act with Richmond, Cairns and Salisbury, see *DD2*, 111.

[773] Hussey Packe, of Prestwold Hall, Loughborough. See Packe's diary, 1872, PkP DE1749. On Kimberley's approbation, see Lady Kimberley to Alice Wodehouse, 5 Sept. 1872, PkP DE1749 38/3.

[774] Robert George Herbert (1831–1905), perm. u.-sec. col., 1871–92. Childers had re-entered the cabinet as Chanc. of the Duchy of Lancaster in Aug. 1872.

[775] Charles Malcolm Kennedy, head of commercial dept., for. office, 1872–94.

talk about local taxation, Irish education, & the necessity of finding something for the P. of Wales to do. On the last subject our deliberations I need hardly say came to nothing.[776]

14 October 1872.   Went back to K. after the Cabinet.[777]

14 November 1872.   Thursday. Went to London.

15 November 1872.   Friday, Cabinet, Talked over our last F.O. muddle, the want of any definition of the Haro Channel.[778] In the evening presided at dinner at Cannon Street Hotel celebrating success of Australian Telegraph. The company were mightily enthusiastic about the integrity of the Empire. I wonder how may of them ever reflected for two minutes on the real difficulties of keeping self governing communities such as Canada &c. permanently connected with England. Of course it does not follow that these difficulties may not be overcome, but the difference between the hard talk about firm ties &c. and the action of the colonial government especially the Australian where home & colonial interests in any way seem to clash is notable.

3 December 1872.   Tuesday. The Cabinet's last month were almost exclusively upon Irish Univ: Questions.[779] We have no serious differences of opinion but Gladstone who does not want to leave town till the 14th. seems to delight in going on just at the pace which will enable him to spread the Cabinets over the times he will be in London. Pleasant for his colleagues who like myself am dying to get away. I am heartily sick of it.

On Thursday[780] I brought the question as to the Canada fortifications Guarantee before the Cabinet who agreed in my view.

9 December 1872.   Monday. Returned to Kimberley. Two cabinets were held after I went away but nothing important took place at them. Gladstone won't really face the local taxation question. He proposes to bring it on after Easter, and to somehow or other shove it off, I suspect,

---

[776] See *Gladstone Diaries*, VIII, 220–1.

[777] See correspondence between Gladstone and Kimberley in *Gladstone Diaries*, VIII, 223.

[778] One of the three straits traversed by the U.S.–Canadian boundary on the western coast around Vancouver Island. Notice of 'F.O. muddle' omitted from *JE*, and from Gladstone's minutes. *Gladstone Diaries*, VIII, 236–7.

[779] After much discussion the government proposed the establishment of a non-denominational Irish University, to which protestant colleges would be affiliated as well as those catholic institutions which wished to join.

[780] 28 Nov. See *Gladstone Diaries*, VIII, 243.

altogether.[781] But the H. of Commons will hardly let him do that. Our Cabinets have been throughout quiet, & no serious difference of opinion has arisen as to the measures for next Session.[782]

1 January 1873. I have much indeed to be thankful for during the past year. Armine's recovery more than balances the misfortunes of the year, chief of which is Johnny's infatuated folly & extravagance. I have begun to feel wear & tear of work. Work alone would not have wearied me, but work with agonizing anxiety at home has made its mark. As to politics all at home looks smooth, but I doubt whether we shall weather the Irish Univ: Question. It was the rock ahead on which we always thought we might make shipwreck, and steer as we will the danger is great, as it is simply impossible to reconcile the pretensions of our Nonconformists & R. Catholic supporters.

9 January 1873. The Emperor Louis Napoleon died at Chistlehurst.[783]

21 January 1873. Went to London.

6 February 1873. Meeting of Parliament. Our measures are all ready except local taxation on which the Cabinet seems quite unable to make up its mind. The Irish Univy. Bill I think promises well. As to the French Treaty the bungling of the F.O. has been only successful by the marvellous insouciance of Lrd G. who treats such matters as easily as if he had no concern with them. The Central Asian arrangement however is a success.[784]

1 March 1873. Saturday. Notwithstanding the delusive calm after Gladstone's speech introducing the Irish Univ: Bill the storm is about to burst over us. At the Cabinet to day no one seemed surprised at this and we were unanimously[785] of opinion that we must fight it out.

3 March 1873. Monday. To a Council at Windsor, where Flo. & I stayed the night. Heard the sad news of the accident at Cannes to Ripon's son. The Queen seemed very cheery. She amused me by her keen perception of Gladstone's character who she said was alternately

---

[781] In the event, legislation was not introduced, but a select committee on local taxation was established. See *Gladstone Diaries*, VIII, 255.

[782] A modified version of this entry included with previous entry of 3 Dec. in *JE*.

[783] Much reminiscence in *JE* on his 'hateful' regime. 'When the secret history of these times is known,' Kimberley wrote, 'it will be found I think that Morny pulled strings in all the most critical moments of Louis Napoleon's strange career.'

[784] Agreement of January 1873 that Afghanistan would be a neutral zone between British and Russian territories, with the Oxus River as the nothern territory.

[785] 'Unanimous' not used in *JE*. See *Gladstone Diaries*, VIII, 293–4.

sanguine & depressed, (alluding to the Irish Univ: Bill). The new Belgian Minister Mr. de Solvyns was at the castle – a rather priggish, self sufficient man, but with some cleverness in small talk such as diplomatists delight in.

8 March 1873. Saturday. The Parliamentary storm has raged fiercely all this week, and our prospects look very gloomy.[786] The combination against us is singular. Fawcett & the free thinkers with the Ultramontanes & the Tories. The Irish R. Catholic members, poor creatures, are ordered to vote against the Bill by their masters the Bishops. It is said 25 will go against us & some 20 stay away. Perhaps we may have 12 or 16 Irish votes for the 2nd reading.[787] The Tories are behaving quite fairly. It is evident they don't want to turn us out but we can't complain of them for taking advantage of the fair opportunity presented by the dissension on our side. At this Cabinet the prevailing feeling seemed to be in favour of dissolution if we were beaten.

12 March 1873. Wednesday. The Govt. beaten this morning by a majority of 3.[788] The Cabinet to day were evidently no longer able to screw their courage up to dissolution. Two or three only including myself were still for it. However it was determined to leave the question for division to morrow. Practically however I look upon resignation as certain.

13 March 1873. Thursday. It turned out as I expected. Resignation was determined upon after very little discussion. So ends the Gladstone ministry. We have been a wonderfully harmonious Cabinet, and after four years of office & power few of us will be sorry for rest. Gladstone seems utterly weary of office. The question ever is, will Disraeli form a Govt.? I think he will and that he will dissolve immediately. I see no advantage to the country or the Liberal party in our having placed the dissolution in his hands. I would have appealed boldly to the country on the ground of the general claims of Gladstone's administration to confidence.[789]

I believe we should have had a strong & compact party in England and Scotland, & that we should have been no worse off, than we shall in any case be, in Ireland. Now we have played into Disraeli's hands, & we shall have all the old discreditable manoeuvres over again. If we

[786] Over University bill.

[787] Prognostications omitted from *JE*.

[788] Commons division of 284 to 287 on Irish University bill. See *Gladstone Diaries*, VIII, 298–9.

[789] Along with Lowe and Goschen. See Kimberley to Ripon, 13 March 1873, in *Liberal by Principle*, 133–4.

had dissolved, we should have put fairly to the test whether the country wishes us to remain at the head of affairs. As it is we have not only lost the confidence of the H. of Commons, but we have shown that we have lost confidence in ourselves![790]

18 March 1873. Tuesday. A meeting of Cabinet at Gladstone's House. We all looked very gloomy, but it was settled that there was no alternative but to resume office.[791] Gladstone's mode of spinning out the time between the vote of the House against us & our 'resumption' was ingenious. What Disraeli wanted was of course that Gladstone should have 'resigned' on Thursday and resumed on Friday when he would have stigmatized the resignation as a sham. This trick has been defeated, but the position in which we are left is very unenviable. Our old programme is completely exhausted, we can hardly hope to escape discredit. Our best chance is to tide over this session, & have no dissolution till the autumn of 1874.

A dissolution now would be very different from a dissolution instead of resignation. The worst of it is that Gladstone is not the kind of man to play the part of a leader in difficulties. He wants a strong tide of opinion in his favour.

20 March 1873. Thursday. Heard the explanations in the H. of Commons. G's statement was dignified and measured. D's ingenious, but like all his manifestos hollow & unreal. What do all the fine phrases about the future come to? Nothing. He has really no policy.

22 March 1873. Saturday. Cabinet.[792] I thought on Tuesday we looked like men who had been buried & dug up again. To day we seemed more alive. I suppose the air of Downing St. is vivifying! Our greatest difficulty is the 25th Clause of the Education Act.*[793]

[Added at a later time, but undated:] *The notion of a big bill is given up, & I hope we may avoid a split with the dissenters.

5 April 1873. Cabinet. A good budget I think. G's first idea was to pay the whole Alabama sum out of this year's revenue. This was broached

[790] In *JE*, 18 March 1873, the reasoning of 13 March is combined with the activities of 18 March and 20 March.

[791] See *Gladstone Diaries*, VIII, 305. Disraeli declined to form a government.

[792] See *Gladstone Diaries*, VIII, 307.

[793] Clause 25 of the 1870 Education Act allowed the boards of denominational schools to pay the fees for parents unable to afford them. Non-conformists objected strongly to the possibility of sectarian boards thus subsidising Anglican schools. Not mentioned in *JE*.

at our dismal assembly after our defeat. Several members of Cabinet protested against this excess of financial virtue. G. was very stiff at first but has gradually come round.[794] The advice of the 'Times' wh. now writes entirely in the Tory interest is amusing. We hear that the writer of the article this morning says that it is clear we are in a hopeless 'fix'. If we take their advice we are ruined without doubt as the country will be indignant that no remission of taxation is given: if we do not, we shall be accused of a popularity hunting budget &c. &c. A pleasant adviser! but I expect they will find themselves sadly disappointed.

We have got over the difficulty about Fawcett's Bill[795] but local taxation looks nasty & we may yet be driven to dissolution which is the object of the Tories.

10 April 1873.   Thursday. Went to Ky.

17 April 1873.   Thursday. To Ipswich, where I made a speech at a Liberal banquet. Stayed the night with Mr Ransome[796] the great machine manufacturer, a very intelligent and pleasant man and a great Liberal light in those parts.

14 April 1873.   Monday. Returned to London. The weather pleasant tho' cold in the country. Now it is most unpleasant and bitterly cold.

26 April 1873.   Saturday. The Zanzibar question looks nasty.[797] Granville sees the necessity of showing fight. Cabinet to day held at Gladstone's house.[798] He has a chill which has touched his liver. We are all getting shaky not only politically but physically.

29 April 1873.   Tuesday. I don't think the Tories will take much by W. Smith's move against the Budget.[799] If we win, it helps us as to local taxation. If we lose, we can go to the country on a popular budget.

[794] The remainder of this entry omitted from *JE*.

[795] Proposal to abolish religious tests in Trinity College and the University of Dublin. Fawcett introduced a third version of the bill on 3 April. The bill received the Royal Assent on 26 May 1873.

[796] James Allen Ransome (1806–75), agricultural implement maker.

[797] Regarding renegotiation of contracts for carrying Cape Mails. Cf. *JE*, 39.

[798] See *Gladstone Diaries*, VIII, 320.

[799] W.H. Smith (1825–91), Cons. MP for Westminister, 1868–85, for the Strand, 1885–91; fin. sec. to treasury, 1874–7; 1st ld. adm., 1877–80; war sec., 1885–6; 1st ld. treas., 1887–91. Smith moved that the govt. inform the nation of its views on direct taxation before reducing indirect taxation

Meeting of Committee of Cabinet at F.O. on Zanzibar question.[800]

20 May 1873. Sunday. Smith's motion as I expected utterly broke down. Gladstone's smashing speech on Emanuel Hospital[801] saved us from defeat on that Question. He made another admirable speech on Miall's motion.[802] Indeed he seems to pour forth his wonderful speeches on every subject with ever increasing vigour.

Our position in Parliament is decidedly improved, with the exception of the O'Keeffe bother[803] I see no ugly rock immediately a-head, but the Bath & Gloucester elections are unpleasant warnings of the weakening of our hold on the country.[804]

In the Cabinet nothing notable lately. The chief business of importance Zanzibar. At the colonial office the Ashantee war[805] is troublesome and the Australian mail question not very 'easy of solution', but I think we (i.e. Lowe, Childers & myself) have hit upon a good plan at last.[806]

23 May 1873. Friday. Alice safely delivered of a daughter a little before 4 o'clock this morning at 4 Seymour Street Portman Sqr.

24 May 1873. Saturday. Ministerial question of importation of arms to Assinee in Cabinet.[807] Got authority to bring in a Bill. On Friday the Australian Colonies duties Bill passed.[808] We had two discussions on 2nd reading & Committee on which Ld. Grey showed himself as impracticable & rash as usual but no one was foolish enough to agree with him.

His theory of course was undeniable that free trade is an excellent

---

[800] To discuss the question of further instructions to Sir Bartle Frere, who in the previous year had been appointed special commissioner to the Sultan of Zanzibar to secure a treaty abolishing the slave trade by sea. Not mentioned in *JE*.

[801] R.W. Crawford (1813–89), Lib. MP for the City of London, 1857–74, had moved the rejection of plan by Endowed Schools Commissioners for future management of Emanuel Hospital.

[802] For the disestablishment of the Churches of England and Scotland.

[803] Liberal objection to ultramontane interference in temporal affairs was aroused when Father O'Keeffe was suspended by Catholic hierarchy as manager of the Callan National Schools in Ireland.

[804] Both May by-elections reversals for the Liberals.

[805] See n. 819, below. For a full treatment of British policy, see W.D. McIntyre, 'British Policy in West Africa: The Ashanti Expedition of 1873–74', *Historical Journal* 5 (1962), 19–46.

[806] See cabinets of 14 and 17 May in *Gladstone Diaries*, VIII, 328, 330.

[807] French port bordering the British Gold Coast. See *Gladstone Diaries*, VIII, 332–3.

[808] Enabling Australasian colonies to establish preferential tariffs. See Kimberley's extended analysis of free trade and imperial integrity in *JE*. Also, Kimberley to Musgrave, 19 July 1875, in *Liberal by Principle*, 140.

thing: but no one can prove that to attempt to force it on the colonies would be either politic or practicable.[809]

2 June 1873. Monday. Went with Hussey Packe to Cornwall.

4 June 1873. Wednesday. To Helston where we stayed the night & in the morning saw the grand scenery at the Lizard.

6 June 1873. Friday. Returned to London.

7 June 1873. Saturday. Cabinet.[810] Settled Fiji inquiry and that no bill could be brought in giving power to issue limited proclamation against exportation of arms &c. This point arose in connection with the imports of arms by British subjects to Assine for Ashantee.[811]

25 June 1873. Wednesday. The town Shah-mad[812] ...

[Eight lines here excised.]

... 'dazed' after his voyage down the river.

28 June 1873. Saturday. Questions as to recall of marines from Gold Coast, and Newfoundland fisheries...[813]

[Some nine lines here excised, verso of previous excision.]

... Ayrton was present and made a dogged resistance.[814] There is something thoroughly 'mulish' about him. The worst of it is the Treasury is in such a state of disorganization that Ayrton (who is as usual utterly in the wrong) is more than a match for them. Were it not for the discredit which it brings on the whole government there would be a grim pleasure in observing the blunder, and disgrace of that insolvent office. Formerly their work was efficiently if unpleasantly done. Now they seem to be both ignorant and negligent: and their insolence to every one who has to do with them is no longer irritating but simply ludicrous.

The Zanzibar contract was a pitiable string of blunders, all caused by the neglect to ask the Colonial Office before the new contract for

---

[809] Additional material added to this entry in *JE*.

[810] See *Gladstone Diaries*, VIII, 336–7.

[811] This entry omitted from *JE*.

[812] Nasr-ed-Din (1831–96), r. 1848–96 as Shah of Persia. Additional material in *JE*.

[813] See *Gladstone Diaries*, VIII, 346.

[814] Acton Smee Ayrton (1816–86), Lib. MP for Tower Hamlets, 1857–74; parl. sec. to treas., 1868–9; 1st com. works, 1869–73; judge-adv.-genl., 1873–4. Cf. *JE* and note.

the Cape mail was made. The anger of the Cape colony at not having been consulted has stirred up all the opposition.

Yesterday whilst the debate on Ld. Stanhope's foolish motion yesterday for a new literary 'order' was going on the D. of Somerset[815] told me that he once asked Lord Melbourne to give some assistance to Carlyle[816] who was then in very poor circumstance. Who is he? said Lord M. A very original writer was the answer. 'D—mn your original writers,' replied Lord Melbourne. 'I hate them'.

6 July 1873.   Sunday. Went tonight to Minley.

10 July 1873.   Thursday. Considering Cairns' objection to Judicature Bill on ground of privilege. We adopted a contrivance for getting out of the difficulty, suggested by Mr. May.[817] Gladstone not on his high horse as I anticipated he would be.[818]

13 July 1873.   Sunday. News of bombardment of Elmina.[819] An end to all peace & quiet for the unlucky Colonial Secretary!

14 July 1873.   Monday. Council of war at War Office. Oddly enough the military authorities seem quite unwilling to move. However at last on my motion it was decided to send 200 marines, and to have a wing of a regiment in England ready to embark if necessary.

24 July 1873.   Thursday. Judicature Bill in the H. of Lords. In spite of the greatest exertions on the D. of Richmond's part to keep back his supporters we were in doubt up to the last whether Redesdale's motion[820] to upset the bill would be carried. As he came out of our lobby, Richmond came up to the Treasury bench & said 'how will it go? I don't know how you feel, but I never was in such a funk in my life. We have been whipping off our men with all our might but it seems all no use'. It was of use however & we had a good majority.

On the amendment to restore £6,000 to the salary of the appeal judges, Cairns lost his temper & actually advised the House to do what

---

[815] Edward Adolphus Seymour 12th Duke of Somerset (1804–85), 1st ld. adm., 1859–66.

[816] Thomas Carlyle (1795–1881), Scottish man-of-letters and historian.

[817] Thomas Erskine May (1815–86), clerk of the House of Commons, 1871–86, K.C.B., 1866.

[818] This passage omitted from *JE*. See *Gladstone Diaries*, VIII, 354.

[819] *The Times* of 10 July 1873 reported the 29 May rout of the friendly Fante at the hands of the Ashanti, who had invaded the Gold Coast in Dec. 1872.

[820] To defer for three months the Commons amendments to allow time for further consideration.

would have been so completely in the teeth of the Commons' privileges that the bill must have been lost.[821] He then walked out of the house leaving Richmond to help us through against Salisbury &c. as best he could! Richmond as he went thro' our lobby kept exclaiming 'what pig headed fellows, was there ever anything like them.' Dizzy was in the House, looking as some one remarked to me like 'the man of fate' watching the suicide of the House. It is more than probable that he wished the bill to be lost.

25 July 1873. Friday. The rating Bill of which I moved the 2nd·reading thrown out with little ceremony.[822] The front opposition Bench tho' speaking against it showed not much animus. I suspect they did not really wish to destroy it but dared not refuse their followers 'blood' a second night. As to our supporters? They are no where.

26 July 1873. Saturday. The third Cabinet in succession to day. Gladstone ill in bed with diarrhoea.[823] We are in a sad scrape. The position of Lowe is become almost untenable. What with Zanzibar contract, Post Office scandal, clerks grievances &c. the Treasury is cut to pieces. The immediate pressing matter is Cross' motion.[824] Gladstone was determined to throw over Monsell,[825] but after a long struggle wiser counsels prevailed. Monsell is inexcusable really, but if we make him a scapegoat, we shall make our position worse, & expose the Treasury to a most damaging attack.

We had another sharp contest as to the answer to the Lords' address as to officers' grievances. Cardwell wished to refuse a Commission entirely, but he was persuaded at last to grant a Commission strictly limited in its terms.[826] The end of all this came at last in a reconstruction of the Cabinet. Ripon told me his real reasons for going out was that he saw that the majority of the Cabinet were for extending household suffrage to the counties, and as he could not consent to this he thought it better to go out now when by so doing he could facilitate the new arrangement than to cause a difficulty in the autumn.

Why Childers went is rather a mystery. Some time ago he told

---

[821] See 3 *Hansard* 47 (24 July 1873), 895.

[822] The Rating (Liability and Value) bill was rejected by 43 to 59 votes.

[823] Hence the imperfect report in *Gladstone Diaries*, VIII, 361.

[824] On 24 July R. A. Cross gave notice of his motion, introduced on 29 July, criticising the Post Office for misappropriation of funds. The motion was defeated by 111 to 169 votes.

[825] William Monsell (1812–94), Lib. MP for Limerick, 1847–74; u.-sec. colonies, 1868–70, post.-genl., 1871–3; cr. Baron Emly, 1874.

[826] The previous two sentences excluded from *JE*. The Commission to consider the purchase of any commissions. See 3 *Hansard* 217 (18 July 1873), 612–47.

Gladstone, that it was not worth his while to hold office at so small a salary as £2000 a year, and it is said that on its being hinted to him that he might take the Post Office he gave Gladstone to understand that he would not undertake so burdensome a business for such small pay, & that he would prefer whenever there was a convenient opportunity to retire. It is supposed that G. wanting a place for Bright took C. at his word. But all this is more or less conjecture. He evidently does not look to coming in again as he has asked me for a colonial appointment: and I have told him that if Gladstone carries out his intention to offer Dufferin Ireland *vice* Spenser who has resigned, & D. accepts, I will appoint him to Canada. Lowe at Home Office is an odd arrangement, but what better could be done?

[Two pages here excised, and the following half-page lightly crossed through: 'neglect is really unpardonable, & he cannot retain his office. The strangest thing is that he seems perfectly unconscious of the position he is in, & would have gone on quite contentedly!'][827]

Just before Parliament broke up at nearly the last Cabinet I obtained the consent of my colleagues to Glover's expedition.[828]

5 August 1873. Tuesday. Parliament prorogued. Truly we go into the country with our tails between our legs as Gladstone long ago said we should.[829] My poor Uncle Edward Gurdon[830] died at Hingham after a long & painful illness, an internal tumour. He was a most amiable excellent man, who discharged admirably every duty of life.

10 August 1873. Alas! We are in great tribulation. Our poor Army has typhoid fever, a victim with so many others of Dairy Reform milk.

20 August 1873. Misfortunes come indeed thick upon us. My dear brother Henry died this morning at 1 o'clock at Athens of typhoid fever.[831]

[827] The final sentence, which had been struck through, included in modified form in *JE*.

[828] Sir John Hawley Glover (1829–85), entered the Royal Navy at twelve; harbour-master of the newly formed colonial government at Lagos, 1857, thereafter pursuing an expansionistic policy in West Africa. Glover was commissioned to mount a flanking expedition against the Ashanti by way of the Volta River.

[829] In *JE* Kimberley adds: 'In fact we have never recovered from the Irish Education defeat. That was a mortal blow.'

[830] On Gurdon's goodness, see 'The Late Rev. E. Gurdon', *Norfolk Chronicle*, 9 Aug. 1873.

[831] On various reports and accounts of Henry Wodehouse's death, see KP1 15/K2/20.

21 August 1873.   Lady Isabella FitzGibbon[832] died. Her death was a happy release from wasting disease. She had been very long ill, & at last had fairly burnt out the candle of life. Her tenacity of life was surprising.

6 September 1873.   At last by the mercy of God Army is convalescent, & we are able to go to Kimberley. He had the fever very severely for 28 days. Our detention in London was so far more bearable that Flo. has been much occupied with winding up the affairs of her Aunt whose Executrix & residual legatee she is, and I have been as busy as possible with this unhappy Ashantee war. Such very unsatisfactory accounts reached us of the state of affairs, the Commodore Commerell and the administrator Col Harley quarrelling & the senior military officers Col Wise reported to be drunken, that Cardwell & I determined to cut the knot by sending out Sir Garnet Wolseley.[833] We first asked Sir Andrew Clarke[834] to go but he declined. We have a heavy responsibility, being obliged to act without the Cabinet. Every one of course was away in August when we had to decide.[835]

22 September 1873.   Monday. Went to London to have a conference with H. R. H.,[836] Cardwell, & Goschen. We decided to send a tramway to the coast, & that a hospital ship should be prepared. Gladstone is aghast at the expenditure & we must have a Cabinet soon.

26 September 1873.   Friday. Deposited my poor brother's remains in the vault at Kimberley. His widow, & her brother Mr. King came here to be present on the occasion.

3 October 1873.   Friday. To London to attend Cabinet.

4 October 1873.   Saturday. After a great deal of discussion to day and yesterday we agreed on a draft to Sir G. Wolseley, which seemed to satisfy those who hope to get out of the war by doing nothing but

[832] Lady Kimberley's aunt.

[833] Sir Garnet Wolseley (1833–1913), col. 1865; commanded Red River expedition, 1870, qtrmst.-genl., WO, 1880–2; occupied Cairo, 1882, and cr. genl.; conducted campaign for relief of Gordon, 1884–5; commdr.-in-chief Ireland, 1890–5; commdr.-in-chief British army, 1895–9. According to Wolseley, Lord Kimberley 'abruptly and angrily' settled the question of 'war or no war' over the objection of several ministers. Wolseley to Fleetwood Wilson, 22 Sept. 1902, Wolseley Papers, Perkins Library, 18–H.

[834] Sir Andrew Clarke (1824–1902), joined Royal Engineers, 1844; served in Ashanti, 1863; dir. engineering works at Admiralty, 1864–73; gov. Straits Settlements, 1873–5; lt.-genl., 1886; agent-genl. for Victoria, 1891–4, 1897–1902.

[835] This passage considerably expanded in *JE*.

[836] Duke of Cambridge.

which really changes nothing in former despatches. On the whole my colleagues swallowed this extremely nauseous pill without many wry faces. Returned to Ky. by mail train.[837]

8 November 1873. Saturday. We all came to town for the 'Cabinet season'.

17 November 1873. Monday. News of Wolseley's success & retreat of Ashantees. At the Cabinet it was determined to day to send off the European troops asked for by Wolseley. I never doubted for a moment that they would go, but Cabinets like to procrastinate to the last moment & to try to persuade themselves that they won't have to do a thing they dislike tho' they know it to be unavoidable. This having been done with the proper amount of reluctance I was desired to prepare a despatch setting forth our 'views'.[838] I wonder what is to be our domestic policy for next Session & whether we have a policy. I suppose Gladstone is busy concocting it with Bright & Granville but we have heard nothing of it yet: and it is understood that Cabinets will end for the present with next week.

3 December 1873. Returned to Kimberley. The result of the Cabinets on the whole shows that Gladstone does not intend to go in for any striking novelty. Local taxation he seems unwilling to take up in earnest and it is too big for Stansfeld. But we must face the question.

31 December 1873. So ends a for us most sad year. Johnny is the cause of our sadness: otherwise the world has gone well enough with us, except poor Henry's untimely death. Army's wonderful recovery from the fever and the improvement of his health is a great blessing.

19 January 1874. Monday. Went all of us to town. Cabinet at wh. Gladstone was not present on account of a bad cold.

23 January 1874. Friday. Cabinet at which Gladstone proposed immediate dissolution of Parliament.[839] Unanimously approved. None of us had heard a whisper previously of such an intention, except three or four who saw him at his house yesterday. The reasons for this step are those stated in G's manifesto. All the stories about dissensions and

---

[837] See cabinets of 3 and 4 October in *Gladstone Diaries*, VIII, 396–7. This passage omitted from *JE*.

[838] See *Gladstone Diaries*, VIII, 412–14.

[839] See *Gladstone Diaries*, VIII, 447.

difficulties &c. amongst ourselves are pure myths. In fact we have agreed on the general scope of the measures to be introduced next session. But it is obvious that hope is stronger than gratitude. The best we could look to would be a successful budget and then a dissolution. It is far better to have a Dissn. with a successful budget in prospect. The Tories wish to drag out the session, feeling with good reason sure that, as Dizzy is reported to have said, 'by July the Ministry will stink'. What is good for them is bad for us, and what is of more consequence it is bad for the country. A dissolution will infuse fresh life into our political system, whatever be the event.[840]

3 February 1874. Tuesday. Moved to 35 Lowndes Sqre.

13 February 1874. Friday. The great fire at the Pantechnicon: a fearful sight. The forked flames darted high above the houses in Lowndes Square. We watered the fire from 4.30 to 1.30 when we went to bed as it had somewhat subsided but we could not sleep for the noise of the engines. During the fire I went into No. 19 & found Mr. Cox and his wife Lady Wood very quietly bringing back their furniture having just been told that their house was safe. It was much scorched at the back. From Motcomb Street to Kinnerton Street one could see nothing but a raging fire and volumes of sulphurous smoke. I saw the fire well from Mr. Cox's windows.[841]

16 February 1874. Monday. Cabinet dinner at Gladstone's house at which we resolved to resign at once. The only dissentient was Lowe who was for meeting Parliament.[842] Gladstone at one time inclined to this course himself.

21 February 1874. Saturday. Went to Windsor to deliver up the seals. So ends the Gladstone Government. The result of the elections was a surprise I believe to nearly every one. I heard on good authority that Lord Salisbury said that when he first learnt that Parliament was to be dissolved he thought it was a bad move for us, but that on reflexion he came to the contrary conclusion. The prevalent opinion was that we should have about 20 or 25 majority. The causes of our fall have been so fully written about that there is little to say. It is clear that the chief cause was that there was a vague general distrust. We had exhausted our programme, and quiet men asked what will Gladstone

---

[840] In *JE*, Kimberley adds 'how entirely these anticipations were falsified by the event'.
[841] See W. D. Mallock and G. Ramsden, *Letters, Remains, and Memoirs of Edward Adolphus Seymour, Twelfth Duke of Somerset* (London, 1893), 388.
[842] Lowe not mentioned in *JE*. See *Gladstone Diaries*, VIII, 461.

do next? Will he not seek to recover his popularity by extreme radical measures? and it must be admitted that there was ground for this view. We had no real policy in the future except the financial measures which Gladstone promised.

As it turned out it would probably have been better if he had brought in his Budget before dissolving, but this could not have saved us long. There is a genuine Conservative reaction, and the other party must have their turn. Of course Bruce's unlucky management of the Beer question, the confusion at the Treasury, Ayrton's offensiveness and a host of other minor causes helped to precipitate the catastrophe, but we might have still fought on, if the country had not been bent on repose or inaction or whatever best describes a state of mind averse to changes. Our people are some of them very dispirited, but I do not believe the country will long be content with inaction. Events in this age move too fast, and men are too fond of excitement to 'rest and be thankful'.[843]

7 March 1874.   Saturday. Meantime we are in great straits about our leader. We had a meeting to day of the ex. cabinet, including Ripon, & Childers at Granville's house. Gladstone, Bright, & Aberdare the two last of whom are out of town, were the only ex. ministers not present. It was agreed that Ld. Selborne, Halifax, and Granville should try to persuade Gladstone to remain leader, telling him that we were unanimous in earnestly desiring it. Nothing was said at this meeting about the choice of a new leader if G. persists in his unhappy resolution to abdicate. But the general tendency is towards Hartington. In fact who else can lead? Lowe no one will follow. Forster is odious to all the Dissenters, Goschen has for some reason no hold on the party. Would the left wing follow Hartington. I hear that Mr. L. Playfair[844] says he & others would not. Every one seems heartily to desire that G. should continue leader, except W. Harcourt who goes about denouncing G. in a manner as indecent as it is foolish.

What a strange thing that Cardwell should run away to the Lords for fear he should be asked to take the lead? and what can have induced Fortescue to extinguish himself under a peer's robe?[845]

[843] Kimberley adds a summation in *JE* admitting the government's numerous mistakes, but believing that even their worst enemies would have to 'admit that the Gladstone Ministry will fill a not un-important page in English history'. The *Journal of Events* ends at this point.

[844] Lyon Playfair (1818–98), Lib. MP for universities of Edinburgh and St. Andrews, 1868–85; post.-genl., 1873; for South Leeds, 1885–92.

[845] Edward Cardwell became 1st Viscount Cardwell, and Chichester Fortescue took the title Baron Carlingford.

8 March 1874. Sunday. Lt. H. Wood,[846] Halifax's son, who brought the despatches from Sir G. Wolseley came to see me. He told me hardly anything worth mentioning. He said Coomassie was a finer town than Cape Coast.

9 March 1874. Monday. Another meeting at Granville's. G. has virtually given in. We asked if he would see us, & on his saying 'yes' we went in a body by the terrace behind the Carlton terrace Houses, so as to prevent the newspaper touters from taking down our names. We have seen them spying about. G. received us kindly. He seemed much depressed, but in fact he has been in a state of depression ever since our beating last year. He made as usual all manner of objections & drew all sorts of distinctions, and said he must have a day or two to consider. He had told Selborne, Halifax, and Granville that he wd. continue to lead till the end of the session of 1875 but that he would not bind himself to go on beyond that time, and indeed would announce that he should then retire finally. He was not so explicit to us, altho' the gist of what he said was much the same as what he said to them. He fancies that he has recd. very bad treatment from the party because Fawcett, & Bouverie & Harcourt have made vexatious attacks on him, as if any leader could expect to be free from the attacks of crotchetty philosophers and disappointed place hunters. He wants to sulk like W. Pitt, & the party he thinks if left to wander in the wilderness for a session without a leader will repent of their sins, and come back pacified and submissive.

How foolish & undignified! To run away when beaten is natural, but the English people expects its leaders to [be] made of sterner stuff. For his own reputation if not for the sake of the party, G. should meet the House & the party as recognized opposition Leader. If he chooses to retire two years hence- *alors comme alors.*

12 March 1874. Thursday. Entry of the G. Duchess into London. What a show, & how I pity the people who are fools enough to go to see the sight. Englishmen are after all very little different from Ashantees whose King made war because his young men wished to see something new.

Last night dined at Lady Waldegraves. The Dc. d'Aumale was there. He looks aged and worse. Lady Molesworth informed me that she had used her influence against us in E. Cornwall, & boasted of having brought in Mr. Tremayne, the Tory. She has some feminine spite apparently against Gladstone, hardly at her advanced old age 'sprite

[846] Henry Wood (1838–1919), a.d.c. on staff of Sir Garnet Wolseley during Ashantee War; gov. of Natal, 1879–80.

injuria forma'. Yet when one saw the painted & bedizened old woman in her frizzled wig, one could imagine even that.

20 March 1874.   Friday. My poor uncle[847] the Admiral's death last Tuesday at Witton shocked us greatly. A most worthy brave old man. He must have been really 'temporarily insane' when he put an end to his life. Suppressed gout and incipient diabetes had thrown him into a state of depression which ended in his fatal act.

Last night the debate on the address, notable only for an outbreak of bitter speech against Gladstone from the D. of Somerset.[848]

27 March 1874.   Thursday. Sir G. Wolseley came to see me. He is he says in perfect health. We had a long talk. He told me he had offered the temporary administration of the G. Coast to four officers in succession saying that they would receive pay at the same rate as himself (£4000 per ann:). One & all replied – 'not if we received £4000 a day!'. The climate is our real enemy.

28 March 1874.   Friday. Met Lady Wolseley at dinner at Halifax's. A pretty pleasing woman.

22 April 1874.   Tuesday. Came back to town from Ky. after staying there 3 wks.

3 May 1874.   Monday. Meeting at Granville's to consider Gold Coast motion on Monday next. Goschen, Hartington & Cardwell present & self. Gladstone is for leaving the Coast – happily he is at Hawarden. Granville agrees with him. The rest all the other way. Forster also very strongly. The motion (Hanbury's) happily came to nothing.[849] K. Hugeni[850] made a good speech. Hunt's escapade about the Admy. is mistake no 1 of the Govt.[851]

8 May 1874.   Friday. Lord Derby's answer to Ld. Russell was an amusing instance of awkwardness. He made so much mystery about

---

[847] Edward Wodehouse. See p. x, above.

[848] 3 *Hansard* 218 (19 March 1874), 39–43.

[849] R. W. Hanbury (1845–1903), Cons. MP for Tamworth, 1872–8. Hanbury's motion called for Britain to withdraw from the administration of the Gold Coast.

[850] Edward Hugessen Knatchbull-Hugessen (1829–93), Lib. MP for Sandwich, 1857 u.-sec. home office, 1860, 1866; u.-sec. col. 1871–4; cr. 1st Baron Brabourne, 1880.

[851] George Ward Hunt (1825–77), Cons. MP for Northamptonshire, 1857–77; chanc. exch., 1868; 1st ld. admiralty, 1874–7. On his demand for supplementary estimates, see *DD2*, 172.

nothing that he actually affected the funds, & has frightened the Parisians consumedly.

14 May 1874. Thursday. F. & I dined at Windsor in St George's Hall at the banquet to the Emps. of Russia. A fine sight. The plate splendid. The dinner indifferent. The Queen was resplendent with diamonds, & wore a small crown on her head.

I have not seen her so fine since Prce. A's death. The Emperor little changed since I last saw him in 1858: but I suspect he has dyed his hair. The Gd. D. Alexis a tall rather ill-mannered youth. It was amusing to see the Emperor speaking to Sir H. Seymour. I did not hear what he said but he looked ungracious. They say he turned round & introduced Genl. Skolkoff to him 'un de ros heros de Crimea, Sir Hamilton' in a significant way.

15 May 1874. Friday. Dined at Marlborough House & afterwards to Stafford House. Had some conversation with M. de Hamburger a humpbacked little man, who is said to be Gortchacow's 'right hand' in the Russian F. Office.

31 May 1874. Saturday. Returned from an agreeable trip (since Saturday last) to Cornwall.

20 June 1874. Saturday. Yesterday the Abp. of C's Bill reached the 'Report' in the H. of Lds.[852] A most remarkable unanimity has been shown in the House against the ritualists who appear not to number more than 30 Peers. The Bp of Peterboro' (Magee) made a lamentable exhibition of rashness and weakness in the proposal and withdrawal of his amendments. The bill is really more Lord Cairns' & Ld. Shaftesbury's, than the Abp's in its present shape. Ld. Salisbury was evidently opposed to it & to Cairns but kept down by his colleagues.

24 June 1874. Wednesday. Meeting at breakfast at Granville's to consider course as to Licensing Bill in the Lords. Present Aberdare, Wolverton, V. Harcourt, Cardwell, Carlingford, Goschen, & Stansfeld. Determined that Aberdare should state moderately our objections to the Bill, and that we should wait for amendments from independent quarters. Harcourt's intense eagerness to sacrifice anything in order to propitiate the public was most amusing.

---

[852] The Public Worship Regulation bill, intended to suppress ritualism within the Church of England.

2 July 1874.   Colonel Packe died.[853]

11 July 1874.   Went to Minley.

14 July 1874.   Maynard Currie married to Lady Mary Cadogan.[854]
     This evening the report on Intoxicating Liquors Bill. We did very little good in Committee beyond jeering the Government: but the Bill after all makes very small changes in the Act of 1872.

15 July 1874.   Wednesday. To day the debate goes on of Public Worship Bill. Gladstone has created a complete breach between him & the Liberal party by his ill judged resolutions, as far as one can tell from the general talk.[855] We are trying thro' Granville to persuade him to withdraw them: and to answer instead he will move amendments in Committee, if he follows this advice he will place Disraeli in a most embarrassing position: but I fear he is altogether wrong-headed about Church matters. The Tory Endowed Schools reactionary Bill, debated last night, is in a party sense a god-send to us: quite providential as Lord Sandon[856] wd. term it. I have omitted to mention that we had a conference at Cardwell's on Evelyn Ashley's ill advised motion about Slavery at the Gold Coast.[857] Forster, Goschen, Harcourt & myself. Forster and Harcourt were equally unreasonable – in opposite directions. Cardwell & I advised moderation. The end was what might have been foreseen, the withdrawal of the motion in a manner, not creditable to the opposition. Goschen who in fact framed the motion at the instance of philanthropist M.Ps alarmed by some expressions of a pro-slavery tendency in Mr Lowther's speech[858] made a mistake in generalship. He should have deprecated a motion, & contented himself with demanding explanations on the report of supply.

[853] George Hussey Packe (1796–1874), entered the army in 1813, serving with the 13th Dragoons at Waterloo; Lib. MP for Lincolnshire S., 1859–68.

[854] Lady Mary Cadogan (1847–82) niece of 4th Earl Cadogan.

[855] Gladstone subsequently withdrew his six vaguely worded resolutions against the bill. See Parry, *Democracy and Religion*, 413–16.

[856] Dudley Ryder, Lord Sandon (1831–1900), succ. as 3rd Earl of Harrowby, 1882; Cons. MP for Lichfield, 1856–9, for Liverpool, 1868–82; v.p. counc. on educ., 1874–8.

[857] Anthony Evelyn Ashley (1836–1907), fourth son of the 7th Earl of Shaftesbury; priv. sec. to Palmerston, 1858–65; Lib. MP for Poole, 1874–80, for the Isle of Wight, 1880–5. On 29 June 1874 Ashley moved that no governmental arrangements on the Gold Coast which recognised slavery in any form could be satisfactory. 3 *Hansard* 220 (29 June 1874), 607.

[858] Jeremy Lowther, as u.-sec. for the colonies declared in the Commons on 25 June 1874 that he could neither confirm nor contradict reports of slave trading on the Gold Coast, 3 *Hansard* 220 (25 June 1874), 420.

16 July 1874. Thursday. Very satisfactory is the determination (almost unanimous) of the H. of Commons last night to pass the Public worship bill & make the clergy understand that they are not above the Law.

21 July 1874. Tuesday. Went to Kimberley. What a mistake the Govt. have committed by their endowed schools bill. It will do much to reunite our scattered forces.

On Friday last Carnarvon made his statement as to Fiji.[859] I think it will be impossible to avoid annexing it: but it will be an unenviable task to govern it for many a year, and I rejoice that the responsibility of the decision does not rest with me.

A tremendous drought here.

1 August 1874. My Uncle Philip Gurdon died at Cranworth.

13 August 1874. Alice safely confined of a boy at 2 Eaton Place West.[860]

21 August 1874. Heard that Alice who had been going on very well was dangerously ill with inflammation of the lungs. Flo. went up at once to town.

Received a letter from Ripon announcing that he has determined to become a R. Catholic![861] How extraordinary. By what train of reasoning can a man of sense & sober mind have brought himself to believe that he is bound to surrender himself into the hands of superstitious priests, and to swallow whole whatever they tell him is divine.[862] It makes one almost despair of the progress of the human race when one sees men still voluntarily enslaving their minds, & debasing their reason before the groveling fables invented by Italian devotees. Fancy a man like Ripon, believing the 'immaculate conception', and on the faith of an opinion expressed by Pope Pius IX![863] Alas! for my poor friend: what hallucination can have possessed him?

27 October 1874. Went to Knatchbull-Hugessen's. No one there. H. as usual very full of himself. He is very sore at not having had a higher

[859] Arguing that Britain had an 'indirect duty' to 'take under our protection a place into which English capital has overflowed, in which English settlers are resident, in which it must be added, English lawlessness is going on.' 3 *Hansard* 221 (17 July 1874), 185.

[860] The child did not survive infancy.

[861] 'I know your strong feelings about the Catholic religion,' Ripon wrote, 'and I feel therefore how greatly you will blame me; but I hope you will at all events give me credit for honesty....' Ripon to Kimberley, 20 Aug. 1874, KP6 MS.eng.c.4473, ff. 11–12.

[862] Cf. his assessment of Evy Currie's conversion to Roman Catholicism, 13 Nov. 1867.

[863] Pope Pius IX, r. 1846–78; forced to flee Rome in 1848, but restored by France, 1850; ultra-montanist; proclaimed dogma of the Immaculate Conception 1854; convened Vatican Council 1869–70, which promulgated the dogma of papal infallibility.

place in Govt. than an Under-secretaryship. He has a good deal of cleverness, but it is spoiled by his excessive conceit, and he gives himself such absurd airs that though really a very good fellow he is unpopular.

31 October 1874.   Went to Prestwold and found Alice much better.

7 November 1874.   Returned to Ky.

25 November 1874.   The Duke of Connaught came here to shoot. He seems an amiable man, and has pleasant intelligent manners: but on the whole does not give the idea of a strong man mentally or physically.

1 January 1875.   So begins a new year. Last year after the resignation of Gladstone's Govt. was a quiet one, for us except poor Alice's illness, her recovery from which has been indeed wonderful.

14 January 1875.   Thursday. Went to London to a meeting of the late Cabinet at Granville's house. There were present Gladstone, Granville, Ld. Selborne, Cardwell, Aberdare, Halifax, C. Fortescue, Stansfeld, Hartington, Lowe, Forster, Goschen, and myself. Gladstone read us his letter (afterwards published) announcing his resignation of the leadership of the party.[864] He also read a short summary of his reasons. They were as far as I can recollect, that if he now resumed the leadership he would bind himself for an indefinite period, that he foresaw difficulties with which in the present state of the party he could not contend successfully, as to denominational education, and as to the Church. The Liberal party approved generally of the Cowper-Temple clause[865] which he thought utterly indefensible. Secular education he might be able to accept but not a colourless system which was neither one thing nor the other. His views as to the Church were that any attempt to narrow the existing basis would be ruinous; he had embodied these views in his resolutions of last session, but obtained no support. He expected that the Scotch Patronage Act[866] of last session would lead to an agitation for disestablishment of the Kirk, and he did not see how such a demand could be resisted, seeing that a majority of the Scotch people do not belong to the Establishment. Further he felt himself

---

[864] See *Gladstone Diaries*, IX, 4–6, for full text of Gladstone's memoranda of resignation. For Granville's response to Gladstone's draft see Granville to Gladstone, 5 January 1875 cit. *Gladstone–Granville Corresp. 1*, II, 463–5.

[865] The Cowper–Temple amendment to the 1870 Education Act prohibited denominational teaching in local Board schools.

[866] The Scotch Patronage Act of 1874 transferred lay patronage within the Church of Scotland to the congregations.

generally out of harmony with the opinions which prevailed on both sides of the house as to the necessity for Govt. interference in a variety of affairs. He had always been for a *laissez faire* policy, a policy now quite out of fashion. He had also been an ardent advocate of economy in and out of office, and no party in the state now desired to economize the public money. He was very quiet but very determined. It was evident his mind was made up. A long conversation ensued lasting two hours, and various arguments were pressed upon him to induce him to continue leader, but without any effect. Granville, Cardwell, & Selborne with whom he had been previously in communication had in fact already said all that could be said. However we wished to leave no stone unturned, and so the arguments were repeated again and again. As he persisted in his resolution, we then considered Granville's answer which was afterwards published with the letter of resignation.

I was not in the least surprised. In fact the step now taken was really inevitable. Gladstone knows that the old questions are used up and that there must be a new departure. He does not (who does?) see what is to be the future basis of the Liberal party, if indeed the present combination can continue in any shape. Weary of public affairs he naturally at his age shrinks from the task of reconstructing the party, and it is obvious that if he did not retire now, he could scarcely hope to be released as long as he had strength for work.

The future is utterly dark. If we can agree on a leader which seems very doubtful, it will be long before he will acquire any real authority. A man of genius might soon become a real leader but we have no such man amongst us; and remove Disraeli the Tories are no better off. Forster is the best man we have. Will the Nonconformists make up their quarrel with him? If not, I anticipate that Hartington will be chosen.[867]

27 January 1875.   Wednesday. Attended meeting at Lewes to present a testimonial to Dodson. The situation was most embarrassing for Hartington, Goschen and me who had to deliver speeches, especially for Hartington.[868] Our orations were as dull and pointless as might be expected. Having nothing to say we said nothing.

12 February 1875.   Friday. Came up to London.

[867] Hartington was elected leader at a meeting of 136 Lib. MPs on 3 Feb. 1875. On the competition for leadership, see Patrick Jackson, *Education Act Forster: A Political Biography of W. D. Forster (1818–1886)* (London, Associated University Presses, 1987), ch. 10.

[868] On Hartington's 'astute' speech in the midst of leadership controversy, see Jackson, *Education Act Forster*, 224.

27 February 1875.   Saturday. Flo: came out with measles. The second time within 12 years!

9 March 1875.   Tuesday. Astounding statement of Cairns in the Lords. The Govt. abandon their Judicature Bill.[869] The speeches of Cairns & Derby were remarkable. Cairns was in a white rage. Every tone in his voice quivered with suppressed fury. Derby, perhaps for the first time, visibly betrayed annoyance. Selborne very good in reply, and Grey applied the cautery in his best vein of bitterness. A curious scene altogether.

Probably Disraeli is the cause of this change of purpose. We always heard that he was much annoyed with Cairns for supporting Selborne's bill in 1873.

Taylor[870] says this proceeding is the first nail in the coffin of the Govt., and doubtless he is right.

11 March 1875.   Thursday. Meeting at Granville's of Ex. Govt. to consider our course. All present except Lowe, & unfortunately Selborne who was sitting on an appeal. Gladstone was there. All agreed that we should make no move till the matter develops itself further. The Govt. have dug this pit for themselves. Let them founder in it without the consolation of being able to ascribe any part of their mishap to any one but their own partisans.

12 March 1875.   Friday. Richmond brought in his tenant right Bill. He made a lame confused statement received with the utmost coldness by the Tory peers. His colleagues except Malmesbury did not think it worth while to come down to hear him.

19 March 1875.   [*sic*] Thursday. Meeting of Ex. Cabinet at Granville's. Harcourt also there. Our course on the Judicature Bill considered.[871] Harcourt wanted to make attack on Govt. on motion to adjourn for Easter. Majority in favour of doing nothing till the Govt. announce what course they will take. Ripon is not asked to these meetings, since he became a R. Catholic.[872]

---

[869] The Conservatives failed to pass a Judicature bill in 1874, revising Selborne's Judicature Act of 1873, for lack of parliamentary time. In March 1875 Derby noted that nearly all the Conservative peers and half of the Whigs opposed Cairns' Judicature bill and at a cabinet on 6 March 1875 it was decided to drop the measure. *DD2*, 197–8. On 9 April 1875 a second Judicature bill was introduced which eventually passed.

[870] Probably Col. Thomas Taylor (1812–83), Cons. chief whip in Commons, 1859–68, 1873–4; chanc. Duchy of Lancaster, 1874–80; Cons. MP for Dublin Co., 1841–83.

[871] See *Gladstone Diaries*, IX, 22.

[872] See entry for 21 Aug. 1874.

9 April 1875. Friday. Meeting at Granville's talk about Natal business.[873] Granville, Cardwell, Fortescue & self against Govt. & Colenso. Lowe, who was not present, agrees with us. Forster the other way.... .

[Two pages here excised.]

12 April 1875. Monday. Debate on Lord Grey's motion on Natal.

14 April 1875. Wednesday. Dinner at Fishmonger's Hall. Ld. Hartington made I thought rather a clever speech tho' the jokes were certainly ponderous. I have been sharply rebuked by the newspapers for supporting Grey about Natal. The report of my speech was most incorrect & meagre, and the accusations are to a great extent based either on what I never said or on a total ignorance of the subject. I was made to say that Langalibalele had a full & fair trial instead of that Pine[874] 'intended by introducing English forms into a proceeding under Caffre law to give the prisoner a fuller and fairer trial', and my expression of regret that he should have tried him in so loose and unsatisfactory a manner was not reported. But the fact is the newspapers are determined that only one side shall be heard, & I was a fool for my pains in trying to get a hearing for Pine. Of course if I had agreed with the newspapers, they would have reported my speech fully & fairly. If indeed they can ever bring themselves to give a tolerable report of speeches in the H. of Lords.

3 May 1875. Monday. We had two meetings last week one at Devonshire House and one at Granville's. The budget was discussed, and the privilege question in the H. of Commons as to newspapers & strangers. Gladstone furious against the grossest case of working the figures he had ever known. Lowe is the prime mover on the privilege question.[875] I think after Disraeli's mistake in telling Mr. Sullivan he wd. not deal with it, Hartington may get a little credit by taking it up.

On the 29th went to a dinner at Willis' rooms in glorification of Sir G. Bowen. The hottest atmosphere, and most intolerably wearisome speech making I ever endured. I must make an exception for Bowen

[873] Lord Carnarvon, Disraeli's Colonial Secretary, was pursuing a policy of removing control of native affairs from the settlers in Natal. This was intended to allow the natives to be handled with greater justice, but equally the policy was guaranteed to create disaffection within the colony. Derby thought that although Carnarvon's plans were well meant they did not allow for the strength of colonial opposition. *DD2*, 207.

[874] Sir Benjamin Pine (1813–91), gov. of Natal, 1849–56, 1873–5; gov. Gold Coast, 1856–9; lt.-gov. St. Christopher, 1859–69; gov.-in-chief, Leeward Is., 1869–73.

[875] On 9 April 1875 *The Times* and the *Daily News* published proceedings of the Commons Select Committee on Foreign Loans. On 13 and 16 April Lowe, Harcourt and Hartington argued this to be a breach of privilege.

who really sounded his trumpet very effectively. But what a curse these dinners are to public men! A disordered mucous membrane made me I admit more cynical than usual.

7 May 1875. The Jew is getting intolerable but I doubt whether our credit rises tho' the Tory credit certainly shows symptoms of waning. I fear the 'Times' is right that Parliament itself is losing its authority or 'prestige' if one must use a foreign word.

27 May 1875. Returned from Kimberley where we have been for Whitsuntide. It is more evident every day that the nation has deliberately descended into sleepy hollow, and that they wish for a Government which does nothing. The tide seems stronger than ever against Liberals. We have now literally no paper unless it be the 'Spectator' which supports us as a party.[876] This shows how strong is the antipathy of the public to us. Gladstone's attack on the budget was a fiasco. *More suo* he enormously exaggerated the defects of Northcote's finance.[877] The public which has now no sympathy with him, was ready to condone much worse errors.[878]

As to Fawcett's motion on rating[879] it was of course certain that the Tories some of whom are really discontented with the Govt. on this matter, would have nothing to do with the Professor, but I don't think his motion did us any harm. Indeed it would be difficult for our position to be made worse than it is by anything.

22 June 1875. Tuesday. Wodehouse married to Isabel Stracey at St George's Church. Hanv. Sqr.[880]

Yesterday we had a meeting at Granville's, & Agricultural Holdings Bill talked about. Then County voters (household suffrage). Much

---

[876] The *Spectator* was a Liberal Sunday newspaper founded in 1828 and owned in 1875 by Meredith Townsend and Richard Holt Hutton.

[877] Sir Stafford Henry Northcote (1818–87), Cons. MP for Dudley, 1855–8, for Stamford, 1858–66, for N. Devon, 1866–85, when cr. 1st Earl of Iddesleigh; pres. b. of t., 1866–7; India sec., 1867; ch. of exch., 1874–80; leader of opposition, 1880–5; for. sec., 1886–7.

[878] By general report Northcote got the better of Gladstone in the budget debate. Derby saw Gladstone's attack on Northcote as an attempt quietly to resume his old post as party leader. Gladstone criticised the handling of income tax, the brewers' license and the debt. *Gladstone Diaries*, IX, 35; *DD2*, 215.

[879] On 24 May 1875 Fawcett moved a hostile motion against the Public Works Loan Acts Amendment bill. Fawcett's motion was defeated by 249 to 175 votes. See 3 *Hansard* 224 (24 May 1875), 796–862.

[880] For a model of marriage negotiation, particularly in light of Lord Wodehouse's earlier bankruptcy, see letters between Kimberley, John Wodehouse and Sir Henry Stracey. KP6 MS.eng.c. 4475.

difference of opinion about the latter, and it was agreed to meet again about it before Trevelyan's bill comes on.[881]

15 July 1875. By accident I missed Granville's next meeting. It was decided that Hartington should speak against the bill but not vote. Our left wing were very angry when this was done, but on the whole I think it was the wisest course. My own opinion is in favour of giving the county voters the franchise but it must be accompanied by a redistribution of seats, and if Hartington had voted with Trevelyan he would have frightened all the Whigs & probably broken up the party without really advancing the question.

It is quite certain that the arbitrary line between town & country votes cannot long be maintained. The real contest will be between the two parties to get the conduct of the measure in order that they may have the manipulation of the rearrangement of seats. The Whigs & the Tories too will yield easily enough to pressure when the leaders think the time come. Goschen who is against Trevelyan, was very angry with Forster for speaking so vigorously for the bill. Lowe was the only ex-minister who voted against the bill. It was curious at our meeting to see how eager Gladstone was for it. He becomes more Radical daily. If he were a younger man, he would I believe come out with a flaming Radical programme, disestablishment of the Church, & extension of the suffrage.

The govt. are in an uncomfortable position as to the money for the P. of Wales' journey to India.[882] They have left themselves so small a surplus that they are afraid to ask for a sufficient sum. They used to accuse the late Govt. of meanness. They find now that economy is a virtue not to be despised, especially when you have no money to spare!

28 July 1875. Went to Kimberley. Very little to remark on this session. As some newspaper observed, the Govt. have lost, and the opposition has not gained credit. The two most notable features in politics are the utter indifference of the public to economy or rather the general desire for extravagant expenditure of the public money, and the little interest wh. is taken in the proceedings of Parliament, both bad signs. It is also remarkable that the London newspapers are persistently seeking to stir

---

[881] In 1875 county franchise reform (extension of the household suffrage to the counties), as well as temperance reform, championed by radicals (in the case of the county franchise by G.O. Trevelyan) did not help party unity. Trevelyan subsequently made annual motions for county franchise reform which, by 1877, secured broad Liberal support.

[882] The Conservative cabinet originally allowed £50,000 for the Prince of Wales's visit to India. In July they reluctantly increased the allowance to £60,000. By mid-July sections of the Royal Household and the press were demanding twice that amount to enable an appropriate Royal progress to be undertaken.

up the nation to a policy of large armaments, interference in continental affairs, & extension (any where, any how) of our Colonial possessions. This indicates no doubt that they believe that there is a growing desire for such a policy amongst their readers. It looks as if John Bull were hankering after his old follies, and like a green boy at school, want to fight some one in order to show that he 'won't take a licking'. Will he be fool enough to get himself into a fever, which will only be abated by copious bleeding of his purse & person? It will not [be] the fault of his newspapers, if he does not lose his senses.

14 August 1875. Began harvest. Hay only just got up!

4 February 1876. To London to attend meeting at Granville's. All members of late Cabinet there except Bright & Childers. Long discussion on Fugitive Slave Circulars. We also discussed c/y Andrassy note (as to which it was agreed that Ld. Derby had done right), and the Suez Canal shares purchase.[883] As to the latter Gladstone gave sound & moderate advice, to question the Govt. & draw out the details so as to enlighten public opinion but to make no direct attack. Gladstone, Granville & Lowe decidedly hostile to the purchase, & Granville evidently looks on it as a mere piece of 'chauvinisme'.

7 February 1876. Monday. We all went to town. To another meeting at Granville's. Present the same as on Friday and in addition Harcourt, James,[884] & Whitbread.[885] We agreed on a resolution of wh. Whitbd. is to give notice in the H. of Commons.

8 February 1876. Tuesday. Opening of Parliament. Granville made an admirable speech on the address. I think I never heard him speak so well. Derby was as effective as a man can be who reads a prepared

---

[883] Count Julius Andrassy was Austrian foreign minister. The Andrassy Note, 30 December 1875, called on Turkey to concede reforms to their subject Serbs so as to avoid a Russian aggression and diplomatic intervention by other European powers. Although Derby, as foreign minister, thought the Note moderate in tone Disraeli instinctively disliked Britain being seen as only a secondary party in the settling of the vexed Eastern Question and favoured an independent British initiative. The Andrassy Note was accepted by Turkey on 3 February 1875. In November 1875 the Conservative cabinet agreed to attempt to buy the majority shares in the Suez Canal being sold by the Khedive rather than let them be acquired by a French company. The £4 million for the purchase was provided by Rothschild.

[884] Sir Henry James (1828–1911), Lib. MP for Taunton, 1869–85, for Bury, 1885–95; cr. Baron James, 1895; atty-genl., 1873–4, 1880–5.

[885] Samuel Whitbread (1830–1915), Lib. MP for Bedford, 1852–95; member HC Committee of Selection.

speech like a sermon from a written paper. The Govt. will have no easy task to defend in argument their Suez purchase tho' they have undoubtedly the country with them. This general approval is indeed quite unreasoning, a mere impulse arising from the wish to assert in some way the power of England, a protest against a tame foreign policy. Myself however I am inclined (not without much doubt) to think the Govt. were justified in buying the shares. In consequence of Lord Palmerston's ill-advised opposition, the canal fell entirely into French hands, and we have never since been able to assume the position in Egypt which our preponderating interest in the success of the canal clearly entitles us to. The step now taken gets us out of the wrong groove once for all, and repairs as far as it is now reparable the consequences of Ld. Palmerston's mistake. I do not know that this could have been done in any other manner, and moreover if the Khedive's shares had passed into French hands, our position would have been still worse than before.

21 February 1876. Monday. Meeting at Granville's to consider a communication he has had from the Queen as to the 'Titles Bill'.[886] It has been the custom for many years when any proposal was to be made to Parliament, affecting the Queen personally, for the Govt. to communicate with the leaders of the opposition. This was not done by Disraeli in the present case. We all agreed that the title of 'Empress' was most objectionable, & that before the Bill goes further, the H. of Commons ought to be informed what title the Queen will be advised to take if the Bill passes. Granville is to write to H.M. accordingly, pointing out also the offense which may be given to the Colonies if they are left out. It is said that the Queen is foolish enough to wish for the title of Empress, in order that her family may be put on an equality with the Continental Imperial Highnesses!

1 March 1876. The opposition are jubilant at the defeat of the Solicitor General at Horsham.[887] What with the Fugitive Slave Circulars and the Admiralty blunders the Govt. are getting into a mess. But their strength is the country.... .

[Two pages here excised.]

---

[886] At a cabinet on 25 January 1876 the government, in response to royal pressure, agreed to a measure giving the Queen the title Empress of India. The proposal was not popular. Derby considered it 'a royal whim indulged, and that is about all the comment it requires'. *DD2*, 228.

[887] Sir Hardinge Giffard (1825–1921), Cons. MP for Launceston, 1877–85, when he was appt. Lord Chancellor as Baron Halsbury; sol.-genl., 1874–80; ld. chanc., 1885, 1886–92, 1895–1905. Was defeated by the Liberal J.C. Brown at the Horsham by-election of 29 February 1876.

30 March 1876.   Thursday. Titles Bill, 2nd reading. L. Salisbury as usual vulgarly abusive.

8 May 1876.   Nothing but Titles Bill. I am sick of it. It was a real blunder of the Government to start the question, a worse blunder to persevere, but after all even if the Queen should be called 'Queen Empress', nothing very serious will happen. As Gladstone said at one of our meetings, 'It is a piece of tomfoolery' [*ill.*].

I am sorry for Lowe.[888] This escapade too does us harm as a party. He could not however get out of the scrape, & the only thing left was to make as he did an ample apology.

We went to Kimberley on April 12, & the next morning there were six inches of the snow on the ground!

15 May 1876.   Monday. Interesting debate in H. of Lords on Burial of Dissenters.[889] Ld. Granville made an admirable speech. It is singular how much he has improved in speaking in the last three or four years.

3 June 1876.   Went to Falmouth and afterwards made a charming little tour in North Cornwall & North Devon, returning on June 13 from Ilfracombe to London.

3 July 1876.   We had a small meeting at Granville's to consider what steps should be taken in Parliament to question the government as to their policy in Turkey.[890] Forster very anti-Turk, the rest for remaining quiet & waiting for papers. The Govt. are for the moment masters of the situation. The people generally are delighted to see England 'cutting a figure' in foreign politics. Provided only we make a splash, they seem to care little how or where. A sort of petty vanity is the motive, just as a public man often makes speeches for no reason except to get himself

[888] Who publicly implicated Gladstone in previously refusing a change of title. See Winter, *Robert Lowe*, 310–11.

[889] On 15 May Granville brought forward a resolution giving Non-conformists right to burial in a churchyard without Church of England rites. Resolution was defeated by 148 to 92 votes. 3 *Hansard* 229 (15 May 1876), 558–666.

[890] During April 1876 Turkey began a vicious repression of insurrection in Bulgaria. In May 1876 Disraeli's government rejected the Berlin Memorandum outlining Bismarck's plan for pacification in the Balkans. In June Serbia and Montenegro declared war on Turkey. By early July Derby was urging Disraeli to use moderate language, without sensation and swagger, so as to avoid government policy being seen as too pro-Turkish. It was Forster, rather than Gladstone, who was urging Hartington to attack the government over reports of Turkish atrocities against Bulgarian Christians in the *Spectator* in early June. Not until late July did Gladstone become deeply disturbed over continuing reports of atrocity. See R. Shannon, *Gladstone and the Bulgarian Agitation 1876* (London, 1963), 93–5.

talked out. However there is a considerable current of opinion against
another war on behalf of Turkey, & if Disraeli gets the country into
such a war, there may be some feeling around against him, if any[x]
thing will arouse feeling on any subject.

[Undated annotation]: [x](Obviously wrong this – Witness the autumn
agitation. K)[891]

February 1877. The autumn was spent very quietly & happily at
Kimberley and on Feb 8 the day before the meeting of Parliament we
went up to town.

I was not present at a meeting of the old Cabinet at Granville's on
the 8th.; I attended one a few days later at which the Turkish question
was talked over.[892] On Tuesday the 20th we had a debate on Eastern
affairs started by the D. of Argyll, who made a very fine speech. I spoke
for a short time, & made a poor speech.[893] The violent effervescence of
feeling about the Bulgarian atrocities has now cooled down, & the
sentiment of the country is for peace at almost any price. It is amusing
to see the Tories who taunted us when we were in office with want of
spirit in our foreign policy, obliged to be even tamer & more peaceable.
At the meeting at Granville's, Adam,[894] our 'whip', told us that if we
attempted any division in the H. of Commons against the Govt. on
the Turkish question we should not muster more than 200 men, &
should be beaten by 150. No doubt the country is somewhat more
favorable than the present Parliament but for all that I believe the
great majority is against us: nor do I see any prospect of our improving
our position to such an extent as seriously to weaken the government.

I say nothing as to the appearance of the great charlatan in his new
character as an Earl.[895] The newspapers have given nauseously full
accounts of his poses and attitudes.

[891] During the autumn Gladstone headed a powerful extra-parliamentary agitation
denouncing Turkish barbarity and Disraeli's pro-Turkish policy. Yet Hartington, in
December 1876, believed Whigs and moderate Liberals in parliament were 'a good deal
disgusted' with Gladstone's popular agitation which, if it continued, would break up the
Liberal party. See Jenkins, *Gladstone, Whiggery and the Liberal Party 1874–1886*, 59.

[892] Granville and Hartington pursued a moderate policy concentrating their criticisms
of government policy on the failure to act in concert with other European powers, as
when they refused to sign the Berlin memorandum. See Jenkins, *Gladstone, Whiggery and
the Liberal Party*, 59.

[893] Kimberley followed the Granville–Hartington line in this speech, while also
supporting Palmerston's Crimean policy of the 1850s of propping up Turkey as a
constraint on Russian expansionism.

[894] William Patrick Adam (1823–81), Lib. MP for Clackmannan and Kinross, 1859–
80; lib. whip, 1874–80; gov. Madras, 1880–1.

[895] In August 1876 Benjamin Disraeli assumed the title Earl of Beaconsfield.

9 March 1877. Went with Flo. to Windsor to dine & sleep. H.M. was in uncommonly high spirits. Sydney has got a story that she vowed after the 'Empress' affair last year never to receive one of the late Cabinet under her roof. If so, her vow like many others was only made to be broken. Aberdare told me a rather amusing anecdote of Dizzy. A. asked him how he liked the H. of Lds. 'I feel' he said 'that I am dead; but I am in Elysium'.

Sir Bartle Frere,[896] the new Governor of the Cape has just started for his post. I went to a dinner at the Langham Hotel in his honour. Like most 'banquets' the food was nasty & the atmosphere stifling. The speeches were good except the new governor's wh. was very feeble. My impression is that Sir Bartle is far from a 'strong' man. Those who know him best say his administration at Bombay was a failure, that he is conceited, and not by any means wise. He will probably please at first at the Cape as he has a popular plausible manner.

28 April 1877. Meeting at Ld. Granville's to consider Gladstone's resolution on the Eastern Question.[897] Most of the late Cabinet there and James & Harcourt. Gladstone was not well & was unable to come. Everyone except Forster against moving any resolutions. Bright undertook to tell Gladstone & to try to dissuade him from going on. He is however not likely to give way, as Granville and Bright have already done all they could to keep him quiet. He thinks of nothing but disburdening his own conscience & is blind to the disastrous effects he will produce. The pro-Turkish party can claim nothing better than the opportunity he will give them. The whole Liberal party, as far as I can hear, with the exception of a few Radicals, strongly disapprove any Parliamentary action at this moment on the part of the opposition. I met Carnarvon in the evening at dinner at Ripon's. He expressed the strongest regret at Gladstone's proceeding, as tending to give strength to the anti-Russian party who wish to get us into war for Turkey.

One thing is certain. The wave of feeling wh. swept the country last autumn is spent & there is great danger of a flood rising from the opposite quarter.

[896] Sir Henry Bartle Edward Frere (1815–84), gov. Bombay, 1862–7; negotiated suppression of the slave trade in Zanzibar, 1872; gov. of Cape and high com. of South Africa, 1877; censured by govt. for exceeding instructions in relations with the Zulu and superseded as high com., 1879; recalled by Lib. govt. in 1880.

[897] On 27 April 1877 Gladstone indicated his intention to move five resolutions in the Commons on 7 May declaring the Turkish government to have lost any claim to moral or material support; calling for the British government to seek local liberty and self-government in the disturbed provinces in concert with other European powers: and demanding such changes in the provinces as necessary for humanity and justice. Gladstone described his decision as 'a severe one, in face of not having a single approver in the *Upper* official circle'. *Gladstone Diaries*, IX, 214.

2 May 1877. Meeting at Granville's where it was decided (*nem:con:*) to support Sir J. Lubbock's motion of the 'previous question' on Gladstone's resolutions.[898]

5 May 1877. I went to the academy dinner & sat next to Gladstone who seemed in great spirits. After the dinner most of the Ex-Cabinet met at Granville's to consider a compromise wh. Gladstone is willing to consent to in order to prevent the threatened split in the party, namely to withdraw or rather not to divide on his third & fourth resolutions, and to amend his second resolutions. On these conditions we all heartily agreed that the first & second resolutions should be supported by Hartington & his friends.[899] We are well out of a very great perplexity.

Everyday the pressure on Libl. members to vote for G. has been increasing & probably a majority of the party would have voted against Hartington, who would then have resigned. The Radicals, such as Mr. Chamberlain, would have been delighted at this. They have been hoping to get back G. as leader of a Liberal party from which all Whigs should be excluded. They will be furious at their disappointment. It is quite evident however that there were more Liberals who wished for some Parliamentary actions than we supposed. It is remarkable that a few weeks ago when Granville & others hinted at coercive action against Turkey, they met with no response. Now, our leaders are greatly blamed for feebleness & want of a policy. What do the Liberals mean? It seems to me that they have no common opinion on the question. There is a vague desire to disconnect England from Turkey & to keep out of war, but no distinct view as to how this is to be done.

4 June 1877. Returned to town from a pleasant tour of a fortnight in Cornwall & Devonshire. I went to Falmouth to open the 'Kimberley Park' on the 24th of May.[900] The affair went off very well.

---

[898] Sir John Lubbock (1834–1913), Lib. MP for Maidstone, 1870–80, for London University, 1880–1900, when he was cr. 1st Baron Avebury. Following the meeting Granville informed Gladstone 'that it was not opportune at this time to move resolutions'. Granville to Gladstone, 2 May 1877 in *Gladstone–Granville Corresp. 2*, I, 36.

[899] See *Gladstone Diaries*, IX, 216: Morley, *Gladstone*, II, 564–5; and Jenkins, *Gladstone, Whiggery and the Liberal Party*, 61–2. When Gladstone moved his modified resolutions on 7 May 1877 he noted the opposition front bench were 'virtually silent. Such a sense of solitary struggle I never remember.' *Gladstone Diaries*, IX, 217. On 14 May his resolutions were defeated by 223 to 354 Commons votes.

[900] Having donated 7½ acres and spent £2,000 in laying out the grounds. City leaders thanked Kimberley for the 'generous and philanthropic spirit of contributing to the health, the recreation, and the general benefit of Falmouth and its neighbourhood'. No doubt Kimberley and his land agent were equally interested in increasing the value of surrounding properties. *Falmouth Packet*, 26 May 1877, 1.

Gladstone's proceedings at Birmingham seem to have rather disappointed the local Radicals who thought they would entrap him with some declaration of a new programme including a crusade against the Church.[901] I hear he is quieter since he came back.

17 June 1877. Monday. The Govt. defeated on Ld. Harrowby's[902] motion on burial Bill. We had an impression that 'Dizzy' whipped off, but I hear now that the Govt. really did its best against Harrowby. The whole matter has been uncommonly well managed by Granville from the first.

26 June 1877. Tuesday. Meeting at Carlton Terrace to discuss what course to take if Govt. propose vote of credit. Agreed that no Parliamentary action can be taken at present. Hartington announced that he had determined to speak & vote for Trevelyan's motion.[903]

1 July 1877. Sunday. Met Comte de Paris[904] at dinner at Strawberry Hill. He spoke with great apprehension of Bismarck's schemes to involve Austria & England in the Turkish war.[905]

2 July 1877. Monday at Carlton Terrace to consider a letter which Gladstone has made up his mind to publish against the vote of credit. Hartington & Granville & every one else against it, but *cui bono?* Gladstone had made up his mind to go his own way. He will neither lead nor follow. After all when the letter was published, it made no sensation whatever.[906]

---

[901] On 31 May 1877; at Joseph Chamberlain's invitation, Gladstone spoke in Birmingham at the inaugural meeting of the National Liberal Federation. In his diary Gladstone noted he was given 'a triumphal reception' and spoke to 'a most intelligent orderly appreciative audience' of 25,000 in the Bingley Hall. *Gladstone Diaries*, IX, 223. Gladstone commended party organisation, counselled greater unity of action, and 'went off in my accustomed strain about the Eastern question'. Gladstone to Granville, 1 June 1877 in *Gladstone–Granville Corresp. 2*, I, 43.

[902] Dudley Ryder, 2nd Earl of Harrowby (1798–1882).

[903] On 29 June 1877 Trevelyan proposed a Commons motion calling for a uniform borough and county suffrage, and further redistribution. Hartington closed the debate supporting the motion. 3 *Hansard* 235 (29 June 1877), 488–588.

[904] Louis Philippe Albert d'Orléans, Comte de Paris (1838–94), pretender to French crown before renouncing claims to the throne in 1873.

[905] On 30 June 1877 the Conservative cabinet agreed to move a British fleet to Besika Bay at the mouth of the Dardanelles.

[906] The government proposed a vote of credit for increased military expenditure. On learning of Gladstone's intention to oppose the vote of credit Granville responded that Hartington and others would 'have reason to be surprised, if you now take the lead, and without further consultation, do that which you proved to them to be inexpedient'. Granville to Gladstone, 28 June 1877 in *Gladstone–Granville Corresp. 2*, I, 47. In the event votes of credit passed on 2 July 1877.

Parliament went out with a 'stink' this year, completely checkmated by Biggar & Parnell.[907] As there was nothing of any kind to do in the House of Lords, I determined to get away early for once & enjoy the summer. We went to Kimberley on the 18th of July.

3 October 1877. Went to dinner of the Agricultural Assn. at N. Walsham where I was chairman in the absence of Ld. Suffield, the President. Made a speech principally on the Turkish war. No one cares to hear of any thing else. I avowed myself somewhat pro-Russian. As all the newspapers are now furious 'Turcophils' or furious 'Russo phils', they were no doubt little pleased with my remarks as I took neither side strongly. At all events they took no notice of what I said whether for this, or whatever other cause. Perhaps I said nothing worth notice. I seemed to myself to talk good sense, but who can judge his own performances?

16 January 1878. Dined with Lord Granville & after dinner the ex-Cabinet remained & had a long desultory talk about the Queen's speech & the state of affairs.

17 January 1878. Meeting of Parliament. General relief on our side & disappointment amongst the Tories that no vote of money or war preparations are announced. I heard on good authority that Carnarvon & Derby were 'out' a few days ago, but I suppose they were persuaded to remain on condition that no immediate warlike steps are taken.[908] We went back to Kimberley on Saturday.

26 January 1878. The news arrived of the resignation of Derby & Carnarvon.[909] I heard it too late to attend the meeting at Granville's on the event.

28 January 1878. Monday. Went to town and on Tuesday attended meeting at Granville's. It had been agreed by those present on Saturday

---

[907] Joseph Gillis Biggar (1828–90), Home Rule MP for co. Cavan, 1874–90; and Charles Stewart Parnell (1846–91), Home Rule MP for co. Meath, 1875–80, for Cork city, 1880–91, who had obstructed debate on the votes of credit.

[908] During a cabinet meeting on 12 January 1877 both Derby and Carnarvon came close to resigning over the proposal to send a British expedition to occupy Turkish territory at Gallipoli. A ministerial rupture was avoided when Salisbury brought forward a compromise proposal. *DD2*, 483.

[909] Derby, having offered his resignation, by the end of the day was prevailed upon to stay, following long conversations with Sir Stafford Northcote, Conservative leader in the Commons. He remained, however, profoundly uneasy and did not think he would remain in office much longer. *DD2*, 493.

that an amendment should be moved on the vote of credit, but to our surprise and dismay Hartington to day objected. Every one else was in favour. Goschen rather wavering.

Hartington was finally persuaded, after we separated, by Granville to support the amendment, Forster moving it. It wd. of course have been much better that H. had moved it, but it is fortunate we have avoided a split. If H. had refused to support it, Gladstone wd. have moved it & we should have had the Radicals going with him, the Whigs with H.

27 January 1878.   I went off to Ky. again to wind up things there before our great move.

5 February 1878.   We all went to town.

9 February 1878.   Saturday. The history of the amendment is very shortly told.[910] On the arrival of the alarming announcement that the Russians had entered the lines of C[onstantino]ple. the leaders of the oppn. held a meeting at which it was determined not to pass Forster's amendment. The fact is that Gladstone's most ill timed violent speech at Oxford had frightened all our Whig supporters, & any pretense for backing out was largely seized.[911] It is said however that this was a miscalculation & that with a little pressure most of them wd. have voted with us. Adam told me if the news from Cpl. had not arrived we should have mustered about 220, & the Govt. would have had a majority of 130.

The truth is Gladstone's proceedings make Hartington's position & all union & reorganization of the party impossible.

22 February 1878.   I had some conversation with Lord Carnarvon a few days ago. He told me he had been in constant disagreement with his colleagues for the last nine months. A pretty comment on Salisbury's declaration at the beginning of the Session that the Cabinet was united! The 'lying spirit' which Mr. Cross[912] spoke of seems to be a Cabinet

---

[910] On 31 Jan. 1878 Forster moved an amendment that, as the government declared Britain not to be engaged in war in Eastern Europe, there was no need for additional taxation. Afer five nights debate the amendment was withdrawn on 7 Feb. 1878.

[911] Confirming Derby's opinion that the opposition were 'far weaker than before' and could not unite on a question of foreign policy. *DD2*, 504. At the Corn Exchange, on 30 January 1878 Gladstone delivered his most controversial speech on the Eastern Question. See *Gladstone Diaries*, IX, 287.

[912] Richard Assheton Cross (1823–1914), Cons. MP for Preston, 1857–62, for S.W. Lancashire, 1868–86, when he was cr. 1st Viscount Cross; home sec., 1874–80; 1885–6; India sec., 1886–92; ld. privy seal, 1895–1900.

'familiar'. What Carnarvon said entirely confirms the opinion that discussion in the Cabinet has been the cause of the vacillating inconsistent policy of the Govt. throughout.

All the ignorant folly of the country is now rampant for war. It will be lucky if we avoid it. The Govt. really deserve some credit for resisting the pressure of their supporters. It is curious to observe in both Houses how any indication of a warlike spirit is cheered by the Tories, & how sullen a silence reigns on their leaders when any announcement tending to peace is made from the Treasury bench. Our best course now is to sit still & give what support we can to Derby, who weak as he is, still is the chief obstacle to Disraeli's plans.

25 February 1878.   Went over Millbank prison.[913] Observed nothing to find fault with except perhaps the ward where men suspected of being lunatics are kept under 'observation' which seemed small & crowded. Captn. Harvey, the Governor, a very intelligent pleasing man.

2 March 1878.   Visited Pentonville prison.

9 March 1878.   My aunt, Mrs. Phayre[914] died at West Raynham.

13 March 1878.   Visited the new prison building at Wormwood Scrubs: on the 16th Brixton and on the 23rd Fulham prisons.

29 March 1878.   Meeting at Granville's to consider Derby's resignation & the message as to the reserves.[915] General opinion in favour of cautious action. The fact is the opposition is powerless & the nation madly eager for war and war for what? *[Two lines heavily struck through.]* As a man said to me in a club 'I have no notion of paying 2/6 in the pound Inc: Tax & having no war for my money!'

4 April 1878.   Di Wodehouse married to C. Thornton at St Peter's Church Eaton Square.[916]

5 April 1878.   A meeting at Granville's where it was decided to move

---

[913] As part of his work, as chairman of the Royal Commission on Penal Servitude. See L. Radzinowicz and R. Hood, *The Emergence of Penal Policy in Victorian and Edwardian England* (Oxford, 1990), 433–5, 546–72: T.W. Moody, *Davitt and Irish Revolution 1846–82* (Oxford, 1981), 146–7, 211–20.

[914] Charlotte Laura Wodehouse married the Revd Richard Phayre.

[915] In cabinet on 27 March 1878 Derby resigned over the proposal to call out the Reserves. Derby announced his resignation in the Lords the following day. *DD2*, 532–3.

[916] Mary Diana, da. of rear-adm. Edward Thornton Wodehouse, m. Charles Conway Thornton.

no amendment on the Queen's message on Monday. The opinion of most people I see is that there will not be war. I am afraid they are wrong.

8 April 1878.   Great debate in our House on Message calling out reserves. Ld. Derby made a most remarkable speech. Extremely bitter against the Govt. I spoke after Lord Salisbury but it was too late to produce any effect & the newspapers reported very little of what I said.

It is believed that an expedition will shortly be sent to the East, & dissent from this measure was the cause of Ld. Derby's retirement. He would have done better for the country & his own reputation if he had resigned upon the vote of 6 millions.

17 June 1878.   Returned from a very pleasant ten days tour in the S. West. On Friday the 7th. we went to Falmouth. On Monday spent a day at the Lizard. On Tuesday to Tavistock. Wednesday visited the prison at Dartmoor. On Thursday to Weymouth. Friday to Portland prison. Saturday saw the fleet, & to Salisbury. Sunday saw Stonehenge & the Cathedral, & Monday home.

9 July 1878.   Tuesday. Jubilee celebration at Univ: Coll: speeches &c.

10 July 1878.   Wednesday. Meeting at Granville's to discuss the Treaty with Turkey.[917] Bright, Lowe, Cardwell & Selborne not there. Harcourt talked in a wild strain about the defensive Treaty with Turkey. He said he always desired the downfall of the Turk: that by this Treaty his downfall was made certain: that Asia Minor, Syria & Mesopotamia must be governed by British Residents, & the Sultan reduced to the condition of the Indian Princes: that it was no doubt a vast undertaking, but that this nation was equal to the task &c. &c. Gladstone said the Treaty was one which might have been appropriately signed by Don Quixote and a dancing Dervish in Bedlam. This is exactly what I think. Gladstone however proposed that we should evade the main issue, & move a resolution condemning the Govt. for having concluded the Treaty without consulting Parliament. No one agreed in this view. It is true that the Govt. have strained the use of the Prerogative very far in what they have done, but I do not see how we can maintain that they have actually gone beyond the power of the Crown: besides we recently raised an issue of the same kind about the India troops, and the country

[917] The Anglo-Turkish Convention of 4 June 1878 divided Bulgaria into two parts, the northern section to be autonomous, the southern section subject to Turkish rule. On 26 May, in return for a defensive alliance with Britain, Turkey agreed to the cession of Cyprus to Britain, under the terms of the Cyprus Convention.

will care for nothing but the real question, is the Treaty wise or not? Goschen spoke tho' with much more moderation than Harcourt on the Jingo side. Childers also leans that way. Hartington gave forth a very uncertain sound. The rest of the old Cabinet including those who were absent, strongly condemn the Treaty.

14 July 1878. Saturday. At a garden party at Marlbro' House I had some conversation with Musurus. He was much excited at the schemes for reducing Turkey in Asia to the condition of our Indian feudatories. He said that if the Sultan were to give his consent, he wd. be deposed & that the Turks wd. resist by force such an attempt to deprive them of their power. 'We would rather,' he added,' throw ourselves into the arms of Russia.' This is just what I expect. If we try to make the 2nd article of the Treaty a reality we shall have to use force. Of course nothing of the kind will be done, & the 2nd article will turn out to be a sham, more philanthropic buncombe for home consumption. Whenever, perhaps some ten or fifteen years hence, Russia is ready for a fresh move, it will be easy for her to find a pretext in the disorderly state of Armenia, the depredations of the Kurds, oppression of Xtians & c. We shall be appealed to by the Sultan to defend him. We shall reply that as Turkey has failed to fulfil her part of the engagement viz Article 2, we are absolved from the engagement of article I. The Russians will take the rest of Armenia, & we shall perhaps take Mitylene as a further security for our 'Oriental' interests.

We went on July 24 to Homburg, & returned on August 27 to Kimberley. We dined one day at the Schloss with the Crown Prince & Princess of Germany. The Princess has grown wonderfully like her mother the Queen. She talked of the unreasonable panic in Germany about Socialism. It is well known that there is no love lost between her & Bismarck. The Prince & Princess lived in a quiet homely manner, but I was told that since the attempts on the Emperor's life they are really surrounded by secret police. I had curious proofs that freedom of speech does not exist in Germany; Germans are afraid to say anything against Bismarck wh. may be overheard by the police. As a lady said to me, you may find yourself before you can look round, hurried off to prison. It put me in mind of Russia. There seems to be much discontent at Bismarck's internal administration, but all, even his enemies, acknowledge that as Foreign Minister he is indispensable.

We met here the Countess Usedom (née Miss Malcolm)[918] whom I had not seen since we were at Rome after our marriage in 1847. Her husband, the former Minister at Rome, was not with her. A clever but most fatiguing noisy woman. Her daughter the Countess Hildegarde is

[918] Wife of Count von Usedom, of an old Pomeranian family.

a strapping handsome girl, who would have done for a wife to one of
the Elector's grenadiers. Homburg swarmed with English: who behaved
with their usual vulgarity. They mobbed the Prince & Princess at the
Springs, so that they were obliged to hide themselves in the by walks &
have their glasses of water brought to them. An old peasant whom I
talked to one day, said he heard that the Princess was a 'brave frau'
'gar nicht stolz' like the old English Landgravine Elizabeth.

5 December 1878.   Thursday. Parliament suddenly called together for
the Afghan war.[919] I went up on Monday for two sittings of the Penal
Servitude Commission, & staid till Friday.

9 December 1878.   Monday. Went up again for the debate on the war,
wh. was very dull, and returned Wednesday. We did not divide till near
three o'clock. I was not at all surprised at our small minority. If we
had divided at any time during the last five years upon any question
of foreign policy, the result would have been the same or worse. Disraeli
wound up the debate in a jocular rollicking speech. I thought at first
he was drunk. But he was quite in the vein to suit his audience which
is no compliment to them. In point of fact the peers on our side are
almost as 'Jingo' as the Tories: indeed some of the most furious Jingoes
'sit' with us.

I attended a meeting last week on Tuesday at Granville's. We were
all quite agreed to divide against the Govt. The only doubt was whether
there should be a resolution or an amendment to the address. The
decision against the latter was virtually taken on the Monday before
when I could not be present. It was a mistake. The real reason I was
told was that Hartington had not had time to read the papers for the
address.[920]

The division in the Commons was an improvement on the divisions
last session & rather better than we expected. It is from many signs
that the position of the Govt. is somewhat weakened. This war is far
from popular & the distress in the iron, coal, & cotton districts, tho' I
suspect exaggerated, is beginning to tell.

12 February 1879.   Went to town for the meeting of Parliament on the
13th.

[919] In November 1878 the Second Afghan war broke out, in large part because of the
unauthorised initiatives of the Indian Viceroy, Lord Lytton, who precipitated the war
against Afghanistan to remove Russian influence in the region.
[920] Hartington was initially cautious about attacking the government over the war in
Afghanistan. Gladstone and many radicals, meanwhile, fiercely denounced government
policy. A split, similar to that over the Bulgarian question, threatened. This was averted
when in the Commons debate Hartington attacked the government with far greater force
than anticipated. See Jenkins, *Gladstone, Whiggery and the Liberal Party*, 82.

15 March 1879. Hear that it is perfectly true that the Queen refused to ask Gladstone to the D. of Connaught's wedding, altho' the Duke himself pressed her to do so. How very foolish.

1 May 1879. We have had several meetings of the usual kind this year to discuss opposition tactics. Nothing particular took place at any of them except that the alteration of the motion about the Zulu War by adding an opinion that Frere should be recalled was made at the instance of Wm. Harcourt.[921] Granville was against the change but Hartington stepped in & supported Harcourt with more of the air of a leader than I ever saw him show before.[922] The result showed that the two Hs were right. We had an excellent division in the H. of Commons. As to the Lords, we are permanently in the position of not being able to count on (at most) more than 100 votes. A large part of those who sit behind us are as 'Jingo' as the Tories. The debate in our House was not very effective.

16 May 1879. Friday. The Duke of Argyll made a most eloquent oration of two hours on the Eastern Questn. generally. He made a mistake however in bringing in the Afghan question. Lord Beaconsfield rather weak, evidently put out at the thinning of the House for dinner. I followed as a buffer between Lord B. & Salisbury, a disagreeable duty wh. I got thro' tolerably in an empty house. I did what was wanted namely to enable Granville to keep himself in reserve for Salisbury.

20 May 1879. Tuesday. Meeting at Devonshire House[923] to discuss the O'Conor Don's University Bill.[924] Every one for caution except W. Harcourt who fancies he sees a golden opportunity for catching Irish votes, forgetting that for every Irish vote we gain we may lose two English votes. We decided to wait to see what the Govt. will do. It would be folly to commit ourselves before we know the opinions of the

[921] On circumstances surrounding the recall of Frere, see C.W. DeKiewiet, *The Imperial Factor in South Africa: A Study in Politics and Economics* (London, 1965), 246–53; D.M. Schreuder, *Gladstone and Kruger: Liberal Government and Colonial 'Home Rule', 1880–85* (London, 1969), 60–72. See entry for 2 Aug. 1880, below.

[922] As noted by T.A. Jenkins, by January 1879 Hartington's stock as leader, particularly after the Afghan debate the previous month, was rising. Chamberlain was courting Hartington, and Harcourt had emerged as the main mediator between the Whigs and radicals. See Jenkins, *Gladstone, Whiggery and the Liberal Party*, 97–8.

[923] During the 1879 session, as a further sign of his growing assertiveness as Liberal leader, Hartington began to open up Devonshire House for social and political gatherings. Granville's residence in Carlton House Terrace was damaged by fire in March 1879.

[924] The Irish University Education bill, introduced by O'Conor Don (Lib. MP for Roscommon, 1860–80), proposed the establishment of a new National University for Ireland. 3 *Hansard* 246 (15 May 1879), 475–92. The bill was withdrawn on 23 July.

Irish R.C. Bishops, & the course of the Govt. Gladstone was there, and seemed still sore about the question & disinclined to commit himself.

[Undated annotation:] A subsequent meeting had much the same result.

27 May 1879.   Tuesday. Announcement that Frere & Chelmsford[925] are superseded in Natal & Transvaal. Better late than never!

27 June 1879.   Friday. Meeting at Hartington's about Chaplin's motion as to agricultural distress.[926] Agreed that Hartington should move an amendment drawn up by Dodson specifying entails, tenancy, game, distress, and local taxes as subjects of inquiry.

30 June 1879.   Monday. Another meeting on same subject. Our county M.P.s who have been sounded, have taken fright. They think if Hartn. moves the proposed amendt., it will be taken as a manifesto for the elections & terrify the country gentlemen. We determined to get it moved by some quite independent M.P.

1 July 1879.   Tuesday. Last meeting of Penal Servitude commission.[927]

4 July 1879.   Friday. Meeting at Devonshire House about Univy. Ireland Bill. Granville proposed to move a resolution that money should be given from Church Surplus. I & others opposed & it was given up. Arranged that we should only sharply criticize & move nothing, Carlingford to open the ball.

5 July 1879.   Saturday. Sudden death of Lady Waldegrave.

8 July 1879.   I had to open the Univy. debate instead of Carlingford. Marvellous stuff is written in the newspapers about Lady W. According to them she was a paragon of women, lovely, witty, accomplished, wise, good &c. &c. &c. &c. &c. &c. &c. &c. I have known her more or less intimately for more than 30 years, & can confidently say she never was lovely since I knew her. She was once rather good looking, but always coarse and had a fat ill-shaped figure. For many years she had painted her face almost scarlet. She was undoubtedly clever in her way, & could when she pleased talk readily and agreeably. It would be absurd

---

[925] Frederic Augustus Thesiger, 2nd Baron Chelmsford (1827–1905), maj.-genl., 1877, commanded troops in Kaffir and Zulu wars, 1878–9; superseded by Wolseley.

[926] Chaplin's motion called for a Royal Commission to investigate widespread agricultural distress. See 3 *Hansard* 247 (4 July 1879), 1425–1544.

[927] See report of 14 July 1879, along with minutes of evidence *Parliamentary Papers*, Crime and Punishment, Penal Servitude, 2 vols., Sess. 1878–9.

to call her witty, nor was she accomplished. She fancied she understood politics and that she exercised a great influence on statesmen who behind her back only laughed at her. She was, as might be expected from her birth, decidedly vulgar, and quite without the manners of a grande dame. She was good natured to most people, very cheerful, and took a lively interest in everything & every body, whatever might be her motive. Her success, such as it was, was due to great animal spirits, unblushing self confidence, energy, perseverance, and wealth. It would be ridiculous to call her success that of a 'leader of society'. Most of the people she gathered around her were rather below the first social rank, especially the women. She was untiring in cultivating the writers for the press who repaid her by gross flattery of both her & Lord Carlingford.

Perhaps the oddest thing in her career was the way in which she patronized the Orleans family, and latterly to some extent even our own Royal family. As to her entertainments the food & wine were always bad, and I never heard of any one except her immediate clique who wished to endure a second time the weariness of a Sunday at Strawberry Hill.

22 July 1879.   Meeting at Devonshire House about Univy. Bill. Nothing important.

23 July 1879.   Harcourt who it seems was mainly consulted by Hartington as to his 'volte face' upon the 'cat' question, told me that the cause of H's sudden resolution was simply that he had to choose between going into the lobby with 40 or 50 Whigs for or 180 other Liberals against the cat.[928] This is a good reason but it is a pity he did not announce his course a week sooner.

2 August 1879.   Went to Ky. Laid up with an accident at tennis on July 16 to my leg. This night a tremendous thunderstorm, which lasted from midnight till near six o'clock. In many parts of England the storm did great harm; here not much. The rain was prodigious. At 9 o'clock the flood in the river was higher than ever before seen here either in winter

---

[928] The debate over flogging in the army had, in early July, brought on an attack on Hartington by Chamberlain for lack of vigour in the practice. The immediate effect of Chamberlain's attack, however, was to prompt Liberals to rally round Hartington. Moreover, once it became clear that the government were not prepared to accept a compromise resolution of the issue, flogging being confined to those offences otherwise punishable by death, Hartington himself moved an amendment to abolish flogging: the 'volte face' referred to by Kimberley. Again, note Harcourt's prominence as an intermediary. See Jenkins, *Gladstone, Whiggery and the Liberal Party*, 94–5.

or summer. It was over the footbridge at the garden ford. We are only just beginning to cut the park hay.

25 August 1879. One or two farmers began harvest here, by cutting barley wh. is more forward than wheat.

1 September 1879. We begin to cut our barley on the Home Farm. Wheat not ready. Still at our hay, a good deal not carried, some not cut. We have had one fortnight's fine weather: the rest, violent and incessant storms of rain. To day looks fair.

20 September 1879. Saturday. Finished harvest on the Home Farm. Some hay still uncarted in the park. I hurt my leg, playing tennis at Prince's on July 16, & was unable to walk for many weeks. Towards the end of the year I began to walk a little, but am still very lame.

17 December 1879. Went to town on account of the very serious illness of my mother.

25 December 1879. A dismal Xmas: the blackest fog in London all day, I ever saw.

1 January 1880. Mother a little better. Went back to Ky.

3 January 1880. Gerald Dillon (Fitzgibbon) died.

10 January 1880. Mother worse, returned to town.

14 January 1880. My dear Mother died after a lingering but not painful illness which she bore with great fortitude. She was in full possession of all her faculties, & conscious till nearly the last. She was in the 78th year of her age (born Sept 7.1802)

21 January 1880. My Mother's funeral. She was buried in the family vault at Kimberley Church. We had no procession from the house but met the hearse which came straight from Wymondham Station at the Church. Robert, Charles, Frank, & Evelyn Gurdon were there, & Hector Rebow. Also Maynard Currie, Lady Mary Currie, Mrs Edward Gurdon, Wodehouse, Armine, Constance, & Florence & myself. Mr. Upcher read the service. The funeral was at 3 o'clock.

4 February 1880. All went to London.

5 February 1880.   Thursday. Meeting of Parliament. Granville made an excellent speech on the Address: Beaconsfield feeble. His Grace of Argyll very violent. His violence does us harm, in spite of his eloquence.

13 February 1880.   Friday. Meeting at Granville's about Herat.[929] Decided not to have a motion. Harcourt made some foolish observations, amongst other things professing that he had no fear of an advance of the Russians beyond Merv, because Schouvalow had assured him they meant to go no further. Knowing nothing about foreign affairs, he speaks as rashly and confidently of them as if he was on a platform.

17 February 1880.   Old Miss Mellish of Hamels died at 11 Stanhope St. aged 84.[930]

8 March 1880.   Announcement of the dissolution which took every one by surprise.

10 March 1880.   Wednesday. Meeting at Devonshire House to discuss Hartington's election manifesto. The result of the discussion was that every one agreed that we had better leave it entirely to H. to draw up his address. It was not read, & as far as I know it was altogether H's own composition.[931]

20 March 1880.   Elections are now the only subject of conversation. Sober men on both sides acknowledge that the event is quite uncertain. Sanguine men prophecy each according to his wishes and party. On the whole what seems least improbable is that there will be something like a tie: that is, the Tories will be no more than half the whole House. This will have the Liberals in a miserable position. With some 70 Home Rulers the opposition, tho' nominally equal in strength to the Govt., would be really far weaker. Sanguine men on our side hope that we shall at least run the Tories to a tie in Gt. Britain. In such a case of

[929] The massacre of the British mission at Kabul by Afghans in September 1879 brought on the Third Afghan War. After a severe struggle, British forces under the command of General Roberts secured a military victory.

[930] Catherine Martha Mellish of Hammels Park. On Charles Villiers' proposal to her, see Kimberley Memoir, herein, 495.

[931] Hartington's election manifesto linked the Gladstonian moral condemnation of Conservative foreign policy with a call for a reform in local government and land tenure. During the election Hartington undertook an extensive speaking tour in Lancashire, making twenty-four major speeches, as opposed to Gladstone's fifteen speeches in Midlothian. Hartington's election manifesto and speeches were subsequently published. See Marquis of Hartington, *Election Speeches in 1879 and 1880: With Address to the Electors of North East Lancashire* (1880).

course the Govt. will be upset, but I shall believe it only when I see it. All parties however seem to be agreed in expecting that the Govt. will lose heavily in Scotland & Ireland. The spirits of the Liberal party are undoubtedly rising, & a considerable change in our favour may be reasonably expected.

Ld. Derby's defection though no surprise, is nevertheless a grave loss to the Tories,[932] & Ld. Beaconsfield's age must ere long lead to his retirement. To set against all this and other difficulties present & the many failures impending of their administration, the Govt. have only the 'Jingo' feeling, and the vague terror of Gladstone. But this feeling is still very strong, and may yet carry them through, at all events for the moment.

24 March 1880. Went to Kimberley & stayed till April 20. My prognostications of the election were utterly wrong. The constituencies have swung clear round.[933] The bad times have I believe been the primary cause of the fall of the Tories.

22 April 1880. The Queen has sent for Hartington, a foolish step. Evidently she has been advised to do this by Beaconsfield who has taken advantage of her dislike of Gladstone to endeavour to sow discord in the Liberal party.[934]

The maneuver will fail and Gladstone will be at the head of the Govt, but it is none the less mischievous. All sections of Liberals are united in desiring that Gladstone should resume the leadership, the Radicals because they hope much from him, the moderates because they think he will be far more dangerous as an independent force. Every one will regret the unmerited affront put on Granville by the Queen in not sending for him first. He would no doubt have declined in favour of Gladstone but as our chosen leader, his advice ought to have been first taken. His abdication should have been his own act.

23 April 1880. Friday. The great question is settled in the way every one wished & expected, & Gladstone is once more at the head of the Govt.

25 April 1880. Received a letter from Gladstone offering me the great post of Governor-General of India. Went to see him at Lord Granville's

[932] During 1879 Hartington and other prominent Whigs visited Knowsley preparing the ground for Derby's going over to the Liberals.
[933] 354 seats won by Liberals with the Conservatives gaining only 238 seats. Irish Home Rulers won 60 seats.
[934] See J. Morley, *The Life of William Ewart Gladstone*, (3 vols., London, 1903), II, 621–4; *Gladstone Diaries*, IX, 504–5.

house in Carlton House Terrace in the afternoon and declined.[935] In the evening received a letter from him offering me the Colonial Secretaryship which I accepted. For the moment I was almost dazzled by the splendid vision of the Indian Viceroyalty: but I was never really in doubt. The separation from home and all that is dear to me would be too great a sacrifice. My wife courageously offered to go: all honour to her for her willingness to face such an undertaking. But she does not & cannot know what the undertaking is, and I am bound in duty not to expose her to risks to which she is really unequal: and as to separation from her, I could not endure it for months, much less for years. Nor is the Viceroyalty on reflection attractive to me. As a matter of duty, if there had been no domestic sacrifices to make, I might have prevailed on myself to go: as a matter of choice I prefer employment at home.

26 April 1880.   Wednesday. Sworn in at Windsor. Queen looked tired but gracious. Mob at Windsor.

3 May 1880.   Monday. First Cabinet.

12 May 1880.   Wednesday. Went to Windsor with Flo: for a night. Queen gracious and in good spirits. Spoke to me about S. Africa & Ireland. Cowper & his wife & Childers also there.[936] Sat next to Princess Victoria of Hesse at dinner, a nice quiet very German girl, speaks English well. In billiard room talked a long time to Grand Duke of Hesse, who seems an intelligent man.

27 May 1880.   Thursday. Poor Hamilla Taylor[937] died after her confinement at Dunkirk.

28 May 1880.   Friday. My dear Aunt Henrietta died at 38 Hill Street.[938] What a sad year for us!

9 July 1880.   I have been too busy to make any entry. Ld. Lansdowne's resignation announced this morning is an ugly shake to the government.

[935] Kimberley's refusal of the governor-generalship left Gladstone 'rather stunned'. Gladstone to Kimberley, 25 April 1880 in *Gladstone Diaries*, IX, 509. Cf. Kimberley's attitude when first considered for the Viceroyalty of India, entry for 31 Dec. 1863.

[936] Lord Cowper had been appointed Lord Lieutenant of Ireland, and Childers Secretary of State for War.

[937] Hamilla Wodehouse, da. of Kimberley's uncle Alfred Wodehouse, on 8 Nov. 1876 had m. Edward Taylor, British vice-consul at Dunkirk.

[938] Wife of Brampton Gurdon.

He has been preparing to go ever since the introduction of the Irish Bill.[939]

Is it the first step in a schism between the Whigs & Radicals? It looks like it. The storm which raged so furiously for some weeks about Sir B. Frere's recall has somewhat abated. The H. of Commons has been too much occupied with other things. We get on badly in Parliament. The symptoms point to a break up at an early date of both Govt. and Parliament. The fact is members were very ready to promise Liberal measures on the hustings but when it comes to the redemption of their promises their Liberal principles prove to be only skin deep. The detestable Bradlaugh affair spoiled our short session utterly.[940]

18 July 1880. Still hammering at the Irish bill.[941] The bill is in my judgment right in itself, but the case for it is imperfect. If Forster had more nerve he would have waited to see what happened in the autumn. Nothing very serious was likely to happen, tho' some riots & perhaps bloodshed might have been expected. But in Ireland you never have anything but a choice of evils. I would have faced the chance of disturbances and let the case make itself clear. Parliament always requires very strong facts before it will do anything reasonable in Irish affairs. As it is, if the bill fails in the H. of Lords, what shall we have gained? I am very sorry for Dodson who was unseated on petition at Chester yesterday. He has been unlucky all through with his elections. He paid, some £25,000 for Sussex elections & after all could not hold the seat, because a foolish attempt was made to bring in two Liberals.

2, 3 August 1880. Debate on 'Irish Disturbance Bill' in Lords, 2nd reading. Enormous majority against us. I made rather a dull speech at close of first night. Cairns intolerably prolix: Argyll brilliant: Beaconsfield rather senile. Lansdowne made an excellent speech against us: Derby a speech so nicely turned that a hair would have turned the balance: Salisbury a speech of characteristic incisiveness full of bitterness against Derby. The long & short of the matter is that Forster was prematurely alarmed. He had not strong enough facts to prove his case. No doubt in theory prevention is better than cure, but the average

[939] Lansdowne resigned as under secretary at the India Office in protest to the Irish Disturbance Compensation bill, which penalised Irish landlords for evicting tenants, even for non-payment of rent. The bill subsequently passed through the Commons, but was overwhelmingly rejected by the Lords.

[940] Charles Bradlaugh (1833–91), an avowed atheist, was elected MP for Northampton and refused to take the parliamentary oath. He subsequently agreed, but publicly declared the oath to be meaningless. A parliamentary uproar followed and Bradlaugh was not allowed to take his seat. He was later allowed to sit for Northampton, 1886–91.

[941] The Irish Disturbance Compensation bill.

Englishman has not imagination enough to perceive coming evils, and it is almost always necessary that some disaster should happen before he will consent to any strong measures. In the Fenian troubles of 1865–6 I was able to avoid actual disaster but I went to the brink of it, & only the incredible folly of the conspirators in leaving on paper ample proofs of the conspiracy & the luck of seizing those proofs saved us from the charge of undue alarm and precipitation after all. Forster will grow less sensitive after a longer experience of Irish affairs. We are going the usual weary round and in due time shall have to recur to the old coercive policy.

On Monday Aug: 2 I announced Frere's recall. I am well satisfied with the course of this affair. We have allowed the Confederation policy time to be fairly brought before the Cape Parliament under Frere's Governorship, & whatever chance there was of its success cannot be said to have been marred by us, and we have managed, though with difficulty, to stave off the Radical attack until the question was fairly decided at the Cape. Frere committed a monstrous error in not resigning at once, as Lytton did, on the change of Government.[942]

12 August 1880.   Thursday. Went to Osborne. The Queen had nothing particular to say to me. She behaved well at the last about the recall of Frere whom she greatly patronised & admired. Came back on Friday.

14 August 1880.   Saturday. To Minley till Monday. Found my old uncle uncommonly well.

5 September 1880.   At length ends this most wearisome session. We have carried our bills with but little damage to them after all by the Lords, except the unlucky Irish Disturbance Bill which never ought to have been proposed. Nor would such a blunder have been made, if Forster had a little more nerve. Unfortunately though an excellent honest & able man, is full of sentiment, a quality of which the less an Irish Secretary has, the better. He has been terribly tormented by the wild Irish M.Ps and latterly has quite lost his head, witness his foolish onslaught on the H. of Lords. However on the whole we end well, and may go on well, if we do not shipwreck on Irish affairs.

Gladstone came back yesterday looking much better but not his former self. Meantime Hartington has led admirably & risen immensely

---

[942] See entry for 1 May 1879.

in general estimation. The passage of the Ground Game Bill[943] thro'
the Lords was rather amusing. The Tories were like hungry wolves
eager to tear the bill to pieces. They were with difficulty kept back by
Beaconsfield who made an admirable speech in his half jocular, half
solemn & oracular style.

8 September 1880.   Went down at last to Kimberley, this weary session
having at length come to an end. We had however no alternative but
to go hammering on. If we had given up on account of Gladstone's
illness, we should have lost all authority & have been justly looked on
as mere clerks to Gladstone. *[Two lines relating to Hartington heavily struck
through.]* After all the Burials Act, Employers' Liability Act, & Game
Act are very fair achievements for a broken session.

30 September 1880.   A sudden Cabinet. Foreign affairs. Surely the weary
have no rest.

8 November 1880.   All went to London for the November cabinets &
stayed three weeks. All these three weeks the air has been full of
rumours that the Cabinet was on the point of breaking up about
Ireland. We had our differences, but they were much exaggerated. The
Irish difficulty seems hopeless. Turbulence and disrespect of law have
been bred in them for generations till they have become part of the
Irish nature. Our philanthropists cannot see that no remedial measures
can for generations produce a change in the character of men, any
more than you can by good feeding suddenly change the character of
a sheep or an ox. That is no reason for not taking measures to improve
the breed, but it is a reason for unlimited patience. Coercion by itself
is of little use.

4 December 1880.   To Windsor for a night. The Queen very cheery &
gracious.

13 December 1880.   To London for a Cabinet.

29 December 1880.   All went to town.

6 January 1881.   Parliament opened, nothing very notable in debate on

---

[943] The Ground Game Bill allowed concurrent hunting privileges for owners and
occupiers in order to prevent destruction of crops. Also, see Kimberley to Ripon, 4 Oct.
1880, in *Liberal by Principle*, 150–1.

Address in our house. My own troubles greatly increased by the outbreak in the Transvaal.[944]

16 January 1881. House of Commons still debating address. Obstruction is rampant. But we must have patience. The country & the House must be worked up to a white heat before we can interfere to any purpose.

18 January 1881. Extraordinary snow storm and very severe frost. London quite blocked up.

28 January 1881. Received news of Sir G. Colley's repulse by Boers.[945] An unfortunate event, but ups & downs in war must be expected. Of course there will be the usual unmanly Shriekings in our newspapers.

The Tories who had been rather disposed to support us in proposing the cloture have now drawn back.[946] So I suppose our great talking machine must go grinding at wind until it has made itself thoroughly ridiculous. The country as yet shows but little signs of impatience.

2 February 1881. Wednesday. Dinner at Westminster Palace Hotel of Chambers of Commerce. 'Cherry' Monk in the chair.[947] I had to return thanks for HM's ministers as Hartington did not come which after the 41 hours sitting of the House of Commons was excusable enough. The audience was very enthusiastic when I spoke of the necessity of putting an end to the scandalous scenes in the H. of Commons. The Speaker's *coup d'etat* took place at 9 o'clock this morning.[948]

3 February 1881. Thursday. The great Irish Shindy in the H. of Commons. We may truly say 'The Lord delivered them into our hands.'[949]

[944] Following Gladstone's return to power the Boers had expected the annexation of 1877 to be reversed, as Gladstone had indicated in his election speeches. When this did not occur the Boers, led by the formidable President Kruger, rebelled and in December 1880 inflicted a quick defeat on the Connaught Rangers. For full details on British policy surrounding the war and its settlement, see Schreuder, *Gladstone and Kruger*, 60–224.

[945] Maj.-genl. George Pomeroy Colley (1835–81); gov. of Natal, 1880; repulsed at Laing's Nek on 23 Jan. 1881; defeated and killed at Majuba Hill, 27 Feb. 1881.

[946] The proposal enabling the Speaker, after a minister declaring that the business was urgent, to call an immediate division without amendment or adjournment.

[947] Charles James Monk (1824–1905) Lib. M.P for Gloucester, 1859, 1865–85; then Lib. U., 1895–1900; pres. Associated Chambers of Commerce, 1881–4.

[948] The Speaker, on his own authority, intervened in Common debate to prevent further Irish obstruction on the Protection of Life and Property (Ireland) bill.

[949] A recurring Old Testament theme.

21 February 1881.   Monday. Long speech by Brabourne on Transvaal in H. of Lords, with his usual meanness carping at Gladstone &c.

22 February 1881.   Tuesday. Killigrew Wodehouse[950] married at St Augustin's Church Queen's Gate to Miss Katherine Wood.

7 March 1881.   Monday. To Windsor where dined & slept. The Queen in excellent spirits. As usual a very bad dinner.

12 March 1881.   Saturday. In the thick of the Transvaal difficulty – an enormous mess. At a Conference at the War Off: today H.R.H. and the other soldiers crying out for blood to salve the wounded honour of the army. Gladstone told rather a good story of the D. of Wellington *a propos* of the 'point of honour'. The Duke said: 'the Spaniards were always talking of the "punta d'onor." I said that is all nonsense. The point of honour is to do your duty.' The Queen stirred up by Pc. Leopold and her other sons is immensely warlike. Between the clamouring for peace at any price, and war at all hazards, my position is, to say the least, uncomfortable.

I feel the truth of Lord Sherbrook's pen. Some one saying I must be 'bo(e)red'. He replied let him take care he does not get 'overbo(a)rd'.

12 March 1881.   Saturday. We came to a determination as to the terms to be offered to the Boers which much relieves my anxiety.[951] If we remain firm on the present basis, we shall be able to justify our course to the country.

13 March 1881.   The horrible murder of the Emperor of Russia.[952]

22 March 1881.   Heard news of settlement of terms with the Transvaal Boers.

31 March 1881.   Lord Cairns made a vigorous and brilliant speech against us in the H. of Lords on our Transvaal policy. He spoke for three hours and the only fault in his speech was that it was too long, & that his minute analysis of the telegram[953] was rather pettifogging than

---

[950] Second son of Kimberley's uncle, Major Berkeley Wodehouse.

[951] In February 1881 the Boers had inflicted a small but humiliating defeat on British forces at Majuba Hill. Gladstone pressed upon the cabinet the terms of what would become the Convention of Pretoria, an armistice leading to the granting of independence to the Boers under the suzerainty of the British crown.

[952] Aleksandr II.

[953] The telegram was from Sir George Strahan to Kimberley regarding peace negotiations in the Transvaal.

statesmanlike. I did my best in reply, speaking for an hour and a quarter, but I had undoubtedly the worst of it.

8 April 1881.   Argyll's resignation is a great calamity especially to us in the Lords, where in rhetorical power we are distinctly overmatched. I fully expected it as he had been long saying that he could not be responsible for the Land Bill.[954]

19 April 1881.   Lord Beaconsfield died. It is almost impossible for a strong political opponent to fairly estimate his character. My honest belief is that whilst his personal success was brilliant, his career was most injurious to this country. His malignant assaults upon Peel, his advocacy of Protection, his Reform Bill, and his foreign policy whilst First Minister were the most conspicuous acts of his public life. Which of them constitutes his title to credit, or foresight as a statesman? Protection is dead long ago, the Reform Bill has made the artisans masters of our destinies, in direct opposition to every principle of the Conservative party which he led: and his foreign policy has failed on every point. His admirers say he raised England again to a position of influence in Europe. Where are the proofs? Cyprus, the Anglo-Turkish convention may answer. What he really did was to pander to the base passions of Chauvinism under the guise of patriotism, and to make no solid provision for maintaining the position he so loudly claimed for this country. Mere talk and flourishes of oratory and paper Conventions, which cannot be observed, will never make a country respected or powerful tho' they may tickle for the moment the ears of the mob.

28 April 1881.   My poor old uncle Brampton Gurdon died at 38 Hill Street in his 84th year. He had been quite childish for the last two years.

4 to 10 June 1881.   Made a most pleasant trip to Falmouth. Alice & Hussey went with us.

5 July 1881.   An intensely hot day. Followed by a a violent thunderstorm.

6 July 1881.   Went to dinner at Freemason's Tavern given by Middlesex Liberal Association.

---

[954] On 5 April 1881 Argyll resigned from the cabinet over the terms of the Irish Land bill, which granted Irish tenants the '3 Fs', fair rent, free sale of leases and fixity of tenure.

15 July 1881.   Another prodigiously hot day – 98 in the shade!

16 July 1881.   To a Lord Mayor's dinner, a gathering of colonists. An assembly interesting & curious. I sat next the King of the Sandwich islands, a quiet well mannered man, speaking excellent English. I had to speak & made as in duty bound a 'Spread Eagle' oration.

The Irish land bill drags on with much abuse of Forster & outpouring of vulgar personalities by Parnell & Co.[955] Is it surprising that the universal feeling of Englishmen is if they tell the truth one of profound contempt and loathing for this scum. It is comforting that some Irish members e.g. Shaw[956] have shown this session good sense and moderation. But the 'irreconcilable' faction has the sympathy of the Irish masses whom they represent only too faithfully in all their worst qualities.

1 August 1881.   Land Bill second reading. I was very ill with a feverish attack on Sunday & could scarcely travel to the House to day where I only stayed till dinner-time.

2 August 1881.   Ld. Granville being laid up with gout, I had to act as deputy leader: & wind up the debate, a very unsatisfactory proceeding in a tired House at 1 o'clock at night.

4, 5 August 1881.   Committee on Land Bill. We got much knocked about. Carlingford was feeble and inaudible. The Chancellor on whom age is telling, generally inaudible.[957] Also: and as to myself tho' I can make myself heard, I could not be of much use, as I have no authority in the House, and people there or elsewhere care very little for what I say. However we fought on and muddled through the Bill somehow. Fortunately (to my surprise I must confess) the House was very good-humoured.

The signing of the Transvaal Convention[958] will I hope bring me some rest, which I sorely need.

6 August 1881.   Lord Mayor's dinner to Ministers to wh. I went. The usual heat, bad food, and eloquent speeches.

[955] By mid-July Commons debate on the Irish Land bill had reached Committee stage. Gladstone informed Granville on 15 July 1881: 'we came to blows, so to speak, with the Irish last night, and I made (with advice) a most violent speech which followed up one of Bright's'. *Gladstone-Granville Corresp. 2*, II, 284.
[956] William Shaw (1823–95), Home Rule MP for Co. Cork, 1874–85.
[957] Lord Selborne was then sixty-nine.
[958] Convention of Pretoria. See n. 951 above.

16 August 1881.   Final stage of Irish Land Bill. Its end was peace. I think Lord Salisbury is not open to much criticism for his conduct except on the night when the answer of the Commons to the Lords' Amendments was considered. On that night he was rash in his proceedings & what was much worse insolent in tone & manner. He ran a dangerous and unnecessary risk of provoking a serious collision between the Houses which was only averted by the admirable skill and calmness of Gladstone.

So practically ends the Session as far as the Lords are concerned. We have had singularly few debates. In fact there have been no discussions of any interest except on the Land Bill and the Transvaal. Foreign affairs have been almost a blank.

27 August 1881.   Prorogation: we went to Kimberley. Found harvest much further advanced than in the South not nearly so much rain having fallen here.

28 September 1881.   Heard the sad news of Airlie's death at Denver, Colorado U.S. – Poor fellow he was one of my oldest and best friends. We had been very intimate ever since we were at Christ Church together. A more honourable, warm hearted excellent fellow never lived. He was by no means the hidden genius which some of the obituary newspaper notices make him, but there was good stuff in him & more than appeared on the outside.

10 October 1881.   We went to Prestwold and on the 11th I went to London to attend the Cabinet on the 12th where we settled Parnell's arrest,[959] & the refusal of the Boer demands without any of the dissension on either point between Whigs & Radicals which the newspapers imagine. As to Ireland I fear the effect of the coup will be spoiled by Forster's want of vigour. He should have not only arrested Parnell but all the leading agitators great & small in Dublin and the provinces as nearly as possible, simultaneously. Instead of this he will potter over it, arresting here a man, & there a man & wholly fail in producing the effect on Irish imagination of fear which alone can have the result of paralysing the League. Pottering and hesitating will bring inevitably failure & ultimately in all probability serious bloodshed.

Cowper seems to be a perfect cypher.[960]

[Undated annotation:] Note: Forster showed far more vigour than I or any one gave him credit for.

---

[959] Parnell and two other Irish MPs, Dillon and O'Kelly, were arrested and imprisoned in Kilmainham Gaol for breaches of the new Irish coercion legislation.

[960] Lord Cowper was lord lieutenant of Ireland until May 1882.

14 October 1881.   Friday. A violent gale which has done great damage to trees everywhere. At Kimberley we have suffered severely.

15 October 1881.   Saturday. Back to Kimberley.

16 October 1881.   My dear Uncle Raikes Currie died at Minley after a short illness. From my childhood I received constant kindness from him which I can never forget. Indeed he was almost a father to me. His prosperous & happy life ended by a peaceful death in a ripe old age.

7 November 1881.   Went all of us to London. Only one Cabinet (on the 10th).[961] Afterwards attended several meetings of a Committee of Cabinet consisting of Dodson, Harcourt, Childers, Spencer, Chamberlain & myself to prepare a Local Govt. Bill and on the 19th returned to Kimberley.

4 December 1881.   Ever since my return I have been in hot water about Mr Sendall's appt. to Natal.[962] He was recommended by Sir H. Robinson and Herbert & I thought I had pitched on the very man. The event proved that I was wrong. This is the first appointment of mine which has ever been questioned.

11 January 1882.   Went up to town for good.

20 January 1882.   Armine broke out with measles, a sharp attack.

2 February 1882.   Cabinet dinner at Gladstone's. Basuto questions principal subject of discussion.[963] Our Cabinets have been mostly occupied with H. of C. procedure, once with county local Govt. bill, and several times Egypt. Very little happily about Ireland.

[961] See *Gladstone Diaries*, X, 159–60, for Gladstone's note of cabinet meeting, 10 November 1881. The intention to legislate on local government in Ireland and Scotland, followed by a plan for London, was leaked to the press. Gladstone failed to find the source of the leak.

[962] Walter Joseph Sendall (1832–1904) sec. to local gt. bd., 1878–82; gov. Windward Islands, 1882–5, after failing to take up appt. as gov. at Natal; gov. Barbados, 1885–9; high com. for Cyprus, 1892–8; gov. of British Guiana, 1898–1901.

[963] Following the Gun War of 1880–1 between the Basutos and the Cape Colony, Britain reluctantly agreed to resume responsibility for governing Basutoland, leading to repeated conflicts with both the Cape Colony and the Transvaal.

7 February 1882.   Parliament met. Dull discussion on address in H. of L.

11 February 1882.   We are likely to be hard run on the 'closure' Resolution.[964] No thoughts of giving way. We shall fight it out. Ridiculous statements in the 'Times' about the Cabinet not having considered the Resolution. We have in fact done scarcely anything else since the first cabinet in January. Also a great deal of nonsense about Gladstone's 'dictating' –

3 April 1882.   Went to Kimberley & stayed till 18th. Very fine spring. The week before I forget the day (Wednesday I think) to a dinner at Willis' Rooms in honour of Sir H. Irving outgoing Govr. of B. Guiana.[965]

20 April 1882.   Cabinet. Gladstone had a cold, looked worn & dispirited. A very disappointing budget explained. There is no scope for large financial changes of any kind. The fact is till we have an abundant harvest, trade will remain slack and the revenue languid.

22 April 1882.   Cabinet. Ireland. Some of our colleagues in the old Fool's paradise of soothing, conciliation &c. &c. &c. as a remedy for the woes of Ireland, superseding the necessity for the hateful coercion. Why can't they see that both are necessary? *Rumours that the Irish irreconcilables wish to come to terms with the Government. If they were not (most of them) men who cannot be trusted, this might be good news. At all events it looks as if they felt the game was going against them.

[Undated annotation:] *These rumours came true.[966]

27 April 1882.   Flo. & I went to the marriage of Prince Leopold at Windsor: a pretty, interesting sight. In the evening I went to the banquet (166 persons) in St George's Hall. Fancy the 'Daily Telegraph' taking Lord Sydney[967] for John Brown, and announcing that J. B. proposed the toasts at the banquet!

[964] Formalising procedure for use of the 'clôture' in closing Commons debate. See report of 9 Jan. 1882 cabinet in *Gladstone Diaries*, X, 191.

[965] Sir Henry Irving (1833–1923).

[966] In late April, through Joseph Chamberlain and the Irish MP Capt. O'Shea, Gladstone established indirect communication with Parnell. This quickly led to the understanding called the 'Kilmainham Treaty' by which Parnell was released in return for encouraging constitutional behaviour in Ireland. The decision to release Parnell was made public on 2 May 1882. See H.C.G. Matthew, *Gladstone, 1875–1898* (Oxford, 1995), 202.

[967] John Townshend, 3rd Viscount Sydney (1805–90), cr. Earl Sydney, 1874.

28 April 1882.   Friday. Dinner at Willis' Rooms in honour of Sir Henry Parkes,[968] 'Premier' of New S. Wales. Sir H. P. who is a vulgar and excessively vain man, who murders his h's in the most excruciating manner, made a bumptious speech full of his own importance & achievements, and boasted that the colonies had nothing to learn from the old country. This was too much for the audience who applauded vociferously some observations of mine, gently protesting on behalf of our 'used up' old country against this 'tall' talk.

Sir H. P. gravely assured me that his work as a Minister in N. S. wales (750,000 pop:) is as much as that of an English Minister (35,000,000 pop)!

1, 2 May 1882.   Tuesday & Wednesday. Important Cabinets. Forster resigned at the second, & the Chancellor with difficulty persuaded to stay.[969] The rumours about my possible resignation pure invention.

3 May 1882.   Wednesday. To Hertford (dinner of Liberal association). My speech very well received.

6 May 1882.   Saturday. We dined with Austrian Ambassador. After dinner when we rose to leave the dining room, Harcourt took me aside & showed me the telegrams announcing the horrible assassination at Dublin of Lord F. Cavendish & Mr. Burke.[970] We agreed not to tell Gladstone who was dining there, or any one else: and H. went off at once to tell Hartington who was dining at the Admiralty.[971]

7 May 1882.   Sunday. Cabinet. Monday do. – We resolved to bring in at once the measure for Repression of crime &c. which has been for some time preparing. The usual difficulties in bringing the Chief to the point. However by Wednesday they were all overcome, & on Thursday Harcourt brought in the bill.

Harcourt who has been all on the 'conciliation' tack, now breathes nothing but 'blood & thunder' against secret societies &c. &c. Lamentably ignorant of Irish affairs & history, he imagines that by some

---

[968] Sir Henry Parkes (1815–96), free trader and col. sec. of New South Wales.

[969] For Gladstone's report of the cabinet of 2 May see *Gladstone Diaries*, X, 248–9. Forster, as chief secretary for Ireland, objected to the release of Parnell, Dillon and O'Kelly. Cowper, after objecting, signed the order for releasing the three Irish MPs and was persuaded not to resign.

[970] Lord Frederick Cavendish (1836–82), within hours of arriving in Dublin as Forster's successor as chief secretary of Ireland, was murdered, along with T.H. Burke (1829–82), the permanent under secretary. Cavendish was Lord Hartington's younger brother and Gladstone's former private secretary.

[971] Harcourt first went to Edward Hamilton, asking him to 'break the news' to Gladstone upon his return. *EHJI* 1, 265.

conclusive effort secret societies can be 'rooted out'. As if you could suddenly change the nature of Irishmen, who have for the last century or more been working their dark conspiracies of assassins. Stern repression is the right course, but it is hopeless to expect suddenly to extirpate practices wh. are engrained in the habits and character of the population. Another melancholy delusion is that we can rely on the good feeling of the Irish to assist us in discovering the assassins. Fear in some, sympathy in others will prevent any active cooperation with the police. A still more dangerous mistake will be to give in to the cry against the Irish police. This is an old device of the anti-English agitators.[972]

13 May 1882. Courtney[973] appointed to be Secy. to Treasury. I am very sorry to lose him. He is an admirable worker. E. Ashley succeeds him: a good choice I think.

16 May 1882. Algernon Wodehouse died (son of my gt. uncle William Wodehouse).

31 May 1882. Wednesday. Cabinet suddenly summoned for Egypt. My Cetywayo telegram to Sir H. Bulwer approved.[974] Gladstone proposes to give up Ch. of Exch: to be filled by Childers if Goschen will take War Office. Goschen however declined to join us. The County franchise I conclude the obstacle.[975]

27 June 1882. The Egyptian mess occupies all our attention.[976] We have had much discussion and there is a good deal of difference of opinion between those who are for decided measures and those who are for 'Micawber'. I belong to the former section.

Whether we shall prevail remains to be seen.

29 June 1882. Thursday. To a Council at Windsor. Had audience of

---

[972] Contrast his letter to Spencer one week later, in which he refrains from mentioning Harcourt's about face. *Liberal by Principle*, 157–8.

[973] Leonard Henry Courtney (1832–1918), Lib. MP for Liskeard, 1876–85; Unionist MP for Bodmin, Cornwall, 1885–1900; u.-sec. of the Colonial Office, 1881–2. Kimberley's compliments came despite their differences of opinion. See *Liberal by Principle*, 151–2.

[974] See Gladstone to Kimberley, 27 May 1882, in *Gladstone Diaries*, X, 259.

[975] For Gladstone's offer of the War Secretaryship which was refused by Goschen see Gladstone to Goschen, 1 June 1882, in *Gladstone Diaries*, X, 271–2.

[976] Egyptian u. sec. for war, col. Ahmed Arabi, having led a successful military revolt in September 1881 against Anglo-French financial control and the pliant Khedive prompting June riots in Alexandria which led to the deaths of some fifty Europeans.

HMy. who talked of Ireland, Egypt and Cetywayo.[977] She seemed in good spirits and humour.

1 July 1882.   Saturday. Cobden dinner at Willis' Room, a hot & wearisome function. The H. of C. engaged in a violent contest with Parnell and Co.[978] Cabinet at Gladstone's room at H. of C. The MPs very weary and angry. No wonder. Meanwhile Egyptian affairs need careful consideration by the Cabinet, & no time to discuss them properly!

8 July 1882.   Saturday. Govt. beaten last night on search for arms clause.[979] Served us right. Gladstone talks in a really wonderful way about Ireland & Egypt. He has 'submitted' to the Prevention of Crime Bill in deference to Spencer & others!, and he will not hear of any warlike preparations having been authorised for a possible expedition to Egypt!!

(vide newspapers passim as to said preparations)

12 July 1882.   Bombardment of Alexandria.[980]

15 July 1882.   Flo. & I went to Windsor for a night. Bright resigned.

25 July 1882.   To Osborne. Received the seals of the Chancellorship of the Duchy of Lancaster which I am to hold provisionally without salary, till it is convenient to Gladstone to fill up Bright's place in the Cabinet. Childers was to have taken it, but it was found that it wd. vacate his seat. What a piece of constitutional pedantry! Bright seemed out of spirits, & evidently is very sorry to leave us. No one can blame him however. His position as a member of a Ministry engaged in a war after his many violent peace manifestos would be intolerable. I doubt if he much condemns our policy at heart. He certainly made very little resistance to it in the various stages up to the very last. Yet he must have seen long ago that it was all along tending to war.

We had some conversation about the extension of the county

---

[977] The Zulu king, captured and deported in 1879; brought to England in 1882 'to make a useful impression on his mind', Kimberley to Gladstone, 25 Aug. 1882. GP 44227, f. 225. See Schreuder, *Gladstone and Kruger*, 294–5.

[978] On 30 June the Commons was drawn into a prolonged sitting on the Crimes bill, leading to twenty-five Irish MPs being suspended.

[979] Gladstone recorded in his journal: 'we were beaten today on the Search clause through Whig defections and Irish abstentions. A blow to me, very welcome if it displaced me; but from the nature of the case it will not.' 7 July 1882, *Gladstone Diaries*, X, 293–4.

[980] On 11 July 1882, a British fleet despatched to Alexandria bombarded the city, prompting Bright's resignation.

franchise. He thinks we could pass it without re-distribution. I do not. The Lords would throw it out.

3 August 1882.   Cetywayo arrived.

7 August 1882.   Had my first interview with him at the Col: Office.

14 August 1882.   Went with Cetywayo to Osborne. C. is neither so big nor so fat as I expected. He is not quite so tall as I am (just under 6 ft.) and not very broad shouldered: but he has legs and hind quarters like an elephant. The 'cousin' Ngongwana is rather a foolish looking man. Unkozana is the chief spokesman of the three chiefs, and a very intelligent man. Gobozana is the most European looking. He has an aquiline (large) nose, and no trace of the prognathous thick lipped negro type. His colour also is more that of mahogany than black. C. is the blackest of the party. The tint is olive. C. has a most unpleasing countenance. He looks a thoughtful, determined man, somewhat inclined to sulleness. When animated, his countenance lighted up wonderfully. A certain glare of the eye when anything was said which displeased him reminded me of a bull.

Many wives have told upon him, & he is now quite impotent. His age is about 45. He and the chiefs were dressed in European clothes in which I need not say they looked rather uncomfortable. I observed that in true negro fashion, C. had always put on his hands a pair of new kid gloves which he flourished about. His hands & feet are large and coarse. The general effect both C. & his chiefs produced on me was that they were men possessed of much shrewdness, self possessed, thoughtful men, reminding me of what I have read of the old Red Indians: a very superior type to the ordinary negro.

The interview with the Queen went off very well. C. and his three Chiefs made the Zulu salute by holding up each the right hand, & saying 'Hah! Quini!'. The Queen was extremely dignified & at the same time gracious. She said that the Zulus were a brave people; we had encountered them in war, but she would far rather see them as friends. This little speech pleased C. much. After some ordinary conversation about his voyage, his proposed visit to Windsor &c. the interview terminated having lasted about 10 minutes. The Queen and all present were standing. Nothing was said as to business. This was arranged beforehand. C., when he was told, merely observed 'I quite understand that the Queen leave the business to her Headmen' –

After the Audience C. was by the Queen's desire taken into the garden, where he saw Pce. Leopold who is ill as usual, at a window.

He & the Chiefs were greatly struck by Landseer's[981] admirable picture of a Deer drive wh. is in the room called the Council Room. 'The deer' they said 'look as if they were alive'. They recurred with expressions of pleasure again & again to this picture. Pictures have a great attraction for them. C. was delighted with his reception. Never had he been more kindly received by any one. On our way home he begged me to tell the Queen how sorry he was to see one of her sons ill. 'As she was now his Mother, he felt for all her family.'

I had some talk with Unkosana. I asked him how many wives he had? Fourteen – and children? – ten boys, ten girls! Cattle? he had lost nearly all his cattle by the war & lung disease: only five were left. C. had a tall hat for the first time: his chiefs new wide-awakes. I asked Ngongwana if he did not find a hat uncomfortable? Oh! no! he should stick to his hat when he went home. We had a special train to go down. It cost £50. C. & his chiefs eat no meat but beef of which they consume enormous quantities. One morning they actually ate (four of them) 13 lbs. of solid beef steaks for breakfast. Their ordinary meal is about 2 lbs. a piece. After the beef steaks C. had an indigestion & the doctor was sent for & administered a black dose. This was C's newspaper cold.

Lady F. Dixie[982] sent C. a fat buck: but he wd. not touch it. I asked him why. He said he had never seen such a beast before. The King, it seems, only eats two particular kinds of deer in Zululand. Besides beef they eat potatoes & a little bread. Fruit and flowers were sent them by several admirers. Fruit they care little for. Flowers, like true savages, they utterly despise.

They are very clean, take a bath every morning: & I observed have none of the usual negro odour. I am told they do no damage to their house: wh. is fortunate as it is a nice house, belonging to an artist. Their language is pleasing in sound, rather long drawn, & plaintive. They make an odd sort of moaning sound, rather, like that of wild beasts when just fed. C. can write his name in printed characters. The others can't write.

The day after the Osborne interview I saw C. & the chiefs at the Col: Off: & told him that he would on certain conditions be restored. He said very little at this interview, reserving, like a sensible man, his observations till he had digested my communication. He showed signs of pleasure when he went home, but the newspaper story that he danced with his Chiefs a wild dance of joy (what the penny a liner calls a 'break dance') is pure invention.

[981] Edwin Henry Landseer (1802–73), famous painter of animals.
[982] Lady Florence Dixie (1855–1905), da. of 7th Marquess of Queensberry; m. Sir Alexander Dixie, 1875.

I had one more interview with him. On the whole I think his visit has been satisfactory & will be productive of good. C. was of course much struck by the various sights, specially by the Zoological gardens. When he saw a big snake swallow a little snake, he broke out, & clapped one of his chiefs on the back saying that is splendid! He has a great idea of his own dignity & an extreme horror of being made a show of. We had great difficulty in protecting him from the British sight seer. It is unconscionable what fools the British public can make themselves about a 'Lion'.

C. departed on Sept 1, much to my relief.

18 August 1882. Parlt. adjourned.

19 August 1882. Saturday. Went to Kimberley. The close of the session was marked by the great Conservative fiasco about the Arrears Bill.[983] This and the Egyptian war wh. is popular, have quite set the Govt. on its legs again, notwithstanding the general failure of our Parliamentary campaign.

13 September 1882. Wednesday. Cabinet at 3 o'clock. News of the victory of Tel el Kebir[984] arrived just before the Cabinet.

24 October 1882. Tuesday. All went to town for the Session.

9 November 1882. Saw Lord Mayor's procession for the first time in my life, a most ludicrous spectacle, and to the Guildhall dinner, a dull affair.

17 November 1882. We are much disturbed & perplexed by Gladstone's very foolish promise of a Committee on the 'Kilmainham Treaty'. We were unanimously against it in the summer when he had a strange hankering after an inquiry. The Committee will satisfy no one, & will do some mischief.[985]

18 November 1882. Saturday. The parade of the troops in honour of

[983] The Arrears bill, providing public money to pay off rent arrears in Ireland and so enabling tenants to make use of the land courts created by 1881 Irish Land Act, was subjected to Lords amendments. After negotiation in early August the Arrears bill received the royal assent 18 August 1882.

[984] Where Wolseley routed Arabi's Egyptian force.

[985] With difficulty the cabinet persuaded Gladstone not to second Sir Stafford Northcote's motion for a select committee of enquiry into the Kilmainham negotiations of earlier in the year.

the Egyptian campaign. A very pretty sight. We saw it from the Admiralty windows.

20 November 1882. Some talk has been going on in the newspapers about the unending 'reconstruction' of the Ministry. I suppose the vacant places will be filled up before next session, but I have heard nothing about it yet. Lord Harrowby's death vacates another Garter. I suppose the Queen will let this one be filled up. The public is naturally much puzzled at Ld. Beaconsfield's Garter remaining still vacant. The explanation is that Gladstone recommended Ld. Derby for it long ago. The Queen refused and there the matter has stood ever since. Gladstone was excessively vexed at this refusal, & the refusal to make Sir G. Wolseley a Peer which occurred at the same time. I hear that the Queen remarked the other day to one of [sic] 'So after all Sir G. Wolseley's peerage has come of itself', alluding to her former refusal.

We are in a great 'fix' about Arabi.[986] The trial has become a farce. The wisest thing to do in my opinion is simply to exile him, dropping the trial. Baker Pasha[987] too is an embarrassment. He must be thrown over, but we ought never to have allowed the Khedive to take him up. Dufferin is our 'deus ex machina', & we must hope he may drag the coach out of the rut. The French are nasty about the dual Control, but go it must.

23 November 1882. Thursday. Laura Wodehouse married to Major Charles John Wyndham at the Church in Eaton Sqr. *A propos* of the wedding some one told me a good saying of Lord Beaconsfield – that 'on the whole a wedding was perhaps more dismal than a funeral, as at a wedding you made an acquaintance, at a funeral you got rid of one' – cynical!

2 December 1882. Saturday. To Council at Windsor. Afterwards attended as one of Commissioners to prorogue Parliament. The 'procedure' session has been a marvellous success beyond all expectation. All due to Gladstone.

4 December 1882. Meeting of Cabinet Ministers (eight) still in town. Settled to send Arabi to Ceylon. Gladstone said 'I am quite worn up' – no wonder.

[986] During the summer Sir Garnet Wolseley, with a force of 40,000 troops, had occupied Egypt and captured Arabi.
[987] Valentine Baker (1827–87), British calvary officer; entered Egyptian service as commander of police, 1882–7.

5 December 1882.   We all went to Kimberley.

11 December 1882.   To my infinite surprise I received a telegram from Gladstone saying that difficulties had arisen in 'high quarters', and asking if I should object to change to the India Office if he could settle matters on that basis. I replied of course assenting.[988] I had no wish to leave the Col: Office, but the India Office being rather superior in importance, I could have no ground for refusing. I received another telegram saying exchange was less likely. On Friday however Gladstone telegraphed to me to come up to London as it was possible I might be wanted for the Council. On the next day Saturday the 16th Dec. I accordingly went up, not knowing my fate even then. I telegraphed to have the seals of the Secy. of State sent to Paddington Station if wanted. On my arrival there I found a messenger with a box, & this told me that the exchange would take place. At the Council I received the seals of the India Office. It had been settled before we left London that Derby was to go to India, Childers the Exchequer, & Dilke (probably) to the Duchy. I do not know the precise nature of the objection to Derby as Indian Secretary, but I gathered from various sources that The Queen objected to him as wanting firmness to resist Russian designs†. The appointment of Dilke to the Duchy she objected to on the obvious ground of his opposition to the grants to the Royal children. The consequence was great difficulty in placing Dilke. A pause ensued in order to see whether Fawcett would recover. Then Chamberlain offered to resign B. of Trade & take Duchy: but HMy. would not agree to this. Finally poor Dodson was asked to become the scapegoat which he did, not as may be supposed, very joyfully.[989] The sacrifice was duly consummated at Osborne on Thursday Dec 28th, where I gave up the Duchy seals.
[Undated annotation:] †This was the reason as Gladstone told me afterwards.

22 January 1883.   Monday. Poor old Henry Hutchinson died aged over 80. A kindly excellent man.

25 January 1883.   Thursday. Went to Witton till Saturday & found Johnny & Isabel very comfortably established.

[988] Ministerial rearrangements were undertaken, in part, to bring Lord Derby into the cabinet. On 11 December 1882 Gladstone proposed appointing Derby to the India Office, but the Queen opposed the appointment. On 15 December Derby was offered, and accepted the Colonial Office, which required Kimberley's transfer, on Saturday 16 December, to the India Office.

[989] J.G. Dodson was moved from the Local Government Board to the Duchy of Lancaster, which had been held by Kimberley since July 1882.

5 February 1883.   All went to town. Gladstone uncertain as to his return, thinks of staying till Easter at Cannes – talks of resigning, all which very serious.[990]

15 February 1883.   Parliament met.

1 March 1883.   H. of Commons concluded debate on address!!

2 March 1883.   Gladstone returned to London. It is to be hoped he will not go back from the position we have taken about the Kilmainham 'Treaty' inquiry.

16 March 1883.   The dynamite explosion at the public offices.[991]
Nothing of much note in public affairs. Our chief still clinging to his plan of giving over the police to the new London municipality. The explosion will I should think blow up this plan: but the unguarded public utterances of the Chief on the subject will make it awkward for him to retreat. It is fortunate we persuaded him not to touch the Irish Land Act this year.

17 March 1883.   Dined at United Service Club at dinner to Lord Alcester.[992] Speeches short, and to the purpose. Lord A. told me it was his first speech! Lucky man. Met Baron Mohrenheim the new Russian ambassador at the drawing room. I remember him one of Gortchacow's 'devils' at the Russian F.O. in 56–58. I hear he is a bore of the first class.

22 March 1883.   Went to Ky. for Easter and came back April 3. Horribly cold most of the time.

7 April 1883.   Dined with Civil Engineers, speeches.

9 April 1883.   Long Indian debate in Lords. I got through pretty well. Harcourt came up to Lords in a state of wild excitement about explosives bill, and positively raged at the mere mention of putting off the bill to next day: so we pressed it through, but we might just as well have passed it the next day, as it was too late to get the Royal assent.

[990] See Gladstone to Granville, 22 January 1883, in *Gladstone–Granville Corresp. 2*, II, 9. On 3 February 1883 Gladstone declined the Queen's invitation to take a peerage and go up to the Lords *ibid.*, 16.
[991] On 15 March 1883 a dynamite explosion occurred near the Local Government Office causing extensive damage but inflicting no fatalities. See *EHJ1*, I, 409.
[992] Frederick Seymour (1821–95), com.-in-chief Mediterranean fleet, 1880–3; commander at the bombardment of Alexandria, 1882; cr. Baron Alcester, 1882.

5 April 1883.   Gladstone told me that the Speaker will positively resign in July. G. looks much aged...

[Some four lines here excised.]

24 April 1883.   A Mr Pritchard Morgan a passenger from Queensland (where I heard he is an attorney) wrote to me that Charles Wodehouse, who has been long living at Rockhampton in that colony) had died on board the 'Dorunda' steamer in the Red Sea on his passage home on April 5. Mr. M. was in the same cabin with him. We had not heard from C. W. for many years, & no one of his family here knew he was coming home. He had a Govt. employment at Rockhampton, & Mr. Archer, the Agent Genl. for Queensland, says he knew him well & much esteemed him. He leaves a wife & family.

3 May 1883.   Thursday. Govt. beaten by 3 on affirmation Bill.[993] We expected a majority of something under 10. The bill must have been abandoned & is better to have had a small majority against, but it gives us a very ugly shake.

12 May 1883.   Saturday. We all went to Falmouth, and thence to St Ives. Saw the Botallack Mine, Cape Cornwall, (St Just), and Gurnard's Head from St Ives. Charming weather and charming scenery. Returned home May 19.

26 May 1883.   Saturday. Dinner at I. Off: for Q's birthday. Cabinet decided to give up L. Corp: Bill.,[994] go on with the rest except Crim: Code Bill. Chief more full of fight. Apart from time, differences between Gladst: & Hart. as to whether Police shall be put under new Corp: made it impossible to go on with Corpn. Bill.

I forgot to mention that on Tuesday May 22 I went to Windsor for a Council & had rather a long audience of H.M. – I did not see any change in her. She spoke cheerfully about her strain, tho' the improvement has been very slow. She now moves about a little in the room. She talked about Indian affairs.

5 July 1883.   Thursday. The sudden death of the D. of Marlborough[995]

---

[993] The bill amended the 1866 Parliamentary Oaths Act. The government were defeated by 289 to 292 votes.

[994] The London Corporation bill was dropped by the cabinet on 26 May 1883 because of Gladstone's differences with Harcourt and lack of time in the parliamentary schedule. See *Gladstone Diaries*, X, 453.

[995] John Winston Spencer Churchill, 6th Duke of Marlborough (1822–83), ed. Eton, 1835–8.

has shocked people very much. I remember him at Eton a singularly disagreeable boy: and for the first four or five years after he grew up he was rather a 'fast' young man. Then he took a strong religious turn, and greatly altered for the better in every way. He was a very worthy useful man, rather dull, but with respectable abilities, steadiness and perseverance. He played a not inconsiderable part in the Tory ranks. Sir A. Helps[996] told me that when the Duke was President of the Council he surprised him by his intelligence & business capacity. Helps thought him rather an underrated man.

7 July 1883. Saturday. We selected in Cabinet the 'innocents' to be massacred on Monday, a goodly list, but there will remain bills enough to keep us here till September.[997] I find I have noted nothing about Ld. Rosebery's resignation which excited a good deal of attention.[998] The cause was simply his disappointment at not being put in the Cabinet. He was very angry when Carlingford was put in, furious when Derby joined us,! and now, not getting the Privy Seal, has left us in great dudgeon. He could not be Privy Seal as another Peer in the Cabinet would have made the Peers a majority. We are now 7 Peers & 7 Commons. His proceedings do not raise my opinion of his judgment & good sense. No one can doubt that he is a very caustic, clever speaker, but he has shown no signs yet of buckling* to official work, and I fear he may never become anything more than a speaker. If so tho' he is seen to be a member of future Cabinets, he will never exercise much influence in them.

The Duke of Argyll is a striking example of this. The primary duty of a Cabinet is to do the business of the Govt.: and however clever a speaker a man may be & belauded by newspapers, he will always play a minor part unless he will work hard and can dominate a department. Of course the most powerful man is he who is both a clever orator and a capable administrator. Such men lead Govts. and parties, but they are very rare.

[Later undated annotation] *He has since abundantly proved at the F.O. his capacity for hard work.

14 July 1883. Saturday. Florence went to Windsor to receive the C. I.[999] from the Queen.

[996] Sir Arthur Helps (1813–75), clerk of the Privy Council, 1860–75; man of letters.

[997] Gladstone recorded that eight bills were dropped, while the cabinet agreed to go on with the Grand Committee bills, the National Debt bill, the Medical bill, the Scottish Local Government bill, the Irish Registration bill, the third reading of the Poor Relief bill, the Police Reorganisation bill, and the Tramsway bill. *Gladstone Diaries*, XI, 3.

[998] In June 1883 Rosebery resigned as under secretary at the Home Office, an office he had taken up on 8 August 1881.

[999] Companion of the Indian Empire.

Yesterday a Cabinet in Gladstone's room at the H. of Commons (*not* as the newspapers say, 'hastily summoned'). It was arranged for Friday because nearly every one wanted to shirk having a Cabinet on Saturday in order to run out of town. To my mind these hurried Cabinets are very prejudicial to the Govt. Very few things are properly considered, where half the Ministers are running backwards & forwards to divisions in the House. Three hours a week (the usual time of Cabinets) is not too much to devote to the business of the Cabinet; and the only convenient day for our ordinary meetings is Saturday. It looks as if we might soon be relieved of attendance on Cabinets by the Suez Canal imbroglio.

I have all along thought that Childers was not firm enough in the negotiation, but the public objectors utterly disregard the question which is far more importance [sic] than the precise amount of shipping dues, how amicable relations with France are to be preserved.[1000] A quarrel with France would cost us in six months more than the decreased shipping through the Canal for many a year.

17 August 1883. Went with these Indian Thakoors, Morvi, Gonda, and of Kattiawas to Osborne. The Queen in apparently good spirits, talked some time about Dhuleep Singh.[1001]

25 August 1883. Parliament prorogued and we went to Kimberley. Altogether we ended the session stronger than could have been expected. The inconceivable stupidity of the opposition got us out of our Suez Canal mess. By proposing a feeble and illogical resolution they united our whole party, shipowners included, in our favour. Never was a greater fiasco. The concluding weeks of Parliament were an unedifying spectacular. The H. of Commons after wasting months in idle questions, and personal bickerings, 'rushed' through a number of important bills, the House of Lords being thus practically set aside. The only business transacted there was the Agricultural Holdings Bill on which Lord Salisbury & the Tory tail displayed their usual blundering hostility. The other measures were simply passed without discussion.

11 September 1883. Went to Witton. Weather clearing. Very early & on the whole prosperous harvest here.

[1000] Discussed at the 7 and 13 July cabinets the provisional agreement with Ferdinand de Lesseps to build a second Suez Canal with canal rates to be considerably reduced. There was strong opposition to the proposal which was subsequently withdrawn on 23 July 1883.

[1001] Bahadur Duleep Singh (1837–93), Maharaja of Punjab from 1843 until British annexation in 1849. Lived extravagantly in England on an annuity, and from 1886 attempted to regain independence for the Punjab. For Kimberley's correspondence regarding Singh, see KP6 MS.eng.c. 4209.

26 September 1883.   The new bridge was finished. Mr. Burton the county surveyor of highways was the architect and the work was done by [ill.] of Wymondham under the superintendence of Tubby my carpenter.

We are well satisfied with the work. The water was turned off the river for some time during the construction of the bridge.

25 October 1883.   Thursday. Sudden Cabinet.[1002] Mentioned despatch on 'Ilbert' Bill. The cause Madagascar and diminution of troops in Egypt. Some preliminary discussion on measures for next session. Returned to K. same day.

31 October 1883.   Went to London to see D. of Connaught[1003] who is starting for India, and attended council.

5 November 1883.   We all went to town. A series of the usual Cabinets. Transvaal and measures for next session discussed.

11 November 1883.   Johnny's boy born at Witton.[1004]

24 November 1883.   Saturday. Returned to Kimberley.

26 November 1883.   Monday. Went to Witton to see Isabel and her babe. The babe (or 'pup' as Johnny calls it) a very nice one.

3 January 1884.   Suddenly to London for Cabinets of which we had two. Egypt the immediate cause, but the opportunity was taken to settle our Reform programme, and we had Transvaal, of course. Hartington gave up his objections on the understanding that Gladstone will remain in office to take charge of Redistribution after the Franchise

---

[1002] Gladstone's verdict on the cabinet was 'very good'. The first item of business was Madagascar and the issue of compensation for the British missionary G.A. Shaw arrested there by the French. The reduction of troops in Egypt to 3,000 men was agreed in cabinet. C.P. Ilbert's Criminal Procedure Amendment bill allowed certain Indians jurisdiction over Europeans. Ripon proposed a compromise bill, which was passed in January 1884. A preliminary discussion of franchise reform also undertaken, the overall feeling of the cabinet in favour of dealing with the question. *Gladstone Diaries*, XI, 48. On the 'Ilbert Bill', see *Liberal by Principle*, 161–8.

[1003] Arthur William Patrick Albert, Duke of Connaught and Strathearn (1850–1942), 3rd son of Queen Victoria; m. Princess Louise of Prussia, 1879; comm. Royal Engineers, 1868; genl., 1893.

[1004] Also John Wodehouse.

Bill has been carried, and that the minority question remains open. So we are a 'happy family again'.[1005]

I never thought that anything serious would come of Hartington's scruples.[1006] Moreover as far as I know he stands alone. Arthur Peel[1007] is to be proposed as Speaker. Herschell first and then Goschen declined. There was no question James. I am sorry for Dodson who would have had a good chance if not in the Cabinet but Gladstone was I think right in laying down that all eligible candidates outside the Cabinet must be exhausted before any one in the Cabinet was proposed.

Came up to London on Monday Jany. 21.

5 February 1884. Tuesday. Parliament met.

12 February 1884. Tuesday. Sudden Cabinet at 11 to consider Tokar & Sincat &c. After an hour's stubborn resistance the chief consented to measures being taken.[1008] Pity they were not taken immediately after Baker's defeat. Hartington proposed an expedition two or three days ago.[1009]

22 February 1884. Friday. Meeting at F. O. at which Gladstone, Hartington, Granville, Dilke & self present with Fitzmaurice & Cross to consider Merv business.[1010] News arrived just before we met that Tokar had surrendered: an untoward event, but not so bad nearly as Sincat. Lucky for us that Tokar did not fall before the division on Tuesday (the 19th) Our majority (49) was as good as we could wish & rather better perhaps than we deserved. Two admirable speeches were made on our side by the Chief and Hartington. The opposition speeches were poor, as was the debate last week in the H. of Lords.

[1005] Gladstone noted in his journal on 3 January 1884, referring to Hartington's threatened resignation over reform: 'Today our little crisis was virtually over: a great mercy, though in one sense I had to pay the piper by an extended engagement.' *Gladstone Diaries*, XI, 94.

[1006] On Hartington's scruples, see P. Jackson, *The Last of the Whigs: A Political Biography of Lord Hartington, Later Eight Duke of Devonshire (1833–1908)* (Rutherford, NJ, 1994), 163–73.

[1007] Arthur Wellesley Peel (1829–1912), Lib. MP for Warwick, 1865–85, for Warwick and Leamington, 1885–95; youngest son of Sir Robert Peel.

[1008] Having decided to evacuate the Sudan, which had been badly governed by Egypt, the government still had to arrange for the successful evacuation of Egyptian troops. The cabinet agreed to collect a force at Suakin in the Sudan with the object of relieving the Tokar garrison. *Gladstone Diaries*, XI, 112.

[1009] On Kimberley's opinion, see Kimberley to Hartington, 10 Feb. 1884, in *Liberal by Principle*, 168. The unfolding crisis in the Sudan is succinctly covered in Jackson, *Last of the Whigs*, 149–60: also in Morley, *Life of Gladstone*, III, 156–60.

[1010] This conclave at the Foreign Office agreed to the delimitation of the Afghan frontier, Merv having been annexed by Russia. *Gladstone Diaries*, XI, 117.

29 February 1884. Went with Flo. to Windsor for a night. The Queen looked pretty well, but sat down after dinner. The Russian ambassador Bn. Mohrenheim bored me with profuse assurances of Russian friendship *a propos* of Merv. 'Credat Judaeus: non ego'. Mr. Waddington[1011] talked long in the billiard room about French affairs. He struck me as rather a common-place man. The 'Tel' battle was fought to day.

13 March 1884. My aunt Mrs. Edward Thornton Wodehouse died at Mentone.

15 March 1884. Saturday. On going to Downing Street where a Cabinet had been summoned, found the H. of Commons Ministers in much excitement as the Govt. was threatened with defeat on Labouchere's motion on the Soudan.[1012] We adjourned to Mr Gladstone's room at the H. of Commons & after some time we heard that members enough had been whipped up to pull us through. Our whips had been caught asleep, & we had a very narrow escape.

16 March 1884. Sunday. A Cabinet to decide as to Soudan business wh. was very pressing & would not be settled in consequence of the interruptions caused by our perils yesterday. The Chief still confined to his rooms with his bad cold. All sorts of silly rumours afloat that he's 'sulking', his 'resignation' &c. &c., all without the smallest foundation.

29 March 1884. Saturday. A Cabinet at Bertram's villa at Coombe.[1013] The stories about our dissensions are all falsehoods. Differences of opinion of course we must have on a matter of such supreme difficulty as the Soudan, but thus far we have been able always after discussion to come to an agreement. Upon one point there is no sort of difference, that our prospects as a Govt. are bad and likely to grow worse. We shall have to come to a Dissolution before very long, & all the signs point to our defeat. Even if we were not in such great difficulties as those connected with Egypt, we should be here to meet the usual fate of Govt. after some years of office. The country gets tired as a matter of course of all Govts., which never can perform the promises made in Opposition.

The Tories will, I expect, not have an easy time of it when they

---

[1011] William Henry Waddington (1826–94), French ambassador in London, 1883–9.

[1012] Henry Labouchere (1831–1912), founder and editor of *Truth*; Rad. MP for Northampton, 1880–1906. Labouchere's motion stated that the necessity for military operations in the Sudan had not been shown. The motion was defeated by 111 to 94 votes. See 3 *Hansard* 285 (15 March 1884), 1662–1728.

[1013] Commemorated with an engraved brass plate. Currie, *Recollections*, II, 160.

come in, and very possibly they may be compelled to propose a Reform Bill, which with the help of the Radicals they would carry, but, which, as in 1867, would probably give a majority to the Liberals in the subsequent Parliament. Meantime our position, as is always the case with a tottering Administration, is far from pleasant.

I wonder what fate is in store for our Parliamentary system. The H. of Commons is becoming a mere machine for embarrassing the executive action of the Govt. It is rapidly ceasing to discharge any useful function. It does not enforce economy, but rather promotes extravagance. The speeches of its members, delivered for the most part to benches almost as empty as those of the H. of Lords, with rare exceptions interest no one. It is unable to legislate except on one or two great matters in each session, & then only after the most ridiculous expenditure of time in fatuous talk and wrangling. The few minor bills it passes are generally not discussed, & almost always careless and ill-considered.

It is evident that this nation cannot permanently be governed by such an Assembly. No man seems to know of a remedy, or to be able to forecast the future.

28 March 1884. Prince Leopold's[1014] death is a sad event, but as he had been subject to constant epileptic fits not surprising. What could have induced a man with such an affliction to press to be made Govn. Genl. of Canada, & when this was refused, Govr. of Victoria? The fulsome adulations in the newspapers of their young prince, who had done nothing, & never had the opportunity of doing anything, is infinitely disgusting. He was undoubtedly a studious, cultivated man, & would possibly have hereafter exercised some useful influence in matters of art & taste. He had some political influence with the Queen from constantly living with her, the cessation of which is by no means to be regretted. As far as it went, it was mischievous.

22 April 1884. Extraordinary earthquake at Colchester. It was very distinctly felt at Witton, and slightly here in Lowndes Square. It did no damage in Norfolk or London.

13 May 1884. Tuesday. Govt. had a narrow majority (28) in H. of C.

[1014] Prince Leopold, Duke of Albany (1853–84), fourth son of Queen Victoria.

on (Soudan) vote of censure.[1015] Our position gets worse daily, & I see no escape from it. The London newspapers and the Tories clamour for an expedition to Khartoum, the former from ignorance, the latter because it is the best mode of embarrassing us.[1016] We shall hardly I fear succeed in baffling the combination of Exeter Hall fanatics, bondholders, and Tories. The interest of the nation is to get quit of the Soudan and the Egyptian occupation as soon as possible. But Gordon is a tremendous obstacle. If he cannot be got out in any other way, an expedition, (a frightful undertaking) is inevitable. Of course it is not an impossible undertaking, but is melancholy to think of the waste of lives and treasure which it must involve, and except the rescue of Gordon & Stewart,[1017] no good end to be attained. We shall have to fight the Soudanese with whom we have no quarrel and to support the rascally Egyptians whose cowardice and cruel Govt. have been the cause of the whole calamity.

29 May 1884.   Thursday. Went to Falmouth & then to Dartmouth. Home on June 5. A very pleasant little trip.

8 July 1884.   Tuesday. Representation of People Bill rejected by H. of Lords after two night's debate by 205 to 146.[1018] I moved 2nd reading on Monday. The debate was remarkable. Ld. Rosebery especially made a powerful & eloquent speech. The majority against us was evidently smaller than the opposition expected. They looked very blank, and scarcely cheered at all. I received two compliments on my speech which pleased me: one from Cairns who told me he thought it judicious and conciliatory: the other indirectly from Lady Salisbury who told Lady Spencer as she sat by her in the Gallery, that she felt almost persuaded whilst I was speaking, that we were in the right.

[1015] On 18 Jan. 1889, Genl. Charles George Gordon (1833–85), who previously had served in the Sudan, 1873–6, 1877–80, was sent to relieve Egyptian garrisons in the Sudan, leading to widespread debate over the probity of sending English soldiers into territories being threatened by Islamic fundamentalists under the Mahdi. The voting was 303 against and 275 for the motion of censure. Gladstone noted the prolonged cheering from the Liberal backbenches with which the result of the division was received. *Gladstone Diaries*, XI, 144.
[1016] On 9 May 1884 Kimberley sent Gladstone a cutting from *The Times* of an interview with Gordon at Khartoum. Gladstone noted his firm opposition to sending any British expedition to reconquer the Sudan. *Gladstone Diaries*, XI, 144.
[1017] Sir Herbert Stewart (1843–85), led relief column to Khartoum; mortally wounded in Feb. 1885.
[1018] The House of Lords rejected the government's Franchise bill on its second reading. Lord Cairn's amendment that franchise reform must be accompanied by a redistribution scheme was subsequently passed. See A. Jones, *The Politics of Reform 1884* (Cambridge, 1972), 153; *Gladstone–Granville Correp. 2*, II, 211–12.

4 August 1884. The great Reform demonstration has come & gone: the Tory 'picnics' have had their fling. What is the result? It is difficult yet to say. The Radicals no doubt are in earnest & will work heartily in the cause. What is the feeling of the indifferent 'many' who turn elections? We have yet to see. I doubt whether the country will agitate itself as much as partisan newspapers imagine. The lowering the franchise all now know to be certain. Will the country work itself into a fury on the question whether the Tories or we are to have the management of the Re-distribution? Will there be a real campaign against the H. of Lords? I fear more that the exertions of Rosebery & the younger Peers may improve the House off the face of the earth, than that direct assaults will destroy it. There are some in the House itself who would not I suspect care much if they lost privileges which they seldom use, and others who, being ambitious, chafe at being excluded from the H. of Commons.

On Saturday (Aug. 2) the Conference on Egypt came to an end – a complete fiasco: and we are again face to face with the (insoluble?) difficulty, how to keep France out of Egypt without annexing it ourselves.[1019] It is singular that so many people imagine that annexations would add to our strength. Few things I believe would weaken us more.

Bismarck decries annexation by England in order that we may be permanently embroiled with France. As we would not annex he took care that the Conference should fail, as the next best move for Germany. In any case he secures a bad feeling between us and France, which is one of the chief aims of his policy.

9 August 1884. The circumstances about New Guinea are very curious. A few days ago it was at last decided to move in this matter, and to establish a Protectorate over the whole of the non-Dutch part of the island.[1020]

To day Ct. Munster by order of Bismarck inquired our intentions about the South Sea Islands generally, & also New Guinea. Bismarck has no objection to offer to our having the South Coast of N. Guinea, but thinks the North Coast should be left open to German settlement. This is in one way convenient, as it amounts to a recognition of our right to take this Southern part: but what a commentary on Derby's

[1019] Gladstone announced the failure of the Egyptian Conference in the Commons on 2 August 1884. Gladstone noted in his journal: 'This day for the first time in my recollection there are three *crises* for us all running at high tide at once: Egypt, Gordon, and franchise.' *Gladstone Diaries*, XI, 182.

[1020] On 9 August 1884 the cabinet agreed to limit the Protectorate to the south coast of New Guinea. Northbrook reported to the cabinet Granville's conversation with Munster that the Protectorate was for the part of the island of special interest to the Australian colonies. *Gladstone Diaries*, XI, 186.

assurance to the colonies that there was no reason to fear interference with N. Guinea by any Foreign Power. We are just and only just in time. We shall only take the part which really signifies to Australia, leaving the question of the other part for further consideration according to circumstances. The colonies will be angry at not getting the whole but without reason I think.

14 August 1884.   Went down to Kimberley, where there is a very severe drought. On Monday the 11th we had a day of extraordinary heat – 94 degrees in the shade at Greenwich. I do not remember ever to have felt such heat in England. Parliament prorogued to-day, the 14th.

Before we left London, the question of the successor to Ripon as Viceroy of India was settled.[1021] All who were consulted thought Spencer the very best man. Gladstone specially strong in his favour. Granville and Hartington objected to his going to India on ground that his absence would seriously weaken our party here. Eventually it was determined to ascertain whether he wished to go. The result was that he did not wish it, but would consider it if an offer were made to him. On learning this we determined that Granville's & Hartington's objections must prevail.

Lansdowne was mentioned as a very fit man, but we thought it out of the question to remove him so soon from Canada, as it might give offense to the Canadians. Morley was also talked about. We felt however that his political positon hardly warranted so great an employment at present. Finally our choice fell on Dufferin. He is an admirable diplomatist; it is not so certain that he possesses the qualities necessary to govern: Canada is no safe criterion, as the Govn. Genl. does not govern there nor did his recent Egyptian proceedings tend to reassure us. On the other hand he performed his Syrian mission admirably: his knowledge of Russia and Central Asian affairs, and his experience of Cple. will be most valuable. Above all he has hitherto succeeded well in all his employments, (except perhaps his Egyptian mission). His appointment will be popular in India, and will cause no difficulty on a change of Govt. here. The last is important, as it is very undesirable that the Viceroyalty should come to be regarded as a strict party appointment, and that a change of Gr. here should cause the Viceroy to resign or be recalled. On the whole I am well satisfied with our decision. I have no doubt he is the best man available.

[1021] The government, nervous over Ripon's handling of the Ilbert Bill controversy and the potential for a rapid change of government, decided in July to replace Ripon before the end of the year. Kimberley to Gladstone, 23 July 1884, GP 44228, ff. 144–6; *Gladstone Diaries*, XI, 178.

27 August 1884. Odo Russell's[1022] death is a sad event. Every one who knew him must regret him personally and the diplomatic service suffers an immense loss.

Harvest was finished on my home farm on the extraordinarily early date of Aug: 19.

6 October 1884. Summoned suddenly to a Cabinet. The cause the Bechuana difficulty[1023] and New Guinea. We resolved to take active steps to expel the freebooters, but first to ask the Cape Govt. what is the nature of the assistance they are pressed to give.

New Guinea has nearly been a nasty mess. Just before we left London (see Aug: 9) we determined to annex the South Coast and so much of the N.E. as is necessary to include the East Cape. Instead of doing this at once, a communication was made to Bismarck who objected, as he alleged it did not leave enough open for German colonization. Thereupon nothing was done & the matter was left to drift. At last however I think we shall act and take the South coast simply.

I don't understand why we should be so wonderfully compliant to Bismarck about these colonial questions. The Germans have behaved with scant courtesy to us in their proceedings. They seized the Cameroons tho' they must have well known that the arrangements had almost been concluded for its cession to us. The loss of the Cameroons is not of any consequence, but it never need have become German, if the Col: & For: office had not gone to sleep after the decision to annex it was taken by the Govt. I suppose the Treasury was the cause.[1024] Of course the object in Kotowing to Bismarck is to buy his support in the Egyptian question. This I suspect we shall not get, however much we humble ourselves. Germany is no doubt very powerful in Europe by land. I hope before long she may be reminded that we are her master at sea.

8 October 1884. Another Cabinet. I went home in the interval & got a day's shooting. Desultory talk about the franchise Bill.

It is interesting to observe how well Dufferin's appointment is

[1022] Odo William Leopold Russell, 1st Baron Ampthill (1829–84), asst. u.-sec. at f.o., 1870; amb. at Berlin, 1871–84; nephew of Lord Russell. Kimberley wrote to Granville, 'I cannot think how you are to fill his place; adequately to fill it is impossible.' 1 Sept. 1884, GrP, 30/29/136.

[1023] The Boers in declaring a protectorate in certain districts of Bechuanaland, and in granting railway concessions to Germany, led the British government to declare a protectorate there in January 1885. *Gladstone Diaries*, XI, 219–20; A. J. P. Taylor, *Germany's First Bid For Colonies, 1884–1885* (London, 1938).

[1024] On circumstances surrounding the loss of the Cameroons, see *Liberal by Principle*, 172 and n. 74.

received, and it is curious to note, how far higher the press estimate of him is than the opinion of the 'inner' political world. Gladstone was reluctant to appoint him, & only made up his mind on receiving a decided letter from me pressing the point; and Granville by no means favoured the choice, tho' he acquiesced.

12 October 1884.   My uncle William Gurdon died this morning at the age of 80, a kindly good man, whom all who knew him will regret.

21 October 1884.   We all went to town for the session, much lamenting to have to leave the country for foggy, grimy London.

22 October 1884.   Cabinet. Nothing notable. Talk about French and Chinese.[1025]

23 October 1884.   Parliament met. A lively, jocular speech from Salisbury, neat reply by Granville.[1026] No signs of surrender on either side. House thin and dull.

26 October 1884.   Took a walk with Dodson. He told me that in the summer, finding his seat for Scarborough insecure, he asked for a Peerage at the close of the Parliament, saying at the same time he wd. retire sooner if it were any convenience to the Govt. He was in pursuance of this offer, asked a fortnight ago to make room for Trevelyan. Dodson was unlucky in missing the Speakership, which was the object of his ambition. I think he ought to have been offered it, when Brand retired, considering how he had been pushed out of the L. G. Board.[1027] He would have made a good Speaker. I am very glad Trevelyan has got out of the Irish Secretaryship. He has been in a nervous condition, pitiable to witness, & could not have gone on much longer. He is too sensitive for such a *galère*. A tougher man would not have cared what the Irish MPs said of him. To be abused by such men should be rather encouraging than otherwise to any decent man. What would be alarming, wd. be to be praised by them.

[1025] It was feared that war between France and China was imminent, although it did not in fact transpire. *Gladstone Diaries*, XI, 228.

[1026] On the franchise, Kimberley believed Salisbury to be 'quite indifferent to the consequences to the House of Lords, and in fact rather to look forward with satisfaction to its possible abolition'. Kimberley to Ripon, 24 Oct. 1884, in *Liberal in Principle*, 172–3.

[1027] Cf. entry of 3 Jan. 1884.

31 October 1884.   Cabinet. Hicks-Beach[1028] has made known to us in strict confidence that the re-distribution scheme wh. would satisfy him would be as follows:

No constituency with less than 25,000 to have a member: constituencies not exceeding 80,000 to have one member; all towns of 10,000 to be grouped: single member constituencies throughout. This is a tolerably radical programme. It is very doubtful however whether this plan represents any general Tory view at present. But we may be sure that if we propose a moderate scheme, the Tories will trump us by something of this kind: and that if we proposed such a scheme as this, the Tories will denounce it as revolutionary. Either game will suit their tactics.

1 November 1884.   Dinner of Northbrook Club to Dufferin, audience not very enthusiastic except when there was an allusion to the Russians, and the necessity of trusting to our own strength not to their promises or good will. The Anglo-Indians who are mainly Tories and Jingoes wanted to have Salisbury in the chair. This was warded off by Barrow Ellis[1029] taking the chair as V.P. in the absence of the President. The P. of Wales, I hear, is strongly against the H. of Lds. rejecting the Franchise Bill, and the same view prevails in a still higher quarter. No wonder, considering what the consequences may be.

13 November 1884.   Thursday. Went to Bristol to the Anchor dinner where I addressed an easily pleased & enthusiastic audience. The candidate who is to take S. Morley's[1030] place at the general election, Mr. Weston[1031] late Mayor, outdid any one I ever heard in misuse of the letter H. Hi if Hi ave the Honour to get into the Ouse &c.

15 November 1884.   Cabinet. Everything now points to the Tories again rejecting the Franchise Bill in the Lords. We settled a declaration of our position to be made in both Houses on Monday.[1032] Good news

---

[1028] Sir Michael Hicks Beach (1837–1916), Cons. MP for East Gloucestershire, 1864–85, for West Bristol, 1885–1906; ch.sec. Ireland, 1874–8, 1886–7; col. sec., 1878–80; ch. exch. and leader of the Commons, 1885–6; pres. b. of trade, 1888–92; ch. exch., 1895–1902; cr. viscount, 1906, Earl St. Aldwyn, 1915.

[1029] Sir Barrow Helbert Ellis (1823–87), ch. sec. Bombay, 1865–70; member council of India, 1875–85.

[1030] Samuel Morley (1809–86), Lib. MP for Nottingham, 1865–6; for Bristol, 1868–85; proprietor of the *Daily News*.

[1031] Joseph Dodge Weston (1822–95), industrialist, mayor of Bristol, 1880–4; Lib. MP for Bristol South, 1884–6; for Bristol East, 1890–5.

[1032] A ministerial statement for 17 November 1884 was agreed stating the aim of passing the Franchise bill without delay. Gladstone subsequently slightly modified the statement adding 1 January 1886 as the effective start of the Franchise bill. *Gladstone Diaries*, XI, 242.

from Gordon. I hear Ct. Munster has been going about saying that the German Gt. has certain information of Gordon's death. The wish is father to the thought. It is singular how hostile the Germans are to England. If they quarrel with us, their new colonies won't be worth many weeks purchase: and they would find it no easy matter to get at us. What on earth can be their object in what on the face of it seems to be a senseless policy.

18 November 1884. Tuesday. The 'compromise' as to Franchise Bill announced in both Houses: & Bill read 2nd time in H. of Lds.

22 November 1884. Cabinet. The difficulty with Northbrook about his Egyptian Report settled.[1033] He had talked of resignation because we would not accept his views en bloc. After this, Gladstone, Hartington and Dilke met Salisbury and Northcote about the redistribution Bill. I hear that Salisbury is determined to keep R. Churchill[1034] 'out of it', & that the latter is very angry.

The Garmoyle-Finney case[1035] settled & the young woman gets £10,000 as a consolation for the lost coronet. The Cairns family did not behave well to her: but I hope the time will come when no such suits will be allowed: and English middle class girls will have to bear their jilting like the rest of womankind, without having a price set on their wounded hearts.

27 November 1884. Thursday. Our 'negotiators' reported to day to the Cabinet that the Redistribution Bill is virtually settled with the opposition leaders without any serious difficulty.

Hot & tedious dinner yesterday at that home of colonial Jingoe's and windbags, the 'Empire' Club in honour of Sir John Macdonald,[1036] the Canadian first Minister. Sir John made a very sensible speech. He is a

---

[1033] The cabinet rejected Northbrook's report for submitting the Egyptian settlement to the endorsement of interested European Powers.

[1034] Randolph Henry Spencer Churchill (1849–94), 3rd son of the 6th Duke of Marlborough; Cons. MP for Woodstock, 1874–85, for S. Paddington, 1885–6, 1892–94; India sec., 1885–6; ch. exch. and leader in the Commons, 1886. Resigned office Dec. 1886 over budget disagreements with the Cabinet.

[1035] In July 1883, Arthur William Cairns, Viscount Garmoyle, proposed to Emily May Finney, actress and daughter of a coal merchant. In order to please the Cairns family, she gave up the stage, but within six months, Garmoyle stopped all communications, leading Finney to sue for breach of promise. See *The Times*, 21 Nov. 1884, pp. 4,9,12; J. Stedman, ' "Come, Substantial Damages!" ', in *Victorian Scandals: Representations of Gender and Class*, ed. K. Garrigan (Athens, OH, 1992), 69–91.

[1036] Sir John Alexander Macdonald (1815–91), member of Canadian House of Assembly, 1844–54, 1856–91; leader of federation movement; pr. min., Dominion of Canada, 1867–73, 1878–91.

singular instance of a successful man of great ability and industry who is subject to fits of drunkeness. I believe he has been more sober lately.

2 December 1884. Cabinet. Gladstone spoke strongly of his intention to retire. I hear he is continually speaking of this. Much discussion about the Navy. It is curious how very reluctant Gladstone is to increase expenses even for the most urgent wants of the army or navy. The public are perfectly ignorant of the pertinacity with which he opposes all plans for increasing our military or naval power. He is really the sole obstacle & I admire his financial consistency: but his objection, to expenditure of all kinds are carried to an extent, mischievous to the public interests.

After all Hicks Beach's plan was in substance the Tory plan of re-distribution, tho' it has been watered down to a somewhat less Radical Bill. The grouping we have happily resisted: the bill is an improvement on our original scheme, and will be a fairly satisfactory settlement. The one member device will give some protection to minorities, & is infinitely better than the 'proportional' crotchet. The worst blot in the scheme is the increase of members, and the leaving Ireland with its present number of members. For this latter I see no defence but the H. of Commons convenience of avoiding Parnell's opposition.

6 December 1884. Last night the Franchise Bill passed without remark from any one. What a singular result after the storms of the autumn! We ought to have had a Cabinet to day before separating for the recess, but the Chief eager for the country, would not hear of it.

10 December 1884. Went to Kimberley.

In the first week in January we had two Cabinets.[1037] Gladstone was ill, and much out of spirits. A very useless proposal to the French Govt., was resolved on that they should enter at once on a discussion of our Egyptian proposals instead of making their counter-proposals, as has been announced to be their intention, on the 15th. However Gladstone was bent on making this communication and altho' every one else in the Cabinet saw it was quite futile, no one liked to cross him in his present state of health. Then we had some unpleasant discussion about colonial affairs and Bismarck. I protested strongly against our attempting to conciliate Bismarck by humility; I am certain that the more we give way to his bullying, the more cavalierly he will treat us. If we could pluck up courage to show a bold front, he would respect us & deal

[1037] The cabinet meetings took place on 2 and 3 January 1885. *Gladstone Diaries*, xi, 269–70.

with us accordingly. It is astonishing what terror he inspires.

7 January 1885. Another Cabinet to consider whether a fresh expedition should be sent to Suakim. It was left to Hartington to exercise his discretion after consulting Wolseley. Gladstone remains at Hawarden & did not attend.[1038]

The newspapers are full of abuse of Granville and Derby, and imagine that if Gladstone took foreign & colonial policy in hand, he would be more vigorous. The fact is Gladstone has again & again refused to agree to proposals made by Derby for active measures; e.g. Derby wished to add Zululand, up to the Black Umvolozi, to the reserve: also to annex the coast from Natal to the Portuguese border.[1039] Both these proposals were vetoed by Gladstone. I supported Derby. We should have taken all New Guinea in time to prevent the German annexation, if Derby's views had been followed: but he was thwarted by Gladstone & others. Harcourt is the most strenuous supporter of Gladstone in opposing all action. In Egyptian affairs again Gladstone has always been opposed to any decisive policy such as the newspapers clamour for. I by no means imply that he has never good reasons for his policy which I have sometimes cordially agreed in, and sometimes with reluctance: but it is hard that his colleagues should be charged with not taking measures, which it is supposed Gladstone would take if left to himself, when the contrary is the truth.

7 January. A discontented & unsatisfactory audit at Kimberley. I am obliged to reduce various rents. At Witton the audit the following week passed off extremely well. It is difficult to account for the difference.

20 January 1885. Cabinet. French Egyptian proposals discussed: and answer to be given to them. Strong objections of Hartington, Childers, Northbrook, and Carlingford to the proposed inquiry into Egyptian finance.[1040]

21 January 1885. Further Cabinet & discussion on answer to France, which was settled. Determination to proclaim sovereignty instead of Protectorate in New Guinea.[1041] Went to Witton.

[1038] Granville reported on the cabinet meeting to Gladstone at Hawarden noting 'Kimberley warlike against Germany'. Granville to Gladstone, 7 January 1885, in *Gladstone–Granville Corresp. 2*, II, 315.

[1039] See Kimberley to Chamberlain, 25 Sept. 1884, in *Liberal by Principle*, 172.

[1040] Kimberley, in agreement with Gladstone and Granville, supported French proposals as a reasonable basis for settlement. *Gladstone Diaries*, XI, 280.

[1041] On Cabinet discussion, see *CJ*, 55–6.

10 February 1885. To London for the reassembling of Parliament.

8 March 1885. I have been so busy since we came to town that I have had no time to make any entry in this diary. On Friday Feb 27. the Govt. had a majority of only 14 on the vote of censure.[1042] On the next day we had a most extraordinary discussion in the Cabinet lasting 4 hours & 3/4 on the question whether we should resign or not. There were the evident differences of opinion and more than one Minister changed his mind during the discussion. Finally we divided 7 to 7 one not voting, & Mr. G. gave the contrary vote in favour of not resigning.

For resigning 7.	Against 8.
S.	Gl.
G.	C.
Sp.	Hc.
D.	Cha.
Hn.	Dil.
N.	L.
Ch.	K.
	T.

I am persuaded we were right. Our party has stood by us and we owe it to them not to run away – : The Irish votes do not count for anything on such a question. A change of Govt. would have caused great confusion. The Tories would have dissolved at once, the Redistribution Bill would have been postponed indefinitely, and the chances of a war with Russia much increased. These were the main arguments for staying on.

Those for going out were that we are divided amongst ourselves about our policy in the Soudan, that there is danger therefore of our breaking up from internal dissensions, that we could now retire as a united Cabinet, and that we should go to the elections with better prospects than if we remain in, & get into further discredit with our party: also that the Tories would be able to make it up with Bismarck. Weariness, & eagerness to throw off responsibility for all the difficult questions which press daily upon us, had more influence I believe with those who wanted to resign, than any reasoning on the advantage or disadvantage of either course.

13 March 1885. Cabinet at G's room in H. of Commons where we settled the reply to the Russian note of Feb 3.[1043]

[1042] Northcote's censure motion following the fall of Khartoum and General Gordon's death, 288 for the motion, 302 against; Goschen and Forster voted with the Conservatives, Bright voted with the government. See Morley, *Life of Gladstone*, III, 175–6.

[1043] The cabinet agreed that without further inquiry Penjdeh and other districts should not be excluded from Afghanistan. *Gladstone Diaries*, XI, 307.

24 March 1885. Cabinet at G's room at H. of C. when we settled answer to Dufferin's telegrams as to an expedition to Herat. The Turk recalcitrant & declines at the last moment to sign the Egyptian Financial Convention. Evidently inspired by Russia.[1044]

27 March 1885. Friday. Govt. had majority of 48 on Finance (Egypt) Convention. I dined at Ld. Rosebery's dinner to Colonists. How strikingly middle class, & vulgar the trading colonists are.

4 April 1885. Saturday. Cabinet to consider Russian answer about Afghan frontier.[1045]

9 April 1885. Thursday. News arrived yesterday morning of the fight between the Russians and Afghans at Penjdeh.[1046] Cabinet to-day to consider it.

11 April 1885. Saturday. Cabinet Soudan. I read telegram about Amir's interviews with Dufferin. This evening Lady Cremorne died, a great loss to Flo. to whom she has ever been a kind friend.

13, 14, 15 April 1885. Successive Cabinets principally about Soudan. Hartington with the greatest difficulty at last persuaded not to resign.[1047] A sort of compromise has been made & Parliament is to be informed that the expedition is suspended only in order that our troops may be available for service, if required, 'elsewhere'. For all that the Soudan campaign is a thing of the past: and happily. No good reason can now be given for an advance in the Soudan, unless we intend permanently to occupy the country: and that would be madness. It is urgently necessary to extricate ourselves from a situation which exposes us to affronts from all sides.

24 April 1885. After prolonged discussions we at length agreed as a

[1044] The cabinet agreed that a Russian move against Herat would be a *casus belli*. It was also decided that Turkey's refusal to sign the Egyptian Financial Convention should be met with a suspension of diplomatic relations. Turkey signed on 30 March 1885. *Gladstone Diaries*, XI, 312.

[1045] The Russian proposal as a basis for settling the Afghan border question was rejected by the cabinet, the Russians having previously rejected the British government's proposed settlement of 13 March 1885. *Gladstone Diaries*, XI, 317.

[1046] For details on the Russian defeat of the Afghans at Penjdeh, see Rose Louise Greaves, *Persia and the Defense of India, 1884–92: A Study in the Foreign Policy of the Third Marquis of Salisbury* (London, 1959), chap. 5 and appendix 1.

[1047] Hartington was pressing for a resumption of the Khartoum expedition in the autumn. The compromise noted by Kimberley kept Hartington in the cabinet.

note to Staal[1048] proposing arbitration in the Penjdeh affair.[1049] I remained till 8 o'clock (and past) at Gl's room at H. of C. discussing it with Gl, Granville, Hartingn. and Harcourt. I thought we should never agree.

The Bosphore 'incident' immensely increases our embarrassments.[1050] Why in the world did F. O. choose this particular moment to suppress that scurrilous print? & why did they not ascertain what was the proper legal procedure. As the case stands, dirt we must eat, as the proceedings are clearly illegal. Freycinet's[1051] insolent menaces make the operation peculiarly unpleasant. I would we were clear of Egypt, and were a little less timid.

7 May 1885. Thursday. Met Staal and Lessar[1052] at F. O., retired with Lessar to P. Currie's room where after about two hours discussion we agreed on a project of the Afghan N.W. boundary.

[8 May 1885.] Friday. Lessar called with Currie at my house & said Staal agreed with a slight modification & had recommended it to the Emperor of Russia.

9 May 1885. Saturday. Cabinet. Budget, Irish question, and Registration (Local tax) seems to portend an early fall. Yesterday I went to Windsor to present the Regent of Kolapore. Long audience afterwards of the Queen who was very gracious and seemed satisfied with the avoidance of war with Russia.[1053]

15 May 1885. Irish quarrel in Cabinet patched up at last after many days discussion. Spencer was *very* near resignation.[1054]

[16 May 1885.] Saturday, another 'resignation' Cabinet. This time

---

[1048] Baron Georgi de Staal, Russian amb. in London, 1884–1902.

[1049] Following a cabinet meeting on 25 April 1885, Granville saw Baron de Staal to tell him that only the German Emperor would be acceptable as an arbitrator.

[1050] French protest of 16 April to British suppression of a hostile Egyptian newspaper.

[1051] Charles Louis de Saulces de Freycinet (1828–1923), French premier, 1879–80, 1882, 1886, 1890–92; for. min., 1882, 1885.

[1052] M. Lessar (1851–1905), min. to Russian embassy in London, serving under Staal.

[1053] For a review of a 'severe' week regarding Russia, see Kimberley to Halifax, 10 May 1885, in *Liberal by Principle*, 175–6.

[1054] Lord Spencer, lord lieutenant of Ireland 1882–5, objected to a proposed Irish Land Purchase bill. On 15 May 1885 Spencer withdrew his opposition to a modified measure.

Childers about his budget. He has since the Cabinet been persuaded to postpone his decision till after Whitsuntide.[1055]

21 May 1885. Thursday. More threatened resignations! Dilke & Chamberlain are 'furious' at Gladstone's announcement of a Land Purchase Bill. They object to this remedial measure without a 'grand' local Gt. scheme for Ireland. Postponed till after Whitsuntide also!! What a ridiculous situation.[1056]

1 June 1885. Received sad news of 'Zak' Currie's death yesterday.[1057]

4 June 1885. Returned from a two days sojourn at Kimberley. Lessar came down for a few hours on business concerning the Afghan frontier.

8 June 1885. Govt. defeated on Budget by 12.[1058]

9 June 1885. Cabinet. Ministry resigned. We had last week an extraordinary exhibition of temper and obstinacy on the part of Childers. At the last moment he proposed to increase the Wine duties. Every one was against him on the ground that it would probably give great offence to France, and might cause us to lose most favoured nation treatment for our trade with that country. Nothing however would content C. altho' he had already succeeded against much opposition in getting consent to his beer and spirit duties, and at last he wanted out of the Cabinet and was only persuaded afterwards with great difficulty not to resign. He made himself in the opinion of us all supremely ridiculous.

The battle as to the Coercion Bill raged all the week and nothing was finally settled when we resigned. Spencer would not give way, nor wd. Chamberlain and Dilke. The nearest approach to an agreement was on the plan of leaving it optional with the Ld. Lt. to bring the Act

---

[1055] On 16 May 1885, Gladstone noted: 'Very fair cabinet today – only three resignations.' During the previous four weeks Selborne, Northbrook, Hartington, Chamberlain, Dilke, G. Shaw-Lefevre, Spencer, Harcourt and Childers had, on differing grounds, all threatened to resign from the cabinet. See *Gladstone Diaries*, XI, 339.

[1056] On 21 May 1885 Gladstone circulated a minute to cabinet colleagues laying out the circumstances under which a Land Purchase bill for Ireland might be introduced and explaining the misapprehension that had arisen between Chamberlain, Dilke and himself. Dilke and Chamberlain had indicated their surprise and objection to the modifications required by Spencer's earlier opposition to the measure. Gladstone also noted that Kimberley had seemed surprised by the change to the measure. *Gladstone Diaries*, XI, 343–4.

[1057] Isaac Edward Currie (1861–85), Bertram Currie's eld. son.

[1058] The government were beaten over the Budget by a Commons vote of 264 to 252 on an amendment moved by Hicks Beach.

or any part of it into force by proclamation. Spencer wd. have consented to them as to the 'changes of venue' and the inquiry into crimes on oath when there is no one charged; but he refused as to the boycotting clause. All the rest of the present Act was to be dropped.

I think he might safely have agreed to the whole plan. It has always almost been the practice in these Acts to give the Ld. Lt. a discretion, another suggestion was to make the new Act last one year only, but this was not much supported. There was no difference of opinion as to resignation. Grosvenor told us before Whitsuntide we should certainly be beaten on the Budget, when we came back after the recess, he thought we should win. On Saturday last he told us that the division looked worse, & a majority was doubtful. How absurd it is for Liberal MPs to pretend they were taken by surprise at our making the question vital. How could a resolution aimed at nearly the whole Budget be anything else? They appear to consider themselves mere pawns to be moved by the whips mechanically. They even declaim against the notion that they are bound to know what is going on in the House. Wretched creatures! According to their own excesses without any will or opinion of their own.

But what could the Tories be about to beat us on the Budget, when we were on the point of falling to pieces on the Irish difficulty.[1059] What tactics!

16 June 1885. Salisbury still forming his Cabinet. To day we had a meeting of ex-Ministers to consider a curious verbal communication from Balfour on the part of Salisbury to Gladstone asking whether he will promise to support the new Govt. in taking every day in the House for Supply & Ways & Means, and to raise the money wanted by Exchequer Bills. It was decided only to give a general answer that we would not embarrass them by factious opportunism. Mr. R. Churchill & Co. asking for forbearance will be an edifying spectacle.[1060]

17 June 1885. It is evident that R. Churchill has beaten poor Ld. Northcote along the whole line. A mem: sent round to day by Gladstone saying that he will take the place of leader of opposition during

---

[1059] At cabinet meetings on 5 and 8 June 1885 deep disagreement about an Irish Crimes bill had emerged, with reports of wider differences within the parliamentary party over the issue also being received. On 7 June 1885 Gladstone noted 'a formidable division in the *party* (quite apart from the cabinet) is to be anticipated; and such a division can only end in one way'. *Gladstone Diaries*, XI, 353.

[1060] On Lord Salisbury's behalf A.J. Balfour called on Gladstone seeking an understanding which Gladstone described as 'very pointed and peculiar'. *Gladstone Diaries*, XI, 357. Lord Randolph Churchill was appointed chancellor of the exchequer in Salisbury's cabinet.

remainder of this session, but that after this Parliament he will retire from 'active political life'.[1061] Curious commentary on Sir W. Harcourt's speech last night at St James Hall.[1062] Will Gladstone adhere to his resolution?

20 June 1885.   The crisis continues. Harcourt, Granville, Dilke, Trevelyan, the Atty. Genl. and self met yesterday to consider what to do on the Redistribution Bill in the Lords. We decided to persist and divide, if resisted. It is evident that R. Churchill has prevailed, and that they mean to hold dissolution on the present constituencies as a threat, over our heads. To day we met at 11 o'clock at 10 Downing Street (all present except Spencer, Rosebery, Hartington). We decided unanimously to give a final & stiff answer to Salisbury's demands.[1063] Will he now go on or throw up? It is said R. Churchill having overthrown Northcote wants not to go on. But everything is in uncertainty. Harcourt, Chamberlain & Dilke's rash speeches since our resignation have done much mischief.

21 June 1885.   It appears to be certain that the Tories contemplate as a possibility 'Dissolution' on the old constituencies. Northcote has used language which proves this. On Friday some of our supporters scouted this as a mare's nest, but we know better. If this should happen, the Liberal M.Ps who absented themselves from the Budget Division will have brought a catastrophe on the country.

23 June 1885.   Ld. Salisbury at length definitely accepted office. Redistribution Bill finally passed Lords.

24 June 1885.   Delivered up seals at Windsor. Had rather long interview with The Queen who talked of Ireland and Afghanistan. She was very gracious.

25 June 1885.   Explanations in H. of Lords. It is entirely untrue that Mr. Gladstone wd. in no case have undertaken to reconstruct his Govt.

[1061] Text of memorandum in *Gladstone Diaries*, XI, 358. See also Jenkins, *Gladstone, Whiggery and the Liberal Party*, 241–2.

[1062] On 17 June 1885 Gladstone described Harcourt's speech to Lord Grosvenor as 'admirable' and fully justifying his increasing political prominence. Harcourt was 'dancing upon poor and ill-used Northcote's prostrate body'. *Gladstone Diaries*, XI, 359; see also A.G. Gardiner, *The Life of Sir William Harcourt* (2 vols., London, 1923), I, 529–30.

[1063] Gladstone read the agreed response to the Commons on 24 June 1885.

On Sunday last he summoned his colleagues to Downing Street.[1064] The notice was so short that only Dilke, Chamberlain, & myself attended. The Chancellor arrived after we had finished. Gladstone read us his proposed answer to the Q's last letter in wh. we all agreed. He then asked me if I did not think that Spencer should be asked to come over immediately, as nothing could be done, if Salisbury threw up, without consulting him. I quite concurred & at Gladstone's request I wrote to S. pressing him to come. He arrived in London in consequence, before the crisis was over. My letter went with one from Gladstone to the same effect.[1065] It was quite understood that if Salisbury failed, G. wd. endeavour to form a Govt. Of course the Crimes Bill wd. have been the difficulty, & very probably three or four of the members of the late Cabinet might have declined to resume office unless a Crimes Bill was brought in. This after the Tories had practically announced their intention to let the Act lapse, wd. have been obviously impossible. Happily the case has not arisen.

G. has very kindly offered me the Garter, a pleasant recognition of my services.

28 June 1885. Looking back on the career of the late Govt. I should range our doings under these principal heads
1. Reform of Paliament in which we have had a brilliant success. The Franchise and Re-distribution Bills are great & solid achievements.
2. Ireland. The Land Bill was a well conceived measure, and the Govt. showed much firmness and decision in carrying it through against violent opposition. It is too soon however to pronounce an opinion on its results. Our first coercion Act was on the whole a failure, owing mainly to the clumsy, injudicious manner in which it was administered by Forster, the worst Irish Secretary in my time. Our second Coercion Act succeeded. It was a well drawn measure, and had the advantage of being administered by Spencer, as good a Ld. Lt. as Forster was a bad Chief Secy. – Trevelyan, who I am told shows little aptitude for administration, did not count for much in the administration of Irish affairs. In the one case Forster, in the other Spencer conducted the Govt. of Ireland. Nothing could be more admirable than Spencer's conduct.

[1064] On 21 June 1885 the late cabinet met and during the discussion Gladstone indicated that, if recalled, he might form a ministry without Hartington and Spencer. This would clear the way for further Irish reforms, Ireland being the great issue left unresolved by Gladstone's second ministry. See *EHJI* II, 894.

[1065] Kimberley to Spencer, 21 June 1885 in *Liberal by Principle*, 176; *Gladstone Diaries*, XI, 360–1.

3. Foreign affairs. Here was our weak point, & no doubt Egypt & the Soudan were the chief cause of our ruin.[1066]

4. Colonial affairs. These have been less prominent lately. At one time South Africa largely occupied the public mind. Notwithstanding the violent abuse of us for the Transvaal Convention. I doubt its having weakened us in the country.

5. The settlement of Afghan affairs by Hartington gave general satisfaction, and our recent dealings with Russia are, I believe, in accordance with the predominant feeling in this country. Taking Indian affairs as a whole, the late Govt. conducted them, I think, with fair success.

Mr. Gladstone predominated in this as in his former Cabinet: but in neither was he the dictator which newspapers supposed him to be. Hartington, Harcourt, & Chamberlain all in their separate ways exercised much influence in his last Cabinet. The least influential member of it was certainly Childers, who seldom expressed an opinion, and, when he did, was usually so indistinct & muddled that it was difficult to know what he meant. Rosebery during the short time he was with us scarcely opened his mouth, & remains quite a dark horse. The impression is that he will run very cunning.

On Saturday June 27 Ld. Salisbury cabled to me to receive an account of the Afghan negotiations. I have avoided seeing R. Churchill, whom I do not consider fit company for a gentleman after his letter about Granville in the 'Times'.[1067]

6 July 1885. Salisbury made his statement of policy in the H. of Lords, & Carnarvon spoke on Irish affairs. The latter's speech received in dead silence. I followed in Granville's absence from govt.[1068]

19 July 1885. To Windsor to receive Garter.

22 July 1885. Went to Kimberley.

7 August 1885. Sir H. Stracey died.[1069]

9 August 1885. This morning I saw Ld. Halifax's death announced in

---

[1066] See Kimberley Memoir, where Granville is regarded a 'complete failure at the F.O.', herein, 498.

[1067] On Churchill's 'brutal' letter to *The Times*, see R. Foster, *Lord Randolph Churchill* (Oxford, 1981), 177. In a letter to Dufferin, Kimberley referred to Churchill as a 'reckless swashbuckler'. 14 May 1885, DfP Eur.F/30/3, ff. 68–9.

[1068] From early June to mid-July 1885 Granville was frequently confined to his bed with severe gout.

[1069] Sir Henry Josias Stracey (1802–85), Cons. MP for Norfolk E., 1855–7, for Yarmouth, 1859–65. Lord Wodehouse's father-in-law. See entry for 22 June 1875.

the newspapers. He was I think the quickest witted man I ever knew, and a most indefatigable worker. The newspaper writers always ludicrously undervalued his abilities & services. Today I see a foolish Radical writer in the 'Echo' ascribes his constant high official employ-ment to his family connections. Doubtless his family connections greatly helped him to get an early start: but in any walk of life he would soon have distanced most competitors. The reasons for their false estimate were his utter want of the oratorical faculty (he was really the worst speaker I ever heard), a certain flippancy & hastiness of manner, and above all his ingrained habit of telling a fool that he was a fool. Hence he naturally offended a great many men. But to those who knew him well, he was one of the kindest hearted of friends. His mind was, as keen as ever, to the last. *Requiescat in pace.*

14 August 1885.   Began harvest on Home Farm.

30 August 1885.   Finished it. Drought excessive.

8 October 1885.   Liberal meeting in the evening at Norwich in the Agricultural Hall. Trevelyan and I made speeches, neither of them very effective. Several other speakers afterwards, the only speech worth notice was that of Arch[1070] which was short, judicious and in the concluding part really eloquent. About 3000 persons in the Hall, men and women. An excellent place for speaking.

13 October 1885.   Tuesday. Went to Knowsley, and staid till Friday. A large rambling House with no good room except the dining room wh. is handsome. The Duchess of Bedford with her daughter Lady Ella, (a clever girl), Ld. & Lady Arthur Russell, Sherbrookes &c were there. Ct. Munster came the next day but one. Poor old Sherbrooke is quite twaddling, his memory gone: he was led about by his new wife, a stiff uninteresting woman. Derby and I took a long walk the next day about the grounds, and went as far as Croxteth (Ld. Sefton's)[1071] wh. adjoins Knowsley. It is lamentable to see the trees dying of the smoke from the collieries. D. said it would be soon necessary to migrate & that he was preparing for a new seat in North Lancashire. We had much talk about politics. He seemed not to wish for office again. He fears (not perhaps without reason) Gladstone's plans about Ireland. When he saw him lately he found him inclined to make large concessions in the Home

[1070] Joseph Arch (1826–1919), organising secretary of National Agriculture Labourers' Union at its inception, 1872; Lib. MP for North-West Norfolk, 1885–6, 1892–1902.
[1071] William Philip Sefton, 2nd Baron Sefton of Croxteth.

Rule direction. Ireland, we both agreed, was the pivot on which the political future turned.*

On the following day we went to Liverpool & passed a day in seeing the wonderful docks and other sights. Our cicerone was Mr Lystic the Engineer of the docks, a very pleasant and intelligent man.

[Undated annotation:] *He evidently expects some measure in the direction of Home Rule. He made this prophesy (since come true). If such a policy is adopted by Mr G. you will be for it, I against. K

18 November 1885. Parliament dissolved.[1072]

14 December 1885. The elections are now virtually over and the result being nearly a tie between the Liberals, and the combined Tories and Irish Nationalists is most unsatisfactory. On the other hand the elections have been decidedly disappointing to the extreme Radicals.[1073] We should have done very well, if Chamberlain had not frightened away many of our more moderate supporters, and the cry of the Church in danger had not been stirred up by the violence and rashness of the Liberationists. If the Church takes advantage of the opportunity and reforms itself, its position will be very strong, perhaps inexpugnable. The extreme Radicals hope by overthrowing the church to attain the secret object of their aspirations, a Republic, and they are right in their policy: the House of Lords and the Monarchy would not long survive the church. Happily England shows as yet no signs of being ripe for Revolution.

How is the Irish difficulty to be dealt with? solved it cannot be. I hope we shall let Salisbury and R. Churchill try their hands. They have made themselves responsible by turning out the late Govt. by means of an alliance with Parnell. It is for them now to govern the country in conjunction with their ally. I don't envy them the task.

12 January 1886. Went to London

[Undated annotation:] Flo. came on the 14th.

13 January 1886. Called on Granville at his house: afterwards on

---

[1072] Kimberley used the break to continue research into his family history. See his memorandum of 27 Nov. 1885. KP7.

[1073] The 'smash in London', which Kimberley attributed to the 'Radical programme', went 'far beyond' his expectations. Kimberley to Monk Bretton, 28 Nov. 1885, MBP. The general election held in late November and early December 1885 under the terms of 1884–5 Franchise and Redistribution Acts resulted in 334 Liberal, 250 Conservative and 86 Irish Home Rule MPs being returned.

Gladstone & in the afternoon on Spencer. The situation seems to be that Gladstone will reserve his opinion on Irish affairs on the address and wait to see what move the Govt. make. This is quite right for the moment, but it won't carry us far.[1074] Gladstone, it is evident, would like to give the Irish a local Parliament, under some restrictions; and Spencer inclines decidedly in the same direction. Granville will follow Spencer. Derby with whom I had a long conversation at the Club declares he will never agree to a Home Parliament in any form. Hartington is of course against any Home rule plan, but I have not heard what line he means to take when Parliament meets. Chamberlain I am told says nothing will induce him to agree to a Parliament on College Green. He is naturally very sore at the way the Irish treated him. *[Four lines heavily struck through.]* Carnarvon's retirement portends I think some responsible measure of coercion.[1075] Such a measure would be quite in the usual course of affairs. As the Whigs turned out Peel with the help of the Protectionists on the Arrears Bill, & had before long to propose repressive legislation for Ireland, so now the Tories having turned us out with the help of the Parnellites, will naturally recur to the measures of coercion which in order to get the Irish vote at the elections they would not propose in the last Parliament. Such is political morality!

20 January 1886. Wednesday. Dined with Granville. Queen's speech read. A feeble production.

21 January 1886. Thursday. Meeting at Granville's House, present Gladstone, Hartington, Spencer, Granville, Rosebery, Northbrook, Chamberlain, Dilke, Harcourt, Trevelyan & self. All agreed that no amendment would be moved on the Union paragraph in the Queen's Speech. It is a transparent attempt to prejudge the question of the policy to be pursued towards Ireland. Obviously the Queen's Speech is not the proper opportunity for parliament to decide this most grave question.[1076] Great was the disappointment of the Tories at finding that no one wd. walk into the trap they had baited for us.[1077]

[1074] On Gladstone's avoidance of opposition to Salisbury's government and any public commitment to Irish Home Rule during December 1885 and January 1886, see Matthew, *Gladstone, 1875–1898*, 232–3.

[1075] Lord Carnarvon, lord lieutenant of Ireland, was both ill and known to be opposed to Irish coercive legislation. Despite his deep discomfort he did not resign prior to the end of Salisbury's government in late January 1886.

[1076] In the Commons on 21 January 1886 Gladstone stated that the responsibility lay with the government to state clearly their Irish policy.

[1077] Cf. Kimberley to Grant Duff, 22 Jan. 1886, in *Liberal by Principle*, 181–2.

26 January 1886. Tuesday. Salisbury made a strong announcement last night that their Irish policy would be produced in 48, perhaps 24 hours. They are evidently frightened & dare not wait for Smith's report.[1078]

27 January 1886. Wednesday. Last night the Govt. announced their Irish policy: a mere manoeuvre preparatory to their defeat on Collings' amendment.[1079] Their blundering and vacillation have been inconceivable. But this, tho' it makes their position hopeless, does not solve the enormous difficulties of the situation. Can Gladstone form a Govt.? and if not who is to govern?

28 January 1886. Thursday. Govt. have resigned. They were defeated by 79: of the majority 72 nationalists.[1080] Hartington voted & spoke for Gt. with a view I believe to not joining a Gladstone Cabinet.

29 January 1886. Friday. Sir H. Ponsonby[1081] did not arrive at Carlton House Terrace with the letter from the Queen to Mr Gladstone till 12.30 at night. It is surmised that in the afternoon he must have paid visits to some other leading men. But I cannot hear whom he saw, if he did see any one.[1082]

1 February 1886. Monday. Gladstone went to Osborne to kiss hands. Hartington has, I am sorry to say, declined to join him, tho' in a very friendly manner. I never before at a change of Govt. saw nobody pleased. Long faces everywhere, except in the Parnell camp.

3 February 1886. Wednesday. Cabinet making going on all yesterday. The newspapers persistently put me in the new Govt., but I have had no offer of any kind, and I suppose am not now likely to receive any.[1083] I thought at one time from the persistent rumours I might possibly be

---

[1078] On 23 January 1886 W.H. Smith succeeded Sir William Hart Dyke as Chief Secretary for Ireland.

[1079] On 26 January the radical MP Jesse Collings moved an amendment to the Address regretting that there was no mention of allotment reform, the 'three acres and a cow' cry comprising part of Collings and Chamberlain's 'Radical Programme'.

[1080] At the end of the Commons debate over Collings's amendment on 26 January 1886 the government were defeated by 329 to 250 votes.

[1081] Sir Henry Frederick Ponsonby (1825–95), maj.-genl., 1868; private sec. to Queen Victoria from 1870.

[1082] At the Queen's request Ponsonby visited G.J. Goschen and Salisbury to explore the possibility of a Whig–Tory coalition government.

[1083] Originally Gladstone had hoped to appoint Kimberley to the Foreign Office, but on 29 January 1886 Sir Henry Ponsonby, on Queen Victoria's behalf, made it clear that Kimberley would not be acceptable and Lord Rosebery was subsequently appointed. See *Governing Passion*, 340.

asked to take the F.O., which would have been very distasteful to me: but Rosebery will now, I hope & presume, be the man, & it will be I think the best appointment that can be made. Apart from all other considerations I conceive it would be a great mistake to appoint an unpopular man like myself. I would be received with a chorus of newspaper denunciations, & where there is a determination not to place any confidence in a Minister, the battle is half lost before it is begun. Rosebery's appointment on the other hand would be universally approved.

4 February 1886.   Thursday. Gladstone offered me, and I accepted the India Office, which I much prefer to any other.[1084]

6 February 1886.   Saturday. Went to Osborne to be sworn in and kiss hands. The Queen seemed placid and undisturbed.

8 February 1886.   Monday. Shameful riot in the West End of London.[1085]

15 February 1886.   Monday. First Cabinet.

16 February 1886.   Tuesday. Decision not to make Burmah protected State.[1086]

13 March 1886.   Saturday. Cabinet. Gl. explained scheme for buying out Irish landlords, and for Irish Govt. (the latter only in general terms).[1087] Chamberlain strongly against both schemes. Trevelyan same side.[1088] They will probably leave us. Harcourt talked wildly & does not seem to have any definite opinions.

26 March 1886.   Friday. Cabinet. Chamberlain & Trevelyan resigned. The position of the latter is simple. He objects to handing over the charge of 'law & order' to a local Irish executive Govt. acting under

---

[1084] According to Grant Duff, Kimberley's acceptance of the Home Rule 'experiment' reassured *'thinking'* skeptics. 'You at least are not prepared for any wild courses.' Grant Duff to Kimberley, 14 Feb., 31 March 1886, KP6 MS.eng.c. 4223, ff. 5, 68.

[1085] In cabinet on 16 February 1886 Chamberlain claimed to have evidence that linked the Conservative leadership with certain *agents provocateur* who instigated the riots. *Gladstone Diaries*, XI, 498.

[1086] Kimberley spoke in cabinet supporting the proposal of the Viceroy Lord Dufferin that Burma be formally annexed.

[1087] For the full text of Gladstone's proposals see *Gladstone Diaries*, XI, 668–71. During cabinet discussion Chamberlain openly opposed Gladstone's proposals forcing a confrontation over Home Rule. Gladstone noted that Kimberley also expressed reservations about Irish land purchase proposals. *Gladstone Diaries*, XI, 508.

[1088] Trevelyan not mentioned in *Governing Passion*, 383–4.

the control of a local Legislative Body. Chamberlain's position is difficult to understand. He is ready to establish a Local Representative Body with considerable but united powers, and also to offer certain terms of purchase to the Landlords. His objections are therefore rather to the details than the principles of Gladstone's policy. A plan of semi-Home Rule, leaving the Irish members of Westminster seems to me to combine every disadvantage. What can be his real motives? Does he hope to overthrow & supplant G.? This is inconsistent with the overtures he has made to Hartington, as he wd. hope when H. goes to H. of Lords to succeed to the leadership.

31 March 1886. Wednesday. Meeting at Gladstone's to discuss finance of new Irish plan.[1089] Harcourt, Childers, Granville,[1090] Spencer, Morley, and self. Harcourt violent & ridiculous; declaimed against Bill, & never made a single suggestion for amending it.[1091] He is becoming little better than a 'farceur'. Nevertheless good progress was made in settling final details.

1 April 1886. Thursday. Cabinet at 2 o'clock, resumed at 5.30 in G's H. of Commons room. Long discussion on Irish Gt. Bill. Harcourt & Childers so dissatisfied, that if they were not Harcourt & Childers I should expect them to resign.[1092]

2 April 1886. Friday. Another meeting at Gladstone's to discuss details of Irish Govt. Bill. Granville,[1093] Spencer, Morley & self. After the House Ripon, Granville, Spencer & self went to Chancellor's room, & had a rambling talk on Irish Gt. Bill. We succeeded I think in somewhat reassuring the Chancr.[1094] who was getting alarmed.

17 April 1886. Saturday. Both the Irish measures are now fairly

---

[1089] For Kimberley's annotated working copy of Gladstone's proposal of 20 March 1886, see KP6 MS.eng.c. 4070, ff. 70–1.

[1090] Granville not listed in *Governing Passion*, 394.

[1091] At this meeting it was decided that the future Irish contribution to imperial expenditure should be fixed at one fourteenth. A contentious issue was whether control of the Customs should be handed over to the Irish, Gladstone being firmly in favour of doing so. Sir Edward Hamilton noted: 'Harcourt was not in an amiable mood. He was bent on fault finding and holepicking; taunted Mr G. with converting Ireland into a colony "*pur et simple*".' *EHJ3*, 32.

[1092] Gladstone hoped that this cabinet meeting need be the last devoted to discussing the Irish Home Rule bill, the main elements of the measure now being agreed. At this suggestion Harcourt violently objected and talked of resigning. In his diary Gladstone noted he was being 'solely tried' by Harcourt. *Gladstone Diaries*, XI, 522.

[1093] Confirming the inaccuracy of a press report omitting Granville from the meeting. *Governing Passion*, 396–7.

[1094] Lord Herschell.

launched. Harcourt wasted a great deal of time at our last Cabinet, as usual, in protestations.[1095] He is now very angry at Gladstone having left open a door to possible reconsideration of the exclusion of Irish members from the H. of Commons. This was done after consulting myself amongst others. Much as I desire to get rid of the Irish members, who are like a cancer eating away our Parliamentary life, I considered that having put in the Bill a provision for bringing them back to the House for a particular case, the amendment of the Irish Gt. Act, we cannot at this stage set our feet down & absolutely refuse any liberty to examine whether other cases may not arise for their presence at Westminster. On the whole in spite of the furious opposition of the London Press & Club society, I think we stand as well as could be expected.

The coalition against us is no doubt most formidable, but Gladst. said 'His measure holds the field'. If we fail, it will be after a sharp struggle, and our policy will I am convinced survive us, & force itself on the country before long. On Thursday the 8th Flo. & I went to Windsor for the night. The Queen very cheerful & gracious. The malicious say she is in such high spirits because she thinks the fall of the present ministry imminent. Hartington's position is logical and his honesty of purpose commands universal respect. His influence is deservedly high at this moment. It is supposed that he would form a Gt. with Salisbury at the F.O. under him. This however seems to be uncertain, and some say he will only support a Salisbury Gt., himself remaining outside. This does not to me appear to be a very hopeful scheme.[1096] Chamberlain has declined in public estimation. His newest plan, produced at the last moment, (we never heard anything of it from him in the Cabinet) a wholly impracticable and unworthy of his reputation for sagacity. He is too able a man however not to recover himself.

Trevelyan is nowhere.

20 April 1886. Went to Kimberley for Easter. Very cold weather. Spring a fortnight behind.

3 May 1886. Returned to London.

4 May 1886. Opening of Colonial & Indian Exhibition.[1097] A fair ceremony. I attended as a Commissioner.

[1095] In cabinet meetings on 6 and 14 April 1886 Harcourt raised constant difficulties and objections over Ireland. See *Governing Passion*, 400–4.

[1096] A plan of limited Home Rule which might be extended to each of the four nations, and requiring retention of Irish MPs at Westminster.

[1097] Held in the Royal Horticultural Society Gardens, South Kensington. See Findling, ed., *Historical Dictionary of World's Fairs and Expositions*, 95–7.

7 May 1886.   Friday. Dined with P. Currie. Tseng[1098] outgoing Chinese Ambassador, Lord Rothschild & others. Tseng speaks fair English but said little: an intellectual looking man with pleasant manners. He will, I hear, occupy a high position at Pekin. I fear he was too much under the influence of Sir H. Macartney,[1099] his Secretary, a rather vulgar, intriguing person. Lord Rothschild told us many stories about the early intelligence obtained by his House. They are much better served in this respect than the Govt., no doubt because it is worth their while to pay handsomely for information.

The newspaper intelligence is not often of much value, as it is hardly ever accurate, tho' sometimes earlier than Govt. news.

14 May 1886.   Prospects of the Irish Bill & the Govt. bad. Some attempts, hitherto without much success, have been made to detach Chamberlain's following, wh., tho' not large, is quite enough to upset us.[1100] Chamberlain himself, it is clear, would prefer no reconciliation & that the Govt. should be turned out. His object, I am convinced, is to break up the Whig-Radical combination, & let the Tories in for a time. He hopes then, that a purely Radical opposition will be formed, of which he will be the Head. He showed pretty plainly in the autumn campaign that this is his real aim. I have no belief in the sincerity of his objections to Home Rule. He opposes Gladstone's measure for two reasons (1) in order to ovethrow Gladstone; (2) in order to make the Irish members, whose contemptuous treatment of his own scheme he has not forgotten, feel his power.

Hartington on the other hand & his followers are perfectly honest in their objections to Home Rule. Another reason probably for Chamberlain's dislike of our Bill is that he does not wish the Irish members to be removed from Westminster, because, as long as they remain, they are sure to vote for all the extreme Radical motions to spite the Tories & Whigs. Chamberlain wants to produce a revolutionary state of affairs, tending to the abolition of the H. of Lords, & the Church Establishment. this might (I believe, certainly would) bring us near to a Republic. On the other hand, if the Govt. will 'climb down' to please him, he will accept such a victory over Gladstone as sufficient. Will G.

[1098] Tsêng Chi-tsê (1839–90), min. to Great Britain and France, 1878–80; envoy to Russia, 1880–1; negotiated convention with Britain concerning opium traffic, 1885; member of Tsung-li Yamen, 1886–7.

[1099] Halliday McCartney (1833–1906), British army med. dept., 1858–62; sec. to Chinese legation in London from 1876.

[1100] On 12 May 1886 Chamberlain held a meeting at his South Kensington house attended by fifty-two MPs at which Chamberlain declared that, unless Irish members be retained at Westminster, Gladstone's measure must be opposed. See Cooke and Vincent, *Governing Passion*, 418. Chamberlain's information was that 102 Liberal MPs were intending to oppose the Home Rule bill.

'climb down'? I think not. He is very angry with Chamberlain, whose real objects he sees plainly enough. They have long been apparent to those who were behind the scenes.

22 May 1886. Labouchere, asked by Chamberlain what people thought about the Dilke scandal,[1101] replied: 'They say it would have been a d—d sight better if it had been you'.

30 May 1886. The talk last night at the F.O. reception was that the Gt. wd. have a majority of 12. Nothing however is certain, as Chamberlain & his tail have not declared themselves. J. Morley told me he thought we should be beaten. They say that Gladstone gesticulated so violently in the House on Friday night that he tore his shirt!

8 June 1886. Govt. beaten this morning on Irish Home Rule Bill *341–311*

9 June 1886. Cabinet. Determined to advise Dissolution. No difference of opinion. The Queen, it is well known, will raise no objection. She is much wiser than the foolish people who talk of her possibly refusing. If she refused, she would do herself infinite harm, and play directly into our hands. The fact is that on every account immediate Dissolution is best for all parties concerned, and for the highest interests of the nation at large.

24 June 1886. I went to day to Osborne Morgan's[1102] near Wrexham to make a speech to his electors (Denbighshire). The meeting was at a village called Rhos in the open air. A large number of colliers attended, & the proceedings were very enthusiastic. Mr. Abraham[1103] the miner who is M.P. for Glamorganshire made a speech in Welsh & sang a song which he told me was the Welsh national air. The whole meeting, men & women, joined in the chorus: the air was plaintive & solemn, the voices melodious & the effect very touching.

26 June 1886. Yesterday Parliament was prorogued & to day it was dissolved.

29 June 1886. A remarkable gathering of colonists (with a few Indians)

[1101] Charles Dilke's political career was ruined by his adulterous involvement in the Crawford divorce case.
[1102] George Osborne Morgan (1826–97), Lib. MP for Denbighshire, 1868–85, and Denbighshire East, 1885–97; parlt. sec. to CO, 1886.
[1103] William 'Mabon' Abraham (1842–1922), Labour MP for Glamorganshire, Rhondde div., 1885–1918.

at a dinner at the Mansion House to the P. of Wales. They showed immense enthusiasm for the 'Empire'.

30 June 1886. In Childers' absence attended the Queen at the opening of Holloway College at Egham. A very large handsome building, most luxuriously fitted up. What will the young women educated there be fit for?

Ld. Granville having been a month in bed with gout, I have charge of Colonial office, as well as my own work. The stupid Tories in Denbighshire put out a handbill saying I held a sinecure office!

8 July 1886. Great heat for several preceeding days. To day much cooler.

5 July 1886. A reception of Indian & Colonial visitors at Windsor. Flo. & I went to it: ill-managed but gave I am told much pleasure to the guests.

17 July 1886. Cabinet dinner at Gladstone's. Very little business discussed. There is to be a Cabinet on Tuesday, when we shall know the result of all the elections except Orkney & Shetland. It is quite understood that we shall then resign. Gladstone told us that Cabinet dinners which used to take place once a week during the Session each minister giving a dinner in turn, were first discontinued by Palmerston, he did not know exactly why. He said he rather regretted them, as they enabled discussions to be held which it was not necessary to report to the Queen, to whom all important matters discussed in a regular Cabinet were reported, and also because much fewer Cabinet were then required.

He also told us that in Peel's Govt., the H. of Commons members of the Cabinet used to meet once a week, generally on Saturday, to determine on the course to be taken in H. of Commons matters during the ensuing week.

There was some conversation about Burke.[1104] Gladstone said that he had heard the old Ld. Lansdowne,[1105] who was nearly contemporary with Burke, declare that it was absolutely out of the question to put Burke in the Cabinet, as he was a man with whom no one could get on on account of his impracticable temper. There were also grounds

[1104] Edmund Burke (1729–97), MP for Wendover, 1765–74; for Bristol, 1774–80; for Maton, 1781–94; advocated peace with America and opposed French revolutionary principles.
[1105] Sir William Petty, 1st Marquis of Lansdowne (1737–1805), throughout the 1770s pursued a policy of peace with America; home sec., 1782; 1st ld. of treas., 1782–3.

for suspecting that Burke was not altogether pure in money matters.

Will Hartington join the Tories? Opinions differ. The majority, I think, expect he will not. Gladstone is (naturally) much exasperated at his defeat. He shows no sign of retiring from public life, but I doubt if he will go on long as leader of Opposition at his great age.

20 July 1886.   Cabinet. It was resolved to resign at once. There was no difference of opinion. Gladstone will continue to be leader of the Opposition.

1 August 1886.   The Salisbury Cabinet not yet entirely formed. Granville told me yesterday that he believed Stanhope wd. go to Col. Office, & that Cross & Stanley were fighting fiercely for the India Office.[1106] Meantime the Office wishes for neither: Stanley especially is looked on as hopelessly inefficient. They would have liked Stanhope who was, I am told, a very good Under Secy. but of course as he is well fitted for the round hole, he will be put in the square one. The public does not seem to be much edified by these squabbles.

3 August 1886.   Went to Osborne to deliver up seals. The Queen very gracious & seemed to be in immense spirits, no doubt at getting rid of us. I had rather a long audience. Granville being too ill to go down, I delivered up his seals as well as my own.

4 August 1886.   Went to Windsor with Granville. He told me Hartington had written to Gladstone, saying he proposed to sit on the front Opposition Bench. Gl. who I hear is in a very irritable temper, appears to have given a rather ungracious answer.[1107]

5 August 1886.   We went to Kimberley. Yesterday morning Sir R. Cross called on me to receive my account of affairs at the India Office. Rosebery is gone down to Scotland, & does not mean he told me to come up for the Queen's Speech. He is evidently running cunning as usual & wishes to avoid committing himself about Ireland, as far as he can.

18 August 1886.   Wednesday. Began harvest on Home Farm.

19 August 1886.   Went to London to attend the debate on the Address.

[1106] On 3 August 1886 Edward Stanhope was appointed to the Colonial Office, Sir Richard Cross to the India Office and Col. F.A. Stanley to the Board of Trade.

[1107] Informing Hartington that he could not 'materially contribute to relieve you from embarrassment.' *Gladstone Diaries*, XI, 602.

Oddly enough the Govt. could not find five Commissioners to deliver the Queen's Speech & after I had taken the oath & my seat, the Chancellor asked me if I would oblige them by acting as Commissioner, wh. I willingly did. The debate short: Lord Sy. made a prudent speech, Argyll a fuming oration. Granville still weak, but put his points in his old puss-like manner, very neatly. Altogether I should say Govt. made a fair start in both Houses. Went back to K. next day.

4 September 1886. A fortnight's unusually hot weather ended in a violent thunderstorm this evening.

7 September 1886. Finished harvest on the Home Farm.

29 September 1886. The short Session ended on Saturday the 25th. The Govt. is very strong, and likely I think to remain so for some time. It is evident however that they are contemplating coercive measures in Ireland, and the resort to them will tend to strengthen the Liberal party in this country. Looking back now on the course of politics since the beginning of this year, I have come to the conclusion that the misfortunes of the Liberals have arisen in no small degree from the too precipitate overthrow of the last Tory Govt. The vote on Jesse Collings motion took most of us completely by surprise, and I have never clearly understood why Gladstone did not prevent it. Up to that time it was ageed on all hands that our best policy was not to drive the Govt. out of office till they had brought forward their Irish policy. They must have foundered on that rock and we should probably have had the inestimable advantage of uniting all sections of Liberals against their measures. This critical mistake having been made, I do not see what better course could have been taken by the late Cabinet; our Chief's management however of his relations with Chamberlain was inexplicable to me, & certainly unfortunate. Why did he not take him more completely into his confidence about the Irish Bills? and, if he was for good reasons unable to treat him with such confidence, ought he to have attempted the formation of a Govt? The general result of our Irish policy has been in my opinion most beneficial to the relations between England & Ireland. It has shown the Irish that they have the sympathy of a very large part of the English people, and it has paved the way for Home Rule in the near future. The vast change which it has produced, is no where more apparent than in the language of the Tory Govt. on the subject of local institutions for Ireland. They will do in two steps what we proposed to do in one.

1 October 1886.   Isabel safely delivered of a boy at Witton.[1108]

26 October 1886.   I was weighed. (16 st: 8lbs.).

31 October 1886.   I have been reading Sir Francis Doyle's Reminiscences, a disappointing book.[1109] Much of it consists in acrimonious remarks on Gladstone, such as may be read every day in the Tory press, & the rest is made up of anecdotes most of which are very stale, & some inaccurately told: e.g. the ancient diplomatic story about Metternich & Castlereagh. Doyle makes the former say 'il est bien destinque.' Of course the right version is that a young diplomatist having asked Metternich to point out Castlereagh to him, exclaimed 'Conneut: il a joint de decoration' to which M. repled: 'Hic for c'est bien destinque'.

10 November 1886.   W's[1110] very disagreeable lawsuit, brought against him by one Empson for slander during the last election, but one for East Norfolk, settled in Court by an apology. A trumpery business. The costs which are heavy of course fall on me. No doubt the Tories are much pleased at inflicting a fine on me. I doubt however whether they will gain much by it in E. Norfolk in the long run.

11 January 1887.   My cousin George Currie died on the 8th. He had been failing for a long time. A clever man, excellent in business, who wasted his life and talents.

I have had nothing to record lately. Living quietly in the country, I only know what is going on in the world from the newspapers, an untrustworthy source of information. As far as I can judge at a distance, the Govt. since R. Churchill's resignation have been in a 'muddle'. Their treatment of Ld. Iddesleigh has been mean and shabby, and their arrangements generally very weak.[1111] If they found it necessary to take in Goschen, they should have made him leader.[1112] A stopgap leader, which it is said Smith is to be, will give no confidence to their party. I am glad the attempted 'coalition' has miserably failed. No one seems to have really wished for it but the Editor of the 'Times'

[1108] Philip Wodehouse. On his birth, see Kimberley to Monk Bretton, 17 Oct. 1886, in *Liberal by Principle*, 187.

[1109] Sir Francis Doyle, *Reminiscences and Opinions, 1813–1885* (1886).

[1110] John Wodehouse, who served as Liberal agent for E. Norfolk.

[1111] Forced into resignation of the Foreign Office. See Foster, *Lord Randolph Churchill*, 302–15.

[1112] G.J. Goschen succeeded Lord Randolph Churchill as Chancellor of the Exchequer in Salisbury's cabinet following the latter's precipitous resignation over defence spending on 20 December 1886. W.H. Smith was made leader in the Commons.

newspaper. So Holland[1113] is be Colonial Secretary; not a very strong man, but sensible, and painstaking. He will work well with Herbert and Meade both of whom however are better men, in some ways: perhaps Holland has a sounder judgment than Herbert. The principal objection to Holland is that he will supply no new ideas from outside.

What absurd things are written about R. Churchill! He is lauded as a successful leader of the House of Commons. Now he undoubtedly showed good promise during the five or six weeks of the session for which he led, but five or six weeks trial is ridiculously too short to determine whether he can lead the House successfully. He will be a sharp thorn now in the side of his late colleagues.

13 January 1887. Heard the news of Lord Iddesleigh's sudden death yesterday. Though not in the first rank of political men he was above mediocrity. A vein of humour gave life sometimes to his speeches which were generally rather dull and commonplace, and his remarkable good sense and unvarying amiability of temper made him a fairly successful leader of his party in the House of Commons. He was more efficient in office than Opposition: indeed his was too fair and candid a mind to stoop to the ordinary rhetorical exaggerations of an Oppositon orator. His party used him shamefully, when he was kicked up to the House of Lords, and supplanted as leader by Hicks Beach, who has since deservedly shared the same fate at the hands of R. Churchill, his fellow intriguer. The latest indignity which Lord Iddesleigh has been subjected to by his summary eviction from the Foreign Office wh. doubtless hastened his death.

26 January 1887. To London. Meeting in the afternoon at Granville's house. All the members of the late cabinet present with Sir C. Russell[1114] and Fowler.[1115] Nothing of importance took place. We were all agreed that beyond general talk in favour of Home Rule, no move should be made till we see the Govt. measures. They are embarking in the old coercive policy, and our policy is to let them plunge deep into the inextricable embarrassments which await them.

27 January 1887. Thursday. Meeting of Parliament. Short uninteresting debate on Address in H. of Lords.

28 January 1887. Returned to Ky.

[1113] Sir Henry Thurstan Holland (1825–1914), Cons. MP for Midhurst, 1874–85, for Hampstead, 1885–8, when he was cr. Baron Knutsford, 1888; col. sec., 1887–92.

[1114] Sir Charles Russell (1833–1900), atty. genl., 1886, 1892–4; Lib. MP for Dundalk, 1880–5, for Hackney S., 1885–94; made life peer as Baron Russell of Killowen, 1894.

[1115] Henry Hartley Fowler (1830–1911), Lib. MP for Wolverhampton E. 1880–1908; financial sec. to treas., 1886.

9 February 1887. We all moved to town. The H. of Commons is still maundering on over the Address, a sorry spectacle.

10 February 1887. Found Brooks' Club in a great state of excitement about the recent blackballing. Primrose,[1116] as a Gladstonian, & Lord Wolmer,[1117] as an Unionist, excite much sympathy. The managers of the Club have wisely determined to suspend the Ballot till after Easter. The Unionists are said to be infuriated at Gladstone having dined with Harcourt at the Club the day before the opening of Parliament! However we Gladstonians, are quite strong enough in the Club to bring them to reason.

11 February 1887. Met Trevelyan in street and stopped & had some talk with him. He evidently longs to find a way back to us.

When I was in town for the opening of Parliament I had rather an interesting conversation with Count Corti, the Italian ambassador, about Dilke's article in the 'Fortnightly' on foreign affairs.[1118] He told me that Dilke was mistaken in his assertion that in 1878 our Govt. proposed a 'Mediterranean League' to Italy, (Corti was then Italian Foreign Minister). The Italian Govt. was sounded by Paget as to their willingness to act in concert with England in the affairs of Turkey, but nothing was said about a league, and he (Corti) at once told Paget that he would enter into no engagement which could involve Italy in war. Corti said the relations between France and Italy are now as bad as possible. He does not think there will be war between Germany and France. He feels sure no actual alliance was proposed by Salisbury to Austria against Russia: the communications between the two Govts. were vague, and the Austrian Govt. is dissatisfied at the failure of our Govt. to give them more specific promises of support.

15 February 1887. Meeting at Ld. Cranbrook's to consider memorial to Ld. Iddesleigh. Most of present, and past Cabinets, Salisbury, Granville, Hartington &c. Interesting as an example of good feeling between our opposing parties. Gladstone declined to join Committee, a very

---

[1116] Sir Henry William Primrose (1846–1923), Gladstone's priv. sec. and Rosebery's cousin.

[1117] William Waldegrave Palmer, Viscount Wolmer (1859–1942), eldest son of Earl of Selborne; Lib. MP for Petersfield, 1885–92, for Edinburgh W., 1892–95; m. Salisbury's da. Lady Beatrix Cecil, 1883, but also voted for Labouchere's motion in March 1886 against the House of Lords. See Henry Eeles and the Earl Spencer, *Brooks's, 1764–1964* (London, 1964), 124.

[1118] On the series of articles published collectively as *The Present Position of European Politics* (London, 1887), see S. Gwynn and G. Tuckwell, *The Life of the Rt. Hon. Sir Charles W. Dilke* (2 vols., London, 1917), II, 245–63.

ungracious and unwise act. Granville in his most puss-like manner hinted that Iddesleigh was not quite as great a man as Ld. Russell and that it might be well to reserve the Octagon lobby between the Houses of Parlt. for first Ministers of distinction.

11 March 1887.   I called a few days ago on Gladstone, the morning after his adventure in the fog, of which he & Mrs G. spoke very lightly.[1119] He seemed to be in good spirits, and rather sanguine as to the prospects of Home Rule, tho' he inculcated patience which I hope rather than believe he will exercise himself. He observed that there was an ominous flutter in the ranks of the Liberal dissentients. No wonder, considering the weakness & embarrassment of the Govt. Chamberlain's pettishness & violence shows plainly which way the wind is blowing. He will have soon to trim his sails.

I was rather amused by an anecdote told me of Gladstone, by Quaritch, the bookseller.[1120] On the day of the resignation of the late Govt., Gladstone made an appointment with Quaritch at his shop. An American woman who was at Quaritch's when G. came, improved the opportunity by getting Q. to introduce her & then asking G. to write her name in her birthday book, which he did with much good humour.

22 March 1887.   Tuesday. Meeting at Harcourt's in Grafton St. to consider course to be taken to-morrow on demand of the Govt. for postponement of all business to the Coercion Bill.[1121] Harcourt had drawn up a very clever amendment to wh. we agreed; Morley is to move it. There were present Gladstone, Granville, Harcourt, Morley, Childers, C. Bannerman, and myself.

6 April 1887.   Went to a Home Rule meeting at Chelsea Town Hall, where I spoke for half an hour. T. P. O'Connor M. P. made an eloquent and humorous speech. Meeting of course enthusiastic. Such meetings always are. Every day it becomes more and more evident that political power is being transferred from Parliament to the platform.

7 April 1887.   Thursday. Went to Ky. for Easter & stayed till April 21. Weather bitterly cold. No sign of spring.

[1119] Kimberley visited Gladstone on 4 March 1887. In his diary for the previous day Gladstone notes: 'journey to Dollis at night was cut short by fog.' *Gladstone Diaries*, XII, 16.

[1120] Bernard Quaritch (1819–99), offices at 15 Piccadilly from 1860; reputed to have attended, either in person or by proxy, every important book auction in Europe and America during his later career.

[1121] On 22 March 1887 the government indicated the urgency of introducing an Irish Coercion bill. Balfour introduced the measure to the Commons on 28 March 1887.

24 April 1887.   Debate in H. of Lords on Irish Land Bill which lasted two nights.[1122] Every speaker was moderate in tone & applied himself to the merits of the Bill, except D. of Argyll and Ld. Selborne, the former of whom emptied his vials of wrath on his old colleagues for nearly an hour & 1/2, quite omitting to notice the bill till at just the end of his declamation when he made a few observations on it for the space of exactly seven minutes! I replied to him, speaking to a cold and sullen house. I suppose not more than 20 Peers support us, the official 'opposition'. Lord Selborne followed with great violence. As usual the (Liberal) perverts are far more passionate than the orthodox (Tories). The fury of recrimination which goes on now all over the country, is sufficiently disgusting, which our side indulges in.

30 April 1887.   Academy Dinner. Two good speeches, Ld. Salisbury's & Trevelyan's. The rest dreary beyond description. G. Hamilton's[1123] a dull official statement: Huxley's[1124] a long prosy lecture: & the Archbishop of Canterbury,[1125] who outdid everyone, a string of flat pulpit commonplaces. The exhibition better than last year, as it might well be.

11 May 1887.   Poor dear Maynard Currie died this morning very suddenly: an excellent good kind creature, & most active clergyman: a great loss to us all.

13 May 1887.   Went to his funeral at Hingham.

26 May 1887.   Went to Falmouth, and on our return spent two days at Exmouth, &c. Sunday at Bath. Exmouth a charming seaside place. Much struck with Bath. The town is handsome, and it is now again thriving, its baths having come into fashion. Her old Roman bath is most curious.

6 June 1887.   Back in town.

7 June 1887.   A short time ago I resigned the Presidentship of University College in consequence of the petition to the Crown adopted by the Council, asking that Kings' & Univy. Colleges should be constituted a

---

[1122] The Irish Land bill, following the report of the Cowper Commission into Irish land holding, was presented by Salisbury as the counterpart to the government's coercion bill. The Land bill generated much discussion in the Lords.

[1123] Lord George Francis Hamilton (1845–1927), Cons. MP for Middlesex, 1868–84, for Ealing div., 1885–1906; 1st ld. adm., 1885–6, 1886–92; India sec., 1895–1903.

[1124] Thomas Henry Huxley (1825–95), biologist; foremost exponent of Darwin's theory of evolution.

[1125] Edward White Benson (1829–96), archbp. Canterbury, 1883–96.

new University for London.[1126] This foolish move arises from jealousy of the new Victoria Univy. & the desire of the Professors to get the examinations into their own hands, the worst possible system.

21 June 1887. Jubilee. We went to B. Currie's at Richmond Terrace to see the procession. The crowd was, as far as we saw it, very orderly, the cheers not enthusiastic. The number of people in the streets disappointed me. I expected to see many more. The great mass of working men were not there. In the morning we started at 8.30, but the block of carriages at Hyde Park Corner was hopeless: so we walked down Constitn. & through St James' Park. In the evening saw the illuminations in Piccadilly &c. (walking) an immense but quiet mob.

23 June 1887. The streets continue to be extraordinarily full of people most of them apparently from the country.

2 July 1887. Meeting of ex-Cabinet at Ld. Granville's. Some discussion as to our general attitude on Home Rule question. It was agreed that it would be unwise to attempt to frame details of a measure, based on the principle of retaining the Irish members in our Parliament. We then considered what course should be taken in the H. of Lords on the Crimes Bill. Rosebery wished to divide: Granville was strongly against dividing on the ground that we could only muster 20 or 25 supporters. This view prevailed. Granville is to make a protest in the name of all his late colleagues, & we are to avoid if we can, a general debate. I expect our Dissentient 'friends' will make a virulent attack on us.

Lastly we saw & approved the resolution, which is to be moved by Campbell-Bannerman on the Land Bill.

6 July 1887. At a garden party today at Coombe (B. Currie's). Harcourt, who was absent from the meeting on the 30th, broke out in one of his ridiculous tantrums, complaining that Gladstone will not agree with Hartington, which he might easily do &c. &c. Our election successes will set him straight again, but he is a strange 'inconsequent' creature, always swaying about from side to side, and equally violent whatever side he takes at the moment.

13 July 1887. A propos of the absurd title 'Magheramorne' taken by

---

[1126] For a printed statement of Kimberley's reasons for resignation, complete with marginalia, see KP 6 MS.eng.c.4466, item 16. Kimberley nevertheless remained member of the Senate, to which he was appointed in 1859, and eventually served as Chancellor of the University of London, 1899–1902. See also W.H. Allchin, *An Account of the Reconstruction of the University of London*, Part I (London, 1905), 176–80.

Sir James Hogg,[1127] I hear that his brother-in-law Ld. Penrhyn's butler was so puzzled by it, that he announced him as the 'late Sir James Hogg'!

Our position, as a party, is improving. Trevelyan comes back (rather illogically) to the fold, and the Liberal voters who abstained or went against us at the Dissolution, are evidently returning to our side. But we have an uphill battle still to fight & probably a long one.

15 July 1887.   A thunderstorm with a shower of rain after an unbroken drought & great heat for six weeks. An amusing scene yesterday in the House of Lords. In pursuance of our view that as it was of no use dividing on the Crimes Bill, Granville made a protest on our behalf against the Bill.

19 July 1887.   Meeting at Granville's to draw up Protest against Crimes Bill: present, Granville, Spencer, Rosebery, Herschell, Thring & self.

28 July 1887.   We went to Kimberley.

3 August 1887.   To a meeting at Lynn, where I made a speech to about 1,100 people which was well received.

4 August 1887.   Harvest begins on Park farm.

8 August 1887.   Do. on Home Farm.

11 August 1887.   To London for a night to attend debate in Lords on Commons' amendments to Irish Land Bill. Argyll began with his usual declamation against us, rambling over all manner of topics: *moutarde apres diner!* Then we discussed the amendments till 12.30. The Tory Lords afraid to strike, tho' they swallowed their pill with very wry faces. On the whole bill not much altered from the Commons' version. Govt. is much weakened by these bungling affairs and the cynical admissions of Lord Salisbury.

23 August 1887.   Harvest finished on Park Farm.

17 September 1887.   Went to Chippenham to address a political meeting. An open air meeting: 3000 said to be present: they did not look so many. The rainy morning no doubt diminished the attendance. All the

[1127] Sir James Macnaghten M'Garel-Hogg, 1st Baron Magheramorne (1823–90), Cons. MP for Bath, 1865–8, for Truro, 1871–85, for Hornsey, 1885–7; chairman of Metropolitan bd. of wks., 1870–89.

talk of course about Ireland. Mr Dillwyn,[1128] Mr John O'Connor, (M.P. for Tipperary) and self the principal speakers. We were very well received, and O'Connor's harrowing descriptions of evictions &c. evidently made a deep impression. These Irish M.Ps will do infinite harm to the Tories by stirring up the English labourers and artisans against them. Mr J. Fuller, eldest son of Mr G. P. Fuller M.P. for Westbury div. of Wiltshire, made a first appearance & was unanimously approved as candidate for the Chippenham Divn.[1129] I stayed two nights with the Fullers at Neston Park. Very pleasant people. Mrs F. a sister of Hicks Beach but a strong Liberal.

25 October 1887.   Snow lying on the ground!

27 October 1887.   To a meeting at Louth Lincolnshire. Some 1500 people in town hall. Usual Home Rule Speeches: meeting very enthusiastic. I suppose this 'stumping' is useful: it is certainly not an agreeable occupation. I stayed the night with Mr Bennett, lately M. P. for Gainsboro' Div.[1130]

25 January 1888.   To a meeting at East Dereham where I made the usual Home Rule speech. The other speaker was a fluent Irishman, Mr. Patrick Power, M.P. for a divn. of Waterford county.[1131] The audience seemed to be much pleased with our orations.

6 February 1888.   Moved to London.

9 February 1888.   Parliament met. Ld. Crawford[1132] moved the address in one of the dreariest speeches I ever heard, and Lord Armstrong[1133] read a speech, as seconder, principally remarkable for its advocacy of expenditures on fortifications, to be armed of course with Armstrong guns. Ld. Granville was pungent occasionally, rambling generally, & Ld. Salisbury neat and quiet in reply. Then we adjourned.

Last night the members of the last Cabinet except Lefevre, with two

---

[1128] Lewis Dillwyn (1814–92), Lib. MP for Swansea, 1855–92.

[1129] George Pargiter Fuller (1833–1927), Lib. MP for Wiltshire West, 1885–95; John Michael Fuller (1864–1915), Lib. MP for Wiltshire West, 1900–11). In 1892 J. Fuller was defeated as Lib. candidate in Wiltshire Chippenham division.

[1131] Joseph Bennett (1829–1908), Lib. MP for Lincolnshire Gainsboro' division, 1885–6, 1892–5.

[1131] Patrick Power (1850–1913), Home Rule MP for Waterford, 1884–1910.

[1132] James Lindsay, 26th Earl of Crawford (1847–1913), Cons. MP for Wigan, 1874–80, when he succeeded to the title.

[1133] William George Armstrong, 1st Baron Armstrong of Cragside (1810–1900), arms manufacturer.

or three others (Trevelyan, Fowler & C. Russell amongst them), met at
9.30 at the house Gladstone has taken in James Street. That extraordinary old man having just arrived from Cannes, & swallowed some
dinner, discussed business for an hour or so with as much briskness as
if he was 50 years old, and had been staying quietly at home, instead
of being just off a long railway journey. Nothing was said worth
recording.

Much surprised to hear that Dufferin has resigned the Viceroyalty
of India. I am told on very good authority that the reasons for this
strange step are pecuniary. He was afraid of being left without sufficient
means on the termination of his Indian appointment, & therefore
applied for an Embassy, and Rome being vacant, is to go to that not
very important post. If this is true, it is rather a pitiable affair from
every point of view.

8 March 1888. Meeting at Rosebery's to discuss on reform of the
House of Lords. Granville, Spencer, Ripon & myself. Harcourt came
in later. Rosebery propounded his scheme. Ripon swallowed the whole
eagerly. G. threw cold water on it, Spencer & I favourable to reform
generally without pledging ourselves to R's details. It was agreed that
R. should bring his proposals forward on his own responsibility, we
giving general support to inquiry.[1134] The time is certainly ripe for
discussion of this extremely difficult question. The Radicals wish for no
reform of the House, which they would let perish, as the power of the
Crown has perished, by senile decay. For my own part I disbelieve in
the possibility of governing this Empire by a single elected assembly
without any checks. Either there must be an effective second House,
or some other system of restraint upon the action of the single House.
The latter would be very difficult to devise, as we have no such
materials as the Americans have in their separate States. If, as is not
impossible, the outcome of the Home Rule agitation should be some
system of federation, the case might be different. At all events I do not
think any important measure for altering the present constitution of
the House of Lords could be safely adopted until we have settled the
'Home Rule' question. Meantime it will be useful to discuss any plans
which may be suggested for reform, tho' I do not expect any present
practical result.[1135]

In the afternoon meeting of ex-Cabinet (and H. Fowler) in Gladstone's

---

[1134] Rosebery moved for a select committee to consider reform of the House of Lords.
3 *Hansard* 323 (19 March 1888), 1548.

[1135] Rosebery subsequently moved for a committee of enquiry into reform of the House
of Lords.

room at H. of Commons to consider Barttelot's motion on army.[1136] The opinion was that, whilst economy should be supported, the wild schemes for putting the expenditure into the hands of soldiers,[1137] freed from parliamentary control, should be strenuously opposed. It was agreed also that on Labouchere's motion on H. of Lords, such general approval should be given as is implied in voting against the Speaker leaving the chair (to go into Supply). This will pledge us to consider reform of the hereditary basis of the H. of Lords without tying us to any particular proposition. Harcourt talked great nonsense, as usual, on both questions.

9 March 1888. Death of German Emperor. Went to Kimberley on March 28 and returned to town on April 12. Very cold weather; constant North wind & snow storms. (in the last new slang, 'blizzards').

13 April 1888. To a meeting of Liberal members at the Nat. Lib. Club under the presidency of Stansfeld to talk over Locl. Gt. Bill[1138] – sensible talk, unanimous desire for long & full discussion on 2nd reading. Some one however opportunely reminded the meeting of Mr Smith and the closure.

19 April 1888. Thursday. St Beaconsfield's Day. A mob of worshipers with offerings of primroses round the statue of the saint in Palace Yard. Can it be true that the primrose was not his favourite flower, but that the label attached to the primrose wreath sent by the Queen to his funeral on which was written 'his favourite flower' meant Prince Albert's?
  'These by thy gods O Israel'!

19 May 1888. Went to Falmouth: then to Newquay, where is a fine bold rugged coast, & from Newquay to Wells, where we stayed three days, & saw the lovely cathedral, & the curious picturesque old Bishop's Palace. Made excursions also to Glastonbury (remains of the Abbey) and the pass through the Cheddar Rift, a magnificent piece of rock scenery. Fine weather throughout.

30 May 1888. Returned to town.

[1136] Walter Barttelot (1820–93), Cons. MP for Sussex W., 1860–85, for Sussex N.W., 1885–93. Barttelot's motion called for an increase in military expenditure. 3 *Hansard* 323 (5 March 1888), 239.
[1137] On the curious turn to which such thinking led, see Wolseley to Kimberley, 4 Oct. 1893, in *Liberal by Principle*, 213–13.
[1138] Bill reforming structure and powers of County Councils.

15 June 1888.   Friday. The unfortunate Emperor Frederick[1139] died after 3 months reign.

16 June 1888.   Isabel safely confined of a girl at Witton at six this morning.[1140]

10 July 1888.   Singular scene in the H. of Lords. Salisbury's Life Peers Bill (2nd reading) was debated for some time, no one saying much in its favour.[1141] The last speaker was Rosebery, who made a very amusing sarcastic answer to Argyll: then Salisbury rose and informed us that he had just heard that Smith had told the H. of Commons that the Bill wd. not be proceeded with. It evidently took Salisbury as much by surprise as it did every one else. As for the bill, no one cares any thing about it, one way or the other.

12 July 1888.   Thursday. If the collapse on Tuesday was singular, to day there was a still more extraordinary scene. A very full House assembled to hear Argyll move a vote of confidence in the Govt. about Ireland. He made rather a poor speech & no one answering him, the debate collapsed. The whole thing was a farce, & very properly declined to be trotted out in order that Selborne & the other Dissentient Liberals might deliver orations on Ireland. We had our say a few nights ago on Camperdown's motion,[1142] when Spencer made an excellent speech: & I also discussed for a few minutes. But all these discussions are stale, flat & unprofitable, as mere academical discussions always are.[1143]

17 July 1888.   Dear Army engaged to Miss Arnold.[1144]

11 August 1888.   The session closed with an admirable speech by

[1139] Frederick III (1831–88), king and German emperor; husband of Victoria Adelaide Mary Louise, eldest da. of Queen Victoria.

[1140] Isabel, third child of Lord Wodehouse.

[1141] The measure provided for the appointment of a number of life peers, no more than fifty in total and never more than five in one year.

[1142] Camperdown called attention to the involvement of the National League in crimes in Ireland.

[1143] Cf. Kimberley to Ripon, 7 July 1888, in *Liberal by Principle*, 191.

[1144] On the marriage of Armine Wodehouse and Eleanor Arnold, da. of Matthew Arnold, see J. Powell, 'Parenthood and Politics: Some Reflections on the Shared Values of Matthew and Eleanor Arnold', *Nineteenth-Century Prose* 16 (1988–9), 35–46.

Herschell against the Parnell Commission Bill.[1145] Lord FitzGerald,[1146] the law lord, a hot Unionist, told me he entirely disapproved of the Bill, and I heard from Herschell that Lord Watson[1147] was loud in condemnation of it. Ld. Bramwell[1148] took the same view, and I hear that most of the leading lawyers of whatever party are averse to the employment of judges in this partisan business. Of course the whole matter has from the beginning been a mere party battle. Parnell in the judgment of many people made a false move in demanding inquiry after the Atty. General's speech in the O'Donnell case.[1149] His position was excellent: he had asked for & been refused inquiry by a Committee. The whole Gladstonian & Nationalist party was on his side & treated the 'letters' as forgeries. What more could he want? By demanding again inquiry, he gave the Govt. the opportunity of making the clever move of the Commission. A good deal of damage was done to them in the discussions on the bill, but on the whole, the advantage remains, I think, on their side. The further progess in the game will be interesting to watch, but in no case can any good result to the country.

Harcourt has been outdoing himself in violence. Great as is his rhetorical ability, it is difficult to say whether on a balance he does our party more good or harm. I doubt the justice of accusations against him of insincerity. I believe at the moment he says what he really thinks, but then he changes his opinions as fast as the chameleon its colours. I have often known him within 24 hours to argue with equal vehemence on opposite sides on important questions, and this not in orations but in private consultations. How can he ever lead a party?

15 August 1888.   Went to Kimberley.

22 August 1888.   Finished getting up park hay to day!! Harvest scarcely begun any where in this neighbourhood.

27 August 1888.   Harvest began on Home Farm. Disastrous weather.

[1145] The Parnell Commission confirmed that letters linking Parnell to the Phoenix Park murders were in fact forgeries, written by Richard Pigott (1828–89) and published in *The Times* in 1887.

[1146] John Fitzgerald (1816–89), Lib. MP for Ennis, 1852–60; sol. genl. Ireland, 1855–6; atty.-genl. Ireland, 1856–8, 1859–60, when appointed to the Queen's bench; cr. Baron Fitzgerald, 1882.

[1147] William Watson (1828–99), Cons. MP for Universities of Glasgow and Aberdeen, 1876–80, when cr. Baron Watson; Lord Advocate, 1876.

[1148] George Bramwell, Baron Bramwell (1808–92), ld. justice of appeal, 1876–81; cr. Baron Bramwell, 1882.

[1149] Frank Hugh O'Donnell (1848–1916), Home Rule MP for Dungarvan, 1877–85; unsuccessfully sued *The Times* for publishing 'Parnellism and Crime' in 1888 which led to the setting up of the Parnell Commission.

15 September 1888.   Finished harvest on Park and Home farms except raking. Much corn has been got up in bad condition.

22 September 1888.   Harvest now over here. The last week we had fine weather.

20 October 1888.   I was Chairman of Committee of magistrates to settle the new county Divisions.[1150] Our sitting to day sufficed, the matter having been thrashed out by an informal Committee wh. met several times.

13 November 1888.   Went to Bristol to attend Anchor dinner. Usual speeches, by Wilfrid Lawson,[1151] Asquith[1152] & self. The 'Dissentient Liberals' were eliminated from the dinner for the first time, but a full attendance notwithstanding. Stayed two nights with Stafford Howard[1153] at Thornbury Castle, a very curious old house, a small part of a great ruin the remains of a house built by the Duke of Buckingham in Henry the Eighth's reign. We drove over to Berkeley Castle, a splendid example of a genuine feudal castle. It has been most elaborately furnished by the present owner, Ld. Fitzharding,[1154] best known as the 'Giant', 'lucus a non lucendo''.

January, 1889.   Elected without opposition C. C. for the Wymondham Divn. on the 24th. Virtually I was elected on the 16th, the nomination day. On the 9th I made a political speech at Wymondham wh. was well received.

7 February 1889.   Thursday. 1st meeting of Provisional County Council at Norwich.[1155] Coulton[1156] of Lynn proposed me as Chairman: Ld. Walsingham[1157] proposed R. Gurdon. Gurdon who was elected by 37

[1150] County divisions pursuant to the creation of County Councils by the Local Government Act of 1888.

[1151] Sir Wilfrid Lawson (1829–1906), Lib. MP for Carlisle, 1859–65, 1868–85, for Cumberland, Cockermouth division, 1886–1900, 1906).

[1152] Herbert Henry Asquith (1852–1928), Lib. MP for East Fife, 1886–1918; home sec., 1892–5; joined Lib. Imperialists, 1899; chan. exch., 1905–8; pr. min., 1908–16.

[1153] Edward Stafford Howard (1851–1916), Lib. MP for Cumberland, 1876–85, for Gloucestershire, Thornbury division, 1885–6.

[1154] Francis Berkeley, 2nd Baron Fitz-Hardinge (1826–96), Lib. MP for Cheltenham, 1856–65.

[1155] For an expanded account, see Kimberley to Monk Bretton, 8 Feb. 1889, in *Liberal by Principle*, 191–2.

[1156] J.J. Coulton, solic., Middle King's Lynn.

[1157] Thomas de Grey, 6th Baron Walsingham (1843–1919) Cons. MP for W. Norfolk, 1865–70, when he succ. as 6th Baron.

votes to 18. Every J. P. but Johnny voted against me. The 18 for me were all Liberals but one (Mutimer).[1158] Two Liberal J.Ps against me, L. Buxton[1159] & Lee Warner,[1160] and one other Liberal. Total of Liberal Councillors 21, including myself. The Tories are 25, the lib. Unionists 11. It was therefore nearly a pure party vote. No doubt also the Squires (who don't love me), were glad to give me a snub. The Aldermen (19) were then elected, 11 Tories, 3 Lib. Unins., 5 Liberals. What nonsense it is to talk of the elections not being political! Even if in some cases on this first occasion, politics have been kept out, in future the elections will be just as political as in the towns. Of course any one could foresee this. It was quite inevitable.

20 February 1889.   Went to London. Dined with Rosebery. Gladstone & other ex Ministers there. Decided that amendment should be moved on Address.

21 February 1889.   Thursday. Meeting of ex Ministers at Spencer House. Form of amendment agreed on.[1161] Gladstone wonderfully vigorous, but getting very deaf. Debate on Address short & unimportant in House of Lords this evening. Smashing evidence against 'Times' on Parnell inquiry today.[1161a] It looks as if Buckle & Co. & the rest of the crew will get their deserts.

24 February 1889.   Sunday. My dearest wife alas! taken very ill. Terrible anxiety about her.

29 March 1889.   Last week a meeting at Granville's to discuss course to be taken on Naval Estimates. Gladstone not there. Agreed to press for reasons of Govt. for increased expenditures &c. &c. but not as a party to oppose, except as to proceeding by bill instead of the ordinary manner. The Radicals will vote against all increase, but many of our party would not go so far, and rightly. Harcourt harangued us in his finest vein of peace at any price rhodomontade, after which J. Morley quietly asked, is not the question whether one naval force is sufficient or not?

On the 27th John Bright died. A great orator, a most honourable upright man, a kind and loyal colleague. He was not a good man of

---

[1158] J.H. Mutimer, farmer.
[1159] Louis Buxton, J.P.
[1160] Henry Lee-Warner, J.P.
[1161] Morley gave notice in the Commons of an amendment to the Address on Ireland.
[1161a] Under cross examination Richard Pigott collapsed, subsequently confessed to forging letters incriminating Parnell, fled the country, and on 1 March 1889 committed suicide in Madrid.

business: indeed I have often heard him say that he felt his deficiency of administrative experience. His strength lay in his oratory, but he was also a calm and judicious adviser in Cabinet deliberations.

The Duke of Buckingham died, very unexpectedly, at the same time. He was a man of very mediocre abilities, a total failure as Chairman of the N. Wesn. Ry., as Secy. for the Colonies & Govn. of Madras. His merits were his simplicity, industry, and upright character; and he discharged the duties of Chairman of the House with fair success.

13 April 1889. Went to Norwich to preside at a meeting at which Rosebery was chief spokesman. A very successful affair over 5,000 people in Agricultural Hall besides an overflow meeting. Stayed the night at Carrow (Colman's M.P.).[1162]

17 April 1889. To Althorp for a night to attend meeting at Daventry where I made the usual speech.

25 April 1889. My dear wife is (thank God) at last recovering from her terrible illness. Sir Oscar Clayton,[1163] who attends my wife, told me a good story *a propos* of a new opiate, sulphonal, which has been given every night with great success to my wife. He was called in to attend 'the most eminent man in our profession' (obviously Jenner) who could get no sleep. He gave him sulphonal and the effect was 8 hours good sleep. At his next visit the 'eminent man' said to Clayton: 'your draught almost makes me believe in medicine.' 'What,' replied Clayton, 'don't you believe in your own medicines?' 'Not a a bit' –

11 May 1889. Lord Malmesbury's death announced this morning. A shrewd man of the world, with a singularly blundering way of talking when on his legs. His celebrated saying, 'knowledge of reference is knowledge itself', a good specimen of his awkward utterance in the H. of Lords. Every one liked him.

29 May 1889. To Lord Mayor's dinner to Dufferin on the occasion of his receiving the freedom of the city. Dufferin ill, & his speech dull.

3 June 1889. Conversation in H. of Lords about Sir H. Robinson's resignation of Cape Governorship.[1164] Carnarvon & I spoke. I have

---

[1162] Jeremiah James Colman (1830–98), mustard and starch manufacturer; Lib. MP for Norwich, 1871–95.
[1163] Sir Oscar Clayton (1816–92) surgeon to the Prince of Wales and the Duke of Edinburgh.
[1164] Sir Hercules Robinson (1824–97), Governor of South Africa, 1881–9.

since learnt from Carnarvon that he communicated in writing to Knutsford these conditions on which Robinson would return to S. Africa: (1) that his policy should be supported; (2) that his term of office should be for three more years certain; (3) that he should receive some mark of distinction (meaning a peerage). He demanded an immediate answer, his reason for this being, that he had been offered certain lucrative directorships, which could not be kept open for him beyond a certain time. This was putting a pistol to the head of the Govt., & I cannot say I am surprised that they declined to give way to such arrogance. There has been some bad feeling between Knutsford and Robinson about the Pope Hennessy inquiry, Robinson being angry that Knutsford would not publish the papers on that subject.[1165]

6 June 1889. Armine married to Miss Arnold at St Peter's Church, Eaton Square.[1166] After the marriage they went to Tunbridge Wells, to the Wellington Hotel. If good wishes can make them happy, they will be happy indeed. God bless them.

8 June 1889. Saturday. Went to the Deacons at Poynters.[1167] Very bad weather. Stayed till Tuesday, & then went to Tunbridge Wells to see the bridal pair. On Thursday to Dover to see them off. Back to London from Tunbridge Wells on Saturday June 15. The Hotel in a fine situation & good clean rooms, but very bad food and very dear. The air of Tunbridge Wells delightful & the environs, Penshurst &c. charming.

25 June 1889. Thursday. With other ex-official people to Buckingham Palace to make our Kotow to the Shah. What a ridiculous fuss is made about this semi-barbarian. Does anyone suppose that the shows and gaping crowds here will weigh a feather with him against the Russian myriads which overshadow him. Why indeed should they?

26 June 1889. Friday. Govt. beaten on an amendment moved by Lord Bath on 3rd reading (or rather after it) to Land Transfer Bill,[1168]

[1165] John Pope Hennessy (1834–91) was suspended as governor of Mauritius in 1886 following an open quarrel with his lieutenant-governor. Reinstated despite censure for partisanship and poor judgment, Hennessy successfully sued *The Times* for libeling his administration. See Pope-Hennessy, *Verandah: Some Episodes in the Crown Colonies, 1867–89* (Toronto, 1964), 285–302.

[1166] See entry for 17 July 1888.

[1667] The home of Bertram Currie's sister, Mary.

[1168] On 25 June 1889 Bath opposed the third reading of the Land Transfer bill claiming opponents of the legislation had not had sufficient opportunity to amend it. 3 *Hansard* 337 (25 June 1889), 656.

whereupon, Salisbury, looking daggers, withdrew the Bill. We of course supported the Bill. I sat all last session and half this on the Select Committee to which the bill was referred. A waste of time, as it turned out. The bill was however greatly improved in the Committee by Lords Selborne & Herschell. As to the Chancellor, he seemed to know little about the bill and to care less. What geese the Tory peers are who followed Bath!

9 July 1889. Tuesday. Meeting of ex-Ministers at Spencer House to discuss Royal grants. Gladstone made the best fight he could for liberality, but the predominant feeling amongst the M.P.s was fear of their constituencies.[1169] There is no doubt a wide-spread dislike to any further grants, arising largely from the belief that the Queen has saved large sums of money, and from a just dissatisfaction at the Queen's retired life. The people think that as they pay highly for the maintenance of a court, they are entitled to some return for their money in the form of courtly show & magnificence. Whether the Queen has large savings, no one seemed to know. The Court officials say she has only saved £400,000. That her expenditure on Balmoral & Osborne has swallowed up a great part of her income, is very probable.

The result of our consultations was that no one was in favour of grants to any of the Sovereign's grandchildren except the children of the heir-apparent. A majority, I think, was for making a grant to the Prince of Wales' eldest son. Gladstone & two or three more would extend the grants to all the Prince's children. A suggestion that any Grants should take the form of an addition to the Prince of Wales' income out of which the Prince should provide for all his children married or unmarried, met with a good deal of favour.

There is of course much talk everywhere about the Fife marriage.[1170] Personally I have no objection to it: I would much rather that the Royal family should ally themselves with British peers than foreigners. What a relief it would be to have Princes who did not speak English like all our present Princes, with a German accent. On the whole the marriage seems to be popular.

8 August 1889. Began harvest on Home Farm. Corn terribly laid, & bad stormy weather. Every prospect, I fear, of a disastrous harvest. The crops are however good, as far as we can judge. (This seems doubtful Sept 2)

[1169] The Liberal leadership were unwilling to support new grants for younger members of the Royal Family, though Gladstone hoped something might be done for the family of the Prince of Wales. *Gladstone Diaries*, XI, 216–17.

[1170] Alexander Duff, 6th Earl of Fife (1849–1912), cr. Duke of Fife, 1889, married Princess Louise of Wales (1867–1931), da. of Prince of Wales, on 27 July 1889.

What a sorry exhibition my old colleagues made of themselves on the Royal Grants Bill! Gladstone was straightforward, consistent & courageous: so, it must be admitted, was Labouchere whatever one may think of his opinions. The maneuvering of J. Morley was a futile attempt 'to run with the hare & hunt with the hounds', to have at once the credit of supporting G. and voting against the bill. Trevelyan who voted with Labouchere was consistent in his desertion of G. The rest really deserted G., and managed also to be inconsistent.

16 August 1889.   Spent our 42nd wedding day with great contentment & thankfulness for my dear wife's recovery.

26 August 1889.   Monday. Went to Prestwold & stayed there till Saturday. On Tuesday after deluges of rain the weather at last cleared in Norfolk, and the harvest is going on well.

Whilst at Prestwold went to Derby, to see the Crown Derby china manufactory. The china now made is quite equal to the old, but somewhat different in the style of painting. I was surprised to find that no foreigners are employed for painting. Most of the work people are young women and girls. They are taken on at 14 to learn the business.

Derby a very uninteresting town. It has some of the most hideous buildings I have seen, even in English towns.

11 September 1889.   Harvest at last finished on Park & Lodge farms. On the Home farm on the 6th.

1 December 1889.   Lord Blachford's death reminds me of the important era in my political life when I became Secy. for the Colonies.[1171] He was about to retire when I was appointed but very kindly stayed on a year, that I might not have to begin my Secretaryship with a novice under me. When he did go, I felt as if an avalanche of business had suddenly descended on me. Blachford was a most able permanent Under Secy., quick, accurate, and indefatigable in work. He is, I think, the only permanent official I have ever worked with who could write a really good despatch. Except when he was under me, I have always had to write really important despatches myself. The only fault of his despatches was that he was so logical & incisive that he confuted an adversary too completely.

I remember apologizing to him for softening his drafts, and he said I was quite right to put some water in his wine. It is seldom politic to crush an opponent in argument in dealing with foreign or colonial

---

[1171] Sir Frederic Rogers, 1st Baron Blachford (1811–89) was perm. und. sec. of the Colonial Office, 1859–71.

Statesmen. They are sure to take their revenge. Blachford told me that when he was first employed under the Colonial Office, Lord Grey, then Col. Secy. told him he was hopelessly inefficient, and that he could not but acknowledge that Lord Grey was then quite right.

5 December 1889. Went to a political meeting at Dereham, made the usual speech. White, the Norwich Shoe-manufacturer, presided & spoke remarkably well. Kilbride M.P.[1172] (one of Balfour's criminals) was the other speaker, not an eloquent man, but spoke sensibly & was well received.

5 February 1890. We all went to London.

8 February 1890. Meeting of ex-Cabinet with Sir C. Russell & A. Morley at 10 St James Sqre. where Gladstone is for this season. The old man was in wonderful vigour & spirits, but he made the significant remark, that his memory failed him as to recent events, & he is increasingly deaf.[1173] He gave us a brief account of his conversation with Parnell about the Home Rule Bill, of the future on the occasion of Parnell's recent visit to Hawarden. The points of these discussions were enumerated by G., as far as I remember, as follows

1. Are the powers to be given to the Irish Parlt. to be enumerated in the bill, or the reserved powers, all powers not reserved being given to the Irish Part.? G. inclines to the first alternative.

2. Is the supremacy of the Imperial Parliament to be reserved in express terms?

3. Would the Irish party object to Ireland paying a fixed percentage on all Imperial expenditure? G. evidently inclines to this arrangement. He said that fairness to Ireland required that better financial terms should be given her than those of our bill of /86. Giffen, Bd. of Trade,[1174] and Treasury officials, he said, both take this view.

4. Retention of Irish members in Imperial Parliament. G. is disposed to prefer the retention of a limited number of Irish members, say 1/3 of present number, with power to vote on all questions, to retaining the whole number with power only to vote on 'Imperial questions'

[1172] Denis Kilbride (1848–1924), Home Rule MP for Kerry South, 1887–95, for Galway North, 1895–1900, for Kilkenny South, 1903–18.

[1173] See *Gladstone Diaries*, XII, 271, for the detailed account of the meeting in Morley's diary.

[1174] Robert Giffen (1837–1910), chief of the statistical dept., bd. of trade, 1876–97; edited *Journal of the Royal Statistical Society*, 1876–91; Lib. U. from 1886.

(with the exception that the whole number should be entitled to come & vote on any amendment of the Home Rule Act). G. makes the retention of any Irish members dependent upon its being clearly shown that public opinion in Gt Britain absolutely demands it as a *sine qua non*: & he would propose that in the Home Rule Bill this provision should be enacted 'so long as Parliament shall not otherwise determine', in order to show that the Impl. Parliament may at any time repeal it without any breach of faith with Ireland. In short this provision would be wholly dependent on British opinion.

5. Police. He would propose that recruiting should cease for the Constabulary, who should be gradually replaced by an ordinary local police.

6. That for some specified time the Imperial authority should have a veto on the appt. of Judges.

7. That the Irish Parliament should be prohibited from passing laws invalidating contracts in the same way as the U. S. Congress is prohibited.

Parnell was ready to concede any of the points mentioned above, if necessary to pass the Bill.[1175] A little talk followed, but nothing material was said, as it was well understood that no final determinations will be come to at present on the subject. Parnell entirely agrees with G. that it would be unwise to make any further public explanations of the plan. Harcourt made some rather foolish observations, *more suo*, with which nobody agreed. Subsequently it was determined that a bill should be introduced in the Commons, relieving R. Catholics of the disability to hold the offices of English Ld. Chancellor & Lord Lieut: of Ireland, and that a motion should be made about privilege re the forged 'Times' letters.

Mr. C. Russell told us that Parnell's costs in the Commission were not more than £30,000, that the 'Times' costs are at least £80,000; some people say as much as £160,000. Its circulation has fallen from 60,000 to 30,000 a day, & the shareholders get no dividend. This is the appropriate punishment for the shameful conduct of Walter & Co. If the pillory were still in fashion, they would rightly deserve to be put in it.

11 February 1890.　Meeting of ex-Cabinet & others at Gladstone's to hear Queen's speech read. Nothing passed of importance. Meeting of Parliament.

March.　Isabel and my two grandsons have had influenza at Witton:

[1175] Cf. Gladstone's private memorandum of the conversation, 23 Dec. 1889, in *Gladstone's Diaries*, XII, 256.

the two children badly; Philip was at death's door. They are now, thank God, all convalescent. This extraordinary epidemic has been very prevalent near Witton, as in most other places.

13 March 1890. Dined with civil Engineers in the splendid new Hall at Lincoln's Inn. A colleague of Rosebery (who was there) in the London Cy. Council was behind our chairs, the caterer of the dinner looking after the waiters & dishes!

21 March 1890. Debate in H. of Lords on Salisbury's motion to inscribe Report of Parnell Commission on Journals, wh. lasted till 12.30. Salisbury, evidently suffering from ill health, not quite so forcible as usual, but his speech full of scorn & bitterness against the Irish. Herschell somewhat laboured & too long, not nearly so effective as in his speech on the Commission Bill two years ago. Rosebery spoke excellently; nothing else remarkable. I had no intention of uttering a word, but at Granville's request I answered Selborne, & managed to get through half an hour at dinner time without a fiasco. There was a tolerably full & attentive House all the evening.

I was glad of the opportunity of expressing my strong condemnation of the 'Times', & their article next morning showed that the anonymous slanderers have a hide not quite impenetrable.

16 May 1890. To Norwich for the Gladstone 'demonstration'. Dined at Carrow Abbey, & afterwards to the Agricultural Hall, which was packed from top to bottom. Seven thousand persons are said to have been there. G. had a magnificent reception. He spoke for about an hour and ten minutes & with all his usual eloquence. His voice, though at times rather husky, was wonderfully clear & strong, and reached to every part of the immense assembly. After the meeting, I went to H. Birkbeck's[1176] at Stoke, a charming place, for the night, & returned next day to London.

14 June 1890. Saturday. We went to Falmouth, and stayed till Friday: a pleasant visit.

24 June 1890. Meeting at Gladstone's. Everyone in great spirits at the almost incredible blunders of the Govt. about their public house compensation Bill. Abandonment of the scheme, now inevitable, will not retrieve their position. They will lose heavily in the country wherever there are Liberal Unionists who are also temperance fanatics. I hear

[1176] Henry Birkbeck (1853–1930), Norfolk Liberal; dir. of Barclay's Bank.

these are coming back to us freely, Caine[1177] means, I am told, a real return to our fold. His apology in his address to his Constituents for his change of front on the Irish question is feeble enough, but what could he say? We discussed the East African & Heligoland agreement.[1178] No one wishes really to oppose it though there will be some deserved criticism. Harcourt was in his most characteristic mood. In his eyes at this moment the Irish question is insignificant as compared with the great pot house controversy. When he descanted on this theme, Mr G. drily said 'I do not agree with you'. The twinkle in Mr G's eye was keenly satirical I thought.

16 July 1890. Wednesday. Attended Liberal meeting at Aylesbury, made usual speech. Lawson M.P (young 'Daily Telegraph') presided & spoke very well.[1179] Power M.P. for Waterford poured forth usual Irish eloquence. Enthusiastic reception of speeches, as usual. Are these eternal meetings any real use? I am told we have no chance at Aylesbury. The Jews (Rothschilds) are far too strong for us. We slept at the George Inn, good plain food.

19 July 1890. Dear little Jack went away, after staying with us a week.

7 August 1890. Went to Kimberley.

16 August 1890. Began harvest on Home Farm to day. Park Farm on the 14th., Lodge Farm on 15th., very fickle weather.

19 August 1890. Heard that Isabel has measles (with a quinsy). Parliament is at length prorogued. A dull and profitless session. The Govt. is damaged by its utter failure to conduct its business through the H. of Commons, but Lord Salisbury's very successful settlement of the African questions[1180] will go some way to neutralise the effect of this failure.

[1177] William Sproston Caine (1842–1903), Lib. MP for Scarborough, 1880–5, Lib. U. for Barrow-in-Furness, 1886–90; Lib. for Bradford E., 1892–5.

[1178] Heligoland-Zanzibar Treaty, in which Germany recognised Zanzibar as a British protectorate and Uganda as British sphere of influence, in return for the North Sea island of Heligoland.

[179] Harry Levy-Lawson (1862–1933), Lib. MP for W. St Pancras, 1885–92, for Cirencester, 1893–5; Unionist MP for Mile End, 1905–6, 1910–16; succ. father as managing proprietor of *Daily Telegraph*, 1903–28.

[1180] Since October 1889, the government had signed a commercial convention with Egypt; agreed with Germany, France, and Portugal to the General Act of the Brussels Conference establishing guidelines for abolition of the interior slave trade and for regulating trade; and reached separate agreements with Zanzibar, Germany, and France resolving a variety of boundary and sovereignty disputes.

28 August 1890.   Since my last entry the settlement with Portugal has been added to Lord Salisbury's diplomatic achievements.[1181]

7 September 1890.   Harvest on Home farm is finished except a few rakings. On the whole notwithstanding the uncertain weather, the corn was got up in good condition.

15 September 1890.   Went to Prestwold and stayed till Saturday: beautiful warm weather.

24 September 1890.   Received the good news that Nelly[1182] was safely confined of a boy this afternoon at 21 Sloane Gardens.

24 October 1890.   Went to Gilbey's[1183] Elsenham Hall to attend meeting at Bishop Stortford. Sir Ch. Russell & I spoke, and were well received. Next morning we saw Gilbey's stud, a wonderful show of shire cart horses & Norfolk trotters. We saw a two year old shire cart stallion for which G. had just given 1500 guineas.

24 November 1890.   Went to town for opening of Parliament on the 25th. Dined with Arnold Morley in Stratton Street. Gladstone & all late Cabinet present except Rosebery, Ripon, & Stansfeld. Discussed at much length question of Parnell's positon. It was unanimously agreed that looking to the strong feeling in the Liberal party against Parnell on account of his conduct in the O'Shea divorce affair, it was essential that he should cease to be leader of the Irish party.[1184] No one seemed to doubt that he would retire on learning from Gladstone that his retirement was essential for success of Home Rule measure. Nothing else was discussed.

25 November 1890.   Meeting of Parliament. I went to H. of Commons after our House was up & heard Gladstone speak, but all spirit was taken out of him by the news that Parnell had been re-appointed leader. No one talks or thinks of anything else.

26 November 1890.   Went back to Ky. I stayed at Almond's hotel the

---

[1181] Agreement of 20 Aug. 1890, formally ratified in a convention of 11 June 1891, confirming British claims to Mashonaland and Nyasaland; granting a wider sphere of influence to Portugal in her East African colony; and providing for free navigation of the Zambezi River.

[1182] Eleanor Arnold Wodehouse.

[1183] Sir Walter Gilbey (1831–1914), wine merchant.

[1184] Parnell was cited correspondent by Capt. O'Shea in his divorce from Katherine O'Shea, Parnell's mistress. See accounts in *Gladstone Diaries*, XII, 340.

two nights I was in town. How shamefully Parnell is behaving! He will wreck Home Rule, & the prospects (up to this time) very bright of the Liberal party are completely over clouded. What a curious evil destiny seems always to cross every effort to pacify Ireland!

It began to snow on this day Nov. 25, and there was snow & frost till the 4th Decm. when there was a thaw. On the night of the 9th Dec. the frost returned &, with slight thaws on one or two days, lasted till the 23rd of January, when it finally broke up. The ice on the Lake was 10 inches thick. The cold, though continuous for so long, was not very severe. The lowest reading of the thermometre in the flower garden was 22 degrees of frost. After one day's thaw during this frost the roads were so completely frozen that a man skated from Carleton to Wymondham, & the Wademan's boys skated from the stable down the path to Carleton.

January 1891. The Duke of Bedford's death by his own hand was the occasion of a disgusting outburst in the newspapers about the alleged non-publicity of the inquest: but it turned out that the Coroner pursued the usual course, & gave all the customary notices. The Duke, whom I knew when he was Hastings Russell, was a cynical but pleasant man. He had a vein of dry humour, and possessed many accomplishments. In his latter days he became rather eccentric. I often met him at Grillions & he was a regular attendant in the H. of Lords.

4 February 1891. Went to London for the season.

9 February 1891. I hear from Herschell, who was present, that at a meeting of our ex-colleagues in town it was resolved to give no assurances to the Irish party, going beyond the lines of our old Home Rule policy, but in some form to repeat the old assurances to Dillon[1185] & McCarthy.[1186] Of course Parnell & the Tories will cry out that we have surrendered to Parnell, whatever we say.

10 February 1891. There is a hitch in the negotiations of McCarthy & Co. with Parnell. (which finally broke down).

9 March 1891. Went to Levee. In the evening began the snow fall,

[1185] John Dillon (1851–1927), Home Rule MP for Tipperary, 1880–3, for Mayo E., 1885–1918; Nationalist Party leader, 1896–1900.

[1186] Justin McCarthy (1830–1912), Home Rule MP for Langford Co., 1879–85, N. Langford, 1885–6, 1892–1900, for Londonderry, 1886–92; leader of Irish Nationalist Party, 1890–6.

which was so extraordinary in the South & South West of England.

18 March 1891.   To Darwen, where I made a speech to about 2,000 people in the theatre. I spoke for an hour & ten minutes. The audience was attentive & enthusiastic. I stayed for the night with Mr Huntington,[1187] a large wall paper manufacturer at Darwen, who is the Liberal candidate against Ld. Cranborne, the sitting member. Mrs. H. a pretty, talkative woman.

26 March 1891.   Went to Kimberley for Easter.

31 March 1891.   Lord Granville died. In him I lost an excellent & constant friend. His character has been so fully drawn in speeches and newspapers, that it is needless to say anything as to his many admirable qualities. His defect was inatten on to details, and a certain poc-ocurantism. This often made his work in Office defective in execution, in plain words 'sloppy', and was the cause of many of his failures. No man could give better advice or discern more clearly the wisest course of action, but the execution was often not equal to the design, and he was conscious of this himself. No greater mistake could be made than to impute weakness to him. His grasp was strong, and no one who knew him well, would have trifled with him for a moment. He was universally beloved, & he deserved it.

9 April 1891.   We returned to town. The weather was miserably cold & the country extraordinarily backward.

11 April 1891.   Saturday. Oxenbridge[1188] came to tell me that Mr Gladstone thought a meeting of Liberal Peers should be called to consider what should be done with regard to appointing a successor to Granville as leader in the Lords, but wished me to decide. I authorised Oxenbridge to call a meeting at his house for Tuesday next. We are a very select body 38 in all! In the afternoon I called on Mr G., & we had a long talk about the leadership. The upshot of it was that Mr G.'s opinion is that no leader should be appointed at present, & that I should go on managing business for us, as far as may be necessary as I did in Granville's absence. He had heard nothing from Rosebery who has gone abroad! Mr G. has summoned a meeting at his house of Peers who were members of his last Cabinet.

[1187] Charles Philip Huntington (1833–1906), Lib. MP for Darwen, 1892–5.

[1188] William Monson, Viscount Oxenbridge (1829–98), Lib. MP for Reigate, 1858–62, when he succ. as 7th Lord Monson; junior Lib. whip, 1874–80; Lib. chief whip, 1892–6.

13 April 1891.   Meeting accordingly at 18 Park Lane. Present, besides Mr G, Ripon, Spencer, and self with Oxenbridge. Herschell is unfortunately in France, & will not be back till Saturday. Mr G. repeated in substance what he had said to me. He had consulted Harcourt & J. Morley & Arnold Morley, who agreed with him. After some discussion we decided to follow Mr G's advice. Looking to all the circs. I think it is the best course. Next year there must be a dissolution, wh. possibly may result in a change of Govt. For many reasons it is better not to anticipate the choice of a leader which would then be made, & which would depend on the distribution of offices & many other considerations. Ripon told me he thought I ought to be definitely leader but against this much is to be said. I know well that I have not any influence with the party generally or in the country. Rosebery & Spencer both more or less fulfil this condition & I would most willingly serve under either of them. I imagine that the behind the scenes is that G. would like to appoint Spencer but that this might not be accepted by Rosebery.[1189] I am told that Harcourt has declared that if, after Mr G. is gone, Spencer were chosen as leader of the party, he would serve under him as leader of the H. of Commons, but not under Rosebery. This is probably true, as Harcourt & Rosebery did not get on at all well during the short time R. was under him at the Home Office.

14 April 1891.   This morning we had our meeting of Peers at Oxenbridge's. I explained why meeting called.[1190] Spenser then proposed our arrangement. I gave some further explanation. Cork[1191] thereupon said he thought the peers present would accept the arrangement as satisfactory, using some civil expressions towards me. Ripon expressed his entire concurrence, & no one else offering to say anything, I said I concluded I might assume the approval of the meeting, adding a few words as to my willingness to do whatever would best serve the interests of the party; and the meeting separated. Fifteen or sixteen peers were present. Eight sent excuses. Herschell is abroad, as well as Rosebery.[1192]

At the meeting of the House Ld. Cranbrook, in the absence of Ld. Salisbury, passed an eulogium on Granville. Myself, Derby, & Selborne followed.

[1189] On Gladstone and his high view of Spencer generally, see *Private Diaries of Sir Algernon West*, ed. H. G. Hutchinson (London, 1922), 114; Morley, *Life of Gladstone* III, 512; *PMP: Gladstone*, I, 164–5; *Personal Papers of Lord Rendel*, ed. F. E. Hamer (London, 1931), 143.

[1190] To consider the Liberal leadership in the Lords following Granville's death, Kimberley agreed to act as leader for the immediate future, without foreclosing other options in time.

[1191] Richard Boyle, 9th Earl of Cork (1829–1904).

[1192] To whom Kimberley wrote with a report, Kimberley to Rosebery, 14 April 1891, in *Liberal by Principle*, 195.

15 April 1891.   Went to see Mr G. about the Newfoundland Fishery Bill.[1193]

23 April 1891.   Meeting at Mr G's about Newfoundland. Spencer, Herschell, self, Harcourt, J. Morley & Mr G.

25 April 1891.   2nd reading of Newfoundland Bill in H. of Lords. Herschell & I made speeches. On the next stage, going into Committee I moved a resolution to proceed no further with Bill till time had been given to Newfd. legislature to pass the necessary Act. This was of course defeated by a large majority but I think we took up a very defensible position.

7 May 1891.   Meeting (which I summoned) in Committee room of H. of Lords to consider memorial to Ld. Granville. It went off very well. Men of all parties attended, & the proposal to raise money for a statue was most cordially adopted.[1194]

19 May 1891.   We went to Falmouth, with Army & Nelly. Very cold for the time of year but nice sunshine and not much rain. We enjoyed ourselves on the whole.

25 May 1891.   Returned to town.

29 May 1891.   Harcourt summouned us to a meeting at Gladstone's room in the Commons (G. himself is away at Hawarden nursing his convalescence from influenza) after the speech of Sir Wm. Whiteway[1195] at the bar on Newfoundland. But on Herschell & myself going to the Commons we found that the speech of Sir Wm. W. was not to be much, and a strange debate was going on, the 2nd reading of the Newfd. bill having actually been moved by the Govt., after it was announced that the Colonial Office had accepted the Bill passed by the Newfd. legislature! What inexplicable fatuity!
Harcourt spoke, too violently as usual. The adjournment was moved

---

[1193] The government introduced the measure on 19 March 1891 giving greater power to the Imperial parliament following Newfoundland's unwillingness to submit various questions to arbitration. On Kimberley's role in the Newfoundland question, see W. Wyndham-Quin, *Past Times and Pastimes* (2 vols., London, 1922), I, 109–15; also A.T. Bassett, *Gladstone to his Wife* (London, 1936), 255.

[1194] Kimberley was instrumental in organising the committee for raising memorial funds. See Kimberley to Rendel, 12 May 1891, Rendel Papers, Natl. Library of Wales, 1338.

[1195] Sir William Vallance Whiteway (1828–1908); premier, and atty. genl. of Newfoundland, 1878–85, 1889–94, again premier 1895–7.

from our side and defeated by the usual party majority, but it was obvious that the Tories were dissatisfied, & later in the evening the Govt. accepted a sensible resolution suggested by Bryce. The moving of the 2nd reading was evidently a fad of Salisbury's who had an idea that it wd. give satisfaction to France!

After the division on the adjournment we went to G's room, & discussed Manipur.[1196] Harcourt read a letter from G. in which, amongst other things, he said that it was just as well he should be away when the 'Free Education' Bill is brought in. Significant! He has always been unwilling to adopt 'Free Educn'.

2 June 1891. It is an amusing example of 'sic vos non vobis', that the resolution which the Govt. accepted on the Newfoundland question and for which much laudation has been bestowed on Bryce in the newspapers, was suggested by Roby,[1197] M.P. for Eccles, and as Harcourt could not speak a 2nd time, was put into the hands of Bryce who had no particular merit in the matter.

2 June 1891. Dined at Lincoln's Inn. I asked to be introduced to the Bishop of Oxford (Stubbs)[1198] when to my surprise he said 'the last time we met was at a lecture of Liddell's[1199] on Aristophanes'. He was little Stubbs of Christ Church!

The following is going the round of the town –
1st. Tory – 'we shall have to throw overboard our Jonah (Goschen).
2nd. Tory – 'but shall we find a whale to swallow him?'

Tories are very down in the mouth after the recent elections & the manifest failure of the 'free education' bid for the labourers' votes.

20 June 1891. Lord Coleridge told me that whilst the baccarat trial was going on, he met the D. of Connaught who asked him if he had any interesting business on hand! He did not know that C. was trying the case! This trial has been a very ugly affair for the Prince of Wales. Of course in 'society' his loose living, and gambling have long been notorious, but 'puritan' England was in blissful ignorance. If he does not pull up sharp now, the consequences will be serious. I hear he is very low in spirits, and he well may be.

[1196] Regarding British policy in the wake of a revolution in the Indian hill state of Manipur. See T. Legh, Lord Newton, *Lord Lansdowne: a Biography* (London, 1929), 80.

[1197] Henry John Roby (1830–1915), Lib. MP for Eccles, Lancashire, 1890–5.

[1198] William Stubbs (1825–1901), bp. of Oxford, 1888–1901. It is curious that Kimberley would not have placed Stubbs, especially as he had read his *Constitutional History of England*, See Reading Journal, Oct.1887, KP1, 15/ /10.

[1199] Henry George Liddell (1811–98), tutor, 1836, censor, 1845, of Christ Church, Oxford; White's prof. of moral philosophy, 1845.

23 June 1891.   Ripon raised an interesting debate on Manipur. Cross made a temperate & satisfactory speech, throwing over Gorst[1200] completely. Argyll ridiculously acrimonious, & even Northbrook who generally takes non-partisan views of Indian affairs, rather sour in his answer to me. But there was really unanimity on all important points apart from Argyll's rhetorical platitudes.

25, 26 June 1891.   Thursday & Friday. 2nd reading of Irish land Purchase Bill. I spoke on the 2nd evening. On reflection I think for an Opposition leader I went rather too far in approval of the Bill. But then (apart from the absence of Home Rule) I really do approve the principle of the Bill. Is it not more honest to say so plainly? After being a party to the Bill of 1886 I never could disapprove of English credit being employed to promote the transfer of the landlords' interest to the tenant. The Radical cry that the bill is merely a means of enabling landlords to sell their estates at prices above their value at the cost of the British taxpayer is mere factious calumny.

7 July 1891.   Went to Windsor to the banquet in St George's Hall in honour of the German Emperor. A bad dinner, but a very fine sight. I was presented to the Emperor & Empress.

8 July 1891.   Wednesday. Wymondham for the Agricultural show. Torrents of rain.

9 July 1891.   Thursday. To Garden party at Marlborough House. Women in hideous staring dresses. Harcourt saw Mr G. before he went to Hawarden, & thought him better in health, notwithstanding the shock of Wm. Gladstone's death.[1201] The defeat of Parnell's candidate at Carlow by a crushing majority is a good omen for the Dissolution.[1202] It is amusing to see the Tories, who the other day were Kotowing to the Pope in order to get him to interfere on their side against the Irish nationalists, now howling about 'priestly influence'! Such is faction.

5 August 1891.   Went to Kimberley. Very wet cold weather. Much hay out. Cover crops green. Miserably cold wet weather all this month except the last 2 or 3 days. Only 2 days during which hay could be carried, in the whole month.

[1200] John Eldon Gorst (1835–1916), Cons. MP for Cambridge borough, 1866–8; for Chatham, 1875–92; for Cambridge University, 1892–1906; sol.-genl., 1885; u.-sec. India, 1886–91; Fin. sec. Treas., 1891–2; v. p. com. Council, 1895–1902.
[1201] Eldest son of W.E. Gladstone, who died of a brain tumour.
[1202] John Hammond (3,747), A.J. Kettle (1,532).

12 September 1891.   Began harvest on the Home Farm on Aug: 26 finished on Sept 12. Hay still out in the Park! Since Septr. began the weather fine & now very hot.

Received the unpleasant news that our house in Lowndes Sqre. was broken into last night by thieves.

18 September 1891.   Finished getting up hay at last in the park! It appears that the thieves did not get much, an umbrella, some old clothes of the butler, and a few plated spoons from the basement. They went into the drawing rooms, and dining room, where they took nothing. Upstairs they only entered my dressing room, & the little sitting room adjoining. From my room they carried off my civil service uniforms, worth very little to them, but which cost me a pretty sum to replace. Evidently they were not practised burglars as they opened no locks.

22 October 1891.   To Watton where made a speech in support of Lee Warner,[1203] the Liberal candidate for S.W. Norfolk. Very dark, wet night, notwithstanding which a good attendance in the Wayland Hall where the meeting was held.

3 November 1891.   To Gainsborough. Made the usual speech in support of Bennett, the former member & present candidate for that Divn. of Lincolnshire. Oxenbridge presided, & made a long speech. Pickersgill, M.P. for Bethnal Green,[1204] followed with a very frothy oration, some good points though in it. What a terrible nuisance this platform speaking is! I feel half inclined to give up public life. The same weary grind, the same old topics again & again. Can anything be more appalling?

A discussion with one's opponents face to face in Parliament on some practical question is the only public speaking which gives me any satisfaction. Yet I do not go to half the places which I am pressed to visit! The only novelty just lately has been Chamberlain's attack on the Cabinet of which he was a member. What a mean creature he is! I hope he may join the Tories altogether. Who knows that he will not take a peerage some day?

14 January 1892.   The tragic death of the Duke of Clarence.[1205]

21 January 1892.   Influenza terribly bad everywhere. Army who has had it at Prestwold getting better, thank God.

[1203] Warner was defeated in July 1842 by T.L. Hare, 3,739–4,077.
[1204] Edward Hare Pickersgill (1850–1911) Lib. MP for S.W. Bethnal Green, 1885–1900.
[1205] Albert, Duke of Clarence (1864–92), eldest son of the Prince of Wales.

21 January 1892. Went to Lowestoft to political meeting on opening of Liberal Club. Usual speech. Mr Judd[1206] is our candidate, & was pleased with success of meeting.

5 February 1892. Went to London. Found Armine quite convalescent after his attack of influenza at Prestwold. Influenza very bad at Wymondham, & in the surrounding villages.

17 February 1892. To Barnstaple to attend political meeting. Usual speech. Mr Billson the Liberal candidate is a Liverpool Solicitor, a man apparently of some ability. He has good hopes of winning the seat.[1207]

24 February 1892. Made speech at a meeting in Walworth. Saunders our candidate seemed to be a shrewd quiet man.[1208] Usual enthusiasm. A delightful Salvation Army man perorated thus – 'and then we shall have the Grand Old Man, and there will be heaven upon earth'.

1 March 1892. Made another speech at a meeting in Fulham. Barnett,[1209] our candidate, is an Irishman, very 'mixed' in his talk. I think I made rather a better speech than usual on these occasions.

4 March 1892. Called on Mr G. who is at his son-in-law Mr Rendel's in Carlton Gardens:[1210] found him in wonderful health & spirits, full of fight. He discussed the future Home Rule Bill: he is still strongly of opinion that no separation of subjects in the H. of C. into Imperial and English local is possible: & holds to the plan of a reduced number of Irish members, empowered to vote on all questions.

9 March 1892. My aunt, widow of Edward Gurdon died of pneumonia at Hingham aged 68. She was a Miss Frere: an excellent good woman.

12 March 1892. Dinner given by Causton M.P.[1211] at Reform Club to 60 County Cl. (London) members & candidates & others. Indifferent food and dingy hot rooms, but company in high spirits. Campbell

---

[1206] James Judd (3,909), defeated by H.S. Foster (5,099).

[1207] As he did in July: Alfred Billson (4,383), Leedham White (4,236).

[1208] William Saunders (1823–95), Lib. MP for Newington, Walworth division, 1892–5; established *Western Morning News*, *Eastern Morning News* and Central News Agency. Elected in July: Saunders (2,514), L.H. Isaacs (2,218).

[1209] W.D. Barnett, unsuccessful Lib. candidate for Fulham, July 1892.

[1210] It is unclear why Kimberley refers to a son-in-law. Stuart Rendel (1834–1913) Lib. MP for Montgomery, 1880–94; friend and confidant of Gladstone, lived at 1 Carlton Gardens. Rendal's da., Maud, was married to Gladstone's son, Henry Neville.

[1211] Richard Knight Causton (1843–1929), Lib. MP for Colchester, 1880–5, for Southwark W., 1888–1910.

Bannerman & I had to make little after dinner speeches.

27 March 1892.   Wrote to Mr G. as to Indian Councils Bill, which comes on in the H. of Commons to-morrow.[1212]

2 April 1892.   Went to dinner of Civil Engineers held at the handsome new St Martin's Town Hall. Sat next to Lincoln[1213] the U. S. Minister a very pleasant man.

13 April 1892.   Went to Kimberley, very cold, extraordinarily late spring.

25 April 1892.   Political meeting at Wymondham to support Mr. Higgins, Q.C. our candidate.[1214] Well attended. Higgins made a solid but rather dull speech. Strong marks of applause when he said he was for disestablishment of Church. Macfarlane[1215] (who hires Cossey), formerly M. P. for an Irish constituency, spoke well. I made usual speech.

28 April 1892.   Back to London. Horribly cold.

30 April 1892.   Academy dinner, most wearisome. I think I shall avoid this function in future.

3 June 1892.   To Falmouth where stayed till 11th. Armine & Nelly with us a delightful trip. On the 8th made a speech in the Polytechnic. Crowded & enthusiastic meeting, but I fear our candidate (Serena) a poor timid creature, no chance.[1216]

28 June 1892.   Parliament dissolved. The prevailing opinion is that we shall have a majority; whether small or big is another matter. I don't think it can be very large.

13 July 1892.   Spencer called, having just returned from Homburg. Long talk on the political situation. We agreed that if as is probable we have a majority of (say) 20 the Gt. cannot go on. Harcourt he tells

---

[1212] See Kimberley to Arnold Morley, 27 March 1892, GP 44229, ff. 17–19.

[1213] Robert Todd Lincoln (1843–1926), US sec. of war, 1881–5; min. to Great Britain, 1889–93; son of Abraham Lincoln.

[1214] Clement Higgins (1844–1916), Lib. MP for mid-Norfolk, 1892 until March 1895, when he declared himself a Liberal Unionist. The Council of the Mid-Norfolk Central Liberal Assoc. agreed to thank him for past services and invite him to sit until the next general election. On negotiations to avoid a by-election, see letters of Jan. and Feb. 1895 from John Wodehouse to Kimberley, KP 1 3/2.

[1215] Donald Horne Macfarlane (1830–1904), Lib. MP for Carlow, 1880–5, for Argyllshire, 1885–6, July 1892–5.

[1216] W.G.C. Bentinck, cons. (1,218), A.D. Serena (880).

me talks in his loon way about giving up Home Rule, but this is out of the question. Even if we were not in honour bound to propose a Home Rule Bill, it is certain that the Irish nationalists wd. vote with the Tories against us, if we were false to our pledges: and they would be quite right.

Rosebery is it seems in a very strange state of mind and talks of not coming back to public life! But he must yield to the pressure that will be put upon him. If such a great blow were to befall us, I fear I should have to undertake the F. O., but happily there can be very little probability of such a a *pis-aller*. We should be terribly weakened by losing Rosebery. Not only, because he is by far the most acceptable man for the F. O., but because next to Gladstone he is much the most influential man in the country of our party.[1217]

14 July 1892. Presided at dinner at Criterion in honour of G. R. Dibbs, first Minister of N. S. Wales. Dibbs is six feet four, and gives me the idea of a strong self possessed, but not brilliant man, neither is he eloquent: altogether a good sound specimen of the Australian democracy. He spoke in very plain terms against the Imperial Federation craze: & I was glad to hear Sir C. Tupper the Canadian Commissioner speak in the same sense. Dibbs however is a Protectionist & believes in an Imperial Customs Union.

I have forgotten to mention that some days ago the Guicowar of Baroda called on me, a very pleasing intelligent young man. He and his Minister who accompanied him both speak excellent English.

Great triumphs in Mid & East Norfolk where Gurdon and Birkbeck both lost their seats.[1218]

19 July 1892. Elections over to day, except Orkney & Shetland polling for which takes place on 25th. & 26th.[1219]

28 July 1892. The death of poor old Sherbrooke announced (aetat:81). He was a close & excellent friend of mine.[1220] For the last 12 years his mind had given way, & latterly it was quite gone. I saw the first signs of his mental decay before 1880.

Indeed it was but too plain to every one but himself when Mr G.

[1217] Gladstone himself freely suggested Kimberley as a potential foreign secretary. See Henry Primrose to wife, [10 Aug. 1892], Primrose Papers, Perkins Library, Duke University.

[1218] R.J. Price (4,743) defeated Sir Edward Birkbeck (4,308) in E. Norfolk; Clement Higgins (4,069) defeated Robert Thornhagh Gurdon (3,599) in mid-Norfolk.

[1219] In the 1892 general election 270 Liberals, 47 Liberal Unionists, 268 Conservatives, 81 Irish Home Rulers, and 4 Labour MPs were returned.

[1220] Lowe and Kimberley had lived next to one another in Lowndes Square since 1874.

formed his govt. in that year, & did not include him. He asked me to
tell him as an old friend why he was left out. I could only reply I knew
nothing as to Mr G's reasons for the way in wh. he had formed his
Cabinet, but the reason was evident enough.

Last week we dined with the Thakur of Gondal and his wife at the
Grosvn. Hotel. The first time I should think that a Rajpoot lady of
high caste appeared at a dinner party with Europeans. She is not
particularly good looking but has a very pleasing expression. She
understands English well, but was too shy to talk. She wore her native
dress, very gorgeous. They have been living at Edinburgh for two years,
she having come here to have an operation performed on her head,
which quite succeeded. He is a very enlightened man, & is said to
govern his State admirably. They are going to leave their children here,
when they return to India in the autumn, & the son is to go to Eton!

30 July 1892.   Went to Prestwold & returned to town Aug. 3.

3 August 1892.   Meeting at Mr G's. Present Mr G., Ld. Spencer, Ld.
Ripon, Ld. Herschell, Harcourt, J. Morley, A. Morley & self. Mr
G. explained to us the arrangements come to with Messrs. Dillon,
McCarthy, & Sexton,[1221] who had an interview with him on behalf of
the Irish Nationalist party this morning.[1222]

4 August 1892.   Meeting of Parliament.

8 August 1892.   Queen's Speech read. Debate began in H. of C. on
motion of want of confidence moved by Mr Asquith, seconded by Mr
Burt.[1223]

9 August 1892.   Mr G. made his speech in the H. of C. I hear he was
shaky tho' he made an effective speech. The fact is, he is far from well,
not having recovered from his cold. But what a prospect for the new
Govt.! It will be a marvel if he lasts out next Session. Rosebery has, I
hear, at last come to town. He is in a strange state of mind; and had
not on Monday consented to join the new Govt. I have not heard
whether he has since come to a resolution to join, but I feel confident

---

[1221] Thomas Sexton (1848–1932), Home Rule MP for Sligo Co., 1880–5, for Sligo S.,
1885–6, for Belfast W., 1886–92, for Kelly N., 1892–6.
[1222] See *Gladstone Diaries*, XIII, 54.
[1223] Thomas Burt (1837–1922), Rad. MP for Morpeth, 1874–1918; parl. sec. bd. of
trade, 1892–5.

he will overcome his reluctance. It would be a very heavy blow to the new Govt. if he refused.[1224]

11 August 1892. Thursday. Govt. beaten on vote of confidence 350–310. Extraordinary division only one absent member & (a Nationalist in Australia), one pair which with the four Tellers & the Speaker makes up the whole House.[1225]

13 August 1892. Satuday. Meeting at Mr G's to discuss appointments. Present Mr. G., Spencer, Harcourt, J. Morley, Self, and A. Morley & Marjoribanks[1226] the Whips. We have still hopes of getting Rosebery. I called on him yesterday. He seemed glad to see me. There is apparently no reason for his not joining us except his morbid fear of returning to public life. He wished, he said, to pass his life in solitude!

Much discussion about Labouchere. It was decided that he could not be recommended for an appointment. 'Truth' is an insuperable obstacle in high quarters.[1227] I fear I shall be sent to the Council Office wh. I detest.

14 August 1892. Meeting at Mr G's. Present Mr G., Ld. Spencer, J. Morley, Harcourt & self with the whips A. Morley & Marjoribanks. Mr G. offered me the India Office wh. I gladly accepted. I am to hold the Presidentship of the Council provisionally in commendance as Mr G. said. This is very tiresome but of course I could not refuse. Spencer is to be first Ld. of the Admiralty, Ripon Colonial Secy. Much discussion followed. Harcourt violently objected to so many good places being given to Peers. Mr G. was very decided and insisted on his right to form his Gt. in the way he thought best – Harcourt then sulked.[1228] J. Morley agreed with him, and strong as I think Ripon's claims, and

---

[1224] As plans were being made for a Liberal cabinet during early August 1892 Rosebery repeatedly declared his disinterest in and unfitness for public life, and suggested that Kimberley would make an admirable foreign secretary. At a meeting with Gladstone on 11 August 1892 Rosebery refused office.

[1225] Gladstone noted that the vote was an 'astonishing muster'. *Gladstone Diaries*, XIII, 57.

[1226] Edward Marjoribanks (1849–1909), Lib. MP for Berwick, 1880–94, when he succeeded as Lord Tweedmouth; ld. privy seal and chan. D. of Lanc., 1894–5; 1st ld. adm., 1905–8.

[1227] According to Gladstone, 'a journal rather of comment and animadversion than at record'; known for its republican sympathies. On Gladstone's manner of handling the communication, through Bertram Currie, see correspondence between Gladstone, Currie, Labouchere and Algernon West. GP 44515.

[1228] Gladstone recorded in his diary after this meeting: 'I am sorry to record that Harcourt has used me in such a way since my return to town that the addition of another Harcourt would have gone far to make my task impossible.' *Gladstone Diaries*, XIII, 58.

much as I wished him as an old friend to have the Colonies, an office for wh. he is admirably qualified, I should have given way to the protests of our H. of Commons colleagues if I had been in Mr G's place, and I have no doubt Ripon wd., if needful, have accepted a minor office. Unfortunately his being a R. Catholic is an objection to his holding the Ld. Presidentship; as it is connected with Education. Harcourt however was quite intolerable, & enormously exaggerated *more suo* the importance of the point. After all Mr G. is the best judge & has a right to decide as he pleases. Campbell Bannerman was sent for to advise as to the Scotch Secretaryship. We have good hopes at last of securing Rosebery.

19 August 1892. Friday. First Cabinet. We went (Thursday) yesterday to Osborne to be sworn in. In returning from Cowes to Portsmouth a furious thunderstorm.

26 August 1892. Went to Kimberley. Harvest begun on the Lodge Farm on August 22.

29 September 1892. Cabinet on Uganda. The result a dilatory 'fishing' policy which will end in our retaining the country without taking efficient steps to maintain our authority there. Why can we never do anything thoroughly?[1229]

30 September 1892. Second Cabinet (very short) to settle the terms of letter to the Company. Slept at Brooks' & returned to Ky. this afternoon.

25 October 1892. We all moved to London. Cabinets on 27th, 31st, Nov. 2 & 7. Nothing particular except Uganda on which Rosebery will have his way in spite of a loud but really feeble opposition by Harcourt.[1230] The rest of the time spent in rather vague talk about bills.

[1229] During 1892 the Imperial British East Africa Company which had been trading in Uganda and encouraging missionary activity indicated it was going to evacuate the region. Pressure arose to formally annex Uganda so as to honour the Company's commercial, religious and humanitarian commitments. The cabinet became deeply divided over the issue, Rosebery arguing hard for annexation, Gladstone and Harcourt being strongly opposed. At the 29 September 1892 cabinet meeting a compromise was agreed whereby the government supported the Company in Uganda for a short period, evacuation being postponed. Peter Stansky, *Ambitions and Strategies: The Struggle for the Leadership of the Liberal Party in the 1890s* (Oxford, 1964), 5–12. On Kimberley's position, see his memorandum of 21 Sept. 1892, in *Liberal by Principle*, 203–4.

[1230] On 7 November 1892 the cabinet agreed to send Sir Gerald Portal to Uganda as Imperial Commissioner to inquire and report on the situation. In fact, when the Imperial British East Africa Company's rule in Uganda ended on 1 April 1893 Portal, without cabinet authorisation, raised the British flag in Kampala.

At the first meeting Russell's remonstrance against the prohibition of the Law Offr. to take private practice was disposed of.

9 November 1892. Lord Mayor's dinner. For my sins I was chosen to return thanks for the Govt. as Mr G. was forbidden to go by Sir A. Clarke, and Rosebery, Harcourt & John Morley shirked.[1231] I resisted as long as I could, having declined the invitation. I made a dull speech to a hostile audience.

11 November 1892. Irish H. Rule Bill mentioned for the first time by Mr G. A vain attempt was made to discuss it. Mr G. in spite of protests from Harcourt & others insisted that the bill must first be drafted & that we should meet in the first week of Decr. to discuss it. Every one except Mr G. & J. Morley disapproved, I believe, of this extraordinary mode of proceeding. Surely the main principles of the bill should be discussed & settled, and then a bill drawn accordingly.[1232]

10th, 11th, & 12th Nov. extraordinary fogs. I was dining at Queen's Gate on the 10th with Mr Knowles,[1233] & had to walk home. It was so thick one could hardly grope one's way even with a lantern which my footman carried. I met at Knowles' Dr. Vaughan[1234] the new Abp (Catholic) of Westminster, a pleasant man.

12 November 1892. 'Morrow of St Martin's'. Attended the strange ceremony of nominating the Sheriffs in the Ld. Chief Justice's Court.

21 November 1892. Mr G. has wisely changed his mind, moved no doubt by the discontent of the Cabinet, & to day we had a discussion on the H. Rule Bill. A Committee, Mr G., Herschell, Spencer, J. Morley, Bryce,[1235] & Campbell-Bannerman were appointed to draw up the bill which is to be ready when we meet again early in Jany.

25 November 1892. Went to Windsor to dine & sleep. I sat next at Dinner to the G. Duchess Sergius (born Hesse), the Queen's grand-

---

[1231] Cf. Rosebery's assertion that 'Gladstone was determined that I should *not* go for fear I suppose of some Uganda declaration', Kimberley Memoir, herein.

[1232] On Kimberley's attempt to influence the initial draft, see his letter to Gladstone, 12 Nov. 1892, in *Liberal by Principle*, 205. For Gladstone's proposition regarding a Home Rule bill see *Gladstone Diaries*, XIII, 139. See also Gladstone's correspondence with Kimberley on Home Rule on 12 November 1892 in *Gladstone Diaries*, XIII, 141.

[1233] James Thomas Knowles (1831–1908), founder and editor of *Nineteenth Century*.

[1234] Herbert Alfred Vaughan (1832–1903), archbp. Westminster, 1892–1903; made cardinal, 1893.

[1235] James Bryce (1838–1922), historian; regius prof. of civil law, Oxford, 1870–93; Lib. MP for Tower Hamlets, 1880–5, for S. Aberdeen, 1885–1906; ch. D. of Lanc., 1892–4; pres. b. of trade, 1894–5; ch. sec. Ireland, 1905–6; amb. to U.S., 1907–13.

daughter, an exceedingly pretty & very agreeable woman. The G. Duke, whom I did not speak to, is like his father. He looked sour. The last time I saw him was at Tsarskoe-Selo when he was baptized!

Mr and Mrs G., Rosebery, & the Russn. Ambr. (Staal) & his wife were the other guests.

26 November 1892. Council. I had an audience of H.M. who was in good spirits & very gracious. Parlt. prorogued to Jan. 31.

1 December 1892. We returned to Kimberley. At Windsor I had long talk with Rosebery. He gave Mr G. to understand he would resign if we did not agree to his Uganda policy. He says he saved the Cabinet from a hostile vote, as soon as Parlt. met. I am sorry to say I agree with him. The majority of the nation is suffering from violent Jingo fever. In such circs. argument is useless. It would be absurd to upset the Govt. on such a question as Uganda, so there was nothing for it but to acquiesce, tho' what possible good we can get from Uganda I cannot conceive, & we may have serious trouble there. But what are a few millions of money, & a few thousands of lives when a sacrifice must be made to the great god Jingo in the name of Xtianity & philanthropy!

Rosebery said he must decline to lead the Lords. I did all I could to persuade him. It is silly to make me lead. Rosebery has weight with the nation, wit, & eloquence. I have none of these requisites, Mr G. will press him very strongly, & will I hope prevail upon him not to Shirk our obvious duty.*

[Undated annotation:] *This matter was left unsettled till shortly before the meeting of Parliament in the hope that R. would consent but he finally refused & I had to undertake the leadership.[1236]

12 December 1892. Monday we went to Witton & stayed till Friday. On Friday the 16th I went to London, & attended a Cabinet next day. Why it was held I can't conceive as there was no business of importance. After the Cabinet I returned to Kimberley.

10 January 1893. We all went to town to day. Thaw began yesterday after a fortnight's hard frost & some snow.

13 January 1893. Heard that Francis Cavendish died last night at Eastbourne.

[1236] On 12 January 1893, following Rosebery's refusal to continue in the position, Kimberley agreed to become Liberal leader in the Lords.

6 January 1893.   Cabinets Wednesday (4th): & to day. Irish H. Rule Bill.

9, 11 January 1893.   Cabinets on same.

16 January 1893.   Do.

17 January 1893.   Sudden Cabinet at 5 o'clock on Egypt. Cromer's violent proposals not approved but firm language to be held to Khedive.[1237] Harcourt on the rampage as usual, & full of terror at the possible consequences of maintaining a firm attitude. We came however at last to a wise conclusion, & I have little doubt the Khedive will give in. Harcourt was at the old game of disdaining responsibility for Egyptn. Gt., wh. had such disastrous results in the Gt. of 80. J. Morley naturally on same side, with more discretion however.

18 January 1893.   The Egyptian bubble burst, as might be expected, Cromer fulfilling our instructions with much discretion.
    Cabinet to day on Irish Bill.

19 January 1893.   Committee of Cabinet on wh. I have been sitting at L. Gt. Bd. finished Registration Bill.

20, 23, 25, 27 January 1893.   Cabinets on Irish and other Bills.

25 January 1893.   Ripon being ill who was to have presided, I took chair at dinner at Nat. Libl. Club on presentation to club of Oxenbridge's portrait.

30 January 1893.   To Council at Osborne. The Queen was in very good humour. The 'Speech' was approved after Council. It is not, as is supposed by ignorant newspaper scribblers, settled in Council. The Privy Council has nothing to do with the 'Speech'. How singularly inaccurate & ill informed the press is on every subject!

31 January 1893.   Tuesday. Meeting of Parliament. Salisbury made one of his incisive speeches, this quiet in tone. I followed and, having a very bad cold, was even duller than usual. The debate went maundering

---

[1237] Following a *coup d'etat* in Cairo and the installation of Anglophobe ministers advising the Khedive, Lord Cromer proposed that ministerial buildings be occupied unilaterally, telegraphs fixed and new provisional ministers appointed. Cromer's plan was rejected by the cabinet. See *Gladstone Diaries*, XIII, 182.

on without any striking feature till Friday. Brassey[1238] & Thring, the mover & seconder of the Address, really did very well, and Monkswell[1239] came to our aid with a smart little speech.

14 February 1893.   Tuesday. Cabinet. Harcourt on the high horse about Irish finance. After a disagreeable discussion we thought we had settled the difficulty, but on Thursday the differences all broke out worse than ever.[1240] We were at almost a moment's notice summoned to a Cabinet. Harcourt was, if possible, more cantankerous and violent than usual. We sat from 2.30, till the H. of C. met, and determined nothing. We were to meet again in Mr G's room at the House at Six o'clock. We Peers went there accordingly but our colleagues were detained in the House by the privilege discussion on the disgraceful article in the 'Times' on Ld. Wolmer's[1241] very discreditable speech at the 'Liberal' Unionist dinner. We went into J. Morley's rooms & smoked, until by degrees most of our colleagues came in except Mr G. who was still in the House.

Then a most extraordinary scene ensued. Harcourt & J. Morley both worked themselves into an absurd state of excitement about the 'excise' clause in the Irish Bill. It is difficult to say which of these behaved most foolishly. Neither would listen to reason. At last Mr G. came in, and it was agreed to send A. Morley to sound the Irish members. The point at issue was the amount to be borne by Ireland in the event of excise duties being increased. Harcourt insisted that Ireland should pay over the whole increase without any reduction (wh. J. Morley considered indispensable) in the case which excise is augmented in order to defray some charge for a purely British purpose. I did not get home till nearly 8.30. Harcourt has never given the smallest assistance in framing the bill, and by raising objections at the last moment when the bill was about to be distributed, he has caused the greatest embarrassment. He is certainly the most perfect example of the 'mauvais coucheur' I have ever seen. Mr. G's patience with him is angelic.

On this since Thursday I had a special Council to pass my 'juries'

[1238] Thomas Brassey (1836–1918), Lib. MP for Hastings, 1868–86, when cr. Baron Brassey; parl. sec. Adm., 1884–5; gov. Victoria, 1895–1900; cr. Earl, 1911.

[1239] Robert Collier, 2nd Baron Monkswell (1845–1908), ld. in waiting, 1892–5; u.-sec. war office, 1895. For an account of the evening, see E.C.F. Collier, ed. *A Victorian Diarist: Extracts from the Journals of Mary, Lady Monkswell, 1873–1895* (London, 1944), 217–9.

[1240] For Gladstone's notes on the events of 16 February 1893 see *Gladstone Diaries*, XIII, 202.

[1241] William Waldegrave Palmer, Viscount Wolmer (1859–1942), priv. sec. to Childers, 1882–4, to his father Lord Selborne, 1884–5; Lib. U. MP for Petersfield div., Hampshire, 1885–92, for Edinburgh W., 1892–5, when he succ. as Earl of Selborne.

despatch which was agreed to by the Cabinet on Tuesday.[1242] I ought to have mentioned above that just before the meeting of Parlt., Mr G. asked me to lead the Lords, Rosebery having absolutely refused. It is a bad arrangement, but I could not decline, and I must do my best.[1243]

23 February 1893. Went to Windsor to officiate as Secy. of State (in uniform) on the occasion of the Queen receiving an address from Convocation. Asquith could not go as he was moving the Welsh preferment Suspensory Bill. The Convocation was presenting an Address against it. The ceremony was very amusing. After presenting the address & receiving the answer, the deputation backed out in a row, the Abp in the middle, to the door. Sumner, who appeared as Prolocutor & who is Archdeacon of Winchester, & a Bishop suffragan, I knew well as a boy at Eton.[1244] We had not met for 50 years! A very old boy friend also, W. W. Douglas, an Hon. Canon of Worcester was there. I think I had only seen him once before since we left Eton. He was with me at T. K. Arnold's as well. How curiously one's ways part after boyhood![1245]

18 March 1893. To Windsor to dine & sleep. The Empress Frederick was there and said a few words to me after dinner. She looks old and sad. On the 11th (Saturday) I had my Sheriff pricking dinner. Of 14 who accepted only nine came, the rest being detained at the H. of Commons. On Wednesday the 22nd I went to the Council at Windsor for the real Sheriff pricking by the Queen, a strange old ceremony.

24 March 1893. Cabinet. Harcourt propounded his Budget which will be very unpopular.

28 March 1893. A hurried talk with Herschell & Mr G. about Indian currency.[1246] Mr G. seems to be not unfavourable to closing the Indian mints to the free coinage of silver. This conversation took place in Mr G's room in the H. of Commons. Harcourt ran in & out and presently Mr G. was sent for & moved the closure.

[1242] Lord Lansdowne, the Indian viceroy, had sanctioned the withdrawal of jury trials in cases of murder and culpable homicide, raising an outcry in India. The government agreed to a Commission of Inquiry. See Legh, *Lord Lansdowne*, 110–12.

[1243] For Gladstone's notes on the events of 16 February 1893 see *Gladstone Diaries*, XIII, 202.

[1244] George Henry Sumner (1824–1909), appt. archdeacon of Winchester, 1884.

[1245] See p. 43, above.

[1246] In August 1892 Kimberley received from the Indian government a despatch arguing for the adoption of bimetallism or the introduction of a gold standard for the Indian currency. Kimberley disliked bimetallism, but was willing to consider the proposal for a gold standard.

This currency of question [sic], being of first rate difficulty and importance, will probably never be seriously discussed by any member of the Cabinet except Herschell & myself. As usual the whole energies of the Govt. are concentrated on carrying the babble of the H. of Commons. I am convinced this cannot last. The House has been for some years visibly losing importance & authority in the country. It will decline more & more, and ultimately the whole system of Govt. will be changed: but how? Time only can show. On the 28th the H. of Lords adjourned till April 18. We went to Witton on the 29th & stayed till April 5: then back to town.

20 April 1893.   An extraordinarily hot day: 80 in the shade.

22 April 1893.   Lord Derby died yesterday. He was a good friend of mine and I had a great regard for him. His character is admirably described in the 'Times' biography of him this morning. Perhaps the newspaper writers hardly appreciate sufficiently his besetting weakness, indecision. He was painfully unable to make up his mind to action. No man saw both sides of a question so clearly or could state the arguments pro and con with such perfect impartiality: but this very clearness of vision seemed to deprive him of vigour of will in determining what course to pursue. Hence his failure as an administrator, and as a statesman to attain the highest rank. He never recovered from two severe attacks of influenza.

Home Rule Bill read 2nd time last night by a majority of 43.[1247]

5 May 1893.   Cabinet. At length after a long interval. Amendments in Home Rule Bill considered.

10 May 1893.   Opening of Imperial Institute. The ceremony took place in a very shabby temporary wooden shed, such as is erected for a landowner at an Agricultural Show. Intensely hot in the shed. Flo. & I duly attended. The multitude of people sitting at the Albert Memorial were really a pretty sight.

18 May 1893.   Went to Falmouth and stayed till 26th. A delightful week.

5 June 1893.   The Irish Bill and nothing but the Irish Bill.[1248] The old man's vigour is astounding. The opposition cackled very shrilly over

[1247] Home Rule bill passed its second reading by 347 to 304.
[1248] According to Hamilton, who was present, Kimberley was brought in to discuss Irish finance, and took in Gladstone's new plan with 'surprising quickness'. *EHJ3*, 202.

the insertion of words in the body of the Bill, preserving the Supremacy of Parliament. The fact is we had decided there would be no harm in inserting a declaration to that effect tho' we held that the motion in the preamble was sufficient. J. Morley however did not like it, & it was his reluctance, wh. caused some hesitation in the House. I fear he has not very sound judgment, able as he is. Between him & Harcourt our Chief has a 'bad time'.

On Friday last we were beaten on a resolution moved by Mr Paul[1249] in favour of simulataneous competitive examinations in England & India for the civil service.[1250] A very foolish vote. How are we to govern India if the House of Commons follows on Indian subjects the lead of Paul, Wedderburn,[1251] Caine, Naoroji[1252] & such like. It is a lamentable exhibition of ignorance & folly. Since this vote we determined to send the resolution out to India for opinion of Indn. Govt.

18 June 1893.[1253] Cabinet at wh. it was decided to adopt recommendation of Committee on Indian currency.[1254] The new financial clauses of Irish Bill were also considered & agreed to.

19 June 1893. My Council made a very wry face to day on the despatch to India sending the Resolution about competitive examination. They voted against it 7 to 4. One did not vote, & Mr Owen Burne[1255] is away.

30 June 1893. After we had agreed on the amendment on the anti opium resolution, Mr G. wanted at the last moment to come to terms

---

[1249] Herbert Woodfield Paul (1853–1935), Lib. MP for South Edinburgh, 1892–5, whom Kimberley described to Lansdowne as 'a very clever young member'. See *Liberal by Principle*, 208.

[1250] For Gladstone's correspondence with Kimberley on this vote on 2 and 3 June 1893 see *Gladstone Diaries*, XIII, 245–6.

[1251] William Wedderburn (1838–1918), entered Bombay civil service, 1860; Rad. MP for Banffshire, 1893–1900.

[1252] Dadabhai Naoroji (1825–1917), pres. Indian National Congress, 1886, 1893, 1906; Lib. MP for Finsbury-Central, 1892–5.

[1253] The cabinet was held on 19 June. *Gladstone Diaries*, XIII, 253.

[1254] In favour of closing Indian mints to unlimited coinage of silver. Details of committee deliberations can be found in KP6, MS. eng.c. 4357. See also Currie, *Recollections*, I, 69–71, II, 261ff; A. Kaminsky, '"Lombard Street" and India: Currency Problems in the Late Nineteenth Century', *Indian Economic and Social History Review* 17 (1980), 307–27.

[1255] Owen Tudor Burne (1837–1908), maj.-genl.; priv. sec. to Lord Mayo, 1863–72, to Lord Lytton, 1876–8; head of pol. and secret dept., India Office, 1874. 'Under Lord Kimberley's regime', he wrote, 'matters worked very smoothly with us. ... He was very particular as to phrases in despatch-writing ... keeping me, for one, up to late hours in the evening in attendance at the office. Both now and in after-years I got to like him very much, *Memories* (London, 1907), 262–3.

with Pease by inserting 'when' instead of 'whether' in the first par. so that it should run to report 'when it was to be expected that the manufacture of opium &c. should be prohibited'. This of course begged the whole question at issue, and I refused to agree saying that if this change was agreed to by the Govt., I must part company.[1256] Harcourt came up to the H. of Lords to try to persuade me to give in. He was as usual in a terrible 'funk' of a beating, and ready to concede anything and everything to the anti-opium fanatics. However I would not be moved & the result was a very satisfactory majority for our amendment, thanks to Mr G's admirable speech, in which he utterly pulverized the Resolution.[1257]

[Undated annotation:] The amusing thing is that afterwards Harcourt said 'This shows what a good effect a stiff backbone has'!!

5 July 1893. Wednesday. A short Cabinet at Mr G's Room at the Commons. We decided to propose 'omnes omnia' and the reduction of Irish M.Ps to 80. This seems on the whole to be the line of least resistance.

6 July 1893. Thursday. Marriage of D. of York. We went to the Chapel & Palace afterwards. Contrary to the inventions of the penny-a-liners of smiles, bows &c. &c. &c., the pair after the marriage walked out looking neither to the right nor left, both of them with very sullen faces. They looked inexpressibly bored.

The Palace 'banquet' was a very poor luncheon, scrambled for standing up. Barring the wine, wh. is always good at the Palace, it was hardly on a par with luncheon at an agricultural show.

13 July 1893. Went with Flo: to Windsor to dine & sleep. The four Indian 'Princes' were there.

20 July 1893. Cabinet to Windsor. Siam difficulty.[1258] We were all in a pacific spirit but not prepared to follow Harcourt's advice to sit still and make no diplomatic communication to France.[1259] Harcourt talked utter nonsense as he usually does on foreign affairs.

28 July 1893. Went for Council to Osborne. Also presented the

---

[1256] See Gladstone to Kimberley, 30 June 1893, in *Gladstone Diaries*, XIII, 256; Kimberley to Gladstone, 30 June 1893 in *Liberal by Principle*, 210.

[1257] For fuller context on Kimberley's threat to resign, see *Liberal by Principle*, 210–11.

[1258] See Kimberley to Lansdowne, 21 July 1893, LP MSS Eur. D 558/6, no. 39.

[1259] The cabinet agreed to send Lord Dufferin to Paris to discuss the declaration of the French government as to the integrity and independence of Siam.

Sawbown of Thibau (a Shan Chief) and his son. This old Shan chief has a curious history. He was summonded to Mandalay a short time before our occupation of Upper Burma, the King intending to kill him. He escaped to our Burmese territory. Two emmisaries from the King who he believed were sent to murder him, were shot by him. For this he was tried & sentenced to be hanged, but the sentence was commuted to imprisonment. After a year he was released, and on our conquest of Uppper Burma he returned to his state, & was the first Chief who gave in his allegiance to us. His son who speaks English well, has been for a year & some months at Rugby School. The old Chief has come over to be operated on for cataract.

On entering the Queen's presence they both prostrated themselves with their faces to the ground. It was some time before they could be got on their legs. The Chief is a well-mannered & apparently intelligent man. He is the first Shan Chief who has come to England.

29 July 1893.   Saturday. We went to Conybor & stayed till Monday.

11 August 1893.   Went to Prestwold and stayed till 15th. Tremendously hot weather.

16 August 1893.   Great difficulty in finding a Viceroy for India.[1260] Spencer has declined: he would have much liked to go, but relinquished the idea in deference to pressure form Mr G. & other colleagues who think his presence here more important. After much consideration we can think of no one but Elgin[1261] and Sir H. Norman,[1262] the former too inexperienced, the latter too old.[1263] Cromer after his extraordinary want of discretion in the late Egyptian crisis, the Cabinet won't hear of. Also it is believed he would not go. What an extraordinary dearth of fit men! Carrington[1264] & Sir H. Loch[1265] have been mentioned but not approved.

[1260] For detailed references to the search, see *Liberal by Principle*, 212n; also entry for 16 Oct. 1893, below.

[1261] Victor Alexander Bruce, 9th Earl of Elgin (1849–1917), 1st Com. of Works, 1886; col. sec., 1905–8.

[1262] Henry Norman (1826–1904), genl. 1882, gov. Jamaica, 1883–9, of Queensland, 1889–95.

[1263] After further discussion, Spencer's refusal and Sir H. Norman's ill health forcing him to decline the offer, Lord Elgin was appointed Indian viceroy.

[1264] Charles Wynn-Carrington (1843–1928), ld. chamberlain, 1892–5; succ. as Viscount Wendover and Earl Carrington, 1895. Later chairman of the Home Counties Liberal Federation.

[1265] Henry Brougham Loch (1827–1900), gov. Victoria, 1884–9, of Cape Colony, 1889–95; high com. of South Africa, 1889–95.

17, 18 August 1893. Two very short Cabinets to settle 'guillotine' Resolution on Report of Irish Bill.[1266]

19 August 1893. Harvest on Home Farm &c. finished. Very poor crops.

21 August 1893. Mr J. D. Chambers my Aunt Harriet's husband[1267] died at Princes' Gardens in his 89th year. He was what wd. be called now a days a man of considerable 'culture', fond of art, literature, and ritualism. He had formerly some practice as a barrister, & was Recorder of Salisbury.

26 August 1893. To Osborne for a Council. The Queen seemed very well & cheerful notwithstanding her deep grief at the death of the D. of Saxe Coburg.

31 August 1893. Cabinet. Autumn session &c. discussed & decided to meet on Novr. 2.

1 September 1893. Home Rule passed 3rd reading in Commons by 267/301 = 34, after (altogether) 82 days debate![1268]

5 September 1893. Home Rule Bill (2nd reading) debate & continued every day till Friday when we divided 41 for/419 against – majority against 378. The best speeches were Argyll's & Rosebery's. The latter most ingeniously evaded saying much in support of the bill. Salisbury's speech was more measured in tone than usual. I made but a poor reply tho' my colleagues appeared or professed to be satisfied with it. However I did my best, more I could not do, and it is not my fault that Rosebery is not, as he ought to be, leader. Still my position is a very irksome one for many reasons.

14 September 1893. At last we have been able to go to Kimberley.

19 September 1893. Summoned to town by a telegram from Harcourt. Found him in a ridiculous fuss about Naoroji's amendment on the Indian Budget. He fumed and raged for an hour, after which we went quietly together to luncheon. He really is quite intolerable as well as absurd. The amendment as I expected came to nothing, and was withdrawn. But it was lucky I went up as on my arrival I received a surprising & very unpleasant telegram from Sir H. Norman, informing

---

[1266] Regarding notice of closure. See *Gladstone Diaries*, XIII, 280.
[1267] Henrietta Wodehouse had in 1834 m. John David Chambers.
[1268] Gladstone noted in his diary: 'This is a great step'. *Gladstone Diaries*, XIII, 285.

me that he withdrew his acceptance of the Viceroyalty on the ground that his strength was not equal to it.[1269] We must now find another man. It was difficult enough before, & will be worse still now, when every one is dispersing. There is a rumour in the newspapers, for which there is no foundation whatever, that Norman withdrew for political reasons. I have had no communications with him except as to his movements, since his acceptance, and I simply sent him a telegram offering him the post to which he replied by a simple acceptance.

22 September 1893.   Parliament was adjourned.

23 September 1893.   I returned to Kimberley.

16 October 1893.   After much difficulty and consideration we have at length settled again on a Viceroy. Rosebery has a very high opinion of Elgin and I trust much in his judgment.[1270] He persuaded Elgin to accept.[1271] It is no doubt somewhat of an experiment but I think he will do well. A shrewd Scotchman experienced in business, is not likely to fail. Of course it wd. have been more satisfactory to appoint a first class statesman but none such were available. Were the Tories any better off? They had no one in view but G. Hamilton. The dearth of suitable men really extraordinary. Elgin was asked before Norman but then declined, not thinking himself equal to the office. No offer was made to any one except Spencer, Norman, & Elgin.[1272]

2 November 1893.   We went to town for the autumn session.

4 November 1893.   Cabinet. Long talk about Stansfeld and his cantonments inquiry.[1273] This miserable agitation is of course of greater importance than the imperial questions of which we have a large crop. Foreign affairs we never talk about but leave entirely to Rosebery. Our trifling difficulty in S. Africa[1274] was disposed of in a few minutes at the end of the Cabinet with about as much discussion as a Bd. of Guardians would give to the application of an old woman for relief.

[1269] See Gladstone to Kimberley, 20 September 1893, in *Gladstone Diaries*, XIII, 300–1.

[1270] Rosebery to Kimberley, 2 Oct. 1893, KP2, 10247, f. 20.

[1271] Kimberley received Elgin's acceptance of the viceroyalty on 10 October 1893.

[1272] See entry for 16 Aug. 1893, above.

[1273] This was with regard to Indian Contagious Diseases legislation, this question being a particular concern of the radical James Stansfeld.

[1274] The status of British authority in Matabeleland and Mashonaland was unclear. The cabinet agreed to give the administration of the area over to Cecil Rhodes' British South Africa Company.

6 November 1893. Met Stansfeld at Mr G's to discuss whether he is to have a day for discussion on his cantonments inquiry. Harcourt was also present, & Marjoribanks. We spent an hour in persuading S. to be content with such discussion as he could get on a motion for adjournment. He wanted to move a resolution. It is melancholy to see a man of some ability like Stansfeld, grow up to this wretched agitation, which, if I were to copy his own language, I should term wicked & immoral.[1275]

What wickedness can indeed be greater than deliberately to refuse to take measures to prevent the spread of a horrible disease? I forgot to mention that at the Cabinet we determined to advise H. M. that it would be wise not to ask Parliament to continue any part of the allowance of the D. of Edinburgh, now that he is D. of Coburg. We also spent a considerable time in discussing who should go to the Ld. Mayor's Feast!

11 November 1893. Lord Mayor's Guildhall Feast: I responded to toast of HM's Ministers & got through pretty well.

15 November 1893. Went to Bedford to attend a political meeting: stayed the night at the charming house of the Rev: Paul Wyatt a very agreeable man, and *mirabile dictu* an advanced Liberal. The meeting presided over by Howard Whitbread[1276] was well attended & enthusiastic, about 1500 people present. I made a speech wh. was well received, & was followed by Waddy M.P.[1277] His buffoonery was amusing. An old fellow (I forget his name) over 94 yr. old spoke afterwards. S. Whitbread & G. Russell both ill and could not attend.

21 November 1893. A short Cabinet, principally about the D. of Coburg's allowance.

23 November 1893. Council at Windsor. Queen looked well & was very cheerful. I forgot to mention that on Nov. 13 I attended the silly proceeding of settling the roll of sheriffs at the High Court.

[1275] Kimberley had succinctly stated his opinion on the immorality of the repeal movement in his letter to Lansdowne at 17 June 1893. See *Liberal by Principle*, 209–10. On the longstanding dispute between Kimberley and Stansfeld, see J.L. Hammond and B. Hammond, *James Stansfeld: A Victorian Champion of Sex Equality* (London, 1932); James Stansfeld, *Lord Kimberley's Defence of the Government Brothel System at Hong Kong* (London, 1882).

[1276] Samuel Howard Whitbread (1858–1944), Lib. MP for S. Bedfordshire, 1892–5; for S. Huntingdonshire, 1906–10.

[1277] Samuel Danks Waddy (1830–1902), Lib. MP for Barnstaple, 1874–9, for Sheffield, 1879–80, for Edinburgh, 1882–5, for N. Lindsey, Lincolnshire, 1886–94.

1 December 1893. Cabinet about H of Commons business, and the 'unemployed'.

2 December 1893. Flo. & I to Windsor to dine and sleep. At dinner I sat next to the Duchess of Connaught, a very pleasant lady. Carrington was summoned in the middle of the day from Mentmore where he was shooting to dine, & Lady C. from Brighton. How very agreeable a Court place must be! The Queen seems to be growing very infirm. She can hardly walk from rheumatism. She was gracious & cheerful. A sharp frost.

14 December 1893. Cabinet. Navy.

21 December 1893. We went to Kimberley.

26 December 1893. Caught a cold which developed itself into a very severe attack of bronchitis which touched both my lungs. I recovered slowly after many days severe illness. I was attended by Dr Barton of Norwich, and Hughes of Wymondham. Many people kindly sent to inquire after my health. The Queen sent more than once to inquire.

29 January 1894. We are going to town to morrow. I am quite free of the malady, but still weak. Whilst I was ill, there were important Cabinets about the Estimates for the navy.

[Undated annotation:] to which Mr G. would not agree.

1 February 1894. Thursday. Went into Committee in the H. of Lords on Local Govt. Bill.

6 February 1894. An extraordinary message brought me by Algn. West from Mr G. who is abroad. He suggests immediate Dissolution & asks opinion of colleagues in town. We answered unanimously by telegraph that we strongly objected.[1278]

12 February 1894. Cabinet. Very short. Settled our course as to Employer's Liability Bill. The rumours of differences with Asquith utterly untrue. Also discussed the Lord's amendments in L. Gt. Bill.

17 February 1894. Dinner at Mr. Gladstone's. The invitations were 'Cabinet dinner' but to our amazement Mr G. never said a word about

---

[1278] Kimberley to Gladstone, 7 Feb. 1894, GP 44229, f. 213.

any business, & very soon after dinner we separated![1279]

23 February 1894.   Cabinet to consider our course as to the amendments of the Lords on the L. Gt. Bill. At the close Mr G. mentioned the great *matter.** He will announce it to the Queen after the prorogation speech is agreed to by her. Thus virtually ends this extraordinary suspense, wh. has continued ever since the Cabinet of January 9. Indian budget also considered. Long sitting afterwards in H. of Lords (till Midnight) on L. G. Bill amendments.

[Undated annotation:] *his resignation

25 February 1894.   Harcourt came to see me for the second time & remained for two hours talking over the situation. Various conversations with my colleagues, specifically, Rosebery, J. Morley, Spencer, Ripon and Acland all prove that the succession to Mr G. is surrounded with difficulties.

26 February 1894.   Monday. Cabinet. L. G. amendments of Lords considered. Mr G. mentioned after the Cabinet a communication he had with Sir H. Ponsonby. Everything thus far at sea. Saw C. Bannerman, after the Cabinet with Ripon & Spencer. It seems to be the prevailing wish that we should come to some understanding amongst ourselves as to the future. All agree in determination to continue the Gt. if possible, but suppose H. M. sent for Salisbury?

28 February 1894.   Wednesday. Amusing to read the evidently inspired article on Mr G. in the 'Daily News'. Rosebery is clearly first favourite, with Harcourt to lead Commons. Will they be able to agree? Harcourt blusters now loudly, but if R. is firm he will 'more suo' give way. Will R. insist? That is the question. I think he can hardly shrink when it really comes to the point, whatever he may say now, but he is a 'Sphynx' whom no one can interpret.
   To night Salisbury rather to the surprise of many tho' I rather expected it, moved & carried two amendments on the L. G. Bill. He evidently is encouraged by the impending resignation of Mr G.

1 March 1894.   Thursday. Last Cabinet of Mr G's Govt. We agreed not to continue the contest with the Lords. It is all essential to terminate the existing ministerial crisis as soon as possible. At the end of the Cabinet at the request of my colleagues I said a few words of farewell

---

[1279] Gladstone noted in his diary: 'I believe it was expected that I should say something. But from my point of view there is nothing to be said.' *Gladstone Diaries*, XIII, 378. Colleagues anticipated Gladstone making an announcement about his retirement.

to Mr G. but quite broke down. Harcourt followed, reading a long pompous letter which he had addressed to Mr G., accompanied by much blubbering.[1280] This was unedifying. Mr G. replied in a very kindly manner with wonderful self possession. So ends a marvellous career. Of course the real cause of his resignation now is his difference with the rest of the Cabinet on the naval Estimates, but, as he himself said, the increasing failure of his eyes would render his much longer continuance in office impossible.

2 March 1894. I saw Rosebery at the F.O. I fear he will not take the Premiership, & will hand us over to Harcourt. He has already made known to the Queen his reluctance to accept the post.

3 March 1894. Council at Windsor. Before the Council I had rather a long audience of the Queen. She talked generally about the political situation without alluding to particular persons, in the Govt. She spoke sympathetically of Mr G. The only allusion she made which might seem to indicate her intentions, was to Labouchere, whose mischievous proceedings she strongly condemned. This points to her sending for Rosebery, which I have little doubt she will do. After the Council Mr Gladstone had an audience & resigned. Ripon, Spencer, & Harcourt with Mr G. & myself attended the Council. Mr G. had expressed a wish that the three I have mentioned should be summoned. Harcourt looked like a whipped schoolboy. He is now off the blustering tack, & is thoroughly down in the mouth.

I hear that if Rosebery succeeds Mr G., the F. O. will be between me and C. Bannerman. I most devoutly hope C. B. will get it. There is some talk also of J. Morley for F. O. Spencer told me that he feels sure now that Rosebery will accept. I gave Sheriff's dinner in the evening.[1281]

[Undated annotation:] Mr G. there in excellent spirits apparently.

4 March 1894. Sunday. Rosebery came to see me just after breakfast.

[1280] See Morley's account in *Gladstone Diaries*, XIII, 439–40. Kimberley spoke first on behalf of the cabinet and when he left the room had tears rolling down his cheeks. John Morley noted in his journal: 'Kimberley cleared his throat, amid profound stillness, and began his words of farewell. But almost in an instant the [brave] honest fellow's voice gave way, and he could not get on. However, he bravely forced out a few broken sentences – [and] with many tears – and good honest sentences they were. [The sight of] such simple and unaffected emotion was as manly as could be, and touched everyone of us to the core.' Morley diary, 1 March 1894, in *Gladstone Diaries*, XIII, 439.

[1281] On Harcourt's and Morley's opposition to Kimberley's appointment, see Stansky, *Ambitions and Strategies*, 88–95. Also, Journal entry for 22 Feb. 1898; Rosebery annotations on the Kimberley Memoir, 502–03 below.

He has accepted the offer of The Queen & is forming his Cabinet. He makes my acceptance of the F. O. a *sine qua non*. He evidently has unfeigned reluctance to be Prime Minr. I observed to him how curious it is that both he and I should be most reluctant to accept the great offices open to us. Harcourt is dead beat, and now sulks absurdly. In the afternoon to Rosebery's where other colleagues and talk about minor offices.

5 March 1894. Monday. News of Ld. Tweedmouth's death, a heavy blow to us.

6 March 1894. Tuesday. Dined at Buckingham Palace, the first time since Prince Albert's death. Only Rosebery & myself besides household & Royalties; the dinner execrable. The Empress Frederick spoke to me some time about foreign affairs. She takes a very gloomy view: thinks all the Powers will be ruined by their expenditure on armaments. I fear this is too true. The Govts. are playing the game of the Socialists & Nihilists and some day there will be a 'cataclysm'.

8 March 1894. Thursday. First Cabinet under Rosebery. Cotton duties and Queen's speech. It went off well. Harcourt's continued sulks too ridiculous.

10 March 1894. Saturday. To Windsor where Council, and I received seals of F. O.

12 March 1894. Meeting of party at F.O. R. made good business speech wh. was well recd. Harcourt pompous.
  Debate in Lords on Address. R. made a fine speech, but a slip about H. Rule.[1282] Salisbury very clever. His eulogy of Mr G. in perfect taste. His chaff of Swansea's[1283] ponderous oration in moving address delicious. Hawkesbury as seconder spoke very nicely.

13 March 1894. Tuesday. Grand 'row' in Commons. Labouchere beat

---

[1282] Cautiously supporting Home Rule, but suggesting 'that before [it] is conceded by the Imperial Parliament England, as the predominant member of the partnership of the three Kingdoms, will have to be convinced of its justice and equity.' For a full discussion see Stansky, *Ambitions and Strategies*, 100–4.

[1283] Sir Henry Hussey Vivian (1821–94), Lib. MP for Truro, 1852–7, for Glamorganshire, 1857–85, for Swansea district, 1885–93, when cr. Lord Swansea, 1893.

us by two.[1284] His amendment about Peers, H. of Lords ridiculous enough, but for all that an ugly shake.

14 March 1894. Wednesday. Cabinet at 11.30 at H. of Commons to consider our positon. Harcourt's proposal to move that address as amended be negatived agreed to unanimously. No difference whatever of opinion.[1285]

In the afternoon held my levee of diplomatic corps wh. lasted 3 hours & 1/2! and all in full uniform!

15 March 1894. Cabinet. H. explained Budget. Good I think.

30 March 1894. Violent dispute with Harcourt about Uganda papers, Rosbery being also in the engagement. On March 22 when there was a Cabinet, we discussed the Uganda question. Of course the retention of Uganda was a foregone conclusion. Rosebery carried his point in the Gladstone Cabinet, when it was decided to send Portal[1286] out. It is an ugly business, but it was no doubt certain that we should be driven by the H. of Commons into this adventure, and we could not have resigned upon it, so that really there was no option.

2 April 1894. Cabinet. Budget again. Harcourt pompous & long winded.

6 April 1894. Cabinet. Uganda.[1287] Harcourt on the rampage. How can we possibly go on with such a man for leader in the H. of Commons. He does not possess a single quality wh. fits him to conduct the business of a Govt. except smart speech. He said to me 'thank God this can't go on much longer. The ship has got a hole knocked thro' its bottom.' I replied laughingly 'you are no better than a wrecker' –

[1284] Labouchere moved an amendment to the Address deploring the powers of the House of Lords, clearly intended as a vote of censure on Rosebery. Labouchere harboured a deep grudge against Rosebery for refusing him the Ambassadorship at Washington in 1892. Labouchere's amendment passed by 147 to 145 votes. See *EHJ2*, 122–3.

[1285] With Conservative and Liberal Unionist help the original Address, without Labouchere's amendment, was passed by the Commons. But this was a disastrous beginning for Rosebery's ministry apparently demonstrating their internal party divisions and reliance on the opposition. See Stansky *Ambitions and Strategies*, 104–5.

[1286] Gerald Portal, commissioned by Rosebery in 1892 to arrange 'the best means of administering Uganda'. See G. Martel, *Imperial Diplomacy: Rosebery and the Failure of Foreign Policy* (Kingston, 1986), 86–8. Kimberley found Portal's *Mission to Uganda* (1893) 'very interesting'. KP1 15/K2/10, p.151.

[1287] Harcourt objected strongly to the declaration of a British protectorate in Uganda. Harcourt described the Uganda issue as a bomb which would probably blow up the cabinet. Stansky, *Ambitions and Strategies*, 120.

(wh. is true). I cannot say how low an opinion I and I believe every one of his colleagues have of him as a minister. Privately he has a good heart & when in a fair humour is excellent company.

13 April 1894.   Friday. Cabinet. Welsh Disestabt. Bill

18 April 1894.   Wednesday. Cabt. Evicted Tenant's Bill.

23 April 1894.   Monday. Cabt. Great row with Harcourt about agreement with K. of Belgians (Congo State).[1288] Afterwards Welsh Dist. Bill.

25 April 1894.   Wednesday. Welsh Bill again. Harcourt's proceedings look like resignation after budget. He is as nasty as possible.

4 May 1894.   Friday. Cabinet. Continuance of Great row with Harcourt about Unyoro, Upper Nile &c. &c. &c. and King of the Belgians (Congo State).[1289]

7 May 1894.   Monday. Row still going on. Harcourt quite intolerable. Uganda. Went to Windsor for the night.

17th to Witton & stayed till 21st.   The Cabinets are one continual wrangle with Harcourt about Uganda & the Belgian Agreement besides various interviews with him at which he fumes & rages wasting time & breath. At last we arrived at the Uganda debate. The day before the usual storm & wrangle which ended in Harcourt declaring he would not speak in the debate: so it was left to Bryce & Grey & went off well enough.

But of course the whole policy is spoiled by the pulling both ways which results in a weak compromise. I was originally against retaining Uganda but now that we have determined to retain it, nothing can be more unwise than to refuse to take the necessary measures, & so get the advantages of neither policy.

[1288] Kimberley and Rosebery were engaged in secret negotiations with Belgium over the 'sphere of influence' in the Upper Nile. On 28 March 1894 Kimberley informed Harcourt of these negotiations by letter. On 12 April 1894 Kimberley and King Leopold's representatives secretly signed a treaty in London. When Kimberley sent Harcourt a copy of the treaty on 21 April Harcourt was enraged. At the 23 April cabinet meeting Harcourt abused Kimberley for keeping the treaty secret. Most of the cabinet seemed to side with Harcourt.

[1289] In an attempt to placate Harcourt both Kimberley and Rosebery agreed to the withdrawal of the Belgian treaty. A modified treaty was signed on 12 May 1894.

7 June 1894.   Cabinet. Discussed instructions to Col. Colville.[1290] Harcourt in calm temper but harangued us uselessly for an hour or so. At last we got to business & agreed pretty well on the course to be taken.

Cabinets June 14, 18, & 22, all devoted to my unlucky Congo Agreement. Naturally I got more 'kicks than half pence' which I must say I deserve. The fact is I found the matter in progress: I trusted to Rosebery and Anderson[1291] & thought I had done a pretty stroke of business. Imperfect knowledge & blind trust in other people, these are the reasons for my fiasco, but they are no valid excuse for my blunder, & my reputation will suffer accordingly, besides what signifies much more the damage to the public interest. I have eaten the German leek, & have now got the French onion in prospect.[1292] Pleasant!

19 June 1894.   Went to Oxford to be made D. C. L. Stayed the night with the Dean of Ch. Ch. (Paget)[1293] an agreeable man. The other visitors in the house were the Bp. of Peterborough (Creighton)[1294] and Sir John Mowbray,[1295] M.P. for the University. The Bishop very chatty and cheery.

20 June 1894.   To day duly 'doctored' in the Theatre.

25 June 1894.   Horrible assassination of French President[1296] last evening. I heard it by telegraph about 11.30. Called on M. Decrais to condole this morning.

26 June 1894.   Tuesday. Short Cabinet, business in H. of Commons. Harcourt placid.

29 June 1894.   Friday. Went to Windsor in the morning with M.

[1290] Henry Edward Colville (1852–1907), acting commissioner of Uganda, 1893; commander of Unyoro expedition, 1894.

[1291] Henry Percy Anderson (1831–96), enforced F.O., 1852; senior clerk, 1873; asst. u.-sec. to F.O., 1894–5.

[1292] During June 1894 both Germany and France attacked the terms of the Anglo-Belgian treaty. Amendments were made to satisfy Germany, but discussions with France remained difficult. Morley thought the matter had been 'grossly mismanaged'. J. Garvin and J. Amery, *The Life of Joseph Chamberlain* (6 vols., London, 1932–69), II, 598. For fuller accounts of the debacle, see Martel, *Imperial Diplomacy*, 203–15; G.N. Sanderson, *England, Europe and the Upper Nile 1882–1899* (Edinburgh, 1965), chs. 8 and 9.

[1293] Francis Paget (1851–1911), dean of Christ Church, Oxford, 1892–1901.

[1294] Mandell Creighton (1843–1901), bp. of Peterborough, 1891–7; bp. of London, 1897–1901.

[1295] Sir John Mowbray (1815–99), Cons. MP for Oxford University, 1880–99.

[1296] Sadie Carnot (1837–94), elect. 1887; assass. by Italian anarchist.

Decrais who had an audience of The Queen to thank her for her condolences on M. Carnot's murder. He made a very pretty little speech & H. M. gave a most graceful sympathetic reply. How admirably the Queen does these things!

(On the 23rd Duchess of York delivered of a son. Much satisfaction that this will prevent a 'Duff' dynasty –)[1297]

Remained at Windsor to dine and sleep. The Archduke Franz[1298] of Austria there, an amiable mannered young man. He does not look very bright, but like his uncle he may turn out to be a capable ruler. His manners pleasing, free from affectation or haughtiness.

17 July 1894. Tuesday. Cabinet. Very quiet. Business of Commons. Pamirs, only lasted an hour.

8 August 1894. Went to Osborne for a night. The German Emperor spoke to me for some time after dinner and was very civil but did not allude to politics. He looked uncommonly well. Rosebery who was at Osborne the previous day told me he had an hour's conversation with him on various political matters. He was very friendly but did not appear to be quite 'posted up' in current foreign affairs & seemed rather indifferent to them. We dined (54) in the handsome new Indian room.[1299]

13 August 1894. Cabinet. Congo Treaty. Went off quietly for once, decided on answer to Brussels, as to Congo negotiation with France.[1300]

14 August 1894. Turkish Convention, & instructions to Dufferin (Congo). Saw Dufferin in afternoon. He goes to Paris tomorrow. Had some thoughts of speaking on Evicted tenants Bill but I was so harried with F. O. business that I could hardly listen to the speeches: so gave it up. I was not really wanted.

15 August 1894. The tiresome Whitebait Dinner revived. I excused

---

[1297] A son (later King Edward VIII) to George, Duke of York (later King George V, r. 1910–36), secured the succession, which otherwise would have passed to the issue of Princess Louise and the Duke of Fife, family name Duff. See entry for 9 July 1889.

[1298] Franz Ferdinand (1863–1914), nephew of Francis Joseph, emperor of Austria; became heir apparent to the crown by the deaths of Crown Prince Rudolf, 1889, and of his own father, Archduke Charles Louis, 1896.

[1299] The Durbar Wing, added in 1890.

[1300] The cabinet agreed with Belgium, in response to demands by France, to abandon the treaty.

myself. Why not dine together comfortably in London instead of going to an Inn at Greenwich? It would be pleasanter in every way.

18 August 1894.   Went to Conybors for two nights.

23 August 1894.   Cabinet for Queen's Speech. Parliament prorogued.

28 August 1894.   Went to Kimberley.

4 October 1894.   To London for a sudden Cabinet & stayed till next day. There was an extraordinary scare caused by this Cabinet. The cause of the summons was to consider the order to the Admiral to prevent a Japanese attack on Shanghai.[1301] This of course the public did not know.

8 October 1894.   Rosebery is in a prodigious fuss about China & Japan, & has gone up to town to look after the proposed negotiation for peace. I do not believe in the necessity for hurry tho' of course no time should be lost. These matters are not dependent upon a few hours more or less, and fussiness always impedes the real progress of business: but I must not be ungrateful, as Rosebery's presence in London enables me to stay here a little longer.[1302]

Dalmeny is too far off for a Prime Minister's residence, but how did Ld. Salisbury manage to live in France?

23 October 1894.   Tuesday. All moved to London.

31 October 1894.   Wednesday. Cabinet. I.B.E.A. Company's[1303] claims; French negotiation[1304] – Bills – House of Lords. Harcourt being in good humour all went easily.

Cabinets ended for the present with two in the last week of November. We settled what bills should be proposed & also the line we should take as to the H. of Lords. We had of course differences of opinion as to the Lords, but discussion cleared the air, & we ended by agreement

[1301] Japanese advances in Sino-Japanese war were demonstrating her superior economic and military strength.

[1302] Rosebery, in looking back, observed that Kimberley's 'was rather the old fashioned view of ministerial responsibility'. Kimberley Memoir, 503, herein. On the other hand, Rosebery was being criticised in the press for having moved 'too precipitately'. *EHJ2*, 178. For an excellent assessment of British policy, see Keith Neilson, *Britain and the Last Tsar: British Policy and Russia, 1894–1917* (Oxford, 1995), 147–60.

[1303] Imperial British East Africa Company.

[1304] Rosebery and Kimberley having agreed that 'a little delay and less eagerness' would be useful. Kimberley to Rosebery, 18 Oct. 1894, RsP 10069, ff. 67–8.

on the essential point namely what is now possible to be done.

27 November 1894.   Went to Windsor for Decrais the French Ambassador's audience to present his letters of recall. He is very sorry to go and it is not clear why he is displaced.

28 November 1894.   Dined & slept at Windsor Castle.

7 December 1894.   To Windsor with Count Tornielli to present his letters of recall.[1305] He too is very sorry to leave London: and the causes of his recall are obscure. He has been here five years. I regretted Decrais' departure as he is a pleasant and conciliatory man. My relations were excellent with Tornielli but he is rather heavy in hand, and long winded. All this week I have been incessantly occupied with the Armenian question.[1306] Prodigious scolding letters of the usual kind from Harcourt. Truly he is incorrigible. I am told Mr G. used to say that he really could not read them: he had no time to spare!
   It is inconceivable that a man of Harcourt's abilities should write such ill-tempered ignorant rigmaroles. Poor Rustem Pasha[1307] who is in wretched health, will I think almost die of the vexation the folly of the Sultan causes him. I really pity him. He does his best to keep up good relations between us & his Master but in vain.
   On Thursday Dec 6 I dined with the 'Eighty' Club and made a speech which was very cordially received.

19 December 1894.   Wednesday. Went to Kimberley.

21 December 1894.   Friday. The great beech on the terrace blown to pieces by a furious gale. Not much damage else.

31 December 1894.   Elected Chairman of District Council & Board of Guardians.

7 January 1895.   My birthday. What a contrast to my last birthday when I was very ill. I enter my 70th year. *Eheu fugaecs*! but I have much to be thankful for, altho' I am fast losing my income & ruin stares all Norfolk landowners in the face.

[1305] Count Tornielli was the Italian Ambassador.
[1306] Following the massacre of Armenians in Turkey, Rosebery and Kimberley made vigorous though careful protests to the Turks and sought a coordinated response with France and Russia. Harcourt led the cry in cabinet for more forceful action. See Harcourt to Kimberley, 2 December 1894, in Gardiner, *Harcourt*, II, 327–8.
[1307] Chimelli de Marini, Ottoman amb to Great Britain.

8 January 1895. We went to London leaving much snow at home.

23 January 1895. Sharp thunderstorm with snow.

24 January 1895. Unimportant Cabinets since we came to town. Spencer & Harcourt have agreed as to Navy Estimates. A lull in foreign business after heavy pressure till a week ago.

25 January 1895. Cabinet. John Morley in a state of feminine irritation about Irish affairs, accuses us of being lukewarm &c. &c. &c. He deserves immense credit for his Irish administration; but his craving for flattery is his weak point. It is a pity that Rosebery does not 'lay it on thick'.

29 January 1895. Cabinet: for Queen's speech. Harcourt in his absurd dismal vein. I think worse of him every day as a statesman. Continuous frost & snow.

1 February 1895. Cabinet. Nothing of much importance. Harcourt in great exultation at the prospect of our being driven out of office.

5 February 1895. Parliament met.

11 February 1895. Cabinet. Long talk by Harcourt about 'unemployed' Committee who should be appointed to it &c. &c. No earthly reason for troubling us to sit there.

19 February 1895. Cabinet suddenly summoned for this morning.

19 February 1895. Rosebery made to us this morning a most surprising announcement, no less than this, that he had made up his mind to resign because he was not supported by his colleagues in the H. of Commons. He read to us a somewhat long paper, recapitulating his grievances. They were he said of long standing: he could endure it no longer. He had never sought his present position, & the Govt. wd. only be one member the less by his withdrawal. What he especially complained of was that no notice was taken by his colleagues of the virulent

speeches against him of Labouchere & Dilke in the recent debate.[1308]
The whole thing came on us like a thunderbolt, no one having the
slightest idea that he would contemplate such an amazing *coup de tête* –

Harcourt followed with judicious soothing remarks such as he can
use on occasions as well as any man. After all the members of the
Cabinet (except Tweedmouth who did not utter a word) followed in
the same strain, strongly urging him not to take a step which wd. ruin
his own reputation, and inflict an almost irreparable blow on the party.
As to the Govt., we all agreed that it could not go on, but must at
once come to an end if he resigned. Of course technically it no longer
exists when the Prime Minr. resigns: in this case it could not be reformed. With much difficulty we at length persuaded him to suspend
his determination till the Cabinet on Thursday.

He is not without ground of complaint. Harcourt's talk is most
objectionable. What can one think of a Minister who ostentatiously
and publicly expresses his delight at the prospect of the Govt. being
beaten & coming to an end? Nor can I be surprised that Rosebery is
sore at no notice being taken by any of our colleagues of Dilke's &
Labouchere's venomous attacks. It may have been excellent tactics to
treat them, as Harcourt said with contempt, so far as the debate in H.
of Commons was concerned, but Harcourt must know perfectly well
that, if he wished to oil the wheels of the Gt., he should have not left
the attacks entirely unnoticed. He has from the first done every thing
to make Rosebery's position intolerable, tho' quite recently I must
admit they have apparently been on better terms. Rosebery actually
went one day to his house to consult him! But making every allowance
for Rosebery's natural irritation, the folly of this sudden resignation is
inconceivable. 'Casimi Periu' as Ripon observed to me. It would make
him, & his colleagues and his party look simply ridiculous. As for his
vituperators, he would give them a triumph. They would justly boast
that they had driven him out of office. All that they have said against
the 'Peer Premier' would be amply justified. I have written to him very
strongly, entreating him not to persist in resigning.[1309] I can't believe
on reflection he can commit such an insane act.

The long frost going at last. It has been uninterrupted for four

---

[1308] In speaking on Chamberlain's amendment to the Address on 15 February 1895
Labouchere commented on the disadvantage of having a peer as the head of a radical
party. On 18 February, as the debate continued, Dilke made similar observations and
declared that the old Whig element remained too influential in the Liberal party. In
closing the debate Harcourt did not try to defend Rosebery against Labouchere's and
Dilke's attacks. Rosebery later claimed that his threat of resignation was a ruse intended
to frighten his colleagues and bring the party into line. See Kimberley Memoir, 504,
note 45, herein.
[1309] 19 Feb. 1895, in *Liberal by Principle*, 228.

weeks, & at times the cold has been intense. First drawing room to day.

21 February 1895.   Thursday. Cabinet. Rosebery announced very quietly that he had decided not to resign. 'All's well that end's well' but it would be vain to disguise that he has considerably shaken confidence in his judgment, and the extreme sensitiveness which he shows to personal attacks, indicates a certain weakness of character.

We had to consider our course to night on James' motion about the Indian cotton duties.[1310] We were unanimous in our determination to resist it to the utter most, making it a vote of confidence. Fowler[1311] wanted to sing rather small, but we told him it was essential that he should take the highest ground at once. He has very little back bone, but after what was said to him, I think he will screw himself up to the point. Can the opposition be so idiotic as to support James? They could not play our game better from a party point of view, set aside the want of patriotism they wd. show.

22 February 1895.   The opposition utterly routed last night.[1312] As Harcourt wrote to me, 'there has been no scene like it since Sennacherib' —[1313] Fowler made a capital speech, & gets just and universal praise. He figures now as the 'man with a back bone'! This is amusing to those who know him. The 'Spectator' says it would rather like to know what I said to him. It wd. no doubt be surprised that I should exhort him, as I did most strongly, to stand to his guns. I had conclusive reasons for postponing the cotton duties last year till we had time to see the result of the currency experiment, for a moderate rise in the exchange would have rendered the duties unnecessary. Now however that the exchange instead of rising has fallen further, there cannot be the smallest doubt that the duties are indispensable. Had they been put on last year, Lancashire could not have been resisted, and a most disastrous effect would have been produced on public opinion in India, far more serious than the irritation caused by the postponement. It is curious how blind our newspaper writers have been the [sic] real difficulties of the case.

[1310] Liberal Unionist Sir Henry James moved to impose a duty on cotton imported into India.

[1311] Henry Hartly Fowler (1830–1911), Lib. MP for Wolverhampton, 1880–1908, when cr. Viscount Wolverhampton; pres. loc. govt. bd., 1892–4; India sec. 1894–5; chanc. Duchy of Lancaster, 1905–8.

[1312] Vote on James' motion producing a majority of 195, 304 to 109.

[1313] Around 700 BC, the Assyrian King Sannacherib conquered much of Judah. According to the Biblical account, God slew 185,000 Assyrians who had been laying siege to Jerusalem: 'and when men arose early in the morning, behold, they were all dead corpses.' II Kings, 19:35.

23 February 1895. Laurence Currie[1314] married to Miss Finch at Burley on the Hill. This is interesting as he is the last of his race. I am glad to say he has had the sense to cease to be a R. Catholic, much I hear to the grief of his mother.

General Edmond Wodehouse is dead.

[Undated annotation:] *Note My old Aunt Harriet (Mrs. Chambers) says he was baptised in Ch. of Engld., Chambers being godfather & that he never was a R.C.

27 February 1895. To Windsor to present Mr. Kato the new Japanese Minr.

28 February 1895. Asked to Windsor to dine & sleep.

1 March 1895. Stayed till the afternoon in order to be present at audience of Chinese Minr., who brought the presents from the Empress of China to The Queen in return for those sent by the Queen on the occasion of the Empress' jubilee. The presents consisted of some most beautiful embroidered silks, two large china vases, a splendid jade ornament and a piece of silk embroidery designed by the Empress herself (more curious than pretty). The Queen's presents were a dressing case (very handsome) a big musical box & two sets of photographs of H M & her family. Presents to Chinese must always be in even numbers. Odd numbers are unlucky. After the audience the Chinese Minst. was taken to see the Mausoleum. This highly delighted him.

6 March 1895. In consequence of Rosebery's illness I at his request presided at his 'Sheriffs dinner'. Only 10 ministers present, many are ill with this horrid influenza.

9 March 1895. To Windsor to present Genl. Annibale Ferrero the new Italian Ambassador.

8 March 1895. Heard of death on March 6 of Lady Elinor widow of Rev: Algernon Wodehouse, my cousin.

9 March 1895. To Windsor for Council where I officiated for Rosebery. A funny thing happened when the Queen pricked the Sheriff. She has first to sign the roll, but the inkstand contained no ink & another had to be fetched. The Ld. Chamberlain (Carrington) who was at the Castle

---

[1314] Laurence Currie, only son of Bertram and Caroline Currie. On catholicism in the Currie family, see J. Powell, 'Testimony in High Places: The Conversion of Bertram Wodehouse Currie', *Recusant History*, 19 (Oct. 1988) 198–207.

was well chaffed about this. He remonstrated with an attendant, who said he knew there was no ink but did not venture to interfere as it was not his business, but the business of the page of the backstairs!

11 March 1895. Cabinet at Berkeley Sqr. as to Speaker. Rosebery looked less ill than I expected. No member of Cabinet to be proposed. Courtney probably.[1315]

15 March 1895. Friday. Meeting without R. in C. of Exchr. room at the H. of C. Decided that Courtney should be asked at once.

19 March 1895. C. having refused, Cabinet to consider next move. Decided to address the resolution that no Cabinet Memr. shall be proposed. C. Bannerman was very anxious to be Speaker but in compliance with wish of his colleagues renounced gracefully and good humouredly. Nothing further settled.

24 March 1895. Sunday. A furious gale from the West. Great damage at Kimberley. The Alma plantation wrecked.

25 March 1895. Monday. Dined at Grillions. Mr Gladstone there. The old man was marvellously well & vigorous. He talked long with me about Armenia,[1316] & still longer about A. Balfour's new book.[1317] He thinks it very clever but the argument wanting in depth & solidity. He is thinking of editing Bp. Butler's works & is studying all that has been written on the immortality of the soul!

28 March 1895. Thursday. Grey's speech on Nile Basin[1318] &c. in H. of Commons. It made a great stir. Grey had no written speech as was generally supposed, only some rough notes. Grey & I had some conversation on the subject in the afternoon, as he thought it possible something could be said on the vote on account. But he did not feel at all sure anything would be said.

[1315] A.W. Peel (1829–1912), Speaker since 1884, resigned because of ill health. Leonard Courtney was an independent-minded Liberal Unionist.

[1316] Agreeing that the Eastern question should not be raised 'in an acute form'. Kimberley to Rosebery, 26 March 1895, in *Liberal by Principle*, 228–9.

[1317] *Foundations of Belief.* Kimberley found it 'very clever, and not at all convincing like all arguments about the "unknowable"'. KP1 15/K2/10, p.153.

[1318] Warning that a French expedition to the Nile valley would be regarded by England as an unfriendly act.

30 March 1895.   Saturday. Cabinet thereon.[1319] Harcourt made a stir but was for him moderate. Morley announced that he would resign. The amusing thing was that Harcourt went out of the House & would not come back tho' Grey sent for him.

1 April 1895.   Sunday. Morley at my suggestion came to see me. I somewhat pacified him. I don't think he will resign. I have had a series of letters from Harcourt in his usual style about the relations of F.O. to himself and the Cabinet.[1320] He is quite intolerable.

3 April 1895.   Wednesday. Cabinet. Settled that Gully[1321] was to be proposed as Speaker.

11 April 1895.   We went to Witton & stayed till the 17th when we went back to town.

[Undated annotation:] Made speech at N. Walsham on 13th.

Much bother about the Nicaraguan affair.[1322]

18 April 1895.   Thursday. My darling Flo. seized at night with a brain attack. Alas! Alas! What could I do without my darling wife? In the afternoon next day she was a little better.

2 May 1895.   Alas! After making apparently good progress she has relapsed into almost complete unconsciousness. I am most miserable.
   Cabinet. Harcourt very absurd about Nicaragua. J. Morley supported him – no one else.

4 May 1895.   Saturday. Ah. blackest day in my life. My own love, my pet, my angel, my adored wife passed peacefully away at 14 minutes to three this afternoon. Dearest Johnny & Army were there with me by her bedside. They have watched her incessantly for the last three days, almost day & night. How they loved her and how she loved them! So ends a happy wedded life of nearly 48 years. I must not repine. To the lot of how few falls such happiness in this life. She died

---

[1319] Harcourt requested cabinet to discuss Grey's speech of the previous day. Morley, H.H. Asquith and James Bryce supported Harcourt in criticising Kimberley's policy and Grey's statement.
   [1320] See KP6 MS.eng.c. 4377; a number of these are included, in edited form, in Gardiner, *Harcourt*, II, 334–6.
   [1321] William Court Gully (1835–1909), Lib. MP for Carlisle, 1886–1905.
   [1322] Surrounding the expulsion of the British vice-consul. See R. Naylor, *Penny Ante Imperialism: The Mosquito Shore and the Bay of Honduras, 1600–1914* (London, 1989), 204–8; *Liberal by Principle*, 238.

of apoplexy, the result doubtless of weakening of the tissues of the brain by her terrible illness in 1889,[1323] and her constant rheumatism and suppressed gout.

8 May 1895.   My dear wife's funeral at Kimberley Church.

13 May 1895.   Cabinet.

20 May 1895.   Cabinet. Uganda Railway. Harcourt climbing down. J. Morley on the rampage. Will resign &c. &c. we adjourned till to morrow to give time for reflection.

21 May 1895.   Harcourt climbed down in his best style.[1324] He was quite right that it would be absurd to break up the Govt. on this question: but why such 'tall' talk for the last six months! J. Morley will 'take time to consider'. As he has 'resigned' ever so many times and 'reconsidered', I suppose he will do this time as usual.

[Undated annotation:] which happened

11 June 1895.   Cabinet Armenia. Harcourt, J. Morley & Fowler for running away at once! (We went to Poynters on June 1 & stayed till June 3. Weather lovely. St George's Hill beautiful. But I can enjoy nothing. Alas! for my dear lost love. I am most miserable.)

19 June 1895.   Wednesday. D. of Cambridge's retirement. He asks for a pension! This we will not give. Armenia.

22 June 1895.   Saturday. Govt. having been beaten by 7 last night on the question of the supply of ammunition (formally on motion for reducing Campbell-Bannerman's salary) the Cabinet met this morning to consider what course we should take.[1325]

We rejected at once the alternative of attempting to reverse the vote, and the only question really at issue was resignation or dissolution of Parliament. We met at 11 & discussed this question for about three hours. Rosebery & Harcourt were strongly for resignation.

[Three lines heavily struck through.]

[1323] See entry for 24 Feb. 1889, above.

[1324] Over the issue of House of Lords reform. *EHJ3*, 298.

[1325] The opposition motion indicating disapproval of Campbell-Bannerman passed by 132 to 125 votes. The government whips were caught unawares, the Liberal Unionists making great efforts to ensure a strong showing in the division lobby against the ministry. Harcourt immediately informed Rosebery: 'It is a *chance* blow but in my opinion a fatal one.' Gardiner, *Harcourt*, II, 363. See also *EHJ3*, 302

... After a long discussion it was agreed to meet again at four o'clock. Ellis (our chief whip)[1326] was decidedly against dissolution on the ground that the Opposition were better prepared with candidates. Tweedmouth took strongly the same line. But I cannot see much force in this argument, as the Tories if they come will dissolve almost as soon as we could.

[Seven lines heavily struck through.]

... J. Morley told us that the Irish party *[ill. from ink blots]* prefer dissolution. Harcourt was in the sulks. He could hardly be got to say anything. What he did say was really absurd. I had as usual some sharp passages with him. His principal argument against dissolution was that he could not after the Govt. had been placed in a minority wind up the business, which was simple nonsense. However Rosebery & he were for once agreed, being both eager to get out of office as soon as possible. When we met again at 4 o'clock, after further discussion it was resolved to resign.

[Two pages here excised.]

24 June 1895.   Our resignation accepted & Salisbury sent for. Meeting of late Cabinet to talk over election prospects: harmonious discussion but with no particular result. In the afternoon I received the diplomatic Corps & took leave of them: a very wearisome business.

29 June 1895.   Saturday. We went to Windsor and gave up the seals. So ends the Rosebery Govt.
  I acted in Lord Rosebery's absence as President of the Council, & before the Council had an audience of The Queen. She was exceedingly kind. She shook me by the hand & spoke with the greatest sympathy of my great sorrow. You will find, she said, thinking doubtless of herself, that your life never can be the same again. Alas! too true. It was a very painful interview.

1 July 1895.   Armine has embarked in a contest against the Attorney Genl. for the seat in the Isle of Wight.

4 July 1895.   Went with Army & Nelly to Ryde (Royal Pier Hotel). Armine went to meeting of delegates where he was accepted as candidate. In the evening we both made speeches at a meeting. We were well received. Armine spoke with much effect.

[1326] Tom Ellis (1859–99), Lib. MP for Merionethshire, 1886–99.

5 July 1895. To Newport in the morning, & on to Cowes to attend a meeting. Armine spoke really brilliantly for about 3/4 of an hour. I also spoke. Usual enthusiasm – but I fear he has no chance of winning.[1327]

6 July 1895. Returned to London & dined at Austrian Embassy. The Prince & Princess of Wales were there. The Princess spoke very kindly to me about my dear wife.

The Austrian Archduke the brother of the Emperor & next heir to the throne dined there. He is a stupid looking man. They say she was once handsome. The Crown Prince of Denmark was also there. Parliament was prorogued to day. I sat next to Mrs George Curzon,[1328] a very pretty and agreeable American.

8 July 1895. Parliament dissolved.

21 July 1895. Complete smash of our party at the elections.[1329] Harcourt's defeat[1330] will I hope be a lesson to him. What egregious folly he has shown about his precious local veto bill![1331] Notwithstanding his great abilities in debate I believe it would be a real blessing to the Liberal party if he disappeared altogether from the political stage. Utterly without principle, an arrant coward & a blustering bully, he combines every quality which unfits a man for the conduct of the affairs of a nation. Happily we successfully resisted his interference in foreign affairs, but it was one continued fight with him. Without him we should have been usually a very harmonious Cabinet: and with Asquith or C. Bannerman to lead the Commons we should have done I believe better on the whole. Mr G. found Cabinets so unpleasant & unprofitable with such a colleague as H. that he almost ceased at last to hold them. On one occasion Harcourt behaved so outrageously at an interview with him that Mr G. requested him to leave the room! There was hardly any communication between Harcourt & Rosebery: in short it was a perfect cat & dog life, and it is well for all of us that the end has come.

    J. Morley's curiously feminine temper made him very captious &

[1327] Sir R.E. Webster (5,809) A. Wodehouse (5,363).

[1328] Mary Curzon, neé Leiter (1870–1906), da. of an American millionaire.

[1329] The general election resulted in 177 Liberals, 70 Liberal Unionists, 341 Conservatives and 82 Irish Home Rulers winning seats.

[1330] Cons. H.H. Bemrose (7,907) and Geoffrey Drage (7,046); Libs. Harcourt (6,785) and Thomas Roe (6,475) at Derby.

[1331] The cabinet had been warned that the measure went 'beyond' public opinion and would ruin the party. See, for instance, Henry Spring to Rosebery, 20 Dec. 1894, RsP 10146, ff. 216–17; *EHJ2*, 86–7.

obstinate at times, but he is as honest & straightforward as the day, & never rancorous or personally disagreeable. Harcourt alternated between loud bluster and childish sulks. But he always gave way when it came to the push. If you agreed with him, he was sure to leave you in the lurch when the pinch came, turning his back on himself without compunction. If you disagreed, you had at least the satisfaction of knowing that his bark had really no practical result: but what a colleague!

25 July 1895. Thursday. Went with Constance to Kimberley. Oh! what a blank without my darling!

Heard that Robert Gurdon was beaten yesterday by Wilson. Curious reversal of the bye-election![1332]

7 August 1895. Wednesday. Went in the evening to Wymondham to a 'celebration' of Wilson's victory. Was very cordially received: made a short speech on the 9th. Harvest began on Home farm.

12 August 1895. Monday. Parliament met.

15 August 1895. Thursday. Queen's speech. Rosebery made very good speech. I did not go up, tho' much pressed by Spencer. It would have been too melancholy just at the anniversary of our wedding day. Besides I could have done no good. Rosebery has written to Harcourt that he can hold no communication with him on political matters. I think he is quite right after all that passed in the late Govt. If he had let Harcourt quietly assume the leadership of the Opposition in the Commons without saying anything, it would have been answered that he acquiesced. By entering a decisive caveat at once, he has prevented this.

Nothing further can or ought to be done now. The party must decide, & it would be quite premature to consult them now. Probably we shall drift on with two 'leaders' who have no communication with each other! I do not see how I can act again with him, but it does not signify much what I do, as my political life is drawing to a close. This Govt. will last I expect till the next century. In the present state of Liberal party it is much the best for the country that the Tories should be in power with a strong majority at their back, & especially as regards foreign affairs. It is almost impossible to carry them on effectively

---

[1332] Gurdon had defeated the Gladstonian Lib. Frederick W. Wilson (1844–1924) in the April by-election by 208 votes, but lost in the general election by 134, thus confirming Wodehouse's intelligence that the Tories would likely gain some 400 votes in a by-election. See John Wodehouse to Kimberley, 8 Feb. 1895, KP1 3/2.

with such divergent opinions as existed in the late Cabinet, between Rosebery & me, and Harcourt and to a less extent J. Morley. I am heartily glad to be out of it.

16 August 1895. The anniversary of my wedding day. How joyous a day it was, how melancholy now! It is a comfort to have dear Armine & Nelly with me.

10 September 1895. Constance & I went to Studley & stayed there till the 16th., a very pleasant visit.

2 October 1895. The extraordinary spell of hot weather & drought ended here last night.

14 October 1895. Lord Spencer came over from Creake to see me before he starts for India. We talked over the political situation. His opinion in which I entirely agree, is that nothing can be done now to appease the quarrel between Rosebery & Harcourt. Things must drift as best they may. I cannot for my part say that after Harcourt's intolerable conduct in the late Govt., Rosebery can be blamed for refusing to act with him.

6 December 1895. First fall of snow to night.

23 December 1895. To Prestwold and stayed there till the 30th. A melancholy Xmas: but my grandchildren who were all there, were so merry that it was a pleasure to watch them, dear things.

31 December 1895. So ends this to me saddest of years. May God comfort me, and enable me to pass my remaining time here, wh. can be but short, with resignation, & grant me trust in His infinite mercy & love, and a peaceful death, when I go to be by my darling.

7 February 1896. Went to London for the season.

8 February 1896. To Mentmore and stayed there for Sunday (till the 10th). Ripon, Fowler, Asquith, Campbell Bannerman, Tweedmouth, Herschell, E. Grey, & T. Ellis were there: also Waterfield Rosebery's private secretary. Much consultation about public affairs: but no difference of opinion between us. On foreign affairs we shall avoid attack on the Govt., and also on South African affairs.[1333] We shall however criticise Salisbury's impudent threats against the Sultan & point out the disastrous result of the 'peace with honour' negotiations at Berlin. Chamberlain's action we shall applaud except his premature publication of his scheme of reforms in the Transvaal an obvious blunder.[1334] With regard to education we shall take up the position that increased subsidies of public money to the voluntary schools must be accompanied by popular control in some form of those schools, & that there must be no interference with the board schools by levelling them down to voluntary schools: on the contrary the increased subsidies to the latter must be employed to level them up.

The breach between Rosebery and Harcourt remains unhealed. An arrangement however has been come to by which Rosebery will communicate through Asquith with H. Harcourt I hear professes much indifference, and feigns astonishment. This is all very pretty fencing with the situation, but there is really no solution possible as long as Harcourt is Harcourt.

11 February 1896.   Tuesday. Meeting of Parliament. Rosebery made a smart speech. Salisbury appeared to be ill & was unusually feeble in answer. Argyll made a few trivial remarks & promised us a lecture on Turks & Armenians on another day.

19 March 1896.   John Morley came to talk to me about his speech to morrow about Egypt & the Soudan. We were quite agreed about the main lines on which criticism of the Govt. policy should be framed. I asked him if he had seen Rosebery. Oh! no, he replied. R. boycotts Harcourt & me.

Saturday.   Morley's speech last night excellent. Evidently the Govt. are drifting into a campaign for the reconquest of the Soudan. They can't stop at Dongola. What infatuation!.

2 April 1896.   To Witton & staid till the 9th when we returned to town. Easter Sunday was on the 5th, pleasant weather: a very early spring.

21 April 1896.   Went to Kew Gardens with dear Army: a grey cheerless

---

[1333] On 29 Dec. 1895, Leander Starr Jameson, backed by Cecil Rhodes, had led 660 South African Company men into the Transvaal, hoping to raise an insurrection among the Uitlanders. They were forced to surrender on 2 Jan. 1896, and three days later Rhodes resigned as pr. min. of the Cape.

[1334] See Stansky, *Ambitions and Strategies*, 243.

day tho' warm. It could not be gloomier than myself under the black shadow of my sorrow.

13 May 1896.   Went with Army to the Tower Bridge, very warm.

14 May 1896.   Rosebery asked Herschell & me what notice we thought he ought to take of the Irish vote on the 2nd reading of the Education Bill.[1335] He seemed inclined to speak rather sharply on the subject. We advised him to say only just enough to mark his regret at the incident, leaving the matter to develop itself naturally as it is sure to do, only too quickly. We all then agreed that it was a fatal blow to Home Rule for many a year.

R. afterwards in speaking at Newton Abbott alluded in prudent terms to the vote.

20 May 1896.   Went with Constance & Army to Canterbury where we had luncheon with that charming man, Canon Holland,[1336] who showed us over the beautiful cathedral and its interesting precincts. What a noble picture! Truly our architecture of to day is a startling proof that all is not 'progress' upwards in this modern world.

23 May 1896.   Saturday. Went to Minley & stayed till Tuesday.

4 June 1896.   To Eton. Luncheon with Provost (Hornby).

22 June 1896.   Extraordinary collapse of the Govt. The education Bill wholly abandoned.[1337] This a most damaging blow to them, as C. Bannerman said when a horse has broken his knees, it leaves scars which are indelible.

Harcourt has distinguished himself by his 'slogging' speeches against the Bill. He would be admirable if he could be retained only as counsel to a Govt. to fight their policy in the H. of Commons, without any voice in the determination of the policy. He has just given a specimen of his folly & cantankerousness. We Peers were asked to give our opinions to our H. of C. colleagues on the question of the promised inquiry into the Chartered Compy. Chamberlain having asked them

[1335] The Education bill offered voluntary schools increased financial support, exemption from liability to rating, proposed education committees in each county and county borough, and granted permission to parents to secure denominational religious instruction for their children. Irish Catholic Nationalist MPs supported the second reading of the bill.

[1336] Henry Scott Holland (1847–1918), canon of St Paul's 1884–1911.

[1337] Abandonment of the Education bill was the result of disarray within Conservative Unionist ranks in the Commons over the issue.

their views on the matter. We unanimously* advised that they should decline to incur any responsibility and leave it to Chamberlain to take his own course.

In the evening Herschell met Harcourt who was furious & said he was not going to be dictated to by the Peers! Then why ask our advice? But what idiotic conduct!

[Undated annotation:] *(Tweedmouth was absent)

27 June 1896. Went to Cobden Club dinner at Greenwich, room unbelievably hot. Courtney made a telling speech but much too long. Altogether I can't say I enjoyed myself.

10 July 1896. 3rd reading of Deceased Wife Sister Bill carried by 142 to 104 (H. of Lords). The debates on this Bill were remarkable for the strong manifestations of dislike of the 'priest' movement among the clergy, & opposition to the Bishops – a very wholesome sign that the old English feeling of 'no priest' is not dead.

22 July 1896. Attended marriage ceremony of Princess Maud with the Danish Prince.[1338] Everything was well arranged, the spectacle was pretty, and the Princess looked charming & beaming with happiness. Govt. beaten to day on a clause of Irish land Bill. Their muddling of business is inconceivable.[1339]

25 July 1896. Went to Kimberley.

30 July 1896. Began harvest on Home & Lodge Farms. Great drought. An hour's rain on 26th.

17 August 1896. Harvest finished Home Farm.

7 September 1896. Went to Wallington, Trevelyan's charming place.

8 October 1896. I received a letter from Rosebery announcing his resignation of the leadership of the Liberal party.[1340] I cannot blame

[1338] Princess Maud (1869–1936), youngest da. of Prince of Wales; married Carl (1872–1957), 2nd son of King Frederick VIII, who became King Haakon VII of Norway, 1905–57.

[1339] The bill was intended to make the terms of purchase of their holdings more attractive to tenants. The former Conservative Lord Lieutenant for Ireland Lord Londonderry led a rebellion against the measure in the Lords. Only Arthur Balfour's strenuous efforts and diplomacy kept the bill alive. It appeared that many Conservative MPs agreed with the obstructionist peers.

[1340] Rosebery to Kimberley, 6 Oct. 1896, KP2 10247, ff. 26–8.

him. His position was really intolerable. In any case it is hardly possible for a Peer to lead our party, especially if he has had no opportunity of making his mark in the Commons, but it is a hopeless position unless there is cordial cooperation between him & the leader in the Commons. In the present case there is no cooperation and there can be none between Rosebery & Harcourt.

9 October 1896.   Spencer & Lady Spencer came to Kimberley to luncheon. He thinks that R. ought not have resigned without consulting his former colleagues. Perhaps not; still I can guess the reason. He was resolved to resign and did not wish to face colleagues who would have begged him to remain. The Armenian question gave him his opportunity and he was determined not to let it slip.[1341]

18 October 1896.   It now seems to be settled that no step shall be taken to elect a leader of the party. This is obviously the wisest course. An attempt to elect one would probably have split the party. Harcourt is in possession of the leadership in the Commons, and can go on without difficulty. Spencer assumed that I shall take the leadership in the Lords. I suppose I shall be asked to do so and I can't well refuse. It is a miserable position, almost absurd, to be a leader with a handful of (at most) forty men to lead − and it is most unpleasant to me to have to act with Harcourt, in whom politically I have no confidence, & whose odious temper makes all business relations with him detestable.

1897.   After passing Xmas at Prestwold I went with Armine for two nights to Mentmore from the 30th to the first day of the New Year. Fowler was there for a night & we had a talk about the Irish financial question. He thinks that the provision in the Act of Union, renewed in 1816, gives Ireland a right to special treatment; on the practical question what does justice now require to be done, he is as much puzzled as other people.

Rosebery seemed to be in fair spirits. We talked about affairs generally but nothing passed between us worth recording, except that I asked him whether anything had ever passed between him & Harcourt with respect to Harcourt's Budget which indicated any disagreement between them on that subject. I never heard anything when we were in office, which could make me suppose that Rosebery had any objection to

[1341] Rosebery seized upon a speech made in Liverpool by Gladstone on 24 September 1896 on the continued Turkish massacre of Armenians as rendering his own position untenable. See Stansky *Ambitions and Strategies*, 212–23. See Kimberley to Ripon, 9 Oct. 1896, in *Liberal by Principle*, 247–8.

Harcourt's Budget but something might have passed unknown to me. As I expected, R. replied that he had never opposed the Budget in any way. There was some discussion amongst us on a minor detail, but the Budget was generally approved & accepted by all of us.[1342] So much for the lie promulgated in the *Pall Mall* statement & made the ground for severe condemnation of R.

4 January 1897.   I have expressed my willingness to act as Leader in the H. of Lords if (which I am told it certainly will be) it is the general wish of our supporters. It is an ungrateful duty but I could not refuse. I wrote a civil letter to Harcourt & have received an answer from him in his most suave style expressing his satisfaction that I am to be leader in the Lords, and his desire to cooperate with me. How long will this temper last? However having undertaken the task I must do my best to fulfil it, & above all try to keep the peace with H. Alas! my darling wife being gone, I feel very little desire for active public life or energy to work. My thoughts are always fixed on the hope that on some blessed day I may in another world be reunited to my sweet love. In that hope I live & in that hope I shall die.

13 January 1897.   Dear Army has been here to day for a day's shooting & brings better accounts of little Roger.

16 January 1897.   We went to town for the season.

18 January 1897.   Meeting of Liberal Peers at Spencer House where I was, on Cork's proposal seconded by Thring, unanimously requested to be leader. Some 20 were present; about half our little band.

19 January 1897.   Tuesday. Parliament met. I spoke at some length on the Address & was very kindly received by the House. Salisbury answered. Some of his statements on the Turkish question were remarkable. On Sunday Harcourt called on me & we had a long conversation on the topics likely to be touched on in the Queen's Speech. We were quite agreed on all points, and his speech in the Commons was precisely on the same lines as mine in the Lords. So we begin most amicably. The only allusion he made to Rosebery's retirement was that it must have been a sad disappointment to R. to find that his (Harcourt's) speech to his constituents showed no point of difference between them on the Armenian question. R. was therefore

---

[1342] See Kimberley's report to Ripon, Jan. 1897, in *Liberal by Principle*, 250; Robert Rhodes James, *Rosebery* (London, 1963), 341–7.

unable to use that speech as a reason for his retirement & was obliged to fall back on other reasons.[1343]

21 January 1897.   Harcourt proposed meeting of ex-Cabinet either at my house or his. I assented to Harcourt's house thinking it was best in order to show at once that we accepted the position as regards him, to meet at his house, he having proposed the meeting. I was wrong. Jealousy of H. manifested itself at once. Herschell said he would not attend. I persuaded him to do so, but it was rather an unlucky beginning.[1344]

28 January 1897.   Thursday. We had our meeting which went off well. Harcourt on his best behaviour. We talked about Turkey & education. It was agreed that as the Turkish papers presented showed that Salisbury had been so far successful in bringing the Powers together, there would be no advantage in raising a discussion on them at this moment. As far as we can anticipate, the education measure will be very unsatisfactory. No aid, it seems, will be given to poor Board schools. If so, we shall stoutly oppose. From what I hear confidentially there is a good deal of ill feeling in our party towards Harcourt & the malcontents look to me to keep him from mischief! This is indeed a pleasant outlook for me.

7 February 1897.   Sunday. Called on Bayard,[1345] the U.S. ambassador. Mrs. Bayard, a very pleasant, well bred lady, whom one would not take for an American, spoke to me so nicely about my dear wife, that it brought tears into my eyes. She said she should never forget her kindness to her when she first came to London as the U.S. Amassadress.

8 February 1897.   Monday. Went to see Harcourt to consult about the news from Crete. We agreed on a question to be put by him in the Commons & me in the Lords. Salisbury was reticent as to policy of the Powers but outspoken against Greece.[1346]

Last Tuesday week I had a talk with H. about the Norwich meeting wh. we are to attend on the 17th March. I warned him not to be too strong about local option wh. is very unpopular with many of our

[1343] Harcourt had made a speech on Armenia to his constituents on 5 October 1896 arguing that Britain could not act independently of the other European Powers.

[1344] See Kimberley to Herschell, 25 Jan. 1897, in *Liberal by Principle*, 251–2.

[1345] Thomas Francis Bayard (1828–98), U.S sec. of state, 1885–9; amb. to Great Britain, 1893–7.

[1346] Greece and Turkey were in dispute over Crete. With both Philhellinists and Tucophiles in the party and the cabinet Salisbury pursued a moderate intermediary policy with considerable dexterity.

supporters in Norfolk. He said he should avoid the subject. He had told the L. Optn. people that as his bill had been disapproved, he was no longer pledged to it, though he adhered to the general policy, some popular control of licensing.

He showed us his correspondence with Rosebery on the subject of R's refusal to hold any communication with him on political affairs. With this I was already acquainted, tho' I am not sure I had seen all the letters. In my mentioning that I was surprised at the 'Pall Mall' statement that R. had opposed his budget, & I had never at the time heard of any disagreement between them on that subject, he said I was quite right in supposing there never was any 'disagreement'. R. did raise some objections, but after discussing the matter with him, he withdrew them. Of course such a discussion between two colleagues, which results in their agreement, is a common occurrence, & as H. said, did not imply any friction betwen them. If they had disagreed the matter must have been brought before the Cabinet, which it never was. Some one however must have told the 'Pall Mall' that R had raised some objections.

As I walked home from the House I met Ct. Dehm[1347] who stopped me, & asked me whether I thought there would be a popular movement here in favour of Greece. I said I thought it quite possible, and that if the Powers wished to prevent a general explosion in the East they must not only consult but act. The truth is their jealousies & shilly shallying have brought us into a dangerous crisis. In another conversation which I had with Dehm a few days ago: he told me he felt certain that France would not support Russia in an attempt to get free passage from her fleets through the Dardanelles. This, if true, is important.

18 February 1897. Thursday. Meeting of ex-Cabinet in Harcourt's room at the H. of C. We agreed on answers to be given to the Liverpool Association telegram to H. & me about Crete. On the 16th I met Mrs Humphrey Ward[1348] at dinner at Army's in Sloane Garden. After dinner I had a long talk with her. She has learnt Greek and is enthusiastic about Greek poetry, especially Sophocles. She reads Spanish novels, & we found ourselves there on common ground.[1349] She greatly admires Galdos' 'Doña Perfecta'. I mentioned Dickens. She did not seem enthusiastic about him. His later works, she said, she had never read.

The other Guests were de Courcel the French Ambassador. Lady Malmesbury (who was looking pretty) & her husband, Sir Jn.

[1347] Austrian amb. in London.

[1348] Mary Augusta Ward (1851–1920), novelist; niece of Matthew Arnold.

[1349] On Kimberley's interest in Iberian literature, see especially his reading of Galdos, Calderon, Alarcon, Valera and Mendoca. KP1 15/K2/10, 106–8, 113, 122, 136, 140, 151, 166–7; 15/K2/13, 1, 20.

Ardagh,[1350] & Mr Humphrey Ward,[1351] who did not prepossess me. He was formerly an Oxford don, & is donnish still. He is the art critic of the 'Times'.

25 February 1897.   Statement by Salisbury in H. of Lords as to Crete. All this week consultation with Harcourt & other ex-colleagues as to whether we should bring on a discussion on Crete & what we should say. H. is terribly longwinded & hammers away at the same points again & again. He is terribly afraid of the 'tail' of our party in the Commons.

26 February 1897.   Went to levee – very full.

4 March 1897.   Thursday. Meeting at H's room at H. of C. to consider what line we should take to morrow in H. of L. on Castletown's motion on Irish Finance.[1352] Agreed to take as little part as possible.

8 March 1897.   Monday. Meeting at my house of ex-ministers to discuss Crete. All present except Herschell. We were very harmonious. Harcourt read us most of the speech he intends to deliver to morrow in the H. of C. He declaimed it, especially the peroration, in his most pompous tone. I felt a malicious inclination to laugh, but I only said that I should say the same thing in substance in the Lords tho' I could not aspire to such a flight of eloquence. He looked daggers, but I made it all up by saying to him as we broke up, that it was all very well for him who would have some 150 men behind him to cheer him, to indulge in eloquence: I who should have to speak (as Lord Grey said, to 'dead corpses'), must adopt a tone suitable to them.

9 March 1897.   Tuesday. I spoke in the H. of L. on Crete, and was followed by Salisbury. It was very perilous stuff to handle, & I never felt more weighed down by a feeling of responsibility for my words. Harcourt introduced the subject in the Commons, speaking I was told with portentous solemnity. A good debate followed.

8 March 1897.   Monday. Meeting at Harcourt's House. Harcourt wanted to move address against coercion of Greece. He agreed however

---

[1350] Maj.-genl. John Ardagh (1840–1907), priv. sec. to Lansdowne, 1888–94; dir. of Military Intelligence, war office, 1896–1901.

[1351] Thomas Humphrey Ward (1845–1926) Fellow of Brasenose College, Oxford; ed. *Men of the Reign* and *Men of the Time*; miscellaneous writer.

[1352] Lord Castletown proposed that the refences to the proposed commission on financial relations between Britain and Ireland be laid before the Lords. 4 *Hansard* 47 (5 March 1897), 1.

to defer a decision of this till we see Greek answer, & know more of what Powers are likely to do thereupon. He was full of nothing but the necessity of following the lead of the tail of our party. We are not he said 'our own masters' – characteristic this! I protested strongly. I was I replied 'master of myself' & meant to remain so. General assent to this protest: but we were good humoured & we may not split this time.

9 March 1897. Tuesday. Harcourt came to my house. Wise counsels prevailed, & in view of the proceedings in the French chamber we determined to ask the Govt. not to use British forces against Greece before Parliament has had an opportunity to express its opinion. All of our colleagues agreed to this. Obviously the best policy is to keep in line as far as possible with France.

10 March 1897. Wednesday. Dined with Mr Horniman MP for Falmouth[1353] to celebrate the termination of the 'Rector's Rate' Controversy. Horniman is a ridiculous looking little man with a bald head and a bottle nose like Sir R. Temple's famous nose. He proposed the health of all kinds of persons from the Queen down to a man who was engaged to sing for our recreation. This last toast not a little astonished the guests, but it turned out that the singer was what Mr H. called an 'employee' in his tea business, and it was evidently a prearranged mutual admiration scene, Mr H. enlarging on his kindness to his 'employees' and the 'employee' explaining that 'singing' was only an evening occupation, which did not interfere with his service of the 'best of masters'. Fortunately Horniman can't put two words together on his legs or we might have remained there till breakfast time, & the entertainment, wh. was at the Metropole Hotel, ended at last about 11.30. There were about 30 guests. I sat next to Jenkins, the Penryn town clerk who piloted the bill through, a very intelligent man.

17 March 1897. Wednesday. Went to the meeting of the National Liberal Federation, stayed the night with Geoffrey Buxton and returned to town next day. Harcourt & his son Lulu[1354] went with me. We had a most successful meeting in the Agricultural Hall. I presided & made short speech (15 minutes).[1355] Harcourt made the speech of the evening. He had it all written out but delivered it very effectively. He began with some good banter. The rest was clear & strong, but he has no

---

[1353] Frederick John Horniman (1835–1906), Lib. MP for Penryn and Falmouth, 1895–1906.
[1354] Lewis Harcourt (1863–1922), priv. sec. to his father through 1904.
[1355] On the impact of Kimberley's speech, see *Pamphlets and Leaflets of 1897* (London: Liberal Publications Dpt., 1898).

oratorical fire. He spoke for an hour & 25 minutes & was enthusiastically cheered. Some of his utterances about Crete were imprudent but on the whole he kept within safe limits, as he had promised to do. We had a meeting of ex-Ministers in his room at the Commission on Tuesday to consider what should be said.

19 March 1897.   Friday. Salisbury attacked me about my speech at Norwich on the point of the integrity of the Ottoman Empire. I stuck to my guns.[1356]

30 March 1897.   Tuesday. 2nd reading of Education Bill in H. of Lords. I followed Creighton the new Bishop of London. I was much disappointed by his speech which I expected would be an argumentative one with points on which I could answer him. He made a very poor speech: in fact it was little more than a rather dull sermon. We had a ridiculously small minority; only 15! voting against the second reading. However my speech seems to have given satisfaction to our party outside.

I had a little amicable conversation with Ld. Salisbury after our encounter on the 19th about my speech at Norwich. On my saying that I quite admitted his objection to important declarations on foreign policy being made on platforms, but that I had been waiting in vain for some statement from him on the policy of the Govt. which wd. have given me an opportunity of expressing my views, he made this curious observation. 'If you want a statement from me, you must make some statement yourself to which I can reply, as I always feel a difficulty in leading off.' I told him this was unfortunate, as I was in the same predicament. He was visibly agitated during his speech which was obviously caused by his influenza cold which showed itself next morning. He is I hear quite worn out, which is not surprising & I cannot blame him for going away, tho' it is a misfortune at the present crisis. What an example of the inconvenience (to use a mild word) of uniting the offices of Prime Minister & Foreign Secy.!

31 March 1897.   Wednesday. Dinner in my honour at National Liberal Club. A large attendance. Fowler proposed my health & I had a very warm reception.

1 April 1897.   Thursday. Meeting at Harcourt's house of Ex. Cabinet. Harcourt has been ill with 'influenza' & is obliged to keep at home.

[1356] *Liberal by Principle*, 278; 4 *Hansard* 47 (19 March 1897), 1019. Arguing that it was 'in the interest of this country ... that we should be disconnected, forever from regarding the integrity of the Empire of Turkey as a basis of British policy.

We discussed whether a vote of censure should be moved & agreed that if blockade of Greece is declared, we can't avoid it, but it will do the Govt. more good than the Opposition.

Many people are ill with so called influenza. The doctors say that it is not the true 'influenza', but ordinary feverish cold. I remember the same thing in former epidemics. For a long time all bad colds were called 'influenza'.

4 April 1897. Talk with Harcourt about moving vote of censure. He was in a very reasonable humour, & I agreed generally with him on course to be pursued. Had luncheon with Reay[1357] & met there McVeagh[1358] an American who has been ambassador at Rome. He thinks the Senate right about the arbitration Treaty.[1359] He sees no necessity for an 'automatic' Treaty, as the U.S. has always been willing to arbitrate, and the 'automatic' Treaty wd. deprive the senate virtually of its Treaty making rights.

5 April 1897. Monday. Meeting of ex-Cabinet at Harcs. house. All there but Tweedmouth who is in Spain. Agreed unanimously on notice of Address to the Crown.

8 April 1897. Thursday. Attended dinner at Cafe Monico in honour of Mr Baker[1360] the Liberal candidate for the Chertsey Divn. of Surrey. Sydney Buxton[1361] & I made speeches. Leveson Gower[1362] in chair. Dinner good.

13 April 1897. Tuesday. My dear old Aunt, Mrs Chambers, died this morning at 15 Princes' Gardens, aged 92. She was well as usual on Sunday afternoon, and received [sic], chatting with them in her pleasant way. After they were gone she became suddenly ill & soon unconscious. She remained so till the end, dying from sheer old age! What a happy death! She had been for some time nearly blind but her mind was as bright as ever & she took an interest in all that was passing in the

[1357] Donald James Mackay, 11th Baron Reay (1839–1921), u.-sec. India, 1894–5.

[1358] Isaac Wayne MacVeagh (1833–1917), U.S. amb. to Rome, 1893–7.

[1359] The U.S. and Britain signed a general Treaty of Arbitration which the U.S. Senate rejected.

[1360] Lawrence James Baker (1827–1921), Lib. MP for Frome, Somerset, 1885–6; defeated on 18 Feb. 1897 by H.C. Leigh-Bennet for Chertsey, 4,845–3,977.

[1361] Sydney Charles Buxton (1853–1934), Lib. MP for Peterborough, 1883–5, for Poplar div. of Tower Hamlets, 1886–1914, when cr. viscount and appt. gov.-genl. of South Africa; u.-sec. col., 1892–5; post.-genl., 1905–10; pres. b. of. t. 1910–14.

[1362] George Granville Leveson-Gower (1858–1951), asst. priv. sec. to Gladstone, 1880–5; Lib. MP for Staffordshire N.W., 1885–6, for Stoke-upon-Trent, 1890–95.

world. She was a most kind, & pious woman, full of life & intelligence to the last. Peace be with her.

14 April 1897.   Went to Witton for Easter & stayed the 22nd, then back to town.

30 April 1897.   The Budget last night. Harcourt made some unwise remarks on South African affairs, to wh. Chamberlain made a fiery & equally unwise reply. I warned H., when I saw him a day or two ago, against violent language on this subject. This nation is firmly resolved to maintain at all costs our supremacy in S. Africa and violent language such as Harcourt used, is sure to be interpreted as meaning 'peace at any price'. H. always speaks in an exaggerated tone on foreign and colonial policy (neither of which with all his cleverness, he really understands).

8 May 1897.   Attended funeral service at the French Chapel in Little George Street for the victims of the terrible calamity at the burning of the charity Bazaar at Paris.

18 May 1897.   Conversation with Ht. at his house. He told me that Chamberlain had asked him to agree to put off the Transvaal discussion on Friday, as he had seen Leyds[1363] and he thought there was a prospect that the differences with S.A.R. Govt. would be amicably arranged. H. thinks that C., perceiving that Rhodes was out of the running at the Cape, has gone round to the peace tack. H. is convinced that C. had calculated on Rhodes maintaining his influence in wh. C. would have backed him up in his anti-Kruger designs. I told H. that I had seen Rosebery a few days ago and that his attitude was very friendly. H. expressed himself much pleased at this.

18 May 1897.   Dined with Bryce & met Col. Hay,[1364] the new U. S. Ambassador, a quiet unassuming well bred man. We talked about the Indian currency. He seemed still to have hopes of the 'rehabilitation' of silver.

25 May 1897.   My old friend Monk-Bretton died to day. He had been long ailing. His last illness began with bronchitis, & he had been for nearly two months in a very precarious state. We were at Eton & Christ

---

[1363] Dr. Willem Johannes Leyds (1859–1940), atty.-gen. of South African Republic, 1888 Boer representative, 1899–1902.

[1364] John Milton Hay (1838–1905) U.S. man-of-letters; priv. sec. to Abraham Lincoln, 1860–5; amb. to Great Britain, 1897–8; sec. of state, 1898–1905.

Church together. We both read with Mansel, and he took a first class in the next examination after the one in which I took a similar degree. His career rather disappointed me, as it never seemed to me to be commensurate with his abilities. He was clear headed, industrious, shrewd, and extremely well read. He could speak fairly, though he was certainly no orator. He had a remarkable knowledge of languages & foreign literature. He was proficient in French, German, Italian & Spanish; had a fair knowledge of modern Greek, & some Arabic. I think his failure to attain a higher position in politics arose partly from his dry, cynical manner, & still more from the total absence of passion in his nature. He was too uniformly 'drab' to exercise any commanding influence. He was true & honest to the back bone, and a most trustworthy staunch friend. To me he is a great loss. I have now scarcely an old friend left.

18 June 1897.   Dinner at Imperial Institute to Colonial Premiers, P. of Wales presiding. Laurier[1365] & Reid[1366] (Canada & N.S. Wales) made good speeches, the latter especially. Salisbury spoke well as he always does: Chamberlain's speech was rather thin and strangely enough he confined himself to some commonplace chaff of Salisbury's remarks on the H. of Lords and a eulogy of the H. of Commons, never making any allusion to the Colonies. Keen-witted and clever as Chamberlain is, he shows no depth of feeling in his speeches.

I thought Rosebery's speech rather below his usual level. Altogether however the gathering was very striking & impressive. I sat next to Seddon,[1367] the New Zealand Premier, a well mannered, & as far as I could judge from his conversation an able far-seeing man.

The dinner was given in a wretched shed, reminding one of a luncheon at an agricultural show in some little provincial town, except as to the food & wine which were excellent.

21 June 1897.   Address of H. of Lords to the Queen moved by Salisbury, & seconded by me. House full & cordial. As I went into the House the 'Times' reporter asked me for the MS. of my speech. I don't think he believed me when I told him I had no MS. nor note of any kind.

22 June 1897.   Tuesday. Commemoration of the completion of the 60th year of the Queen's reign (absurdly called the 'diamond jubilee'). I went with Constance & Sybil Packe to the Travellers' Club where we

---

[1365] Wilfrid Laurier (1841–1919), Lib. pr. min. of Canada, 1896–1911.
[1366] George Houston Reid (1845–1918), premier of New South Wales, 1894–9.
[1367] Richard John Seddon (1845–1906), prem. of New Zealand, 1893–1906.

had an excellent view of the procession, a very fine & striking 'sight'. We started from house at 7.45 and went (without any obstruction) by Victoria Street to Queen Anne's gate & then across the Park on foot by Marlborough House to Pall Mall.

3 June 1897.   Lords and Commons presented their addresses to the Queen at Buckingham Palace: a hurried and ill-managed ceremony. A large number of Peers attended. The Chancellor walked up first with Lord Salisbury on his right & myself on his left. After reading the Address he kissed the Q's hands, as also did Lord S. and I. The Chancellor bowed so low that I thought he would fall flat on his face. The rest of the lords having hurried out of the room, the Commons followed but many members I was told never got into the room. They are of course very angry. The fact was too much was attempted to be done in a very short time, but it was a serious mistake. The Houses of Parliament are bodies too important to be treated lightly, & the Commons especially. It is not for the interest of the Crown to give them offense. The block of carriages was prodigious. I waited an hour before I got away.

The Queen, when our Address was presented, said simply 'I thank you very much' & handed us written answers to the Chancellor. Our Liberal newspapers comment upon Ex. Cabinet Ministers not being asked to the St Paul's ceremony. Rosebery & I received an intimation (very late in the day) that if we wished for tickets for a stand at Paul's two would be placed at our disposal (two for each of us). Harcourt, I conclude, recd. the same letter as he attended the ceremony. As this was not an invitation to attend, R. & I did not think it necessary to go. For my part I was very glad to get off, as I had made arrangement to go with Constance to the Travellers.

14 July 1897.   Harcourt came to see me. We talked of the Turco-Greek affairs & the S. African Committee's report.[1368]

16 July 1897.   Meeting H's room H. of C. of ex. Cabinet. Slight talk about Foreign Affairs. We agreed that there was no use in attacking the Govt. in present state of Turkish negotiations. Some remarks were made on S. African Committee. It was evident that every one not on the Committee thought it had been a lamentable 'fiasco'. I believe C. Bannerman thinks so too. Harcourt has suffered seriously in public

---

[1368] A Commons Committee of Inquiry was established in 1896 to investigate the Jameson Raid of December 1895. Harcourt, Campbell-Bannerman and Buxton were Liberal members of the Committee. The inconclusive report of the Committee was presented in July 1897. See Stansky, *Ambitions and Strategies*, 245–7.

estimation from what is considered to [be] his mismanagement of this business. The fact is he was too ready to make a 'deal' with Chamberlain. He never should have originally taken any responsibility in the matter. He agreed with C. that there should be a Committee against the opinion of Rosebery & all his colleagues in the Lords, & now he has given himself away by not insisting on the Rhodes telegrams being produced. There is probably nothing important in them, but the public will never believe this. H. came to terms with C. on C. agreeing that the report should condemn Rhodes.[1369]

20 July 1897. Tuesday. Workmen's Compensation Bill 2nd reading, very dull debate. Belper[1370] who moved 2nd reading in a speech of an hour & ten minutes, inexpressible dreary; Dunraven not much better; Londonderry not effective; even Sarum[1371] caught the infection, though his remarks were dexterous. He brushed aside some observations of mine without an answer. Could they be answered? Several Peers, amongst these Tories, told me they entirely agreed with me.

23 July 1897. Friday. Motion of Abercorn to enlarge scope of Irish Land Commissioners. Irish peers made speeches full of sound & fury, and it was rumoured that the Govt. would be beaten, but Sarum put his foot down finally & the whole thing collapsed (motion withdrawn!) A ridiculous exhibition of weakness (not the first time).

29 July 1897. Last Monday's (26th) debate in the Commons on the S. African Committee was most damaging to Harcourt & the prospects of our party. Very few Liberals followed him into the lobby, and I don't believe there is a single Liberal who does not condemn him. The net result of his proceedings is the triumph of Chamberlain, and the setting up again of Rhodes. In fact his policy throughout has been a miscalculation. That he honestly believed he was taking the best course I have no doubt: but his judgment was at fault from the beginning to the end.

I am amused to see the general belief that the late Cabinet were always quarrelling amongst themselves. The fact is we had very few differences except Harcourt who led us a 'cat & dog' life.

The Committee on the Compensn. to Workmen's bill on Monday did not last long. The only important amendment was the striking out the provision as to the liability of employers in case of insufficiency of funds of a voluntary assocn. We divided against it, & mustered the

[1369] See entry for 22 June 1896.
[1370] Henry Alexander, 2nd Baron Belper (1840–1914).
[1371] Lord Salisbury, the pr. minister.

number of 19, of whom only 13 belonged to our little party! Truly our position is little short of ridiculous.

4 August 1897.   We went to Kimberley, very hot weather.

9 August 1897.   Began harvest on Home farm.

12 August 1897.   W. Cubitt's buildings Bacton Abbey Farm burnt down.

7 September 1897.   Went to Studley & stayed till the 15th, a very pleasant visit. Ld. de Grey (wife & child), Lulu, and Primrose & wife there.

13 January 1898.   Meeting at Wymondham of Liberal Assn. (Local) where I made a long political speech.

3 February 1898.   Moved to town.

4 February 1898.   Meeting of ex Cabinet, settled the amendment on Address by Mr. Walton.[1372]

8 February 1898.   Parliament met. Called on Harcourt in the morning. We were 'Knocked all of a heap' by the appearance in the Blue Book of Fowler's Waziri despatch.[1373] He never said a word about it at our meeting on Saturday! We determined to put a bold point on it, but our attack on Govt. is much weakened. I spoke for an hour on address to a crowded & attentive audience. Salisbury made a clear & impressive reply. I hear that he had a sharp conflict with Chamberlain and put his foot down on 'Pushful's' Jingo projects. His emphatic warning to the nation was no doubt mainly directed at C. He treated the China business very dexterous but for all that it is a very serious matter.

10 February 1898.   Ex Cabinet meeting. Redmond's Irish amendt.[1374] & Indian frontier discussed.

22 February 1898.   Rosebery called on me & told me a curious story about the formation of his Govt. The day after Mr G's leave taking of

[1372] John Lawson Walton (1852–1908), Lib. MP for S. Leeds, 1892–1908. On Walton's amendment and Fowler's previous policy in providing 'effective control of Waziristan, on India's North West frontier, see E. Fowler Hamilton, *The Life of Henry Hartley Fowler, First Viscount Wolverhampton* (London, 1912), 353–63, 444–8.

[1373] See Hamilton, *Life of Fowler*, 357–60.

[1374] On 11 Feb. 1898, John Redmond (1856–1918), Irish Nationalist MP for Waterford city, 1891–1918, moved an amendment to the Royal Address calling for Irish Home Rule.

the Cabinet, R. had a meeting of several of our colleagues to discuss the situation. R. said he was willing to become head of the Govt. if his colleagues all desired it: but he must make two conditions (1) that he should have the choice of the leader of the Govt. in the Commons, and (2) of the Secy. for Foreign Affairs. Morley was very cordial, but enlarged on the advantage of having the Foreign Minr. in the Commons. When subsequently he heard that the Foreign Off: was to be held by a Peer (myself) he turned quite rusty & R. was convinced that he wanted to be Forn. Minr. himself. Harcourt who was not at this meeting, R. said, blustered at first, as usual, & as usual soon gave way.

26 February 1898. To Oxford, made a speech to Eighty Club & Russell Club at a dinner at the Randolph Hotel where (with Armine) I stayed the night. Paul, who was in the chair, spoke excellently. My speech was well received.

5 March 1898. Met Gould,[1375] the caricaturist, a pleasant man at luncheon at Armine's. Mrs Stewart Hodgson the night before told me this good story. A South African 'richard', a German, who had taken a shooting near Balmoral was presented to the Queen. It seems he came from Bavaria, & H. M. having heard this asked him in German 'Sind sie ein Bayer'. He in his confusion thought she said 'bear' & replied 'no ma'am, not at present prices.' (*bien invente??*)

7 March 1898. Monday. Lord Roberts made a speech in H. of Lords of nearly an hour on the Indian frontier question. He set forth in clear language his well known views.[1376] The speech was already in print, but he delivered it excellently, and one was hardly conscious that it was an 'essay' learnt by heart. The House was very full, & numerous ladies were in the gallery, eager to hear the 'hero of Candahar'. Ld. Onslow[1377] (Under Secy.) spoke well tho' with a somewhat too pompous utterance. He dissented entirely from Robert's extreme 'forward policy.' Northbrook made a speech in the same sense, excellent in matter, but wretched in delivery. Lansdowne, who was a mere tool in Robert's hands when Viceroy, showed unmistakeably his sympathy with Roberts.[1378] Reay said a few words; also Ripon, Devonshire & self, some ten or

---

[1375] Francis Carrothers Gould (1844–1925), asst. ed. of *Westminster Gazette*, Kimberley's favourite journal.

[1376] As a 'powerful representation of a forward policy'. See Kimberley to Campbell-Bannerman, 7 Oct. 1892, in *Liberal by Principle*, 205.

[1377] William Hillier, 4th Earl of Onslow (1853–1911), u.-sec. India, 1895–1900, for the Colonies, 1900–3; dep. Speaker House of Lords, 1905–10.

[1378] See Kimberley to Campbell-Bannerman, 7 Oct. 1892, in *Liberal by Principle*, 205.

so peers remaining to hear us. After which I went to Spencer House to discuss 'en famille'.

19 March 1898.   Presided at dinner of E. Anglian Society. A terrible 'function' lasting four hours. Constance with me.

30 March 1898.   Meeting of Ex. Cabinet to discuss China.[1379]

1 April 1898.   Called on Harcourt. China &c. again.

5 April 1898.   Tuesday. Statements on China by D. of Devonshire in Lords, Balfour in Commons. D's speech very solemn but clear & well delivered. I followed. I was bound to say practically the same thing as Harcourt. This tied me to a discourse which was not particularly effective; it was of course essential not to let any difference appear between us.

E. Grey made an excellent speech. Balfour's statement was, I am told, very coldly received by his followers. There is much discontent with the Govt. who have managed by blustering & yielding to create the impression that our 'bark' will never mean 'biting'. Wei-hai-wei does not satisfy our Jingoes, & its value to us is doubtful: but it has done something to restore our 'prestige' in the East, & in Europe ('valeat Quantum')–

Houses adjourned to day for Easter.

12 April 1898.   Received telegram this morning at 9 a.m. to say that Isabel was delivered of a son this morning, born at 6 a.m.; weighed 9 lbs. 12 oz.[1380]

13 April 1898.   Wednesday. Went to Althorp (till Saturday) – Constance to Prestwold.

27 April 1898.   Meeting of Ex. Ministers in H's room at H. of C. to discuss Chinese Blue Book.

[1379] In November 1897 the Germans seized Kiochow and the following month the Russians occupied Port Arthur. Because of Salisbury's illness Balfour was in charge of the Foreign Office and faced the choice of insisting that the British receive territorial compensation in China (thereby condoning the Russian and German annexations), or risking war by insisting that Russia withdraw. In April 1898 it was decided that Britain should 'lease' the port of Wei-ha-wei.

[1380] Edward, fourth child of Lord Wodehouse. See Lord Wodehouse to Kimberley, 12 April 1898, KPI 15/K2/21.

30 April 1898.   To Academy dinner. A long dull speech from D. of Devonshire in the absence of Salisbury.

4 May 1898.   Lord Salisbury's remarkable speech to the Primrose League.[1381] In audacity he surpassed himself: but 'polite withdrawal' too accurately described his own attitude. The phrase will stick. His speech will not improve his position which is much weakened. Still, however ill-managed the China negotiations were, I do not see that any serious harm has resulted to this country. Of course the advance of Russia who has virtually annexed Manchuria, weakens our position in the Far East: but that advance was inevitable. There will I expect before long be a reaction from the Jingo fever which has for the last few months possessed this nation.

The war between Spain & the U.S. now engrosses attention, and there is a vast deal of 'gush' about friendship between us & the Americans. I do not quarrel with the feeling of sympathy with them in their effort to free Cuba from the miserable & oppressive rule of Spain: but I have no belief in the permanence of a friendly disposition on the part of the U.S. towards this country.[1382] Ever since I have been connected with public affairs, the U.S. has never missed an opportunity of doing us an ill-turn. Witness the 'Maine' boundary question, the Canadian fisheries, the abrogation of the reciprocity Treaty, the San Juan question, the monstrous disregard of all the obligations of a friendly State on the occasion of the Fenian raid on Canada, the Behring seal fishery, & lastly the wholly unjustifiable interference in our dispute with Venezuela. On all these occasions we have more or less 'caved in' and however much we may disguise our actions under the cloak of 'love for our dear kinsmen', the true cause of our long-suffering is our fear of the consequences of a war with a strong Power which can always by invasion of Canada inflict a tremendous blow upon us. At the present moment it is of course for the interest of the U.S. to be on good terms with us, as we are the only European Power which does not sympathise with Spain. (Russia must also, I suppose, be excepted tho' she does not sympathise I imagine with either party) but as soon as Spain is crushed, I feel convinced that we shall find the U. S. as unfriendly as ever, & her arrogance will be immensely increased.

19 May 1898.   Mr Gladstone died.

[1381] Meeting at the Albert Hall, where he contended that international cooperation alone could solve future problems, and suggested that 'the living nations will gradually encroach on the territory of the dying'. See J. A. S. Grenville, *Lord Salisbury and Foreign Policy: The Close of the Nineteenth Century* (London, 1964), 165–6.

[1382] On attempts to induce Kimberley to support an Anglo-American alliance, and Kimberley's reaction, see *Liberal by Principle*, 255.

On the 17th I made a speech in the Lords about Wei hai Wei. Since I gave a notice to ask a question on that subject Chamberlain made his extraordinary speech (on the 13th) on foreign affairs.[1383] My ex-colleagues wished me to endeavour to 'draw' Salisbury on this remarkable utterance. I did my best but he was too crafty for me. It was plain enough however that he did not share C's opinions. It is quite certain that C. spoke entirely off his own bat. One of his colleagues expressed no doubt the feelings of all of them when he said, 'Joe has behaved d—d badly'.

Mr G's death has so completely engrossed the public mind that my speech attracted little notice, & we have lost the opportunity which C's escapade wd. have given us for attack.

20 May 1898. Address to the Crown moved in both Houses for public funeral to Mr G. (Commons adjourned on news of death yesterday; Lords being Ascension day were not sitting.) Rosebery made an admirable speech. Curiously enough I hear it was not appreciated by the House. This arises from the general want of sympathy between him & the Peers. Salisbury was evidently much affected. His own speech was pathetic. He spoke from the heart. I was too short, but I should have broken down if I had attempted more.

Harcourt's speech read well, but his habit of reading his speeches spoils their effect on the hearers. I am glad he denied that Mr G. was dictatorial to his colleagues. I never did business with any man who was more patient, less meddlesome, and more ready to listen to the arguments of those who disagreed with him. I remember that soon after I became a member of his 1868 Gov. I was on one occasion so pertinacious in arguing against him at a Cabinet, that on thinking it over afterwards I felt that he must have been vexed with me and meeting him in the evening I apoligised for my undue pertinacity. He seemed quite surprised, & said 'Pray don't apologise. There is nothing more useful than that a question should be thoroughly thrashed out by argument.'

Unlike most men I have known, he positively liked a full statement setting forth all the arguments, where there was a difference between him & a colleague. I was much amused by his private Secy. telling me that he particularly liked my numbering my paragraphs. He was quite convincable but to convince him it was essential to persevere and not to be repelled by his first answer which was sure to raise every conceivable argument on his side. I never saw him lose his temper, however sorely tried: yet he had he told me himself, naturally a quick

---

[1383] On 13 May 1898 Chamberlain made a speech in Birmingham attacking the Russian seizure of Port Arthur and Talienwan.

temper. As to interference with the business of his colleagues, my own experience, which was I believe that of others, was that he interfered very rarely, except of course in matters on which it was necessary to consult the Cabinet.

21 May 1898.   I had luncheon with Rosebery.

28 May 1898.   Attended as one of the pall bearers Mr Gladstone's burial in Westminster Abbey, an extremely well managed & impressive ceremony. Went afterwards to Ky. & staid there till June 7, when back to town. On June 2 over to Witton, where saw the infant (Edward) a very fine child.[1384]

4 June 1898.   Marchesa della Rocella,[1385] my sister in law, died in a flat at Addison Mansions, aged 72. She had long been quite bed-ridden. My dear wife & after her death I supported her during the last years of her life as she was absolutely penniless having ruined herself by reckless extravagance.

We buried her in accordance with her wish in the R. Catholic cemetery, at Carisbrooke, I. of Wight, by the side of her eldest son.

4 July 1898.   Attended dinner at Hotel Cecil in celebration of U. S. Independence Day. Bryce & the U. S. Ambr. [?] Hay made excellent speeches. I responded for the Guests in a short speech which was very well received.

30 July 1898.   Bismarck died. Parlt. prorogued on the 12th.

3 August 1898.   Went to Kimberley.

18 August 1898.   Began harvest on home & Lodge farms. My aunt Mrs Philip Gurdon died at the age of 93. She was a Miss Pultenny, a pretty delicate woman when she was young whom one would have thought the last person likely to live to so great an age.

I should have mentioned above that I was not in the House when the Govt. were beaten in Committee on the Vaccination Act.[1386] I left London after the 2nd reading thinking that the Govt. must be able to overcome any Opposition. Had I been there I should have voted with Govt. Strongly as I am opposed to the anti-vaccination craze, I do not

---

[1384] See entry for 17 April 1898.
[1385] See 'Louisa FitzGibbon', p. xii.
[1386] On 4 Aug. 1898 the Lords passed numerous amendments to the government's Vaccination bill.

think after the Report of the Commissioners it wd. be possible to compel the 'conscientious' objector.

This has been a most unsatisfactory session. The Govt. is much weakened in the country partly (perhaps principally) by dissatisfaction with the conduct of Ld. Salisbury of foreign affairs especially as regards China, partly by a good deal of blundering in the H. of Commons. The stupid mismanagement of the vaccination Bill was universally condemned.

On the other hand the opposition is miserably weak. Harcourt is generally mistrusted by the Liberal M.P.s. Nor do I see any prospect that he can better his position. He has beat the Protestant drum loudly, and it is possible that the outcry against the Ritualists may become so strong as to procure him some support in the country.[1387] I made a moderate speech on the subject in the Lords. I begin to think too moderate as I have been complimented on it by two Bishops. No one can more utterly abhor priestcraft in every form than I do, and I feel nothing but contempt for the votaries of 'incense, lights & vestments'! It all makes for disestablishment.

What a melancholy spectacle! & all this in the name of religion! My own part in the business of the Session has been humble enough. I have been able to ask a few timely questions on Chinese affairs which have drawn important statements from Salisbury. I asked him for information about Chinese railways a few days before I left town. But in any case what could I do? As 'leader' of some 40 peers of whom perhaps 15 attend the House (usually much less), my position is almost ridiculous, & the necessity of keeping touch with Harcourt does not make the situation more agreeable.

Meantime people talk of the probable defeat of Govt. at the general election. A nice mess our party will be in if that should happen, withhout any leader who commands the confidence either of the party or the country.

8 September 1898.   Finished harvest on Home Farm.

9 September 1898.   Saw an Aurora Borealis, not very bright, this evening.

10 September 1898.   Horrible murder of Empress of Austria.

11 October 1898.   Extraordinary drought. Up to this time only a little more than 15 inches of rain here this year! For many weeks practically

---

[1387] In July 1898 Harcourt launched an attack on the Anglican bishops over the Benefits bill which extended into an onslaught against ritualism. See Stansky, *Ambitions and Strategies*, 252.

no rain. Watercourses & ponds, & wells drying up everywhere. This morning thunder and only a wretched little sprinkle of rain. More rain in the afternoon & the drought broke up.

27 October 1898. Went to Studley & stayed a week. The other visitors were Sir John Barran[1388] & wife, Spence Watson[1389] & wife, John & Lady Margaret Bickersteth.[1390] No one talks of anything but Fashoda.[1391] From N. Creake Ld. Spencer came over to see me before I went to Studley. He said he had heard that Harcourt was so discontented at the little support he received from the party that he contemplated resigning the leadership in the Commons. 'Credat Judaeus, non ego'. Meantime Rosebery is evidently returning to political life, & many of our party wish him back again as leader.

S. Watson & I talked over our difficulties; we agreed that however unsatisfactory it is to drift, nothing can be done at present to mend the situation.

14 November 1898. Presided at East Anglian dinner to Lord Kitchener[1392] at Cecil Hotel.

28 November 1898. My old friend Lord Henley died at Watford yesterday.

6 December 1898. I received a very foolish resolution from the Committee of the Home Counties Liberal Association stirring up the question of the Leadership of the Liberal party. I hear that this is

---

[1388] Sir John Barran (1821–1905) mayor of Leeds, 1870–1; Lib. MP for Leeds, 1876–85, for Otley division of W. Riding of Yorkshire, 1886–95; m. Elizabeth Bitton, 1878.

[1389] Robert Spence Watson (1837–1911), m. Elizabeth Richardson, 1863; pres., National Liberal Federation, 1890–1902.

[1390] John Bickersteth (1850–1932), barrister, m. Lady Margaret Ashburnham, da. of 4th Earl Ashburnham, 1882.

[1391] Standoff between British and French troops on the upper Nile between 18 Sept. 18 and 3 Nov., when French troops were ordered to be evacuated.

[1392] Horatio Herbert Kitchener (1850–1916), com. in Royal Engineers, 1871; served under Wolseley in expedition to relieve Gordon, 1884–5; destroyed power of Khalifa in the Sudan, 1898, and in the same year forced the French to withdraw from Fashoda; cr. Baron, 1898; gov.-genl. Sudan, 1899; com.-in-chief, South Africa, 1900–2.

intended as a move in favour of Harcourt (probably an intrigue of 'Loulou's').[1393]

12 December 1898.   Harcourt wrote to me announcing his intention to resign his leadership of our party in the Commons.[1394] I was not altogether surprised. The growing discontent in the party with his leadership must have been extremely galling to him. On the whole I think his retirement is a fortunate thing for the party. He will be a serious loss as a powerful debater but the want of confidence in him which arises from the belief that he is not really in earnest, is fatal to his influence both in Parliament & in the country. Add to this that his conduct in the last two liberal Governments made it almost impossible that he should be at the head of a Govt. The outside world is necessarily ignorant of this, & imagine that he has been the victim of some base intrigues. He is a genial agreeable man when not in his 'tantrums', and I found it possible to act harmoniously with him during the last two years, when we have been as it were 'joint' leaders. What has damaged him more than anything has been his mismanagement of the Jameson Raid business, in which he was completely the dupe of Chamberlain. The new leader will, I suppose, be Campbell-Bannerman, or Asquith.

25 January 1899.   I made a speech at Wymondham (at a meeting of the local Liberal Assocn.) on political affairs generally.[1395] It was skating on very thin ice. However what I said seems to have been well received by our party & my ex-colleagues warmly approved.

1 February 1899.   We moved to London. Jack stayed with us a few days at Kimberley & came up with us. He was away from Eton for a week as an 'infected' person, having been in contact with his sister who was taken with scarlatina at the Northcote's house in town. What a charming boy Jack is! He is getting on comfortably at Eton.

4 February 1899.   Meeting at my house of ex Cabinet: only six were

---

[1393] The Executive Committee of the Home Counties Liberal Association passed two resolutions, the first of 7 Nov. 1898 calling for early settlement of the leadership question; the second of 23 Nov., asking Kimberley 'to consider and advise' the Executive Committee regarding the first resolution. On 25 Nov. Kimberley declined an interview with the committee, though acknowledging 'the feelings of the younger members' as expressed in the resolutions. Harcourt recognized the favourable intent, but observed 'a great deal of underhand machination' at work. *Liberal by Principle*, 256–8; Armine Wodehouse to Kimberley, 27 Nov. 1898, KP2, 10249, ff. 38–9; Kimberley to Harcourt, 28 Nov. 1898, HP 53, ff. 32–3.

[1394] Harcourt to Kimberley (secret), 12 Dec. 1898, KP2 10245, ff. 87–8.

[1395] *Liberal by Principle*, 258–63.

able to come. Herschell is in America, Asquith in bed, & Bryce gone to Cambridge. We had a very friendly talk about things in general. On the 6th C.B. was duly chosen our leader in the Commons by the Liberal M.P.s.[1396]

18 February 1899. Everything went on swimmingly for us in the Commons till last night, when C. B. made a mess of it by voting with J. Morley & Labouchere on the Soudan question, Grey & several others including McArthur[1397] one of our whips!! voting with Govt. C. B. made a weak speech and gave no decided lead – result chaos again. The position it must be admitted was very perplexing, T. Ellis away ill, & Asquith & Fowler both away also, but no possible good can result from C. B. playing into the hands of Labouchere, Dilke, & J. Morley.

27 February 1899. The vacancy in North Norfolk[1398] would have given a capital chance for dear Army to get into Parliament: but besides the objections to his competing with E. N. Buxton & W. Gurdon, there were other very serious obstacles nearer home. What a pity! I am much vexed.

The H. of Lords dismally dull. On the address there were the usual speeches by Lord S. & myself, no one else except the mover & seconder (D. of Bedford & Ld. Cawdor),[1399] who both spoke very well.

The next day but one we had a Church discussion. The Bp. of Winchester Davidson[1400] opened followed Kinnaird,[1401] in a gentlemanlike speech without much force. Bp. of London (Creighton) was flippant & made a bad impression. The Ap. of C. spoke with dignity & earnestness. Halifax[1402] was fierce & uncompromising. Kinnaird, who opened, was ridiculously weak. A short speech by me was, I think, well received. We shall now have to wait to see whether the Bishops will take any effective action. I doubt it much.

1 March 1899. The sad news of Herschell's sudden death at Washington, an immense loss, especially to me. I have now no one in the Lords to advise me on legal points, not to speak of the invaluable assistance of Herschell in debate.

[1396] On the negotiations surrounding Harcourt's successor see Stansky, *Ambitions and Strategies*, 277–92.

[1397] William McArthur (1857–1923), Lib. MP for St. Austell, Cornwall, 1887–1908.

[1398] The Lib. H.H. Cozens-Hardy having been appointed judge of chancery division. William Brampton Gurdon subsequently was elected.

[1399] Frederick Campbell, 3rd Earl Cawdor (1847–1911).

[1400] Randall Davidson (1848–1930), bp. of Winchester, 1895–1903; archbp. of Canterbury, 1903–28.

[1401] Arthur Kinnaird, 11th Baron Kinnaird (1897–1923).

[1402] Charles Lindley Wood, 2nd Viscount Halifax (1839–1934).

23 March 1899.   Meeting of ex-Minists. in C.B's rooms at Commons. Tax on sugar bill considered, decided to wait for full information. Our present intention is to move Address to the crown to disallow the bill. This inroad on Free Trade is the prelude to others.

5 April 1899.   Went to Welcombe & stayed two days with the Trevelyans. The spot (near Stratford on Avon) is charming, but quite spoilt by a huge pseudo Elizabethan house built by Lady T's father. Dr Butler the master of Trinity[1403] & his pretty young wife were there. Both were very agreeable. The lady, notwithstanding her learning, quite unaffected, & free from blue-stockingness.

12 April 1899.   Appointed Chancellor of London University.[1404]

20 April 1899.   Attended marriage of Crewe[1405] & Lady Peggie Primrose at Westminster Abbey, & afterwards the 'breakfast' at Ld. Rosebery's. A most extraordinary demonstration by the public. Not only was the Abbey completely full, but besides an immense crowwd outside the Abbey, the streets & park were lined with people, mostly of course women, all the way from the Abbey to Berkeley Sqr. The day before I dined at the yearly dinner of the Colonial Institute (Aberdeen[1406] in the chair): & made a speech.

10 May 1899.   Went to Birmingham where I addressed a large & enthusiastic audience in the Town Hall. The occasion was rather awkward as I had to steer clear of the imbroglio caused by Rosebery's speech to the City Club which has spread in our party an exaggerated feeling of dismay. It will do more harm to R. himself than to the party. I stayed the night at Geo: Cadbury's[1407] villa (5 miles from Birmingham), and in the morning visited his cocoa &c. works.

11 May 1899.   Dined with Ld. Wandsworth[1408] where I met Rosebery & had some talk with him. He professes that he is out of politics; but why

---

[1403] Henry Montagu Butler (1833–1918) Master of Trinity College, Cambridge, 1886–1918.

[1404] For a brief summary of Kimberley's involvement with the University of London, see Univ. of London Minute 1644, 16 April 1902. Kimberley was member of the Senate, 1859–1902; and Chancellor, 1899–1902.

[1405] Robert Offley Ashburton Crewe-Milnes (1858–1945), viceroy of Ireland, 1892–5; succ. as Earl of Crewe, 1895; Rosebery's da. twelve years after the death of his first wife.

[1406] John Campbell Gordon, 7th Earl of Aberdeen (1847–1934).

[1407] George Cadbury (1839–1922), chocolate manufacturer.

[1408] Sydney James Stern, 1st Baron Wandsworth (1844–1912), Lib. MP for Stowmarket, Suffolk, 1891–5, when raised to peerage.

then become President of the Eighty Club & make enigmatical political speeches?

13 May 1899. Went to Cambridge and stayed with the Master of Trinity till Monday. Mr Choate[1409] the new U. S. Ambassador with his wife & daughter were there.

15 May 1899. Heard that poor old Hardy died at Kimberley yesterday from inflammation of the lungs after a short illness. A great loss to us. She was with us 21 years & a most excellent servant, so fond of all the children & grandchildren of the family. Another link with my past life gone!

23 May 1899. Went to Witton & stayed till the 30th. On my way down I was waylaid by W. B. Gurdon and persuaded to attend a meeting at Cromer on the 25th to celebrate his return as M. P. for N. Norfolk.[1410] I made a short speech.

3 June 1899. To Eton ('4th of June' day). Vote of thanks &c. in H. of Lords to Kitchener proposed by Ld. Salisbury. I followed & received many compliments on my two little speeches, one on the concurrence in the vote of money to Ld. K, the other on the vote of thanks. Afterwards we had a meeting of Ex Ministers in C. B's room, & talked about China.

16 June 1899. Tweedmouth came to my House to talk about the London Govt. Bill. C.B. & Ripon afterwards joined us, & we had a conversation about the Transvaal. We agreed that C.B. should allude to the question in a speech he is to make to morrow at Ilford, indicating cautiously our aversion to forcible measures at the present juncture, however much we sympathise with the grievances of British subjects.[1411] Kruger seems to be rather more disposed to make concessions and surely the true policy now is patience till we see what he does. If he gives five members of the 1st Rand to the Johannesberg district, this, if it is true, as Loch tells me, that there are some six 'Progressives' among the existing members, this would be a good beginning. Everything depends on the temper of the Dutch in our colonies & the Orange

---

[1409] Joseph Hodges Choate (1832–1917), U.S. amb. to Britain, 1899–1905.
[1410] See entry for 27 Feb. 1899.
[1411] In March 1899 British subjects living on the Rand goldfield in the Transvaal sent a petition to the Queen complaining of the refusal of the Transvaal to give them full political rights.

Free State. If they go against us, we should have a war of races, a terrible prospect.

21 June 1899.   C. B. came to my house this morning & gave me an account of a curious conversation wh. he had yesterday with Chamberlain: (at the latter's request). Ch: said he had no complaint to make of C. B's speech on the Transvaal quarrel that he was glad to observe that C. B. did not wish to make it a party question, but he was anxious that C. B. should know exactly how matters stood, and he hoped that the Opposition would do nothing to weaken the effect of what was contemplated by the Govt. All their information was to the effect that Kruger wd. not give way on the franchise unless such strong pressure was applied, accompanied by a show of force. This was Milner's[1412] decided opinion. The Govt. therefore intended to send out a force of 10,000 men besides making at once arrangments for providing transport for the troops now in Natal. If however the Opposition were to pronounce strongly against these measures, their effort wd. fail. He (Chn.) was far from wishing to go to the extremity of war, but he was persuaded that the only way to obtain a remedy for the grievances of British subjects in the Transvaal & to check the growing disaffection of the Dutch in the Cape Colony was to make such a display of force as would show we were in earnest. In short the Govt. are playing a game of bluff.

We had a meeting of Ex. Ministers in the afternoon at the H. of Commons. We all agreed to enter into no bargain with Chamberlain. It is the business of the Govt., not the Opposition to determine on the policy. We shall remain quiet & not embarrass them, reserving our liberty to take the line we may think right when they have announced the course they intend to take. We have not forgotten the 'understanding' so rashly entered to by Harcourt with 'Joseph' about Rhodes & the Commission on the Raid. 'In vain (now) is the net spread: the birds will not walk into it'.[1413]

14 July 1899.   To. C. B. in the morning, & in the afternoon meeting of ex Ministers at H. of Commons – on Transvaal.

15 July 1899.   To political garden party at Sir W. Pearson's pretty place in Sussex, near 'three Bridges'. Went back to the station on a motor car, my first experience of that horrible vehicle.

29 July 1899.   Discussion in both Houses on Transvaal. On this very

---

[1412] Alfred Milner (1854–1925), high com. for South Africa, 1897–1905.
[1413] Proverbs 1:17.

thorny subject I had many consultations with C. B. & we had much difficulty in so framing our language so as to deprecate war, & at the same time not to play into the hands of the peace at any price party. I think we on the whole avoided both 'Scylla & Charybdis', & our speeches were therefore successful. In our House Ld. Selborne made a clear & forcible statement, & Lord Salisbury wound up with a short speech studiously moderate in tone, but firm & decided; leaving no possibility of doubt that the Govt. will insist on the redress of the grievances of British subjects. This practically ended this very uninteresting & unproductive Session.

4 August 1899.   Constance & I went to Kimberley. We found a severe drought but the grass not so much burnt up as last year. The lake & river are lower than I have seen them: the Hingham stream is actually dried up.

7 August 1899.   Harvest begun on Home farm. The worst fruit year in our garden I ever remember, thanks to 16 degrees of frost in March.

16 August 1899.   Our tame doe has just had twin fawns. Palmer says he never knew before of a case.

26 August 1899.   Saturday. Office wing burnt down. Fire wh. originated in a beam adjoining the kitchen discovered by groom, out exercising, at 6.15 a.m. Butler, who slept in wing, looking out of window, saw groom, who called out fire: groom galloped to Wymondham for fire engine which soon arrived. Butler after waking inmates of wing called me at 6.30, & I was in courtyard at 6.40, and Constance soon followed. Most of the roof was then in a bright flame! Had it occurred in the night, the lives of inmates would have been in great danger. As it was they had to be taken down by ladders out of the windows, all other exits being cut off.

The butler, when he first heard the alarm, went at once to the next room wh. was unoccupied, & saw fire just appearing at a corner of the ceiling. This room & the butler's room were next to Kitchen chimney. Till he heard the alarm, the butler had perceived no sign of fire. On arriving in courtyard I directed the roof of the colonnade to be broken down to prevent the fire from extending to main house. This was not carried far, as I saw that the fire was not likely to extend far in that direction before the fire engine arrived. All danger in that quarter was soon put an end to by the firemen, the wind, of wh. there was not much being fortunately from the West. We had a plentiful supply of water, as luckily the fire-engine had recently been provided with a 300 yard hose, wh reached to the river. The servants wisely rang the dinner bell immediately, which brought up the gardeners & many labourers. Every one worked with a will & the servants, who were wonderfully active, saved nearly everything of any value. The maidservants specially distinguished themselves, showing great presence of mind & courage. My guns were unfortunately overlooked, till it was too late, the servants supposing they were in the main house. I am insured but cannot tell yet whether the insurance will cover the loss.[1414] Harvest over on Home Farm.

28 August 1899. Monday. We went to Witton & stayed there till Sept 4. On Saturday I presided at the unveiling of the portrait by Shannon of Cranworth wh. is to be put in the Gd. Jury Room. This little function wh. was largely attended went off very well.

5 September 1899. The heat extraordinary, thermometre 84 in shade. The next day the weather broke & we had a good rain. I have many letters condoling on the fire. The Transvaal question & Dreyfus case[1415] are in full swing. The newspapers furnish every morning a string of telegrams from the Cape, most of them containing news deliberately invented or falsified by intriguers & speculators. Not a word can be trusted, except what is official.

2 October 1899. Went to London & next day attended meeting of Ex Ministers & H. Gladstone at C. B's in Grosvenor Place. All there except Tweedmouth. We agreed on the line which C. B. should take in a speech which he is to make at Maidstone. No serious difference of opinion, but Spencer & Ripon over-peaceful. Fowler very bellicose!

4 October 1899. Wednesday. Returned to Ky.

16 October 1899. Monday. Went to Lowndes Sqre. for the meeting of Parliament & attended meeting of Minister's at C. B's house to consider what line we should take on the Address & the subsequent

[1414] For an extended account, see 'Kimberley Hall on Fire', *Eastern Daily Press*, 28 Aug. 1899, 5.
[1415] In Dec. 1894 Alfred Dreyfus, a French military officer, was found guilty of spying and sentenced to life imprisonment on Devil's Island. In 1896 documents were found supporting Dreyfus's plea of innocence. Military stonewalling led to the involvement of many prominent French citizens, including Émile Zola, who helped in securing a new trial in 1899. Anti-Jewish sentiment in the military produced another conviction, though the trial was generally considered a mockery of justice and Dreyfus was pardoned by the French president.

proceedings.[1416] All there: and also E. Grey & Sydney Buxton & H. Gladstone. There was considerable difference of opinion. Fowler & Grey, as at last meeting, very warlike. Spencer, & Ripon peaceful & Bryce vehement against the war. C. B. sat on the fence. It was evident from all we heard that the party will split on this question, whatever line we take. Finally after three hours discussion, carried on with much good temper, we agreed that on the Address C. B. & I should criticise the negotiations, declaring at the same time that we would support the Govt. in the measures necessary to carry on the war.

17 October 1899. Debate on Address in both Houses. My speech appears to have given satisfaction. I received indeed much praise for it, more than it deserved. Salisbury was very civil to me. His answer to my criticism of the 'new diplomacy'[1417] was extremely ingenious, but in his heart I am convinced he agreed with me. The House was very full.

There were no further debates in the Lords. In the Commons on a motion by Phil: Stanhope[1418] answering the negotiations, Grey & Fowler voted with Govt., Bryce for the motion; C. B., Asquith & S. Buxton walked out, a party split! Most of our party voted with Stanhope, including of course Harcourt who made a very able and temperate speech, & John Morley.

On Friday Oct. 27 Parlt. was prorogued. We returned to Kimberley on the 23rd.

Our party prospects are now very bad. The whole mind of the country, naturally, is occupied by the war & all other questions are in abeyance. Meantime our differences amongst ourselves most seriously weaken us. Our heavy beating at the Boro election shows what we may expect.

7 November 1899. Went to Studley & thence on the 13th to Newcastle, where I stayed two nights with Spence Watson. I made two speeches on the 14th, one at luncheon at the Liberal Club of which I am President for the year, and another at an evening meeting in the Town Hall. Both were well received. On the 15th returned to Studley & went home the next day.

[1416] On 9 October 1899 Kruger issued an ultimatum demanding the withdrawal of British forces from the frontiers of the Transvaal. When no answer came from the British government the Anglo-Boer war began.

[1417] Observing the development of 'the new diplomacy' and wondering 'what is to be said for the manner of conducting a negotiation which is practically *coram populo*'. 4 *Hansard* 77 (17 Oct. 1899), 12.

[1418] Philip James Stanhope (1847–1923), Lib. MP for Wednesbury, 1886–92, for Burnley, 1893–1900.

22 November 1899.   Went to the State Banquet in St George's Hall at Windsor in honour of the German Emperor, and Empress: a fine sight & what is rare at Windsor, a good dinner. The Empress spoke to me for a few minutes. She has very pleasant manners & more dignity than when I last saw her at a similar banquet 8 years ago.[1419]

We went down with the Ministers and other distinguished guests in a special train & returned after dinner. I did not get home till past midnight. The journey was not very pleasant in breeches & silk stockings! Fortunately it was not a cold night.

1900.   This new year begins miserably. We seem to be unable to make any progress with the war in S. Africa. I fear it will be a very long struggle.[1420] The only cheering feature is the loyal support given us by all parts of our Empire: a most happy augury for the future. We went to Prestwold for Xmas & stayed till Jany. 1.

The newspapers are full of the silly controversy about the beginning of the century. I am one of those who think that a century means 100 years & that you cannot begin the 20th century till the 19th is completed, but what can it signify to any body what we call 1900? It will make no difference in the scope of time, whether it is called the first year of the 20th or the last of the 19th.

23 January 1900.   Moved to London.

25 January 1900.   Meeting at C.B's: settled amendment on the address in the Commons. It was agreed that it wd. be useless to move one in the Lords. Our discussion showed all the old differences of opinion about the war, but we were able to frame an amendment which we could all vote for. All the ex-ministers were there (except Spencer who is poorly with results of influenza) with Grey, S. Buxton & Sir R. Reid,[1421] and H. Gladstone. The disorganisation of the party generally seems to worse [sic] than ever.

30 January 1900.   Debate on Address. Salisbury made a singularly feeble reply to my speech. It is inconceivable that he should not have taken the trouble to ascertain from his colleague Ld. Lansdowne, sitting on the same bench, whether the Intelligence department had supplied

---

[1419] See entry for 7 July 1891.

[1420] The Boers invaded the Cape and Natal and besieged Kimberley, Mafeking and Ladysmith. During 'Black Week' in December 1899 three British armies were decisively beaten by the Boers at Stormberg, Magersfontein and Colenso.

[1421] Robert Threshie Reid (1846–1923), atty.-genl., 1894–5; Lib. MP for Hereford, 1880–5, for Dumfries, 1886–1905.

adequate information as to the military preparations of the Boers and should have exposed himself to a flat contradiction to his statement that the Govt. had not been duly informed. Both Lord L. and Wyndham[1422] the Under Secty. of War (in the Commons) declared that full information had been supplied! The fact is Salisbury evidently attends to nothing but F.O. business. There is practically no Prime Minister.

Rosebery denounced him in no measured terms: I never saw him so angry before. His speech made a great impression. The govt. are seriously damaged in the eyes of the country, but of course they are practically unassailable by our discordant & disorganized party.

8 February 1900. Lansdowne with Rosebery. We had a long conversation about politics. He is open mouthed against the Govt., but seemed to be quite undecided as to his own course. He talks as if he would remain quite aloof: and evidently does not see his way to taking any decided part at present. Will this last? I think not.

17 February 1900. To day he burst out with a vehement speech (in our House) on the dangerous position in wh. the country is placed. It was overdone, & laid him open to the charge of 'panic'.[1423] I followed with a short speech, pointing out the possible danger on the Indian frontier & in the Soudan. My principal object was to get up Salisbury, who replied to me in a very poor speech, quite below his old form. I am afraid that hard work & domestic grief is telling heavily on him.

I have been elected (on Feb: 14) President of the 'Eighty' Club, after much discussion in the Club. It is a very disagreeable position, but I could not refuse, as my election was it appears generally desired. The discord in the club between the 'Forwards' & the Roseberyites threaten to deprive the club of all usefulness.

20 February 1900. Tuesday. Debate on Ld. Wemyss' motion on Militia Ballot. I supported the Govt. on the ground that at the moment it is inopportune to deal with that thorny question. Rosebery supported Wemyss in a caustic speech. He is playing for leadership of the war party. The motion was rejected by 69 to 42.

The success of Roberts at Kimberley causes great rejoicing.[1424]

The debate in the Commons on a motion to renew the 'Raid' inquiry was 'moutarde apres diner'. Harcourt now sees what blunders

---

[1422] George Wyndham (1863–1913), Cons. MP for Dover, 1889–1913; parlt. u.-sec. war, 1898–1900. ch.sec. Ireland, 1900–5.

[1423] See Kimberley to Spencer, 19 Feb. 1900, in *Liberal by Principle*, 266–7.

[1424] On 15 Feb., relieving a siege of 124 days.

he made in the Committee in 1897: but it is too late now. The mischief is irremediable. Chamberlain made a blustering speech, which will not do away with the impression that the business, as far as he is concerned, was 'fishy.'

21 February 1900. Dinner at Nat: Liberal Club. I made a speech which was well received, but what a hopeless condition our party is in! Our cranks are now busy setting up an Anti-Imperialist Club!

1 March 1900. At last good news from Genl. Buller that Ladysmith is relieved. This coming just after Cronjé's surrender is immense relief from our long anxiety.

21 March 1900. Met Lord James at dinner at Ld. Dacre's.[1425] From some conversation which I had with him about S. Africa I gathered that there is a question of suspending or putting an end to responsible Govt. in Cape Colony, a very dangerous policy, if really intended.

22 March 1900. At dinner with Ld. Carrington met Mr Barton[1426] the Delegate from N. S. Wales.

3 April 1900. Dinner given by 80 Club at Cecil Hotel. I made a speech wh. was not very effective. I felt tired & not up to the mark & I had really nothing but stale topics.

7 April 1900. The war drags on, and since Roberts' great success, things have gone very badly for us. First we lose 7 guns, and a large number of men by walking like blind men into a trap, & next a detachment is surrounded by a large force of Boers and all captured. Our men are heroes, *[two lines heavily struck through]* but our officers sadly wanting in tactics & vigilance. This war will I fear drag on for many weary months yet.

People are beginning to speculate on what will happen after the dissolution. It is the general belief that Salisbury will retire. Will Chamberlain succeed him? & Balfour be Foreign Secy. in the Lords? The Tories who made an idol of the great Jew adventurer, will find no difficulty in submitting to be led by C. They will grumble for a time but he will soon be received in the Tory pantheon. Gladstone was once a High Tory, but he died the idol of Radicals.

[1425] Henry Brand, Baron Dacre and 2nd Viscount Hampden (1841–1906).
[1426] Sir Edmund Barton (1849–1920), led delegation presenting Australian Commonwealth Constitution bill to British parliament; first pr. min. of Australian Commonwealth, 1901–3.

25 April 1900.   The Duke of Argyll died, the last of the Aberdeen Cabinet. I am now the last surviving member of that Administration in which I was Under-Secy. for Foreign affairs. That Argyll was a great orator no one can dispute: otherwise he was not a great man. He had less influence in the Cabinets in which he & I were colleagues than perhaps any other member of them. Indeed it would not be too much to say that he had no influence at all. Ld. Granville asked me once what I thought was the reason for this, which he had never been able quite to understand. I believe the reason was that Argyll harangued us like a Professor giving a lecture, with a touch of the Presbyterian preacher. But whatever was the true reason, the fact is beyond doubt & not a little curious: for he was a man of great ability & straightforward, upright character, & tho' haughty in manner not unpopular with those who knew him. As to his writings I must confess I never could esteem them highly. A smattering of metaphysics mixed with a narrow religious orthodoxy characterised most of them and the confidency, or rather 'cocksureness', with which he laid down the law & confuted to his own satisfaction the most eminent scientific men of the age struck me as almost ludicrous.[1427]

21, 22 April 1900.   After a long spell of very cold weather, two days of extraordinary heat but soon cold again.

25 April 1900.   The publication of Roberts' despatches, censuring Buller & Warren[1428] has produced a sensation: & in many quarters much blame is thrown on the Govt. If Warren is relieved of his command I do not see that anything but good will have been done. As to Buller the censure does not seem to me very severe, and his subsequent successes in relief of Ladysmith may be held to have fairly redeemed his military character.

What a strange thing is the resignation by the D. of Norfolk[1429] of the Postmaster Generalship! He was doing excellent work here, and to throw up his office because he had some connection with a Yeomanry regiment going to S. Africa seems to me absurd.

We did not leave London during this Easter recess.

2 May 1900.   Dinner at Natl. Libl. Club in honour of Australian delegates. It was curious how enthusiastically Rosebery was received.

[1427] Cf. Kimberley's comments on *Reign of Law* (1867), *Eastern Question* (1879) and *Unity of Nature* (1884). KP1 15/K2/6, 14v; 15/K2/10,53,105.

[1428] Sir Charles Warren (1840–1927), lt.-genl., 1897.

[1429] Henry Fitzalan Howard (1847–1917), 15th Duke of Norfolk, special envoy to Pope, 1887; post.-genl., 1895–1900; served in S. Africa, 1900.

There were some cries of 'No' when he approved the Boer War, but they were drowned in cheers. C. B. was also well received, & E. Grey. The function was intolerably long, from 7.15 to 11.45!

4 May 1900.   A smart little debate in the Lords on publication of the Spion Kop despatches. Lansdowne made a weak defense & in both Houses the Govt. cut a poor figure.

8 May 1900.   Resolution moved by Bp of Winchester. Salisbury made an amazing speech, trusting the report of Peel's Commission as a matter not concerning the Govt. & generally sneering at all proposals for reforming the licensing laws. On a division Govt. had only majority of 3.

9 May 1900.   Presentation for degrees of the London Univy. at their new abode in Kensington in the Impl. Institute building. The Prince of Wales was present & a very large assemblage. In the evening I attended dinner in honour of Sandhurst[1430] & proposed his health – a rather hard day's work.

Dear little Roger went to school (Mr. Locke's) for the first time last week.

24 May 1900.   Dinner at Colonial Club to Australian delegates. Made a speech proposing the Empire. What an intolerable bore constant dinner speaking is!

26 May 1900.   Dinner at Swedish Legation to meet King of Sweden.[1431] H. M. is a very tall good looking man with a gracious & pleasant manner. He remained after dinner till 11.30. He is young in appearance for 72.

30 May 1900.   Long talk with Sir H. de Villiers[1432] about S. African affairs. He takes a gloomy view, dwelling especially on the bitter feeling between the Dutch & English Cape colonists.[1433]

[1430] William Mansfield, 2nd Baron Sandhurst, of Shotesham Park, Norfolk; u.-sec. war, 1886, 1892–4; gov. Bombay, 1895–9.

[1431] Oscar II (1829–1907), king of Sweden, 1872–1907, and of Norway, 1872–1905.

[1432] John Henry de Villiers, 1st Baron de Villiers (1842–1914), member of royal com. which drew up the Pretoria Convention, 1881; first col. judge on judicial com. of Privy Council: chief justice of the Cape Colony, 1874–1910.

[1433] In June 1900 the British occupied Johannesburg and Pretoria, the Transvaal government departing by railway for Delagoa Bay.

2 June 1900.   Went to Witton and stayed till the 8th. On the 9th we went to Falmouth & returned to town on the 16th.

30 June 1900.   Friday. Carrington made a violent attack on Chamberlain on the 2nd reading of the Australian Commonwealth Bill. Not content with criticising his clumsy management of the bill which was a fair subject for some caustic remarks, he wandered off into S. Africa & other matters which had nothing to do with the bill. The Chancellor gave C. a severe dressing with the manifest approval of the House. I did my best to defend him which was no easy matter. C. is an excellent good fellow and not wanting in cleverness. What he does want is discretion.

30 June 1900.   Saturday. Went with Armine to see [*ill.*] where Roger is at school. I thought Mr Arnold, the master a very interesting man.

18, 19 July 1900.   Meetings of Ex Ministers in C. B's room at the Commons. Our 'confabulations' did not come to much. Some vague talk on the first day about China & South Africa: and on the second about a manifesto by C. B. when the dissolution takes place.

25 July 1900.   Debate in Commons on S. Africa, result an electioneering speech by Chamberlain, and an ineffectual & feeble appeal by C. B. to our 'party' to walk out on a motion by W. Lawson to reduce C's salary by £100, whereupon E. Grey and 39 other Liberals voted with the Govt: Bryce and 30 other Liberals against the Govt: 35 walked out with C. B. (Asquith amongst them); Fowler was absent from town. So we are now a tripartite 'party'. A pretty kettle of fish!

We had two meetings of Ex. Ministers to consider this very awkward situation, but no one could suggest any way of mending matters. C. B. unfortunately has not been able to establish any authority over his miscalled 'followers'. Could any one have succeeded in leading such a broken & distracted party?

29 July 1900.   Atrocious assassination of the King of Italy[1434] at Monza. On the 30th the D. of Saxe Coburg (D of Edinburgh) died. He had latterly taken to drinking wh. no doubt hastened his death. He had many good qualities, and his ability as a naval officer was unquestionable.

On the 27th Rosebery made a curious speech in the Lords in the course of which, in commenting on Salisbury's alarmist speech to the Primrose League, he said 'I should be more satisfied with a single

---

[1434] Umberto I (1844–1900), king of Italy, 1878–1900.

sentence' from the Commander in speech answering us that we are amply prepared for all contingencies 'than with a thousand speeches from Primrose L. orators'. This brought up Lansdowne who strongly protested against such an appeal to Wolseley as undermining the authority and responsibility of Govt. I spoke next agreeing with L. on this point. Rosebery raised the question again on Aug 2, but in my opinion did not mend his hand.

5 August 1900. For the last fortnight or 3 weeks, the war has ceased to occupy public attention, which has been engrossed by the alarming situation in China.[1435] Harcourt made a remarkable speech in the Commons last week, in his best fighting style. He has been absent for a long time on account of ill-health.

8 August 1900. Parliament prorogued. A dull unprofitable Session. Had it not been for the war the outlook would have been far from favourable to the Govt. Salisbury engrossed with foreign affairs is evidently unable to perform the duties of Prime Minister. There being therefore no control over his colleagues, there has frequently been a pitiable exhibition of want of concert between the Ministers. Salisbury himself, though he revived somewhat towards the end of the Session, is evidently not the man he was since Lady S's death & A. Balfour has singularly deteriorated in tact & temper as Leader of the Commons. Two under-secretaries, Brodrick[1436] & especially Wyndham, have done well, but the Govt. as a whole shows symptoms of being worn out. As to the one vigorous & pushful Minister, J. Chamberlain, he is reaping what he has sown, & as long as the Khaki fever lasts his position is unassailable. The Opposition is in a pitiable condition & likely to remain so.

As a so-called 'Leader' in the H. of Lords, I keep up the pretence of criticising the Govt., but it is really a farce to pose as a leader when I have only about 15 followers who attend the House when whipped up! It is weary work & I am heartily sick of it. There is a general expectation that Parliament will be dissolved in October. Nothing can be worse than the prospects of the Opposition, but if the Govt. get an enormous majority, will it strengthen them? I doubt it.

18 August 1900. Saturday. Went to Prestwold where we stayed till the

---

[1435] As a part of a widespread anti-foreign campaign of violence, European legations were besieged by Chinese troops in June. International military units counterattacked from Tientsin on 4 Aug. and on 14 Aug. captured Beijing.

[1436] William St John Fremantle Brodrick (1856–1942), Cons. MP for W. Surrey, 1880–5, for Guildford, Surrey, 1885–1906; u.-sec. war, 1895–8; u.-sec. f.a., 1898–1900.

27th then to Lord Ripon's at Studley. We came back to London on Sept 1. We had arranged to go to Ky. on the 5th, but we found to our annoyance that our offices wh. are rebuilding cannot be ready for us till the 12th. We had a day's grouse driving at Studley – four guns, & bagged 372 birds of wh. DeGrey killed 202. He is a marvellous shot. Ripon says it is a bad year for grouse on his moor.

8 September 1900.   Two remarkable men passed away this summer. The D. of Argyll had for some time been failing in health and took but little part in public affairs. He was the last of the orators, though we have still very clear speakers. The newspapers never understood how little real influence he had in the political world.

Lord Russell, the Chief Justice was a man of a very different type & is a serious loss to the nation.

12 September 1900.   At last got down to Kimberley.

25 September 1900.   Dissolution of Parliament on the day before, being the last on wh. according to the etiquette of elections can speak, I went to a meeting at Saffron Walden to support Armine's candidature for North Essex.[1437] He made a very good speech, wh. was well received. Burghclere, the former liberal M.P., was kind enough to come all the way from Scotland to support A. He made an excellent speech. I stayed the night at Stansted with Mr Gold[1438] who unfortunately was ill in bed & unable to attend the meeting.

15 October 1900.   Armine elected M.P. for the Saffron Walden Divn. by a majority of 110. It was a very tough fight. Nelly's unfortunate carriage accident deprived him of her aid which was a great loss.

18 October 1900.   The elections are now over, with a result practically of 'as you were'.[1439] I never expected any thing better. In Norfolk we retained five of the six county seats, & almost won the 6th. The staunch Liberalism of the Norfolk voters is very remarkable. Our strength lies with the agricultural labourers, nearly all the landowners & most of the farmers being against us.

The conduct of the contest in this county was not marked by the

---

[1437] For a succinct statement of Wodehouse's Liberal position, see his election circular, 25 Sept. 1900, PkP DC1 749/19/1.

[1438] Charles Gold (1837–1924), wine merchant; Rad. MP for Saffron Walden, Essex, 1895–1900, when he retired.

[1439] The general election gave the Liberals 186, the Liberal Unionists 68, the Conservatives 334 and the Irish Nationalists 82 seats in the Commons. See Kimberley to Harcourt, 17 Oct. 1900, HP 43, f. 40.

extreme bitterness which prevailed elsewhere. Anything more disgraceful than the conduct generally of the Ministerial candidates cannot
be imagined. Led by Chamberlain who outdid himself in violence &
unfair statements, they used very poisonous weapon without scruple.
Every Liberal vote they cried was a vote given to the Boers, & the lies
which were freely circulated & formed the staple of many of their
speeches were infamous. No such exhibition of party violence has ever
taken place in my time. At the last moment the Norwich Liberals
(comprising both sections of the party) to our great surprise asked
Wodehouse to stand. It is very seldom that both sections unite; when
united, they have generally carried the election. Wodehouse, who was
not at all anxious to stand, gave them a civil answer, but it was
impossible without any time for preparation to embark in a contest.
Hoare[1440] of course was quite safe, but W. might have beaten Bullard[1441]
who lost his popularity.

31 October 1900. Attended meeting at Wymondham to celebrate Wilson's return for Mid: Norf. & made a speech. Armine could not be
present, a great disappointment. He was laid up with an abcess in the
ear, wh. gave us some anxiety, but under Dr Barton's excellent treatment
he happily recovered after more than a week's illness.

3 December 1900. To London for the short & unexpected session. On
arrival I was summoned to a meeting of Ex Ministers at C. B's to
consider a most embarrassing communication which he had received
from Harcourt. It was a request to be admitted to our 'ex Ministers'
conclave. He professed an ardent desire to give hearty support to
C. B. as leader, and claimed on that ground to be readmitted to our
Councils, especially as he had never done more than resign the
leadership in the Commons. He proposed to write a formal letter to
this effect & if he were refused he should be compelled to publish
Rosebery's (old) letter 'ostracising' him. Those of us who were present
at the meeting came after considerable discussion to the conclusion
that we must refuse, but as Spencer, Fowler, Asquith, Bryce & Grey
were not present, we postponed any decision till they had been
consulted. A second meeting was accordingly held, which every one
attended. There was a lively discussion & Spencer was in favour of
admitting Harcourt. He however ultimately gave way to the general
opinion which was for refusal. It was manifest that if we admitted H.
we should stultify our more recent actions in holding out 'the olive

[1440] Sir Samuel Hoare (1841–1915), Cons. MP for Norwich, 1886–1906.

[1441] Harry Bullard (1841–1903) Cons. MP for Norwich, 1885–6, 1895–1903. Sir Samuel
Hoare and Bullard were returned unopposed.

branch' to Rosebery, as it was certain that he & Harcourt wd. not act together, and we should infallibly cause an open split in the party. In the interest therefore of the unity of the party it was clearly our duty (however unpleasant) to refuse H's request. Tweedsmouth gallantly undertook to communicate our decision to H. This course was taken as being most friendly to H., and giving him an opportunity to let the matter drop without the promised 'formal' letter. The result justified our diplomacy. H. accepted our refusal with a good grace in a friendly letter to C. B.

We heard that J. Morley had advised him not to press his request, & had pointed out to him the embarrassment in wh. he would be placed if Rosebery should return to us. So ends what first appeared to be likely to cause much trouble, but what a miserable position the quarrel of H. & R. has placed us in. That quarrel is the 'fons et origo' of our difficulties.

On Thursday the Address was moved & I made the usual speech. Next day I returned home as I had been unwell for the last fortnight, & required rest & quiet. The session ended on the 15th.

On the 21st we paid our usual Xmas visit to Prestwold & returned home on the 31st. There was a very heavy flood when we started. Our train to Peterboro' got through without obstruction: later in the day the line was blocked. So ends another year & I have reason to be thankful for good health except just lately and many blessings but real happiness without my dear wife can never be my lot in this world.

5 January 1901. Johnny was blackballed at the Norfolk Club.[1442] I was not surprised. He was proposed by R. Gurdon & Sir Wm. Folkes, & could have had no two better men at his back. Gurdon (I ought to write Lord Cranworth) was so anxious that he should be put up that in deference to his wishes we agreed, perhaps, as it turned out, unwisely. There was a very large assemblage.

7 January 1901. My birthday, spent quietly & happily at home.

21 January 1901. Sad news of the Queen's serious illness. 22nd got telegram in the afternoon summoning me to London, & I went up by an early train next morning.

22 January 1901. The Queen died at Osborne at 6.30 P.M.

23 January 1901. I attended the Privy Council at St James' Palace at

---

[1442] On Wodehouse's aggressive temperament, see p. xii.

2 o'clock (having gone up to London from Kimberley in the morning). The new King made an excellent short speech. As to the rest of the proceedings they can only be described as 'hugger mugger'. After the Ministers & a few others had taken the oath in the usual manner, the oath was administered to the rest in a body, but there was so much confusion that I could not make out exactly what was going on. I believe some 120 P.C.s were present.

25 January 1901. House of Lords met at the usual time. Ld. Salisbury moved Address to the King, condoling &c. I seconded & was followed by Abp of Canterbury. The House was very full, and listened to the Speeches in profound silence. Rosebery rather to our surprise did not speak.

I felt real sorrow for the Queen's death. She treated me with such unvarying kindness that I always regarded her as a dear personal friend; and how many of her subjects high & low can say the same! A better and a wiser woman never lived.

On Saturday *Jany. 26,* I went back to Kimberley.

27 January 1901. Monday. A most extraordinary thunderstorm. The lightning was extremely vivid & the peals of thunder deafening. It began after a fine bright morning soon after 3 in the afternoon. I was in the flower garden & took refuge in the greenhouse. The storm ended with a blinding fall of snow. The wind (from the Northwest) was piercingly cold.

The newspapers bestow much commendation on the speeches of Lord Salisbury, & myself in the Lords & Balfour & C. B. in the Commons. I never performed a more painful duty, and very nearly broke down from emotion.

30 January 1901. I was invited to the funeral ceremony at St George's Chapel but not having been very well the last day or two I excused myself as I was afraid of the cold which is piercing.

13 February 1901. Went to town for opening of Session. Soon after I returned to Ky. I felt ill, & sent for Barton who found that I had congestion of a lung caused by a singular accident. In the lavatory carriage in which I travelled to Wymn on the 26 Jan. I inadvertantly sat down where the door is to the lavatory and struck the lower part of my back violently against it. I had a good deal of pain at the time but thought nothing of it. It however had caused congestion of a lung. After some days keeping my room the lung was pronounced sound and I went to town, tho' feeling miserably weak. I attended a meeting of ex Cabinet &c. at C. B's; & next day managed to make a short speech on the Address since which I have been very poorly.

28 February 1901.   I took to my bed.

18 April 1901.   Dear Armine was taken suddenly ill. An operation was performed successfully by Mr Bennett, but he died on May 1. A twisted bowel supposed to be the cause. He appeared to be doing well after the operation, but a clot appeared wh. went to the heart, & killed him. A previous clot had gone to the lungs. He was in excellent health when this sudden illness seized him. He was buried on the 4th at Kimberley.

What a terrible blow! He had made a successful maiden speech in the House of Commons,[1443] and everything seemed to smile upon him. The sympathy expressed for him was extraordinary. There was a memorial service largely attended by MPs at St Margaret's and a number of his friends attended his funeral. Dear boy! his loss to me is irreparable.

25 May 1901.   I was myself slowly recovering. The kindness of my friends to me is extraordinary. Dear Johnny is most useful to me. I cannot be too grateful to him and dear Constance. Avery too has been kindness itself. I was also at first attended by Sir Douglas Powell one of the Queen's physicians.

12 June 1901.   Went to Falmouth with Constance, Johnny, Isabel & little Isabel. Cold weather, but sunny & the trip decidedly did me good tho' I am very weak.

25 June 1901.   The prospects of the Liberal party worse than ever. Asquith & his 'tail' seem to be determined to play into the hands of the Govt. Will they like the Libl. Unionists drift into the Tory party?[1444]

29 June 1901.   Mrs Arnold,[1445] Nelly's mother died at Cobham; one of the most charming women I ever knew; she was a daughter of Judge Wightman.

2 July 1901.   The squabbles of our wretched party continue without abatement.

[1443] 12 Dec. 1900.
[1444] On Kimberley's fears and Asquith's reassurance, see Kimberley to Asquith, 29 June 1901, in *Liberal by Principle*, 270.
[1445] Frances Lucy Arnold, née Wightman; m. Matthew Arnold, 1851.

17 July 1901.   Still squabbling. The meeting of the party passed off well but the old difficulties remain, & will remain. This morning appeared Rosebery's letter in the 'Times', a very unsatisfactory document.[1446] He professes to stand aloof! (His speech in the City worse)

18 July 1901.   Lord Russell's trial. I of course could not attend. C. B., Spencer, Tweedsmouth, Bryce, & H. Gladstone came to my house to discuss R's letter. Spencer wanted us to take some action to protect against it, but the rest were for letting it alone.

25 July 1901.   Went to Kimberley.

5 August 1901.   The Empress Frederick died: a charming & most accomplished woman. Her only failing was that she was outspoken about political affairs beyond what was prudent.

9 September 1901.   A good rain at last. Since we have been here it has only rained once, when 1/2 an inch fell. The drought has been most severe. Harvest was all over at the end of August: much of it some days earlier. Hussey & Alice came here on the 7th for a few days.

14 September 1901.   The atrocious murder of Mr McKinley,[1447] the President of the U.S., shocked the whole civilised world.

25 October 1901.   The weather has a[t] last changed & we have had good rains. Very cold on this & the following day. Nelly came on a visit on the 5th.

24 November 1901.   News of the death of Ct. Hatzfeldt who had just on account of ill health resigned the post of German Ambassador in London. He had long been in very bad health. He was a thorough German, hard and rough, but he was thoroughly honest & straightforward, & a man of considerable ability. We had some rough passages when I was Foreign Secy. but were always good friends.

10 January 1902.   We moved to town.

[1446] Saying that he would not return to party politics, but arguing that the 'great Liberal force in the country' must 'make up its mind about the war.' For the circumstances of this and his speech of 19 July 1901 at the City Liberal Club, see Rhodes James, *Rosebery*, 425.

[1447] William McKinley (1843–1901), pres. of U.S., 1897–1901; assassinated by an anarchist.

Appendix: The Kimberley Memoir

(National Library of Scotland, Rosebery Papers, 10186, pp. 252–81)

By the 1890s, when Kimberley prepared his Memoir,[1] he was recognised by a younger generation of Liberals as a respected member of the 'old guard', an old-fashioned but essential feature of the Liberal landscape – 'Uncle Kim' as Herbert Gladstone fashioned him. Rosebery too was fond of Kimberley, but for more personal reasons which often have been obscured. In many ways, the two were very different. Kimberley (b. 1826) had come of age amid the political and international turmoil of the 1840s; Rosebery (b. 1847) entered public affairs in the flush of British ascendancy a generation later. Kimberley was garrulous and straightforward, Rosebery aloof and complex. And though both were landed aristocrats, Kimberley had spent his first score of adult years repairing the fortunes of a troubled estate, wondering whether he even ought to be called a 'large' landowner, while Rosebery was 'supremely ignorant of the worries and compromises which dominate the lives of most men'.[2] Nor did they ever fully transcend the gulf imposed by differences in circumstance and personality. Kimberley, for instance, never pretended to fathom the depths of Rosebery's opaque manner, and frequently urged him to be less secretive in political relations. Rosebery, for his part, bemoaned Kimberley's social habits, observing that his elder colleague 'remained in seclusion' out of the parliamentary season, 'asking nobody, seeing nobody, indeed repelling visitors'.[3] Rosebery was also rather too willing to believe in Kimberley's political naïveté. Kimberley's political opinions were less sharply defined than Rosebery's, and thus required less overt defence, but generally he was well informed of political developments by Ripon, Spencer and a host of others through his position as Liberal leader in the Lords.

If their differences were substantial, a number of factors nevertheless strengthened the bond of friendship between Kimberley and Rosebery. Personally they shared fundamental assumptions about character, valuing personal discipline, family devotion and public duty. Rosebery's

[1] On the nature and preparation of the Memoir, see above, 7–13.

[2] According to Bateman in 1883, Kimberley owned 11,147 acres valued at £25,000; Rosebery 32,411 acres valued at £36,479. *The Great Landowners of Great Britain and Ireland* (4th edn, London, 1883), 251, 386. After Rosebery's marriage to Hannah Rothschild in 1878, his annual income increased by more than £100,000 pounds. R. Rhodes James, *Rosebery* (London, 1963), 84.

[3] Kimberley Memoir, 488, below.

well-known antipathy toward public office, for instance, was matched by Kimberley (and not by many other high Liberals), who observed 'how curious it was' that both 'were reluctant to accept the great offices' open to them in March 1894.[4] Both were intelligent and well read. Their political gifts had been recognised early, and both had risen rapidly to cabinet rank. Kimberley's interest in, and general support for, Rosebery's foreign policy during Gladstone's third and fourth ministries, was at times less enthusiastic than Rosebery would have wished. Yet their general agreement left no ground upon which dissenters such as Harcourt, Morley or even Gladstone might rally, as long as Rosebery and Kimberley were the only foreign policy experts in the cabinet. Kimberley's self-effacement, even accompanied by a notorious loquacity and a straightforward simplicity, was a positive blessing to a prime minister besieged by little Englanders who seemed to care so little about the good name of Great Britain. When the acrimonious Rosebery–Harcourt feud threatened to wreck the party, Kimberley, with considerable equanimity, tried to calm the waters. For this Rosebery was thankful.[5]

Kimberley was well placed by age, temperament and official experience to understand in some fullness the public and private pressures which Rosebery felt. Rosebery was personally sensitive, and few among the front ranks were prepared to tolerate his willful coolness. Kimberley could accept Rosebery's manner because he was not seeking approval or preferment, while his long experience had taught him that personal idiosyncrasies frequently shielded astute political minds. Their curious friendship was the result of an imperceptible and probably unconscious weakening of personal defences. Rosebery continued after the Liberal defeat in 1895 to express concern for his elder colleague, inviting him to Mentmore and asking after his health. With Rosebery's resignation as Liberal leader in October 1896, however, the two drifted apart politically. Kimberley held the nascent Liberal League in 'absolute contempt', yet made every allowance for Rosebery's erratic behaviour and continued to occupy the narrow middle ground between the Rosebery and Campbell-Bannerman camps.[6]

Rendered almost irrelevant by the Liberal victory of 1905, Rosebery might naturally reflect with nostalgia upon the life and times of a 'model' public servant, who in an earlier age could earn his position in the highest counsels of state through simplicity, rectitude and devotion to duty. In reading the Kimberley Memoir in 1906 Rosebery was drawn, as Gladstone had been in another context, to this 'older type'

[4] Kimberley Memoir, 503, below.
[5] Rosebery to Kimberley, 7 April, 24 June 1895, RsP, 10070, ff. 33, 157.
[6] See Liberal by Principle, 247–8, 251–2, 267–8, 273.

of Cabinet minister, naïve perhaps, but honest, straightforward and extremely competent.[7] The 'conversational fault' and egoism, even the naïveté itself, seemed unimportant beside the integrity and sense of duty which had characterised Kimberley's long career. Rosebery undoubtedly was seeking information about the circumstances of his own career as well. His extensive notes are all one is ever likely to see of the Kimberley Memoir.[8] In the last surviving reference to the original, Rosebery invited Kimberley's son to 38, Berkeley Square, so that the 'precious deposit' might be personally delivered. 'If anything could increase the affection and regard that I feel for your father', he wrote, 'it would be this autobiography.'[9]

Rosebery's extracts and annotations are herein fully transcribed. Ellipses are Rosebery's as are quotation marks which he used when quoting directly from the Memoir. Otherwise, Rosebery either annotated or paraphrased Kimberley. One set of bracketed numbers standing alone at the end of an entry – [253] –refers to pagination in the original Kimberley manuscript, as indicated by Rosebery. Where two sets of numbers appear in the same bracket divided by a slash – [345/501] – the first refers to pagination in this edition of the Kimberley Journal; the second to the corresponding page in the original Kimberley manuscript Memoir. A dagger '†' indicates material in the Kimberley Memoir not found in the Journal.

KIMBERLEY'S MS MEMOIRS

Are half of them spirited and interesting but become somewhat senile towards the close.

He himself was a fine fellow – intolerably conversational, an egotist without vanity, but very attractive as he got older from a certain humility. He bored me and everyone else to extinction for he had a torrent of talk mainly but unconsciously about himself; his health, his family, his estates &c.[10] And yet I was sincerely fond of him. He was

---

[7] See below, p. 487–8; *Gladstone–Granville Corresp.* 2, II, 421–2.

[8] There is no record of anyone other than Rosebery having been allowed to see the Memoir, and the lack of any reference to it in the successive divisions of the Kimberley Papers suggests, as has been rumoured, that it may have been burned along with other papers shortly after the second world war.

[9] Rosebery to 2nd Earl of Kimberley, 26 Oct. 1906, RSP 10120, ff. 33–4.

[10] Kimberley's loquaciousness was legendary. Edward Grey recalled a typical experience while serving as undersecretary to Kimberley at the Foreign Office: 'In conversation, or perhaps it would be more accurate to say in talk, Lord Kimberley was the most copious of men ... When the Under-Secretary went to ask him to read and approve drafts and answers to questions that were to be asked in the House of Commons in a quarter of an hour's time it was sometimes embarrassing that he would embark on an

an honest straightforward able old Whig, without much backbone (though he prided himself on it) or much initiative but an excellent lieutenant. However when he was second to Granville and was left in charge he always lost his temper. When he became leader he was conciliatory and popular to the last degree. This seems to tell the other way, but the truth is as I have stated. I think his best piece of work was his lord lieutenancy of Ireland, where moreover he was supposed to have lived within his salary. He went as S. of S. to the Foreign Office too late.

This memoir raises my high opinion of him. The second half is feeble and shows the marks of age and confusion. He has then taken his journal and copied pretty much at random. But I doubt if he ever knew much except of the surface of political proceedings – he was not told secrets – he was the last man to whom people would go to tell what was going on. And so, engaged in honest work, he knew little else.

His judgements are not profound but sincere. The whole record is the honest, humble and sincere record of a hardworking, simple life. *Simple* not in the sense of plain living but of a certain innocence as compared with worldliness. As regards office he went loyally where he was told to go.[11] But at the end of the session he departed for his home in Norfolk and remained in seclusion there till parliament or cabinets called him to London, asking nobody, seeing nobody, indeed repelling visitors. Of course this placed him out of touch with politicians who regarded him too much as a torpid but hungry Whig who only appeared when there were loaves and fishes to be got.[12] Nothing could be more unjust. He lived a model life at home, devoted to his family, shooting, farming, reading the classics.[13] [252–3]

account of the ravages wrought among trees by a great gale in Norfolk; though the weather and the trees were topics not uncongenial to the Under-Secretary.' *Twenty-Five Years, 1892–1916* (2 vols., New York, 1925), I, 17–18. See *Liberal by Principle*, 44.

[11] Cf. Gladstone's surprise at Kimberley's refusal of the Indian viceroyalty in 1880. *Gladstone Diaries*, IX, 508–9.

[12] Labouchere, for instance, complained that of the 33 Gladstonian Lords, '30 are more or less codgers after place or office.' Labouchere to Dilke, 12 Nov. [?1891], DkP, Add. MS 43892, 163.

[13] A writer for the *Eastern Daily Press* noted that Kimberley's 'home life was simple. He did not entertain largely, but gave occasional shooting parties over his well preserved woods'. 9 April 1902, p. 2. Kimberley was well read in the classics, having taken a first in *literae humaniores* at Christ Church, Oxford, in 1847. However, thereafter he in fact read more generally, focusing on history, biography, contemporary issues and, later in life, German and Spanish literature.

KIMBERLEY MS

On the first page he speaks of 'the strong sense of duty which has been the touchstone of my life'. [†/1]

Ld Lansdowne – a very efficient leader of the H of L. Universally courteous and an effective speaker without eloquence. The finest speech that K. heard of Lord *Derby's* was on Don Pacifico.* The Duke of *Wellington* on account of deafness sate at the table in the place of Chairman of Committees. He rarely spoke.

* (It was in this debate that Ld Canning broke down.) [44–5, 242/36–42]

K only just knew Peel before his death. 'His manner of speaking was very measured and rather pompous. The bitterness against him was extraordinary.' [46/55]

Old Nesselrode said of Palmerston (to K) 'c'est la premiere plume diplomatique in Europe'. Palmerston's 'golden rule' for good handwriting was that it lay in the complete formation of each letter. [†/75]

K was very coldly received in Russia. He says the Emperor Alexander II was supposed to drink and spend his time with mistresses. But this K doubts. [47–8/78]

Ly K talking before her presentation to an officer told him that as Peterhoff was so far off it would have been more civil to ask her to stay the night. The officer was the Emperor! [50/102]

Kimberley disliked Morny. A sensation was produced at a party of M's by he and his staff after the Emperor had gone, taking off their uniform coats and appearing in dress coats with uniform trousers! [50–1/106]

Regina was Neapolitan ambassador at St P. He had married his niece but the dispensation had not arrived. As she was well in the family way she went to Rome to hasten matters. 'Enfin' she said 'j'ai vu le Saint Pere mais, avant que je l'ai dit un mot, il s'est ecrie'. 'Ah, madame, je crois qu'il etait bien temps'. [53/114]

Gorchakow sent a message to Bombas through Regina that he wanted a Neapolitan order. Bombas replied that he should prefer waiting till G had done something to deserve it. [54/124]

The owner of a serf wetnurse sent for her home. The father of the baby who was made ill by her departure brought an action against him. This dragged on so long that when it ended a young officer in the guards was informed that his wetnurse was restored to him. [58/135]

Halifax said of Lord J Russell 'You never can tell what he will be up to. When he was P.M. I used to get him as often as I could to meet 3 or 4 colleagues at luncheon at my house that we might find out what he was after and put a stop to any [ill.]'. [†/157]

Clarendon's fault was a certain tendency to intrigue, paying too much attention to details and to a courtesy of language that led to the impression that he was a man of smooth words, not to be trusted. In private often bitter about people he disliked. [†/161] Once when Ld Derby was making an attack on foreign policy Cn said to Ky 'you must answer this. I cannot do it. I should have to say sharp things, and I have such a bad opinion of Derby that I believe he would vent his anger on my daughter who is about to marry his son'. He always hated Derby.[14] [†/501]

In 1860 K was offered the governorship of Madras, in 1861 of Canada and in 1862 of Bombay; and in 1880 the g. gship of India. [61/170]

When Ly Selina Vernon was asked how she could marry such a bad man as Bidwell she replied that she could not bear to meet both her husbands hereafter. Another explanation was that she wanted a rake to get rid of her weeds. [62–3, 64/173]

Dec. 7, 1862. K notes '... my political prospects about which I am foolishly discontented and miserable. In fact I am selfishly ambitious instead of trying humbly to do my duty. It is provoking to find oneself shelved in the prime of life when I am boiling over with energy and longing for opportunities of action on the great stage of the world' & c. &c.[80/187]

As to the Danish affairs in 1864, K says DeGrey was in favour of strong measures. (I always understood from DeG just the reverse.)[15] The Chancellor told K that the govt plan would have been to send our fleet to Kiel and 10,000 men to the Dannevirke.[126, 127/227, 230, 249]

[14] M. Grant Duff, *Notes from a Diary, 1886–1888* (London, 1900), 131–2; *DD3*, 216 and n. 30.

[15] Ripon appears to have wavered. Cf. Sandiford, *Great Britain and the Schleswig-Holstein Question, 1848–64*, 78, 112, 146.

Granville, Milner Gibson, Cardwell, Wood, Villiers and Gladstone were for peace at any price; Palmerston, the Chancellor, Somerset, de Grey, Stanley and Argyll would have run the risk of war. [138/249]

Garibaldi coming to the H of L. The Bp of Oxford shook hands warmly with him. Bath who had resigned the whipship because Derby had met Garibaldi at Stafford House expressed to the Bp his surprise that 'he had shaken hands with the champion of revolution and infidelity'. [133–4/240]

Sir Erskine Perry[16] was called Sir Irksome Perry – not bad. [†/242]

Lord Lieutenancy of Ireland. The idea of the Lord Lieutenant riding into Dublin is that he rides in all booted and spurred from a journey and assumes his functions without even waiting to change his clothes. The yells and hisses predominated at K's entry. 'The uproar was indescribable'. [†/265]

Resignation of Sir R Peel as Chief Secretary.[17] He had been offered the Chancellorship of the Duchy without the Cabinet. [178/348]

Earldom of Kimberley. 'On May 14 I received a letter from Lord Russell whom I had told I should like to be promoted to an Earldom, assuming that he had obtained the Queen's approval and that HM had been pleased to say I well deserved the honour ... my new title. Lord Russell suggested Norwich unto which I was disposed to agree but on enquiry I found that the Howard family claimed this title and that it would give offence to them if I took it ... Some of my relatives, especially the Curries, wanted me to keep the title of Wodehouse. I shrewdly suspect that the eagerness of my relatives for "Earl Wodehouse" arose from the fact that the world would not so easily recognise their connection with the "Earl of Kimberley".' (a curious and unusual spice of vanity.)[18] [186–7/379]

Northbrook told me that his father never consulted him as to the peerage and that he was much amazed at it. Sir F. Baring's reason for taking a peerage was, K believes, that Tom Baring[19] disliked the head of the

[16] Thomas Erskine Perry (1806–82), Lib. MP for Devonport, 1854–9; member of the Council of India, 1859–82.

[17] 7 December 1865.

[18] For Kimberley's *apologia* see Kimberley to Currie, 31 May 1866, KP1 3/1; Kimberley to Anne Wodehouse, 31 May 1866, KP1 15/K2/18.

[19] Thomas Baring (1799–1873), financier and Con. MP for Great Yarmouth, 1831–7, and Huntingdon, 1844–73.

family having less rank than Lord Ashburton of the younger branch, and had promised to lend his money to the elder branch if Sir F. became a peer, hoping this would lead to an earldom. [†/385]

Raby.[20] as K went to Raby in Nov 1866. Nothing could have been more agreeable. 'All that was wanting was a tolerable cook, drinkable wine, attentive servants and a comfortable bed'. [194–5/393]

D of Marlborough was at Eton with K. 'A more ill conditioned disagreeable fellow I never knew there'. [336–7/403]

Gladstone in 1867. 'It is curious now to reflect upon his unpopularity at this time as leader'. [201/405]

Disraeli. 'I remember when it was the general belief that as long as Disraeli was leader of the Tories they could never be formidable'. [†/405]

Stanley (in 1868) 'appeared to regret not having joined the Liberal party when Palmerston offered him office'. 'If it had not been for my father' he said. [228/450]

C. Fortescue (1868) (whom Jezebel his wife stirred up) 'made an egregious ass of himself by pressing for the Colonial Secretaryship'. [228/452]

Halifax was offered (1868) the viceroyalty of Ireland with a seat in the Cabinet. He declined but not without doubt and was not offended. This viceroyalty was in doubt between Spencer and Dufferin. [228/452]

As to Mayo's appointment 'the unanimous opinion of Mr. Gladstone and his colleagues was that no better choice could have been made by a conservative Govt'.[21] [†/455]

Westbury introduced a copyright bill with some very [ill.] statements. These were challenged by K on the select committee to wh it was referred, and w. cd produce no authority. After the sitting was over K. went to W's room to talk it over. 'My dear young friend' he replied 'I am weary, very weary. I do not think I shall go on with my bill'. K

---

[20] Seat of the Duke and Duchess of Cleveland, County Durham. According to Robert Rhodes James, Raby was 'grandiose, bleak, and freezing cold in winter'. *Rosebery,* 42.

[21] Richard Southwell Bourke, 6th Earl Mayo (1822–72), ch. sec. for Ireland, 1852, 1858–9, 1866–8; Viceroy of India, 1868–72. Cf. Kimberley's annotation of 1877, *JE,* 27; Grant Duff, *Notes from a Diary, 1896–1901,* (2 vols., London, 1905) I, 189–90.

then went to the House. W. came in and sitting down behind him tapped him on the shoulder, saying, 'Kimberley, you stripped the husk off my argument very prettily today, you ought to have been a lawyer'. 'The "husk"' adds K 'was a charming euphemism for his misstatements'.[22] [†/473]

A long account of Gladstone's wish to throw up the Irish Church Bill if the Lords carried their amendment on the preamble. A fierce conference in his room at the H of C. Granville adjourned it to debate in the Lords and arranged a compromise. 'Cairns did a great service to the country by preventing the serious perhaps dangerous crisis which would have arisen from the rejection of the Bill, but the Tories never forgave him for his moderation'. [239–40/479]

Lord Derby 'I never can forgive him for the (politically) dishonest course he pursued as Prime Minister both on Protection and Reform. So far as my experience goes, and I sate opposite to him for twenty years, he was with rare exceptions ungenerous and unscrupulous in debate'. [241–2/483]

General Grey not a good adviser, hated the French and John Brown. [247/493]

Persigny (Nov 2. 1870) in talk with K 'laid all the blame for the misfortunes of France on the ex Emperor and Empress, the former for not following his advice to put down the republican party in another coup d'etat, the latter for refusing as Regent to use Bazaine[23] and his army to restore the Empire'. [253–4/514]

The Queen told K that the Empress Eugénie 'had much to answer for in the encouragement she had given to extravagance and luxury. The Q hoped that one good result of the fall of the Empire wd no longer be an evil example to society in England which had much deteriorated of late'.[24] [258/520]

Gladstone in 1871 had a scheme for abolishing the Ld Lieutenancy and

---

[22] On Westbury's recollection, see *The Life of Richard, Lord Westbury* (2 vols., London, 1888), II, 201–2.

[23] François Achille Bazaine, Marshall of France from 1864, and Commander-in-Chief of the Imperial Guard.

[24] In a similar vein, Lady Kimberley urged her daughter not to read 'any French novels. I assure you they do more harm than you imagine. Their tone is false and their sentiment bad. Moral and principle they have none ...' 5 Sept. [1872], DE 1749, PkP 38/3. Cf. 2 Nov. 1870, *JE*, 19.

getting the P of Wales to reside in Ireland for 2 months annually instead. [261/524]

The Royal Warrant ending to the Army Purchase Bill was wisely due to Cardwell. [262/526]

'My position at the Colonial Office is not made easier by the undisguised opinion of Gladstone, Lowe and Cardwell that the wisest policy would be to disembarrass ourselves of our colonies at the first available opportunity'. (1872) [266/530]

He condemns Granville as Foreign Secretary for he trusted to the chapter of accidents and never took trouble to reason out any matter completely or master details. He gives an extraordinary instance of leaving Argyll to see that a telegram of the first importance to the US on the Alabama claims was the correct version and asked him to give it [ill.]. 'Unfortunately Argyll substituted by mistake some words ... wh materially altered its effect'. [267-8/535]

'D of Somerset told me that he once asked Lord Melbourne to give some assistance to Carlyle. "Who is he?" said Lord M. "A very original writer" was the reply. "Damn your original writers – I hate them".' [279/549]

'Ripon told me that his reason for resigning was that he saw that the majority of the Cabinet was in favour of extending household suffrage to the counties to which he could not consent. I never clearly understood why Childers resigned. Evidently he did not look forward to coming in again as he asked me for a colonial appointment'. 1873 [280/551]

Gladstone's dissolution in 1874 a complete surprise to his colleagues; undoubtedly caused by the embarrassment as to his seat. [283/558]

The reason for the Liberal defeat in 1874 was 'a vague but widely spread distrust. We had exhausted our programme and quiet men asked with alarm "What will Gladstone do next"?' [284-5/561]

There was a meeting of Gladstone's colleagues in 1874 (March 9) to persuade him not to resign the leadership.[25] 'We asked if he would see us, and on his saying "yes" we went in a body by the terrace behind

<hr />

[25] See M.R. Temmel, 'Gladstone's Resignation of the Liberal Leadership, 1874–1875', *Journal of British Studies* 16 (Fall 1976), 153–75.

the Carlton Terrace House so as to avoid the newspaper touts whom we saw spying about'. [286/564]

'A letter from Ripon (July 21, 1874) announcing that he is about to become a R Catholic'. K's stupefaction. [290/565]

Jan 14. 1875. Gladstone reads his letter of resignation. He added that he foresaw difficulties with which in the present state of the party he could not grapple successfully – as to denominational education and the Church. 'The party generally approved of the Cowper-Temple clause, which in his opinion was absolutely indefensible. Secular education he might be able to accept, but not a colourless system which was neither one thing nor the other. His views as to the Church were that any attempt to renew its existing basis would be ruinous. These views he had embodied in his resolutions of last session which had obtained no support. He expected that the Scottish Patronage Act would lead to an agitation for the disestablishment of the Kirk and he did not see how such a demand could be resisted seeing that a majority of the Scottish people did not belong to the Establishment. Further he felt himself to be generally out of harmony with the tendency on both sides of the House to favour the interference of the government in a variety of affairs left till now to private enterprise. He had always been for a "laissez faire" policy, a policy now quite out of fashion. He had also been an ardent advocate in and out of office of economy in the expenditure of public money which no party in the State now desired to practise'. [291–2/570] This was on Jan 14. On July 15 K notes 'It is curious to see at our meeting how eager Gladstone was for it (Trevelyan's County Suffrage Bill). He became daily more Radical'. [296/575]

Aberdare asked Disraeli how he liked being in the House of Lords. 'I feel I am dead but in Elysium'. [†/584]

Feb 1880. Old Miss Mellish died, only child of Joseph Mellish (the last man killed by a highwayman on Hounslow Heath). Charles Villiers[26] proposed to her in vain as she thought he was after her money. When they both became old they became very intimate again, and she left him all her fortune for life. [314/624]

K thinks that 'bad times had more to do than anything else with the defeat of the Tories' in 1880. [315/678]

'The refusal of the Portuguese Govt (caused by popular fury in Lisbon)

[26] MP for Wolverhampton, 1835–98.

to proceed with the Delagoa Bay Treaty was a great misfortune, for had we proceeded as was intended when the treaty came into effect to make the railway from Lorenzo Marques to Pretoria it would have greatly reconciled the Boers to our rule'.[27] [†/698]

K discussing the Majuba treaty says that it was dictated by policy. President Brand declared that he could restrain his burghers no longer, and 'we had strong reasons for believing that a considerable number of Dutch in the Cape Colony would also take part against us.'[28] [†/702]

K once helped Disraeli on with his great coat at Marlborough House. 'This is indeed an honour' said D 'to be helped on with one's coat by a belted Earl'. (A good specimen of D's style.) [†/709]

K becoming Chancellor of the Duchy finds it necessary to hold a council, exempting himself from the fee on accepting the office. 'Hold one at once' said the Secretary 'you are the Council'. And so it was done.[29] [†/729]

Cetywayo on being shown the statue of Achilles opposite Apsley House said to his chiefs 'Ah you see it is not so long since the English fought as we do' (naked) thinking it represented Wellington. [†/729]

People were much puzzled at Disraeli's garter remaining vacant. The truth was that Gladstone recommended Derby for it long ago and the Q refused.[30] She also refused to make Wolseley a peer.[31] Gladstone much put out. [333/749]

Disraeli said that 'on the whole a wedding was perhaps more dismal

[27] Kimberley to Granville, GrP, 30/29/135, ff. 1-2. On Portuguese opposition, see Minutes, 10 July 1880, on FO to CO, 8 June 1880, CO 179/136. Also, Kimberley to William Gurdon, 26 May 1881, CwP, HA54 970/2713.

[28] Kimberley consistently maintained this line and probably referred to his correspondence when preparing statements thereafter. See Kimberley to Ripon, 12 April 1881, in *Liberal by Principle*, 153-4. Cf. the wording of Rosebery's summary with Kimberley to H. Gladstone, 25 November 1899, GP, Add. MS 46057, ff. 218-20; also Kimberley to Herbert Gladstone, 30 November 1899, HGP Add. MS 46057, f. 223.

[29] For a fuller account see Grant Duff, *Notes from a Diary, 1896-1901*, I, 210-11.

[30] The Queen confided to Ponsonby that she 'utterly despised' Derby, who had 'no feeling for the honour of England'. *Queen Victoria: Letters and Journals*, ed. C. Hibbert (New York, 1985), 278. He was finally invested with the garter in 1884.

[31] Wolseley finally was created viscount in 1885.

than a funeral, as at a wedding you made an acquaintance, at a funeral you got rid of one'.[32] [†/753]

Arthur Peel to be Speaker. First Herschell and then Goschen had declined it. Dodson was excluded by being in the Cabinet. [340/762]

'The succession to Ripon as Viceroy. Everybody thought Spencer the best man, but Granville and Hartington objected on the ground that his absence would seriously weaken the Govt. here. S on being asked said he did not wish it but would consider it if the offer were made to him. So Granville and Hartington prevailed. Then Morley was thought of. At last Dufferin was appointed, though Granville was reluctant and Gladstone very reluctant'. [345/776]

New Guinea 'nearly' a nasty mess. It was resolved to annex the South and part of the East coast, and a communication was weakly made to Bismarck who objected alleging that it did not leave enough open for German colonization. 'Derby and Granville showed deplorable weakness in dealing with these questions'. [346/780]

But later K throws all the blame on Gladstone supported by Harcourt. Derby it appears wished to annex Zululand up to the Umfolozi, the coast from Natal to the Portuguese border and all New Guinea, but Gladstone vetoed all. [351/790]

It is to be noted that the memoir in all this latter part sensibly deteriorates is confused rambling and contradictory, and sure sign of decay narrates great things and small with equal emphasis.

May 15. 1885 Irish row in Cabinet. Spencer very near resigning. *May 16* Childers near resigning. *May 21* Chamberlain and Dilke threaten resignation because Gladstone proposes land purchase scheme without first local govt. scheme. [354–5/796]

About this time Childers just before his budget proposed to raise the wine duties. This generally opposed. 'At last he walked out of the cabinet and was with difficulty persuaded not to resign'. (How well I remember this ridiculous scene.) [355/797]

---

[32] Cf. Disraeli's response to Gladstone's letter of sympathy on the death of his wife: 'Marriage is the greatest earthly happiness when founded on complete sympathy. That hallowed lot was mine ...' A. Bassett, *The Gladstone Papers* (London, 1930), 112. The truth of Disraeli's attitude is surely somewhere between these extremes. See R. Blake, *Disraeli* (London, 1967), 160–1.

'The battle on the Coercion Bill raged all this week (June 18) and nothing was finally settled when we resigned. Spencer wd not give way nor would Chamberlain and Dilke. The nearest approach to an agreement was on the plan of leaving it optional with the Lord Lieut to bring the Act or any part of it into force by proclamation. There was no difference of opinion among us as to resignation'. [355–6/798]

'Gladstone announced to us that he wd take the place of leader during the remainder of this session but that after that he wd retire from action'. (June 17) [356–7/799]

June 20. 'Today we met at 10 Downing Street and resolved unanimously to give a final and stiff answer to Salisbury's demands. (All the ex-cabinet present except Spencer, Rosebery and Hartington). [357/799]

June 25. 'It was entirely untrue that G. would in no case have undertaken to reconstruct his Government. On Sunday last (June 21) he summoned his colleagues to Downing Street. The notice was so short that only Dilke Chamberlain and myself attended. Herschell arrived after we had finished. G. read to us his proposed answer to the Queen's letter to which we agreed. He then asked if I did not think Spencer should be requested to come over immediately as nothing could be done without him if Salisbury threw up.* I quite concurred and at G.'s request wrote to Spencer pressing him to come. G. also wrote. He arrived in consequence in London before the crisis was over. It was quite understood that if Salisbury failed G. would endeavour to form a government'. [357–8/800]

*This is most important, as it shows that G meant in the event of reforming his govt to throw over Dilke and Chamberlain and stick to Spencer and that wing.[33]

K looking back on the Govt of 1880–1885 brings its doings under six heads. 1. Reform of the H of Commons 'in wh we had a brilliant success'. The franchise and redistribution bills were solid achievements. 2. Ireland. Land Bill well conceived but has disappointed expectations. First Coercian Act a failure owing mainly to its clumsy administration by Forster 'the worst Irish secretary in my time'. 3. Foreign affairs 'our weak point'. 'It is impossible to deny that Granville with many admirable qualities was a complete failure at the F.O.' 4. Colonial Affairs. Doubts the Transvaal Convention having done the Govt. harm in the country. 5. Settlement of Afghan affairs by Hartington gave general satisfaction.

---

[33] Cf. E.J. Feuchtwanger, *Gladstone* (London, 1978), 229; contrast *EHJI*, II, 894.

6. Indian affairs conducted with fair success. [358–9/801]

K discusses personality of Cabinet. Gladstone predominated but Hartington, Harcourt and Chamberlain exercised much influence. The least influential member Childers who rarely opened his mouth and when he did was so muddled as to be incomprehensible. 'Rosebery during the short time he was with us scarcely opened his mouth and remained quite a dark horse'.[34] [359/803]

K refused to see his successor in the usual way. 'I avoided seeing R Churchill whom I did not consider fit company for a gentleman after his letter about Granville'. [359/803]

Ld Halifax the quickest witted man, most indefatigable worker and the worst speaker known to K, but suffered by his bad speaking and his incurable habit of telling a fool he was a fool. [359–60/804]

Feb. 1 1886. 'Gladstone went to Osborne to kiss hands ... I never before at a change of government saw nobody pleased. Long faces everywhere except in the Parnell camp. There were persistent rumours that I might be asked to take the F.O., but Rosebery I hoped would be the man. He would be the best choice that could be made. Apart from all other considerations it would have been a great mistake to appoint to the F.O. so unpopular a man as myself. My appointment would have been received with a chorus of newspaper denunciations, and when there is a predetermination not to place any confidence in a minister the battle is half lost before it is begun. Rosebery's appointment on the other hand was sure to be universally approved'. [363/810]

April 17. 1886. 'Gladstone sent up a note to the H. of Lords to ask if I would agree to a possible retention of the Irish members at Westminster. With great misgivings I gave way. I have never ceased to regret my weakness on this occasion. Subsequent events proved that I had underestimated my influence with our Chief'.[35] [†/814]

Cabinet dinners, Gladstone told K, enable discussions to be held wh would not be reported to the Sovereign, and reduced the number of cabinets. In Peel's time the Cabinet MPs used to meet once a week –

---

[34] Cf. Edward Hamilton's report of 5 April 1885: 'Rosebery puts down Childers and Lefevre as "lag choices" (to use an Eton phrase). Lord Kimberley strikes him as being a stronger man than he ever imagined.' *EHJ1*, I, 830.

[35] See p. 366, above.

generally on Saturdays – to settle the business of the ensuing week. [369/819]

Sept 29, 1886. Looking back on the year K. comes to the conclusion that the misfortunes of the Lib party were largely 'due to the too precipitate overthrow of the Tory Govt. I never understood why Gladstone did not prevent this. It had been agreed on all hands that our best policy was not to drive the Govt out of office till they had disclosed their Irish policy. They must have foundered on that rock, and we should probably have had the inestimable advantage of uniting all sections of Liberals agst their measures'. Simple minded K! Did you never hear of the old man in a hurry?[36] [371/822]

April 6. 1887. 'Every day it became more apparent that political power was being transferred from parliament to the platform – a momentous change'. [375/828]

March 8. 1888. 'Granville, Harcourt, Spencer, Ripon and myself met at Rosebery's to discuss his motion on the Reform of the House of Lords. R. having proposed his scheme Ripon expressed entire agreement with it; Granville threw cold water on it; Spencer and myself favored a reform generally, without pledging ourselves to R's details. Harcourt came in late and as far as I remember did not express any decided opinion. It was agreed that R. should bring forward his proposals on his own responsibility'. [380/833]

'It is curious that when Gladstone finally left office he said to me "I leave you this piece of advice as a legacy – the Government of this Empire cannot be carried on without some efficient Second Chamber".'[37] [†/834]

Feb 8. 1890. 'Sir C Russell told us that Parnell's costs in the Commission were not more than £30,000 whilst the "Times" costs were at least £80,000'. [391/859]

April 11. 1891. As to succession to Granville as leader of the H of Lords. 'Ripon told me he thought I ought to be leader, but against this there is much to be said. I know well that I have not any influence with the party generally or in the country. Rosebery and Spencer both more

---

[36] On the perception of Gladstone's 'old fault – impatience', see *Florence Arnold-Forster's Irish Journal*, ed. T. W. Moody and R. Hawkins (Oxford, 1988), 479.

[37] Remembered perhaps because it concurred with Kimberley's own longstanding view. See W. S. Childe-Pemberton, *Life of Lord Norton, 1814–1905* (London, 1909), 278.

or less fulfil this condition and I would most willingly serve under either of them. I imagine that the "behind the scene" is that Gladstone would like to appoint Spencer, but that this might not be accepted by Rosebery. I am told that Harcourt has declared that if, whenever Mr. G is gone, Spencer were chosen as leader of the party, he would as leader of the Commons serve under him but not under Rosebery. This is probably true as Harcourt and Rosebery did not get on at all well during the short time that R was under the former at the Home Office'.[38] [396–7/870]

Mr. Gladstone had said that he thought no leader shd be appointed at present as there might soon be a new government, so that it is better that the choice shall be left till then when it wd be guided by the distribution of offices and other considerations. So that K was appointed leader pro tem. [397/870]

July 13. 1892. K's talk with Spencer. 'Rosebery appeared to be in a strange state of mind and talked of not coming back to public life. If such a great blow were to befall us, I fear I should have to undertake the F.O. but happily there can be very little probability of such a *pis aller*. We should be terribly weakened by losing R, not only because he is by far the most acceptable person for the F.O., but because, next to Gladstone, he is by far the most influential man in the country of our party'. [404/882]

August 13. 1892. Meeting at Mr G's about appointments 'we had still hopes of Rosebery joining us'. [406/892]

Sept 29. 1892. Dilatory resolution abt Uganda – determined to retain without taking efficient steps to maintain authority there. 'Rosebery, however who was strongly in favour of retaining Uganda had his way in spite of a loud but really feeble opposition by Harcourt'. (and the whole cabinet! AR) [407/892]

Nov. 9. 1892. K obliged to go to the Lord Mayor's dinner because Rosebery, Harcourt and J Morley 'shirked'. (The amusing truth is that Gladstone was determined that I should *not* go for fear I suppose of some Uganda declaration. I well remember this cabinet and Gladstone's dexterous but anxious manipulation in this sense, which diverted me hugely.) [408/893]

Feb 14. 1893. K describes an extraordinary scene at the Cabinet in wh

[38] See entry for 13 April 1891.

Harcourt played the leading part. 'He is certainly the most perfect example of a *mauvais coucheur* that I have ever met with. Mr G's patience with him was angelic'.[39] I may here notice that K's memoir is full of diatribes against and complaints of Harcourt. But he does not describe the far worse scence of Nov 23. 1892.[40] [411/903]

Lansdowne 'was decidedly the weakest of the Viceroys of India with whom I have had to deal as Indian Secretary'. [†/905]

K narrates how though ill he conducted the Parish Councils Bill through the H of Lords (and admirably he did it). 'I may say without vanity that my successful conduct of this bill considerably improved my position both in Parliament and the country'.[41] [†/929]

Feb 23. 1894. 'Harcourt came twice to see me and remained a long time talking over the political situation. He evidently hopes to succeed Mr G. as Prime Minister. Unfortunately (as far as I know) – none of his colleagues favoured his aspirations. His qualifications as a parliamentary leader no one can dispute, but his time-serving, his sudden changes of opinion, and his cantankerous temper put him quite out of the running, in the opinion of those who know him best, for the all important duties of head of the government. It was soon evident that Rosebery was first favourite with Harcourt leader in the H of Commons'.[42] [421/931]

March 3 (at the Council when Mr G resigned.) 'The Queen spoke sympathetically of Mr. Gladstone. ... It was now practically certain that the Queen would send for Rosebery, and Harcourt was quite off the blustering tack and looked like a whipped schoolboy'. [422/932]

March 4. 'Rosebery came to see me just after breakfast. (*N.B. K seems quite unaware of what occurred at his dinner the night before between Harcourt and J Morley with reference to his own appointment to the FO.*) to tell me that he had accepted office as Prime Minister and was forming his Cabinet,

[39] Gladstone nevertheless devilishly wondered aloud to Algernon West if Harcourt might not succeed Lansdowne as Viceroy in India. West, *Diaries*, 183.

[40] He did, however, remark upon it at the time in a letter to Spencer. 3 Dec. 1892, SP, K336.

[41] Formally, the Local Government Act, creating almost 7,000 elective parish councils with wide-ranging but underfunded authority. For a summary of this complex bill, see V. D. Lipman, *Local Government Acts, 1834–1945* (Oxford, 1949), 156–64. For Spencer's assessment see 3 *Hansard* 106 (15 April 1902), 263–4. On Kimberley's parliamentary reputation, *EHJ2*, 116; Bishop of Limerick to Kimberley, 25 February 1894, KP1, 15/K2/24; 'The Crisis in Foreign Affairs', *'Eighty Club' Yearbook, 1899*, 6.

[42] Cf. Journal entry for 25 Feb. 1894.

and that it was a *sine qua non* that I should undertake the Foreign Office. Of course, little as I wished to become Foreign Secretary I could not refuse. It was evident that Rosebery had with unfeigned reluctance consented to be Prime Minister, and I observed to him how curious it was that both of us were reluctant to accept the great offices open to us'.[43] [422–3/933]

K notes a dinner at Buckingham Palace (March 6) at which he and I were present. 'The dinner was execrable'. [423/934]

March 8. 'First cabinet of the Rosebery Government which went off well. Harcourt continued to sulk in the most ridiculous manner.' [423/935]

'Harcourt continued to rampage and I cannot say how low he fell in the estimation of all his colleagues. He said to me "Thank God this can't go on much longer – the ship has got a hole knocked through its bottom".' [424–5/937]

K gives a long account of the Anglo Belgian [ill.] and to the blunder of Anderson abt the road – 'a disastrous one. How could the Germans be expected to believe the truth about this'. [†/937]

K is rather angry with me about my 'fussiness' in coming to London when there was a chance of securing peace between China and Japan. I remember that he declined to come because it was Wymondham Market or some such reason! So I had to go. His was rather the old fashioned view of ministerial duty and responsibility. [428/948]

Dec 1894. 'Prodigious scolding letter from Harcourt. Truly he is incorrigible. I was told that Mr G. used to say that he really could not read his letters to him; he had no time to spare for them. It is inconceivable that a man of Harcourt's ability should write such ill tempered ignorant rigmaroles.' K goes on to remark that one of his private secretaries came to the F.O. with a most offensive message to him and said he did not know what he was to do as he could not deliver such a message. Armine W. said airily that he would take it, that his father was quite accustomed to these messages, &c. [429/951]

---

[43] Rosebery protected himself by reticence from the most extreme forms of criticism. Gladstone's comment upon his tenure at the Foreign Office is a classic of perverse praise: 'Considering what followed I have great satisfaction in recording on his behalf his rather determined resistance.' *Prime Ministers' Papers: Gladstone*, I, 135. Hamilton observed that 'throughout the crisis [Kimberley] behaved like a real gentleman always thrusting his own claims in the background'. *EHJ2*, 117.

February 19, 1895. 'Rosebery made to us the amazing announcement that he had determined to resign on the ground that he was not loyally supported by his colleagues in the Commons. He especially complained that no notice had been taken of the insolent attacks on him by Dilke and Labouchere. His announcement came like a thunderbolt, no one having the slightest idea that he was contemplating resignation. He was with difficulty persuaded to reconsider his determination,[44] and happily on the 21st he told us very quietly that he had made up his mind not to resign. "All's well that ends well" but it would be remiss to deny that our confidence in his judgment was seriously shaken. His extreme sensitiveness to personal attacks indicate a certain weakness in his character. Harcourt joined in deprecating Rosebery's resignation, but his talk was that the sooner we were driven out of office, the better'.[45] [430–1]

Edward Grey's speech on the Nile Basin question. Harcourt complained (*not I think without ground had he been on the ordinary footing with the govt*). However 'the amusing thing is that Harcourt had left the House and did not come back though Grey sent for him. J. Morley threatened to resign but I managed to pacify him'. [434–5/958]

'C Bannerman was very anxious to be Speaker' but cabinet ministers were excluded. [434/959]

May 23. 'J. Morley again about to resign, but this had happened so many times that I felt pretty sure he would reconsider it (as he did)'. [436/961]

[44] See Kimberley to Rosebery, 19 Feb. 1895, in *Liberal by Principle*, 228.

[45] Rosebery recorded this entry separately, outside the notebook, along with the annotation: 'Feb 19. 1895. Under this date Kimberley notes in his journal that I made the "amazing announcement" that I must resign as I was not properly supported in the House of Commons. His amazement shows that the device was successful. It would of course not have been possible for me to resign. But it was the only way in which I could restore any discipline, or deal with the open and insulting disloyalty of one member of the cabinet at least. This shameful exhibition had excited just comment, for the silence of the Govt. under such circumstances was much more damaging than the attacks of my foes. So I called a cabinet to play the last card left to me, and on the whole it succeeded.' RsP, 10147, ff. 159, 161.

INDEX